I0820994

GARY STEWART

ALSO BY JIMMY McDONOUGH

Shakey: Neil Young's Biography

The Ghastly One: The 42nd Street Netherworld of Director Andy Milligan

Big Bosoms and Square Jaws: The Biography of Russ Meyer, King of the Sex Film

Tammy Wynette: Tragic Country Queen

Soul Survivor: A Biography of Al Green

The Exotic Ones: That Fabulous Film-Making Family from Music City, USA—The Ormonds

The Most Exotic One: The Hard, Wonderful, Fun Life of Georgette Dante

GARY STEWART

I AM FROM THE HONKY-TONKS

Jimmy McDonough

WOLF+
SALMON

1 3 5 7 9 10 8 6 4 2

First Edition 2025

HB ISBN: 979-8-9905799-1-0

Collector's Ediion ISBN: 979-8-9905799-4-1

eBook ISBN: 979-8-9905799-5-8

Jacket and book design by Chris Campion

Jacket photographs: Front © Grandal Stewart / Back © Jimmy Snead

Jacket design © Wolf+Salmon

Repro, scanning, and color correction: Dot Editions

Copy-editing and proofing: Susan VanHecke

Photo retouching: Masumi Kobayashi

Manufactured in the United Kingdom by CPI.

EU Authorised Representative: Easy Access System Europe - Mustamäe tee 50,

10621 Tallinn, Estonia, easproject.com, gpsr.requests@easproject.com

Typeset in Benguiat Montage, Benguiat Pro, and Palatino.

Published simultaneously worldwide by:

Wolf+Salmon

www.wolfandsalmon.com

For Mary Lou

"you touch me where I live"

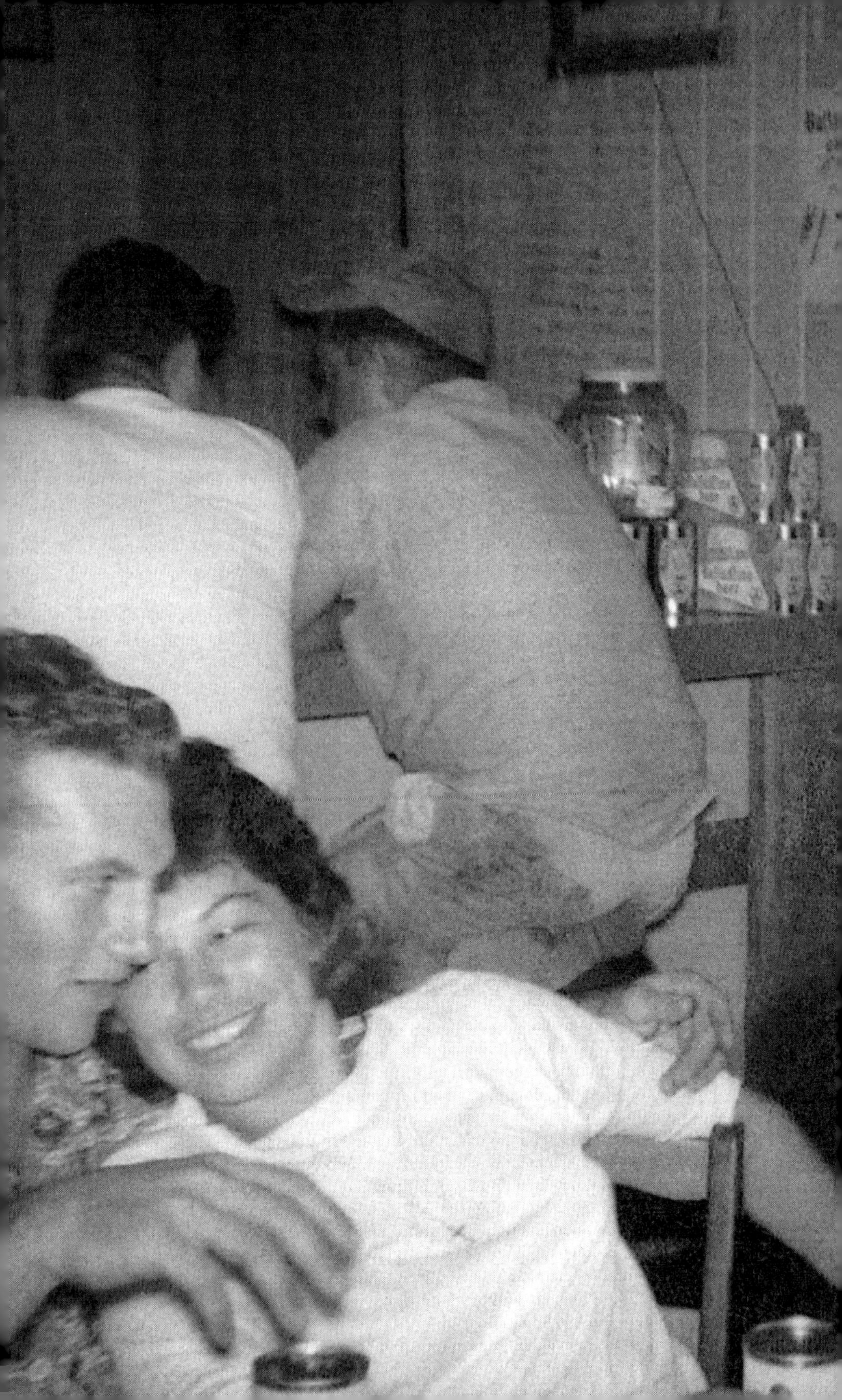

AMI
25¢

What started out as heaven/Got lost along the way

—"Harlan County Highway" (Stewart/Betts)

CONTENTS

introduction: Trailer with Blacked-Out Windows 14
1. Georgia and George 28
2. Long Way out of This Holler 46
3. Florida Man 68
4. Hello, Mary Lou 89
5. Music City Assembly Line 113
6. Better Than Gunsmoke 138
7. Number One with a Bullet 160
8. Animal in a Cage 198
9. Check My Stride 216
10. Griselda 234
11. Only Goin' Through Once 241
12. Ghost Train Slide 264
13. Gerald 296
14. An Irreversible Descent into Major Sevenths 310
15. Bad Attitude 346
16. Jukin' 371
17. Joey 394
18. Dark Place 410
19. Honky-Tonk Bandits 432
20. Find Me 468
epilogue: Somewhere in Time 500
Acknowledgments 510
Photo Credits 514
Source Notes 515
Bibliography 525
Discography 526
Index 530

SOUTH of
ALIENTE

introduction

TRAILER WITH BLACKED-OUT WINDOWS

Man, ain't nobody could ever sing honky-tonk music like Gary Stewart. One of the greatest country singers of all time. The king of honky-tonk music. There was nobody better.

– Tanya Tucker

Gary Stewart, king of the honky-tonks, has just thrown a knife at my head. A mere steak knife, big deal. *Thwap!* It hits the double-wide paneling behind me and falls to the carpet as the clattering air conditioner struggles against the Florida heat. My chuckle only makes him angrier. I'm giving Stewart shit about hiding from the world in his trailer, and it's pissing him off.

Gary's raven-haired wife, Mary Lou, a sharp cookie, sits across from me, intrigued by this dime-store violence. "That's just another one of his personalities comin' out. It's like that movie *All About Eve*. C'mon, Gary, put your chin down and come up another person." I detect a hint of glee in her eyes that someone is giving the lord of the manor a little what for.

"You'll never understand me!" Stewart shouts. He scuttles off to the other room and returns with a scroll, which he proceeds to unfurl and read aloud. "Stranger, you don't know me," he hisses. "You've analyzed my every move, you still go away shaking your head. I remain enigmatic." I listen politely until he gets to the part about "hill folk" who "don't need pills."

"You can't read *THAT*," I sputter, laughing. Gary was a drug fiend. Friends would recount how he'd rip off a sheet of acid and eat all twenty tabs at once. Or down a fistful of pain pills before a show and still deliver the goods. ("Gary was like Keith Richards when it came to drugs," said musician/songwriter/producer Buddy Cannon. "There were no limits.")

Stewart suppressed a chuckle at the line he'd just read. But he still wanted to silence me. He grabbed my battered, black Sony Walkman, intent on erasing the conversation. "Take your tape recorder and *out the fuckin' door with it*!" Murder in the air, I wrestled the device out of his clutches.

A few more rounds and it was over. The atmosphere changed on a dime, as it often did with Stewart. Happy-go-lucky Gary was back in the saddle and I certainly felt relief. He loomed over me with his guitar, singing a number he knew I loved, the mournful "In the Pines," done by Lead Belly, Kurt Cobain, and many others. This time he eyed the recorder like it was a bomb to defuse. It never failed—whatever insanity had ensued between us, he'd donate a performance for posterity. Gary did this murder ballad many times in many different ways over the years. This time it was an elegiac moan from the hills that hit like an icy wind on the back of my neck.

I was a twenty-seven-year-old upstart living in Hoboken, New Jersey, who was intent on dragging Gary Stewart back into the spotlight. Gary was forty-three, a "very complicated" (his words) Southerner, and, to put it mildly, had always been ambivalent about any sort of stardom, let alone a comeback. Abandoned by Nashville, he had fallen off the charts, wasn't recording, and was barely playing live shows having retreated to a pill-fueled existence in a Fort Pierce,

Florida, double-wide with the windows blocked out. Obsessed by his music, I had tracked him down and talked my way into that trailer by finding him an obscure 45 he coveted. Barging into his life, I naively believed I could save him from going to hell in a handbag.

The trailer was Stewart's kingdom, filled with a carefully curated collection of antiques, Western memorabilia, and albums of every vintage. "I got my own little world, see," he told me. "I built this." Few people were allowed in, including relatives. A fabulous museum, a tremendous hang, but also a dim, claustrophobic tomb, like a submarine that never surfaced. At one point I sat on the couch for four days waiting for him to emerge from the bedroom. I went through Gary's archive of unreleased recordings so I wouldn't lose my mind, trapped as I was in the lair of the honky-tonk Dracula.

What I found there would convince me that this was one of the greatest musical geniuses this country has ever produced, and not just a Music City shooting star. "I played country, I played rock, I played psychedelic music—and I dug it all, too. I have no limits in my mind. I've done it *all*, y'know? I am everything."

* * *

Gary Stewart hadn't always been locked away from the world in a double-wide.

The very first time I laid eyes on him in person was at a rare New York City gig at the Lone Star Cafe seven years earlier. Stewart was still flying high on the tail end of his comet ride through the country charts. Not knowing much about him, I expected some pompadoured song salesman in a Nudie suit to waltz onstage and replicate his hits.

Nothing prepared me for the roar that came next. It was like entering a Presbyterian church to discover that Pentecostal snake-handlers had seized the pulpit. This scrawny little guy in jeans, a dark vest, and a billowy, barely tucked-in white shirt ambled out, that gaunt face lost in the shadows of a jet-black hat, a chaos of curly black hair spilling over his shoulders. Gary looked like he'd just slid out of the back seat of Uncle Elmo's moonshine hauler, ready to steal your chickens the minute you turned your head. Not exactly Opry material.

First thing I noticed onstage: no fiddle, no backup singers, and—most surprisingly—no steel guitar, an instrument prominent on many a Stewart hit. It was just three Les Pauls, bass, and drums. And the music was loud as hell.[1] Was this country? "It was a bit like watching Bob Dylan fronting Crazy Horse," countered musician Dale Lawrence, who attended the show with me.

The Drugstore Cowboys, his Texas band, were certainly no Drifting Cowboys. Ten years younger than Gary, they were a lively bunch that seemed more like cowhands than country musicians. What a racket they made! And Stewart drove them hard. When it came to playing live, Gary liked to "kick it in the ass and go with my music, and so do these boys," he boasted. Music was "like fucking, y'know—if they throw it to the left with a little bit of zing, you got to zing it back! Get in the groove, instead of pump, pump, pump, this is my one lick."

This music did not sound like his hits, even when he was singing them. Hell, it didn't sound like *anyone's* music. No—it sounded like someone had backed a burning tanker truck over the recorded version and waited for the explosion. Oh, the singing...*the singing*! Vital, burning, possessed. He fed off an audience, and what was merely extreme on record became unhinged live. Every note felt like a surprise. Perfection wasn't the goal. Gary forgot lyrics, sometimes the pitch went south...he just laughed it off. Whooping it up, such details *just didn't matter*. I have never seen another performer surrender to the moment like Gary Stewart. Whatever he was feeling came straight out of his throat and guitar chords, no filter. Talk about alive! Standing in the audience, you felt if you reached out to touch him, you'd get zapped. My God, it was exciting. "Gary had a groove

---

1 Stewart craved volume. One night when he was playing the Longhorn Ballroom in Dallas "an older gentleman went to the stage and asked Gary if he might turn the music down 'about three decibels,'" said attendee Mike Smith. "Gary thought a second, then asked the gentleman, 'Well, could you just back up about three feet?'"

SAT NOV 16 18

to him like nobody else," said Robert "Cotton" Payne, who played drums that night. "He was so happy when he was onstage."

Amazingly, the crowd at the Lone Star was mostly blasé. Gary had zero presence in New York City and the fact that he didn't give a flying fuck about playing there didn't help. Boozed-up rowdies hollered for "Yellow Rose of Texas," "Cotton-Eyed Joe," and even ZZ Top. "They're a good band," mused Stewart with a wry smile. "But they ain't playin' here tonight." Gary burned the joint down anyway. It remains the greatest live performance I've ever witnessed. I entered that show as a fan and left a cult member. I vowed to track this guy down and find out why he wasn't the biggest star in the universe. Not that Stewart was all that concerned either way. As he told the press early on, "There ain't no big goals to become no big award winner." What was important? "Just my music, that's all. I'm just a country boy that got lucky."

* * *

Gary Stewart's heyday was the back half of the seventies. "Drinkin' Thing," "She's Actin' Single (I'm Drinkin' Doubles)," "Your Place or Mine," "Ten Years of This": these are among the greatest country records ever made—thrilling, exhilarating performances, and if you don't know them I pity you. Stewart at his best inspires awe. "It was as if Hank Williams Sr. and Jerry Lee Lewis had an offspring together," said Dwight Yoakam. Bob Dylan, Willie Nelson, Waylon Jennings, Charley Pride, Alex Chilton, Tanya Tucker, the Allman Brothers, and the Clash were fans. "I adored his records," said Vince Gill. "I never heard anybody with that kind of passion in the way that they sang... that shotgun-fast vibrato. He was country, man."

A singer, songwriter, guitarist, and piano player, Stewart's sound was forged in Kentucky hollers and Florida honky-tonks, and his high, thrilling tenor could tackle rock, ballads, blues, bluegrass, all of it sounding authentic. Writers often compare Stewart to Jerry Lee, one of his early heroes, but I never reference the Killer when I think of his voice. Idiosyncratic stylists like George Jones, Roky Erickson, Jimmy Scott, Bobby Lee Trammell, and Bryan Ferry come to mind instead. When Gary sang, "you *had* to believe it," said Tanya Tucker. Dylan wrote this about Roy Orbison, but it could equally apply to Gary: it's a voice "that made you want to drive your car over a cliff. He sang like a professional criminal."

Playing live with ragtag Texas and Florida bands, unencumbered by the restraints of producers, recording studios, and record company demands, Stewart didn't merely sing a song, he wrestled it to the ground. Depending on his mood, he might coax, snarl, or threaten. Gary was even known to levitate. One night a woman in front of the stage was tugging on Stewart's jeans while he was playing, "and all of a sudden it looked like he did a little tap dance right up the side of her body in midair. Gary suddenly went sideways and danced along her in the air without touching her," according to band member "Boogie" Bob Melton. "I still don't know how he did it. Gary could spook you...music was sexual to him, it was that intense. When Gary was really good, he was the best. Jerry Lee Lewis had nothing on him. There were times I expected his hair to just burst into flames due to his unbridled passion for the music. He'd grin that wide grin, a look of wild ecstasy in his eyes. They seemed to shoot sparks at you."

Yet by the early eighties, after a handful of incandescent albums, it all went south. Gary Stewart was a bona fide outlaw, not the kind concocted by a record company, and one that excelled in self-sabotage. Nashville didn't know how to package (or control) this kind of realness, and Gary's brand of hillbilly was far more downhome than, say, a *Rolling Stone*–friendly Gram Parsons. "Too country for rock and too rock for country," as country music historian Jay Orr put it. "In a way, I think he was too country for country and too rock for rock." Extreme. That's a good word for Stewart, and one reason he's a neglected orphan when it comes to country music history. Gary's not in the Country Music Hall of Fame, there is no career-spanning boxed set, nor a documentary with the requisite Marty Stuart talking head.[2] Yet in the dusty honky-tonks of Texas, Louisiana, and Florida—as well as the boxy civic centers of the Native American reservations of New Mexico and Arizona—Gary remains king, over twenty years after his death.

* * *

"I am from the honky-tonks." That's how Gary Stewart introduced himself to the Austin Municipal Auditorium audience in January 1976 "before blowing them away in a wash of guitar twang," recalled writer Joe Nick Patoski. "The way he said it was proudly in defiance. That was the beauty of him."

At the time, Stewart was just an opening act for Charley Pride, whose family-friendly hits like "Kiss an Angel Good Mornin'" attracted a staid "predominantly middle-aged audience. Charley Pride's crowd was not Gary's crowd," said Patoski. Stewart hated an audience that just sat there politely, didn't dance, and studied you. "Son, they'll pick your ass apart," he told his road manager Terry Porter. "If you're gonna stand there and be in the jury, Gary would just as soon play somewhere else," said Porter. Stewart was too combustible to last as opening act for any country star, anyway. The next time Joe Nick saw him, Gary was commanding an Austin dance hall with a raucous band containing three deafening guitars. "He offered me mushrooms," said Joe Nick.

* * *

Honky-tonks. What are they, exactly? Little roadside buildings (sometimes shacks) built for music, booze, and dance. "A honky-tonk's

2 Sorry, Marty, but you're in a boatload of those things. Stuart had his own run-in with Gary one night when he and his bass player Randy Toman sat in for a raggedy, impromptu set at a Dallas club called Cowboys. "We did 'Rocky Top, Tennessee,' Elvis classics and just about everything else," said Toman. "The electricity around Gary Stewart was so powerful that it was hard to stand next to him," said Marty. "He had so many sparks flying off."

gonna be really dark," instructs singer/sometime Stewart manager Richard McCroan. "Neon's gonna be pretty much the only light in there. It's gonna be pretty smoky. And the dance floor imminent." It is not a dance hall—many of which Stewart also played—as they had higher ceilings and much bigger crowds. Gary preferred small venues packed like sardine cans, where he could reach out and touch the crowd. "They understand me in the honky-tonks. We get close and do it together."

Stewart bass player Curtis Randall laid it out this way: In a honky-tonk, "the guy and the girl get ready and they go out. They walk in the door, they got their boots and cowboy hats on. They go in, grab a beer and shots, and they start dancing. They start hooting and hollering, and all the words to the songs relate to everybody in there. On the jukebox they're playing honky-tonk music, which is Gary *Stewart*."

Gary Stewart slipped through the cracks in country music history, and his music needs to be exalted to the place in history it deserves. Part of that task has involved detective work, as Gary scattered songs around the country like a jewel thief tossing diamonds from a getaway car. He left behind a mountain of unreleased material, including hours of live music recorded by me. Somehow he knew people would eventually unearth it all. "Just remember there's a tape of me in Pikeville" went a cryptic aside to one interviewer. This unheard archive is his untold autobiography, and you can't tell Gary's story without examining these pieces of the puzzle. My hope is that all this music will finally get released as a result. There are so many diamonds in that *dust*.

Gary was the most effortlessly cool individual I've ever encountered. No matter what shape he was in, he remained authentically himself, even while sporting the ugliest bargain-mart Hawaiian shirt imaginable. He favored black hats he shaped himself over a teakettle, vintage Western threads, and because they fit his narrow feet better, ladies' cowboy boots. An ethereal character, he drifted through life in a dream, calling people at 3 a.m., announcing himself in that lazy drawl all who knew him imitated: "Heyyyyy, bud..."

You never knew what kind of state you'd find Stewart in. Robert Gallagher—entertainment director at Billy Bob's, "the world's largest honky tonk" in Fort Worth, Texas, where Stewart packed them in for years—would put Gary up at the swanky old Stockyards Hotel, which had theme suites like the "Bonnie and Clyde Room." One time Gallagher had parked Gary in a Native American–themed suite. "It had all of these damn decorations, like a buffalo head, feathers, an' leather shit hangin' all over the walls." Robert, who had been tasked with babysitting Stewart, snuck out for a food run. When Gallagher returned, he "opened the door an' there Gary was, laid out on the bed in his tighty-whities with a guitar, and he had all that shit from the walls, feathers, leather, and crap tied all over him, even on his head. I said, '*Goddamn, Gary! What the hell are you doing?*' He goes, 'Seekin' inspiration, son. Seekin' inspiration.'"

* * *

Stewart was one of twelve kids raised by George and Georgia.[3] His family fled Letcher County, Kentucky, poverty "like the Beverly Hillbillies," bound for the promised land of the Sunshine State. George was a miner and a cockfighter, Georgia sold Avon products as well as more dangerous substances. His sisters courted (even married) drug dealers; several brothers ran afoul of the law. The Stewart charm is legendary in Fort Pierce. Some say a Stewart could talk you into anything, including activities that could land you behind bars.

Gary's younger sister Gina,[4] the family's documentarian, carried around a camcorder in the late nineties/early oughts, documenting everything Warhol-style. It's a fascinating archive, capturing countless family gatherings where one can observe the Stewarts in their element—

3 All the Stewart children's first names begin with *G*. I had always been informed the count was eleven, but then I saw a family video where Georgia listed a twelfth, Gordon, who died in childbirth. His twin, Gregory, survived.

4 Pronounced "JEH-na."

dancing, imbibing, laughing, loving, feuding, rapping, and occasionally stripping, with brother Gerald even appearing in drag at a kiddie party.

Particularly riveting is Gina's full-moon sojourn to Hillcrest Memorial Gardens with a couple of cohorts to visit the graves of Stewarts gone, Gary's music wafting eerily in the background. Carrying flowers, a picnic basket, a case of Bud Light, and an oversized baby bottle containing "party favors," she pays her respects at the grave of her sister Griselda, who shot herself dead in 1977. Georgia and Gina liked to hit the Outback Steakhouse for a Bloomin' Onion before heading to Griselda's plot, where they'd decorate the grave, "put up umbrellas, sit in lawn chairs, eat that Bloomin' Onion, and just visit for a few hours. That was a ritual every holiday." Gina enjoys a good funeral, making it a celebration of the person. Open casket? "Honey, I'm kissin' ya and takin' pictures with ya." There have been more than a few unexpected deaths in this family. During her lifetime Georgia would bury five of her children.

The Stewarts are a lusty, lively, close-knit bunch, mountain folks who grew weary of winters and mines and rusted-out cars and made the great trek to the land of eternal sunshine only to find another Appalachia already there waiting. Where, as Gary was thrilled to discover, you could go barefoot all year long if you wanted to. This is a family saga as well as the story of a great American artist, because even at the zenith of fame Gary never strayed far from his transplanted kin, who provided a colorful but chaotic backdrop for Gary's time on earth.

Theirs was an American dream. And something of a Florida nightmare. I let those who were present tell the tale in oral history chapters devoted to certain Stewart family members who are no longer with us. Since I like the way these people talk, don't expect much grammatical cleanup. But believe me when I say that this story couldn't have been told in their heyday. I would've been fed to the gators. Gina Stewart got defiant discussing one nemesis of their clan. "We ain't mafia, but you fuck with the family, you're fuckin' with *me*."

* * *

There is a rather ferocious and at times unsettling love story here. Gary and Mary Lou had been childhood sweethearts, Lou the scandalous older woman. They fucked, fought, and finished each other's sentences. An epic country couple, in terms of drama they gave George and Tammy a run for their money. "My wife understands me," Gary told the press. "She's a real lady. She knows I love sex, women and drugs." I will tell you up front that it ends tragically, and in my heart I think Gary and Lou knew it would. "We were always told that if one died, the other would soon follow," said daughter Shannon. "No matter what." They're both long gone, as is son Joey. By some absolute miracle Shannon survived the family carnage, and how she did it is a glimmer of light in this ghost-ridden tale.

This story has haunted me for close to forty years now. No doubt I disappointed Gary as a friend, but I will not fail him as a biographer. That poem Gary read from the scroll? Turns out it's a literary work of some renown, "My Appalachia," written in 1977 by West Virginia native Muriel Miller Dressler and beloved by many a Southerner. Gary was trying to express exactly who he was, but being young and stupid it flew right by me like his knife.

The poem ends by returning to the opening refrain he read that day: "I am Appalachia: and, stranger, though you've studied me, you still don't know." I remember the stare Gary fixed on me as he read the line. He was utterly defiant, as he remained until the day he died.

Maybe he was right, but I'm still going to tell you all I know.

1

GEORGIA AND GEORGE

You take George's chickenfightin' and then you take Georgia's...background, that's where there's an underlying outlaw element that a lot of people never really saw in Gary. People would say, "Gary was no outlaw!" I'd say, "Well, let me introduce you to his sister Gina."

– Terry Porter

All smiles, Georgia Stewart was cheerfully telling me how she carried a rock in a sock for protection. "A pure stone rock! If anybody tries do somethin' to me, if I can't get to my gun, I can get to my rock.[5] Hit somebody in the head with that thing and you'd be 'bout next thing to a gun. I thought somebody stole my rock from me, so I got me a

5 Mention of firearms provoked this mother-son exchange:
"When you gonna let me have my gun back, Mommy?"
"I don't know where it is."
"Yeah," said Gary, disbelieving.

piece of iron and put it in my sock. Don't be sorry—be prepared! For *anything*."

Georgia was a tiny woman, with gray hair neatly tied back and a radiant face. Her friends called her Georgie. Her kids, Mommy. Her grandkids, Meemaw or Mamaw. "I love to talk to people. I like for people to feel like they know me and I know them. Because that's the way we should be in the world. We should do for one another... we started from one man and one woman—we're a little bit of kin, everybody is." She let out a lilting laugh. She had that same infectious enthusiasm Gary did when he was wound up about some record. Georgia knew how to get you on her side. "This is a salesman right here," said Gary proudly. "There is no harder worker than her, son. She still works—you see the Avon in the trunk?" Georgia giggled. "Some days I'll bring me back $100 a day. At sixty-five years old! If I can't go fast, I'll go slow."

A sweet little Kentucky lady with a sing-song voice, I thought. There was a whole lot more to Georgia lurking beneath the downhome exterior, however. It took me decades to uncover it. She was an intricate character, the eye at the center of many a Stewart storm. The tip-off should've been watching Gary interact with her. There was an electric charge between them. He was deferential to her in a way he wasn't with any other woman, even courtly, but with a dancing glint in his eye and measured tone in his voice that somehow hinted at darker shadows. "Georgia was like Ma Barker," said longtime family friend Jimmy Smith. "Outlaw woman. Instead of a kingpin, she was a queenpin! She was the boss, man."

Her husband, George, on the other hand, was an open book, even if nothing fancy was written on the pages. I had been warned he wouldn't say much, besides maybe a grunt "hello" in my direction. He was lanky, with a long, weathered face and big ears. He warmed a bit when I asked to see the chicken pens behind the house. George lived for cockfights. And while he wasn't exactly effusive, what he had to say at the dinner table was telling.

The subject was marriage, specifically his. "We've had a good life together, I think. Fifty years still hangin' together...we always had a home, somethin' to eat, a little money. Raised all these kids. There ain't nobody who has it the way they want it. Nobody. People have to learn to get along and go on. Son, it takes two, two to go together. And that means all the way."

This registered big with Gary, sitting nearby nodding his head, who proudly announced he was "twenty-seven years in" on his marriage to Mary Lou. "When you grow up you have things that stick in your mind. *One time* for Mommy and Daddy. Fights 'n' whatever... Married *one time*."

Like father, like son.

Gary and Georgia. (Shannon Ashburn collection)

TRAMPAS STEWART: We kids spent lots of time with Mamaw and Papaw because our parents used to party. This was in the 1970s, 1980s. There was a lot of partying going on in Fort Pierce and we kids were shielded from a lot. We loved Papaw and Mamaw both.

Georgia talked with a very strong Kentucky drawl—along with talking in third person all the time. If you were to ask her, "How's it going, Mamaw?," she'd say, "Well, let me tell ya, Mamaw's knees hurt. And Mamaw's hands are swollen." If she wasn't tending to the drama that the kids were drumming up all the time, she'd just be sitting on the side of her bed, reading books or *Reader's Digest*. She had an arch in her back, she couldn't walk much. She was in pain all her life, ever since I'd known her. I don't know if it was BS or not. I mean, she always complained.

KAREN PARKER (family friend): Georgia was very sick. She had a lot of things wrong with her...I don't remember any particular ailment, she was just not a well person. But she was so sweet.

BRENDA CASEY (relative): Georgia was uneducated, but she was not ignorant. She had her reality and everybody else had theirs. She would make up narratives to fit the facts that she had.

JASON STEWART: Mamaw was like a typical grandma, always in there cooking. I remember going over there and she'd be cannin' stuff or making desserts. Sea foam candy, that was her specialty. Mamaw was awesome. She was the anchor for the family.

GINA STEWART: Every mornin' she'd make each child what they wanted for breakfast.

NICK STEWART (cousin): I have a lot of fond memories of staying with them. They were very poor. She would cook potatoes for me, boil potatoes then fry them. And all of that family, they were so poor that they would have renderings of meat just to make the vegetables taste better, that's why those Stewart guys were so lean. There was not a lot of big meat-eating. And she'd make mixed pickles, which is basically beans and sauerkraut. It was an old Kentucky thing. They would let it ferment for two or three weeks.

GREG STEWART: Gary loved those mixed pickles. We ate country. She had eleven[6] kids. She fixed cornbread every meal. She always made my daddy a separate thing of bread. He got his own skillet of bread.

GINA STEWART: Daddy wouldn't drink a cup of coffee if we poured it. If Daddy come in that dump truck past the kitchen window, you

6 Greg is omitting Gordon, his twin, who died in childbirth.

better haul ass to the Florida room[7] and get out of the kitchen. He wouldn't eat a piece of cake if he saw us eatin' it.

BRENDA CASEY: George wouldn't eat food that anybody but Georgia cooked. He wanted her to do everything for him. Everything.

SHANNON ASHBURN (Gary's daughter): Papaw used to go to all the dumpsters behind all the schools and the grocery stores. He would go to each and every daughter and son of his and drop us off care packages. And we thought that it was the coolest thing, because we used to love those little hamburgers left over from the school. Pizza. And the little chocolate milks.

They lived like they were very, very poor, and they always lived like that. He used to sell eggs on the side of the road. And Mamaw sold Avon...whatever else Mamaw sold, I don't know.

BRENDA CASEY: George would go to the grocery stores and get food that they were going to throw away. He told them he'd feed it to his pigs. Well, he did feed it to his pigs—after the family had picked through it. I wouldn't eat at their house, because I had seen George bring in a cake left over from the store. It had mold on one end. And Georgia would cut it off and serve the other end. I've seen her do it. Georgie was so frugal—cheap, put it that way. I think it came from the Depression, and having to make do with what you had.

I imagine it was awfully hard to feed all those kids. One of my cousins went to spend a couple of days with them. And Georgia called out that dinner was on the table. He got up and went to the table, but he didn't run, and by the time he got there the food was all gone, because the kids had taken it. You either grabbed it or you weren't gonna get it. There was not seconds.

BILL STEWART: Georgia was a go-getter, but she was tight, tight as hell. She fed *sparingly*. It was tough to get food out of her when you were staying there! Hell, that made it taste good. Because you had to wait so damn long for it. She was that way all of her life.

---

7 The room where the family relaxes, watches TV, and visits.

JIMMY SMITH: Mamaw was tight. She was tight.

GRANDAL STEWART: Buddy, she could take a damn buffalo nickel and make it piss before she turned it loose. I'm serious!

TRAMPAS STEWART: Georgia was a WWF wrestling fanatic. She sat in that Florida room and watched wrestling. She stomped her feet. Dusty Rhodes was her favorite. When you came into the home during wrestling time, all you'd hear was just a little woman yelling, "Come on, come on!!! Get him!!! Get that sumbitch!!!" She was a spitfire.

CANDY STEWART: First time I went to the house, I thought they was gonna kill each other. Her son Glenn would be sitting in front of her and she'd be beating the crap out of him.

BRENDA CASEY: You couldn't sit next to Georgia if she was watching wrestling, because she'd beat you up. She would be hollerin' and waving her arms. She'd hit you, she didn't care. She would get so excited. And I'm like, "Georgie, that's not real." She'd get really upset. She'd get pissed if you told her it wasn't real.

SHANNON ASHBURN: Christmases were awesome at Mamaw and Papaw's. Mamaw and Papaw had, like, their throne. Kids got to pass out the gifts, and everybody was always eyeballing to see what everybody got Mamaw, mostly. Because Mamaw was the queen.

GINA STEWART: Presents corner to corner.

BRENDA CASEY: Georgia was a staunch Republican, she used to work at all the elections for the Republican Party. That was a big deal for her, to be an election worker every four years.

GRANDAL STEWART: My mom was real popular. She knew quite a few people. And she had the personality that she could get along with a snake. Everybody respected my mom. They respected Mom as much as they respected Gary.

BRENDA CASEY: George and Georgie were known for their fights.

TRAMPAS STEWART: For some reason, I've never understood why, Mamaw had a lot of bitterness towards Papaw. She let us know that she wasn't very happy. I think it was just a convenient relationship thing towards the end. Papaw knew to keep his distance. Mamaw was the one in charge of all the finances, all the kids, all the properties they had. Papaw was just trying to exist.

GRANDAL STEWART: One time I went over to Mom and Dad's house after I'd been married. Pulled into the driveway around the side of the house, and all of a sudden I see the ol' man coming out the back door, man. Haulin' ass. I mean, he was hittin' it! And here comes Mommy right after him. She come outta that damn door a-shootin' with a little pistol, buddy, POW! POW! POW! I took the gun away from Mom and throwed it in the damn woods. That's how feisty Mom was.

BRENDA CASEY: Georgie told me this herself. George would go out after payday and get low, y'know, drink too much and spend all their money. And he'd come home and he'd beat on Georgie. And Georgie had had her fill of it. One night while her sister Corsia was staying with her she waited for George to come home. He passed out on the bed. And she took a needle and thread and sewed the sheets together, the top and the bottom sheets, all the way around. Totally sewed him in, and then she took a broom and started beating the shit out of him. And Corsia's sayin', "Don't kill him! Don't kill him!" And she's like, "I don't care."[8]

GRANDAL STEWART: Mommy claimed that the ol' man went off and got drunk. I never seen my ol' man drink a thing. She said she wrapped him up in the damn blanket and beat the shit out of him with a poker, son. Wrapped his ass up and beat the hell out of him! He had black and blue spots all over.

SHANNON ASHBURN: Mamaw was *mean*. Mamaw beat Gerald to a bloody pulp with an Electrolux vacuum cleaner hose.

GINA STEWART: Mommy took a cast-iron skillet to my head. Right in front of Gary.

BRENDA CASEY: You didn't cross Georgie.

TRAMPAS STEWART: One time somebody called her house looking to beat up my dad. Man, Mamaw let him have it on the phone. She

---

8 Willie Nelson, a favorite of Georgia's, tells a very similar story in books and interviews concerning an ex-wife. Some suspect Georgia just lifted the story from him (Nelson was a family friend, and a big favorite of Georgia's).

said, "Garna [Trampas's dad] may be under six feet, but he'll put your ass six feet under if you mess with him." Cocaine was involved in a lot of stuff.

GINA STEWART: Mommy sold Electrolux, Avon, Tupperware, Rally candy bars—you name it, Mommy sold it. She sold Avon for thirty-six years. I still got that shit in my fucking garage.

KIM CARLTON (family friend): Mamaw was always selling something. And God, I bought stuff. Everybody did. She was really good at it. She sold Avon...[pause] among other things. Moonshine would pass our way, out of the hills someplace.

TOMMY SCHWARTZ (longtime family friend, archivist, and musician): You damn sure didn't want to be around her at Christmas, because you may end up buying some kind of fucking Avon for somebody. I used to hate that—"Oh, shit. It's Christmas. She's gonna be looking for me, man." "Oh, you want to buy your wife *this*." Oh my God.

JIMMY SMITH: When I was a kid, I'd hang around with Glenn Stewart. And I'd have to buy Avon products for fucking Christmas. For my whole family. Because you had to. She was a hard seller, man—"Your mama would just LOOOVE this, honey. Now, what's your sister like?" She had this sales pitch, you couldn't tell her no. 'Cause she had this phony sweetness and I was a sucker.

SHANNON ASHBURN: I got a bottle of Odyssey every fucking Christmas. Same perfume every year. And Dad got the white Avon brush.

JIMMY SMITH: Man, everybody got Avon. And if you didn't pay her? You wouldn't get your shit.

TRAMPAS STEWART: I don't know how she kept an inventory on all this stuff. She'd do her little runs, probably two or three days a week around the county. And she'd have all these ladies buying stuff from her. She was a talker. Mamaw knew everybody. She had a lot of customers. I tell you what, when she was sellin' Avon, the back seat of her Cadillac was *packed*. I mean, all the way up to the top of the back of the driver's seat. And the floorboards would be filled with products. I'm telling you, this car was loaded. We used to go on runs with her, but we couldn't fit in the back seat.

JIMMY SMITH: I was, like, on Wife Number Three. Me and her parted ways. And I was getting ready to move out of my little house. So Mamaw comes over. She starts going through my fucking shit—"Oh, those shoes will fit Gerald." She just grabbed my shit. Her and Gina. They fucking raided my house, right before my eyes. I mean, they took my entertainment center! Oh, she wiped me out. And I was always taught to respect your elders, right? But Mamaw took it to the limit.

KIM CARLTON: You could tell that Mamaw was from the piney woods. This woman had cash in $10,000 bills back when they were still printing $10,000 bills. She would stash them places. Georgia would shut money away that you just wouldn't even believe. Gold and silver, lots of $10,000 bills.

JIMMY SMITH: Mamaw fucking loved me, man. I loved her, too. She would make me fucking French toast. And she would sell me her Percocets.

BRENDA CASEY: Gary never was into drug sales, but [some of] the rest of them...drugs were just a means of making a dollar. And they had the personalities for it.

GRANDAL STEWART: Mommy would sell [cocaine], too. And quaaludes. She got in with somebody that had a bunch of quaaludes. Momma got into them damn things! Sold them for a long time. Dad didn't say much. She was the boss. I used to go down and get cocaine from Mom to sell. She didn't *do* it. But, y'know, she had it.

BRENDA CASEY: They used to wrap it up as Christmas presents. And put it in the trunk. So if the car got searched they would just see a bunch of Christmas presents. We weren't talkin' about little amounts. I didn't ask questions. It was a way to make money, so it was totally okay.

DALE THOMAS (musician): We went to their house. And Gary's mom and dad were there. A couple of his uncles. Almost all of his brothers and sisters. The place was jammed. And there was this big round glass table in the living room. It had a pile of white powder, pile of cocaine on it. It was *huge*. I'll bet you it was a quarter pound. It was just, "You go and take what you want." I mean, it was absolutely amazing. Gary's dad was in the kitchen talking to some folks and he introduced me. And I told them, "That's the biggest pile of white stuff I've ever seen." And his dad says, "Well, help yourself. Don't let that stuff get ahold of you. It'll kill you." Of course, after he said that, me and the bass player, we just did a whole bunch.

JIMMY SMITH: They'd take it to Kentucky. They did that for a long time. That's how she came up with all that money. She left the kids $300,000. She didn't make that sellin' Avon!

JO ANN GREGORY (Family friend): Talk about stepping on your coke...Georgia would step on the Avon products, for God's sake! Never buy anything from Georgia—drugs or anything. She would just dilute, dilute, dilute.

BARBARA ANNE PETERS (family friend/Gary and Mary Lou's personal assistant): Mary Lou said one day, "Georgia, don't start no shit with me. Because I will get in your sugar jar. Don't think I won't." That's all I'm saying about that.

GRANDAL STEWART: Papaw would just go into the other room. Didn't want to know anything about it.

FAMILY FRIEND: Georgie was no drug lord. She was buying stuff. Had somebody else totin' it up there to Michigan for her. We had attended a funeral for a friend and after the funeral was over we were headed north on 441. And I was two cars behind Georgia, and when we were got to these railroad tracks she slammed on brakes. We ended up in her ass—the car that was right behind her slammed into her, and I slammed into that girl. It comes back to me through the grapevine that Georgia's wanting to sue me, right? For the wreck! That burnt my ass. Because I was like family. I just sent the message back, "You go right ahead. And I will mess up your shit going on in Michigan. You sue me and that will *all* come out." I never heard another word about it. And we never spoke again—until Gary's funeral.

JO ANN GREGORY: Mary Lou used to say, "Georgia rules the family with a pencil and an eraser." She would have her will in front of her and say, "Okay, today you're in. But I'm erasing Gary's name."

And the next day it was, "All right, Gary, you're back in. And Gina, you're out." Then it would be, "Okay, Gerald, you're in." I laughed over that.

SHANNON ASHBURN: Mamaw always made sure that she had her name on all the kids' houses one way or another—if she purchased it, or they purchased it. I don't know how she did it. But somehow she got her name on it. Mamaw ran all the kids.

GINA STEWART: She didn't ask you, buddy. She'd take your name off the house! It was, "Mommy's changing the names again!" Me and Garna lived at the courthouse, seems like.

BRENDA CASEY: Georgie never could give up control. She was a control freak. One time Gina was on the other side of the state. Georgie had a headache and wanted Tylenol or aspirin. And she made Gina drive all the way back to Fort Pierce, go to the store, pick it up, give it to her, and then drive back home to the other side of the state, three-hour drive each way. She only wanted Gina to do it, she wouldn't ask any of the other kids. Georgie depended on Gina to do everything for her.

Cocaine took away any potential that some of the Stewart kids had. All of 'em were savvy, street smart...but you know what it's like—once you get caught in it, it's hard to get out of it. And they each had talents that they could have pursued that would have probably got them the money that they craved. But they took the easy way. Quick way.

I liked Georgie, but I didn't always agree with the way that she ran her family. She encouraged her kids to do things that were not good for them, for money. She sold a lot of face powder, let's put it that way. I don't see Georgie as a spiritual person, because you can't do that to your family if you really loved them. To go ahead and do it, just because there's money to be made?

ANONYMOUS RELATIVE: Mrs. Stewart said to me one day, "Drugs has ruined my whole family."

* * *

NICK STEWART: George was just George. He would just work his ass off.

TRAMPAS STEWART: Papaw drank coffee all day long. Work pants tucked into boots...he looked exactly like the *Green Acres* farmhand. Papaw had a strong accent, it was all gargled from smokin' tobacco his whole life.

KIM CARLTON: Mr. Stewart was a very good man. A hard man. He would come over and castrate our pigs for us. Seriously, he had a little pocketknife and he whipped it out and went *whip! whip!* and he was done.

GINA STEWART: I never knew Dad played harmonica 'til that day he played "Orange Blossom Special" without stopping in his older age. He can play "Orange Blossom Special," buddy.

GRANDAL STEWART: He'd do it around Christmas every now and then. Just to entertain hisself, really.

TRAMPAS STEWART: Mamaw didn't think too much of it. I don't know that she ever said anything good about Papaw. We loved him anyway.

GAIL STEWART: Daddy was a man of few words. I've only heard him say "I love you" one time. I'm serious. One time.

GINA STEWART: Mommy made him do it for Christmas. She said, "You tell your younguns you love them."

GAIL STEWART: He finally did it. That's all I wanted. He offered money. I said to him, "Keep your money, Daddy. That's all I want." We were in our twenties.

TRAMPAS STEWART: I loved Papaw dearly. He stayed to himself. All these lectures from Mamaw—she'd just drill us with all these old sayings. We wouldn't get any of that stuff from him. It was, "Come on out here and make yourself useful. Feed these chickens." The farm was very active. Cow pasture, plenty of chickens. I would watch the wringing of the chicken's neck. And then he'd chop the head off on the block. And he'd put it right in the scalding water. Then Mamaw'd go plucking. The whole house smelled like bird. It was chicken for the next day or two.

JASON STEWART: George was big on his breeding roosters, because he was an egg farmer. That's what he did after he moved here. And George loved the cockfighting.

SHANNON ASHBURN: I'd always go in the back of their yard where all their rooster pens were and, man, I used to get my ass *beat*. You were not allowed to go back there, 'cause Papaw had fightin' roosters. Me and my cousins would sneak back there and get in trouble. I'll never forget the time I got attacked by one of Papaw's fightin' roosters. He jumped on my back and pecked me all on my head and everything and I couldn't get him off...that was the last time I went back there.

TRAMPAS STEWART: Papaw was the only one who could pick 'em up. I know he gouged his eye out once, feeding the chickens.

GREG STEWART: My dad would fight his chickens and win a lotta times. He had some good chickens. He'd sell 'em to guys in South America, that's how good they were. He'd take them in the house and put 'em right on his lap. He would talk to them, even. And that chicken would listen to what he said. He took care of them chickens like they was his kids.

GAIL STEWART: He'd bring them roosters in the Florida room, he'd be goin' back 'n' forth with them and Momma'd get mad. She let him have his little time with 'em, but enough's enough. "Got to go, buddy, put 'em back!"

GINA STEWART: Me and Grandal did the fights with Daddy. And my boyfriend at the time, Walter Carlton. That's all he lived for. Walter won Southeasternship down in Louisiana, then got invited to Hawaii. We won first place there, then we got invited to the Philippines, but the bets were $10,000 minimum. It was like, "Nope, let's go home with the money."

KIM CARLTON (Walter's daughter): They went to Costa Rica, they went to Manila, they went to a bunch of different places all over the world, fightin' those damn cocks. George taught my dad the chicken fighting trade, got him involved in the breeding and how to check for a good chicken. My dad started raising them because it was easier than goin' into jail. Cockfighting became illegal in the state of Florida. He was still going to Louisiana because they did not outlaw it there.

TOMMY SCHWARTZ: I've been to plenty cockfights. Every Sunday over there north of town at the Draughtys'. Buster Draughty, the old man, he's gone now. He and his wife had a little bitty trailer thing, she cooked and sold hamburgers. There was a tin roof, and some bales of hay around for the cockfight. There would be probably twenty, twenty-five people there. One of them was a judge, Judge DeFriest. I can see his face, because everybody was always afraid. Whenever he bet out there, some people would be...standoffish about betting. But he was just goin', y'know. Nobody ever got busted for the chicken fights in this town.

NICK STEWART: I remember watching these grown men, half of 'em I think were direct descendants of the Hatfields and McCoys. Kentuckians and crackers, fightin' these chickens. Fort Pierce was a bad place back then, y'know, and they were all standing around gambling. And fightin' these chickens. And they would move from one area to another, from one ranch to another, because obviously it was highly illegal. They had it very organized.

TRAMPAS STEWART: It was all fenced off, and everybody went, got seats and sat there and watched. I didn't know that it was illegal. And we'd see the joy out of everybody, and the anguish, and it was just like a scene out of a painting, where everybody's having a damn good time. It seemed so official that we thought, "This is a normal thing." But now I look back...

JASON STEWART: In the beginning, it was like, blacks and whites. Back then things were separated—they kept their side, we kept our side, but everybody got along. There were arguments and stuff, but no guns would come out. A little later on the Hispanic people started to come around, because they were working in the agriculture in the citrus more, like in the '80s. So they started to get more involved in it. That's when things started to get a little hectic. In the beginning, it was all good ol' boys, and then it started to turn more into, like, Mexicans would be the ones that were dominating. And I think a new sheriff got elected. Then it pretty much got squashed.

TRAMPAS STEWART: It went on for like three or four hours. They would never last longer than that. Everybody dismantles and gets the hell out of there. They'd have drums placed here and there for all the victims. We probably went four or five times, Papaw never had to dump a rooster in one of those bins. He always came back with his rooster.

GINA STEWART: We put slashers on 'em. Spurs. And boxing gloves. Grandal still has some of Daddy's spurs.

TRAMPAS STEWART: There's a certain way they run the chickens up on each other to get them all excited. They've got these long spikes, hooked to the back of their ankle, turned upwards. And they will fight to the death.

JASON STEWART: Red roundhead roosters, those were George's prizefighters. He brought them from Kentucky. The only way to breed strong birds is to have the strongest bird. If you want to make the perfect specimen of a bull, you're gonna go and get the strongest bull and use the semen from that, and it's the same with the bird. You want to have the strongest bird. The only way you can find out what the strongest bird is by which one has the most kids, y'know?

GREG STEWART: Daddy had one he called Champ. Because he'd won ten fights. In one of them fights, he lost his eye, the chicken did.

GINA STEWART: He was a big-time winner. A friend of Garna's painted Champ on one of Gary's Les Paul guitars. Gary eventually gave it to me...but then Gary eventually borrowed it back.

GARY STEWART: I can tell you cockfightin' stories...I was about eight or nine years old when Daddy borrowed this big-time rooster from Old Man Johnson. I mean he was a stud. To breed with some of Daddy's chickens. Daddy had him penned up and we had one of our ol' game roosters outside and the damn ol' rooster beat the shit out of him, killed him. The old man, he came home and he was so mad that he took our chicken and wrung his neck. Later he thought, "What a hell of a chicken! *That* was the Champ!"

TOMMY SCHWARTZ: They cut the combs off of the bird so they can't be snatched by the other chicken. They cut the comb and wattle off, anything that another chicken can grab and hold on to they cut off with a pair of scissors when they're young.

Chicken fighters are kind of like witch doctors. Chicken fighters will lie to each other more than anybody else. They're all telling each other what their secret is to raising chickens and they're making it up, trying to screw the other person up by trying to get them to do the wrong thing, tellin' 'em things to screw his chickens up. They'll all be best buddies, but they ain't going to give up any secrets, man.

KIM CARLTON: The last one to peck wins. Chicken's laying there dead, if it pecked last, it won.

NICK STEWART: As a little boy in there I'm watchin' these grown, badass men, they're blowing air up into the asses of these chickens, holding them up like a loaf of bread. And they're trying to revive 'em.

And they're going FOO FOO FOO blowing into the ass of these chickens. Obviously they weren't gonna make it. And then they would throw them all in big piles.

GREG STEWART: They'd be barrels of chickens, dead. Three or four fifty-five-gallon drums of dead chickens.

KIM CARLTON: George was pitting chickens 'til probably the day he died.

TOMMY SCHWARTZ: Ol' George even looked a lot like them chickens. In the face he looked like an old rooster. I liked George. George was a funny guy. He was a good guy. A smart guy.

TRAMPAS STEWART: I smoked a joint with Papaw. Probably about three months before he died. I was trying to instruct him how it could help him with his appetite, because he wouldn't eat. But he smoked it with me. And I seen him smile. He was definitely smiling and laughing and joking with us. So I don't think I obliviated him.

FAMILY FRIEND: The story was that Georgia beat the ol' man. This was after they thought George was gonna die. He went and did his confession with the preacher and, in front of Georgia, confessed to having an indiscretion. What I heard was that she went home and beat George!

2

LONG WAY OUT OF THIS HOLLER

Proud of where I come from – Letcher County, Kentucky. I am from over here, over there, and over yonder, y'know?

– Gary Stewart

"I was born on May 28, 1944 in Dunham, Kentucky, a holler[9] in Letcher County, Kentucky," wrote Gary Stewart in a scribbled autobiography on record-label stationery found among his papers. "My father was a coal miner in Center City Row, a coal mining camp. I was raised on a mother's love, soup beans, corn bread and taters." Gary loved

9 Some say Appalachia was created when Africa collided with North America back in the day, folding and buckling the land into mountain ridges separated by narrow valleys. Ensuing uplift and erosion left a zillion smaller ones known as hollers, often accessed, according to Facebook group "The Appalachian Project," by "a road with no painted lines, and residences dotting either side of the road." "A holler has a head and a mouth," adds the Whitesburg, Kentucky, newspaper *The Mountain Eagle*. "The head is as far as you can go, and the mouth is where the creek runs into a larger stream of water." "The Appalachian Project" points out that a holler "also has plenty of eyes, because if you happen to be a stranger driving up or down the holler, someone has more than likely taken notice."

Kentucky, loved being from Appalachia, and always spoke fondly of the state (as opposed to the city of Nashville, which he seemed less than fond of). "I still dream about it," he told me in 1987.

It's not easy to get to Gary's old stomping grounds in Letcher County. Lexington, the closest airport, is nearly three hours away, and the entire drive is spent dodging pickups and semis on two-lane highways threaded through a maze of forested hills with massive blocks of rock poking through. It's a place of unruly, prehistoric beauty that feels stitched tight to the earth. You have to be resilient simply to survive in some of these tiny, isolated towns, with little more than a Dollar General every ten miles or so for snacks and shampoo, in a state scarred by decades of exploitation by powerful coal companies and prescription drug monoliths. As of 2024, Kentucky was the sixth-poorest state in the nation, with 16.61 percent living below the poverty line. Kentuckians know a thing or two about raw deals.

Kentucky. Say it aloud and it sounds like a plucked banjo. Kentuckians have their own ways of doing and even saying things, like "hotter than a whore's doorknob on dollar day." I'd paint the ones I've met in the muted tones of Edward Hopper. Kentuckians do not seem to come in neon colors. Little Richard isn't from Kentucky. Bill Monroe is. The Bluegrass State has produced a multitude of towering music figures, many from the hills where Gary Stewart was born. "In eastern Kentucky, everybody plays music," explained Sturgill Simpson. "It's never something you ever think for a second growing up, 'Oh, I can do this for a living.' It's what you do after work." Visualize these faces floating across a map of the state alongside Stewart, Monroe, and Simpson: Loretta Lynn, David "Stringbean" Akeman, Keith Whitley, Patty Loveless, the Everly Brothers, the Osborne Brothers, Emma Smith, Dwight Yoakam, Jackie DeShannon, Tom T. Hall, Grandpa Jones, J. D. Crowe, Skeeter Davis, Rosemary Clooney, Lionel Hampton, the Judds—along with many others known and unknown. Larry Flynt, Warren Oates, Tod Browning, Edgar Cayce? Kentuckians. Iconoclastic, independent characters all, dead serious about their work. Kentuckians don't kid around.

That includes crime. Weeks before I arrived in Letcher County in October 2024, it had been all over national news. Over in Whitesburg, the county seat, Sheriff Shawn "Mickey" Stines shot District Judge Kevin Mullins. In his chambers, point blank, killing him.

* * *

"The thing that I found most striking about mountain people over the years is their extreme honesty and willingness to say what they think, and to listen," said Thomas E. Gish, editor of *The Mountain Eagle,* the venerable Letcher County newspaper. I found this to be true of the Stewarts, although you had to know what questions to ask.

The Stewarts were (and remain) a striking, slightly cantankerous bunch. One family genealogist hints at murder and other foul deeds that have gone unrecounted, claiming many a secret has been taken to the grave (in true Stewart fashion, he angrily refused my request to quote from his privately printed book on the subject). The family has had its "idiosyncrasies," admitted Nick Stewart, one of Gary's cousins. He recounted how one aunt refused to speak to her husband for twenty years due to his womanizing. "I witnessed that myself when I was a kid. It seemed so strange. She would communicate through her kids. She'd say, 'Go tell your Daddy supper's ready.' She lived with him, but never spoke to him again. 'Til the day she died."

The Stewart clan in America can be traced back to John Stewart, said to have been born in 1667 in Charleston, Massachusetts. His father, Alexander, a Scottish immigrant, had been captured by English troops in the Battle of Dunbar and held as a POW before being sent to Massachusetts as an indentured servant.[10] Son John found work as a cooper (maker of wooden barrels) before becoming a physician and then a surgeon. The Stewart clan would migrate into Delaware, North Carolina, and Kentucky.

10 There is a lot of conflicting information concerning John Stewart and where he was born (some claim Scotland). I expect requests for corrections, and they are welcome. Alexander played bagpipes and was a chief piper in the Highland Clan.

In recent years it has come to light that the Stewarts are related by marriage to the frontiersman Daniel Boone. John Stewart's great-grandson, also named John,[11] had wedded Boone's sister, Hannah, then accompanied Daniel on a 1769 expedition into Kentucky. In the seventh month of the trip Native Americans absconded with their horses and gear. Boone and Stewart snuck into the Shawnee settlement and reclaimed their steeds, making a clean getaway.

But the Shawnees caught up with them the next day. As Boone recounted in the 1856 biography *The Life of Daniel Boone*, "a number of Indians rushed out of a thick canebrake upon us, and made us prisoners....The Indians plundered us of what we had, and kept us in confinement for seven days, treating us with common savage usage." The Shawnee took them to Ohio, where Boone and Stewart managed to escape. On a later Kentucky trip Boone and Stewart split up to check their trap lines on either side of the Kentucky River. Boone returned, but Stewart did not. Remnants of a fire were found with John Stewart's initials carved into a nearby tree, but he was never seen again (his skeleton was later found in the hollow of a sycamore tree). Boone blamed his disappearance on the Shawnee.

"I returned home to my family, with a determination to bring them as soon as possible to live in Kentucky, which I esteemed a second paradise," said Boone. Apparently some Stewarts felt the same way. By the early 1800s the family began to settle in the Bluegrass State, as there is a record of one Thomas Stewart Jr. marrying in Floyd, Kentucky. A son from this union, Isaac (known as "Blind Ike"), is said to be the first Stewart born in Kentucky. Blind Ike was a blacksmith and the father of ten children. The Stewarts worked as tradesmen, store owners, and midwives. In the late 1800s the railroad came to eastern Kentucky, which would spur explosive growth in the coal mining industry, providing jobs for many of the Stewart men.

George Robert Stewart, Gary's father, was born December 26, 1919, in Etsy, Kentucky. His parents were Harlan McClellen ("Clell")

11 John was the seventh son of Samuel Stewart, who named two of his sons John. The Stewart lineage is a convoluted one.

and Easter Stewart, who were second cousins (given the remoteness of the area at the time, this was not uncommon).[12] The couple, who were illiterate, had nine children and lived in McRoberts, Kentucky, in a small, former coal-company house heated by woodstove with no indoor plumbing. The boys slept upstairs while Clell and Easter slept in the living room with their daughters and, at times, a grandmother. Clell loaded and cleaned coal cars, which paid $9 a day. They shopped at a company store using scrip—private currency issued every payday that was redeemable only at the company store.

Pictures of George and his four brothers show wiry, handsome mountain men with spare, sculpted faces favoring oversized ears and noses. A. P. Carter would've fit right in with this bunch. According to his brother Bill, George was "a nice fella, not feisty. We all were fighters. George was more peaceful, didn't want to start nuthin', being the oldest one. He took care of the rest of us."

"They were poor boys out of Kentucky," said Bill's son, Nick. "And they all used the military to get out. That's what saved them, kept them from the coal mines." Jake Stewart, another brother, lasted one week in the mines. "That was all I needed," he said. Bill had also given mining a go when he was a teen. He'd tell his son Nick he "would come home from the coal mines, sleep in a chair backwards in front of the fire until daylight, then work all night in the mines. It was a horrible life." Bill described working in a mine so narrow you had to "lay down on your side next to two other guys and shovel the coal into a car. It was tough—too tough for a sixteen-year-old. But George went right on through with it. George loaded more coal than anybody else up there in Jenkins for a while. He was a workin' son of a gun."

"He'd go work eight hours, come home, eat, go work eight hours," said Gary. "Working man. Sometimes it would be seldom that I'd see him. He loved work as much as I love picking and singing." George

12 This little fact provided endless ammo for Gary Stewart's wife Mary Lou. "Every time she'd get mad at Gary," said family friend Jimmy Smith, "she'd yell, 'You inbred motherfucker!'"

George (seventh from left) with other employees from Consolidated Coal, Jenkins, Kentucky, 1929. McClellen "Clell" Stewart is fourteenth in line. (Shannon Ashburn collection)

began working at age sixteen. "My dad introduced him to the mines, and George took over," said Bill. George boasted that he was "one of the best operators that Consolidation Coal Company had. They gave me steak suppers, mining caps, I don't know what all."

George would eventually leave Consolidation to operate a few small mines of his own, selling the coal to Consolidation and others. "He'd lease the land and then he'd go in and work it," said his son Grandal, who helped. These smaller mines were known as truck mines, as the coal was hauled away in trucks to a tipple, where it was loaded onto train cars. George would use "timber from a sawmill or a tree to shore up the mine," said Jake Stewart. "They laid track to roll the buggy that carried the coal and built a chute that would load the coal into a two-ton truck. George'd go in and drill holes in the coal and put dynamite down those holes with a fuse on it. After the coal was blown out, they'd shovel it out. He had ponies that would pull the cart out." Some of his brothers occasionally worked for George in his mines, but it didn't always go well. When his brother Charlie failed to unhook a pony, it got pulled down the coal chute. "George got so mad," said Bill. "Charlie said, 'It was gonna break my arm!' George said, 'Your arm will heal. We'll probably have to shoot the damn pony.'"

George would do most of his mining around Letcher County, Kentucky, part of the Elkhorn coalfield, one of the most productive in the state. Mining coal was a harsh endeavor run by overlords with an iron grip. "The companies that mined the coal owned all the mining communities, the company towns, the streets, the houses, the hospitals," noted Letcher County author Harry M. Caudill. "This created a population that was totally dependent." The companies erected rows of spartan, lookalike houses along unpaved roads. Pay was low, the work was dispiriting and dangerous, and if a miner died, his wife would have to vacate the company home so a new worker could move in. Caudill brought national focus to the region with his shocking 1962 exposé *Night Comes to the Cumberlands: A Biography of a Depressed Area,* which laid bare the desperate poverty of the area as well as its exploitation by mining companies, which, he'd point out, were bankrolled from outside of the state. This led to federal aid to the area, not to mention much media attention, which some saw as further exploitation.

In 1967 a Letcher County landlord named Hobart Ison shot and killed English filmmaker Hugh O'Connor, who had been interviewing one of Ison's coal-miner renters about life in one of Ison's $10-a-month shacks. Ison resented the media being there and was unapologetic for the killing. Many of his neighbors supported him. When he was arrested, "the courthouse was full of people who wanted to go his bond," claimed one relative. The first trial ended in a hung jury. Ison pleaded guilty to involuntary manslaughter, got a ten-year sentence, and was paroled after one. While all of this happened after the Stewarts had left the area, Gary understood the suspicion of outsiders many Kentuckians felt. You can hear it in his wryly menacing number "Easy People": "For your own sake, son, I hope you ain't the law / It's a long way out of this holler, and you just might get lost."

* * *

While still in his teens George met a small, striking, raven-haired girl. Georgia Niece had been born March 18, 1923, one of at least eight children. The Nieces were "spunky," according to Trampas Stewart, one of the family genealogists. "That side of the family has got a lot of fierceness. They just had spice, a lot more than the Stewart side. That's where Gary gets his itch."

Jasper "Hoss" Niece, Georgia's father, was an intricate, colorful character, married six (some say seven) times. "Grandpa, he was a rounder," said Gary's brother Grandal. "Grandpa would fight at the drop of a hat. He was full of damn beans." Hoss was known as a trader, "a small-time wheeler-dealer," said Brenda Casey, another family genealogist. According to Casey, at some point Hoss operated a general store. "He got into financial trouble during the Depression because he gave so much credit to people. People would come into the store to get food and he couldn't turn them away. He hid a shoebox full of IOUs. He lost a lot of money doing that."

Niece was a big fan of professional wrestling and was once arrested after jumping into the ring to slip a shiv to a wrestler he favored. A natty dresser, Hoss always wore a suit and hat. And played the banjo. There are many other notable characters in the Niece family, including an Aunt Eveline, who "shot her husband in the crotch," according to Brenda. Another ancestor fought for the Union in Kentucky's 39th Infantry during the Civil War (a relative on the Stewart side of the family fought for the Union as well).

Casey maintained that the Nieces' roots are Scottish, Scots-Irish, Welsh, and English with a dash of Scandinavian. But no Native American ancestry. That piqued my curiosity, since Gary had boasted to several reporters of his indigenous roots. "Everybody says they got it in 'em, y'know," he told me. "I can trace it back. Cherokee on my mother's side." One day Gary prodded Georgia to tell me the story. She spoke of a great-grandfather who lived in the North Carolina hills behind a doorway of rocks. "He was an Indian chief," Georgia said with glee. "Cherokee Indian. He wore that big long headdress. And they lived in them caves, hunted a lot and raised animals to eat. He kept that first fifty cents that he ever made. He had it in a fruit jar."

Nice story, but when I asked Gary's relatives about their Native American blood there were a lot of blank stares. Brenda Casey filled me in. "That's a myth that sprang from a picture of my great-great-grandfather. He had on a huge Indian headdress that came all the way down to the floor on both sides. The piece of paper that came with the picture said that he helped to free the slaves." Casey says other relatives informed her that he was just posing in the headdress for effect. "My family's all been DNA tested. There's no Indian blood."

Georgia's family would scatter following the death of her mother Kate in 1933, "shortly after giving birth," according to Casey. Georgia was ten. "When she died, the kids went to different places." As she later recalled, for a while Georgia "stayed a lot with my grandpa and grandma. Back in them days they was real wealthy. I never seen them take a pill in their life. They done things by the moons. They used herbs." Another wealthy family took Georgia in, and she worked as their maid.

George and Georgia met in church, although Georgia was quick to point out he'd actually sat down behind her with another girl he was interested in. Georgia would tell her grandson Trampas about George walking the long distance to her house to pick her up for their first date. When a man offered him a ride, George told him of his plans to marry this girl Georgia. "This guy says, 'Oh, I know all about that girl. You don't want to meet that girl. This girl, boy, she's got some stories behind her. And I can tell you a few.' George immediately grew upset, snapping, 'You ain't gonna tell me a damn thing about this girl. She's the love of my life, and I won't hear none of it. You can just drop me off right here.' Well, that guy turned out to be Georgia's dad!"

Hoss was so "amazed at his defense of Georgia that he went ahead and let George date his daughter." The couple married January 22, 1938, in Whitesburg, Kentucky. "He was seventeen, I was fourteen," said Georgia. "I weighed 98 pounds, he was 140." George was drafted into non-wartime duty for the army, the only one of his brothers not to volunteer. It didn't last long. "He went into the service and liked to have died," said Georgia. "I had to get him out. He just couldn't stay away from home!" Stewart got a dependency discharge at age twenty-one.

The couple moved to Pound, Virginia, just across the border from Kentucky, where George worked in the mines and Georgia gave birth to her first two children—Glenna Sue in 1940 and Greta Joe in 1942. On December 16, 1943, came tragedy. According to what Georgia told sister-in-law Louise Hudson, she was out in the smokehouse "takin' that thread out of feed sacks—people used it for material then." George had gone "over to Pound to pick up the kids' stuff that they had laid away for Christmas," said Hudson. When Georgia came out of the smokehouse, the house was on fire with her two little ones inside. According to Brenda Casey, when help arrived, Georgia "was trying to get in the house to get her girls out, and they had to hold her back." Both children died in the blaze. Glenna Sue was two and a half, Greta Joe one and a half. Their lamb-topped gravestone, adorned by a small picture of each child, is inscribed, "Gone to be Angels."[13]

Georgia was pregnant with Gary at the time. Eerily, he would be found dead on the same date sixty years later. "There was a lot of tragedy with that family," said longtime family friend Stan Spence. "A lot of heartbreak."

---

13 Georgia rarely spoke of the deaths, and according to some, when she did, it was with a certain vitriol. "I've heard Momma run her mouth about blamin' it on Daddy," said Grandal. "She claimed that Daddy built the fire too big in the fireplace and run off down the road with some girl. When she'd get mad at him, she'd bring that up—'You set that fire too hot, run off with some whore—and I lost my younguns.'" Whether there is any truth to this claim is anyone's guess.

Georgia, George, and baby Gary. (Shannon Ashburn collection)

George and Georgia moved to Dunham, a small mining town built by Consolidation Coal, where they lived in a company house. It was there in Dunham that Gary Ronald Stewart was born on May 28, 1944. According to Grandal, who arrived two years later, he and Gary were both born at home. "Half of the siblings were born at home instead of at a hospital." Georgia named the new son after her favorite movie star, Gary Cooper. Being the first child to arrive after the loss of her first two, Gary would have a special place in his mother's heart. While Grandal would go into the mines with his father at age nine, Gary would not. "I've never been in a coal mine," he said. "I don't know what I could do in there, except maybe holler, 'Take a break, boys, quittin' time!'"

"Dad and me were a team, Gary and Mom were a team," said Grandal. "And I'd do most of the work. Since he was a mama's boy, Mommy let him get away with bullshit. Gary was into that damn music. He wasn't into workin'." Grandal recalled Gary getting a job weeding for a neighbor as a teenager. After ten minutes he came home. "I quit!" he muttered to Grandal. "You do it!"

* * *

When Gary was four the Stewarts moved to nearby Jenkins, a larger, once-bustling town not far from the Kentucky-Virginia border at the base of Pine Mountain. "A City Built on Coal" reads the sign that greets visitors. "It should read 'A City Built on the Backs of Miners,'" counters former resident Tommy Anderson. Many Jenkins old-timers reject such criticisms. "Our family is for coal," one inhabitant told me. "It sent me to college."

Consolidation Coal built the town in 1911, naming it after a company director. They built a thousand homes in the area to house workers. "See, there were no coal miners here," said local author Ked Sanders. "These were woodsman, people who lived off the land. So they had to get workers from all over—all the way down to Mississippi and the African Americans down there, and the Eastern Europeans coming in to New York at Ellis Island looking for a job. They'd say, 'Right, here's your train ticket to Jenkins, Kentucky. There's a job waiting on you down there, a new house, and a company store. You can get credit there.'"

By the time Gary's family moved to Jenkins, "it was a big modern thing," said Ernie Elkins, who grew up with the Stewarts. "A booming place. Streets and all that stuff. They had professional boxers!" According to Elkins, Jenkins had three high schools—"a white high school, a black high school, and a Catholic high school." There was a movie house in town, the Jenkins Theatre. Elkins added, "The white set in the bottom and the black set in the top."

The Stewarts settled in an area called Payne Gap, "along the Kentucky River," according to Elkins. "They called it a two-lane road, but you had to pull over in the gravel to let somebody by." Back in that holler, the Stewarts had a three-bedroom house. "We had fifteen acres up there, on the side of a mountain in the backyard," said Grandal. "We owned all the way to the top of the mountain." One of the kids would have to run up the mountainside to pull in different channels on the family TV. A stream that ran through the property was "the beginning of the Kentucky River," said Elkins. They bathed in the creek and there was an outhouse on the property where they'd "wipe their asses with the Sears and Roebuck catalog," as Gary's brother Garna put it. Georgia would have seven more children by the time the family left Kentucky, and two more after that. "I spent my youth fighting, playing, and loving eight brothers and sisters," wrote Gary. Some felt "fighting" was at the top of that list when it came to his brothers. "They'd get out there and fist-fight like it was a boxing match," said Terry Porter, a friend of the family in later years. They did not battle the matriarch of the family, however. "Those boys all respected their mommy," said family friend Lee Schwartz.

"Georgia was a small lady, but she was tough," said Elkins, who wound up on the receiving end of her discipline after busting Grandal in the nose. "When she put the rod down, the kids got in line. She could line up Mr. George, too. I loved her because she was so good to the children." The Stewarts "were just happy people," said Elkins, who felt they were no poorer or richer than anyone else in Jenkins. "We all just got by. Happy as a lark, but we just got by. Things were pretty tough."

"We never went to the store too often," said Georgia. "We had a big basement downstairs. I would can about seven hundred cans of food. We raised our own potatoes and had chickens for eggs." They'd drive into nearby Wise, Virginia, in apple season, putting twenty bushels in the basement. Gary recalled his chores as being "carrying the coal for a fire, feeding chickens and hogs, washing diapers for the new baby."

The family attended a Baptist church down the road, and the children went to Payne Gap School, a three-room affair that taught grades one through eight. "My children was not allowed to stay at home, not one day that they was sick," said Georgia. According to Grandal, they wanted Gary to skip fourth grade, but his mother nixed the idea. "Gary was smart," she told me proudly. "He was a quiet guy," added Ernie. "Me and Grandal were more like mountain men." Gary was a dreamer who had no interest in sports. "Gary never played a baseball game in his life," said Grandal. "He was not an athletic person at all. Too much trouble."

What was there to do in Jenkins for fun? Not much. According to Ernie, you played sports or you "chased girls. Gary and Grandal and I spent some of our time chasin' those little girls at the Pentecostal church."[14] The believers within were serpent-handlers. "I went in one day, front row. They got the snakes out, I didn't go back. I said, 'It's over, boys!!!'" For pocket money, Grandal and Gary would sell vegetables and wood—one neighbor, Mrs. Hopkins, gave them twenty-five cents a bushel. "Me an' Gary an' Ernie would go up in them woods, drag logs back to the house, and chop the wood up to get money for the picture show," said Grandal, who recalled walking down the hill into town to the Jenkins Theatre with Gary to see Elvis in *Love Me Tender*.

* * *

In the early part of the 1950s, George was badly hurt in a mining accident. He'd been working a vein with a narrow, twenty-seven-inch opening, one man on either side of him, when it collapsed. "I was down on my knees and the top fell on me, six tons of coal." Grandal, who was with Georgia when it happened, recalled that "Mommy had a baby in her arms, one of the siblings. She threw that baby on a pile of clothes that was in the corner and went to the hospital." The accident broke his hip, leaving George in a body cast for nine months and disabling him for life. "He had operations and operations," said his sister Louise Hudson.[15]

Georgia worked selling Watkins products until George was back on his feet, walking with the aid of crutches. No longer able to toil in the mines, George became a field salesman for Watkins, selling pain medication, vanilla extract, herbs, and spices. Grandal accompanied his father, selling candy bars to the kids they encountered on their routes. "We'd load that ol' '48 Chrysler up with them products and go door to door."

* * *

14 As Grandal pointed out, there were countless churches in the area. "Up there in Kentucky, they'd have church under a damn tree."

15 Shortly before George's accident, George took his family with him as he checked on his mine, and a couple of the children were climbing the coal transporting system. "Two of the babies went down the chute," said Louise Hudson. "It's a wonder they didn't get killed."

Right about here, music enters the picture. Where does the music come from in the Stewart family? On Gary's father's side, there isn't much to go on outside of John Stewart playing the bagpipes and one infamous relative: Abraham Stewart. Abe Stewart (1907–1958) is regarded as "the one who may have started the music in us," as a relative wrote in a Facebook post. Abraham, a three-fingered guitar and banjo player who had spent time in jail over a bogus moonshine charge, worked for Consolidation Coal and "was a preacher on the side for a spell." Abe "walked everywhere he went, always wore white pressed shirts." He also drank heavily.

Jake Stewart, Gary's uncle, recalls meeting Abraham in Detroit. According to Jake, Abe had that high lonesome Kentucky sound. All these decades later Jake could still recite the lyrics to a prison ballad Abe sang for him.[16] Abraham "drifted around," said Jake, who thought he was in Detroit "as a session picker." Abraham Stewart would be found dead in a ditch by the side of a Kentucky road in 1958.

On the maternal side, Gary's grandfather Hoss played the banjo, and Georgia told me that guitar-toting gospel shouter Martha Carson, also born in Letcher County, was a distant relative. Georgia would confess to me that she felt she had missed her calling when it came to singing. "I love music better'n anything in the world. I had to work all my life, so I couldn't do what I wanted. I got married too young, because when I was young I could *really* sing. I sang a few places. In school I got up and done programs." Georgia sang in a trio that got together every Friday. "We was the singers for the whole community—they done the playin', I did the singin'. I'd have been in heaven if I had me a guitar. That was my biggest wish in the world when I was a teenager. Children without a mother, they don't get things like guitars."

16 Family legend has it that Abe wrote "Man of Constant Sorrow," the haunting ballad made famous by Ralph Stanley and others, then sold it to someone else who took credit. This is highly unlikely, as this traditional number was first published as "Farewell Song" by Dick Burnett in 1913, when Abraham was five, while others date variations of the song back before that. Stanley himself, who recorded the song in 1950 with his brother Carter, said that he first heard the song as a little boy, and he felt it was "probably two or three hundred years old."

While Georgia may have been unable to achieve her dream as a music maker, she certainly influenced Gary as a passionate listener. She reeled off a long list of favorite artists, including George Jones, Loretta Lynn, the Stanley Brothers, Fats Domino, Willie Nelson, the Hager Brothers, Emmylou Harris, and local favorites the Cooke Duet (later the Singing Cookes). She had reservations about Elvis ("I like some of it" was the best Georgia could muster) and could gossip about local favorites like Bill and Charlie Monroe ("They was both in love with the same girl, and one of them got the woman"). She spoke at length about buying one particular album and how she "played that record for a whole day, over and over and over. George was goin' to the chicken fights and I was there by myself. I never took that record off. I played that record and cried all day. That's how I like to play music, when I'm by myself and I can hear every word. Then I get all the meanin's and stories behind it." The death of Hank Williams in 1953 hit Georgia hard. "We were all around the damn radio listening," said Grandal. "Mama lost it."

* * *

To hear Gary tell it, he practically burst out of the womb singing and playing. "I was small enough to climb inside one of those big Philco stand-up radio jobs singing and talking like a deejay. That's my earliest memory of music." He made a fake guitar "out of cardboard and a stick, at five or six years old." The first song that really grabbed him was Hank Thompson's 1953 country novelty hit "Rub-A-Dub-Dub," and the first number Gary remembered singing in public was "In the Pines," which he'd learned by way of Bill Monroe. At age eleven, he was absolutely transfixed hearing Jerry Lee Lewis belt out "Whole Lot of Shakin' Going On" over a carny loudspeaker while at a Jenkins fair. Lewis, along with the Allman Brothers, were the two influences Gary would name most in interviews.

Grandal and Gary would learn to harmonize singing in church with their mother. One song they all knew: "There Ain't No Grave Gonna Hold My Body Down," a thundering gospel number by

Pentecostal Holiness preacher Brother Claude Ely. A grinning gospel shouter in a white hat, built like a block of ice and sporting a gold tooth, Ely hosted *The Gospel Ranger Show*, a fifteen-minute radio program broadcast on WTCW in Whitesburg, Kentucky. "There Ain't No Grave" was "the theme song of his little show," Grandal recalled. According to Gary, this was before local radio "really started playin' records—the talent came from around the hills." According to his great-nephew (and biographer), Macel Ely II, Claude had written the song at age twelve when he was dying of tuberculosis and "forced to stare death directly in the face." A former coal miner, Ely lived in Letcher County for a time, performing at camp meetings for the miners. "He would put everything into it when he sang," said witness Raymond Williams. "You could hear him three streets down...he could really belt it out."

King Records recorded "There Ain't No Grave" during a Pentecostal service at the Letcher County courthouse in October 1953, with Ely "roaring his way through as if he had a Bible in one hand and a snake in the other," as John Clarke wrote. Gary absolutely loved the song, proudly recounting how he'd finally tracked down an original copy of the King 45, buying it from Mrs. Cora Whitaker, the kindly proprietor of Whitaker Music Shop in Jenkins. He broke into the number on many occasions when I was around, performing it with an intensity that would've given pause to Brother Claude himself. One time, on the way to catch a train with Georgia up in the front seat and Gary in the back with an acoustic, he coaxed his mother into singing it, then leapt in on harmony, quickly adjusting the key to suit her high lonesome sound. Music from the hills! Thrilling.

Gary's first public performances were at the Payne Gap School. "Some of my fondest memories are of school in Payne Gap," he wrote, noting how his class decorated a Christmas tree they'd taken from the woods, "drawing names for gifts." He recalled drinking spring water from a "rock bucket drain" out of a cold spring, using "a paper cup we made from writing paper."

Best of all was "the Friday afternoon shows where all three grades would gather in one big room and make a list of who would get onstage and do what he or she did best—like asking a riddle, reciting a poem, or singing a song. There were solos, duets and trios," wrote Stewart. "Kids in Kentucky loved to sing—and they could sing."

Three of these singers were Gary, Grandal, and Ernie Elkins, who'd impersonate stars for their classmates. Ernie was Little Jimmy Dickens; Gary appeared as Ray Price, Faron Young, and Webb Pierce; while Grandal was Elvis.[17] "We would switch out being Elvis—we could only be Elvis one out of every three weeks," noted Ernie.

* * *

Naturally, Gary wanted a guitar, and his parents didn't have the funds to buy one. Until Lady Luck intervened. A few weeks before Christmas around 1955, Georgia was talking to the lady who owned the Jenkins hardware store. She admitted to the shop owner that it was going to be a meager Christmas as George had been unable to work due to his mining accident. "She said, 'What do your children want?' I said, 'Well, I got a little boy, he wants a guitar so bad.' She says, 'You've got a whole lot of things that I want for my children for Christmas, let's just trade some.' And I got Gary the guitar, Griselda a watch, and Grandal a BB gun. She had everything that my children wanted!" (According to Gary, some of George's Watkins products were "borrowed" to make the trade.) Although Grandal had wanted a mandolin, he got the BB gun instead—it was Gary who got the Sears Silvertone guitar.

"Oh, it was a nice guitar!" Georgia enthused. "Real pretty. Gary took it to a man and he tuned it. And Gary never did need no more help. He started off a-playin'! Gary worked on that guitar every time

17 Georgia said Gary's big impersonation was Faron Young. And that Grandal was so good as Presley that when they moved to Fort Pierce, the kids "didn't know his name was Grandal, they all called him Elvis." Friends at the time thought Grandal was the musical star of the family. "Honestly, I thought Grandal had more talent than Gary," said neighbor Gary Gallant. "He would just hit the bus stop and sing Elvis stuff. The girls loved him."

he didn't have to work! And the first song he ever learned to play was 'Go, Johnny, Go' [Chuck Berry's "Johnny B. Goode"]. Gary just sat down and picked it out. I went somewhere, and when I come back he was goin' to town on it, y'know!" (By Gary's memory the first song he learned was "I'll Go Stepping Too" by Lester Flatt and Earl Scruggs. He would discount the value of any of his guitar playing in Kentucky, saying he only got serious once he got to Florida. "I didn't know how to tune it. I needed some more strings, but we didn't have the money to get 'em.")

Grandal was somewhat less impressed with Gary's new obsession. "Momma told us to clean the bathrooms; I was in there cleanin' and Gary was out there bangin' on that guitar instead of helpin' me. Momma told both of us to do it. I took his guitar and busted it all to hell. So Gary took my damn bicycle and busted all my spokes out."

It was around this time that members of the Stewart clan began migrating to the redneck Riveria - Florida. In 1954 George's sister Susie and her husband Bill Potter had moved down so Bill could clear some land for a Jenkins doctor who ownedproperty in Stuart, Florida. Clell and Easter soon followed, settling in White City. "My parents, bein' illiterate, couldn't get no jobs," said Bill Stewart. (Others say they went seeking relief for Clell's black lung disease or to keep their homesick daughter Susie company.) So they headed south, with more Stewarts to follow. Bill Stewart, who'd founded a trucking company, said he was the one who talked George and Georgia, two of the last holdouts, to move down. "Daddy went into the trucking business, haulin' asphalt and dirt, and that's what brought us to Florida, because all his brothers and sisters were in Fort Pierce," said Gary. They left Kentucky in January 1957.

The Stewarts loaded up a '55 Dodge pickup with their belongings, cramming it full under a funky homemade camper shell George had pieced together from tar paper and chicken wire. Gary and Grandal made the trek lying flat on a mattress in the back with their collie dog Greenie while George and Georgia rode in the cab, with the other five kids squeezed in somewhere. "Even had a couple of chicken coops on the tailgate," noted Gary. Whenever they'd pull into a truck stop, George would back in carefully in an attempt to hide the roosters. "Them chickens would get to crowin' and everybody'd be lookin' around for 'em," said Grandal. The trip took them through Tennessee, the Carolinas, Georgia, then Florida, "drivin' through all little towns," because there were barely any interstates then. "I kept hollering, 'When we're gonna get there? When we're gonna get there?'" said Gary, who remembered the eight-hundred-mile trip taking three days. George would pull off to the side of the road to sleep. "My dad, he drove kinda slow. He was a real mountain man, never had been out of Kentucky."

When they arrived at Clell and Easter's in White City, Georgia wanted to turn right around and go back home. "We come by to tell grandmama bye and they talked us into stayin'," said Gary. "Lord, was we ever homesick." Georgia didn't like the bugs and missed the Kentucky hills. "I liked to cry my eyes out the first year," she said. "I cried off and on for two years." Clell and Easter lived in a "little ol' shack with an outside bathroom," according to Grandal. He and Gary soon relocated to a dilapidated school bus on the property because "there were so many younguns" in the three-room house. "We was poor folks, and they was poorer than we were," said neighbor Gary Gallant. In 1958 or so the family moved to a long, narrow shotgun house in Fort Pierce across from the town dump that had been home to the Bloody Bucket Bar. "No windows in it," said Grandal. "We didn't have nothin'." Georgia would eventually have a new house built on the spot at 2521 South 35th Street. George would hang out in the back with his chicken coops.

Florida was a different world for these Kentuckians. "We left the cold and it was warm. Ran around in bare feet, son," said Gary. "Pickin' them oranges off them trees." No more Kentucky winters! "I had just left the mountains—the hillbilly boy in the big city," Stewart told one interviewer. Fort Pierce would be a place of great extremes for the Stewarts. There would be crazy success, not to mention plain craziness. And much tragedy.

TOM

3

FLORIDA MAN

Fort Pierce: come for vacation, leave on probation.

– Shannon Ashburn

"Disney World, Goofy speaking." That's how Grandal answers the phone. The tone is blasé, the accent pure Kentucky.

Like brother Gary, Grandal is thin as hell and all right angles. He's the Southern gentleman of the family—albeit a rather ribald one—and his drawl and manner conjure up the Bluegrass State more than any other Stewart. His manicured beard and mustache and immaculate wardrobe of pressed jeans and shirts suggest a riverboat captain, or a cardshark lurking in the back corner of some smoky turn-of-the-century house of ill repute. Gary and Grandal had a few things in common. "They both loved music," said Candy, Grandal's wife. "They loved good cars. Women, too."

"In the early days me 'n' Gary was like hoboes 'n' hot dogs—wherever you'd see one, you'd see the other. We were thicker than flies on shit." Grandal shot quite a few of the memorable photos on Gary's album covers. How did he get the gig? By showing his brother some of the slides of local women he'd conned into losing their laundry for his lens, raunchy shots he thoughtfully brought along when I interviewed him. "Hell, who don't want to see a naked woman? I could just about get a damn nun to take her panties off. I was more of a tomcat than Gary was. I'd get more girls than he would!"

Grandal's waters run deep—he got choked up talking about the two sisters he lost to the fire, even though he never knew them. But he can be a sly fox when crossed. "He came over to our house just out of nowhere one day," said his nephew Trampas. Another relative's car happened to be parked there, someone who had somehow pissed Grandal off. According to Trampas, Grandal got out of his truck "with a five-gallon bucket, went over to the spigot, filled it up, walked over to that car, opened the door, and threw the whole bucket of water inside. Saturated the interior. Didn't say nothing, just walked back to his truck and left. That's just how Grandal is."

Grandal's been in a feud with his sister Gina for years. Something to do with inheritance and an antique clock. "I'd trip her in church if I could," he told me. Gina's counting on being interred in the family plot. "Not if I can help it," said Grandal. "I hope I live longer than her, because as soon as she kicks the bucket I'm gonna run down there to the damn cemetery and have them put her ass at the foot of the hill. By herself!" (Stewarts tend to make up...eventually.)

Grandal was Gary's first musical partner, but it wouldn't last long. "I never took to it like Gary. He was so damn ahead of everything. I was full of piss and vinegar, y'know? Shit, me 'n' Gary would get into it." This sibling rivalry would last for decades, with many ups and downs. Gary helped capitalize a clothing store for Grandal in the mid-'70s—Fast Lane, aka Grandal's Boutique. It didn't take, and the investment would be a source of contention until Gary's dying day. Grandal later became a Florida state citrus inspector. When he found out his share of Georgia's estate would be less than his siblings, he asked his mother why. "Because you have a job," she told him.

Two-man band: Grandal and Gary, Florida, May 1958.
(Gina Stewart collection)

What did Grandal miss most about his brother? "His craziness—'What's he gonna do next?'" In Gary's later drug-soaked years, Georgia was always asking Grandal to check on him ("Don't send Grandal," Gary would plead, "he's too mean"). At one point Grandal carted his zonked-out brother off to the emergency room: "He'd been on damn quaaludes or whatever." But by the time Grandal got back to his house to call his mother with a report, Gary had already slipped out of the hospital and returned home.

* * *

There's a statue of Keith Whitley in his little hometown of Sandy Hook, Kentucky. You won't find anything like that in Fort Pierce for Gary Stewart, despite the fact that he lived most of his life there. Nor will you find him in books about the city. There are no parks, plaques, or streets bearing Stewart's name. Local musicians keep his name alive, and that's about it. "The whole city of Fort Pierce did not quite get him," said Wallace Parr, former owner of Russell Music, an instrument shop Gary frequented.[18] "You're never a hero in your hometown."

Fort Pierce, Florida, the Sunrise City on the Treasure Coast. An unusual place, even for crazy-ass Florida, "the land of honky-tonks, Dusty Rhodes, Sacred Steel and snake and monkey farms," as musician and author Reverend Billy C. Wirtz (aka William Wirths) writes. A little over an hour north of West Palm Beach on the ocean side of the state, Fort Pierce looks like any other funky little Southern beach town, but mayhem lurks in the shadows of the swaying palms. "You can leave Fort Pierce, but Fort Pierce never leaves you," states Stewart family friend Bill Hardman. "Everybody that leaves is drawn back." The town is named after a colonel who served during the Seminole Wars, which seems apt. The Fort, as some call it, can be a savage place. "The Baltimore of Central Florida" is how Wirtz describes it.

18 Stewart worked briefly at Russell Music as a teenager, delivering pianos for store owner Marie Russell. According to Tommy Schwartz, "Gary was the only person I remember who got away with calling her by her first name."

"And like Baltimore, [it] has a large population of Southern Whites that moved there when the jobs up north dried up. They quickly found out that Florida comes from an old Seminole word meaning 'Minimum Wage.' The work was here, the pay was brutal."

Some random facts: Several motion pictures have been shot in Fort Pierce, including *Empire of the Ants* (starring Joan Collins), *Invasion U.S.A.* (starring Chuck Norris), and *Dirty Cop No Donut* (starring nobody). John Joseph Houghtaling, inventor of "Magic Fingers," the coin-operated motel bed jiggler, retired to Fort Pierce. The town has a rich African American history. Willie Eason, aka "Little Willie and His Talking Guitar," started the riveting gospel genre known as "sacred steel" by incorporating a lap steel during services in a Fort Pierce Pentecostal church during the 1930s.

Author and anthropologist Zora Neale Hurston died poor in a segregated welfare home there in 1960. The Highwaymen, a fabled group of African American artists who sold landscapes painted on cheap roofing boards from the trunks of their cars, were from the Fort Pierce area. Avenue D hosted many a juke joint in its heyday, most notably Baker's Flamingo Grill, where Little Richard and Ike and Tina Turner played.

Segregation ended in Florida in 1970, but I don't know if Fort Pierce got the message. Whenever the Avenue D area came up in my interviews, it was referred to as "Colored Town" and worse (one of Gary Stewart's nephews, Jason Stewart, maintained that Gary "was the least racist" of his uncles). Let it be said that Trump is a hero with many of the Fort Pierce participants in this story. For them, he's a rebel thumbing his nose at the elite, their White House Elvis. "MAGA all the way," declared Gina Stewart.

* * *

Back when the Stewarts first moved to Fort Pierce, it was nearly a bucolic small-town place, full of hot rods, drive-ins, and hamburger joints. You hung out at Bill's Burger, a central stop on a loop that took you around A&W and South Dixie Drive-In or Higgs Drive-In, "the showplace of Fort Pierce." You caught movies at the Sunrise Theatre or Fort Pierce Drive-In on Route 1, and bought your 45s at the Music Bin or Frink's. It was kids and cars "all night long, burning daddy's gas," as Tommy Schwartz put it. The town had lively, two-fisted honky-tonks and bars like the Merry-Go-Round, Buck Jones Bar ("The Music Is Lousy—the Food Is Even Worse!"), or the Town and Country Tavern. Later came clubs like Frankie n' Johnny's, Rialto's, even a strip joint—the Evil People Lounge.

In those days people made a living in the fishing, citrus, and cattle industries. "When I was growing up, Fort Pierce was orange groves, nothing but orange groves everywhere," said longtime resident Ronnie Baird. But that scent is long gone, along with the Sunrise City's innocence. A new industry developed in the late '60s/early '70s that would radically change the area—drugs. This sleepy, off-the-radar port town with a deep inlet became a favorite spot for smugglers flying in loads or sending them off by boat. First marijuana, then cocaine. Fort Pierce would supply much of the country, becoming a "mecca for drug importation," according to Bill Hardman, a former detective who was with the Fort Pierce police department for thirty years.[19] Swordfish boats would meet up with larger vessels offshore and just "put the bales under the fish," recalled Ed "The Suitcase" Barber, pilot on many a weed-smuggling mission. "Everybody I knew—and everybody that everybody else knew—in this small little town was doin' it."

Even the law, some say. When Bill Hardman was in college, a buddy of his asked if he wanted to see something remarkable. That night they went out to a remote area and watched a plane

19 Hardman decided to moonlight as a stand-up comic while he was still working for the police. His boss on the force said he'd have to use an alias. "I told Gary, because he's the one who kind of pushed me into comedy. No sooner than the words came out of my mouth, he said 'Hank Western.'" "Hank Western" is a song off Gary's 1976 album *Steppin' Out*. Hank Western (the comic) recorded an album in 2012, *Them Tasers Hurt*, which features a mug shot of Hardman on the cover. There are jokes about cops, drugs, Obama, and bestiality. Fort Pierce humor, in other words.

land. Two vehicles pulled up to meet it. "Cop cars," said Bill, who watched through binoculars as the shipment was loaded into the patrol cars. "The plane takes off, the cops drive away," said Hardman. "Every night they fly in a load, and every night them cops unload it," his friend replied. "Back then cops were getting paid off," said another longtime resident. "Everybody knew everybody. I got three DUIs and didn't get convicted of any of them. I mean, it was just fucking wide open. It was awesome." (Hardman maintained that in 1985 the town got a new sheriff "and that shit ended abruptly," although cops vs. robbers remained a unique situation. "Fort Pierce is the only town in the world where the good guys and bad guys get together, break for lunch, then go back to being good guys and bad guys.")

The result of this illicit activity was instant, unexpected wealth. "It was like everybody hit the stock market," said Ed Barber. I was informed there were numerous legit businesses around Fort Pierce that had been funded with drug money. "There are guys here who are doing very, very well today," said Hardman, "who, before all those drugs came in, couldn't put two nickels together." He laughed when I asked how cocaine in particular affected Fort Pierce. "Cocaine didn't 'affect' Fort Pierce. It *defined* it."

Drugs "made Fort Pierce a richer place," said Nick Stewart. "But there were also bad guys that could rival any of the Cubans. I remember watching these grown men, and half of 'em, I think, were direct descendants of the Hatfields and McCoys. It was literally the wild, wild West." Several drug kingpins emerged from the town in this era, among them Donald Raulerson, a one-legged mastermind who oversaw a network of forty marijuana smugglers and was once dubbed "Big Potatoes Man" by *The New York Times*. Then there was the blood-curdling Masters family, three of whom went to prison for plotting to kill a couple of FBI agents. "Everybody in town was scared of Howard Masters," said Hardman. "Howard would hurt you himself instead of having it done. He was rich, very powerful, mean, and dangerous."

Regardless, "everybody wanted to be a drug dealer," maintained Gary's son-in-law Royce Ashburn. "Our group thought it was cool, because all of our parents and aunts and uncles were in the game. Everybody thought it was normal. And it was far from normal. Everybody wanted to be Pablo Escobar or Scarface...what nobody realized, you become something else after you become that."

Over time, the Fort became a popular refueling stop for area delinquents. "All the white kids knew to go to Fort Pierce to get drugs," said Tom Minarchick of nearby Port St. Lucie. "Go to Avenue L for weed and Avenue D for crack and cocaine." Crack in particular wreaked havoc on the city. "That changed everything," said Stewart friend Polly Davis. "There was just so much of that going on, and so much destruction from it."

In 2018, *Business Insider* ranked Fort Pierce thirty-fourth of "The 50 Most Miserable Cities in America, Based on Census Data," stating that "just over half of people there are employed and almost 36% of people [are] in poverty." The *Southern Life* YouTube channel created an uproar among residents in recent years when it declared Fort Pierce a "trashy little town" and "the most hood place in Florida...the whole city is a hood." Recent efforts have revitalized downtown, but one has to wonder if cocaine is just baked into the city's DNA.

The drug history of Fort Pierce is a silent character in this book, because it would shape, alter, and eventually vanquish Gary Stewart. "This town is *known* for its drugs," he told me. "The best of everything came right here. And it was brought to my door."

* * *

Naturally, some very extreme characters traveled in this milieu, and they all gravitated toward Gary. To give you a little whiff of Fort Pierce flavor at the time, let's meet two of them: Walter Carlton and John Wesley Davis.

"My dad was cool. He was a man's man, a cowboy," said Carlton's daughter Kim. "And he liked to beat people's asses." Walter Lee

Carlton was an imposing figure, well over six feet tall, who sported dark muttonchops and mustache and was known to wear a brown hat with a feather in it. "Walter was a mess," said Polly Davis with a slight chuckle. "He wasn't scared of nothing, either. Walter didn't have any fear." Although Carlton came from a long line of ranchers and had inherited a fortune in property, he "wasn't interested in the family business," as Bill Hardman pointed out. "Walter was interested in liquor and chicken fights."

As a teenager, Gary was in awe of the '57 Ford Carlton drove, which sported three carburetors and ran like a bat out of hell. Walter called it "the Wild Boar." "Souped up! I mean as hot as it would go," said Gary. "Walter had money, and whatever was the biggest and fastest, that's what he had to have."

In later years Walter tore around town in a Lincoln Town Car, except when he was driving a limousine full of his roosters to a cockfight. The doors would open and it would be "full of chicken shit," said Tommy Schwartz. Carlton was a champion cockfighter who traveled to fights around the country in a motor home filled with roosters (he even shipped his birds to Hawaii for one match).[20] Walter was "wild as they come, buddy," said Gary's sister Gina, the paramour who accompanied him, sometimes in a full-length mink coat and hat. Gina and Walter would have some epic knock-down, drag-out battles.[21]

---

20 Apparently Carlton wasn't allowed to return to Australia. "Some UFO conspiracy thing happened," said Tommy. "Walter was abducted by aliens in Australia. I didn't ask a lot of questions. Walter was kind of crazy."

21 Some of the most jaw-dropping tales in the Stewart saga revolve around Gina, but many are impossible to confirm, as her memory is rather hazy—although she did recall driving Walter Carlton's station wagon through the front windows of a local Holiday Inn bar. "I heard he was in there with another woman," she recalled. "I went right through the glass." At one point Gina was dating Carlton and local drug dealer José Pena. "Gina would flash her latest pair of diamonds in front of me and say, 'Joe got me this, and Joe got me that. But I just love that Walter Carlton'—in the same breath," said Kim Carlton. "Don't fuck my sister," Gary instructed more than one friend. Gina's boyfriends somehow had a way of running afoul of the law or pushing up daisies. "Every time she'd find a new one, my dad would say, 'Another man done gone,'" said Jimmy Smith, who loves Gina dearly. Gary wrote an unreleased song for her, "Champagne World": "You sure know how to use what you got to get what you want/And the only thing you want is your own way." Gina Stewart deserves a book of her own.

Walter "hated drugs," according to his daughter Kim. "He was a redneck. And he didn't like hippies or bikers. He'd watched all of his friends—like Donald Raulerson, Howard Masters, and all of these people—get rich in the drug game. And he agreed to let some pot be dropped on his property."

Unfortunately the feds cottoned on and were soon in hot pursuit. Kim recalled her dad and Gina showing up at her grandmother's house, desperately incognito. "My dad has a wig on. Gina has a wig on and a big pair of sunglasses. They just bought this Chevy van, they are on the run, and my grandmother's going, 'Walter, what *are* you

Walter Carlton, Gary, and Grandal. (Gina Stewart collection)

Gary in the arms of John Wesley Davis. (Tommy Schwartz collection)

doing with that wig on your head?' He said, 'Mama, hush, don't talk too loud. Y' know, *they* are listening everywhere.' He was completely paranoid, Gina was paranoid. Running from the law." Carlton had previously been arrested as a suspect in an infamous drug-related Fort Pierce shootout that took place in March 1971, "a wild gun battle" outside the Palomino Club that left one man dead and two others in the hospital (Carlton got off). Walter ended up doing a day less than a year's time for the crime.

The years were not kind to Walter Carlton. He drank more, got a little crazier. "He gambled his money away over chickens," said Gina. He also had a one-way feud going with Gary Stewart. "My dad actually thought that Gary had stolen one of his songs," said Kim. Never in a band, nor possessing any music career, "Walter thought he was a songwriter or musician...or something," said Tommy Schwartz. Carlton bought a teepee and stuck it on his property. "I don't know if he was getting back to his Indian roots or what," said friend Ronnie Baird. "Walter lived in that damn teepee for a long time, thinking that the spirit world was talking to him through the teepee."

On February 24, 2003, Carlton crawled into one of the "huge metal boxes he transported his chickens in, taking some liquor with him," according to detective Bill Hardman, who was at the death scene. "He pulled the lid down on it and stabbed himself fifty-seven times. Two of the wounds were not superficial. He bled to death in that box." Was it murder? "Absolutely, positively not. This was a suicide, one hundred percent." His daughter forcefully disagrees. "Sixty-seven stab wounds to the chest and abdomen and enough drugs in him to kill him? I don't know how you can call that a suicide. But the sheriff's department did."

Although they had broken up many years before, Gina Stewart attended the funeral. Gina was "actually trying to climb in the damn coffin with him—she put her leg over the side and was stickin' chicken feathers into his breast pocket," said Kim. Walter Carlton "was the love of my life," Gina admitted.

John Wesley Davis, who made the rounds with a pet pig, "was this big hulking monster of a guy who only wore overall blue jeans, no shoes, and nothing else," said musician Fred Bogert. Indeed. There is an infamous picture of the huge, hairy Davis carrying Gary Stewart in his arms like a rag doll. Davis was another notorious Fort Pierce character well known to everybody, particularly the police.

In 1964 he was arrested for attempting to blow up a Florida East Coast Railway bridge with fifteen sticks of dynamite, part of a labor dispute that would run until 1977. The local papers dubbed Davis "the Barefoot Picket." An enforcer for the union at the time, he had already been arrested for beating up a railroad employee. "They paid him well, I remember," said his daughter Polly. "I was about six years old—I said, 'Where are you goin', Daddy?' He says, 'I'm going to see the fraidy cats.' I asked, 'Who's the fraidy cats?' He never told me, but I found out later it was the union reps who paid him. He was extorting money from 'em." Although David was convicted in the bridge bombing case, it was later reversed. Davis was "arrested a hundred-and-somethin' times and was never convicted," according to Polly. "He always knew somebody." John Wesley was what you might call a polarizing character. "Many people liked him, many people disliked him and his antics," said Jo Ann Gregory. "He loved to get something that he could hold over your head, some negative information about you."

Davis routinely hid out on a nearby island[22] where "two of his favorite things to dine on were the endangered green sea turtle and manatees," said Fred Bogert. Of the latter, he said to Fred, "Why do you think they call them sea cows?" Davis constantly fucked with the status quo. "He'd walk into some store, drink a bottle, break it, cut himself on the foot with it, sue 'em, and win," said Gary Stewart. His main occupation, though, was dealer. John Wesley ran "night and day, trying to supply the Fort Pierce area with their needs," said Polly. In the days of crack, he had a beeper and would get "thousands of calls. He knew everybody's payday, what day they got their check, and he would pull in, give 'em a nibble, and get the entire check." Polly recalled making the rounds with her father when he'd sell $10 gel caps of crack down on Avenue D, "making me weigh it out while he sat on the back porch and smoked pot with this old guy named Hi Molly. I had to hold the gun and all the dough. I was fifteen."[23]

Stewart recounted a wild late-night adventure with Davis back in the early seventies. He'd come back from Nashville with some Thai weed—"the best I ever had." He and Davis commenced to smoke it in John Wesley's funky old Plymouth and got so blitzed that Davis conked out on the hood of the car. He came to, all hopped up, and manned the wheel, running over some garbage cans for an appetizer. "He was ornery!" said Stewart. Next, Davis pulled some binoculars out from under the seat and studied the Fort Pierce police station, "thinkin' 'bout every bad thing he ever done in his life," said Gary in a conspiratorial whisper. "Then, right on the police station lawn, he spins donuts, son. Tears the fuck outta their lawn." They next headed over to the sheriff's department, where Davis was merely content to "look in their window." After they'd pulled over to smoke more pot, an officer approached their car. Gary watched John Wesley eat the joint in one swallow. The officer knocked on the window, said, "Oh,

22 The small island is "actually named after my father now on navigation maps—'Wesley's Island,'" said Polly Davis.

23 Regardless, Polly, who went on to become the director of a local nursing facility, maintained that John Wesley "was a good dad....He taught me everything I know—how to survive, to be independent and never have to depend on anybody."

Wes, I didn't know it was you," then let them go. They drove on, with Davis finding a small building he didn't like, so "he tried to knock it over with his car." Although the escapade left Gary a nervous wreck, he spent the entire time "laughing his ass off." John Wesley Davis "did not conform and would never conform," said Polly. "Gary loved that. That's why they hit it off. Because Gary didn't want to conform, either."

* * *

The Stewart family would thrive in the hotbed, hot-wired atmosphere of Fort Pierce. "They were just unusual. Truly unique," said Lee Schwartz. "All of them." Garna[24] would run an auto body shop in town, with his handiwork shown off "in the centerfolds of automotive magazines," according to his son Trampas. Locals would come to him "to do little things like put a little flip mirror in, with a straw and razor blade holder." Griselda would become a bank teller. Glenn, the youngest, became a trucker. Gina was a sometime chauffeur for Gary, while Greg and Gerald would both play drums for him. According to one nameless observer, Gary dearly loved his family, but "kept them at arm's length." Georgia would never control him like she did the rest of her brood. "He was too independent."

Gary would prove to be the perfect Kentucky/Florida split: one half Kentucky hills moan, one half Allman Brothers twin-guitar boogie-woogie. He'd become the famous member of the family, the anointed one, and the music would first start to flow in Fort Pierce.

* * *

Once the Stewarts moved to Florida, Gary and Grandal began to make music together in the decrepit old bus on their grandparents' property. Grandal made a drum out of "an ol' nail keg with meat-wrapping paper over the top," and Gary, whose battered Silvertone

24 Pronounced "Gar-nee." Garna was the quietest of the brothers, and the one closest to Gary.

was still in Kentucky ("we didn't have no room for it"), bought another cheap guitar with money he'd made mowing lawns, painting it pink and scrawling "rock 'n' roll'" on it, according to Grandal. "I don't even think it had strings on it. It was all for show." Still, they'd sing Everly Brothers songs for the neighborhood kids and "put on little shows, me and him. Charge 'em two pennies or a Coke bottle."

Stewart cadged a few guitar lessons from a friend, a Harley-riding sometime hood named Jerry Lewis Stiles, who, according to friend Joe Parker, "was as ornery as they come." "He taught me how to play a lot," maintained Stewart. "My first chords. I started learnin' and pickin'. I was thirteen." Gary did not let education get in the way. "I'd take my guitar to school, and during lunch I'd set out there and play, harmonizin' with these twin brothers, Ronnie and Donny Brown.[25] Sometimes the teacher would let me play in class." His seventh-grade gym teacher was supportive, allowing Gary to sing "in front of everybody, with just a tennis racket for a guitar. He encouraged me." This teacher also got Gary into band class with all fees waived. "I was poor and he knew it. I liked to play drums."

According to Grandal, Gary even managed to transform the St. Lucie Junior High gym class into a concert. "We had to dress out, put on shorts, and run around the field. The coach was on Gary's ass all the time about not dressin' out. Gary, he'd run and hide. He never was athletic. One day Gary said, 'I ain't dressin' up!' I says, 'Why?' He says, 'I'm gonna go in that auditorium and play that piano.'" When fellow student Cecil Beamsturfer asked Gary if he knew how, he said, "No, but in a few minutes I will." By the time Grandal and the rest of the kids returned from the football field, "Gary was up there just raising hell with that piano, soundin' like Jerry Lee Lewis, damn girls all around him."

Turned out he'd been shown a few chords by the music-teacher mother of a girl he'd been hanging out with after school. "I just sat down, figured it out. I play a few chords on the guitar and I just added

25 Stewart recalled the Brown brothers as fond cohorts. "Hey, we would go down the road in the middle of night, lay down in the middle of the road, and just laugh at nothin'. We'd make up all these doo-wop songs—*bop shee wop bop*."

math to what I knew," Stewart later told Ralph Emery. "Shit, Gary was born musical," said Grandal. "He had it oozin' out of every pore in his body. Gary didn't run across anything that he couldn't pick out a tune on somehow, whether it be banjo or mandolin or whatever."

Grandal and Gary entered a talent contest at the local Sunrise movie theater, but it was Grandal who took home some new footwear for "Blue Suede Shoes." Yet for one brother this was already a serious endeavor. "Gary was on me all the time—'Do it this way, do it *this* way, you're not doin' it *right*!' I just quit. Gary was too good, I couldn't fool with him."

* * *

Gary, a funny, bright kid. B&W snapshots show him next to his bike or playfully standing on his head, like some misty Mark Twain memory. But Fort Pierce was a trial by fire. "I was naive, from the hills of Kentucky," said Gary. He wasn't athletic like Grandal, nor big and tough, but he learned to make up for it. When he first arrived, Stewart "was a real skinny, anemic-lookin', half-a-sissy-actin' kid...then he started whippin' all the other kids," said classmate Joe Parker. "Ol' Gary was pretty good with his fists back then."

Parker would be an important ally. Slightly older, Joe had loads of records as well as musical equipment. They did what had to be done and formed a four-piece band they christened the Tom Cats. According to Gary's handwritten 1960 band bio, "The boys got together about the first of October in the year of 1959, playin' a shoebox as their drum and a piano and guitar and using very small amps. The group has played at school dances, teenage dance clubs, church parties, Stuart night-out-of-town guest appearances, Christmas parties and they even tried to start their own dance....For about six months the Tom Cats couldn't play nothing but fast songs. Then they tried slow songs and now specialize in them."

Who played what? "We all played different instruments," said Gary. "Everybody switched around." Tom Cat number three was Tommy Maxwell. "Tommy had a good voice," said Karen Parker, Joe's soon-to-be wife. "Tommy was the best lookin', and he kind of knew it. Tommy acted a little bit like Elvis." Gary's Tom Cats biography contains some droll bandmate observations. Joe Parker "likes to take naps, not orders. Fine boy, he is." Fourth Tom Cat Carl Johnson "used to not like girls, he couldn't stand them, but we at last got him started... and let me tell you, on his first date he made up for all lost time....He owns a car we call Essie Mae, we have had many good times in the old bomb." According to Gary's notes, the Tom Cats, sporting red shirts with TOM CAT on the back (Gary was a size 14), made their debut at the Fort Pierce Community Center, their first vocal being a cover of Rusty York's 1959 hit "Sugaree." Another early performance came December 10–11, 1959, at a two-day "Stunt Night" at Dan McCarty High School where they did a song called "True Love Rewarded." A Stewart original? No one remembers. With his slicked-back Elvis hair, Gary already had a little bit of a bad-boy presence in the halls of Dan McCarty. "He was like the Fonz," said schoolmate Katherine "Kitty" Parr. "My dad would have thrown him right out of the house."

Karen Parker remembers Gary coming around for guitar lessons from Joe and his Telecaster. Not that it was a walk in the park. "Gary and I were together all the time, but we argued. Argued about music, how to phrase things, how to play songs, or what food to order. Any damn thing!" Gary and the band would congregate at Parker's after school. "Joe had a back porch at his house, and they'd just start jamming," recalled Karen. "High school kids with a dream."

* * *

It's unclear if Gary sang many lead locals for the Tom Cats at the beginning. "I don't really remember Gary being the front man," said Karen. "Tommy had the good voice." Stewart dedicates several pages of his band bio to the Tom Cats' voluminous repertoire of rockabilly / pop / R&B songs of the day. There are "Rockin' Instrumentals" ("Rawhide," "White Silver Sands," "Woo Hoo" and even "One Mint Julep") and "Rockin' Singing Songs" ("Lovin' Up a Storm," "I'm a Hog for You," "Mean Woman Blues," "You Talk Too Much," "I'm Ready") and "Slow

Songs" ("Sea of Love," "Valley of Tears," "The Great Pretender," "Angel Baby," "Blues Stay Away from Me"). From Chuck Berry to Jerry Lee Lewis to Link Wray to the Coasters—quite a range. But no country. "Joe didn't like country music," said Karen. But Parker knew about other music Gary wasn't familiar with. "Joe turned me on to the blues, Jimmy Reed. He was way into blues that far back and I didn't hear it at first. Joe was ahead of it! We did Jimmy Reed and all that shit."

Gary's uncle Jake Stewart dug out a reel-to-reel tape recorder to capture the Tom Cats in all their glory. "Gary had his band there in my livin' room, havin' a ball...they almost run me out of that subdivision because they were making such a racket." The rough, nearly half-hour tape features Gary belting out numbers like "Let the Good Times Roll" and "Johnny B. Goode" and is the first recorded evidence of the wonder that is Gary Stewart. Best of all is the Tom Cat version of Conway Twitty's lusty 1959 pop hit "Is a Blue Bird Blue." The command, swagger, and ease is already evident in Gary's casually tough vocal. The kid already knows: music is his life.

* * *

Gary Stewart would blaze a midnight trail through the honky-tonks, and the first one was a gin-soaked Fort Pierce haunt they called the Merry-Go-Round. Amazingly, the all-underage Tom Cats had a regular gig there. Located at 3626 South US 1 (aka the South Dixie Highway) and partially owned by one Josephine Tobin, the Merry-Go-Round was one of the rougher joints in town. "It wasn't no big hoodoo, just a little honky-tonk," noted Grandal. "Had a Model A Ford up on the roof." The Merry-Go-Round appears quite a bit in the local *St. Lucie News Tribune* under such headlines as "Kicked in Face at Bar, Man Tells Deputies." On Friday nights they'd have a fish fry that would serve over six hundred people, according to Tobin. "It brought in a lot of action," she told the paper. Lesser-known acts such as Slim Bevins and the Hi-Boys ("Guest stars of the Cracker Barrel Hoedown") were Merry-Go-Round regulars.

"I remember seeing a guy get his guts cut out there," said Joe Parker. "He walked out the front, holdin' his entrails in. Blood all over the cement." Bill Ross was the bouncer. "He started more fights than he broke up," said Parker, laughing. "A real likable guy...people came in there just to try him and he'd knock the shit out of them." (The Merry-Go-Round was off-limits for Parker's girlfriend. "Joe wouldn't take me," said Karen.)

"Imagine, now—little kids playin' in a bar!" said hotshot picker and future collaborator Bill Eldridge, who sometimes sat in with the band. "We had no business bein' in there. Technically it was against the law." How did the Tom Cats get around the twenty-one-or-older rule? "They needed a drummer one New Year's, I was about thirteen," said Parker. One of the owners asked Joe's dad if he could sit in. Sure, said Eddie, as long as my son doesn't imbibe—"If he drinks, I'll break your nose." Shortly after Tommy's entrance the Tom Cats were playing regular gigs at the Merry-Go-Round, with Eddie as their chaperone / manager / wheelman. "He was *great*," enthused Gary.

The Merry-Go-Round was an eye-opener for Stewart. It was the first time he saw professional musicians—"real good pickers"—play up close. It was also his first look at those grizzled, quietly desperate, never-quite-made-it veterans he dubbed "Hank Westerns," which he'd later immortalize in song. "They were older guys, a little group of 'em in their thirties, forties. Drinkin' a lot...winos and all that. And they never had gotten anywhere, but they'd talk about the old times...a lot of 'em had quit music and were just hanging around to drink. So I just call them Hank Westerns, y'know, the guys that never got outside of the edge of town."

The Tom Cats were a hit at the Merry-Go-Round, particularly when Gary sang "Alley-Oop" and slipped in the line "Look at that motherfucker go!" "I was fifteen, so I could get away with it. We were little kids makin' dirty music!" That was about as wild as it got for the Tom Cats. At the time, "Gary was completely against drinking and drugs," said Karen Parker. "Joe and Tommy would drink beer. Gary wasn't really into any of that stuff."

The Tom Cats lasted about two years, 1959 to 1961. Grandal maintained his brother had a following even this early on. "Gary was big in our hometown before he was ever introduced in Nashville," he said, noting that he could go into a joint and watch the crowd disperse once word got out Gary was playing somewhere else. "He could empty bar floors. Everybody wanted to be where Gary was."

It was around this time Gary abandoned high school. "He made it through tenth grade and then quit," said Grandal. "I made it to the ninth." Now that they were older, there was little supervision at home. "We could pretty much do what we wanted to, because there was so damn many of us. Mommy couldn't keep up with all of us. Me 'n' Gary just run wild." And the Tom Cats were no more. Why did the band break up? "I got married," said Gary. Did he ever. The name of the dame? Mary Lou Taylor.

Jake Stewart, Gary's uncle, recalled the first time he laid eyes on Mary Lou. It was at the Merry-Go-Round, where he and his wife had gone to see Gary play. "We were sittin' there at a table, and we were watching this couple on the floor. They were swappin' tongues on the floor there, right in front of everyone. No restraint at all. Gary got through playin', he come over and says, 'You seen my girlfriend?' I says, 'You don't mean that one, do you?'" Gary seemed unfazed that she'd been entangled with another fellow on the dance floor.

Not long after that, Jake was over at the Stewarts' house. Gary was leaving. "I says, 'Where you gonna go?' 'I'm gonna go get married.' I said, 'Who you gonna marry?' He says, 'Mary Lou.' I says, 'You ain't gonna *marry* that whore, are you?' He said, 'Yeah, I'm gonna marry her!' I said, 'Okay, well, I think you got a hard bed to lay on.'" But Mary Lou's running around "didn't upset Gary at all. He said, 'She knows I'd do the same thing.'"

"Mary Lou was five years older than Gary. She was twenty-one, Gary was sixteen," said Gary's brother Garna. "Gary liked her because she was WILD. He liked wild women. I guess he found one. Gary never met nobody as wild as Mary Lou!"

4

HELLO, MARY LOU

Gary and Lou? They fed off each other.

– Jo Ann Gregory

What a couple they were, Gary and Lou. She liked to compare their relationship to that operatic coupling of Gregory Peck and Jennifer Jones in *Duel in the Sun*. Over the top enough for you? They were the Romeo and Juliet of Fort Pierce, the Bonnie and Clyde. He called her Pancho, she called him Cisco.

Mary Lou made me laugh. One day, years after I'd been down to Fort Pierce to do my story on Stewart, an envelope arrived. Inside were soft-focus boudoir shots of Mary Lou in lingerie complete with feather boa, taken, no less, by Gary's brother Grandal. On the back she'd scrawled "To Jimmy. You touch me where I live." She then commanded me once more to write this book. It pains me that she isn't here to read it. Lou would've loved it all, good, bad, and ugly. She was a striking figure, with jet-black hair and glittering brown eyes that seemed to burn right through you. She talked nervously, in a foggy little voice that made her sound like she just got out of bed (a distinct possibility), often muttering a sharp, funny throwaway line that didn't register until ten minutes after you left. As Shannon recalled, "People would see her and say, 'Lou, you look amazing. I hope I look as good as you at your age.' She'd say, 'Honey, you're not going to, because you don't look that good now.'" By the time I met her she was a boat who'd weathered countless storms. Battered, a bit creaky, but always game for a cruise to unknown waters. There was unending dignity to her. Lou had been through it all. "She was THE MOTHER," said Shannon. "That's what we called her: THE MOTHER. My brother's girlfriends and a lot of my friends looked up to her and came to her for advice. Mom was wise."

When they met, Lou was the older woman, Gary the younger man, and that sinful cliché never seemed to depart. In the end, I found Mary Lou to be the wilder one. Gary had affairs, so did Lou. Male, female, sometimes with musicians in his bands. She even deflowered one young protégé of Gary's on his eighteenth birthday. "Mama Lou was a sexual being," said son-in-law Royce Ashburn. And she gave as good as she got, which made for a highly combustible union.

"They met their match, both of them," said longtime friend Larry "Mouse" Munson. "They couldn't have done that forty-year stretch with anybody else, that's for damn sure." Gary had no greater defender on earth, even when she was fixing to sock him in the jaw herself. "She was my dad's best friend," said Shannon. "His cowriter. She was his everything. As long as she was here, Dad was good. That was his safety net."

An air of fatality clung to Gary and Lou. Night and its shadows were never far away. "My parents loved to get high," explained Shannon matter-of-factly. As with the rest of us, Gary and Lou were never going to get out of this world alive, but you had the distinct feeling their numbers might come up early. "Jesus make up my dying bed/'Cause I've been stung by the kiss of death," sings Gary in an otherworldly song about the afterlife entitled "Silver Cloud," in which the dead protagonist calls his lover to heaven, "sittin' on top of a silver cloud." It's a morbid little number, pathologically romantic, chillingly prescient. Lou loved the song. "I feel that God has put me here for Gary, just as he's here for me. So I'll never be without him—'til death. And then somewhere in time I'll find him, 'cause that's how much I love him."

* * *

GARY STEWART: Me and Joe Parker went to a dance up to Vero, about twenty miles away. There were some bands playing from Miami. It was seldom you'd get to see a live band back then. That was the first time I saw Mary Lou [whistles]. Oh man, I dug her from the first. She was dancin' and, boy, she could *dance*. Had on a pair of turquoise pants. And I mean, she had the rhythm. It was a year before I saw her again. At Higgs Drive-In.

MARY LOU STEWART: I had my Dad's old '48 red Ford pickup truck. This little kid kept botherin' me [laughter]. I didn't know it, but a year before Gary had seen me at a dance and couldn't take his eyes off me. So I'm sittin' at the drive-in one night with my girlfriend and Gary come up to the car. I had all my 45 records just thrown in the back seat, that's how I took care of records back then. Gary says, "Can I get in the back seat?" And I said, "Watch my records, boy!"

GARY: I said, "Yes, ma'am!" Lou had good taste in records—Chuck Berry, Little Richard, Jimmy Reed, the blues. She ordered her records from Buckley's Discount Record Shop in Nashville and listened to the John R radio show on WLAC. She had even seen Little Richard live at the Showplace. So we had a whole lot in common.

MARY LOU: So then my girlfriends wanted me to go see Gary at this club. He was playin' at the Merry-Go-Round, 'cause Joe's dad would go with 'em. The whole band was, like, sixteen years old! I didn't want to go.

GARY: Just a couple weeks after the drive-in, I saw Lou at a party. I had my guitar, and I jumped up on a stool and said, "I bet I know your name." She said, "Yeah?" And I started singin' that Ronnie Hawkins song, "I'm gonna tell you a story 'bout ol' Mary Lou..."

MARY LOU: Gary told me he was eighteen and I told him I was nineteen [laughter]. I found out about two months later how old he was and about died. But y'know, I already loved him. And I knew Gary had something from the minute he picked up that guitar.

Joe Parker had this white Fender and he had traded it in for something else. It was in the music store. Gary would go and look at it and play it. He knew he could never buy it. So I went in there one day by myself and asked them how much would that guitar be with the Fender amp, 'cause the amp was new. It was either $240 or $280, that was like $28,000 to me back then! And Mom, she didn't have no money, she worked for twenty-eight bucks a week at the cafeteria.

So I said, "Mom, please sign for me at the bank to borrow the money." "I PROMISE TO GOD I'll make every payment," I said. "I want Gary to have a guitar. He's good." She knew he was good. Finally she signed for me, I got the money—and that guitar and amp. I carried it in the trunk of the car all day. I didn't tell Gary I had it.

Gary was playin' a dance in Stuart with the Tom Cats at the community center. Joe Parker and Tommy Maxwell were there in their white bucks. And I carried that guitar onto the stage, set it right in front of Gary, and I said, "There…now *pick*" [laughter]. Gary couldn't believe it. Joe Parker said, "Are you gonna marry her, man?"

JO ANN GREGORY: Mary Lou was just a free spirit. Take her or leave her, she didn't give a damn. Lou was a good jokester, a good teaser. She just had a great sense of humor, and spirit. She didn't let things keep her down. No matter what happened, it turned into a joke. She might not laugh at that moment, and she might be mad as hell, but the next time you talked about it, it would be funny.

Mary Lou was very spiritual, but not in any kind of Christian way. She was interested in shamans, any kind of mystical thing. I'd be walking my little self to Catholic Mass on Sundays—and Mary Lou, she'd probably be getting out her voodoo doll.

MARY LOU: When me and Gary started goin' together, neither one of us could afford a car, but he had $100 saved, so I said, "Okay, you give me your $100, I'll get the car, we'll make the payments, and it'll be *our* car—but it's gotta be in my name, 'cause you're not old enough." The payments were $40 a month and, man, we had it fixed up so neat—'55 Oldsmobile, candy-apple red. We did it all ourselves—stripped her down, painted her, had glasspacks on her. She was *hot*. Called her Apache, written on the back. And Gary had the horns rigged like Woody Woodpecker—da da da DA da!

I would drive by his house late at night. I would start easin' off those glasspacks two or three blocks away from his house. I'd put it in low, and just before I got to his house, I'd take my foot off the gas and those glasspacks would be hummin'—*bububuh, bububuh*. This was midnight or 1 a.m. And I'd turn the car around, turn the headlights off, and drive by Gary's house real slow. And bang! There he'd be!

GARY: How did my folks react? [whistles] Hey, man, they had the police come...I mean, for my parents to go to the *police*, son, that's a big deal. I was a minor and Lou had just turned twenty-one. That's when my parents sent me across state to my uncle to work a job. But I wrote Lou every night.

MARY LOU: What they had done was take Gary out of town to try to get him away from me. Oh, his parents hated me. George hated my guts for years. I can see why now. I was older, that was their little boy and they were from the Kentucky mountains.

JO ANN GREGORY: I never heard Mary Lou speak of George in any kind of venomous way. Now, Mary Lou and Georgia, there were two strong wills at work there. Mary Lou was persona non grata with her, that's just the way it was. There was pretty much always tension, and if it lightened up a bit, Mary Lou still watched her back. She never trusted Georgia. She had it out for Lou. Anytime she could stick a pin in Mary Lou she would. She kept that knife in Mary Lou's back.

GAIL STEWART: Mary Lou had two kids before she got with Gary. And that didn't sit well with my mother.

GINA STEWART: Mommy called her Murray Lou. She never did like Murray Lou. She didn't!

GRANDAL STEWART: Y'know, I didn't have no trouble with Lou. I got along pretty good with her. Lou was there for a good time, she was. And she had a good time.

MARY LOU: Georgia waited for me to turn twenty-one, and as soon as I did, boy, Sheriff Norville came by. Me and my mother lived in a trailer. And he said, ''Take a ride, Mary Lou.'' Lenny Norville, he was a real good guy, I had known him for years. I got in the car and he says, "Now, Gary's mom can really give you some trouble." I said, "Well, I know she don't like me, and I know she's had Gary into court talkin' to the juvenile people." And he said, "No, I'm serious Mary Lou—you're twenty-one now, and Gary's sixteen. If Georgia wants to, she can get you for prostitution—and aidin' the delinquency of a minor. I said, "Prostitution? How?" He said, "With the law, if you go out to dinner, even if you buy Gary a Coke, they can get you for Gary bein' that young–'aidin' the delinquency of a minor.' Georgia could really hurt you." So I told Gary, "Well, it's like this—we've either got to stop seein' each other or *somehow* get married. 'Cause I love you, baby, but I don't wanna go to jail."

JO ANN GREGORY: Gary and Mary Lou were just a great couple. They were both exciting people, exciting to be around. They filled the room with their personality, and you never knew what was gonna happen. Lou didn't give a damn if you liked her or not. Gary? I think he needed to be liked, that he thrived on love and attention. And Mary Lou could give him lots of love and lots of attention—*if* she had a mind to do it.

GARY: We went together about a year.

MARY LOU: Then we acted like we were broke up to put Georgia's hen feathers down, but we were just waitin' for his parents to leave town. They were gonna go to Kentucky for a month's vacation and Gary and several of the kids was gonna stay home. So we thought, "How we gonna get married?" We had less than $100. I thought, "Well, if we go to Georgia, they still might not marry us, 'cause Gary is such a baby face."

So I thought and thought and thought. It took some figuring out, I'll tell ya. Georgia still to this day does not know how I did it. Every once in a while she'll say, "Murray Lou, I know what you did. I know 'cause I was talkin' to the preacher..." And I'll say, "No, Mommy, that ain't it." All these years later and she still ain't found out!

Here's how we did it: A real good friend of Gary's, Norman Sapp—he's dead now, bless his heart—he was maybe twenty. So I says, "Norman, me and Gary want to get married." He knew how much in love we were. I says, "Will you help us?" He said, "What can I do?" I said, "You go to the courthouse with me and say you're Gary."

I said, "I'll write all the info on your hand." So Gary was waitin' in the park across the street from the courthouse, and Norman and me went in there, and they asked him, "What is your name?" "Gary Ronnie Stewart." "What is your mother's maiden name?" "Georgia Niece." "Father?" "George Robert Stewart." "Where you from?" "Payne Gap." So we got the license.

Then me and Gary went to Dr. Browning, this old doctor that would do anything for money. I said, "Dr. Browning, I'll give ya ten dollars if you say that Gary is twenty-one on them blood tests." He said, "Okay." And that's how it worked.

I knew the Vero Beach newspaper only came out once a week, so we got married right after it came out—that way it wouldn't be in the paper for another whole week. George and Georgia were still in Kentucky.

After the wedding we were driving down the road, "Just Married" written on the car and the tin cans tied on, the groom in the back seat with the best man and the bridesmaid driving in the front seat. All of a sudden Gary says, "Oh my God, there's my uncle!" and he gets down on the floor. And I said, "Gary, it's too late now!" Here I am sittin' here with a wedding gown on all by myself!

GARY: Me and Norman, we laughed all the way through it. I mean, all at once it struck me—"Dammit, here I am pulling this off at seventeen years old, gettin' married! *A seventeen-year-old kid* getting married. This is *funny*!" We moved to Vero and I didn't call home

for about a month—"Hey, Mommy?" "Yeah?" "Well, y'know—I'm married." It was a long time before they accepted it.

MARY LOU: Georgia was—furious is not the word. She said, "I'm gonna have it annulled!" And we had that checked out, too. Gary said, "No, Mommy, you can't, because to have it annulled, both parties have to agree and I love her and I ain't divorcin' her. So I'll come home when you let me bring Lou with me."

GRANDAL STEWART: Mary Lou was the older woman. That was Mom's big thing—Lou done took her boy, married him when he wasn't even eighteen, and run off. Mama lost her baby. So she held it against Lou.

* * *

There's this old black-and-white photo of Gary and Mary Lou sitting at a table in some Fort Pierce honky-tonk, a real den of iniquity. It's a fabulous image. Lost in song, his eyes closed, Gary's playing guitar and singing, leaning into Lou, who also has her eyes shut and is smiling. Open cans of Schlitz beers and ashtrays full of cigarettes dot the table. The other couple at the table are entwined and enraptured, nobody's feeling any pain. A couple of patrons perch on stools next to the AMI jukebox in the background. Jukebox, booze, and honky-tonk love. Gary loved playing the "skull orchards," the funkier, rougher joints. "Feller had a crescent wrench, man, and used it on a guy one night," he told one deejay in 1975. "I've played in some wild ones!"

After marrying on July 28, 1961, the newlyweds moved into a cottage in Vero Beach. "Wasn't nothin' fancy about it," said Grandal. "Just a block house with a roof on it." Lou's first child, a daughter named Karen, was already out of the picture. Initially, Andy, her son from another previous engagement, was around. Other Stewarts have dim memories of Andy, whom Mary Lou called Punkin. Garna remembers walking somewhere with the family, maybe out for Halloween, Punkin in tow. "He was still in diapers. And Gary was putting ice down that baby's pants. Gary just didn't like him." Punkin was soon put up for adoption at Gary's insistence. "I wasn't going to raise someone else's kid," he informed one friend a few years later. Lou never discussed giving these children up. Andy would make a dramatic reentry near the end of Mary Lou's life.

And she'd quickly become pregnant again: Gary Joseph Stewart, Gary and Lou's first child, was born October 5, 1962. "I had to make a living now," noted Gary. "So I started playing piano in a country band out west of Vero." He also worked the nightshift at Piper Aircraft (later switching to Grumman in Stuart for better pay). "Gary was a machinist," said coworker Ed Teague. "He was friendly as all get out, cracked jokes. We laughed a lot." On the weekends Stewart played in local joints like Lennie's Lamppost. "We went all over the place to see him play," said Teague. "We knew he was good."

* * *

In late February / early March 1964 a Detroit band landed in Florida that would briefly alter the course of Gary's life. The Impacts—later the Imps—was a three-piece rock band consisting of Alabama-raised blue-eyed-soul shouter Riley Watkins, drummer Larry "Mouse" Munson, various bass players, and Mel Briggs on sax—sometimes playing two at once (Briggs had a routine where he "put on a gorilla mask and played the sax through one of the eye openings"). The Imps had backed Jerry Lee Lewis, Roy Orbison, Del Shannon, Little Anthony, and played "mostly Beatles, light English rock and roll," said Riley. "Nothing hard or heavy." They were playing the Dolphin Inn in Vero Beach, backing hefty country singer / comedian Tiny Jenkins ("He used to say he was '441 pounds of dynamite with a one-inch fuse,'" noted Munson), when Mary Lou, waitressing at the club, caught their act and raved to Gary. "Direct from Detroit! The Impacts! Tiny Jenkins—a ton of fun!" hyped the ad in the local paper. "Jam Session starts 7 PM Sunday, bring your instruments!"[26]

26 Tiny's brand of country didn't mesh well with the rocking Imps and he soon departed. "There was a big hassle," said Munson. "Tiny said, 'I'm gonna kick all of your asses,' and rode away in his big old white Lincoln—man, that car would

Gary did just that, although, according to Munson, he first sat in at a gig at the Flamingo in Fort Pierce, before joining them when they returned to the Dolphin. The Imps' bass player had just quit and Gary stepped into the role. According to Munson, the effect was galvanic. "Man, that lead bass! I never heard that before. It was hot. We just really rocked when he sat in. Gary done a bunch of Jerry Lee Lewis tunes, and it was *exciting*, man. He electrified people. I tried to get Gary to join the band right then." Munson would be the second musician Stewart would weld to. "He used to call me the 'Shuffle King,'" said Larry. "I played with all four limbs, just really crackin' on two and four. Gary loved to hear that backbeat. I'd be banging as hard as I could and he'd say, 'More, man, *more*!'"

A legendary character among this circle, Munson was a "wheeler-dealer, " said later Stewart bandmate Darrell Dawson. "Really smart guy. But you could tell he was from the streets. Mouse was a hustler." Future Stewart soundman Ron "Radar" Griffith thought Mouse was "cool as shit. He didn't say much. Mouse wasn't Southern, he wasn't Northern. He reminded me of Stevie Ray Vaughan because he always wore a hat." One day Munson came out on the road with one little suitcase. "He opened it up and all he had in it was a bottle of Jack Daniels," said Griffith. "Mouse was magical." Mouse would be an off-and-on Stewart running buddy for years to come (unfortunately he'd get tangled in drugs and wind up going to prison in 1992).

At first Stewart said no to joining the Imps, not wanting to lose the security he had with Piper Aircraft. Later, the band was playing in Fort Wayne, Indiana, when yet another bass player left suddenly. They called Gary, begging. "Gary was a little reluctant," said Munson. "We all talked to him." Mary Lou was the deciding factor. "Gary wanted to go real bad," she remembered. "I picked up the phone, dialed their

---

sink to the side when he got in." Jenkins made good on the threat to kick at least one Imp ass when he unexpectedly ran into Munson at a road-stop diner off the Pennsylvania turnpike a year and a half later. "Tiny didn't say anything, not one word," Munson recalled. "CRACK! He banged me upside my head and I flew about two feet to the ground. I was dazed." That was the last sighting of Tiny. "I watched him waddle away," said Munson.

number, and said, 'Here, take the phone. Just go. 'Cause you really wanna go and I think you should.' We sold all our furniture and everything and went on the road."

The Stewarts headed to the Midwest in their maroon Pontiac Bonneville. "Gary and Lou came and joined us in Ohio," said Jo Ann Gregory, soon to be Larry Munson's wife. "I think the first place we went was Ashtabula. It was like a little traveling family. Mary Lou came and brought cooking gear and cooked for everybody in the hotel rooms. That's just the way she was. She loved to cook with a pressure cooker so everything would be really tender. My very favorite thing was her German chocolate cake."

Gary found the band's lead singer/guitarist impressive. "Riley was an old rock and roller at heart. And *sing*? Son, he could scream it out at ya." Watkins was the lead singer, but once Gary joined, the band tilted in his direction. "Gary and Riley sang mostly harmony together," said Mel Briggs. "The Beatles were big at the time, so Gary and Riley sang a lot of their tunes. Gary did some Chuck Berry. I enjoyed working with Gary. He was a hardworking guy, always on time to rehearsals and gigs. Happy-go-lucky." Munson had a lot of laughs with Gary out on the road. Once, while in a high-rise elevator stuffed with terse East Coast types, Gary, in the most Southern accent he could muster, muttered, apropos of nothing, "Man, this fuckin' building would hold *a lot* of corn." Another time, Stewart donned a hat, took the gig money, and enlisted Larry's help to "arrange a little suitcase so there's money stickin' out all around it, some high-dollar bills puffing out. He took the suitcase and made like he was runnin' away like a burglar, like he just snatched it from somebody. Gary's jokes were not in-your-face-type stuff. They were kind of sly. He was real quick."

Stewart spent six months touring with the Imps, tearing all over the country, including gigs backing Gary U.S. Bonds and Ray Stevens in Fort Pierce ("Ray Stevens came onstage with a toilet seat around his neck," recalled Mel Briggs). At one of their first gigs in Erie, Pennsylvania, Munson noticed how Stewart's performances would grow more intense as the night wore on. "It was unbelievable. He was like a generator, man. Through the night he'd charge up, y'know, generating electricity. The first part of the night, he'd be sparkin' and arcin'. And the next set he'd put out a little bit more...Gary would get charged up, charged up, charged up, until he was *all* wound up, and then he'd turn on like he was *electric*. Full-tilt boogie. It would peak at the end of the night. If you came to the last set, you got the best of Gary. He lit the whole place up."

Gary, Jo Ann Gregory, and Larry "Mouse" Munson on the road, Ashtabula, Ohio, 1965. (Courtesy Jo Ann Gregory)

These were not first-class gigs, to say the least. Gary recalled being in Alabama and heading into a restaurant with a band member to raid "their lazy Susan, and steal a pocketful of chicken legs." At one engagement the band stayed above the club in what appeared to be a halfway house for those with mental disabilities, including one denizen named Beanie who'd carry on conversations with his multiple personalities, causing Gary and Larry to address each other by way of "Hey, Beanie" for a few months. Next they stayed in a converted chicken coop. "After that, Lou went home," said Munson. "She was getting tired of it." Mary Lou would seldom travel on Gary's gigs again. "I really don't like the road," she confessed. "I hate bars 'cause I had to work in 'em a lot. I told Gary, 'You go out and see things and do it, come back and tell me about it.' 'Cause he felt real guilty at first about him goin' all the time and me not."

The Imps in Detroit, March 1965. (Tommy Schwartz collection)

The Imps forged ahead. In Revere Beach outside of Boston, Munson and Stewart smoked weed for the first time as a member of the Hollywood Argyles gifted them a joint. "We fired up," said Munson. "And man, we were laughing." A stoned Stewart disappeared, until Munson found him in the closet. And there were women. Even in these early days they flocked to Gary. "He got more ass than a toilet seat, man," said Munson. "It would overflow." Larry vividly remembered a striking redhead pouncing on Stewart at the El Matador in Detroit. "A couple of days later Gary comes back. He said, 'That really good-lookin' redheaded girl? Shit, she gave me the clap.' We found a clinic."

The short stint with the Imps was Stewart's initial taste of touring life, and already he'd had it. "Gary was tired of the road, just burned out with the motel-room thing," said Munson. Not long after the El Matador gig, Gary bailed. "It was two weeks in Detroit, two in Philadelphia, two in Scranton," he told the local paper. "I got so homesick for Florida I headed home." This was the first time he'd abandon ship; it was far from the last. "Gary literally hated the road right up to the day he died," said Riley Watkins. "That's why he quit. He wanted to go back to Florida." Although the Imps fell apart, Munson and Briggs relocated to the Sunshine State and continued to play with Stewart, churning through pop and soul hits at local joints like Good Time Charlie's in Vero Beach. The guys in the Imps would drift in and out of Gary's life. Once Gary had a connection with you, he was likely to pull you back in, even if it was years later. As Munson put it, "You'd get one of those calls—'Hey, man, I need you to come jukin' with me.'"

* * *

Mel Briggs noticed that Stewart had been concentrating on a new skill during his time with the Imps—songwriting. "He was really good at clever lyrics. One of the lines Gary wrote back then was 'Take it easy, Greasy, you've gotta long way to slide.'[27] He was always coming up with lines." Stewart would soon join forces with a Fort Pierce cop by the name of Bill Eldridge and head to Nashville to pitch songs, but it would take playing an outrageous joint known as the Wagon Wheel in nearby Okeechobee for Gary to be pushed in that direction.

27 This line turned up in an unreleased early Stewart publishing demo called "I've Been Known (to Get a Little Stoned)."

Okeechobee was about forty-five minutes from Fort Pierce, but it might as well have been another country. "In those days, Fort Pierce and Okeechobee were enemies," said Stewart friend, archivist, and musician Tommy Schwartz. "Okeechobee was a total redneck town." The Wagon Wheel bar and restaurant on North 441 was a place where Fort Pierce bands "got their asses beat," said Tommy. "We carried a mic stand in one hand and an amp in the other." Fort Pierce people would sit in one part of the club, Okeechobee denizens in another.

"There were times we hid behind the bar after the gig until the shooting stopped in the parking lot," said "Boogie" Bob Melton, future Stewart bandmate. "There wasn't any place in Fort Pierce that was crazier, even though some were close. Once while we were loading out, a cowboy grabbed my girlfriend and threw her over his shoulder. She was screaming as he carried her out the door." One night, fellow musician Fly Hornsby had been chatting with some cowboy's paramour. "He waited for us outside, and when Fly got in his car, the guy came zooming around the building in his truck and T-boned Fly's car," said Melton. "Smashed the whole side in."

The Wagon Wheel was built in November of 1963 by Hubert Thomas, a key influence in Gary Stewart's life. To hear Gary tell it, Hubert was *the* important figure of his early days. There exists a picture of white-suited Gary playing guitar live, appearing quite maniacal—"He looks like he's gonna bite somebody" is how Tommy puts it—and on the picture Stewart has scrawled "Hubert, without you there'd be no Gary Stewart." A steel player, imbiber, and purveyor of substances, a lover of women, Thomas was beloved by all who knew the man. Stewart called him the "Okeechobee Blast." Local pickers had another nickname for him—"Asleep at the Steel." "Many times Hubert would get too much liquor and pass out on his steel," Melton recalled. "When he picked his head up he would have lines in his face from the guitar strings."

One late night on the phone a few years after Hubert had passed,[28] Gary grew emotional remembering him. "He helped me so much through the years. Hubert was a few years older than me, but he was as young in mind as I was. One day I asked him real serious-like, 'Hubert, how old are you?' And he said, 'I never think about it.' He said it so beautiful—and funny, Lord… Y'know, he always had all these young girlfriends…it wasn't because Hubert liked young girls—*all* the pretty girls liked Hubert, 'cause he was such fun. When Hubert was around I always felt I had somewhere that I could go if everything fell under. I had a buddy that I could just go be with and live forever. Because he was a little kid, like me."

Thus far, Gary had played rock and roll, pop, rockabilly, and dabbled in country with a Vero Beach bar band. But Stewart emphasized it was at the Wagon Wheel that he "learned how to play country music. I liked it, was raised on it, and had played it a little bit—but as far as 'Hey, let's do some *serious* country music'? Learning the basics, really gittin' it, doin' it good and doing a professional job? Hubert taught me how. He took me in, turned me on to records, nurtured me...paid me way more money than I was worth." He also bought a few instruments for Stewart. "I know Daddy had bought Gary a bunch of pianos," said Hubert's son David. "Gary tore up so many pianos. He was like Jerry Lee Lewis when he was young. Daddy told him, 'Listen, you got to slow down. Pianos are getting expensive.'"

"Off and on for seven or eight years," Gary played the Wagon Wheel Fridays and Saturdays, joined by Hubert on steel, Nick Collins on bass, and Dale Williams on drums—although Gary's brothers Gregory and Gerald would sometimes sit in on drums despite barely being in their teens. The band also backed up Music City names that blew through town—Carl Butler, Jack Greene, Red Sovine, the Wilburn Brothers. Mel Tillis, then a struggling singer-songwriter

28 Hubert Daniel Thomas died August 28, 1985. "His ex-wife Carolyn took him to Raulerson Hospital when he was feeling bad, and they wouldn't treat him in the ER," Tommy Schwartz recalled. "Said he was 'drug sick.' She loaded him up and headed towards Fort Pierce Lawnwood Hospital and he died about halfway there."

who'd written a few hits for Webb Pierce ("Tupelo County Jail," "I Ain't Never") and had a few minor hits of his own (the Top Ten would elude him until 1969), also frequented the Wagon Wheel when not off in Nashville. "Mel was a writer at the time," said Stewart. "He had made a few records, had him some suits. Him and Hubert were good friends. Mel would come in every now and then to do a show." Tillis grew up in nearby Pahokee, and had developed a stutter after a bout of malaria as a child, which resulted in Mel being very inhibited onstage at the Wagon Wheel. "He wouldn't say nothing over the microphone, he wouldn't talk," said Gary. "Then he started using it to his advantage." That was still in the future, though, and, according to David Thomas, folks at the Wagon Wheel suggested Tillis sing his answers when the staff asked him questions.

Tillis was an early champion of Gary. Stewart "could change clothes in the barrel of a 12-gauge shotgun," he noted to one reporter. "He was as skinny as Hank!" Mel would give Gary a bit of advice that would change the direction of his life. "Mel took me over to the side one night and said, 'I think you could make it in country music...there's a lot of good singers—the key to the door is writin'. Start writin'—and write all you can.'" The instruction registered. Stewart may have been a wildly undisciplined creature in most other areas of his life, but songwriting was an endeavor he got very serious about—in Tommy Schwartz's Gary Stewart archive there are at least five suitcases stuffed with lyrics, lists, and notes written in that unmistakable Stewart scrawl that look "like hieroglyphics," as Tommy cracked.

There is something else important to note about the Tillis connection. Time and again Gary would stress to me he never went looking for stardom, never went knocking on doors, never begged anyone to listen to his demos. "I've always been lucky that way. People have helped me out without me asking. I've always been in the right place at the right time."

Which doesn't mean he always responded to that help, even from somebody with connections like Tillis. According to Georgia, Mel invited Gary to Music City a few times before he actually made the journey. "Mel, oh, he come there to the house and begged and begged Gary—he said, 'Gary, if you'll just go in with me, we'll have plenty someday.' And Gary, I'd get so mad at him. He don't like to leave home too much. He's a lot like his Daddy. His Daddy never would leave home and go get work." (It should be restated here George worked round-the-clock most of his life.)

* * *

Eventually Gary made an impromptu trek to Music City, showing up at Tillis's Cedarwood Publishing company to drop in unannounced. "I wanted to do a Mel Tillis song—he was the one who said, 'Come to Nashville.' So I did—and he was down in Louisiana with the governor!" At loose ends, Gary looked up a friend of Mel's he'd met at the Wagon Wheel. "Fred Burch and Billy Swan came in one time and Fred liked my singin' and said, 'You come up to Nashville and we'll cut a record.' So he set that up with no money. We had no agreement or whatever, but just got to know each other. Fred was a great guy. Funny." Burch was from Paducah, Kentucky, looked "a little like Montgomery Clift" according to *The New York Times*, and was hustling a living writing songs—his big claim to fame was cowriting the 1959 Memphis hit by Thomas Wayne, "Tragedy" (he'd later go on to write Charley Pride's first RCA hit "The Snakes Crawl at Night" with Mel Tillis, "Dream On Little Dreamer" for Perry Como, as well as a number with a short shelf life entitled "How High's the Watergate, Martha").

Gary made a return trip to Nashville by train, and Burch wound up taking him to Muscle Shoals to record his first single—"I Love You Truly," released on Cory Records, a tiny label with no other known releases. "Who Cory was, I don't know," mused Gary. "It was one of those real indie-independent things, no money behind it. Fred was producer. First record I ever made. I was twenty years old." The session was cut at FAME Recording Studios in Florence,

Alabama, a lethally funky studio that cranked out ferocious hits by Wilson Pickett, Aretha Franklin, Etta James, and Arthur Conley. A crack team of musicians played on Gary's track—David Briggs on piano, Kenny Buttrey on drums (both would play on Stewart's classic RCA recordings), Earl "Peanutt" Montgomery on guitar, David Hood on bass. Sandy Posey, who would soon have a few hits of her own, supplied the ethereal voice of the deceased girlfriend on the record. "My first record was a teenage-railroad-track-angel song," is how Gary described it to Ralph Emery in 1978. "This guy and this gal were out on the railroad tracks makin' love...she got bumped off."

Written by Burch, the number was inspired by Mark Dinning's angst-ridden 1959 pop hit "Teen Angel," which was written by Dinning's sister Jean—"my mother-in-law," said Burch. "It was a song about death and a railroad track, and—not to my credit—I thought I'd write something like that." Fred laughed. "It's a weird song." And oddly prescient. A bombastic number of doomed, obsessed love, it could've been written about Gary and Mary Lou—hell, she'd push him out of the way of many a figurative oncoming train, always sacrificing herself in the process. This little two-bit nothing of a record is the perfect introduction to the wild world of Gary Stewart.

The recording opens with a guitar strum as two young women discuss the ghost who haunts the scene of her untimely demise. "I love you truly," she wails. In comes Gary, that high, trembling voice introduced to the world with this unforgettable couplet: "We were walking down the railroad tracks / Your foot got caught between two rails of black." As a train barrels down the tracks toward the two young lovers, Gary sings: "I took my knife and opened the blade / I said, 'My darling, your life I'll save." Instead she pushes him out of the way, saving his life and losing hers.

The flip side was "Walk On, Boy," an uptempo number cowritten by Tillis, Gary fulfilling his wish of paying tribute to his early mentor. The single—the release date is hazy; some sources say 1964, others March 1965—did zilch. "I never heard it outside of my hometown," admitted Gary, although he did get a long-distance call from somebody requesting a photo—"it was gettin' some play in Japan."[29] He sent off a band picture taken with the Imps and heard no more about it. Either at the same session or another at FAME, Gary cut other songs about which little is known, except for "There Goes a Girl" and "No No No," unmemorable pop uptempo numbers complete with horns (Riley Watkins was invited down to the session and also cut some material for Burch but remembered nothing about it—save for a demo for "Sticky Sue," a song later cut by soul singer Mickey Murray).

Gary cowrote some songs with Burch for Cedarwood Publishing, among them forgotten titles "Goin' Up," "Little Miss Hideaway," and "Mr. Peanut Man," a number apparently conceived when, according to a local reporter, Stewart "saw an old Negro selling peanuts and the song wrote itself." Tape exists on a few others Stewart wrote solo—"Kings and Queens," "Big Train," "I've Been Known (to Get a Little Stoned)" among them. Enjoyable if minor, they show him finding his way as a songwriter. Only one of these songs landed—"Poor Red Georgia Dirt," a plaintive ballad cowritten with Burch that opens with the wacky couplet "Had a little gal way down in Alabamy / She grew up, my son, to be your Mammy." You can hear hints of what's to come listening to the song, with its wistful, yearning quality that has one picturing some middle-aged nobody with a pompadour and cigarette eating cold eggs off a white, no-frills plate while he stares out the window of some small-town diner. Stonewall Jackson's recording of it went to number forty-four on the charts in 1965, providing Stewart with his first slight hit. And his first local write-up in the January 9, 1966, *Miami Herald*: "Gary Strikes Pay Dirt with Guitar and Song," illustrated with a big picture of a laughing Stewart holding his 45 while his sister Gail looks on admiringly. The article offers a tantalizing mention of a "six-year contract with Columbia as a recording artist," a claim never heard again.

29 A Japanese picture sleeve apparently exists, and sure enough, it's not Stewart on the cover.

The rest of the Stewart/Burch numbers went nowhere, although he maintained he could always get "$5 for gas to get home on from Tennessee" out of Cedarwood president John Denny. "Hell, that was better than nothin'. Nothing was really good there. When you're learning, you don't know no better. You write it to get it out of your head." For one song, Stewart had another cowriter at Cedarwood—none other than Billy Swan, who'd later score a number-one crossover hit with his fabulous 1974 smash "I Can Help." Swan was a writer at Cedarwood at the time (he'd already penned the Clyde McPhatter hit "Lover Please") and was pals with Tillis and Fred Burch. He had first met Gary at a Mel Tillis gig in Fort Walton Beach, Florida. "We hit it off right away. Gary loved Jerry Lee Lewis and we started talking about how great J.M. Van Eaton's drumming was on those Sun records." The pair wrote one song together—a ballad called "Spare Me" ("Spare me/Because I'm all I've got"), which Gary demoed at Cedarwood. Swan recalled somebody covering the number, but I have yet to find any evidence. Billy never bumped into Gary again, much to his regret. "You just liked the guy. Great smile. And a great singer."

One Cedarwood demo stands far above the rest. It's Gary's first solo songwriting credit, and what a stunner: "A Woman Will Tear the Heart Out of a Man." Unfortunately it wasn't unearthed by archivist/reissue producer Mark Linn until after Stewart's death. Boy, would I have some questions! Over a meandering, lazy acoustic guitar and tinkling honky-tonk piano, Gary wails the words in a matter-of-fact way far too weary for his age. "Give her a chance, there's nothing she won't do/Give her an inch, she'll take a mile or two/She knows how to tear a good man down, make him feel like crawlin' on the ground," he sings matter-of-factly. Who provoked such casual venom? Mary Lou? I'll never know.

Perhaps the bile was inspired by Lou's new (if brief) occupation. During this period Gary continued playing the hits of the day locally—he even sheepishly admitted that he was in a "psychedelic rock band" for half a minute that went by the name Electric Banana—usually with his ex–Tom Cat buddy Joe Parker. When Joe's house burned down in February of 1966, the owners of the Colonial Inn, the joint they'd been playing, offered to hire both Mary Lou and Joe's wife Karen as go-go girls. Gary and Joe weren't thrilled. "Both of them were insanely jealous of their wives," said daughter Chris Parker. "So Gary and Joe said, 'Only way we're going to let them dance is if we're playing the music.'" Mary Lou and Karen go-go-ed at the Colonial as well as Domino's in Vero Beach. "We danced together for a year and a half," said Karen, but "Joe and Gary didn't really like it. So we had to give it up."

Grandal's wife Candy felt Gary was threatened by Lou's independence. "I worked and went out in the world. Gary was old-fashioned, he wanted women to depend on him. He didn't like for Lou to work. He wanted her to stay home, keep the house spotless and clean. That's the way he was. You didn't talk back to him."

Mary Lou, Gary, and unknown go-go dancer.
(Tommy Schwartz collection)

5

MUSIC CITY ASSEMBLY LINE

I took the songwriting thing very lightly. But totally serious at the same time. We were serious about it, but we weren't...'Boy we're in Nashville, we've made it to the big time!' Shit, I'd see people that had acted that way. And they didn't have many friends...Assholes have short careers.

– Gary Stewart

Write songs. The two-word command of Mel Tillis kept rattling around Gary's brain. Songwriting was very much on his mind when he bumped into local cop Bill Eldridge at the local Searstown mall. Three years older than Gary, William "Billy" Eldridge was a Fort Pierce native who'd already had success with an intoxicating rockabilly number cut with his band the Fireballs called "Let's Go Baby," released in 1959 by local record-store owner Irvin Vulgamore on his miniscule Vulco label. Something of a hit, it was rereleased (and rerecorded) by United Artists. Eldridge had sat in with the Tom Cats at the Merry-Go-Round, and was, as Gary put it, "the town hero when it came to rock music." Right there at the mall, Gary made his pitch. "I said, 'Bill, I think we can go to Nashville if you want to write some songs, because Mel Tillis told me so! Why don't we get together and write?'" Eldridge took him up on the offer.

"I used to see Gary, just a little ol' thing, walkin' down the road carryin' a guitar," said Eldridge, who got a little melancholy thinking back to Fort Pierce in those days. "There wasn't nothin' here then. It was just a little dirt town...it was better times, everybody was slowed down. There wasn't all the crap goin' on, crack and all that shit. People killin' people. It ain't nothin' like it was, it ain't home." Thinking about his old partnership with Stewart seemed to sadden Bill.

"Gary still reminds me of a kid. A likeable kid. Always friendly, but he will say what's on his mind. Unfortunately, there have been times when he would've been better off not saying anything. He'll tell some people, point blank, if they rubbed him the wrong way. And some people can't accept that. He was always very honest with me...I tried to write with other people, but they ain't no fuckin' fun to write with." For a second there, Bill and Gary were a hit team. Gary would move on, Bill would be left behind.

A bear of a guy—"built when meat was cheap" as Gary put it during an old local radio broadcast—Eldridge possessed a melodious tenor voice and played unerring rhythm guitar. "Billy was the tastiest player," said fellow guitarist Jimmy Smith. "He didn't use any effects. Just clean, perfect rhythm. And a funny motherfucker. He would say some shit onstage sometimes, it would just make you gasp. Dirty fucking jokes. There'd be some Bible-thumpers in the audience and he'd say, 'Jesus Christ, All Muddy.' I was like, 'Billy, you can't say that!'"

There are a million Eldridge stories. Gary recalled one night when Bill and Walter Carlton were driving Walter's "Wild Boar" hot rod around town. Drunk out of their minds, Carlton and Eldridge decided they'd taunt local lawman Ralph Johnson by tearing up the streets of Fort Pierce. "Bill drove that fucker through town doing over a hundred," said Gary. Finally Johnson caught up with them. "The next thing I know I'm lookin' in the barrel of this pistol stickin' right in my face and I said, 'Hey, goddamn, man, we was just runnin', we ain't gonna fight,'" said Eldridge. "That was my only stint in jail, and needless to say, it did me wonders. I knew right then it wasn't my chosen profession." Funnily enough, Eldridge became a Fort Pierce cop himself in 1964, and it was Johnson who recommended him for the job.

One night in the seventies Billy pulled Jimmy Smith over. Jimmy had a pot plant he'd been growing on Walter Carlton's property in the car with him. Gary's brother Gerald had mistakenly snipped it, so Smith carted it home. "This big-ass fucking plant about twelve feet high! I jammed it in the back seat and pot leaves were hanging out the back window, I didn't give a fuck. It looked like a Cheech and Chong movie. I pull out, and guess who's sitting there in a fucking cop car but Billy Eldridge! And he goes, 'What the fuck is wrong with you, boy? I'm gonna let you slide this time. Get on outta here.' He then pointed at the giant plant and said, 'And put somethin' over *that*.'" Gary added a solemn coda to the tale: "Bill was a good cop, he really was."

When Gary first asked Bill to collaborate, Eldridge was skeptical. "I says, 'Shit, I don't know anything about writin' songs.' We just kind of stumbled on together. Gary's stuff was better than mine, I'll have to admit. The stuff I was writin' wasn't worth a shit!" They started hitting Nashville together in 1966 or so. At first the pair wrote songs separately, bringing them to Cedarwood for consideration, giving them to the publishing company's executive, John Denny. "Poor ol' John would take everything we did and say, 'Oh, this is great!' He didn't know what a hit song was, and we had absolutely no idea of what we were doin'."

A fortuitous event then occurred. Fred Burch had been working with another publisher up the street, Forrest Hills Music, and one day took Gary and Bill over there. The little company was run by Jerry Bradley, son of legendary producer Owen Bradley (Harold, Owen's brother and a fabled session guitarist, co-owned the company).[30] Burch said he mentioned to Bradley that "Gary's got some songs—you wanna publish 'em? He said, 'Yeah.' I said, 'I would like half the publishing.'" Bradley gave Burch half, and got Gary Stewart in return. Another lucky break.

* * *

Born in Nashville, Tennessee, in 1940, Jerry Bradley would later become head of RCA Nashville, signing Gary and making him a star. Jerry would produce many acts at RCA, hitmakers Charley Pride and Dottie West among them. He signed Alabama. Jerry was a marketer as well, as evidenced by his concocted 1973 supergroup the Outlaws. "I'm not a musician," said Bradley. "I didn't try to hide it. I just surrounded myself with the best musicians in Nashville and tried to find the best songs I could."

Not everybody was crazy about Bradley. "I liked Jerry, but he drove me a little nuts," Waylon Jennings wrote in his autobiography. "He didn't have a clue about music, though he always tried to get involved in it, usually by remote control." According to Waylon, Bradley would call him into his office to give him written instructions on what needed to be changed. Waylon would head back into the studio, jiggle a few faders, and bring the exact same recording back to Jerry. "He never knew I didn't fix a thing. We'd have fights so loud in his office that secretaries would be grabbing aspirin bottles and running for cover... He was in the old style.... he fought me every step of the way."

This was not the scenario that would play out between Gary Stewart and Bradley. Gary was not the type to go to war over his

---

30 A rather imperious figure in Nashville history, Owen Bradley was not an easy man to please. "He could dress you down pretty good then turn around and be your pal later," said his son in a 2012 interview with John Rumble. Jerry became emotional when asked about the first time his work was given approval from his father. He'd mixed a record, and Owen "turned to me and said, 'What do you think?' and I thought, 'Man, I've arrived. Owen Bradley wants to know what the hell I think.'" Fred Bogert, a musician who later worked with Gary, mentioned to Owen he knew Jerry. "You've met my asshole son?" was Owen's response.

music—or anything else, unless pushed to the wall. He would prove to be a far more slippery character. Gary was certainly capable of entertaining whatever a record company executive wanted him to do—hell, he might even promise do it. Or he could return to Fort Pierce, change his mind, and not answer your calls for a few weeks. Stewart would be one of Bradley's early successes, and in his view, one of his most painful failures. Jerry sounded like an angry father when I'd ask him about Gary. And Stewart was expert at playing the errant son.

But all that was off in a misty future. Stewart and Eldridge signed with Forrest Hills, which would remain Gary's publishing company for the rest of his life. The first Stewart–Eldridge song to make a little noise was "Charlotte North Carolina," a 1967 release by, as Eldridge put it, "some unknown little shithead named Jimmy Griggs on Boot Heel Records.[31] The song was about some guy who got drafted and was goin' off to the Vietnam War. We started to call it 'Charleston,' crossed it out and wrote 'Charlotte' because it sounded like a girl's name." Bill heard the song on the air and flipped. "I used to leave the radio on WSM all night and here I am sound asleep. I recognized the song, it woke me up and I called Gary. I don't even think we knew the guy had done it."

When it came to songwriting, Bradley certainly wasn't the easy mark that John Denny had been. When Gary and Bill played Jerry a song they'd been working on called "Anna," he rejected it. "Jerry said, 'I don't like it,'" recalled Bill. "Nobody told us that before." Bradley zeroed in on why. "There's a line in there, 'A woman like you could make a man of me'—that's your song title right there. Leave Anna out of it."

"They had good ideas," said Bradley. "But they wrote two songs within one—they'd get a subject and start down one way and they'd get a little off track, stray from the subject. I would critique the songs to help them make 'em better, and they'd listen."

31 The single erroneously lists the writers of the song as Jerry and Harold Bradley.

Inspired by the criticism, Gary and Bill rewrote the song on the drive back to Fort Pierce, Eldridge at the wheel. ("I didn't trust Gary's drivin'," said Bill.) "Before we even got out of Tennessee and into Georgia we had written this thing." A stone classic country ballad, "Only a Woman Like You" would be recorded in 1969 by Jack Greene and was also cut by Billy Walker, Nat Stuckey, and others. Between 1969 and 1970 Stewart and Eldridge songs were cut by a variety of popular country artists, including Stuckey ("Sweet Thang and Cisco," "The Snuff Queen"), Hank Snow ("Vanishing Breed"), and Billy Walker, who hit number three with both "When a Man Loves a Woman (the Way That I Love You)" and "She Goes Walking Through My Mind" in 1970. Maybe the best of them is Jack Greene's version of "There's a Whole Lot About a Woman (a Man Don't Know)," featuring the keening steel guitar of Weldon Myrick.

Gary and Bill developed an immediately recognizable style, writing dynamic, tightly constructed songs with adroit wordplay. Gary and Bill had the rare knack of writing clever country novelty songs that were actually funny, such as "You Can't Housebreak a Tomcat," which was cut by Cal Smith, and one recorded by Del Reeves, "It Takes Me All Night Long" ("I used to get more women than I could put my hands on/Now I put my hands on more than I can get....It takes me all night long/To do what I used to do all night long"). "I used to write 'em dirty," said Eldridge. "Actually, it was easier to just write 'em dirtier than shit and clean 'em up."

When it came to songwriting, Stewart and Eldridge were a perfect match. "I'm an idea and melody man, and Bill can think of a better way to say anything I can think of," Gary told the music press at the time. "He's a polish man." Eldridge stressed the ease of writing with Gary. Songs just flowed out: "If he had an idea, I'd work on it, if I had an idea, he'd work on it with me. It was fifty-fifty. Ideal. And we were having a big time doin' it. We'd get excited, it felt so good."

In February 1969 Eldridge announced to a local Fort Pierce reporter that he and Gary were going to Nashville in a couple weeks with "about ten new songs. 1969 is going to be our year. I just know it." Eldridge was right. "We did a session and three of the songs were placed," Stewart recalled. "That's real good. Jerry Bradley called us up an' says, 'Y'all want to just move to Nashville and work for so much a week and work at Bradley's Barn?' That way we could meet people to pitch songs to and just learn about the whole business...fame's callin', see?" Gary and Bill eventually took the plunge, Stewart relocating his family to the Battlefield Trailer Park in Franklin, Tennessee.

At the same time Jerry Bradley was running Forrest Hills, he was also working as an engineer at Bradley's Barn, situated on a sixty-five-acre farm in Mt. Juliet, Tennessee, that his father Owen had bought. "I thought we were gonna raise cows," said Jerry initially of the large red structure with giant white "BB" on the front. But his crafty father had a plan—instead of enduring a three-year ban on recording in Nashville after selling his hit-factory studio the Quonset Hut to Columbia in 1961, he had a studio built inside the barn, which was twenty miles outside of town. That way he could keep recording, and many an artist followed him there.

"We got so busy," said Jerry, who sometimes overnighted on the couch there. "We were a hot little studio." Loretta Lynn, Jack Greene, Brenda Lee, Kitty Wells, and the Osborne Brothers all recorded there, as did Gordon Lightfoot and Joan Baez (not to mention J.J. Cale, who cut pieces of his first three albums there). "Bradley's Barn was something special," said Eldridge. "It was out in the country, it was laid-back, and the pickers absolutely loved it. They got out of town!" Bill and Gary helped the engineers, set up mics, ran for coffee, swept up, and did whatever else was needed. Being on deck was an amazing opportunity for Gary to study how country records were recorded—handy knowledge for making his own, which was happening at the same time. In March 1969, Bradley got both Eldridge and Stewart recording contracts with Kapp Records, a formerly independent label that'd hit big with Louis Armstrong's recording of "Hello, Dolly!"

"Recording was accidental," Gary said in 1975. "I just wanted to make a go of it as a songwriter." Maybe he wasn't taking the idea all that seriously, but when it came to performing a song, Stewart was already giving his all. Recorded in June 1968 and released in August, "Merry-Go-Round" backed with "Here Comes That Feeling Again" (both written by Stewart–Eldridge), was a tough one-two punch perfect for Gary's debut as a country artist. The A-side was a jukebox-perfect tale of demon alcohol ("the only help I get is through the neck of a bottle") while the flip showed Stewart equally at home with a slow, sad ballad. It would be the first and last record Jerry would produce on Gary.

Steel guitar whiz Walter Haynes entered the picture. Famous for playing groundbreaking steel parts on such hits as Patsy Cline's "Crazy" and "We Could" by "Little" Jimmy Dickens, Haynes later produced stellar recordings on Cal Smith, Wayne Kemp, and Jeanne Pruett. Haynes was running Kapp when Stewart was signed. "He didn't want me to cut Gary," said Jerry. "I got in a situation where it was 'Shit, was I gonna have an artist on the label or not?' so I told Walter to cut him."

Haynes would produce the rest of the Stewart sessions for Kapp, and they are fabulous records with that icy-hot late-sixties honky-tonk sound, hits or not. Both Gary and Bill credited Haynes, who played steel on most of their recordings (and even cowrote a song or two) with further improving their writing. (Despite Stewart and Eldridge lauding Haynes's contributions, Bradley was dismissive. "Walter Haynes didn't play any role in it at all, really. He was a steel guitar player. He worked for me and I gave Walter a place to be reached during the day.")[32]

Kapp put out another Gary Stewart single in June 1969. "Sweet-Tater and Cisco" is a story song about a couple of drunken louts that leaps off the grooves with a roar. When Gary hits that chorus, oh, it's a thrill: "And I said, 'Hello, honey, go borrow some money / Get your sweet man outta the can / Well, it's Saturday night, they've got me locked up tight / Way off I can hear a band.'" Any song that rhymes "Studebaker" with "jailer" deserves our attention, and not

32 Haynes would become Owen Bradley's right-hand man at Decca, and Bradley would turn many artists over to Walter to produce. A low-key guy admired by many, Walter preferred steel guitar over the mixing console. "Making records was OK but I enjoy playing much better!" he said in 2000.

only does this one feature a honky-tonk named Bottom of the Pile, the protagonists stop at a hippie love-in. And Gary sings the hell out of it! I mean, what *more* do you want out of life?

It would take a title change by Nat Stuckey, who had a 1966 hit called "Sweet Thang," to send it chartbound. "Nat came to us and said, 'Boys, I love that damn song. Can I change "Sweet Tater" to "Sweet Thang"?'" Eldridge recalled. They didn't mind, and Stuckey's recording—far less exciting than Stewart's—zoomed to number four on the charts. The B-side of Gary's version, "Little Old Love Light," featured some great singing of questionable rhymes ("Then she ran off with another man/The next I heard they were living in Cheyenne").

In November came the next Stewart single, "Big Bertha, the Truck Driving Queen," an amusing, sitar-driven waddling boogie which details a crass encounter with a voracious trucker ("Save me from this man-sized woman with man-sized arms"). On the flip was "The Lesser of Two Evils," which espoused the same sad, woman-weary outlook of "A Woman Will Tear the Heart Out of a Man"—"The lesser of two evils said goodbye..."

* * *

The boys were on a roll. "It got to a certain point where everything we'd write, people just wanted it," said Eldridge. Gary kept a diary in 1970, mostly listing the many sessions at Bradley's Barn, and one can feel the excitement and wonder bleeding out of his impatient scrawl:

> April 27: "Me, Bill and Bobby Wattrell and Steve cut "Lord Is That Me"....Went to the store and got honey for Jan Howard. She said, 'Thank you, honey, for the honey.'"
> "[W]orked at the Wagon Wheel made $178"
> April 29: "Was with Mel Tillis today. Helped him learn a new song he's cutting in a few days."

April 30: "Met Skeeter Davis in her producer Ron Light's office"

May 4: "Worked Kitty Wells session...went WSM to see Ralph Emery. Eddie Arnold called for one of our songs."

May 6: "Met Little Jimmy Dickens in Decca today. We took him some songs to listen to."

May 25: "Was having lunch with Walter Haynes and Bill Eldridge at Lum's and Chet Atkins came over and set next to me and he remembered my first name."

May 28: "Today I'm 26 years old and did my first background singing at RCA on Nat Stuckey's song 'Caffeine Nicotine and Benzedrine'...<u>Chet bought me a beer</u>" [underlined by Gary, obviously an important event].

June 1: "Just found out by seeing a chart today we have Hank Snow's record."

June 12: "We had a going-away party today for Jerry Bradley who's going to RCA as Chet's assistant. Everybody got drunk, especially Bill Eldridge. Went to the Grand Ol' Opry, sat on stage."

* * *

In April of that year Stewart's next Kapp single was released and it was a stone-cold masterpiece: "You're Not the Woman You Use to Be." "A three-minute soap opera, that's what a country song is," Gary once told me, and here was evidence that he and Eldridge had mastered the form. I believe this is the record where Stewart began getting compared to his early influence Jerry Lee Lewis, because it does have that knife-sharp sound of a mid-sixties Smash Records Jerry Lee number, and Gary's vocal is similar, if you took the murder out of Jerry Lee's voice. If you ask me, it's a superficial resemblance, other than the confidence, authority, and attitude that they brought to a song—once either performed a number, cover it at your own risk, because you're not going to better either. But Jerry Lee would stick to a certain formula he was genius at, while Gary, affected by a newer generation of influences, ventured into more esoteric territory, for better and for worse.[33]

The subject here is infidelity, addressed to the cheating wife, and Gary talks some of the lines to devastating effect: listen to the doom-laden way he delivers "your friend just called." The verses are a classic litany of mundane-details-gone-wrong the betrayed is scrutinizing as he sifts for evidence of the crime, and it's written in that convoluted, indirect style Nashville specialized in at the time: "The clothes you wear leave so little to imagine what you should be hiding," a fancy way of saying his wife looks like a slut. And the postman is bringing "bills for things 'til lately you didn't need."

The pain is palpable, and it is a bravura performance from Stewart. "I got 'Pick of the Week' in Cashbox," Gary wrote in his diary April 14th. Three days later he added "Just learned from Owen Bradley 'You're Not the Woman' is doing good." Inexplicably the record failed to chart. It would take a rerelease after Stewart became a star for this superb record to connect.

As great as they were, none of the Kapp singles hit. As Jerry Bradley put it rather coldly, "Walter cut Gary. Nothin' ever happened." Other tracks were cut that wouldn't see light of day until a 1975 MCA album and they were all crackerjack[34]—like "The Snuff Queen," a humorous number about some trollop who's "got a face like I ain't never seen/ She's been featured on the back cover of a farmer's magazine." If that doesn't grab you, the next line rhymes "baloney" with "matrimony." Yes! The song is rich in absurd details, and on the fadeout he squeezes in, "Man, that gal's gotta face makes a fella wanna carry a sack."

I laugh every time I hear this number and I've been listening over forty years now. So imagine my shock in 2021, long after Gary had

33 Another difference: Gary was not torn between the sacred and the profane. I once asked him if rock and roll was the devil's music. He laughed in my face. "NO, man! It makes you feel good. Makes you want to have a good time. What's wrong with havin' a good time? Hey, one person will hear it and wanna fuck, another person might want to clap their hands. Rock and roll makes you move. Anything that makes you move is good."

34 The title of the collection was *You're Not the Woman You Used to Be*, which, unlike the single, added a "d" to "use."

passed, when Tommy Schwartz pulled out a scratchy Forrest Hills acetate featuring a solo acoustic country-blues version of the song. It's radically different, with most of the humor turned into menace, yet without sounding gimmicky or forced. Gary sounds like he's sitting on a desolate railway platform after the last train has left town, lost in the shadows under a black hat. A performance that could sit comfortably on a jukebox next to Frank Hutchison's 1927 classic "Worried Blues," it leaves you wondering: How did Gary conjure up this version as opposed to the rollicking released one? Did it come to him in a dream? That's what it sounds like to me.

* * *

Back in Florida, Eldridge accompanied Gary onstage for Wagon Wheel gigs on weekends. There are two Wagon Wheel tapes—one a fifteen-minute radio show taped for WOKC in Okeechobee, during which Gary charges through Merle Haggard's "Fugitive," "Hello Josephine," and "Let's Forget That I'm Married," a Stewart original that wouldn't get recorded until over a decade later, rewritten and under a slightly different title. Better still is a very crude live tape from the club itself. Stewart blasts through Lead Belly's "Take This Hammer," his own "Here Comes That Feeling," the Nat Stuckey hit "Joe and Mabel's 12th Street Bar and Grill," Dolly and Porter's "Last Thing on My Mind," plus a vicious rendition of Dale Hawkins's "Susie Q." Gary even hosts a limbo contest ("He wants some girl to hold his pole," cracks Stewart) and sings "Happy Birthday" to somebody named Lucky.

The energy displayed in these tapes is formidable, with Stewart practically vibrating through the speakers. "I love music because it's the best drug there is—it's *adrenaline*," Gary told me once. "Music turns on the adrenaline in me and God blessed me with a big ol' bunch of it." And how. Silent home movies exist of Stewart onstage at the Wagon Wheel backing up Carl Butler, Jack Greene, and playing with Eldridge. Stewart is a whirling honky-tonk dervish, laughing, singing, cutting up, always on the move. It's hard to reconcile this Gary with the moody recluse of later decades. "When I listen to that WOKC tape it makes me want to cry, because I remember that Gary—before hard drugs," said Tommy Schwartz. "He was a comedian, a really funny emcee. Gary was always a great singer and a musician, but there was just something else...you saw star quality in his personality."

Innocent times. Those home movies show it. "We used to laugh our asses off," said Gary, smiling at the memory. Eldridge and Stewart loved a good prank. After hours in the studio they'd pick some hapless individual out of the phone book, call them up, and record it. Like the time they rang one Willie Gilliam in Mt. Juliet to inform him that his elephant had arrived from New Delhi, they were holding it at the airport, and it was time to come get his animal. "Man, I don't want this elephant," said the panicked Mr. Gilliam. "But the bill is gettin' high on peanuts," said Gary, a field recording of an elephant blaring in the background. Another time the pair wrote a song with Stewart's Wagon Wheel buddy Hubert Thomas. "It wasn't really that good of a song as it turned out, but Hubert was thrilled to death he had a part in it," said Eldridge. Unbeknownst to Hubert, the pair had secretly recorded "a vulgar version of this serious song." They summoned Thomas to the studio to hear their creation. "He's sittin' there, and I think the first couple of lines kinda shot by him," Bill continued. "I don't think he believed what he was hearin'. Hubert kinda looked at us...it still didn't hit him, 'cause we were sittin' there real serious, listenin' to this song. And then, of course, we couldn't stand it any longer...We just wanted to pull the ol' boy's leg." "Hubert was no bozo," Gary felt compelled to add.

Then there was Roy Green, the country comedian at the Wagon Wheel. "I was the straight man and he'd do the jokes," Stewart recalled. "He'd get drunk and take his teeth out. Lord, one night I remember the Glaser Brothers were onstage. They was introducing 'em, and we was backstage. Roy was dressed up like a clown. He was drinkin' that whiskey and he'd get wild. We heard 'em say, 'And this is my little boy Jim Glaser, he's twenty-one.' Ol' Roy hollers, 'Is that the first or second time around?' and the whole place could hear it. We was drunk!"

Things degenerated further on the ride home that night. Roy, who was completely schnockered, "drove right through the people's yards to get into his driveway," said Stewart. "Pulled the door open to his house, went into the Frigidaire and pulled every fuckin' thing out, throwed it all over the kitchen. Big ol' breakfast table, picked it up and threw it against the wall, busted up windows. He'd bought him a new Western pistol, boy, he had this thing out—his wife is hollerin', 'Roy, put the gun away!' He tore that house apart. Wild." When I asked where Roy was these days, Stewart's tone grew conspiratorial. "Out of state," he muttered, refusing to say more. "Roy got in...trouble. His old lady's lookin' for him." Just another Fort Pierce legend.

* * *

On April 29, Gary and Lou's second child, Shannon Doah' was born. Making her name sound like Shenandoah, there was some sixties whimsy. "Mom and Dad were gypsies, what can I say," explained Shannon. For the past couple of years the Stewarts had been living at 706 8th Street in Fort Pierce in a mod little pad they'd decorated with African masks, Buddha statues, a leopard-skin couch, and a tiki bar. With the major hubbub happening for Gary in Music City, they headed for the trailer park in Franklin, Tennessee.

* * *

In the midst of all the Bradley's Barn action, Gary had time to record an interesting little side project that was about as far from Music City as you could get. It started with a song: "Grandma's Roadhouse," an entertaining ode to greasy spoons/home-cooking joints accompanied by a nifty descending chorus (Stewart played the song frequently in my presence). "Barbecued pork on cornbread, sure do treat your belly fine/A tall, cool glass of buttermilk, that's how grandma blows your mind," go the opening lyrics, which proceed to extol the virtues of jukeboxes and Wanda Jean the waitress. Stewart cut a version in May 1970 (presumed lost), then recorded a Fort Pierce band called the Nubrume doing it at Bradley's Barn in June.

"Billy Eldridge played a gut-string guitar on the song and Gary was our producer," said Tommy Schwartz, who was in the band alongside Gary's brother Gregory. A tape of the number exists, with the boys screwing around with tape-loop echo after the take, shouting out expletives and corny phrases to amuse themselves. At the very end, Gary chimes in with a rather earnest, "Honey, you got the biggest pussy I've ever seen."

The first thing Tommy noticed on this Nashville visit was that Gary was driving a new car, a '63 Chevy. Schwartz asked what happened to the old one. "Gary said, 'Oh man, I slid that off the side of a mountain.'" Gary took Tommy and his bandmates down to some little roadside stand where they sold cherry cider in gallon jugs. "He told us when you smoke your pot, it takes the burn right out of your throat...so anytime we smoked dope, we had to have that cherry cider." Next it was time to eat, and the "Grandma's Roadhouse" song was no joke. "Gary knew every little place in that area where they had a lunch special for a dollar and a quarter and you got a refill on vegetables," said Tommy. Stewart was such a space case he had to pull over and ask directions everywhere. Once they finally got to his favorite local greasy spoon, Gary started making "these bird calls... he'd make it sound like there was a bird under the table, and he'd get the waitresses going fucking nuts. We were laughing our asses off, man. He was such a character, going out and being with him was such a ball."[35] He told the band they could visit Bradley's Barn the next day—and gave them "Grandma's Roadhouse" to cut.

35 A book could be written about Stewart and food. Robert "Cotton" Payne, a drummer in Stewart's Drugstore Cowboys band, recalled that at restaurants Gary "would order four or five plates of food. I mean, different *meals*. He'd eat one thing off each plate and leave the rest of it."

That version never saw release, but the next one would, barely. Gary had called up his old friend from the Imps, Riley Watkins, and invited him to Bradley's Barn to record. Watkins was working with a new trio that featured Jim Snead on drums and Jim Noveskey on bass. "We didn't have a record deal," said Riley, who recalled Stewart telling him that "Owen Bradley was looking for a soundalike Creedence Clearwater band...Gary was gettin' free studio time plus a free board man." The band was living in Michigan and playing at the Log Cabin Bar in Detroit. "When we got done playing we would take off to Nashville there to Bradley's Barn," according to Jim Snead. "We would record all night Sunday and take off in time to get to work Monday morning." They made several trips to Nashville to record.

Stewart and Eldridge contributed four songs to the sessions, Eldridge played rhythm guitar, and Gary sang and played lead and rhythm, along with piano and harmonica. "Gary had a ton of songs," said Jim Snead. "I mean a *ton* of songs." "Love, Love You Lady," perhaps the most rococo number in Stewart's ouevre, was a ballad Tommy Schwartz had heard Gary writing on piano over at his parents' house during Christmas 1969. Stewart told him he was trying to write a "Neil Young–type song" (aside from the harmonies, it sounds more early Elton John to me). Thankfully Gary abandoned this line of attack. Same for "Drinkin' Them Corn Squeezins," a greasy ode to moonshine that sports a bellicose, overwrought Stewart vocal just this side of Jim Dandy—he's gonna huff and puff and *rock* your house down! Best of all the songs is "Easy People," a fantastic redneck anthem Gary would record later but sung by Riley here.

Their version of "Grandma's Roadhouse" is the most fun of the bunch. The recording starts with a fade-in nearly a minute long as everybody chants "grandma's roadhouse, grandma's roadhouse, grandma's roadhouse." "We were trying to make it feel like a rowdy bunch of good ol' boys, out after a honky-tonk night for a bite to eat," said Noveskey. The band is heard "just chuckin' a bunch of bottles in baskets, y'know, breakin' 'em up and actin' like we're havin' a wild party," added Watkins. "Most records were closing with noise on the end at that time. Well, we decided we're gonna be different. We're gonna *open* with noise."

Then Eldridge's rhythm guitar kicks in ("like the steam drivers on a freight train," said Noveskey) and Riley wails the song, Gary chiming in on harmony. It's a hopping little number fueled by Stewart's electric guitar, which is all over the sessions. ("He played good slide," said Watkins. "Pickin' on his knee.") The song ends as ridiculously as it begins, with everybody saying goodbye to Granny, who tells them "Y'all come back and see me!" Then the door slams (Granny was played by Gary, who had more lines, but the door slam left him speechless, causing everybody to burst out laughing). Jim Snead had a concise answer as to the reason for this obtuse opening/closing overture: "Because we were stoned." There is an alternate version in which Stewart shouts out such lines as "Gimme some o' them beans, Ma!"

It's an odd collection of songs, a lot rock, a little country, a bit psychedelic. But Owen Bradley did not exactly see this motley bunch as the next Creedence. "That was our aim there, but it didn't please him," said Riley. "He didn't want anything to do with it." According to Snead, part of his displeasure was the fact that not only had they recorded a Watkins-penned paean to weed—"Field of Green"—they were caught smoking the green in the studio bathroom along with one of their engineers. "He'd never smoked marijuana ever, and we rolled a big fat joint, I think he had a couple of tokes of it. Jerry Bradley or Owen, one of 'em came in, and said, 'I *know* what you guys are doing in here, because I can *smell it out front*.' Oh man, we got caught!"

Their tenure at Bradley's Barn abruptly ending, Watkins and the band returned to the Motor City and, after Motown honcho Berry Gordy also turned them away, they decided to release an album culled from the sessions on their own non-label, Mo-Fok Records. Titled *Grandma's Roadhouse*, the band was listed simply as Riley; the spartan white sleeve had only stamped lettering on the cover and some stock-art hippie-esque drawings of a band on the back. "We had five hundred copies made and we sold some of them where we played at," said Snead. "That was about it." In 2010 Mark Linn of Delmore Recording Society resurrected this obscure album (complete with compelling outtakes), shedding light on a little-known piece of Gary's history. Looking back, it hints at the many directions Stewart would take in the future.

* * *

In November of 1970 came an unexpected little session that would yet again alter the trajectory of Stewart's career, although it would take a few years. Henry Hurt was a Nashville publishing music executive who'd been contacted by Motown's publishing arm Jobete Music. They wanted to cut a few demos of familiar Motown hits done country-style in the hopes of enticing Music City artists to them. Hurt knew the right man for the job. (Stewart maintained it was because he was cheap!) "I knew Gary well because he wrote for a company across from my office for years," said Henry. "Interpreting a pop song in a country format took a singer familiar with both. Gary was a perfect fit." Stewart went over to D.B.M. Studios in Nashville and for the princely sum of $30—ten bucks a song—he cut country versions of the Four Tops' "Baby I Need Your Loving" and "I Can't Help Myself (Sugar Pie Honey Bunch)" as well as Stevie Wonder's "Yester-Me, Yester-You, Yesterday." Backed by ace studio musicians ("David Briggs, Norbert Putnam, Jerry Carrigan, Billy Sanford, Chip Young, and maybe Jerry Shook," recalled Hurt), they knocked out the songs in an hour and a half. Stewart sang the hell out of these soul hits then promptly forgot about them. But they would eventually make their way to a producer who'd become obsessed with the singer on the trio of demos.

Gary was dropped by Kapp in June 1970 and moved to Decca, where one single was released—"She's the Next Best Thing (To Being There)" and "Something to Believe In." Both were Stewart–Eldridge songs, the A-side a wistful ballad rendered with memorable restraint, making it one of Stewart's finest. Owen Bradley himself produced this session in May 1971, along with a number that saw release a few years later, the ultra-square "You're Everything (God Meant Woman to Be)." The single went nowhere. Though it contains an utterly moving vocal by Stewart, Gary didn't care for the recording, but that might've been colored by Owen's exacting demands. "That's a sloucher to me. I had to sing *every single line* separate. Owen Bradley liked dictation, y'know—'What are you sayin'?' Hey, it's my SLANG." Gary laughed, but the point was made. He had a style, and in that town his delivery, as unique as it was, became a blessing and a curse. It wasn't typical Music City, nor would it ever be.

* * *

Bill Eldridge and Gary, 1971. (Gina Stewart collection)

The year 1970 had been the biggest yet for the Stewart–Eldridge team, and 1971 was shaping up as more of the same. "It got to a certain point where everything we wrote, people just wanted it," said Eldridge. But there was a fly in the ointment: Gary. He had discovered some life-changing music by way of a friend. "We had met some people in Franklin that were real longhairs," said Mary Lou, who pointed out that at the time she'd "never seen a guy with long hair." They prodded Gary into going to a concert. He didn't know who he was gonna go see." The band was the Allman Brothers.

"I wasn't much for goin' to concerts—big concerts," explained Stewart. "I was in the very last row, 'cause my head could reach back and touch the concrete. I smiled and laughed out loud through the concert. From the moment they started playin', they were *gettin' it* and it wasn't no bunch of noise. It was *loud* and *powerful* but it was good. Blues, country, jazz, boogie-woogie, honky-tonk country licks, everything...they incorporated it, took it, and carried it *beyond*. They could get down to a whisper and you could hear the crowd all hushed—and then *build* it, and the audience would go crazy. The first Southern rock, the KINGS of Southern rock. Number one, the *best*."

Stewart came back from that concert a changed man. He came home raving, "These guys picked, Lou, and I ain't never see nothing like it. They blew me away. My face hurts from smilin'!" I believe Stewart saw the Allman Brothers on May 13, 1971, at Tennessee Technological University in Cookeville. Their first two studio albums had been released and the monumental *The Allman Brothers Band at Fillmore East* would come out a little over a month later. Wondrous guitar player Duane Allman was still performing with the six-piece band (he'd die in a motorcycle accident that October). For the rest of his life Stewart would be obsessed with the Allman Brothers, chasing down live tapes and TV performances (particularly with Duane) every chance he got. Even though he became friends with the band and made music with them, he'd never stop being a maniacal fan. I once suggested to Gary his music meant as much to me as the Allmans had meant to him. He scoffed.

"Well, did *you* ever pay somebody to fill in for you on your gig so you could go follow 'em on the road?" (Had me there.)

Seeing the band in concert made him realize this was exactly the kind of music he wanted to make: "I was an assembly-line writer 'til I heard the Allman Brothers." Now that he and Eldridge had perfected their songwriting formula, he rejected it. "I felt like I was selling out. Writing songs wasn't art anymore; it was just for the money." He went straight to Jerry Bradley's office. "I came into work Monday mornin' and I says, 'I know what I want to do. I'm goin' home.' We had four songs in the charts—that's good. Success as songwriters. And to walk away from that? And not even have a job...?" With that, Gary said goodbye to Nashville.

Gary had already been undergoing a transformation while living in Franklin. "I was smokin' grass...I was a country hippie." And he'd been experimenting musically, taping himself with a Rheem Roberts reel-to-reel tape recorder, doing acoustic numbers that were a far cry from "Big Bertha, the Truck Driving Queen." Some are just Gary alone with an acoustic, like "Beautiful River," a wide-open ode that conjures up steamboats and river captains, with Gary whistling the last minute of the song. It could be off an album by the Band.

There are several long, rambling, semi-stoned versions of "The Ballad of Corsia and John," a song he'd consolidate and record in the studio many years later. Carrie "Corsia" Shupe was Georgia's sister, and one of Gary's favorite relatives. "Corsia was this little bitty woman that had been born with a cleft palate," said Brenda Casey. "Back in the Depression, they didn't get those repaired, so when she spoke, she had a very unusual voice, a little difficult to understand. Corsia was kind of feisty. Nobody crossed her." Corsia was married to John Shupe, a miner that worked for George Stewart. "He loved to drink," said Grandal. "He'd get the ol' man to run get him some damn moonshine, but, Lord, when he would get on that shit, son, he'd tear the whole house completely apart. Break every dish. Corsia would come down to our house and Mama had to hide her up in the loft. Then John would come down and say, 'Oh, I'll never touch liquor again.' The same old sad song."[36]

Accompanied by an unknown steel player, Gary taped himself performing for a few friends and family members, talking through the tumultuous story of his aunt and uncle, until the music builds and he wails the lines "Where is my woman/Tell her if she'll come home again/I'll never leave the print of my lips on the neck of a bottle again." Over eight minutes long, it's an indelible portrait of Kentucky life, and Stewart never recorded anything like it again, although he'd turn the number into a shorter, more conventional country song a few years later.

Stewart also recorded a wild version of "Williamson County," a murder ballad that would end up on his first album. Gary had written this song with a neighbor from the Battlefield Trailer Park, Rick Durrett, who'd played keyboards in the California "occult" band Coven, famous for that lovably histrionic flute-laden theme-song hit from the *Billy Jack* movie, "One Tin Soldier." He'd left the band for Tennessee mobile-home life and was hanging with Stewart. "We'd just relax, smoke a joint and fiddle around with songs...we just sat down one weekend in the living room in his trailer and wrote 'Williamson County,' which was the name of the county we were living in,"said Durrett. Mary Lou is also credited as a writer, her first and last credit for many years. It's a stunning performance, radically different from anything he'd been cutting at Bradley's Barn—and, for the matter, anything he's recorded since—but it's best examined much later in this book, recounting the actual moment I discovered it.

Bill Eldridge was no dummy. He saw that Stewart was reconstituting himself, right before his very eyes. Bill was old-school;

---

36 Corsia (pronounced Cor-see) eventually divorced John Shoup and married another man named John "She answered an ad from somebody who was looking for a wife on the back of a detective magazine," said Brenda Casey. "Without knowing this person at all, she moved up her family to California. And they lived on a frog ranch. That was back when they did pregnancy testing with frogs." Corsia "was highly respected in the family," said Casey. Apparently she was also a good sport, as the family "bought her a dildo for Christmas one year," said Jimmy Smith. "It was funny as shit."

Gary was letting his freak flag fly. "One night he called me up an' said, "Bill, I want to do some writin', so I stopped to get a bottle of Scotch. When I got there, there was about fifteen people in the trailer, that fuckin' place was packed. They were watchin' porn flicks...had an old 16mm or 8mm projector rigged up. A *mixed* crowd. Kids were runnin' in and out of the place, and they were burnin' quite a bit of the weed. With all that shit bein' passed around, I got to thinkin' to myself, 'Goddamn, if somebody at the trailer park were to call one o' these redneck cops around here, they're gonna *love* this shit.' And I knew Gary wasn't in any shape for me to tell him. So I just excused myself."

The jig was up for the Stewart–Eldridge writing team. "Gary became disenchanted with Music City, he was kinda bored with what we were doin', fed up with the stereotype hillbilly sound. It got to be routine, it wasn't as much fun writin' in Nashville as it was just hangin' around Fort Pierce. He wanted to branch out, he heard a change in the music comin'." Bill remained in Nashville. "We were gonna try and collaborate over the distance but it just never worked out. He didn't send me anything, I didn't send him anything." Eldridge then returned to Florida at Jerry Bradley's urging. "Jerry wanted me to move down here to see if we could revive it, but we never got it back together. And then when Gary started workin' on the road, I never saw him. He was just gone. We never had a fallin' out, we just quit." The pair never wrote together again.

Mary Lou didn't want to leave Franklin. "I loved it. I cried almost to Atlanta, Georgia. I wanted to stay in Tennessee 'cause I really was happy there. We were away from all our families and we were real close to the kids. But I've always been behind Gary. When I came back, my mom said, 'Why are you doin' this? You're on food stamps, makin' ninety bucks a week, it don't make sense.'

"I said, 'Gary's lookin' for a sound, Mama. A new thing's comin'."

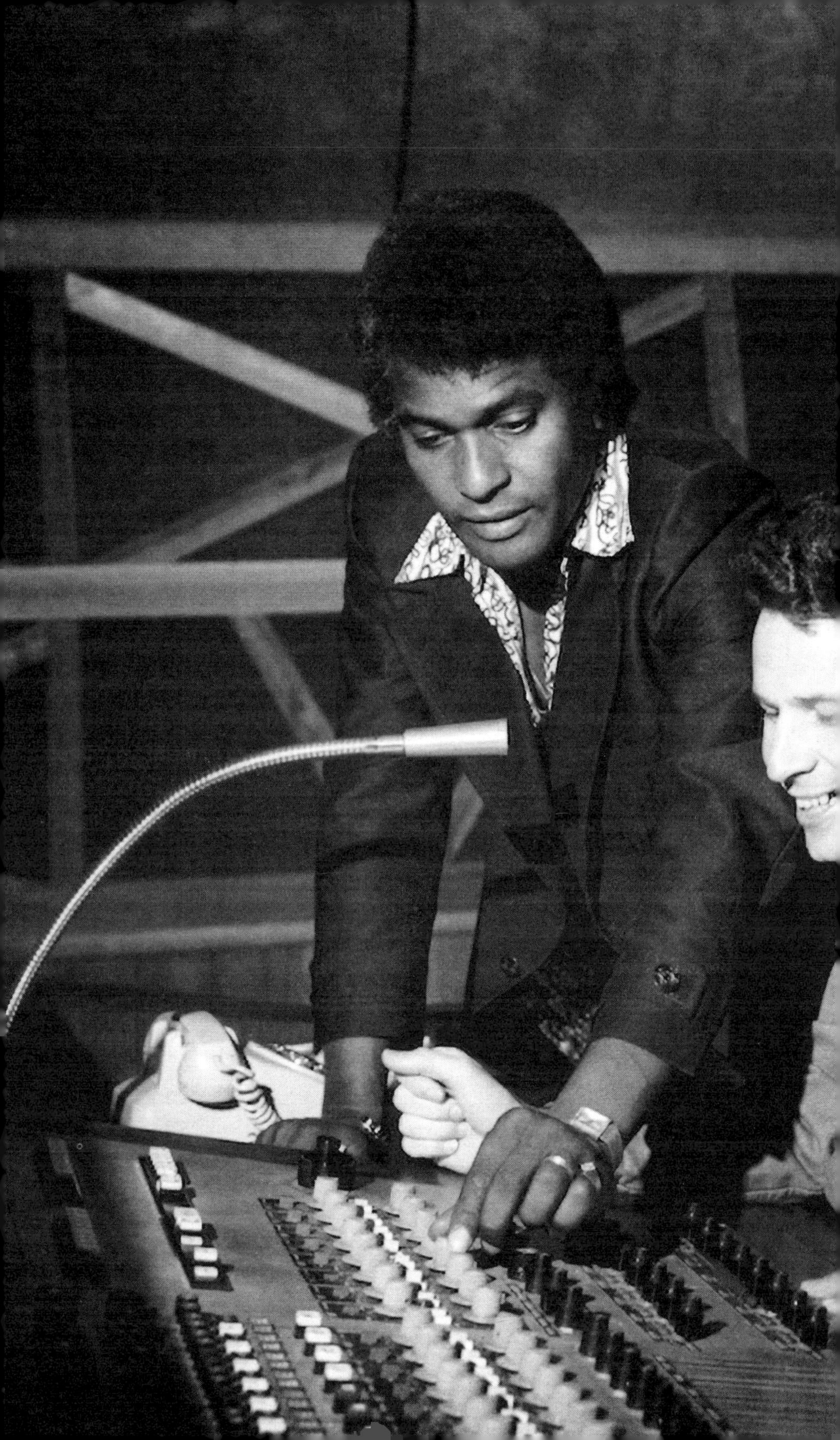

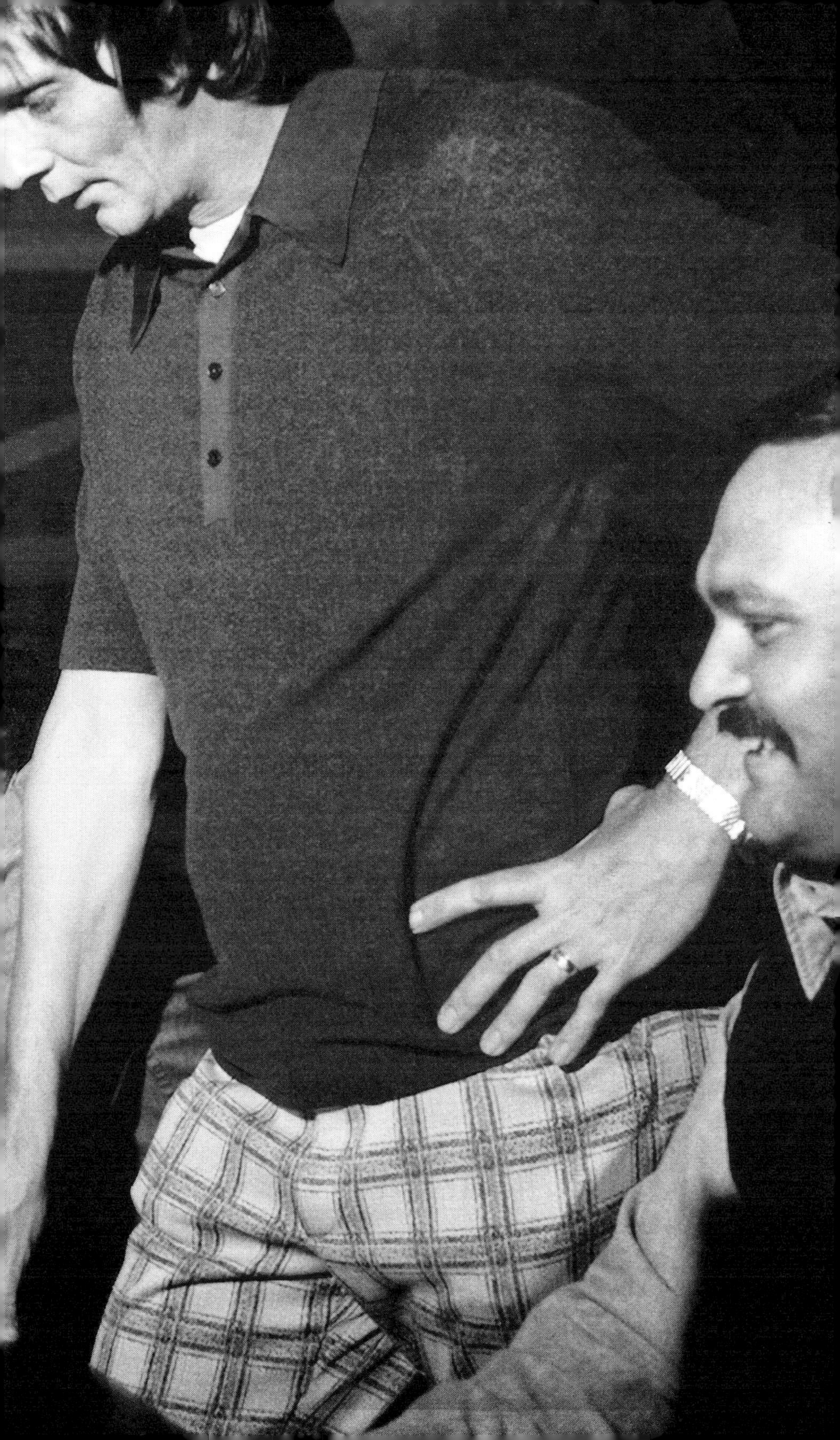

6

BETTER THAN GUNSMOKE

I just loved Roy Dea. I loved the records he cut on Gary. He was all about Gary, and I thought that was so very cool.

– Tanya Tucker

No doubt about it, Roy Dea was one cool cat. Tall, laid-back, and laconic, "Roy never got excited about anything," said rhythm guitar whiz Chip Young, who played many a session for Dea. Roy spoke in a low, Arkansas / Louisiana froggy croak. Dea smoked. Drank. And had little time for bullshit. Most of all he loved music. "Roy was music," explained childhood pal Jerry Kennedy, legendary guitar slinger and producer. "I know you're doing a book on Gary, but I hope that you talk like heck about what a big contribution Roy made."

One thing Roy Dea definitely got excited about: Gary Stewart. "I never knew anybody who blowed me away like Gary—and I seen Elvis, Hank Williams, all of 'em," Roy told me. "You get hooked on Stewart—he's like a damn drug." At RCA, Roy had hits on Dottsy,

Dickey Lee, the Kendalls, recorded a classic 1976 album on Steve Young, *Renegade Picker,* and produced some of Steve Earle's early sessions. When a record is emblazoned with a "Produced by Roy Dea" credit, "you can tell," said steel guitar player extraordinaire Steve Hinson. "Because everybody is playing at the highest level. Nobody's phoning it in." But it is the five-album run with Gary Stewart that earned Dea a place in music history.

When I asked Dea if Stewart was an obsession, he responded enthusiastically. "Oh Lord, yes! Twenty-four hours a day. I told Gary I knew the songs better than he did. I'd learn them on piano *and* guitar. I'd sit around the house, put my feet on the table, play the guitar, and sing it—y'know, a lick will come to you thataway." Once they'd cut a number, Roy would close the door to his RCA office, don a set of headphones, and pop in a cassette as he took a drag off his Kool. "I'd listen to it a million times, all day long. Somethin' might come to me to add on to it, or even take away. Or maybe that I just need to go in and recut it, because it wasn't perfect."

"I like to take country and kick it in the ass," Stewart liked to boast, and in Dea he'd find the guy who could provide the musical boot. "Roy was the guy that captured it," said Hinson. "It's like Phil Walden and the Allman Brothers Band—nobody wanted it. Nobody." Not everybody can recognize a new sound. When it came to Gary Stewart, "Roy could hear it," said Steve. Dea made the world pay attention to Gary's music, and Stewart never forgot it. "Great producer, great man, great friend. Roy liked boogie-woogie *and* he liked country—he was like me. And so easy to work with. We were a team, buddy. If he wanted a song done a certain way, yeah, I'd do it that way—and if I was stuck on a song *my* way, hey, he let me do it. We never had an argument."

Only four years older than Stewart, Roy was nonetheless another father figure to Gary, with all the complexity that implies. Sometimes Gary was a good kid, other times he ran away from home. "Gary Stewart was the best thing that ever happened to me," said Dea, chuckling. "And the worst."

Roy Dea was born Roy Andrew Hayles on April 18, 1940, in Eudora, Arkansas, and moved to Shreveport, Louisiana, after his parents divorced. His mother Doris worked as a $30-a-week waitress. "They didn't have a lot of money," said Delores, Roy's childhood sweetheart and wife, who met Roy at age fourteen at Shreveport's Levy Street Baptist Church. Dea's early years were chaotic. Jerry Kennedy first encountered Roy in the first grade, then "he disappeared for about three years," said Kennedy. Doris remarried her first husband and returned to Arkansas "because she thought that she was doing something wrong for the kids," said Delores. "Roy was the one that told her to divorce him, because he was pretty mean to her—and the kids, too."

Doris left him again, returning to Shreveport to marry Jake Dea. Roy liked his new stepdad, taking his name unofficially before changing it legally in adulthood. Roy was into music early; he got a guitar in the third grade, before the rock and roll frenzy had every kid wanting one. "His mother bought him a Silvertone," said Delores. Jerry's mom got him a Telecaster when he was nine. The two boys would hang out at Kennedy's house, playing along to records, slowing them down on Jerry's Zenith turntable so they could scrutinize the playing on country hits like "You Better Not Do That" by Tommy Collins. "We thought we were pros," said Kennedy. Roy's specialty was bass. "I knew all the country licks and who played on 'em," he boasted.

Kennedy was a child prodigy. At age eleven Jerry signed with RCA (his first record, cut under the name Jerry Glenn, was "Sixteen Chickens and a Tambourine") and by eighteen he was a member of the *Louisiana Hayride* band. (It was at the *Hayride* that Jerry and Roy first saw Elvis. Knocked out by Scotty Moore's guitar on "That's All Right," the boys went to see Elvis at the *Hayride*, so lick-obsessed they were annoyed by "the goofy guy jumpin' around" who was whipping the girls into hysteria and drowning out Moore's guitar.) Kennedy was destined for success, and he was going to drag ol' Roy along with him.

After marrying Delores, Roy made a living playing in Bossier City bands for nearly a decade. "I was one of the first guys in town to acquire an electric bass; before, it was always upright bass. I worked all the time. What I played to make a livin' was black music. People were really into blues/rhythm and blues down there—B.B. King, Bobby Bland, Ray Charles. They dug the black sound. More than even Elvis Presley and rock and roll." He might've been raised on country, but this was the music Roy really loved. "I'm a hillbilly, but I don't have a background in hillbilly pickin'—my background is rock and roll, rhythm and blues. Country's kind of a bore."

* * *

Jerry Kennedy moved to Nashville in 1961 and soon became an in-demand session player as well as a producer for Smash Records, a subsidiary of Mercury founded by Shelby Singleton. He was determined to get Roy to Music City and eventually did, although Dea bailed on both Kennedy and Singleton the first two tries. "We stayed a couple years," said Dea. "I didn't like the hills, I didn't necessarily like the music business...it drew a different type of person. Everybody I ran into was transplants—nobody's from Nashville. You never make any friends, everybody's just an acquaintance. I was worried about my kids growin' up without their grandmas, aunts, or uncles." But Kennedy was persistent. "I thought, 'We could do a duet thing on production that would be cool.' When we would hear a record, we thought alike. We were almost like one mind when it came to music. If Roy came in the office, handed me a tape, and said, 'This song is great,' I would have gone to the studio and recorded it without ever listening. That's how valuable he was to me."

The first single I've come across bearing a solo Dea production credit is a fantastic July 1965 Smash release featuring those Cajun maniacs Rusty and Doug Kershaw belting out a Billy Edd Wheeler song, "I'd Walk a Country Mile (For a Country Girl)." Dea worked for Smash's R&B division in Memphis, producing Gloria Lynne, Junior Parker, and Jesse Butler as well as coproducing Chuck Berry's post-prison return to the studio in 1967. (Rumor has it Dea also provided the whistling on Roger Miller's 1965 hit "England Swings.")

Roy assisted Kennedy on many a session for Charlie Rich, Roger Miller, Roy Drusky, and Faron Young as well as the classic, chaotic Jerry Lee Lewis Smash/Mercury country recordings Kennedy produced in the late sixties/early seventies. "I would find the material, screen songs, hire the musicians—y'know, just do the whole thing," said Dea. Kennedy recalled that Roy's initial trips to go over material at Lewis's Louisiana home were learning experiences. "Roy came back a couple of times wide-eyed—'Hey, that guy's got a Tommy gun in the bedroom. I just left the songs with him.'" Roy was present at the wild February 1972 session where Lewis lunged into an unexpected oldie. "Out of nowhere Jerry said, 'Let's do "Chantilly Lace."' The arranger said, 'We don't have the charts.' Jerry said, 'We're just running it down. Don't worry 'bout the mules. Just load the wagon.' The arranger just about had a heart attack." Jerry Lee whipped off a confining turtleneck sweater and ripped through the number twice. The recording went to number one on the country charts. Sessions with Lewis would be invaluable preparation for Gary Stewart, another idiosyncratic wonder. "Everything was spontaneous," said Dea. "You never could plan Jerry Lee. You never knew what he was gonna do."

In 1972 Roy brought a new country artist to Smash—Johnny Rodriguez. "It tickled me to death," said Kennedy. "I was on vacation in Gatlinburg. Roy called me and said, 'Hey, is it okay if I sign this guy?' I said, 'Are you kidding?' I remember he was hesitant to tell me that Johnny was Mexican."[37] But when it came time to record Rodriguez, Dea suddenly had cold feet. He went in and saw Kennedy an hour before the 10 a.m. session. "Roy said, 'Man, I can't do this. I can't go downstairs and record this guy.' He said, '*You* go do it.'" Finally Roy agreed to do it if Jerry produced the session with him. "Roy would not hear about having his name only on it," said Kennedy, who only found out the real reason many years later. "He just didn't want to

37 Rodriguez, who was born in Sabinal, Texas, is Mexican American. Dea's apprehension gives you an idea of how conservative Nashville was at the time.

compete with Jerry," maintained Delores. "Jerry was too good of a friend." Quintessential Roy Dea—he didn't want to overshadow his pal. Produced by Jerry Kennedy and Roy Dea, "Pass Me By (If You're Only Passing Through)" went to number nine on the country charts, making Rodriguez a star.

Dea was thinking of signing another artist to Mercury. Marty Lacker, an Elvis crony who worked for Jobete Music, Motown's publishing arm, had slipped him a tape of the three Motown demos Gary had cut for Henry Hurt. Talk about right up Roy's alley—soul songs done country, a melding of genres that pointed to the direction he'd soon be exploring himself. The tape blew him away—so much so that he called Hurt. "Roy must have called me a dozen times and asked who was playing what instrument," said Hurt. But what interested Roy the most was the singer. Dea said that when he heard the tape he had the same feeling as when Johnny Rodriguez waltzed into the studio for the first time, auditioning with "I Can't Stop Loving You." Roy was ready to sign him "before he even got through the song." This guy on the tape, Gary Stewart, had greatness in him. "I knew it. There wasn't a doubt in my mind."[38]

Right around this time Jerry Bradley, newly appointed as the head of RCA Nashville, called Dea to offer him a job as A&R man. "I liked Roy's work ethic," said Bradley. "The way he was always looking for songs." Roy leapt at the chance. This would enable Dea to produce artists without the worry of going head-to-head with his buddy and current boss, Jerry Kennedy. "He went to RCA because he did not want to compete with me," said Kennedy, who was sad to see him go but wished his pal the best. "I wanted him to do great. He sure made some great records over at RCA. I was really proud of that."

38 Dea lost the Motown tape and spent the rest of his life looking for it, aided by both Gary (who didn't have a copy) and myself. When Stewart died, Henry Hurt's card was in his wallet. Apparently Gary was planning on calling him to inquire about its whereabouts. Unfortunately, Mark Linn didn't locate the recordings until long after Roy and Gary were gone. Curiously, the song on the tape Roy raved about was a cover of the Marvin Gaye hit "How Sweet It Is (To Be Loved by You)," which isn't among the three songs found, two of which were released by Linn in 2018.

Billboard announced Dea's hire at RCA in the first week of February 1973. Like any guitar player worth his salt at the time, Roy was a great admirer of Chet Atkins, a genius musician and architect of the halcyon early period at RCA, where he'd signed and (often produced) such artists as Dolly Parton, Waylon Jennings, Connie Smith, Willie Nelson, and Jerry Reed. "Roy *worshipped* Chet Atkins," said his wife Delores. Roy described how thrilled he was to enter into such an illustrious history. "I'd walk in the front door and it just felt good—'I've arrived. And I'm gonna make the best of it. I'm gonna give it ten thousand percent.'"

The first name Dea pitched to Bradley was Gary Stewart. "Jerry said, 'I think he's great, too.' Gary wrote for Bradley at that time. I didn't know that." No doubt thinking back to when Stewart had skipped town after having seen the Allman Brothers, Bradley had a few reservations, particularly after he heard an outlandish rumor. "Somebody saw Gary and he had overalls on, no shoes, long hair. Driving a dump truck. Can you imagine that skinny little guy, drivin' a dump truck?"

Jerry Bradley and Gary. (Shannon Ashburn collection)

After Dea's pitch, Bradley spoke to Stewart on the phone. "I said, 'Well, I hear your hair's down over your shoulders, I can't sell that. If you'll cut your hair, we'll sign you.' I'll never forget it—Gary came up, walked in the office, and he had his hair cut—he had it kinda long, but it wasn't hangin' straight down. He spun around and said, 'Well, how's that, boss? Will that work?' I just laughed and said, 'Yeah, it'll work.'" On March 30, 1973, Gary signed to RCA Records. It was a standard one-year contract, two pages long, which called for recording a minimum of eight sides a year. After walking out on Nashville, Stewart suddenly had another chance. "Gary has always been so lucky," said Mary Lou. "*So* lucky." Maybe this time he'd have a hit, maybe not. A roll of the dice.

* * *

The Nashville that Gary Stewart returned to in 1973 still radiated a small-town atmosphere. The country music industry was "a very, very closed business," said Joe Galante, an outsider who moved there in 1974 and would later succeed Jerry Bradley as RCA president and revolutionize the place. "I was moving from *New York*, and people were very suspicious...'What is a guy from New York doing here?' I was ready to move the day after I arrived. I could not believe how provincial and how close-minded everything was...it really was more a cottage business than it was truly the business that we know now, where people hear a name and go, 'Oh my God, you're involved with Kenny Chesney?'"

At the time, RCA was known as the label of Elvis and a few "name" country artists like Dolly Parton, Charley Pride, and Hank Snow. The Nashville division "had something around thirty-six to thirty-eight acts on the label, most of them people you never heard of," said Galante. They were "singles artists" who concentrated on touring the Southwest, Southeast, and Midwest. RCA was cranking out country hits, but just like the other labels in town, "the numbers were insignificant, there really wasn't anything sophisticated about the business," maintained Galante. "It was really just more 'Let's make some records and see what happens.'" The megabucks associated with pop or rock weren't there yet. "Back in those days, country didn't sell, you didn't make any money," said keyboard player David Briggs, session leader for many a hit (and most Gary Stewart RCA recordings). Briggs, a songwriter who also ran a publishing company, lamented that even on a big country hit you'd only pull in fifteen grand or so. "That's one reason I didn't want to write country." Maybe that's one reason music of a certain quality was able to thrive then in Nashville—there wasn't that much at stake.

* * *

RCA country albums had a certain orthodoxy, particularly in the sixties. The covers had an austere, precise look, with muted colors and spartan, elegant lettering. They were square as a Jimmy Olsen DC comic, these covers, sometimes thrillingly so (see Porter Wagoner's *The Cold Hard Facts of Life* or Lorene Mann's *A Mann Named Lorene*). And you knew the playing on the record within that cover would be up to snuff, megahits or no.

For a kid buying records at the Disco Tape in Macon, Georgia, that trademark orange-label, wobbly Dynaflex RCA vinyl was something to keep an eye out for. A formidable steel guitar player whose heyday arrived slightly after Gary Stewart's (although he knew Gary and Roy Dea and played on one of their last sessions), Steve Hinson toured with George Jones, Randy Travis, Dolly Parton, Ray Price, and many others. You can hear him on "Your Man" by Josh Turner and "If the Jukebox Took Teardrops" by Danni Leigh. He loves country music deeply and is insanely knowledgeable about its history. "I bought a shit-ton of records. RCA albums had really good artwork. They sold a well-presented product to me. They had some integrity—that might be because of Chet. They actually had a great musician running the company."

Hinson also points out that by design or by accident, RCA country had been home to some rather atypical singers before Gary Stewart—Willie Nelson, Bill Phillips, and Johnny Bush ("Now, that voice is just *over the top*," said Hinson, who at age sixteen heard Bush's "Whiskey River" blaring from a jukebox and thought, "Man, I gotta be part of this!"). One of RCA's biggest country acts was a truly extreme singer—Hank Snow, whose nasal taffy-pulling of syllables on such ballads as "It's Over, Over Nothin'" is beyond compare. These singers were "a love-hate relationship for a lotta listeners," said Hinson, and the fact that RCA gave such vocalists a shot meant that Gary's Stewart's quivering vibrato would be right at home there.

* * *

It is worth spending a moment describing the well-oiled country music machine Gary Stewart would soon have at his disposal. Dea would cut most of the Gary Stewart sessions at the more intimate RCA Studio B at 1611 Roy Acuff Place, using the much larger Studio A at 30 Music Square West for overdubs as well as an occasional tracking session ("You could fit three or four Bs in the A room, it was just cavernous—you could set the whole band up in one corner," said Hinson, noting it was designed to accommodate a full orchestra). Built in 1957, Studio B was the older of the pair and possessed quite a history. To name but a few of the hits cut there: "Oh Lonesome Me" by Don Gibson, "The End of the World" by Skeeter Davis, "In Dreams" by Roy Orbison, "I Will Always Love You" by Dolly Parton, and "Are You Lonesome Tonight?" by Elvis Presley.

By 1973 Nashville was cranking out country hits with the cool efficiency of a Detroit assembly line. It had a different vibe from other music cities. "Nashville was a lot more positive than Memphis was," said Bobby Wood, who started out at Chips Moman's American Sound Studio in a group of session players known as the Memphis Boys. "Memphis was such a negative place. In Memphis you could ask, 'What about this idea?' and they'd say, 'Naah, that'll never work.' If you ask the same question in Nashville, they'd say, 'Try it.' A world of difference." David Briggs came out of the Muscle Shoals gang that originated at FAME Recording Studios in Florence, and felt similarly about recording in Alabama. "Most of my experience down there was bad, working under terrible technical conditions. We didn't even have headphones in the studio. It was just mono. Dumb engineers that should have been driving a tractor. It was just pathetic. I don't know how we cut the hits that we did." Roy Dea had worked with musicians in Muscle Shoals and Memphis in his Smash days and had encouraged them to head north. "I had been tellin' all the Memphis Boys, 'Y'all come to Nashville, you'll make a shitload of money.' At that time in Memphis, you'd cut all day and just get paid for one session."

Briggs came to Nashville in the mid-sixties and it felt like landing on the moon, partly because of the musicians union there, AFM Local 257. "Owen Bradley and Chet Atkins were strong union guys," said David. "And when they became the most powerful guys in town, they insisted that everybody do everything union." Not that they made it easy for outsiders. "George Cooper was union president, he was a real gruff guy," said Briggs. "And he didn't want any new people coming in. I came up from Muscle Shoals and tried to play on a session, and he stood in the door and said, 'You can't play, we don't want any Alabama rednecks up here.'"

But Music City couldn't ignore the talent coming out of Muscle Shoals and Memphis. "A lot of people knew we'd cut a lot of hits and they just wanted to try us," Briggs went on to say. And with the increase of Nashville studios in the late '60s/early '70s, the town simply needed more musicians. "The explosion of Nashville recording is the thing that gave everyone else a break," said harmonica master Charlie McCoy, who came to town from Miami. "They had it locked, and were doing it so well, but they physically couldn't do it all. Some people thought, 'Those guys are R&B guys, they can't play country music,' but they blended right in."

* * *

Drummer Jim Isbell had been to Nashville as a kid and wasn't impressed. "It was just a hot, dirty town of old red brick. Coming from Miami with the breeze, palm trees, and sunshine, that was hell. And it was the last place in the world I thought I'd ever end up." But when Isbell came to Nashville in 1960 with pal Charlie McCoy, who was cutting a session at Cadence (and would go on to play harmonica on many a session, including Gary Stewart's), he found himself "completely mesmerized by the town because of its music. I had studied the people that were playing on the records. I thought, 'Well, it must be the people who put a band together.' I was shocked to find out that it was a regular *job*. That was a mindblower—that these guys could live at home, have a family, go to the studio and work with a different artist every day. And make *records*! What a dream job! Nashville was a whole different ballgame for me. I wanted to be one of those guys." Isbell soon was, and his influences made him a natural for Roy Dea. "I was into blues, rock and roll, R&B—everything *but* country. But when I got here, what I had learned in the blues was so easy to adapt to country it was ridiculous. I had a very good shuffle, because that was a blues beat. I was playing the black blues, and country is the white blues—a different sound, but the same beat, y'know."

Sessions were booked 10 a.m. to 1 p.m., 2 p.m. to 5 p.m., 6 p.m. to 9 p.m., 10 p.m. to 1 a.m. In those three hours you were expected to get four sides. "You could get stuck on one song," said Jim Isbell. "Charlie McCoy came up with this thing—'Boys, we're burnin' the beans.' That means that we're not getting it. By the time you got two hours and forty-five minutes into your session, everybody had their act together. In that final fifteen minutes, the producer would come out and say, 'Guys, I gotta have this last song, I gotta have it.' They would throw that last song at us, and I swear to you, we would knock it out in one take. BAM, it was done! And for some crazy reason, more than once that last song was their hit."

Roy Dea's primary engineer at RCA, Bill Harris, recalled that Roy was more relaxed about expectations than others, and many times cut less than three numbers during a Gary session. "Roy didn't try to rush anything. If we got one or two good songs in a three-hour session that was enough. Roy wasn't one of these guys to fumble around. He knew what he wanted, he was able to motivate the musicians to perform what he wanted. He never pressured anybody. I don't think I ever saw him get mad or angry in the studio."

Roy liked spontaneity. Once on a session, Fort Pierce singer Bruce Hunter asked if Dea had a demo they could listen to. "Roy said, 'I got something, but you're not gonna hear it.' He wouldn't let the pickers hear it. I asked him why. Roy said, 'Well, then they'll just play what they hear on the demo. This way, they'll find something different. They'll hunt for it.'" Dea's "tracks on Gary were really loose," said Dean Dillon, who'd later record with Stewart. "The track, the sound Roy got out of him and the whole band. All that stuff is so frickin' good. That's when Gary really shined."

"There was a certain group of people that each producer would use," said Jerry Kennedy. "You pretty well stayed within the same group." Dea had worked with many musicians during his Smash Records days with Kennedy, and for Gary's sessions he put together an eclectic mix of players drawn not only from Nashville A-Team veterans but from Muscle Shoals and Memphis as well. He and Stewart were particular about players once they started recording together. "Between me and Gary, we knew how each guy picked. On one song you'd need, say, Reggie Young on guitar. On another, Dale Sellers. 'Cause it depends on the song. Now, other producers, they'd do a session, and if one guitar player couldn't make it, hell, they'd just call another. We never would do that. We'd hold out, whether it was bass, drums, or guitar. If they weren't available, we'd wait 'til they was. We'd just move the session date."

* * *

Like great character actors enriching a movie, Nashville session players provided the color—"musical commentary," as Steve Hinson calls it. A session player was a different kind of cat than some road dog who played

live (although certain musicians excelled at both). You had to be able to think on your feet and pluck licks out of the air that complimented the song without overshadowing it, unlike one well-known hotshot guitar player who auditioned for Chet Atkins and failed the test. "Maybe he thought we were payin' him by the note," Atkins cracked.

"A lot of guys came in here, really hot players, and they didn't get the sessions," said Jim Isbell. "They thought they were better than these hillbillies, y'know? Nashville has always been a good ol' boy town. From the first time I got here, they told me that you have to be a good ol' boy, because you got to fit in. And if you got some kind of ego thing going on, or you think you're better than anybody else, it will show up, and it turns them off. There was a certain way you had to conduct yourself, because everybody was watching. You just can't be a good musician—you've got to be a good person and get along with people. You either fit in or you didn't."

Another drummer Dea was partial to: Nashville-born Buddy Harman, an A-Team legend famous for his playing on Patsy Cline recordings and a zillion other Music City hits. Buddy "was a human metronome," said drummer Isbell, who idolized him. "Solid as a rock. His licks were tasteful and precise. And clean. You could hear everything he did. He was the man." "Drummers just play what they want to and ignore you, but Buddy Harman would listen to what everybody was doing," said David Briggs. "He would play something that would make you sound even better, play *with* you."

Dea also used Kenny Buttrey on drums, who'd played with Neil Young and Bob Dylan, as well as Louisiania-born Karl Himmel, famous for his work with Young and J.J. Cale. He might decide he needed Memphis Boy Hayward Bishop—or Jerry Carrigan, who played on many a Gary Stewart session. Carrigan was a passionate drummer who liked to "really get into it, until your emotions are raw and coming out through your hands." He was part of the group that emigrated out of FAME, where he'd played on R&B records by Arthur Alexander and Jimmy Hughes. Carrigan brought a bigger drum sound to Music City. "I started playing real loose, deep-sounding snare drums on country records...I bought the first set of concert tom-toms that were in Nashville."

On piano Dea frequently had David Briggs, who would often act as session leader. Dea also used Hargus "Pig" Robbins, Bobby Wood, and Bobby Emmons on keys. Robbins, who was blind, created some of the most memorable piano parts in country music, like the intro to Charlie Rich's "Behind Closed Doors." "The best piano player in the history of country music," said Buddy Harman. "He could play a shuffle like you wouldn't believe." Charlie McCoy concurred. "Pig's played the same set of chord changes so many times, y'know, because a lot of country music is very similar. But he always came up with something different, something new. And when he was on a session, everybody else played better." "Pig was *scary*," said Briggs. "He could play anything in any key, and did it better than anybody else. He was just the tastiest guy of all."

Emmons and Wood came out of Memphis, where they'd been an essential part of producer Chips Moman's American Sound Studio band, playing on classic recordings by Elvis, Wilson Pickett, and Dusty Springfield. "When I moved here Roy started using me on about everything that he did, because he just liked my feel," said Wood. "And he knew I wasn't really gonna play 'Nashville,' which I didn't really know to know how to play." Dea picked players "that would get the groove thing underneath, take it to a little bit different place," explained Wood. "The tracks were really kind of funky—and country at the same time."

On guitar Roy favored two heavyweights: Reggie Young, another Memphis Boys export, and Alabama wild man Dale Sellers. Beloved by everyone, Young left an indelible mark on records like Elvis's "Suspicious Minds." Discussing Reggie with Steve Hinson, rhythm guitar ace Jimmy Capps said, "He's such a gentleman as a musician. He never played over anybody. Boy, I wish he wasn't so *nice*!" "Reggie could play on anything that you were doing and make it fit," said Briggs. "He played a lot more soulful R&B. Not funky, necessarily.

Dale was funky." It's Young who supplies the smooth soul on Gary Stewart's "Shady Streets" and Sellers who brings the gutbucket mayhem on "Your Place or Mine."

Young had no bigger fan than Sellers. "Reggie was one of my heroes, buddy, I loved him. I stole a lotta shit off of him. I'm more edgy. I always tried to play up to the edge and get away with as much ridiculous crap as I could, but keep it in context with the song. One guy told me I should have a mother-of-pearl inlay on my guitar with a rat laying on its back and eyes crossed out. He said I played rat-killer guitar."

Dale Sellers "is cutting edge, man," said Hinson. "He's always lookin' for somethin' new to play." If session men actually were character actors, Dale Sellers would be Warren Oates. He went back to the Smash days with Jerry Kennedy and Roy. One of many a picker who got into the session business via steel-guitar god Pete Drake, Sellers would be hanging out at Drake's Stop Records headquarters when Kennedy rang. "Jerry used to call Pete and say, 'Hey, send that boy from Alabama over here just to hang out with us.' I guess I was kinda funny. When Roy went to RCA, I was his boy.'"

On rhythm guitar Dea used Nashville super-picker Jerry Shook; another A-Team member, Harold Bradley; and a Georgia transplant, Chip Young. "Roy wanted the rawness of everything," said Young. "He didn't want to be polished or slicked up—he wanted first takes, mistakes, whatever was there, y'know." Dea used a trio of bass players, both acoustic and electric—Mike Leech, another Memphis Boy, as well as A-Team legends Bob Moore ("Bob was a dandy," said Chip Young, "he put the beat where it needed to be")[39] and Birmingham, Alabama-born Henry Strzelecki. ("It seemed like Strzelecki was always the first call," said Jim Isbell. "He worked on a ton of records in Nashville.")

39 Moore is something of a controversial character in Nashville. David Briggs declared Moore "a very good friend over the years, but he read books during sessions—usually a sex book. The only records you'll hear that he played on that don't have a mistake were anything Owen Bradley did—y'know, like Patsy Cline, Brenda Lee. A lot of the things he did—including the majority of the Elvis records—there's mistakes on all of them." He knew better playing for Owen. "Bob read no books on Owen Bradley sessions."

If there was one instrument that tipped a Gary Stewart session into classic country, it was steel guitar, and the first name that leaps out here is A-Team superstar Roddis Franklin "Pete" Drake, whom Dea hired frequently. Drake had created the indelible steel guitar licks on Tammy Wynette's "Stand by Your Man," Lynn Anderson's "Rose Garden" and Bob Dylan's "Lay Lady Lay," and he'd do the same on such Stewart classics as "She's Actin' Single (I'm Drinkin' Doubles)" and "Out of Hand." "Some of his licks almost became a part of the song," said Charlie McCoy. "Pete played where you need to play, and he played with a lot of conviction. He sold it."

Every Nashville picker I talked to held Drake in high regard. "First of all, Pete couldn't read music, so you couldn't dictate anything that you want him to play," said Harold Bradley. "If you said, 'Hit an A,' I don't know if he could. But if you told Pete 'Play fills in this verse,' he'd play fills that just fit *perfectly*. My brother Owen said that he was the only steel guitar player he was never disappointed in, because Pete would always come up with somethin' that fit the record. Some steel players in town, they don't want to play his style, they think it's too corny. But his licks fit. They went right with the song and the mood. Pete was special. Because he could play commercial licks the song required and never tried to get in the way or be flashy. And that is the secret to being a session player right there." Other steel players Dea used were Hal Rugg, famous for his hot licks on Loretta Lynn records, and Weldon Myrick. ("Weldon was really good at doubling himself, playin' harmony with himself, that's somethin' Pete didn't do," said Hinson. "Weldon had the most beautiful tone.")

Sometimes Dea augmented Gary's tracks with fiddle, played by Tommy Williams (who'd started playing for Ferlin Husky at age thirteen and went on to be a part of the *Hee Haw* house band) or Texan western swing legend Johnny Gimble. Other times he'd use harmonica, usually Charlie McCoy and occasionally Terry McMillan. Vocal accompaniment was provided by the Jordanaires (famous for their work with Patsy Cline and Elvis) joined by Lea Jane Berinati and, at times, pre-solo-career Janie Fricke. Like Pete Drake, the Jordanaires had a sound that was practically a brand.[40] David Briggs cut a Charley Pride record in England with some members of the Philharmonic that were a little on the pop side, so afterward they "overdubbed Pete Drake and the Jordanaires to make it more country. The DJs didn't know the difference—'Oh, that's country. It's got a steel on it.'"

* * *

There were others who played on Stewart sessions, to be sure, but you've now met the principal players. The point here is that Roy Dea had a small army of seasoned, talented pros ready to cut world-class records. Roy respected the pickers, because he remained one. "Even though I was workin' at RCA, I still picked on weekends out in bands in Nashville, just to be around people and get in tune. I didn't need the money. I just wanted to see what people were into. That's the best way to find out."

After a session, Dea sent each picker each a copy of the record they'd played on with a thank-you note. "I know what Nashville does to musicians, having been one," Dea told me. "Say you're a drummer, bass player, whatever. You do sessions for a livin'. You have to be helpful on the sessions, but at the same time, if you're too helpful they won't call you back. You gotta walk a fine line. And before you even got to town somebody told you, 'Well, now, in Nashville, they just play with a brush and a stick, and don't beat no cymbals.' Because there were producers that didn't use cymbals, like Owen Bradley. So when you go to do a session, you're told, 'This is the way you do it' and pretty soon you forget how to pick. You forget how to kick ass, because that's not what country was all about. Nashville is a song town—the voice mixed way up, the band mixed way down. Music was never a part of the Nashville sound, to me. It was the singer and the song." Roy wanted to shake that up a bit.

---

40 Owen Bradley let David Briggs in on a little secret when it came to the Jordanaires. "Gordon Stoker would always sing a little out of tune, a little sharp. And he was always the loudest one. But Owen said, 'I've found a way to keep the tuning problem down is to double it.' So he always doubled the Jordanaires on all their parts."

In Gary Stewart he had a singer who was more than up for the challenge. Gary had just turned thirty-one and had been in some form of the music business for nearly two decades, playing rockabilly, rock, pop, and country. He'd been out on the road, in sessions at Bradley's Barn, and had taken a stab at recording for Kapp.

Roy Dea had a hunch there was something about Gary, something entirely original. He wasn't from the same batch as most country stars. "I couldn't go to Faron Young, Roy Drusky, and Dave Dudley and say, 'Hey, man, I got this idea...' All of a sudden I done landed me a guy that I don't have to tell my ideas, it's in him like it's in *me*. I don't have to sell him on nothing. He hears the same thing I do."

The pickers I talked to were crazy about Gary Stewart. These musicians played on hundreds of sessions, but Stewart stood out from the pack. "We did some great records with Gary," said Harold Bradley. "Such a nice guy. I just loved recording with him. He put his heart and soul into it. When you watched him sing he was giving everything, which was a lot. He was just really a great country singer." Jerry Carrigan got excited when I brought up his name. "He's one of my *favorites*. Gary was the coolest, boy. He was *the coolest*. When I got booked on his session I was all smiles. The *attitude*! I always thought he was the Mick Jagger of country music."

* * *

Gary Stewart and Roy Dea. Together they'd make some of the greatest country records ever recorded, and do it their way. "It was band music, y'know?" said Dea. "You could hear cymbals on the records." For Roy, recording Stewart "was as good as *Gunsmoke*. And I been watchin' *Gunsmoke* for forty years."

7

NUMBER ONE WITH A BULLET

I never set out to be a country star...I just don't have the itch. I never went lookin'.

– Gary Stewart to Bob Allen, 1990

Turned out Chet Atkins knew of a few songs. Because he played golf with Wayne Carson. Carson—who'd written "The Letter" for Alex Chilton's Memphis teen combo the Box Tops after his dad gave him the line "Give me a ticket for an aeroplane"—had some demos of country numbers he wanted cut. "Chet called me and asked if I'd listen," said Roy Dea, who liked two songs on the tape: "Drinkin' Thing" and "I See the Want To in Your Eyes." He told Si Siman—Carson's publisher and a song-plugging legend at Earl Barton Music who'd also discovered Chet Atkins and Porter Wagoner—that he was determined to cut them.

"Sometimes people say, 'Let me play it for the artist.' I said, 'I *will* cut the songs, but with a new artist.' A lot of times publishers don't like that. They'd rather it was somebody established. Si said, 'Hey, you believe in the guy. That's good enough for me.' I sent 'em to Gary and said, 'Now, learn these.'" Carson would go on to write a string of classics for (and sometimes with) Gary, among them "She's Actin' Single (I'm Drinkin' Doubles)," "Whiskey Trip," and "Ten Years of This." Most were booze-related, written from personal experience. "I not only wrote songs about whiskey, I did somethin' about it," Carson told Michael Gray.

Singer/guitarist/songwriter Carson was a wild one. "I was baptized in music," he told Gray. Carson was the son of country duo Shorty and Sue Thompson, "great musicians that played all the tunes, not just country and western or western swing, but pop, showtunes, things like that." This would enable Carson to write for artists as varied as Johnny Paycheck, Joe Simon, and Ike and Tina Turner. His biggest hit was "Always on My Mind," written, according to Bobby Wood, after a fight with his wife, who was "on the phone, just ripping him up one side and down the other." Begging for another chance, Carson pleaded, "Honey, you were always on my mind." The line registered, and suddenly Wayne had more important things to do. "Well, I gotta go now," he muttered as he hung up the phone, off to write the zillion-seller (finished with two cowriters).[41]

Carson was "absolutely hilarious," said Steve Hinson. "One of the funniest people I've ever been around." Hinson was in John Conlee's band when he played in Alaska, where Carson was also on the bill. "Wayne would go a whole day talking like Johnny Cash. I have actually seen him make stewardesses think he was Johnny." Conlee was sitting next to Carson on the flight there, but quickly abdicated his seat to Hinson, telling him, "I can't laugh like this." Wayne "loved to play golf. That's all he cared about, golfing and songwriting." Despite being a Gary Stewart fanatic, Steve never asked Carson about

41 According to what Roy Dea told a mutual friend, Bruce Hunter, Stewart called up Carson one day, asked him how he was doing, and after Wayne said "'Fine,' Gary said, 'Go in there and slap the hell out of your wife.' Wayne said, 'Excuse me?' Gary says, 'I need a hit fuckin' record, and every time y'all have an argument, she leaves, and you write a hit song.'"

the songs he'd written for Gary. "Wayne was like Pete Drake. They didn't think what they were doin' was a big deal. It was their job. Like, they wasn't curin' nothin', know what I mean?"

* * *

Stewart recalled that three songs were cut for Gary's first RCA session (May 30, 1973, by one source). "Drinkin' Thing," "I See the Want To in Your Eyes," and "Rednecks, White Socks and Blue Ribbon Beer." That last number went to number four on the country charts in July 1973, but sung by Johnny Russell and produced by Jerry Bradley. One wonders what would've happened if Stewart's version had been released. Russell "cut it the same day I did, but they gave me a chance at it," said Gary, whose version has yet to surface.

"I See the Want To" was an unusual number—a searching paean to infidelity, or at least being on the edge of it. Will they or won't they? From the evocative opening couplet—"I see the sparkling little diamond on your hand / I can see you've already got a man"—Gary nails this ballad, his tender, understated delivery full of empathy for a woman on the brink. One has to wonder how many marriages this song has demolished. Unfortunately there was some cheating going on when it came to the record itself.

Jerry Bradley had gotten a call from Jimmy Jay, one of Conway Twitty's people, who was on the hunt for new blood for Twitty's band. "He said Conway was lookin' for somebody who could play harmonica and guitar, sing harmony, just do everything. And I said, 'I got just the guy.' Jimmy said, 'Well, send me a copy of a record over, let me hear what he sounds like.' I sent Conway a copy of 'I See the Want To'—Gary didn't get the job, and the motherfucker stole the song and recorded it." Conway released the song as a single in July 1974 and it shot to number one. "It was a big hit," said Bradley. "And I was sick." (Stewart was unfazed: "Conway heard it, really liked it, and waited until it wasn't gonna do anything, then he went in and cut it. Real nice of him.") It's amusing to contrast the two recordings.

Twitty might have nabbed the hit, but his bombastic treatment has none of the delicacy of Stewart's, and he practically bludgeons the song with sweaty jumpsuit angst. While Gary sounds slyly seductive, you feel Conway might be charged with assault.

And then there is the monumental "Drinkin' Thing." "Every day I tell myself / It's temporary..." Gary laments, immediately conveying the fact that it is anything but. The singer is obsessed with a woman, she has betrayed him and continues to do so, thus he has a "drinkin' thing / To keep from thinkin' things." On the surface the song is about addiction, a subject that would turn out to be grimly fitting for both artist and producer. Contrary to popular belief, booze was never really Stewart's poison, although he would occasionally tie one on if pills were out of reach. Alcohol was Dea's vice. He'd hang out at Music City drinking hole the Longhorn with business crony Pat Carter and the spirits would flow. "Roy, he'd get fucked up from the floor up quick," said Bruce Hunter. "Jack and Coke. I tried to get him to drink it with water. I said, 'You'll feel so much better, you can drink more of it.' Roy looked at me. He says, 'I don't fuckin' think I need to drink *more* of it!'" Neither Roy nor Gary would live to see sixty.

But in 1973 that darkness was some distance away. The pair threw themselves at this number like men possessed, not realizing it would outline their fate. Desperation was the real subject. "What RCA never understood is that I never cut 'Drinkin' Thing' or 'She's Actin' Single (I'm Drinkin' Doubles)' 'cause they were drinkin' songs, they were just songs that happened to be *about* drinkin'—drinkin' is secondary to the real subject matter," said Dea. "They're about a *loser*, a guy bein' shit on, man." And Gary knew just how to express it. The singing here is on another level from his Kapp / Decca sides. The delivery feels more conversational, the abandon more real. He sings like a man with nothing left.

Not that the performance came easy. "Gary was really sort of timid when he first started out," said David Briggs. "He was always courteous, and nice. But you got the feeling that he thought maybe he wasn't quite good enough." Dea concurred, noting that this particular stellar company of musicians unnerved him. Stewart "was nervous 'cause his voice was gonna have to be played back, and he was gonna hear it right in his face loud...everybody's gonna hear it and it's gonna stick out like a sore thumb—'I'm awful, people aren't gonna like me.' But about halfway through that session, when the pickers were startin' to get knocked out by the playback, he didn't worry about that no more—'Oh you like that? Looky at what else I got.' Gary wasn't holdin' back. He just let loose." Stewart was just "very soulful," said Briggs. "He sang it more like a pop singer would do. Most country singers in those days didn't have much soul."

Once in the studio, Dea became even more enamored with his new artist. "I thought that Gary looked different from anyone I'd ever seen. He was so skinny that turned sideways you almost couldn't see him. And when he'd set down and sing, he wiggled all over, just sittin' in a chair both legs would be a-bouncin'. He'd find him a little spot where he wanted to sing. Oh Lord, he'd sing in every different position known to man...Stewart's just weird, real weird. It was like he was in another world. He had drive—that's why I liked that song 'Drinkin' Thing,' 'cause I could do a break, then go into that chorus and let him *drive*."

But wouldn't you know it: RCA hedged their bets on Gary's first single. They went understated rather than betting the house: "I See the Want To" was picked as the plug side, and "Drinkin' Thing" was the flip. Released in July 1973, the 45 "didn't do nothin'," as Gary admitted. But due to a disc jockey's wager, "Drinkin' Thing" would rise again.

* * *

In his diary, Gary Stewart does not note his signing to RCA, nor his recording of "Drinkin' Thing." Maybe he didn't want to jinx things. Maybe he thought it would be like Kapp and no one would care. On his twenty-ninth birthday, May 28, 1973, his entry states, "I left for Nashville to start my new job playing piano and fronting Nat Stuckey's band." This would be the first attempt to yoke rising star Gary to an established one. It would not go well either time.

* * *

"We had a pretty good thing goin' at RCA where we used some of the bigger artists to develop the small ones—like we put Ronnie Milsap with Charley Pride," said Roy Dea. "It was just a plan of action." Nat Stuckey was in the middle of a seven-year run at RCA. A sonorous-voiced Texan who turned a bit mod in the seventies by sporting tinted shades, shaggy hair, and a beard, Stuckey could demolish a ballad ("Leave This One Alone") and yuk up a novelty song ("Sweet Thang," number four in 1967, his highest-charting single). Nat would even have the temerity to cover Zager & Evans's angst-ridden dystopia-rock smash "In the Year 2525 (Exordium & Terminus)." As previously mentioned, Gary had provided Nat with his second-highest chart hit when he and Eldridge allowed Stuckey to revise "Sweet-Tater and Cisco" to "Sweet Thang and Cisco," which hit number eight in 1969. No doubt Jerry Bradley, who'd produced Stuckey, thought he and Stewart would be a perfect fit.

"Jerry asked Nat if he could make a place in his band for Gary to be the opening act," recalled Stuckey's wife Ann. "Gary was very good with his segment of the show, which was fifteen minutes, playing the piano and keeping the audience entertained." Once Gary was on the road, he would reach out to the drummer from the *Grandma's Roadhouse* sessions so he would have a little musical support in the Sweet Thangs band. "Nat had good players, man," said Jim Snead, who packed his drums the minute Stewart called. "Good pickers. Herby Wallace played steel guitar, he was bad to the bone." They played state fairs and Moose lodges as well as support dates with Conway Twitty and Loretta Lynn. "Hot as hell," was Gary's diary review of an August show with Twitty in Lenoir, North Carolina. There is a great snapshot of Gary on the tour bus, his wavy hair piled a mile high on his head, looking dangerously serious as he sits with Snead, country singer Karen Wheeler (also part of the Stuckey show), and *Bonanza* star Michael Landon.

At first, "we had a blast," said Snead, who recounted a tale of the bus breaking down in Arkansas. "Gary threw his guitar on his back and said, 'Come on, man.' And we started walking down these little roads...we just kept walking. All of a sudden we came up on these black guys up on the porch singing. They had wine. We got up there, sang some songs with them and just had a blast, man." There is a Polaroid of Gary, guitar under one arm, his other around David Hines, a dapper African American gentleman in a fedora. The date on the photo: July 14, 1973. Hines scrawled his North Little Rock address on the back of the picture. In his hand is a bottle of cheap hooch. Both men look drunk—on music, not booze.

The good times didn't last. When it came to the grind of the road, Stewart was the first to crack. "We'd go out for twenty-four days, come home for three, and go right back out again," said Snead. "Gary loathed it. He just had his way of thinking, and a way he does things. If he don't want to play that night, he ain't gonna play! He'll take off and go home. He could do that when he played with Riley. With Nat Stuckey, we were on a bus. We didn't have a choice."

Furthermore, Stewart couldn't be contained as a mere opening act. "Gary had the energy of ten men," said Snead. "He was always going." Things came to a head rather hilariously one night during an Atlanta gig at the Southernaire Club. "Quite a big venue," noted David Thornhill, who was fill-in guitarist with Stuckey's band at the time. The afternoon before the show Stewart had been drinking with the band and by the time they hit the stage, "Gary was feeling his Cheerios," said Thornhill. "Instead of singing three songs, Gary just kept on singing."

The crowd went nuts. As Gary told his cousin Nick Stewart, "we got up there, we were playin', the crowd was on their feet. We were just gettin' into it. And we forgot all about bringing Nat Stuckey on!" Stuckey was at the side of the stage, motioning for Gary to finish. "Gary was getting a lot of attention," said David. "Nat wasn't happy about that. He said, 'Get him *off*!" The aftermath wasn't pretty. "We went back to the bus and he fired every one of our asses," said Gary.

Well, two asses, anyway. "Nat got a little mad," said Snead. "And when we got back on the bus, him and Gary got into it a little bit. Gary said, 'Hell with ya! Just drop me off right here.' On the highway! I had to get my drums out, his keyboard, his guitar amp, our clothes. On the highway. Luckily we were by Fort Pierce and somebody came by with a truck and took us home."[42]

Apparently this happened more than once. "A couple of times Gary went over his allotted time, and at one point on a forty-five-minute show Gary performed thirty minutes," according to Nat's wife Ann. "Nat was not a happy camper. The second time this happened, Nat talked with Jerry Bradley and said it was time for Gary to have his own band. No bad feelings—Gary was ready to headline his own show."[43] There is an August 13th diary entry from Gary tersely describing what must've been a tense meeting: "Went to RCA talked with Jerry Bradley about my departure with Nat Stuckey. Everything looks for the best." Stewart continued to finish out dates with Stuckey for a bit, and even wrote a song with him—the twin-guitar ecstasy of "Draggin' Shackles," a tale of an imprisoned Georgia thief pining for his paramour, which wound up on Stewart's first album. "I got the idea from Paul Muni in *I Was a Fugitive From a Chain Gang*," Stewart told the press.

* * *

A momentous occasion happened just four days later, which Gary recorded in his diary. "Today I'll never forget. I met my heroes Greg[g] Allman and Jai Johanny Johanson of the Allman Brothers band in the

---

42 The next time Thornhill encountered Stewart he was opening a show for Conway Twitty and Loretta Lynn. It was Gary's birthday and a friend had brought a cake, "only it was loaded with marijuana," said Thornhill, who was Lynn's guitar player. "A bunch of people got a piece of Gary's birthday cake. Needless to say, the celebration went on a while."

43 Years later Stewart band member Randy Toman asked Gary about playing with Stuckey. "He's a horse's ass," said Toman. "Exact words out of his mouth."

Atlanta Airport. I talked with Gregg about 45 minutes. He gave me his address and told me to come see him." This was the beginning of a close friendship with Gregg (a bit later Gary would bump into Dickey Betts as well). No doubt this provided the impetus for Stewart's next RCA single: a slightly countrified cover of the Allmans' just-released "Ramblin' Man," cut in early September.

"Overdubbed my session 'Ramblin' Man' and 'Draggin Shackles,'" Gary wrote in his diary September 13. "I really like them more than anything I've ever done. They're more me." There is no denying Gary's exuberance on the "Ramblin' Man" vocal, but the recording strikes me as more Allman than Stewart, like he's too awestruck to make it his own. This is one of those rare instances where Gary failed to better the material. The most interesting thing about it may be the appearance of steel guitar ace John Hughey. "What John played on that record is not what he was noted for," said Steve Hinson. "He was famous for playing that real slow, emotive stuff that he played on Conway Twitty—that quiverin', shaky sound. John's playing jazzy, real fast, single-string runs on the 'Ramblin' Man' record. It's totally out of character." Released in October 1973, "Ramblin' Man" only got to sixty-three (at least beating out another Music City cover of the song by Jimmy Payne). It would not be included on the first Stewart album.

The B-side was the first release of Stewart-penned material at RCA—"Williamson County," the murder ballad cowritten with Mary Lou and Rick Durrett that Gary had cut back in his Bradley's Barn days. Roy Dea never heard that hellacious demo. "He just sang it to me in the office with guitar," said Dea, after he'd stressed to Stewart the importance of writing. "I told him, 'You gotta write, man, 'cause that makes you different from other people. When you write 'em, they're just a little bit left of center.' Gary wasn't a seasoned songwriter, he don't know all the rules.[44] It was just a little bit different." Roy compared Stewart's writing to "the Charlie Rich things written by his wife Margaret Ann, who wasn't no famous

44 For some reason Dea overlooked the many songs Gary wrote with Bill Eldridge.

songwriter. You listen to some of them songs, they don't change chords where you're used to hearin' 'em change. That gets your attention, I like that shit." More was on the way.

* * *

Two flops in, Gary wasn't sweating the scene at RCA. A new world had opened for him upon returning to Fort Pierce, a cosmic hippie-redneck honky-tonk world rather at odds with prim-and-proper Nashville. Stewart swore to me this was when he made the best music of his life—with a five-piece band of sometime hippies called the Phoenix. The band never went in a studio, nobody ever recorded their live shows with Gary, and they only played with him locally. But nobody in the band has forgotten. "We will all say it was a time of magic, because it surprised us all," said Stewart.

The Phoenix was: "Boogie" Bob Melton on guitar, Howard "Bingo" Folcarelli on drums, Darrell Dawson on bass, Fred Bogert on keyboards, and Walter "Fly" Hornsby on...comedy. "We never plugged Fly's guitar in," Melton admitted. "He was really bad back then." All were Southerners save for Bogert, a Pennsylvania boy who'd had serious musical training at the University of Miami and functioned as the Brian Wilson savant of the band.

As always, once Stewart forged a musical bond with somebody, they joined his cast of characters for life (Fly Hornsby, later guilty of an illicit romance with Mary Lou, was a notable exception). Boogie Bob Melton, a Tennessee transplant who'd moved to Fort Pierce at age five, already had a bit of a showbiz career: a stint in local '60s band the Sandtrippers and an appearance in a 1970 exploitation oddity, *Walk the Walk*. Bob was a major running buddy for Stewart; they'd share wine, women, song, and even write a few numbers together. His rugged longhair looks pulled in many a dame. At one joint they played, "every time Bob would go out and take a piss, he'd get a blow job—and y'know, he wasn't even *lookin'* for it. They'd just follow Boogie out!" said Stewart, still incredulous years later. Folcarelli was another Stewart favorite. According to Melton, Folcarelli "was the most honest, straightforward, no-bullshit guy I ever knew. Bingo was a lot like a loyal dog. You could always depend on him to be there. He was also one hell of a drummer."

The Phoenix had been together about a year and had been the house band at Gary's old stomping ground the Wagon Wheel when Bogert came in. He'd been touring with Little Beaver, an African American guitar whiz who'd hit with "Party Down," but Beaver's prodigious chemical appetites had led to chaos, so Fred split, adept as he was at instantly switching gears between Miami soul and honky-tonk redneck rock. At the time Gary ran into them, the Phoenix had a six-days-a-week residency at a beloved Fort Pierce restaurant/bar called Frankie n' Johnny's, "*the* club in Fort Pierce," said Bogert. "This smoky bar, it was hardcore redneck...but it wasn't. Bar fights and just crazy stuff happened on a daily basis. There were nine people shot—either to death, or just shot—in and around the parking lot in the two years I worked there."

One night, Bogert was on his way to the club when a pickup cut him off, forcing him to stop. "I rolled down the window to say howdy and the first thing my face met was a fist coming through the window." Fred managed to get to Frankie n' Johnny'swith a bloody noggin and a fat lip only to have the guy who pounded him show up for the second set. He pointed the offender out to his bandmates, and at break time Fred was led to a table where the owner of the fist offered a contrite apology. "Somebody said, 'What do you want us to do to him?' And I said, 'Just leave him alone!"

Into this joint strolled Gary Stewart, already famous for his Music City success. "I had come home, got my guitar, and found the boys that was playing some good *country* and *boogie-woogie*," he declared. "Gary came and sat in a couple of times," said Bogert. "I didn't know him from Adam." It immediately became apparent this was a match made in heaven. "That band really clicked with Gary," recalled Bob Melton.

The Phoenix was right up Stewart's alley. They covered Allman Brothers, Marshall Tucker, Buddy Holly, Willie, Waylon, and old blues numbers like "Stormy Monday" as well as Bogert originals like "Leave for Norway"—"kind of a hippie-Byrds thing," said Fred. "The first night we played it I brought up a twelve-string and we did it with three guitars and all the harmonies. We played it five times in a row, because the Frankie n' Johnny's audience wanted to hear it again and again." Three-part harmony was a Phoenix trademark. "One of our best covers was the Dead's 'Uncle John's Band,'" said Melton. The versatility of the band—and the fact they could step out on long songs à la the Allmans—pulled Stewart right in. "It was a jam, one continuous song. And it wasn't just straight ol' bah-dah-dah-dah jam, it was every kind of different beat, every different kind of style, any way we could take it—because the pickers were all good in their fields. It was a magic carpet ride," said Gary wistfully. "The kind of music that I like best."

Stewart would sharpen his slide guitar by jamming to the Allmans with Melton. "We would sit around his house for hours working out the twin guitar parts to their songs while he perfected his slide style," said Bob. But Melton learned that it wasn't the only kind of music Gary could play. The band were spending a rare Saturday night off partying at Melton's apartment when Frankie n' Johnny's owner Frank Guerriero called in a panic and asked if they could fill in for a band unable to make a club date across town. "He said we could name our price if we could get there right away," said Melton. "It was at the Elks Hall on 25th Street. We said, 'Heck, yeah' and started loading equipment."

When they arrived, an impromptu beauty pageant was in progress, killing time until the band showed up. "We were the only white people there," said Melton. There was just a sea of black faces before the stage. They didn't know what to expect—and we didn't either." They started playing. "Gary pretty much took control of the event. He started doing every R&B song there ever was." "Our dates were sitting at a table and a couple of black guys from the audience came over and said, 'Say, man—you mind if we dance with your dates?' We said, 'Heck no, man, if they want to dance, have at it!' Everybody had a big time. They kept throwing more money at us, we played almost all night. Gary was loving it. He knew that music and got way into it."

* * *

However unruly a joint Frankie n' Johnny's might have been, the crowd there loved the Phoenix. "The club would be *packed*," said Mary Lou. "They would set on the dance floor. And would not dance...that is good, when people will just set there and watch you pick. Gary got so fast on slide his hands never stopped movin'." Unfortunately the gig would be cut short due to Stewart's thirst for volume. "Gary would bring in this hot little string of amps that he was trying out and let things get just screamin'," said Melton. "It didn't take but twenty minutes to get the place wall-to-wall with cowboys and hippies both. It would get loud and rowdy, and Frank Guerriero would get beside himself. He felt Gary was bringing in the riffraff. He told us either Gary had to go or we did." The Phoenix went. Next stop: the Fort Pierce Hotel.

Located across the street from the Indian River, the "Old" Fort Pierce Hotel was a ramshackle affair dating back to the twenties, and a fabulous venue for the Phoenix. "It was dirty, smelled like urine and booze, and no tourists went there," said Bogert. "There were fishermen and ranchers, drug runners, ne'er-do-wells. Hardcore. So we would go in there and everybody would get totally fucked up. Just a wonderful, wonderful time. Very tribal, very intense. It seemed like the goal on any given night was 'How far out can we get—and bring everybody along *with* us?'" Stewart proudly told me he made "thirty bucks playing three nights a week." A far cry from the Nashville hit parade, but Gary couldn't have cared less. He was whooping it up.

The crazed antics of Fly Hornsby contributed to the vibe. According to Bogert, Fly was "just an acid trip in the front of the microphone. Like somebody from *Animal House*." For his '50s alter ego, Rockin' Ricky, Fly rode in the front door on a motorcycle, got into a tub, and sang "Splish Splash." As bluesman Blind Lemon Chitlins, Hornsby arrived in an ambulance and was carried to the stage on a hospital gurney. "He got drunk to play the part," said Stewart, noting that Hornsby talked way off mic due to the fact he was "blind." Apparently Fly was something of a method actor. "He never lost character," maintained Gary. "Then his exit! He did a somersault offstage. It was an accident that he landed on his feet. He could never do it again." Everybody remembered that jump. According to Bogert, "What was flying through my mind was: 'Oh fuck, now we're gonna have to take the son of a bitch to the hospital. But Fly was so committed to his insanity that he actually landed upright." For another show, the entire band dressed up as "aliens from outer space. We wanted to land outside in a flying saucer, but we couldn't find one," said Melton.

* * *

Back in Music City, Roy Dea was plotting his next move for Gary Stewart. And then the unexpected happened. A Texas deejay (his name lost to time) fond of the "Drinkin' Thing" B-side made a wager. As Stewart told it, "This guy out in Texas said, 'Hey, why don't you turn that single over, add an electric piano, and put it out as a single?' He bet a RCA promotion man $100 he could make it a hit." Dea mused on the matter and went to Jerry Bradley to discuss the next single.

"We put 'Drinkin' Thing' out and nothin' happened," said Bradley. The situation reminded him of a record Owen, his father, had cut with Wilma Burgess after Brenda Lee had passed on it—"Misty Blue." "He said, 'Shit, if you can't make it with this record, you can't make it with the next record, because this one's so much better than what I've got to offer next.' I had a meeting with Roy. I said, 'I don't give a damn—you ain't never gonna cut a record *better* than the one we put out.' And Roy came back and said, 'Hey, what do you think about just putting 'Drinkin' Thing' out again?'" Bradley also maintained that the promo man who took the bet, Wayne Edwards,[45]

45 Both Dea and Bradley named Edwards as the culprit, but Joe Galante, who claimed responsibility for hiring Edwards, said Wayne didn't arrive at RCA until later.

"thought we'd missed it as a company. So we just said, 'Shit, why not? We can do what we want to do, we're autonomous, we don't have to answer to anybody.'"

Jazzy electric piano had crept into Music City via Conway Twitty's 1970 hit "Hello Darlin'," and one of Roy's favorite session players, Bobby Wood, was adding it to many a record. "I had a Wurlitzer that I ran through a Boss Chorus effects pedal," said Wood. "And while the Wurlitzer was mono, the Chorus made it stereo." Bobby's sound became a hot commodity. "A lot of people actually just hired me to overdub that—'I need your Wurlitzer on this.'" Dea did just that, and had Gary come in and tweak the vocals with a few overdubs. Dea scoffed at the idea that the electric piano made it a hit. "It didn't make no difference. Nobody really talks about, 'God, that's a neat electric piano on that record,' like they did 'Hello Darlin'.' It was Gary's drive, his voice." And so in May 1974, nearly a year after it was first released, "Drinkin' Thing" was unleashed again as the A-side. According to Bradley, this time the promotional department "jumped on it. And wham!"

Steve Hinson was an eighteen-year-old juvenile delinquent living in Macon when the *wham* of "Drinkin' Thing" hit him. "I'm ditching school every day, hanging out in beer joints, shootin' pool, listening to the jukebox, and illegally drinking beer. So I'm seeing these guys—they come in about noon and start drinking. And they got on a white belt, white matchin' shoes, polyester pants. Their wife is not treating them good, y'know? They're sitting at the bar, drinking alone, smoking cigarettes...drowning their troubles. That's who Gary sounded like to me. I said, 'I know that guy.' It just drew me in, man."

As it did the rest of the world. "Drinkin' Thing" shot to number ten on the charts. Gary was on his way, and RCA was abuzz. He'd amble the halls in his hat and jeans, hitting on secretaries for free records. "First thing he'd do when he hit town is go see all the girls he knew workin' at all these record companies...he always went home with a stack of albums. They had never seen anything like him at RCA. Nobody could tell what he might do next, and it excited people.

The place almost stopped when Gary was in town. All the secretaries, promotion people, they just loved him to death."

For a brief period RCA was really excited. "At that time, I had a label behind me," said Dea. It wouldn't last long.

* * *

There was an unintentional casualty to the resurrection of "Drinkin' Thing." When Gary returned to Nashville for the overdub session, Fred Bogert, his buddy in the Phoenix, drove him there solo. "Boy, a lot of trouble started, because other people in the band were really, really, really resentful that I had gone with Gary," Bogert recalled. Melton felt Fred had made sure the band didn't come along so he could finagle a solo gig as Gary's musical director. That story had "nothing to do with the truth," said Bogert, who maintained the trip was innocent of any Machievellian maneuvers: "I had no agenda." Whatever the particulars, the situation "really pissed Gary off," according to Melton. "And when he told us about it, it kind of soured the whole thing for the rest of us...the Phoenix dissolved into ashes." Stewart's favorite band had lasted about nine months, then—*poof!*—it was gone. (Melton, Folcarelli, and Dawson went on to play in other bands with Stewart, while Fred Bogert would work on numerous studio projects with him.)

Not that Gary had any time to think about it. He was suddenly in Charley Pride's band. As "Drinkin' Thing" began ascending the charts, Stewart was promoting the record in San Antonio "playin' a radio station party gig, and two of Charley's band members were there. They told me 'Charley is needin' a piano player.' Good timin'!" For Gary, it was just another case of being in the right place at the right time. "I don't know how I got that Charley Pride gig," Stewart told the press. "It wasn't because of my pickin'. Because I am really no piano player. I'm just a ming-bling-gling-and-a-few-chords man."

Right around this time—July 26, 1974—Stewart was in Dallas "for my first gig on the road as an artist," he wrote in his diary. "I get $200.00 a night." If that kingly sum wasn't enough excitement, he noted that "Charley Pride came out to see the show, got up and sang." After the second night in Dallas, Gary went over to Pride's house "and visited about four hours. Listened to Jerry Clower records. Drank and talked." The image of Charley and Gary yukking it up over some cornpone comedy, well, the mind stutters. Stewart auditioned for Charley's band in Houston between the afternoon and evening shows and Pride put him on that night. Despite it being one of the few times Gary had stage fright, he landed the job.

Formerly a Sweet Thang, Stewart was now a Pridesman. Stewart would stay in the band for a rocky two years. Bad idea? Eventually, but not initially. Just days after the meeting at Pride's house, Gary was in Bismarck, North Dakota, with the Pride show, a smooth Nashville package that also featured future hitmaker Ronnie Milsap as well as pop group the Four Guys, a mild vocal quartet who wowed the Opry crowd with their version of "Shenandoah."

Charley Pride was a fabulous anomaly—an African American country singer wildly popular with country fans, he'd eventually claim an insane run of hit singles: fifty-two Top Tens, thirty of which went to number one. One of eleven children born to Mississippi sharecroppers, Pride had played baseball with the Memphis Red Sox before embarking on a music career. Chet Atkins signed him to RCA in 1966 (his first record pointedly sent out without a promo photo) and he stayed for nearly twenty very successful years. Pride endured racial slurs—not to mention Klansmen purporting to be fans—on his way to the top, and dealt with them with the ease of a pro athlete used to winning the crowd over, despite the ugly human failings on display.

"I didn't set out to be a crusader for racial harmony or change anybody's heart or mind, but I learned early that you can accomplish more with tolerance than indignation," he wrote in his autobiography. Pride knew how to address a (mostly) white country audience. "I'm no color unto myself," he said in 1976. "A lot of blacks are very hung up on their blackness." A family-friendly show was central to Pride's approach. "The people that came to see Pride were the people that wear polyester suits and bring their child," said Dea. "They don't like loud." And now Gary Stewart was on the bill. Casualties ahead![46]

* * *

To follow "Drinkin' Thing," Roy Dea had another bomb to drop: "Out of Hand." Another cheatin' song, this time from the point of view of the cheater rather than the cheated upon. The song had improbable roots for a honky-tonk as it had been written by a California folkie, Tom Jans, and a Brooklyn Jew—Jeff Barry, a formidable Brill Building songwriter who'd cowritten such sixties pop classics as "Be My Baby" and "Leader of the Pack." The song "wasn't very country," Stewart admitted to a reporter. "But by the time *we* got through with it, it was." Either Gary or Dea had found the song lurking on an obscure 1974 Mentor Williams album, *Feelings*.[47] Jans released his version a few months after Stewart made it a hit.

Go listen to either previous of them. I DARE you. For you will be amazed at the artistry, the sheer *wizardry* of Stewart and Dea. Mentor's is particularly egregious. He talk-sings the song, which is string-laden, unbearably funky, and features a foul extra verse which might've been too strong for country radio. Jans's blustery delivery on his own version, cut with such LA studio pros like Jesse Ed Davis

46 A few years later Stewart would tell band member Randy Toman that he felt "Charley was kind of an ass-kisser, a little bit more than he needed to be. And Gary decided that he wasn't going to be that kind of ass-kisser."

47 Williams was a Nebraskan who'd written and produced a 1973 megahit for Dobie Gray, "Drift Away." A year later he'd record his only solo album in Nashville using many of Dea's favorite musicians, and it was a bit of a goldmine for Roy and Gary. Not only did it lead them to "Out of Hand," it provided another song for Stewart's first album, "Sweet Country Red," a Troy Seals song. And it almost gave up a third—the title cut, "Feelings"—not the dreaded Morris Albert hit of indescribable white angst, but a Will Jennings/Troy Seals cheating ballad. "I was ready to cut," said Dea. "We had it changed around, worked up and everything. About a week before we could get into the studio, Conway and Loretta cut 'Feelings' and it went to number one. Conway done nailed me again!" (For the record, their version had a gooier title: "Feelins'." Why the apostrophe, I do not know.)

and Lowell George, is country rock but no better. There is no drama to these records, while Gary's performance is nothing but. Dea edits the song down to its essence and the session cats shine, playing parts so thought-out and precise they fit together like a Rubik's Cube. The slam-bang opening provides a curtain-parting intro to Stewart's commanding vocal, which slithers and slides as much as Pete Drake's steel. Gary had gained confidence since the last record. He owns the song—no other versions matter, nor will any future ones—and you believe every word. Released in September 1974, "Out of Hand" shot to number four.

* * *

For a guy who preferred lying on the couch, Stewart was suddenly in the thick of it. On December 12, 1974, he appeared on the *Dinah!* afternoon show with Pride. They did *The Merv Griffin Show* as well. December 14th was his first solo show at the fabled Gilley's honky-tonk in Texas (Gary would be a regular there, always packing the joint). On December 27th, the late-night music show *Midnight Special* broadcast a Pride show with Stewart taped October 8th in Tulsa. Gary was the homecoming hero when Pride played West Palm Beach on January 2. He then went with the Pride gang to London, where he graced the cover of a UK country music mag wearing a long, outrageous fur coat more Parliament-Funkadelic than Pridesman. "After Gary had the first hit, all of a sudden that fur coat showed up," recalled Joe Galante. "He walked out there like he was early John Rich. It was really bizarre." *Playboy*/*Hee Haw* figurehead Barbi Benton was also on the bill, and there exists a photo of a beaming Barbi sitting in Stewart's lap with arms entwined, Gary grinning like a Cheshire cat. Hee-hee-hee-haw-haw!

On January 14 he taped an episode of the *In Concert* TV show Charley hosted at the Grand Ole Opry, which costarred Dolly Parton, Chet Atkins, and Jerry Reed. RCA released a two-record live album from the event with Gary singing "Out of Hand." Pride and Stewart

also taped an episode of *Pop! Goes the Country* at that time, and it's the earliest known TV performance of Gary floating around. Introduced by Pride, who declares him "hotter than a match right now," Stewart belts out "Drinkin' Thing" and "Out of Hand," accompanying himself on piano.

Hair piled so high Esquerita might approve and wearing a denim suit with white overstitching and epaulets over a wide-lapel Western shirt adorned by a turquoise necklace, Stewart is nervous energy on parade. He seems on unsure footing with the camera present and hits a few bum notes, but it sure is fascinating to experience. Gary's live performances (at least in his prime) are worth the trouble to track down. If he's unhappy with something, it registers on his face, and if something strikes him funny, he laughs, even if it's in the middle of the saddest song in the world. And then moves on. As Larry Munson, Gary's old buddy from the Imps (who'd soon be returning to the fold) put it, "Gary didn't seem to think too much about the past, really. He didn't dwell. He was like, 'Right *now*!' Very few people are able to live in that moment."

* * *

The early days with Pride had moments of levity. During a radio interview with Ralph Emery, Gary told an amusing tale about a Halloween mask he took out on the road. It was of an old man and very realistic, "like maybe Hollywood would make." Gary donned the mask, put on his "longhandle" pajamas, put some towels in his shirt "for my hunchback," brought the lights down low and turned the TV to a static channel, then picked up the phone. "I call Charley up and I say, 'Charley, come over here. *I need to talk to you about something*.'" Pride went straight to Gary's room and knocked. Gary threw open the door. "I just lurk out at him. He just jumped back— 'RAHHHHHHH!'—and it just scared the heck out of him." But Charley loved the jolt. "Once he got over the scare...we had to do it to everybody in the band." When they opened the door on Pride's concession man Bobby Smith, he backed away from the hotel room only to "run into a snowbank...and his feet was *still* just gettin' it!" said Stewart, laughing his ass off.

Tour dates and being on time were not Gary's forte, however. Completely absent-minded, he'd miss planes and lose keys on a regular basis. Pride exited his hotel room one night to find Gary standing in the hallway "with his long johns on. He had locked himself out! And he missed his flight twice." The Prides were crazy about Gary—and Lou. "They were a good couple," said Charley's wife Rozene. "Gary was a good human being. We loved him, we really did. He was a lot of fun. Gary was just so carefree. He didn't take things that serious. And he loved his family." Mary Lou went out to join Gary at a Lake Tahoe gig and was petrified of meeting the Prides. "I was real nervous about meetin' Rozene. They had a penthouse suite, you'd have to ring the buzzer, and I had on a long dress. I had borrowed just about everything, 'cause we still didn't have hardly any money. Gary was just startin' with Pride." But the couple put Lou at ease immediately. "Rozene said 'Oh, I'm so glad you wore a dress here, honey. Can you zip me up?' And Charley poked his head around the corner and said, 'Where's my shirt? Oh, hi! You must be Lou.' Rozene really taught me a lot. So did Jerry Bradley's wife. And Bobby Bare's wife. And Willie Nelson's wife, Connie."

* * *

Out on the road, Stewart had to have a crony with him, so he summoned Jim Snead to come play drums for his section of the show. Gary played a gig on August 2 at the Waterloo Village Music Festival in New Jersey with Dolly Parton (according to newspaper reports it was billed "The Gary Stewart and the Dolly Parton Show"). During his segment of the show Stewart called out an old Hank Williams number. "And Gary said, 'Jimmy, I want you to rock and roll this up!'" Snead did. It was a wild show, which prompted an ominous editorial in the local paper: "Waterloo Festival: Traditional Country Music

Challenged." Stewart was described as a rocker upstart who "stomped, shouted, and strummed the bejusus out of his guitar...always mobile, always gyrating, always vocal," while Dolly's more traditional set "drew a standing ovation." A few weeks after the show, an angry fan wrote Charley Pride care of RCA (a letter which Gary kept). Pride had an upcoming show in Waterloo, and the fan wrote, "Gary Stewart sabotaged us all at the Dolly Parton concert...he showed up with some lame excuse about not reading his contract, and proceeded to sing and play *rock music* with a *gang of freaks* from *New York City*! Please see that he does a country act on 8-30 and 8-31-75 in Waterloo!" Stewart had whipped this fan and his friends into such a frenzy they were forming a group to "combat the trend towards rock" called K.I.C.K.—Keep It Country Klub.

It was becoming apparent Stewart was a different breed of country. Steve Hinson remembers the first time he backed Gary after he showed up in Macon at a club called Nashville South. Hinson expected Gary to do his new hits like any other country star passing through town. "We were used to these cats like Narvel Felts, Nat Stuckey...Gary Stewart was younger than them. I said, 'What do you want to do? "She's Acting Single"? "Drinkin' Thing"?'" No. He charged into the Allman Brothers' "One Way Out" instead. "We gave him a Les Paul and he just took off."

Snead didn't last long as a Pridesman. "I got drunk and took this waitress out. Charley said, 'Don't do it.' And I did it." After Snead was let go, Gary rang up Larry "Mouse" Munson. "I get a call. And Gary said, 'Man, I got a sweet gig for you.'" Munson already had a gig going in West Palm Beach. "Gary said, 'No, you gotta quit that job, man. Tomorrow, go to the airport, there'll be a ticket waiting for you. And when you get in Dallas, I'll be there.' Gary could've used Charley's drummer, no doubt about it, but for some reason he had me come out and work for him." Munson would also accompany Stewart on solo gigs, where they'd play with a house band, who'd be given a tape of his songs ahead of time. Sometimes Gary would use the Pridesmen rhythm section in between Pride gigs. Gary had tried to talk RCA into hiring the Phoenix as his road band, but that was ixnayed. Stewart hated relying on unknown musicians of varying quality for these gigs. He would not have his own band until the latter part of 1976, after his initial wave of success.

* * *

One requirement for being a Pridesman was wearing the band uniform. "It was *polyester*," said Stewart, who would sweat uncontrollably in the garment. "I hated polyester. Owen Bradley says to me one time, 'Wear your clothes, don't let your clothes wear you.' I wanted to wear my Levi's, y' know, and did a few times. Charley—who was a great guy, really—said, 'You can't do that.' So I bought me a leather suit in Hollywood. I sit down at the piano bench the first night I wore it and ripped the damn ass out!" Gary returned to his jeans, which didn't escape notice by the Pride organization. Stewart and Munson were outsiders in the band. "We didn't dress like 'em. Gary refused to wear that stuff. We did stay to ourselves a lot. We just were alone."

Even early on Stewart found big venues soulless, like when he played Felt Forum with Pride November 8, 1975. "Coming home, we're both on the plane, talking," said Munson. And I'm telling Gary, 'Madison Square Garden, I would have thought that was the ultimate. We're really in the big time. Why doesn't it feel like it?' Gary said, 'Hey—they're way too worried about the money. Too much money. And not enough music.'"

* * *

Returning to Fort Pierce from Nashville, the Stewarts moved into a corner-lot house on the south side that—save for a few crazy years much later spent in a double-wide trailer—would be Gary and Mary Lou's home for the rest of their lives. Stewart crammed it with antiques and memorabilia he'd bought out on the road. And countless vinyl albums. He'd bought the house off his parents, who'd sold it for the price of "love and affection," a declaration handwritten into the deed. According to Shannon, the actual figure was more like $16,000. When it came to her kids, Georgia "made sure her name was on all their houses one way or another," said Shannon. "But see, my mom would not allow that. She made sure my dad paid that money back. This was their house, free and clear." The Stewart home would be a contentious subject for some of Gary's siblings, who maintained that Georgia, as Gina put it, "paid for that house many times over" by giving Gary money when he was having IRS troubles. A search of the records shows that Georgia's name did not reappear on the deed after she transferred it to Gary in 1974.

* * *

Charley Pride, Gary, the Four Guys vocal group, unidentified others. (Shannon Ashburn collection)

Now that Gary was touring with Pride, the family settled into a routine, with Stewart gone for weeks at a time. His returns home were fit for a king. Lou would be dressed to the nines when he walked through the door. Certain rituals had already taken place. "There was a whole thing that me and mom had to do," said Shannon. Lou, who was cleaning houses at the time, would "make sure the floors were highly waxed and mopped and the house was spotless. And then me and mom would go to Publix," a nearby grocery store. Lou and Shannon "would literally walk out of there with two grocery carts. My dad would want certain things when he came off the road—fried chicken, macaroni and cheese, baked beans, mashed potatoes and homemade gravy. That was, like, a ritual dinner. Then it would be Breyers ice cream."

Whatever antics Gary got into out on the road, family was never far from his mind. He'd burst through the door and always "have something for me and my brother," said Shannon. "A little airplane that he would get at the airport or a little bracelet, nothing extravagant. Just little trinkets." And when he was out on the road in those pre-internet/pre-cell-phone days, he'd send Lou postcard after postcard professing his love. Shannon has stacks of them. "Remember the Alamo," said one. "But most of all, remember I love you. Gary."

* * *

Stewart and Dea upped the ante even further on their next single, "She's Actin' Single (I'm Drinkin' Doubles)." Another Wayne Carson song, it was an absolute wrecking ball of a record. The idea came to Carson after a round of golf, sitting with a buddy in a bar called the Flaming Pit. "One of the classy joints," Carson cracked to Michael Gray. "And this guy walked in, he was probably seventyish, gray-headed, with a youngish bride." There was another younger man with them. "I thought, 'Well, he's probably the chauffeur, the bodyguard.'" The trio took a booth, drank some whiskey, and "next thing I know, she's done put a couple dollars in the jukebox." She proceeds to dance with the "chauffeur." "They're up there cuttin' a fandango, and he's touchin' her in places you don't need to be touchin' another man's wife." Meanwhile the old guy was silently watching them as he tossed back drinks. "I said, 'Look-a-there—he's drinkin' doubles and she thinks she's still single.' And I mulled that over for about half a minute, downed my drink, and said, 'Bob, I'll see ya later, I'm gonna go to my studio.' That was an easy song to write."

"She's Actin' Single" is a bit like Gary's "High School Confidential"—brimming with cheap drama, and kind of preposterous (those aren't criticisms). Oh, that opening salvo: "I've seen men look at her before / And they think I don't see / I'd like to think it makes me proud / But I'm only foolin' me." Another cheating, evil woman is demolishing a weak man: "While she pours herself on some stranger / I pour myself a drink somewhere." The chorus rhymes the title with "My heart is breaking / Like the tiny bubbles," for God's sake! Stewart recognizes the humor, even as he makes you believe every word. Life is a sad-song cliché, buddy—dig in. This was an intricate number for Gary to learn. He called the arrangement "rather confusing." There is an early take where you can hear him working out the tricky verbiage, figuring out the right syllables to accent. Pete Drake's ascending, operatic opening steel licks aren't present either. It's kind of a snoozer, and once again you hear how much work went into getting these records just right. "We did the backing track, Gary sang and it didn't sound worth a shit," Dea told Wade Jessen. "He took the tape home and kept it for two weeks without a vocal on it and finally called me and said, 'I think I've learned how I can sing it where it fits me—and the music, too.'"

In the majestic final cut, Drake's accompaniment is the perfect mirror to Stewart's quavering vibrato, which is center stage like never before. "Pete plays from the top to bottom of the song," said Steve Hinson. "Usually on a county record in those days somebody played the intro, then you'd leave. Nobody else plays any fills on that record."[48] Gary's unruly vocal slithers around from to his lowest growl to his highest register. Like Houdini escaping from a straitjacket, you think, "How is he doing this?" Released in March 1975,"She's Actin' Single (I'm Drinkin' Doubles)" is a tour de force, the topper of the early RCA singles, and it took home the gold. It shot to the top of the country charts, Gary's only number-one single.

* * *

Stewart slipped off the Pride tour and blew into Fort Pierce for a triumphant gig the week he hit number one, an unrehearsed, loosey-goosey show with some members (but not all) of the Phoenix, opening with "Ramblin' Man." A crude tape exists. "We're celebratin' my number-one song this week and we just want to throw a party!" he shouts out before lurching into a sloppy, no-steel-guitar "She's Actin' Single," laughing at his bum notes. "Do we have any rednecks here tonight?" he asks the boisterous crowd as he heads into a shambling cover of Jerry Jeff Walker's "Up Against the Wall Red Neck [Mother]." One of his sisters brings Gary a drink onstage, and he introduces Georgia to the crowd. "Stand up and take a bow, Mom," he says, jumping into a tough version of her favorite, "Hello, Josephine." Stewart, who sounds on top of the world, Ma, informs the crowd his new album *Out of Hand* is number one as well (it actually only made number six on the *Billboard* country chart).

Dea had been made to wait until "She's Actin' Single" was burning up the charts before RCA allowed that first collection. "They would not let me put out an album until you had three hit singles. That was a big thing—you had to have 'Contains the hits' on the cover...RCA never even knew there was an album. They was

48 Hinson maintained that Drake's "She's Actin' Single" lick shows up in his playing during every live gig. "My wife busted me on that, man—I play a little fragment of it in everything I do. She just rolls her eyes. I tell her, 'I've got to do it. I can't stop doing it.' To this day, if I work with some singer, I'll do that in some song and they'll turn around and look at me. They all know it...It's one of the most identifiable licks ever."

in the singles business. I'd say, 'We ain't never gonna make it as a record company if we don't sell albums to people. We gotta develop artists.' They thought people buy songs. Singles, singles—RCA never promoted albums."[49]

Dea put his foot down about one thing: no covers of songs done by a zillion other country artists, and while it may not sound like a big deal now, it was at the time. "Every album I was involved in before this, I wasn't the complete boss, it was Jerry Bradley. They all had the theory that if 'For the Good Times' was a hit by Ray Price, you needed to cut it on the album with the artist you were doin'—'You need to do some titles, you don't have titles in the album.' I don't want no *titles*. Don't nobody want to hear Gary sing 'For the Good Times'! People out there say, 'Now, why don't he write his own songs? Why's he singin' *Ray Price songs*?' I didn't think it made any sense to cut anything that had already been a hit. Since I was in complete control of this project, I could fight—and win. Nobody asked me to do that again—and they quit doin' it, too. It had a big effect on songwriters, because back then if you had a hit song like Don Williams's 'Amanda' you could just sit back, because it was gonna be cut on at least twenty or thirty albums."

Besides the three hits and their B-sides, Gary cut three new numbers, all of them great: an achingly beautiful ballad written by the largely unknown country singer/former rocker Jimmie Helms, "This Old Heart Won't Let Go,"[50] and the nifty "Honky-Tonkin'," first cut by its cowriter Troy Seals in a wonderfully deadpan version a year before. Stewart turns it into a twin-guitar showcase and contributes a wild vocal, aided by some doo-wop touches by the Jordanaires. The song would become his opening anthem on the road. The last of the new trio was "Sweet Country Red," another Seals song, this

49 "I try to shy away from releasing albums first," Jerry Bradley told *Billboard* in 1978. "The easiest thing in the world is to make an album and the hardest thing to do is to sell it."

50 Mr. Helms, who wrote for the Wilburn Brothers, was also responsible for an obscure 1978 single entitled "I Dreamed I Buried Country Music Yesterday." Stewart's longtime bandleader Randy Toman said that "This Old Heart Won't Let Go" never failed to bring the emotion out of Gary when he performed it live.

one about an enterprising Kentucky redhead. Stewart plays hopped-up piano and delivers a spirited, near-rockabilly vocal. Even though it had been patched together single by single, *Out of Hand* holds together beautifully as an album. There wasn't a weak or boring cut. I'll be damned if I can name another debut album where the artist sounds so thrilled to be delivering the goods.

Then there's that laughably square cover shot. Smiling Gary in his denim suit at the piano in front of a solid-color backdrop, looking like a fatally exuberant member of some north-of-Toledo white gospel quartet. Seventies "hippie" drop-shadow lettering announces the title and, yes, the requisite three "hits" are listed. The back cover was much less artificial, a black-and-white candid snapshot by Grandal of his brother relaxing at home in cowboy boots and the hat RCA refused to let him wear on the cover. Music City Gary versus Fort Pierce Gary, with Nashville insistent on the former.

It was easy to wind Roy up about that cover. "I hated it! It's just a standard ol' RCA album cover, a 'Bruno of Hollywood' shot. That cover don't go with that album! That cover shot was in Gary's file, and I learned that every time somebody wanted a promo shot, they'd send out that stupid-ass picture. I went to his file and cleaned out all those Bruno of Hollywood shots. I said, 'I don't want nothin' in here unless it has *motion* in it!'"

Out of Hand came out October 29, 1975. Some of the top country songs that year? Hits by George Jones and Merle Haggard, joined by "I'm Not Lisa" from Jessi Colter. "Blanket on the Ground," Billie Jo Spears. "Thank God I'm a Country Boy," John Denver, and "Convoy" by C.W. McCall. No wonder Stewart was a sensation. "He was making the wildest country music of his time," wrote music journalist John Morthland. "There was nothing else like him. He blew everything else off the radio."

Dea felt vindicated when the reviews of *Out of Hand* appeared. It received ecstatic attention, with Gary getting coverage even in non-country magazines like *Rolling Stone* ("undiluted honky tonk...recalls classic rockabilly") and *Creem*. John Rockwell in *The New York Times* declared the album a "return to the roots of country rock...this is a disk that exists almost as if the whole recent history of Nashville, with its steady domestication of the country tradition, didn't exist—or more likely, it stands as a protest against that domestication." Some singled out the cover—"Don't be misled by that mod look; this man has got to be a little crazy," wrote *Village Voice* critic Robert Christgau, which tickled Dea. "I thought it was so funny. I just rolled on the floor thinkin', 'Oh Lord, there are people out in the world that do understand!'"

Out of Hand has gone on to be recognized as a seminal contribution to country music, for many, Stewart's finest work (I mildly disagree). "One of the greatest honky-tonk albums ever recorded," wrote country music historian Bill C. Malone. Stewart had created a new sound that lovingly referenced the past—Charley Crockett was moved by "how traditional his big hits were, in a time where traditional country music was really vanishing from the landscape...I think he might have been the last guy to have big pop country hits with an upright bass on the recording."

For others, the rewards of *Out of Hand* were more esoteric. "Driven by the crying steel and the 4/4 Ray Price shuffle, it was a magic elixir reeking of Hai Karate, PBR and Marlboros," wrote Reverend Billy C. Wirtz, who heard "a musical speedball of Claude Ely, Jimmy Reed and Jerry Lee Lewis...that moan starts in church, but somewhere along the way, it always ends up in a motel, with a honky tonk angel, cuttin' rails and feeding the Magic Fingers."

* * *

That June, RCA sent Gary and Lou to New York City for a press junket, during which the couple also celebrated their thirteenth wedding anniversary. "They flew me first class!" said Lou, who tried to change the ticket to coach. "That's how we are. But I went *first class*, drinkin' champagne!" Once there, she was overwhelmed by the city skyscrapers. "They had us in a penthouse suite at the St. Regis. Hey, it was as big as a house! Gary was gonna be real busy while we were there and the RCA guy said, 'Anything you wanna do, Mrs. Stewart, you just let us know.' I said, 'I wanna go see a bunch of Broadway shows.' I had never seen one." RCA got Mary Lou into *Chicago* and *Shenandoah,* while Roy Dea accompanied her to *Grease*. "I thought it was about the *country* Greece!" confessed Dea, who was equally unfamiliar with Broadway. "Lou jumped out in the middle of the street and hailed a taxi like she had lived there all her life." There was no stopping her. "Gary would say, 'I gotta go do a thing at RCA. You stay here in the room, now. Don't go nowhere!' and I'd say, 'Okay.' When he'd leave, I'd get down there and say, 'TAXI!'"

Pancho and Cisco, on the loose in the Big Apple. "Sometimes Gary and I would go shoppin' and the limo would follow us. Everybody would be lookin'—here's two people with Levi's on walkin' down the street with a limo followin' them!" Alas, the same Levi's barred them from enjoying the St. Regis dining room.

Gary was a hit with the press. "Every time they'd leave, they'd be shaking their heads," said Dea. "I mean, they had somethin' to write about. Stewart was an interviewer's dream." If you caught Gary in the right mood, he was eminently quotable and frequently uncensored. Talking to a local reporter in 1975 about the stress of being on the road, Gary admitted that he missed "layin' around the house...gettin' high with my friends." In 1981 he'd boast to another country music magazine, "Some night when the lights come up, you're gonna see me with a machine gun and I'm gonna assassinate the whole audience!" Two writers in particular at *Country Music* magazine were champions of Stewart—Bob Allen and Patrick Carr, and they became his friends. Carr went to Fort Pierce in 1975 to do the first serious profile on Gary and was instantly immersed in Stewartworld. "Gary picked me up from the airport in this big, funky old car. And we start driving along, doing drugs immediately."

Carr would be whisked back to Fort Pierce by Gary after a 1982 New York City show. "He said that he wanted me to produce his record," said Carr, who was neither producer nor musician. Once they got to Gary's house, Gary and Lou repeatedly disappeared into the bathroom to do drugs as he sat and watched Stewart favorite *The White Buffalo* on the TV. Gary then introduced Patrick to "this local woman whom he promises is going to fuck me." Carr was off in a car of crazed strangers. "It's nighttime, right, and these little twisty roads in the Florida Everglades...and they were driving really, really fast, skidding around the corners." Patrick did not get laid. Nor was an album produced.

Exceptions aside, Gary soon grew to loathe doing any sort of publicity, weary of glad-handing deejays and the rest of the expectations that went with being a country star. "Sometimes I feel like I just can't do it," he'd moan in 1980. "Shakin' everybody's hand…it just seems so phony." Yet he had a sly sense of delivering the goods upon occasion. "One time we finished the gig, went back to a motel, and there was some guy from a radio station coming over to interview Gary," said Larry Munson. "So Gary tells me, 'Hey, man, this dude's coming over to interview me, I got to have a bottle of whiskey.'" Munson went downstairs, where the bartender told him he'd have to sell the bottle to him by the shot. Stewart wasn't going to imbibe, he just wanted to look the part. "Sixty-four dollars for a damn bottle of whiskey, a damn prop for an interview," said Munson. "Gary just laughed. He hardly ever drank. I drank more and *I* didn't really drink that much. After 'Drinkin' Thing,' Gary was *expected* to be that. That's when the misery started coming."

* * *

While Stewart wasn't knocking back whiskey, he was certainly living the title of that first album. There were "tons of women," according to Dea. "He knocked women out. They'd throw their drawers onstage and he'd autograph 'em! I didn't think of Gary as a sex symbol, but he had more women than all of the pretty boys put together." Lou had zero illusions. She informed me matter-of-factly that she packed rubbers in his suitcase. Lou didn't want her husband bringing home any surprises.

On the *Out of Hand* album cover, Gary is wearing a ring from one of these paramours. "Left hand, little finger," said Kentucky Kate,[51] who met Stewart at a Frankie n' Johnny's show in January of 1975. Twenty-seven years old, Jewish, from Louisville, and "not interested in country music," Kate was a stunner with long black hair. "Gary came over to my table, leaned in, and said I was the most beautiful woman he had ever seen. I was not impressed. I thought he was an old country dude from another era, with his hair slicked back and that damn pointy white collar." But once Kate saw Gary perform a few numbers with the Phoenix, "I was swept off my feet. He mesmerized me." When she saw him at the Fort Pierce Hotel, she found out he was married when he "stopped by and whispered in my ear 'My wife is here.'" (Lou, who was friendly at first, told her she looked like Cher.)

They were soon entwined. Kate was dealing with a falling-apart "semi-hippie" marriage of her own. "Needless to say, I discussed my issue of not wanting to date a married man" with Gary. "He assured me that Lou was aware and okay with him being with other women." She'd meet him in Nashville at the Fan Fair convention in June 1975 along with other clandestine stops out on the road. "He bought me what I wanted. Paid my expenses anywhere we were. He once sent me ten dollars cash to cover a collect call. Gary was from the old school, when men paid for things and refused to accept money from ladies." Gary introduced Kate to shrimp scampi and peanut butter pie. "Gary always said I was like a gentle cat...we laughed a lot back then. He always had great stories to tell. He was attentive, affectionate in private and respectfully affectionate in public. He laughed at himself. I never saw him being mean or argumentative with anyone. He loved to turn people on to new music or artists. He loved jamming with anyone. He was willing to try new things." At a party, Fred Bogert put his boa constrictor around Gary's shoulders. Stewart was unfazed. Kate recalls being at the beach with Gary, who was dressed only in cutoffs, "weary-eyed and half-awake," holding some french fries up so a seagull could snatch them. "He smiled and

51 An alias.

looked like a kid in wonderment. His hair was blowing in the wind and the sun was rising." Gary talked about moving Kate to Detroit and asked how she felt about children. "That threw me off," said Kate. There is a souvenir portrait of Gary and Kate taken at Tootsie's Orchid Lounge, a legendary Music City watering hole. They are both smiling, and look like any other happy young couple. Except that Gary had a family back home, which would soon lead to Fist City.

On a visit to Kentucky, Kate introduced Gary to her husband Jack. He didn't care they were seeing each other, and the two men spent the day stripping and refinishing a table together. "Late that afternoon Gary informed me he never would have started anything with me if he had met Jack first, he thought that Jack was such a nice guy. But Gary being the multisided person he was, continued to sleep with me and spend time with me alone." They wrote love letters to each other. Kate sent them to his parents' house. "Gary would keep them under the front seat of his car....Against my advice, and, of course, eventually found there by Lou."

Early on, Fred Bogert had tried to warn Kate. "Fred told me to forget Gary," telling her that Gary and Lou had read her letters aloud to some house guests for laughs. Kate was unfazed. "I heard the words, but Gary was still behaving affectionately, so I ignored it."

Things came to a head following a Fort Pierce rendezvous at one of Gary's brothers' houses. There was a knock at the door. "I open it and there stands Lou...she hauls off and slugs me on the side of my head." After Lou clocked her, there was heated conversation. Kate explained how Gary had said he was in love with her, that she thought Lou was fine with it, and how Gary wanted to move her to Detroit. Lou informed Kate that Gary had told her "he loved me as a friend." Lou was smoldering. "I thought you were my friend. You are lucky I did not come here with a gun." Kate fled Fort Pierce.

Although the romance faded somewhat, Gary continued to see Kate sporadically throughout 1975. Thereafter they remained friends, Gary seeing her every once in a while out on the road. There are quizzical pictures from a 1982 Texas visit in which a bleary-eyed

Stewart, the least athletic man of all time, is wearing a football helmet given to him by a Dallas Cowboy, and he's stumbling around a hotel room in some sort of invisible game to amuse her. The pair lost touch. Kate felt conflicted about the affair for years, sorry she had hurt Mary Lou. "This is my pain, my shame. I have felt guilty about it for years... then let it go." She felt bad she wasn't in touch with Gary at the end. "I could have been the friend who he talked to when Lou died...when he wanted to die."

One memory of Kate's remains indelible. It happened during the dalliance before Lou came a-knocking at the door. Gary and Kate had smoked weed before coupling. "I had a hallucination of Gary as the devil. I had asked him to pull the blinds, and he ran over to the window. Naked, skinny, and with a huge hard-on. Only he had horns."

* * *

Gary was flying high. Boom boom boom, three hit singles in a row. Touring with Charley Pride. A critically acclaimed album debut. The next single from Gary and Roy Dea would be a stunner, a rocker written by Gary that was just too wild for RCA. And just like that, things would begin to unravel.

8

ANIMAL IN A CAGE

I feed off an audience...I'm only as good as they are.

– Gary Stewart

Another sunny day in Florida. Grandal Stewart, temporarily separated from his wife Candy, is holed up in a Fort Pierce apartment he shares with a roommate. There's a knock at the door, then his brother bursts in with a guitar. "I want to sing a song I just wrote," Gary announces, then blasts through a raucous number entitled "Flat Natural Born Good-Timin' Man," the tale of a honky-tonk lady-killer: "Steppin' out, steppin' high / Step on back, check my stride / I'm ready for anything come Saturday night." After charging through the number, Gary informs his brother he was the reason he wrote it. "I don't think he was bullshittin' me," said Grandal, grinning at the memory.[52]

52 According to Grandal, "Uncle Joe Dan," the "ladies' man" in the song who teaches "the what to do's and when," was based on "Jack Niece, Mommy's brother." Niece named a racehorse after the Gary song "Whiskey Trip."

Cut on August 20, 1975 (the same day as another top-notch Stewart–Wayne Carson song, "Oh, Sweet Temptation"), "Flat Natural Born Good-Timin' Man" was Gary's first (released) solo writing credit. The first thing you hear is Gary's stinging slide guitar, which wails throughout. "There were no slide pickers in town," Roy Dea recalled. "Gary took a pencil from Jerry Bradley and put it under the strings to raise 'em up." His swaggering vocal is superb, snaking around a raunchy, slightly verbose couplet only he could master: "And when I'm through with you, you won't wanna move / You'll lay on back and smile at what you just gone through." The Jordanaires and Lea Jane Berinati add great backing vocals, including some fifties "shoop-shoops" that link it to a rich past while making you laugh. This record sounds like nothing coming out of the Music City hit factory at the time, and it's much closer to who Gary was.

As if to obliterate that dreaded *Out of Hand* cover, the picture sleeve of the promo 45 sent to radio stations was a color version of Grandal's far more relaxed portrait of Gary that had graced the back album cover. And it was a foldout, the inside plastered with rave reviews and interviews. "Gary Stewart Skyrocketing" said the flap. Released in the fall of 1975 on the tailwinds of the trifecta of *Out of Hand* hits, Roy Dea had nothing but high hopes. "You have to move forward in records, in music, in anything creative. You can't stand still. Somebody'll pass you by. I thought, 'This is the one that's gonna cross us over.'"

But the single was just too rock for the powers that be. "RCA, they did not dig it at all," said Dea. "They *cringed*. I thought, 'I'm trapped'—'cause if I don't put it out I'm gonna miss a potential crossover, and if I *do* put it out it's never gonna get a real push, because they don't *believe*, and you can't push somethin' you don't believe in. If you go out to promote a record, if you ain't high on it, the deejays are gonna know it. As a promotion man, you have to take initiative with a record and say, 'This is the future, Joe. Believe me.' Rather than turn around and say, 'Well, OK, I'm sorry. How about *this* one?' 'Flat Natural' was the type of record that radio did not have, so it woulda took some pushin'."

RCA couldn't be convinced. "That single started the frustrations. Because I realized that it didn't look like I was gonna be able to accomplish what I wanted to, 'cause I couldn't get 'em on my side. I couldn't get 'em enthused about what me and Gary wanted to do." All RCA wanted was "another 'Drinkin' Thing,'" said Dea, adding he felt the pressure to replicate Gary's three initial hits "constantly."

When I asked Jerry Bradley about RCA's lack of excitement over the record and the lackluster promotion, he pleaded ignorance. "I don't know about any of those things," he said. For Bradley, rather incredibly, it boiled down to one thing: diction. "Gary started losing his enunciation for words. You *couldn't understand his words.*" He insisted he wasn't alone in this opinion. "I was the interpreter from out in the field to Gary as to what was wrong, and we got terrible friction from disc jockeys and other people wantin' to know what the words were. I talked to him about it *umpteen thousand times*...if you go back and listen to 'Drinkin' Thing' you can understand every word that he says."

Whatever the reason, "Flat Natural Born Good-Timin' Man" only reached twenty on the country charts upon its release, a substantial drop from Stewart's previous singles. The song went on to become a staple of his live act and in February 1976 he performed it on *Pop! Goes the Country* (Charley Pride was the fellow guest). Looking rather odd playing electric guitar with an off-camera band, Gary sounds much less shaky than in his previous appearance, and both "Flat Natural" and "She's Actin' Single" are tremendous. Still no hat allowed, though.

* * *

Gary's second album, *Steppin' Out,* was released in January 1976, a year after his first. The cover is a shot of Gary standing in an old barn next to Grandal's gleaming yellow '49 Chevrolet Styleline Special Business Coupe (Grandal also took the photos). On the back is Gary sitting on the trunk smiling. RCA was beginning to allow a more downhome Stewart groove—and in true seventies fashion, there was a new "futuristic" Gary Stewart logo on the cover and an iron-on Gary Stewart T-shirt transfer inside the album! This was a stellar collection, more varied than his debut. Every song's worth talking about.

"Quits" is a breakup song written by Danny O'Keefe, a singer-songwriter Stewart held in high esteem whose biggest hit was "Goodtime Charlie's Got the Blues" ("I never got to know him but I considered him kindred," O'Keefe wrote of Stewart on his site after learning of his death). Never a single, the performance is beloved by many a Stewart fan who'll no doubt be outraged that I found the ballad wimpy and used to needle Stewart about it. He quite rightly told me to broaden my musical horizons—"Just because you don't like it don't mean it ain't good, Jimmy!" "Oh, Sweet Temptation," another Wayne Carson cheating song, was the second single, which reached number twenty-three.

"Lord What a Woman" is a dynamic ode to Mary Lou cowritten by Carson. There is a rousing version of "Trudy," a Charlie Daniels song (Daniels plays guitar and fiddle on the album.) A ballad Willie Nelson wrote after the suicide of his drummer Paul English's first wife, "I Still Can't Believe You're Gone," shows off Gary's unerring ballad delivery. There's a wild version of the old Lefty Frizzell hit "If You've Got the Money (I've Got the Time)," with Stewart tearing it up on piano. "(I Can't Be) Your Backdoor" is a fantastic anti-cheating song cowritten by Carol and Mary Beth Anderson, two sisters who'd soon provide Gary with an equally fabulous hit single. In "Hank Western," Gary finally paid tribute to the grizzled old pickers that hung around the Merry-Go-Round. "I had a good thing going/I had a weakness, too," sings Stewart, sounding eerily aware of his own fate.

Stewart was inspired to write "Hank Western" after meeting another one of his heroes—Dickey Betts. "Me and my mama was going back to the hills, back home back to Kentucky," said Stewart to Bob Allen. While they were standing in the Atlanta airport, Gary spotted Betts. "So I went out there and told him how much I loved his music...he was on his way to catch a plane. And he says, 'We'll meet again.' We did." As Stewart told Kirk West, he had so "much adrenaline pumping" after meeting Betts he immediately wrote "Hank Western." "I finished the mother right there, on the plane."

Two songs on *Steppin' Out* deserve special mention. Stewart was particularly proud of "In Some Room Above the Street," yet another infidelity number, this one written by Mormon songwriter Sterling Whipple, which was the last and most successful single from the album, reaching number fifteen. The song had been released as a single on RCA the year before by its author (produced by Dea, no less), as a slow, soft-rock ballad in the style of Bread before Stewart and Dea completely transformed it. "I did a laid-back kind of sensitive-type production," Whipple told Bob Allen. "Gary did a real uptempo, sock it to 'em type thing...a better arrangement than mine."

During the recording Dea had to leave to play a gig, so he put Gary in charge of producing the steel solo. "It was a slow song at first," said Stewart. Roy, who'd cut the original, "played me the song and I said, 'Let ME do it, real slow.' I had an idea." While in the studio, Gary hummed the steel part to Weldon Myrick, which quickly changed the song to a faster tempo. "I wanted it to sound like a magic carpet ride," he explained, inexplicably invoking Jimi Hendrix's name to Myrick. "He had a bunch of pedals—and I'm not into pedals, so I didn't know what would work...we tried a bunch of things. Probably lasted a half hour—then it was, 'Yeah, that's it! Do it that way, just keep playing continuously through it.'" To Steve Hinson, this record was the "most produced-sounding" Gary Stewart single and "another attention-grabber. That guitar intro by Reggie Young is spectacular."

"Easy People" is a stellar Eldridge–Stewart composition dating back to the *Grandma's Roadhouse* days. A rich, amusing rumination on Southern life with cockfights and moonshine stills, it begins with the couplet "My nose has been itchin' me all day / Company must be on the way" and only gets better from there. The lilting melody and cheerful vocal are in delightful counterpoint to the friendly menace lurking within. As Stewart sings a line about getting lost in the holler, you imagine him lifting a shotgun to eye level. There is a slower, moodier unreleased version that is not quite fully realized. Dea had added something new to Stewart's arsenal—bluegrass, with Buck White on mandolin, Josh Graves on dobro, Bobby Thompson on banjo, Tommy Williams on violin, and upright slap bass by Joe Zinkan. The great Ray Edenton plays rhythm guitar and Jim Isbell is on drums. It was cut on November 13, 1975, along with two more tremendous bluegrass-infused numbers that were saved for Gary's next album. Listening to them, you dream of Stewart cutting an album called *Gary Sings the Stanley Brothers and Other Mountain Favorites*.

* * *

Stardom brought provocations. Fans would show up at Stewart's house in the middle of the night. One tracked down Grandal by running the plate of the Chevy on the cover of *Steppin' Out* to bombard him with questions about his brother. "It got crazy, real crazy," said Mary Lou. "People would follow him around. He'd have all these 'friends,' you wouldn't know who the heck they are—'I graduated with Gary.' Well, Gary didn't graduate! He would go to a record store and people would be standin' there starin' at him. It kinda flipped him out." As Gary recalled, "I was in downtown one day in the shopping center. And this kid came up to me, said, 'Aren't you Gary Stewart?' I said, 'No.' He said, 'Are you sure?' I never thought about losin' my privacy. I wished I'd known more about that. Y'know, it's hard to scratch your ass out on the street if everybody's lookin' at ya."

Perhaps Stewart's most screw-loose fan was an obsessed Canadian woman named Beverly Shoemaker, who had befriended Georgia, calling and sending letters before she showed up in person with handmade silk shirts for Gary and his band. Shoemaker would make headlines in 1988 for hijacking a helicopter at gunpoint to bust her boyfriend out of prison. "I did it for love!" she told the *National*

Enquirer, informing them she'd met Danny Mahoney "through a personal ad in a country music magazine." Beverly wound up doing two and a half years in the slammer.

* * *

One hit album and already Stewart was sick of stardom. During the "Flat Natural" session, an Associated Press reporter named Matt Yancey slipped in to interview Gary. The result, which ran in papers all across the country a few months later, must've had RCA reaching for the smelling salts. "50,000 a Year, He Hates Self," screamed the headline. "I hate myself," moaned Stewart, who maintained his newfound attention made him feel "like a freak in a carnival show.... Being in this business has turned me into a fellow I don't like....My bank account has become one of my prized possessions, and that's not me....I just want to sing, but I can't hack doing all the other things that you're supposed to like if you're going to be a country singer." Gary pined for the days he played with the Phoenix "for ninety bucks a week...I was really making better music before I had all these records. Maybe I want to be the boy in the back row again."

"After he got his record deal, Gary didn't seem very happy," said Larry Munson. "The more success he seemed to have, the more dismal he seemed to get." Munson felt RCA didn't know how to handle Stewart. "I wish things could have been just a tad different, just tweaked a little bit, man. I think everything would have changed. I know Jerry Bradley liked Gary. But their definition of success was totally different. Bradley's vision of success was a fancy new car, big house, and even bigger bank account. Gary's idea of success was a '49 Mercury to drive, and one parked in the backyard for parts. Plus a big ol' tarpaper shack where all his buddies could come over and jam."

The constant touring with Pride tightened the screws. "I was still playing piano, makin' $250 a week,' said Stewart. "But when Ronnie Milsap left, I had the openin' spot and made more money." Gary was the featured opening act, supported by Nashville's answer to Tony Orlando and Dawn—Dave & Sugar. Stewart and Munson amused themselves by selling contraband to Dave Rowland, the flashy lead singer, whom they dubbed "Rings 'n' Things." "He had all kinds of jewelry," noted Munson. So when the pair got hold of a hot watch, "we sold it to him, made a little profit." But laughs were hard to come by on the Pride dates. Larry would try to cheer Gary up, telling him what an easy gig it was as they only had to play a few numbers. Gary would have none of it, telling Larry, "Man, these concerts—the people aren't dancin', aren't drinkin', they ain't doin *nuthin'*.' Gary didn't like it. He felt he was stared at like an animal in a cage."

The Pride audience had no idea of Stewart's misery, as his short set electrified them. Charley vividly remembered playing the Houston Livestock Show and Rodeo with Stewart. "Forty-four thousand people. I let Gary do two of his songs." He whipped the crowd into a frenzy. Jerry Bradley was backstage, dumbfounded. "Jerry said, 'I ain't never seen nobody do a show like that.' Gary was so talented, man. He was *it*."

* * *

Money began to roll in. Stewart was incredibly generous, giving loads of cash to family and friends in need. As well as possessions. Guitars, clothes, jewelry, records—if you showed the slightest interest, Gary gave it to you. But the loot became a burden. Grandal recalled a fight between Gary and his sister Gina. "Gary says, 'Money don't mean shit to me, Gina. See this?' And he took a stack of bills—I don't know if it was $300 or $1,000—tore them up, and put them down the commode. Gary said, 'The only thing that means anything to me is music.'"[53]

While it was okay for Stewart to blow a pile of dough on guitars or antiques or whatever else struck his fancy, it was nothing but used cars for the family. For Gary, it was about his image. He informed

53 Drummer Robert "Cotton" Payne was helping Gary pack his suitcase one day when he found some royalty checks stuffed into a side pocket. All together they amounted to "about $200,000," Cotton recalled. "Gary said, 'Should I put those in the bank?'"

Time magazine that country music was "a poor man's music that talks about troubles on the home front and hard times on the job" and that his '49 Buick sedan and '65 Dodge Dart were more than enough transportation for the Stewarts. "I might like to walk on a little bit nicer rug, but if I get caught up in big cars and fancy homes, I'll lose touch with the people. My music is simple honky-tonk. It's nothing too eloquent 'cause I'm a simple man." I know Gary meant these words—he said them to me upon occasion—but it was becoming more and more apparent that there was nothing simple about Gary Stewart.

* * *

One day Reggie Young was out back of RCA taking a break from a session. "I heard this rustling and noise goin' on, and looked around to see Gary emerge from one of those big garbage cans. I said, 'Man, Gary, are you all right???' He said, 'When I left yesterday I left my cocaine on the music stand. I got back there today and it was gone.' So Gary crawled into the garbage cans and dadgum, he found it!" The Dipsy Dumpster (aka Dempsey Dumpster) incident, as it came to be known, would have tongues wagging at RCA.

Dea was at lunch when the incident occurred. "I get back, and one of the engineers saw me in the hall and said, 'What in the world's goin' on? Gary's out in the dipsy dumpster, shit's flyin' everywhere. Everybody's askin'—Jerry Bradley, even the secretaries.'" Stewart eventually reappeared, "no shirt on and black shit all over him," said Dea. "Everybody was lookin' at him...but he found the stuff. It was in a piece of cellophane about the size of a nickel...a needle in the haystack."

While Gary's drug intake was still recreational at this point, his reputation as a drug fiend was already cemented by such antics. Eddie Kilroy, who'd later produce Gary, still remembers the potent Florida weed Gary carried—the infamous Okeechobee Purple. "It had so much resin in it I had to rip it off my lips," said Kilroy. "If you dropped it, it would bounce three times." Once when Kilroy was hanging with Willie Nelson, smoking with him on his bus, he asked Nelson if he'd ever imbibed the Purple with Stewart. "Willie said, 'Oh my God, don't even talk about it! I smoked some of that and it messed me up so bad I had to get off the bus and go stand in the rain during a thunderstorm to get straight enough to do a show with him. That was some wicked pot, man.' When it gets too strong for Willie, it's strong!"

Nelson confirmed the tale via email. "I had a couple hits with him before our show. I *hope* it was a good show. 'Cause I don't remember." Willie and Gary did a few shows together and became good friends. Nelson even gave his mother a fancy inscribed Bible. ("Oh, I wouldn't take nothing in the world for my Bible," Georgia told me in 1987. "Willie calls me every once in a while." Gary's sister Griselda was so taken with Willie she added Nelson as her middle name.) "Gary Stewart was a friend of mine," wrote Willie. "We had fun hanging out, playing music and burnin' 'em down. He was a great singer, writer and all-around good guy. I miss him. May he rest in peace and someday come back and do it all again."

Like he did with Willie, Stewart would do shows with Waylon Jennings and Jessi Colter. All were riding high in 1976 with *Wanted! The Outlaws*, an assortment of (mostly) old cuts (which also included Tompall Glaser) held together by "outlaw" hype concocted by Jerry Bradley, whose cover concept put the musicians' faces on a tattered Wild West poster complete with bullet holes. It became a monster hit, the first country album to go platinum, and started the "outlaw" craze in country. Jennings readily admitted the idea of them being Music City banditos was completely manufactured: "About the closest thing that Willie ever did to bein' an outlaw is that he probably came to town and double-parked on Music Row." Jennings thought the idea was "about the dumbest thing I ever heard" until the album went through the roof. Astute enough to realize Jerry's real strength was as "a merchandiser," Waylon went with the plan. Gary was probably too uncontrollable and bullshit-free to join in such an act (although he would've loved being photographed in Civil War garb), but he was the closest thing to a real outlaw RCA had, and why Bradley didn't market Stewart along those lines is a complete mystery.

Gary with Waylon Jennings and Jessi Colter.
(Shannon Ashburn collection)

In the middle of a new album release and doing dates with Pride, Stewart found time to slip into Bradley's Barn to record a six-song demo of all new material. He was backed by a hot new Fort Pierce band—Aberdeen Rockfish Railroad, aka Rockfish. Dubbed "the heretic sons of Bill Monroe" by Patrick Carr, this "progressive bluegrass" outfit featured Darrell Dawson and "Boogie" Bob Melton from the Phoenix days; Ralph Profeta on banjo/steel guitar; Chris Casses on electric guitar/mandolin; and Donnie Coleman on acoustic guitar, vocals, and fiddle. Donnie also found songs for them to do—like "Leah," a song Gary would cut on his next album using Rockfish's arrangement. "It was a unique band for the time," said Melton. "We did not use a drummer, and we did a lot of bluegrass music as well as rock, country, Eagles, Beatles, Dan Fogelberg, John Prine, and Marshall Tucker. Gary loved it." Gary had played around town with the band, and Melton, Dawson, and Coleman had contributed uncredited backing vocals to his recent bluegrass session. In January 1976, Rockfish played their first road gigs in New Mexico with Stewart and a month later hauled ass through a Colorado snowstorm to join him for the Bradley's Barn session. Gary augmented the band with Larry Munson on drums, plus one picker from his studio sessions—Weldon Myrick on steel.

The songs were all written by Gary save for "Hollywood," an enjoyably clichéd tale written with Wayne Carson concerning a young starlet sinking into tawdry Tinseltown abyss that features some of Stewart's most impassioned singing and a nifty descending chorus. The outrageous "Bedtime Stories" is Gary at his raunchiest: "I'm gonna love you four ways, baby / Deep and long and hard and wide." "Let It Burn" is a nifty bluegrass number, and Stewart finally recorded his tribute to his aunt and uncle written back in his early Nashville days, "The Ballad of Corsia and John," done uptempo in a completely different manner from the original half-spoken jam. "Stella Mae" concerns an actual "fortune teller that traveled the South," Stewart said, who'd happened upon a 1938 Farm Security Administration photo taken by Russell Lee of a tough-looking clairvoyant standing next to a post sporting phrases ("Who Will You Marry / Your Friends / Your Enemies") that Gary worked into the lyrics ("I can look at a picture and write a song," said Gary). Stewart plays acoustic guitar on the cut. "Pretty hot," declared "Boogie" Bob.

My personal favorite is a rocker, "4th of July." Only Gary Stewart could make a patriotic holiday sound sexy and dangerous. He manages to mythologize family members in a conversational yet indelible fashion, particularly Lou: "Yonder goes sweet Mary Lou / Looks like she's takin' a walk," with Gary hurling forward the word "walk" as if simply putting one foot in front of the other was a sultry act of civil disobedience. Stewart's untamed piano sparks like a Pentecostal sermon, as does his vocal, and the whole thing just oozes fabulousness. Obviously Gary thought so, too, as he charges into one verse early, barely able to contain himself. I can recreate the whole damn performance note for note in my head, that's how deep this song's hold is over me. Some days it gets played twenty times in a row.

The band knew none of these numbers when they arrived at Bradley's Barn. "We rehearsed and arranged each song in the studio before cutting them," said Melton. "Gary really was on fire. He was very inspirational during that session." I'll say. Although the entire recording is white-hot, one of Stewart's best, precious few have heard it. Apparently this was a publishing demo session done to encourage other artists to do Gary's songs (Alabama would cut "Hollywood" on their 1981 platinum-selling album *Feels So Right*). Stewart was characteristically humble about the session, noting some of the numbers were "not really commercial" (granted, it would be hard to imagine Jack Greene covering the utterly filthy "Bedtime Stories"). He'd also inform me that Rockfish was his best live band. Had these recordings been released, they would've been hailed as some of Gary's greatest. But despite Roy Dea and Jerry Bradley being present for the session, RCA did nothing with it. Nor would Gary ever record in the studio with Rockfish or any of his touring bands again. Lost in time, all of it.

* * *

The gig with Charley Pride imploded in the summer of 1976. First came a lecture from Charley one night during some Canadian dates in April. No doubt aware of the Dipsy Dumpster incident, Pride had heard Gary was now "on the stuff," as he put it in his autobiography. (According to friends, Gary was merely smoking weed and snorting a little cocaine, still on the light side for him.) Pride felt Stewart was losing his way and felt compelled to address it. Something of an astrology buff, Charley noted Gary was a Gemini and when it came to that sign, "you automatically get two of them...you might get four." Knowing also that Geminis "talk a lot," Pride figured he could reason with Gary, sitting down for an intense conversation that he said went from "from midnight to daybreak." Determined to show Stewart the light, he told him he could be "another Hank Williams. You got all the attributes. You're skinny, you're talented." All he had to do was get his shit together, lay off "the stuff," and do what was expected of a country music star. Gary, who had already seen enough of the big time, was unmoved. "Maybe I don't want to be that big," he told Charley.

"I begged, I pleaded," Pride told me. "But at daybreak he just said, 'I don't want to climb that mountain like you. I just want to hunker down in the bars and have me a good time.'" Charley sighed, throwing in the towel.

The last straw came when Pride was planning another tour of England and Ireland that November, and his team demanded that Gary show up in Pridesman polyester. Reluctant to sound like a complainer or badmouth anybody, Gary told the tale haltingly. "The tour manager called. Says, 'We're getting ready to go to England and places over there. And there's one thing I'd like to discuss. It's the clothes.' I said, 'Well, I don't want to go then.' That's when I left the Charley Pride show." And that was all he had to say about it. According to Larry Munson, Gary hadn't wanted to return to the United Kingdom anyway, telling him, "You know what kind of shit they got on TV over there? Shit like 'How to change a tire.'"

One of the few times Stewart publicly addressed playing for Pride was to a Minneapolis reporter in 1978, who asked why he was behind the piano all night when he played there three years before. "I wanted to get up and boogie...I had to play quiet. Charley's audience is, how should I say, not as wild as the people who go in for divorce songs, cheating songs and honky-tonk songs that my music is all about."

* * *

On September 2, 1976, Stewart went into the studio and cut three absolute knockouts. "Woman in Demand," cowritten by the great A.E. "Doodle" Owens, was a tough honky-tonk ballad about go-go-dancer paranoia ("When they see too much of her/Lord, I see too much of them"); "She's Got Lovin' on Her Mind" aka "Play It, Boys," about a man seducing a woman through his jukebox selections, and a lusty, hard-charging, absolutely demonic version of the Willie Dixon blues standard "I'm Ready," with Gary pounding out a piano solo.

Stewart kills all three. None would see release (in fact, Dea forgot cutting them until I unearthed these three ten years later).

Instead of releasing anything from that session, Dea reached back to something they'd started the year before. A pair of East Coast sisters were mainly responsible for Gary's next single. Carol and Mary Beth Anderson had met Gary early on when he sat in for a set at O'Lunney's in New York City. They went on to form Ladysmith, an all-girl band that backed glorious crackpot outlaw David Allan Coe until "it just got too crazy," as Carol put it. Coe, who had several wives at the time, started introducing Ladysmith as his wives as well. "It got so weird. We just...couldn't." The sisters moved to Nashville and signed as songwriters to Chappell Music. After bumping into Gary at a local eatery, they decided to write a number for him, aided by Rory Bourke, most famous for cowriting "The Most Beautiful Girl," a smash hit for Charlie Rich. Carol had a song she'd written a few years before entitled "Some Call It Lonely, but I Call It a Night." She and Mary Beth and Rory worked on it, then called Gary, who was over at RCA. "Hey, we got a new song. You want to hear it?" Stewart told them to head on over.

They pitched it to Gary right in the studio. "I played it on piano, he started singin' it," recalled Carol. Gary seized on the chorus. "And then he starts playing it. And he changes the title to 'Your Place or Mine.' He didn't even take any credit."[54] Stewart immediately declared ownership. He said, 'Boy, this is *my* song. Don't play it for *nobody* else.'"

Dea first cut the song on February 12, 1976, with a stellar bunch of session players including David Briggs on piano, Reggie Young on guitar, and Weldon Myrick. It remained in the can until August 31st, when it was recut with a new crew that included Dale Sellers on guitar, Pete Drake on steel and—at least initially—Bobby Wood on the eighty-eights. "I play the piano on the one that we put out,"

54 The Anderson sisters' father was a minister and was mortified when he heard the song announced on the radio back in New York. "Girls, couldn't you have picked a better title for that?"

said Stewart. "We cut it, it was really good, but it was kinda fast and real polished...we wanted a rougher style. I'm not that polished on my piano, and it made it cruder—like a sexy movie, y'know. More honky-tonk." Stewart's funky barrelhouse was just the ticket, and Sellers mirrored the grit with some vicious licks. Gary's outrageous vocal—one of his absolute best—stretches, elongates, and practically bounces off walls like Plastic Man in a Jack Cole panel. "Your Place or Mine" hit number fifteen on the country charts, his last single in the Top Twenty. It would become something of an anthem in Texas bars. Kim Willingham, a friend of Gary's in later years: "That was the last song of the night at all the bars. When you heard 'Your Place or Mine,' you knew that the lights would start coming on. It's time to clear out and go home."

* * *

With the Pride obligation gone, Gary started doing things his way. From 1977 to 1981, he'd fly high. Too high. During this period he'd tour with two great (and completely different) bands, the music rawer and wilder than on his records. For the most part he'd avoid the fancier stops, rarely venturing north of Oklahoma or west of New Mexico, outside of a few trips to Los Angeles. "The prestigious big-city gigs Stewart could've cared less about," said his sound engineer Steve Cureton. "But get him into some backwoods shithole and he'd really fly. Stewart was just one of those downward-mobility guys."

Gary would record more incredible music, some of it for RCA, much of it still unheard and unknown. But for the first time, there would be periods in the studio where he was less than great. Gary's weirdness oozed out and he became erratic, unreliable. A trainload of drugs intensified everything. 'Til the end of his life, he'd remain unrepentant about his excesses. "I had *earned* that money, goin' down all them roads, playin' all those honky-tonks, and I wanted to spend it—have a *good* time," he told me defiantly. "The plane could crash tomorrow."

9

CHECK MY STRIDE

It's not an easy life at all. There's fame in it, of a sort, and money, and that keeps a lot of them going. But there's some deeper feeling too that keeps them out on the road, with a night here and a night there and a long drive in between, singing their songs, some trash, some gold, about hearts and wrecks and teardrops.

– Charles Portis, *That New Sound from Nashville*

Now that Stewart was on the loose with Rockfish, it was honky-tonkin' straight, no chaser. No more family shows, no band outfits. "Boogie" Bob recalls the only big RCA gig played with Rockfish—a show at the Mobile Civic Center in Alabama opening for Asleep at the Wheel and Willie Nelson. "We did a great show, Gary killed," said Melton. "We could have definitely done more gigs like that, and RCA wanted us to, but Gary did not like doing those big arenas. He was not thrilled to be doing it. Before, during, and after." Thus another door closed, not that

Stewart batted an eye. "Gary didn't give a shit," said Robert "Cotton" Payne, a drummer who'd soon be in his band. He'd say, 'Robert, I just want to play music, make my money, and go home. Is that so much?'"

He lived for a shabby, two-bit joint with a hot crowd packing the dance floor. The stages at these honky-tonks were often low and accessible, so Stewart could reach out and touch the audience if he so desired. "Gary wanted to honky-tonk, and he wanted the people to be right there with him," said Darrell Dawson. And Stewart wanted those bodies moving. "I love for people to dance at my shows," he told Leon Black. "It shows me that you're digging it if you're out scootin' around the floor."

* * *

For a brief moment Gary and Rockfish traveled by Winnebago. Grandal was hired to drive the rig, which got the brothers' rivalry roiling again. "He'd sit in the back of that Winnebago, we'd hit a bump, you'd bounce, and Gary would holler out, 'Watch the bumps!!!' He'd bitch and moan. And tell me how to drive!" Grandal vamoosed. "I got this ol' gal to run me to the airport while everybody was asleep."

Once the band was crossing the Continental Divide in Utah, with Gary's brother Gerald, then-drummer in the band, along for the ride, when Gary unwisely took the wheel. "Gerald was screaming, 'Quit drivin' like a maniac, Gary. We're about to fall out of bed,'" recalled Rockfish sound engineer Ron "Radar" Griffith. "Suddenly it smoothed out, prompting Gerald to say, 'That's more like it.' Then Chris Casses, guitar player in the band, stuck his head out the window of the tilting vehicle and said, 'No, fuckers—we're in MIDAIR!'" Somehow they lived.

* * *

This band was on the prowl, not that they had to look far. Women were everywhere—hiding in the bushes, throwing up on the bus during encounters best left to the imagination. Gary "liked

fancy blondes, and he had a lot of them," said Melton. "He was not that particular...he loved 'em all. Gary got into them like he got into music." The claims in "Bedtime Stories" were no idle boasts. "Gary was hung like a damn Texas mule," said "Boogie" Bob. "He was proud of that."

Even in the early days Stewart was known to instigate sexual shenanigans. Once on the way home from the Fort Pierce Hotel, Gary, "Boogie" Bob, and a couple of others drove past a waitress none of them knew. Gary got her in the car, and they headed over to Boogie's apartment. "Let's everybody get naked and play a game!" said Gary. Soon various couplings were in progress and "Gary was talking to everybody, pokin' 'em in the butt, actin' like a little leprechaun. Things like that happened a lot with Gary."

Unfortunately Stewart had a habit of cultivating actual relationships with some of his flings, and told at least one paramour he was going to buy her a house. Lou would've "liked to kill him many times over it," said Melton. "At one time Gary and Lou decided they were going to have an open marriage, because she couldn't stop him from philandering. It got to where Gary was even having girlfriends in Fort Pierce. That was something he hadn't really done before, and when he did, Lou decided she was going to philander about, too. One of the people she ended up doing the hanky-panky with was our old bandmate Fly Hornsby aka Rockin' Ricky. Gary never forgave Fly for that...I knew that an open marriage would never work with Gary. It just wasn't in him." Shannon Ashburn recalled Fly showing up at the house to "serenade" her mother. "Dad was home and he had to go out there and run him off. I mean, it didn't get violent...a lot of people thought Mom was a hot item, y' know?"

* * *

Cheating was far from the only subject Gary and Lou fought over. Gary possessed his mother's ferocious, sometimes irrational temper and anything could set him off. Relatives talk about him flipping out over having his photo taken—and flipping over Christmas trees. "Gary had a temper, oh hell, yes," said sister Gail. "He could smash shit, throw shit...one year he threw the Christmas tree out after Mother had it all decorated." One time Lou decided to cut back the vines that covered their house while Gary was on the road. "Mom just trimmed a little back—and it killed the plant." As the vines fell away from the house, Mary Lou knew what was coming and was "terrified," said Shannon. When Gary got home and saw his vine-free, naked-looking hacienda, "there was hell to pay. Oh, we had to leave. We got kicked out!" Then there was the white Trans Am with the giant eagle decal on the hood.

"My mom always wanted a brand-new car," said Shannon. "And Dad went out on the road. This was right at the peak of his career, he was doing really good. So she went and got her a white Trans Am with a blue bird on it. She was tickled to death. And she couldn't wait for Dad to see the car. He came home and made her take it back. Dad would never let her have nothing new, like a brand-new car. We'd always buy used cars.

"The whole car thing devastated my mom. That's one of the times we had to pack up and leave...Mom would pack up and leave, Dad would find us, call and beg her to come back. Of course, we came back." Lou and the kids would stay with her mother or her sister Eileen in California until things cooled down. "It happened a thousand times. Mom would come barreling down the hallway and say, 'Pack your shit.' It got to the point that I marched into their bedroom and told them, 'Y'all are gonna pack and unpack my shit. Y'all are CRAZY.'"

Things got so sideways in 1977 that divorce proceedings were initiated. On May 20th, Stewart was ordered by the court to stay away from his wife and pay her $150 a week in alimony. Lou was granted temporary custody of their children and possession of their home. Only a page of the court record survives and there is no indication of when it was dismissed. Neither Gary nor Lou ever mentioned this. However contentious things got, they managed to stay together, even if the relationship hung by a thread at times. "I love my family *as much* as my music," Gary told me more than once.

* * *

Your Place or Mine, the third RCA album, came out in spring of 1977 (some affix the date as March 21). Recorded over a year beginning in February 1976, this is the most fully realized Gary Stewart album. In addition to Nashville sessions, Dea cut in Memphis with a one-off band that included Leo LeBlanc on steel. Roy also sweetened a few cuts in California by overdubbing Nicolette Larson (who hadn't yet hit with "Lotta Love") and Emmylou Harris. Maybe the only weak cut is the album closer "Dancing Eyes," a masochistic, Stewart-penned tale of a pathetic wretch sentenced to watching his paramour dance with other suitors, a situation Gary certainly recognized: "She's all over him / With her dancin' eyes," Stewart wails. "Looks like I'm along just for the ride."

Even the subtler cuts hold your interest. "Leah" is a raucous bluegrass number written by Jack Skinner that Gary learned from Rockfish Railroad, which became a live favorite. "The Blue Ribbon Blues" is an amusing drinking song Gary had been doing since 1975, cowritten by Wayland Holyfield (author of the hit Stewart missed, "Red Necks, White Socks and Blue Ribbon Beer"), but it's more effective in a funkier unreleased version. "Drinking Again" is an obscure, old-school 1966 number dating back to Stewart's days at Cedarwood Publishing. The mere mention of the recording made Gary cringe as he felt his singing was off-key. (He actually insisted on recutting the vocal after the album came out, but it remains unreleased. I've never heard it.)

The *Your Place or Mine* album would be the only time Stewart bumped up against the Texas singer-songwriter contingent, a rarified, folkier breed represented here by Guy Clark and a newcomer named Rodney Crowell, who had three numbers on the album. Although Crowell's "I Ain't Living Long Like This" had been done by Emmylou

Harris, Waylon Jennings (who had a number-one country hit with it), and its author, none come within a country mile of Stewart. He's the only one who sounds like an actual criminal—unrepentant, on the lam and shouting, "Come and get me coppers!" Plus it features the knockout guitar of singer-songwriter Mac Gayden, famous for his wah-wah slide on J.J. Cale's "Crazy Mama," whose rambunctious, vibrating accompaniment on "Ain't Living Long" sounds like the squall of a squad car in hot pursuit. It's hard to pin down what's more exciting—Gary's vocal, Gayden's guitar, or the dynamic way they drive each other. Stewart also nails the two other Crowell songs, "I Had to Get Drunk Last Night" and "Rachel," a ballad that only grew more intimate when Stewart performed it live.[55]

"Broken Hearted People (Take Me to a Barroom)" once again exhibits how adept Stewart was at covering a song and making it his own. Written by Guy Clark, the song boils the honky-tonk ethos down to a few very painful lines: "Take me to a barroom, driver, set me on a stool/If I can't be her man, I'm damned if I'll be her fool." There are those who argue Clark's original is the better cut, many of them displeased with Stewart's uptempo, vibrato-laden delivery. Not being an aficionado of Clark's, I asked musician John Kopf what he thought. "I am a big Guy Clark fan—I have all his stuff, seen him many times and also have heard many covers of his songs. This is the only time a cover of his work was better than the original—and I'm including some heavy hitters, like Willie, Cash, and David Allan Coe. Guy came up with the bones of the song, Gary put flesh on it." Clark's version is slow, mournful, and solitary. Gary picks up the pace and injects a jaunty melody, and while it's no less sad, it's definitely more carnal. Guy's is written after the bar has closed; Gary's is taking place en route. Or as Kopf puts it, "Guy's version says 'I'm heartbroken, I'm drunk.' Gary's is, 'I'm heartbroken, I'm drunk, and I'm gonna go get some pussy.'" And Stewart personalizes one line: "I'm looking

55 Crowell nicknamed Gary "Hank" due to his "alcohol-fueled, teetering on the edge, driving too fast, living too hard honky-tonk thing." Once again, wrong vice for Stewart.

to get silly" becomes "I'm looking to get sloppy drunk," with Gary dragging down on the last two words, pulling on them like they're some kind of poison taffy.

Cut on the same day as "Easy People and "Trudy" back in November 1975, Stewart's interpretation of Willie Nelson's "Pretend I Never Happened" is utterly magnificent. Waylon had been first to cut the song in 1972, and his loping, melancholy version went to number six on the country charts, while Willie himself took a sleepy turn at it in 1974. Neither prepare you for what Gary does with the song. With his voice soaring high over a bluegrass backdrop, Gary delivers the lyric almost defiantly, as if it's the last declaration of a dying man. It is a stunning, spine-tingling performance. "That's when you could tell he was from Kentucky," noted Steve Hinson. "He had that mountain soul." And the mountain voice. "He could sing higher than anyone I ever knew," wrote columnist and songwriter Hank Beach, who recorded with and later wrote for Stewart. "Gary could sing high tenor to Bill Monroe and you would never see a vein in his neck stick out or his face turn red."

And then there is "Ten Years of This," cut the same day as "Your Place or Mine" and the second single off the album, released in April 1977. "You've got to spill your guts onstage," said the great bluegrass singer Vern Williams. "Then you've got to walk around in them." Gary did just that recording "Ten Years of This." Stewart cowrote this unbelievably intense examination of marital despair with Wayne Carson, exchanging lyrics in the mail. There are so many thrills to this song, this performance, this lyric, *where* do I BEGIN? How about the killer opening? The song deceives you with its peppy uptempo intro before Stewart swoops in, already sounding on the verge of a breakdown: "You'd never know by looking/We were ever more than strangers/But we're celebrating ten years/Of wedded bliss," he sings, hissing out the last two words. Already you know this sad couple, coming and going in the night, not uttering a word to each other. "She made the rounds as usual/While I sit here stoned as usual." So conversational, so real, so much pain. Who else but

Stewart would dare rhyme "as usual" with..."as usual"? Then comes some classic tortured country syntax: "If someone else would tell me/What I already know in my mind/I'm afraid I'd start talking/With my fists." His vocal snakes around the tricky wordplay, making it seem not lugubrious but necessary. There in the middle of it all comes a line of aching tenderness: "Maybe you felt cheated/Because you married so young." Such empathy might be expected from, say, Loretta Lynn, but a honky-tonk *man*? Breathtaking. And it plunges right back to increasing desperation: "What in hell kept us together/For ten years of this?" Note the "us," not "me." It's not accusatory, it's "How did we end up here?" Gary and Lou had been married well past a decade and this "wedded bliss" had already circled the drain at least once. A sense of doom permeates the track, its jumpy tempo only notching up the tension. You actually feel Stewart might explode before the song is over. But it wouldn't be a woman on his mind when he sang the song out on the road. He'd confide to his friend Jo Ann Gregory that when he performed it live, "he always thought about his relationship with RCA."

"Ten Years of This" is not feel-good loose like many other Stewart tracks. It's tightly wound, tense as the vocal, and doesn't relent, right up 'til its bug-against-the-windshield climax. One can't discuss the recording without mentioning a couple of the pickers present. Pete Drake's steel guitar dips and dives lick for lick with Gary's vocal, gilding the lily perfectly. Then there's that electric guitar: "Dale Sellers, man," said Steve Hinson. "That's a tour de force for him." The guitar part that follows Stewart singing "a million nights alone" became known as "the Dale Sellers lick" and had pickers in a frenzy trying to figure it out. Hinson remembers hearing "Ten Years of This" after playing a show with Cliff Parker, guitarist on Johnny Paycheck's "Take This Job and Shove It." "It was late at night, the gig's over, we're standing on the stage, they're closin' up, wiping off the tables, and we're handin' the guitar back and forth goin', '*No*, I think it's more like *this*.' That guitar part is otherworldly." According to Sellers, it was done in one take utilizing a Telecaster with "two strings bent at once against a stationary string on the fret. It was a push 'n' pull–type lick." Both guitars—electric and steel—complement each other beautifully, as was the style for Drake and Sellers on Stewart's work. "You might say I'm a frustrated steel player," said Dale. "I don't know shit about 'em, but I always like the licks and sound they got."

Hinson and Parker were not the only musicians awestruck by "Ten Years of This." Stewart later met Bob Dylan for the first and only time on June 22, 1986, in Dallas, while Dylan was touring with Tom Petty. Announcing Gary's presence in the first row from the stage, Bob declared the number "really one of my favorite records" before plunging into "I and I." Afterward, according to a dumbfounded Stewart, Dylan told him he played "Ten Years of This" over and over, so stunned was he by the recording. The record would hit number sixteen on the country charts, and the *Your Place or Mine* album reached number seventeen.

The songs on *Your Place or Mine* hung together in a way that was unusual for an RCA country record at the time. It came at you like a beer-stained telegraph from a honky-tonk foxhole. And the cover was just fabulous—an action shot of Gary in a long leather coat, his brown, wood-finish 195 Les Paul Junior TV Model slung across his chest as he's caught mid-chord in guitar-face ecstasy, standing against a black background with faux stars, that ridiculously ornate "Gary Stewart" logo above it all. He even gets to wear his damn hat on the cover! The vibe was as seventies as "Baby I'm-A Want You" or "Muskrat Love." Glorious. Stewart and Dea had some triumphs left, but as far as albums go, *Your Place or Mine* is the pinnacle. This an album that sounds best blasting from an old jalopy as you tear down some dark country road feeling no pain, with a lusty companion beside you. Come and get me, coppers!

* * *

Rockfish Railroad didn't last. One member didn't want to tour, the band was expensive to maintain, and it just kind of dissolved, although they'd come back later in a different incarnation. Just like that, a new band came along, this one in Texas. The Drugstore Cowboys found Gary, not the other way round. Big fans, they had been on the bill with him when he was part of the Charley Pride show at the Longhorn Ballroom in Dallas in 1975; the Cowboys were backing African American country singer Stoney Edwards, opening for Pride. Willie Nelson was there and he, Edwards, and the band jammed on an old fifties tune. Stewart made a big impression on the Cowboys. "He stopped everything in the middle of the show, ordered four cases of beer up to the stage, and sponsored his own little beer drinking contest," said Dub Robinson, guitarist and leader of the band. "We thought, 'This guy's out of his mind.'"

At the very tail end of 1976, Gary had a gig at Kicker Palace in Poteet, Texas. He'd been playing a few shows borrowing Preston Buchanan and Rudy Gray, the Pridesmen rhythm section, but they had to depart suddenly for a show with Charley, so Stewart was going to cancel the show. "Gary did not want to play with a pickup band," said Randy Toman, bass player with the Cowboys, who'd heard the news and told club owner Jim Schumacher that they could do the gig—unlike any random pickup band, they already knew Stewart's songs. Schumacher begged Stewart to use them, fibbing that it was an eight-piece band. Gary was skeptical, but reluctantly agreed to a rehearsal. "He walked in in that long mink coat of his with guitar and amplifier, just ready to go," said Toman. "And he goes, 'Well, where's the rest of the guys?'" When Randy informed him there were just three of them—Dub Robinson on guitar, Randy on bass, and Robert "Cotton" Payne on drums—Gary got angry. "He let out a couple of f-bombs, directed at the club owner," and walked off.

The band coaxed him into trying a few numbers, and after "In Some Room Above the Street" and "If You've Got the Money" with them, he relented. The Poteet gig was a success—so much so that Gary pulled a few hundred out of his own pay to tip the band. Younger than Gary by over a half dozen years, the Cowboys had energy to burn, knew all his repertoire, and were already in Texas, Stewart's primary gigging area, so he wouldn't have to pay travel expenses. A few weeks later he rang Robinson to ask if they wanted to be his road band. "He proceeds to tell me that there ain't gonna be no bus, no weekly or monthly salary, you might have to run sound sometimes and pretty much you get there on your own," Robinson wrote in an online post. "He wasn't lyin'." Initially Gary paid the band $750 a gig, which was "phenomenal, compared to what a country band that was backing a star was getting at the time," said Toman. "My friends that played with guys like Johnny Bush, who was on RCA Records around then, they got 100 bucks." Stewart was generous, even springing for dinner for everybody out on the road. "Whatever we needed," said Toman.

The Drugstore Cowboys played their first road gig with Gary at a joint called Western Swing in Houston. They'd tour with Gary until January 1981,[56] when Randy formed the Toman Brothers, a new three-piece with brother Russ that remained Gary's primary touring band until around 2000, although early on he'd take a couple of brief but notable detours with post-Rockfish Florida-based lineups. ("It was like a marriage," said Toman. "Sometimes you need to get away from each other.") Not that the Gary Stewart gig came with any security. "You couldn't predict his next move," said Toman. "I always thought that tomorrow might be our last gig—or we might play together for the next ten years. You never knew with Gary."

The Drugstore Cowboys had a radically different sound from the bluegrass-based Rockfish Railroad. "We were an oddity as far as country bands were concerned, because we didn't have the fiddle and the steel," said Toman. Robinson put it this way: "We were kind of a power trio rock-oriented band." I saw this band live, and they were much closer to a honky-tonk AC/DC than any country outfit. At times they'd briefly augment the band with both steel and piano, but Toman laughed off the additions as favors for Stewart's out-of-work pals. "All Gary would end up doing was messing up our rock

56 For a brief period Stewart played with a Randy-less Drugstore Cowboys, which Dub had augmented with more players, but he found himself missing the simplicity of the three-piece and switched to the Toman Brothers.

and roll with a fiddle," Toman maintained. "We were doing ZZ Top, which didn't need no fiddle." It just goes to show: big-band bluegrass or no-frills country rock, Stewart was nimble enough to throw down no matter what the accompaniment. Regrettably no tapes exist of Stewart with Rockfish Railroad, but there are a few live recordings with the Drugstore Cowboys during Gary's prime, and they are raucous, ragged affairs.

* * *

Thus the Drugstore Cowboys were thrown into the exciting, unpredictable world of Gary Stewart. Toman recounts a shambolic New Year's Eve gig in Lafayette, Louisiana, where Stewart sat down at the piano to do a song but couldn't remember the words. Then he asked if anybody in the crowd had any honey for his sore throat. "I'm thinking to myself, 'Oh, yeah, right, somebody in the crowd's got honey,'" recalled Randy. "Here comes this woman, she's, like, a granny. And she's got one of those little packets with honey in it. She was just proud to be bringing Gary some honey. And he goes, 'Well, can you *heat it up*?'"

Eddy Raven and Charly McClain were also on the bill and Gary invited them back onstage to ring in the New Year. "First thing Gary did was give a Happy New Year hug to Eddy Raven. I was next, and he gave me a kiss on the mouth—'Happy New Year, Randy!' And then he just shook Charly McClain's hand! She just looked at me. I don't know if Charly was happy or unhappy."

Some of the craziest Stewart gigs happened on Native American reservations. Along with his rotation of honky-tonks, Stewart would play Navajo, Hopi, and Apache settlements regularly ("Apaches, they would've had us out every weekend," said Toman), traveling with the band to desolate outposts like Window Rock, Kayenta, and Tuba City, Arizona. For these Southerners it was a trip to the moon. After seemingly endless drives, the venues were often nondescript gymnasiums, the hotels were funky, the food bad, and the women not to their liking.

Yet the gigs paid extremely well and the Native Americans loved Gary with a mad passion that scared him and the band both. They knew all his songs and demanded obscure album cuts like "Dancing Eyes" or, much later, "Rainin', Rainin', Rainin'." "He was like Elvis Presley to them," said Toman. "They were maniacs for Gary."

Bob Melton, who also played reservation gigs, agreed. "They would just go bananas, come up on the stage to try to grab him and hug him. Man, they'd just go nuts." Playing the Window Rock reservation was epic. "When we played there, it was an event," said Toman. "We'd do radio ads and interviews." Toman recalled Stewart having a little fun with a Navajo deejay who asked what his next album would be titled. "My next release is called *Betsy the Heifer*," Gary told him straight-faced. "The deejay ran with it—'Gary, we can't wait for our copy of *Betsy the Heifer*, we'll be playin' it,'" said Toman. The police had to escort the band back to their hotel. "All the Navajos came to the station when they found out Gary was there," said Russ Toman. "It was chaos."

Leonard Yazzie, a member of the Thunders, an indigenous band that opened for Stewart and even jammed with him on one occasion, maintained that Gary's music was a staple of reservation radio and that many Native American bands knew his songs—the Thunders did about ten of them live. Yazzie said Stewart invited the band to jam in Florida, but they never made it down there. He also revealed that one night in Window Rock, Gary let him "in on a secret—'This is how I become Gary Stewart.' He spoke normal when I talked with him before he went onstage. Then he says, 'I take *this* pill, and *that* pill, and then I sound like this'—and he sang out. His voice was different!"

Stewart noted that these particular audiences "were hard to play for, because they don't express themselves—they're subdued, laid-back. This deejay who owned his own radio station out there told me, 'Now, they are going to be kinda quiet, so don't think nothin' of it.'" And that's how the evening usually started. "Sometimes it was real spooky—they'd sit there real quiet, and watch every move he made," said Toman. Gary took it as a challenge. "If I was having a good night, I'd get 'em going. They turned into *something else* when I played, because I was a-hoppin' and a-jumpin' and got 'em going—y'know, my energy—YAAAAAAH! I got 'em to roarin'." Alcohol was definitely a factor at some of these shows. By the end of the night there might be patrons "all over the floor, passed out," according to Melton. "They'd just drag 'em out by the ear." One night after a bottle whizzed past Gary's head onstage, he told the audience, "If you fuckers don't *settle down* we're gonna whip out the machine guns!"

One New Year's Eve in Tuba City things spiraled completely out of control. It was a dry reserve, but members of the audience had slipped out of the show to drink and this "created a riot," said Dub Robinson. "They broke a couple of the big glass windows in the front of the gym. In the meantime, the promoter's yellin' at us—'Stop! Don't play anymore!' The audience was drunk." There was a group of large, rather imposing women lining the stage "and they're all goin', 'Gary! Gary! Gary!' Their eyes were rollin' back in their head." Stewart was signing autographs at the edge of the stage and was pulled into the crowd. "Gary got too close to the front of the stage," said drummer Robert "Cotton" Payne. "They got him by his legs, trying to pull him off."

Stewart panicked. "I had to holler at the guys in the band, 'Man, grab ahold of my feet!'" The band tugged on Gary in one direction, members of the audience in another. "Me and Randy have Gary's legs, the girls have got him by his arms and we're stretching this guy out," said Robinson. "And the girls won the tug-of-war. Gary was hollering. He was in this circle of people, goin' all over the gymnasium. You could see his little hat bobbin' up and down. As serious as it was, I was laughing." Stewart was unamused. "You talk about bein' scared...I had a girl jerk me by the hair on my head—just flat jerk me by the head—to the floor, and she was *strong*, son...I couldn't get up, y' know? I mean, 'Let me go!!!'" Payne "grabbed Gary underneath his arms and pulled him up," said Robinson. "And they grabbed his legs and pulled him back down again!" "Gary clamped down on me and said, 'Get me the hell out of here, *right now*!!!'" said Cotton.

After some back and forth, Payne "jerked him real hard and he come loose." Cotton "popped him out like a cork," said Dub. "We got him out, and he says, 'You fuckers were *laughin'*! You fuckers shoulda *done somethin'*!' Hell, we tried!"

In July 1977, Stewart and the Drugstore Cowboys were videotaped at an invitation-only gig at the Luckenbach Dance Hall in Texas for the *Lone Star Texas Music Special*, an hour-long show broadcast that September 12 (Joe Ely appeared as well). A downhome affair, it was the first time Stewart truly felt comfortable in front of a TV camera. Ten years later Gary was still talking about the bales of hay lined up in front of the stage. This was his kind of joint: a honky-tonk with a low stage, exposed beams, and ceiling fans, not to mention a raucous crowd ready to scoot across the floor. Gary comes charging onto the stage in hat and bright red Hawaiian shirt with two bottles of Lone Star beer in hand. The band plunges into "Honky-Tonkin'" and doesn't let up for over an hour. Randy joins in on harmony, his long hair bouncing as he steps up to the mic. Dub, all shadows under a black hat, fires off tough, metallic licks; Cotton pounds the skins with a locomotive beat. Three pieces, big sound, and plenty of room for Stewart to run amok. The band rips through "Draggin' Shackles," "Drinkin' Thing," "Leah," "Trudy," "Flat Natural Born Good-Timin' Man," "Ain't Living Long Like This," and "Quits" (Stewart also performed "Your Cheatin' Heart," which, although it didn't make the cut, had one reporter crying). Gary never stops moving. He snarls, laughs, and slurs his way through song after song, a man at the top of his game. Such innocence, so much life.

Gary had it all. New band, hit album, a beautiful family. It would all come screeching to a halt in the wee hours of the morning of August 29th, 1977. The sister Gary was closest to, Griselda Nelson Stewart, twenty-nine years old, killed herself in her Fort Pierce home. She was the first Stewart that I know of to take their own life. But far from the last.

10

GRISELDA

TRAMPAS STEWART: Griselda was different. She just glowed. She seemed above and beyond.

TOMMY SCHWARTZ: Griselda was a sweetheart. She was the prettiest one of the bunch, just sweet. I loved Griselda to death. She had that country accent...raised in Kentucky.

STAN SPENCE, family friend: Griselda was petite. She was one of the only Stewarts that had a job and made good for herself. Out in the normal world.

NICK STEWART: Griselda was a loan officer at Sun Bank. Living the dream.

TOMMY SCHWARTZ: She changed her name to Griselda Nelson Stewart. Because of Willie Nelson. She met Willie through Gary at some point.

GREG STEWART: Griselda, she was good to Gary. I mean, she helped him, y'know.

MARY LOU STEWART: Everybody loved Griselda. She was so very smart. She worked at the bank, she had a lot of property because she had invested her money. She had about three houses, a Corvette, probably about a fourth of a million dollars.

GINA STEWART: Honey child, at twenty-nine Griselda could have retired from Sun Bank. That's how smart she was.

JIMMY SMITH: I'll tell you, I'm not a thief...too much. But I was one time. Griselda was working at J.M. Fields, a department store. Griselda was, like, the head person in charge. They had a big window overlooking the whole store. And the *Eat a Peach* album just come out. And I wanted that motherfucker bad. So bad that I stuck it in my bag. Griselda was looking over the store and she seen me. She let me get away with it. Griselda was the most precious lady you ever met in your life.

MARY LOU STEWART: Me and Griselda were very, very, very close. She was married to this man and she loved him so much, he was the only boyfriend she'd ever even been with. I think they had been married maybe twelve years or sixteen years, can't remember which. He came home from work one day, real kind of cold, and says, "Uh, sit down, I wanna tell ya somethin'." She says, "What is it?" "I don't love you anymore, I want a divorce. I'm divorcin' you." She called me up, her voice upset, and said, "Is Gary home?" and I said, "No." She says, "Can I come over and talk to ya?" She came over and started cryin' and told me. Griselda never got over it.

GINA STEWART: That blew Griselda's mind to where she tried to commit suicide. She called Mommy to say goodbye. Mommy called Gary—"Go check on her." And we got her saved.

GAIL STEWART: I have to say this was a chemical imbalance. And I think it runs in our family. We've had some issues with mental illness.

GINA STEWART: The second time Griselda did it I went and stayed with her. I divorced my husband over it. He goes, "Either come home, or I want a divorce." Griselda was datin' a lawyer, so the next day I paid him $20 and [told my husband], "Baby, you *done*! See ya!" I lived with her for a while after that.

NICK STEWART: Griselda got to doin' things that she shouldn't. Runnin' with people she shouldn't.

GINA STEWART: Griselda never did drugs that I know of. I never saw her do 'em. Maybe she'd have a drink.

LAURIE RASTRELLI, family friend: My dad was supposed to marry Griselda. But she was in love with this guy, Doug Cargill. I guess he treated her bad.

GINA STEWART: Griselda bought a concrete pumping business for him.

TOMMY SCHWARTZ: I was with Griselda and Gina the day she died. There was a festival with bands and things, and we were hanging out down there. I know that Griselda didn't have it planned that afternoon...at all.

GINA STEWART: After the fish fry, Doug came. Griselda left with him. And I stayed with my boyfriend Walter Carlton.

Griselda had gone. She was living with Doug. He started beatin' her up, y'know, knocking her around. Out in the backyard. She called me to come home and she was crying. I got home, Doug done beat the shit out of her. What the fight was about I couldn't tell ya now to save my life.

MARY LOU STEWART: Gary and I went out to eat that night at Benihana—which we'll never go to again, because that's how Gary is. I had a weird feeling all that night. The moon was full. We went home. I saw Griselda at the bank that day and she said, "I really need to talk to you." I said, "Okay, call me later." We had our number changed that day and I hadn't given it to her. I forgot. My new number was written down on a paper next to the bed.

I couldn't sleep that night. It was like about 3:15, 3:30 a.m., and this station wagon pulled into the driveway. The moon was real bright and the car sat there a few seconds, went into reverse, and backed out. I thought, "Who in the hell do we know with a station wagon?" It was Griselda. In Walter Carlton's car...she did it about thirty minutes after that.

GRANDAL STEWART: Griselda called me, wanted me to come down. I think the ol' boy she was foolin' with got into it. Argument or somethin' or other. I was livin' up in Vero and I came down, stayed with her for about an hour or so. And she says, "Grandal you go on home, I'm all right now." So I went home. About the time I got home the phone rang. And somebody said that Griselda had hurt herself.

GINA STEWART: Walter [Carlton] had an old yellow Chevrolet station wagon, and he always had a gun he kept in the car. Locked up in the glove box. A .357 Magnum.

LAURIE RASTRELLI: Griselda supposedly took Walter Carlton's gun out of his glove compartment and took it in the bedroom. They thought a door slammed, because they heard a gun go off. I remember them telling me about it. They thought a door slammed, but the gun had been fired.

TOMMY SCHWARTZ: We always speculated that she was going to kill Doug, but he didn't come home. When Gina got up to go to the bathroom in the middle of the night, Griselda called out and said, "Doug, is that you?" Just after Gina answered no...she heard the gunshot.

I'm convinced Griselda was waiting there to shoot him. She was probably going to shoot him and then herself. I don't know. We will never know. I do know Walter felt really bad that she did it with his gun.

GINA STEWART: We was hung up on Kool-Aid fruit punch at the time, me and Griselda. And I got up to get me a drink. I went to check on her. I opened the door, she fell in my arms. Blew her brains out, fell in my arms.

Our utility door was so loud you could hear it. How she got out that back door without me hearin' it... Still got that outfit that she had on that night.

STAN SPENCE: Griselda shot herself in the head. She died first, then Elvis died.

TOMMY SCHWARTZ: I was told Gina just held Griselda until she was taken to the hospital.

I helped clean up the apartment where Griselda shot herself. Gregory Stewart and I walked around the backyard and picked up the jewelry that was knocked off her body while Doug was slapping her around the yard a few hours before. We walked into the bedroom to see the three- to four-foot diameter bloodstain on the floor. I never will forget that. Mike Jenkins had a rug cleaning business he ran on his days off at the fire department. Mike got it all out somehow.

MARY LOU STEWART: We went to the hospital, the emergency room, and Gina come to me and she said, "Lou, Gris is DEAD." We just all cried. Took us all out. I grabbed Gina and was holdin' her. I said, "Okay, Mommy will be here in a few minutes. Everybody get their head on and get together for Mommy, 'cause, oh, Mommy is just gonna die." Georgia was real close to Griselda.

GRANDAL STEWART: Mommy never went to the grocery store after that. Daddy had to go get bread and what have you. She'd tell Daddy what she needed, but she wouldn't go into the grocery store for some reason. I don't know why. I reckon it took something out of her.

CANDY STEWART, Grandal's wife: Grandal was devastated. Only like twenty months between their ages, and Griselda was his baby. After Griselda died, we never had another Stewart family Christmas.

GINA STEWART: Mommy never, ever got over Griselda. I mean never. I found a note in Mamaw's writin': "I can see Griselda in her little Christmas dress. I can't wait until I see her again."

MARY LOU STEWART: We left the hospital that morning. We had stayed there up until daybreak. When we got home, Gary took the shirt he had on off and put it in the garbage. And when we had to go to the funeral, he came home, and that shirt he had on, he took off and put in the garbage. He said, "Lou, I know you got shirts like those." He said, "Please. Don't ever wear 'em." I went and got mine and put 'em in the garbage, 'cause that's how Gary is. He just now can talk about her in the last year.

LAURIE RASTRELLI: That funeral, I'll never ever forget it as long as I live. Georgia had Griselda all patched up. And they had open casket. So then, at the funeral, Georgia is trying to pull her out of the casket, screamin', "My baby, my baby." My dad had fallen to his knees, because he and Griselda were supposed to get married. Me and my sister had to hold him.

GINA STEWART: Griselda, I rolled her hair in the casket. She was already dressed.

TOMMY SCHWARTZ: That was a sad, sad funeral. I remember watching Gary walk in with this bright red shirt on. Jeans and his shirt pulled out. I remember Gary walking up to the casket.

SHANNON ASHBURN: I know that Griselda's boyfriend came up missing. The one she committed suicide over. He disappeared shortly after. Disappeared. They said Mamaw had something to do with it. That's like a family secret.

JIMMY SMITH: Mommy. She paid somebody. That's the truth.[57]

ANONYMOUS STEWART FRIEND: [Doug Cargill] was a total piece of shit. Georgia got her money's worth.

MARY LOU STEWART: After Griselda died, Gary had to have a night-light. Finally I asked, "Is it because of Griselda?" and he said, "Yeah." Gary's changed a lot. Back then he was kind of cocky. He couldn't understand why Griselda couldn't get her shit together. Now he can. 'Cause he's paid the dues now.

Griselda was like Gary. Too tender for this world.

---

57 There are those who suggest Walter Carlton was involved in the alleged dispatch of Doug Cargill. "I couldn't say one way or the other about that," said his daughter Kim. "I wouldn't put it past him. If Georgia Stewart told him to do somethin', he probably did it. She was a mother figure to him."

11

ONLY GOIN' THROUGH ONCE

Life ain't worth living if it don't get out of hand sometime.

– Gary Stewart

By the late seventies, a fine, glittering snow was falling on Fort Pierce. You couldn't see it, but it was everywhere. It wasn't just weed being smuggled into the country via the port now, it was cocaine. Stewart friend David Thomas was active in the drug trade. "I used to go down to Miami to get an ounce—I'd have to wait a week or two. We were bringing in lots of pot." When he asked one of the pilots smuggling grass to get some coke, "He said, 'No, they take that serious.'"

Somewhere along the line that changed. "It hit about '78, '79. It started coming easy...pilots knew they could make a lot of money," said Thomas. "Shit, sometimes three planes would come in one night out in Lakeport, where I lived, out there in the middle of nowhere. We almost had to put up a tower out there." Cocaine "was everywhere," said Trampas Stewart. "I had lines rolled out on the windowsill to do on my sixteenth birthday." Gary would tell me a days-long coke-abuse run earned its own nickname in town—"the Fort Pierce jag."

"It was crazy, man," said Larry "Mouse" Munson. "Hell, if you wanted to buy somethin' and one person didn't have it, you could damn near get out the phone book and get it." Easy money, at least in the beginning. "Nobody had to go to work," said Trampas. "That's how people made a living back then." Some Stewarts sold it, some say one or two even died from it. Two of Gary's sisters were romantically involved with José Pena, a major dealer in town. As Munson put it, "First his girlfriend was Gina. And then he traded in for the younger model." Gina only dated Pena; Gail married him and they had three kids. It's said that José paid for both Gary and Gregg Allman to go to rehab. "He was a great man," said Gail.[58]

Pena "was a pretty good ol' Mexican," according to Grandal. "He was makin' big, big money. He was in with them down in Costa Rica or wherever... I've seen half of a damn garbage can full of raw cocaine. If he thought you wanted somethin' or other, ol' Joe would get it for you. He didn't have no way to hide that money, so he had to give it away." Pena bought Georgia Stewart a white Cadillac, which some say was the vehicle she used to transport the occasional shipment to Kentucky and the Midwest. Cocaine would alter relationships within the Stewart clan. "That really put a damper on practically the whole fucking family," said Trampas. "We'd hear the drunken fights in the middle of the night...brothers didn't get along as much...I know for a fact cocaine definitely destroyed all the charisma, all the positiveness that could have happened."

Gary, who never got involved in the business end, certainly did indulge, although it was far from his favorite drug—"I only did it two times in the past year," he'd boast to me in 1986. "Two times!" (Gary "hated Mary Lou doin' cocaine," according to Jimmy Smith. *"Hated."*)

---

58 I have heard tales of José and Gail pulling away in a car with Gina atop the vehicle with a switchblade trying to get at her sister for stealing Pena away, but Gina doesn't recall the incident—although she did admit to "blowing the windshield out with a double-barrel shotgun" after José and Gail had exited the vehicle, a brand-new Silverado he'd bought that day. Both sisters laugh off the conflict now.

José Pena, Georgia, and Gary. (Gina Stewart collection)

Stewart's passion was pills, particularly at that time quaaludes, which he bought in thousand-lot quart jars.[59] Gary and Mary Lou were volume buyers. "I would go on road trips with her to pick up half-gallon-sized plastic bottles of Percocet and Somas," said Royce Ashburn, who'd later marry Shannon. "They wouldn't buy like five, they'd buy five thousand. Blow-your-mind type of shit. I'm a young kid, and I'm like, 'Holy shit, five thousand Soma!'"

Stewart loved the garbage-head high the 'ludes produced, happily turning into a slobbering idiot after downing a fistful. "Boogie" Bob recalled a night Gary went to see his old partner Bill Eldridge play. "Gary got up onstage. He'd dropped a Mexican quaalude, and by the time he got to playing, that thing had hit him. Gary tried to do 'Statesboro Blues'—oh my God, it was the most pathetic thing you've ever heard or seen. He couldn't hardly stand up or stay in front of the microphone. And slow—'Wake...up...momma...turn...your... lamp...down...........low.' It was more like the 'Statesboro Waltz.' We ended up carrying him out of there like a sack o' taters."

59 Quaaludes were also all over Fort Pierce at the time. Tommy Schwartz recalled getting a call from Pena. "He said, 'Tommy, come over, I need you to take somethin' from me.' And he had 250,000 quaaludes in an old beat-up shed behind his house. I said, 'Well, I'll take a couple of bags, but what the fuck am I gonna do with 250,000 quaaludes, Joe?'"

Stewart got so far gone on the pills, he'd hide away in the bedroom for weeks, "playing funeral music, laying flat out on the bed as if he was he was in a coffin, waiting to die," according to Schwartz. The Fort Pierce solution? Try a different drug. José Pena sent a minion over with an eight ball of coke. "Next thing you know, Gary's up and dancin' around the room," said Tommy.

* * *

The vibe is palpable on the front of Gary's 1978 album, *Little Junior,* another memorable cover snapped by brother Grandal. It's a murky soft-focus shot of Stewart standing in his living room surrounded by hanging beads and houseplants, hands on hips. He's dressed in a robin's-egg blue Western jacket with white piping, silk cowboy shirt, hat, and jeans. It feels humid, way past midnight, and like Ruby Starr is about to slink out from the shadows to chop some lines, then hand Gary a mandolin. "'Little Junior' couldn't have been written without pot and quaaludes," Gary informed me of the title track.

"Tequila after midnight drives the loneliness away/Makes you think you feel good when you don't," he sings on another track.[60] Whether it was the recent death of Griselda or just a sign of the times, there were darker, more despairing colors on this album, alongside a lessening intensity to some of the performances. For Roy Dea the album signaled the beginning of the end.

Whereas the previous three albums had been a breeze, coaxing Stewart into the studio was suddenly a challenge. "He'd get high, rollin', and didn't want to cut," said Dea. And when Gary did want to record, he couldn't articulate what he wanted. "He got squirrely,

60 "Tequila After Midnight" was written by Dee Moeller, who'd recorded the definitive version three years earlier in Texas for Dallas independent label Autumn Records. Moeller found out Gary cut her song when she read a review of *Little Junior* in *People* magazine. Stewart shortened the song and took out some of the lyrics, which "didn't rhyme exactly like Nashville likes everything to rhyme—I've always felt that if the thought was there, and it made sense, it didn't matter. But it did to them, and they changed it. Other than that, I thought Gary did a great job on it."

weird, spastic...he was takin' charge too much. He'd say, 'Let's play *this*' and it would be some far-out thing. The pickers, they'd look at me, I'd look at him, and nobody knew what to do. Gary heard *ecstasy* in his *mind* and he couldn't capture that."

Dea felt that Stewart's intake was affecting his voice. "That high crispness was gone." Plus, Gary "would try to over-phrase, and it didn't work." As Dea saw it, what had come naturally was now a bit of a self-conscious trick, "and it ain't the same."[61] Sessions would vary wildly. "He'd cut stuff and sing it and it would just be awful—I mean, *awful*. And he'd go, 'Man, that's great!' Then he'd go home, I'd send him a copy, and he'd call up and say, 'Man, that's awful!' And he'd come back, put his voice on, and it would be like it was when I met him—wired for 440." Dea never knew which Gary was coming through the door.

Dea had a theory—*his* theory, allow me to stress. Roy felt that Gary's background was so core to his being that it doomed any satisfaction from a financially successful career. "Gary thought he was sinful. It comes from growin' up Baptist. He's brought up same way as me. The church'll tell ya blessed are the poor, you never say blessed are the rich. So you come away with this feeling that if you got money, something's bad gonna happen to you, 'cause you must've stepped on somebody to get it, otherwise you wouldn't have it. As a result, you develop a sort of self-destruction—which, if you look at any hillbilly, black or white, you'll find self-destruction. You look at all this money and say, 'I got it, but it's *sinful money*. I made it bein' sinful and I'm gonna die and rot in hell for it.'

"I'd call him and he'd be layin' on the couch, I don't know what state stoned he was. But he'd tell me, 'Roy, I'm rotten on the inside—*rotten*, and I'm gonna lay here on this couch, I ain't gonna bathe, I ain't gonna shave. Until I get as rotten on the *outside* as I am

61 For the record, Gary insisted that as far as recording in the studio went, he was "fucked up on only one song—'Ain't Livin' Long Like This.' I smoked a joint before I went out and overdubbed it." He allowed that he might've done "a couple of lines" of cocaine a time or two, but he maintained he did not go into the studio high.

on the inside. Then I'll look in the mirror and see how rotten I am on the outside, and then maybe I'll get right on the inside.' What a choice of words, right? He's rotten on the inside. His answer? Get rotten on the outside."

* * *

Based on existing session sheets, *Little Junior* was recorded from October 1977 into February 1978. Dea used the usual bunch of stellar pickers, augmented by Terry McMillan on harmonica and New York City–born steel player Hal Rugg, who'd toured with George Jones. "Hal Rugg does a stellar job," noted Steve Hinson. "He played real traditional Buddy Emmons/Jimmy Day–sounding stuff on those songs, a perfect fit for the material." The first single was a drinking song, "Whiskey Trip," written by Wayne Carson with Donn Tankersley. Although the stink of Jimmy Buffett marimbas prevents me from fully embracing this number, Stewart delivers the goods on a powerful chorus that burns into your memory, like it or not. Dea went back to the bluegrass sessions of November 1975 for the last time with "Can't You See," the Toy Caldwell/Marshall Tucker anthem that had been a recent country hit for Waylon Jennings. Stewart bests all previous versions by upping the tempo and bringing that lonesome Kentucky melancholy, opting for a bit of restraint in comparison to the rest. "Little Junior," another honky-tonk boast along the lines of "Flat Natural Born Good-Timin' Man," would quickly become a theme song for Stewart out on the road. Hastily scrawled on a prescription pad for Bendectin, a morning-sickness drug later found to cause birth defects (Lord knows what Stewart was using it for), the lyrics open with the irresistible couplet "My daddy wore a Stetson and a hundred dollar suit/Developed a cravin' for the black man's blues" before moving on to such Garyisms as "Raised without a mother/So I'm a mother myself." Stewart confessed to me the song was inspired by a bit of dialogue snatched off the TV from a late-show movie: "I'll be out on bail before the booking sheet's dry." And the aforementioned "Tequila After Midnight" is a performance that's grown on me in recent years, with Stewart providing understated beauty to another demon-alcohol number.

Best of all are two songs cut on January 24, 1978: "Stone Wall (Around Your Heart)," written by sometime Music City columnist Pat Twitty, and "Single Again," a ferocious Stewart original. On "Stone Wall," an old-school country ballad featuring a sublime vocal by Gary, Steve Hinson praises the "Jerry Lee Lewis piano" played by Hargus "Pig" Robbins, maintaining that between the eighty-eights and Gary's attitude, the song could've leapt off of the Killer's classic *Another Place, Another Time* album.

The tale of a tormented post-divorce honky-tonk prowl, "Single Again" was written "on a bar coaster," as Stewart told Dave Dawson. "I ran into a bunch of my cousins, about four of them. I said, 'What are you doing in here?' It was a strange place for them. One said, 'I'm getting a divorce,' and I went over in the corner and started writing 'Single Again.'" Although uncredited, Mary Lou came up with the line "Now he's got you and I've got two divorce lawyers on my back." Stewart references "Red Cadillac and a Black Mustache," cut in the fifties by rockabilly singers Bob Luman and Warren Smith, to glorious effect.

"Single Again" is a stellar recording capturing Stewart and Dea at the very pinnacle of their powers, and it hits with the pow of a tawdry pulp paperback cover. Allow me to roll-call the players: Dale Sellers, electric guitar! Hal Rugg, dobro! ("The dobro doubled me," said Sellers. "It was just somethin' that happened.") Acoustic guitars, Jerry Shook and Harold Bradley! Drums, Buddy Harman! Bass, Henry Strzelecki! David Briggs and Gary Stewart on keyboards! Vocal accompaniment, Dottie Deleonibus and Bobby Harden! This is Stewart Nashville at its finest, a magical combination of players giving their absolute all. "Those guys were wizards, man," said Hinson.

The songs shunted to side two in the days of vinyl are for the most part a different story. "I Got Mine" was Stewart's first foray into an actual blues number, this one dating back at least to 1928 when it had been recorded by Frank Stokes. Gary knew the song from Ry Cooder's

1976 album *Chicken Skin Music*. His vocal is sly, larcenous, and playful, sporting the kind of extreme vocal stylings that split admirers for and against. "If My Eyes Touch You," a forgettable Carson–Tankersley song that veers into pop crooner territory, is followed by a limp "You're Running Wild." Stewart should've knocked the old Everly Brothers hit out of the park but sounds nearly off-key, as if he hadn't spent enough time with the song to master it. "He could've done 'Runnin' Wild' better," said Dea with finality.

Worst of all is "Honky-Tonkin'," the Hank Williams classic. The tempo is slowed down, the intro and feel duplicate the Troy Seals song of the same name Stewart had cut on his debut album, and Gary, who was known to do affecting solo acoustic renditions of Williams songs during his shows, walks through the performance. Mystifying and pointless. *Little Junior* would only reach thirty-five on the country album charts, while "Whiskey Trip," the kind of drinkin' song RCA could get behind, made it to number sixteen, Stewart's last showing in the Top Twenty ("Stone Wall" hit number forty-one and "Single Again" number thirty-six—both disgraceful showings for such excellent songs, if you ask me). It would all be downhill from here.

To promote *Little Junior*, Stewart appeared on some generic Music City awards show to perform the title song. Originally the Drugstore Cowboys were going to back him, but the expense was deemed too great. Dressed in nearly the same outfit as the album cover, Stewart does the song alone, the show band playing offstage. While this could've been a recipe for disaster—the band does violate the song with a dopey sax—Stewart oozes bravado as he commands the stage, hunched over the mic like a praying mantis as the camera swoops in and around him, the shadows of his hat evoking Luke the Drifter mystery. Lost for years, this was the one TV appearance that Stewart wanted me to find. Lamentably, it surfaced long after he was gone.

* * *

A new album out, Gary hit the road. But in place of the Drugstore Cowboys was Train Robbery, a new Florida outfit featuring his old Rockfish Railroad cohorts "Boogie" Bob Melton, Darrell Dawson, and Ralph Profeta, with old Phoenix favorite Howard "Bingo" Folcarelli on drums and newcomer John Whalen on fiddle, mandolin, guitar, and harmony vocals ("a great addition," said Melton). Profeta, who'd played banjo in Rockfish, was now a novice steel guitar player after Weldon Myrick talked him into buying one following the Bradley's Barn sessions with Gary. "I got this $3,000 steel from Sho-Bud for five hundred bucks. And Weldon tells me, 'If you only play *exactly* what I show you to play, nobody will ever know you don't know how to play steel guitar." Melton thought Train Robbery[62] was "a great little band." They'd been together about half a year when they opened for Mel Tillis at the Fort Pierce Civic Center. "It was the first concert ever held there," said Melton. "It went over huge. I hung out with Gary and Mel on his bus and we had a big time. Mel was funny as hell." The next day Stewart rang Melton to ask him if Train Robbery wanted to go on the road. Stewart would tour with them into 1979. Most of the members agreed this was the best congregation of Florida-based musicians to ever back Gary. "I think we were more polished, and more of that Allman Brothers sound that Gary loved so much," said Darrell Dawson. "We did that better."

One reason for this was Tommy Ray Miller, who arrived toward the tail end of the band's tenure. T-Ray, as he was known, was a tall, gangly kid from Wise, Virginia, not far from Gary's Kentucky stomping grounds. Stories vary as to how Miller got into the band. Ralph Profeta claimed it was a result of Gary and his cohorts enjoying a meal together in some nameless Kentucky joint and hearing "this guitar playing down the holler." So they followed the sound to its maker. "It turned out to be this seventeen-year-old kid sitting in the bathroom, his playing echoing out of the window." Ron Swindall, part of a group of Wise musicians Gary knew, maintained that Gary

62 Gary was fond of calling the band Ghost Train—not to be confused with the song he'd soon write by that name.

heard Miller during a studio jam, then snuck off to strike a deal, stealing him away from the band he was in, Blue Sky. Tommy was obsessed with his instrument and by all accounts a hellacious player in the Allman Brothers tradition, even at that young age. "T-Ray was a guy that went to bed with his guitar," said Dawson. "Some people take a book to the bathroom, he took a guitar."

Once Miller joined, "we had four guitars for a while," said Profeta. "Gary loved that big sound." With T-Ray in place, Melton christened the band the Honky-Tonk Liberation Army—"because we were like a guitar army that blew the roof off the bars we played in." The band traveled by motor home and later by bus, Gary flying to meet them for gigs and riding along for some stretches. "There was a lot of personality in the band," said John Whalen. "It was a fun group to hang around. "Boogie" Bob was our social director, ringleader, head delinquent." One night Melton was photographed at the Longhorn surrounded by seven adoring women; on another he snuck three Playboy bunnies onto the bus. Larry "Mouse" Munson came out on the road for a spell, this time acting as Gary's road manager, while various others tagged along here and there, like a photographer from Georgia no one remembers the name of, and a wild man only known as "Victor the Indian," whose antics led to a group mantra that went "I can't stay here if I can't fuck up!" Victor was not around to talk about the good old ways. "He was found dead in a ditch quite a while back," said Melton. "They never caught anyone for doing him in. It was speculated that he crossed some cartel gentlemen."

Gary flew high musically with this bunch. "We sometimes had a set list, but not always," said Melton. "Lots of times we had the first two or three songs set, but after that it was whatever Gary felt like." For all his looseness, Stewart knew exactly what he wanted. "Gary was all about 'Let the feeling take you'—being able to know what the person is going to play, knowing what the groove is gonna be," said Dawson. "He taught us anybody can play fast. It takes really good musicians to play slow. It was the air in between that made it happen, it wasn't just ten thousand notes and everybody flailing away. It was all about getting it to where it would just groove. And boogie—or as he always used to say, the *booji-wooji*.

"Gary was a guy who never forgot a lick that he played. He never said, 'How did that go?' He was a *great* guitar player. It wasn't a Dickey Betts kind of thing. He had a real feel, a way of structuring chords unlike anybody that I had ever played with. A lot of people will go, 'Oh, you got to play an A chord,' and they played the whole chord. He'd just play parts of it. Just a few strings—enough to give you the feel—and the feeling of the song that he was trying to get out. And it didn't sound rinky-dink, it sounded *great*. If it was a boogie thing, he wanted to get the base of the chord. If we're playing in A, he wanted to make sure that you would hear the low A, but he didn't necessarily play all the high jangly stuff as he went. He would play, like, the middle of a chord. I don't know who else would do that—Eric Clapton?"

Night after night, Dawson was blown away by Stewart. "The most amazing artist I've ever seen in my life. There was nothing like it in the world, the way he could work a crowd." And being a member of the band meant "you wanted to make him grin. If you were makin' him grin with your playin', you were doin' it right."

Stewart and the Honky-Tonk Liberation Army / Train Robbery tore up honky-tonks across Texas and beyond—the Longhorn Ballroom (Dallas), Lady Long Legs (Beaumont), Dance Town USA (Houston), Coldwater Cattle Company (Lubbock), Rio Palm Isle (Longview), Whiskey River (Dallas and Round Rock), Gilley's (Pasadena), Mr. Lucky's (Phoenix), the Cabooze (Minneapolis), Bananas (Macon), and a zillion others.

* * *

Stewart made several forays out to Los Angeles to play the Palomino Club in North Hollywood. These were triumphant affairs, with Waylon Jennings, Rodney Crowell, Ricky Skaggs, and Mickey Gilley paying their respects. Crowell remarked that when Gary played "it was like he just plugged into the light socket, and he was

Reddy Kilowatt." When Gilley got onstage to do a number with Stewart, Gary announced, "Without Jerry Lee Lewis, neither one of us would be here." (According to attendee Michael Ochs, "Mickey Gilley grimaced.") Eagles Glenn Frey and Joe Walsh were there as well. "Frey really wanted to cut Gary's 'Hollywood' song," said Ralph Profeta. According to Stewart drummer Robert "Cotton" Payne, Frey dubbed Gary's music "hillbilly funk."

One reason Stewart might not have minded visiting this particular high-profile city? A new paramour. A lively, long-legged clothes buyer for high-end fashion stores, Mia De Sousa had met Gary backstage after his showcase at the Troubadour in 1976. "We had an incredible chemistry," said De Sousa, who would hit the clubs and go thrift shopping with Stewart. "Gary and I both love quaaludes. Where most people would fall in their food, for us they were a stimulant," said Mia, who sported a necklace with a sterling silver pendant in the shape of a quaalude, complete with "Rohr 714" inscription (Gary, of course, sweet-talked her into giving it to him). De Sousa showed Gary Tinseltown spots like Carlos 'n Charlie's; Stewart took her to Fort Pierce, where George showed her his fighting cocks. It was "almost a cultural exchange," according to Mia, who insisted that "Lou was never threatened by my relationship with Gary. She never asked for details. It never ever, ever came up that I fucked her husband." De Sousa sent Lou boxes of cool clothes; sometimes Lou would hide out at Mia's place. "I loved Mary Lou. She loved me. She'd run away from Gary and stay with me. Eventually she would get in touch with him and let him know where she was."

De Sousa was pals with another of Gary's Los Angeles buddies, Rosie Flores, then an aspiring singer in her twenties (friends called De Sousa and Flores the "Boogie Twins"). She'd first seen Gary playing a bowling alley in San Diego, then at Dance Town USA in Houston. "He had a way of talking to the audience that made you feel like you were best friends. I was just like, 'This guy is cooler than Elvis and Jerry Lee put together.'" She met him in Houston. "He did try to make a pass at me," said Flores, who knew he was married and turned him down. "I said, 'That's not why I'm here. You're my honky-tonk idol.'" He encouraged her pursuit of music, telling her, "We're from the same cookie cutter."

"He was just so considerate. Delicate. Really polite and sweet," Flores said. When Stewart coveted a vintage San Antonio T-shirt Flores was wearing with a cowboy drawing on it, she offered to trade shirts with him on the spot. From then on, he introduced her by saying, "This is Rosie Flores. She'll give you the shirt off her back." Rosie was a regular at the Palomino, and one night was surprised to see an incognito Gary onstage for the talent show. As Flores recalls, "The announcer goes, 'Ladies and gentlemen—Slim Chance and the Sore-Saddle Riders!'" Rosie and Mia remained close friends with Stewart. "We had that love for Gary in common," said Flores. De Sousa still has a little shrine in her home to Stewart, which includes an old moccasin of his. "With a hole in it," said Mia.

* * *

Stewart loved returning to Kentucky for shows. "Whenever I get to feelin' depressed or need something new, something to slow down to, that's where I head for, is the hills," Stewart told Bob Allen. "It's just like a tranquilizer." The big joint to play in Gary's old stomping grounds was Marlow's Country Palace in Pikeville. As described by writer Coyote Wallace, Marlow's was "a place where your odds of finding companionship for the night, getting stabbed, and running into your own absentee father who left to get cigarettes when you were 12 and never came back—all were within spitting distance of one another." The club was run by one Marlow Tackett, an imperious and kingly figure in the area. "The guy had a picture of him and Jesus on the wall, side by side," said Gary's drummer Robert "Cotton" Payne. "It was his place, his gig, his people, his everything."

Marlow Tackett and Gary. (Gina Stewart collection)

"Marlow was a little scary to me," said Ray Wilburn, another Stewart drummer. "A lot of locals we met would talk about him in hushed tones as if he was a gangster." A rather large troglodyte with a manicured beard, mustache, and cash-register jaw who looked more like a professional wrestler than most professional wrestlers, Marlow had cut a handful of oddball singles like "Ride That Bull (Big Bertha)," "Prayer in the Classroom" ("Put the prayer back in the classroom, take the gun from the hand/Get the children high on Jesus, so they will understand"), and even one for RCA, a slowed-down country take on Wilson Pickett's "634-5789," an oversized 45 label of which hung behind the stage. "Marlow's 1970s country music stylings were sometimes at odds with the urge to dance," wrote Wallace. Many country stars of the day played the Palace and it was a rambunctious place, with some bands allegedly paid in moonshine. "Jerry Lee showed up in a limousine," said Sonny Tackett, Marlow's nephew. "We sent him home in a police car." Then there was the time quizzical baroque outlaw David Allan Coe arrived for a show and somehow insulted Marlow, who was really looking forward to meeting him and took it personally.

"Marlow walked back to the back and got a M16 machine gun," said Sonny. "I pulled out my Glock 45 and put it down the back of my pants. The other guys had guns, every fuckin' one of 'em. Marlow poked Coe in the back with the rifle barrel, then stuck it right underneath his chin, pushing his head back. He said, 'This is a fuckin' machine gun and it's fuckin' loaded. And I'm going to blow your brains out if you even open your mouth to speak. If I hear one word come out of your mouth I'm going to pull this fuckin' trigger. Guess what? You're on my turf now, I can shoot you and get away with it.'

"I could see fear in David's eyes. Marlow was so mad he had tears comin' out of his eyes and his gun was shakin'. He backed Coe out the back door, across the gravel, and into the bus. He said, 'If you're not out of this parking lot within ten minutes, I'm gonna start shooting.'" Coe and company fled without playing a note.

Sonny Tackett had first met Gary when they were both working at Bradley's Barn, but they grew close once Stewart started playing Marlow's, bonding over records. Sonny had a room upstairs at the club with three thousand records in it. "Gary freaked out that I was a young guy that knew who Little Walter was," said Tackett, who added that Stewart insisted on sleeping in the record room whenever he played there.

The first time Gary played the Country Palace, "it was just him and a guitar," according to Sonny. By the time Stewart returned after "She's Actin' Single (I'm Drinkin' Doubles)" hit, there was "such a huge crowd that we had to take all the tables out of the club completely. We ran out of chairs, we had to get 'em from the local funeral homes all around. To this day, Gary holds the record at Marlow's—twelve hundred people. Gary Stewart is a legend in Eastern Kentucky, and the people of Kentucky love Gary Stewart."

On his Facebook page Sonny Tackett describes himself as "a hardridin' outlaw, to-the-core Kentucky Mountain Man." Nine years Gary's junior, Tackett grew up in Dorton, about ten miles from Stewart's hometown. A songwriter and guitar player, Sonny became a running buddy for Gary, who called him "Little Brother." Tackett is a font of information, from how Stewart would shape his hats over a steaming teakettle to get the creases just right, to why he talked so quietly ("you'd lean in, he'd talk even softer—it made people come to him"), to the way Gary agonized over the lyrics he scrawled in an endless assortment of yellow legal pads. "When Gary would write a song, he was very reluctant to turn loose of it. Gary would sweat and worry hisself to death over one word. He was never satisfied."

Yet Stewart always found time to inspire others. Gary "would listen to my songs. And he would encourage me. Instead of discouraging people, he'd always try to get the most out of everybody." Sonny would write with Gary, and Stewart would cut a few of his songs. As well as giving Sonny such logical but curious advice as: do drugs, but don't buy them. "Don't buy it, don't get the habit. I followed his advice and it worked out great. There was never a time I didn't learn things from the guy. He always knew how to handle people...he knew when to leave it alone and walk away."

Although Stewart was a top draw at the Country Palace for the next few years, it didn't end well. Gary showed up to play one date with the house band and was in "bad shape," according to Tackett. The waiting crowd grew restless. Marlow, a straight arrow when it came to substance abuse ("his problem was all them women," said Sonny), "put Gary down desperately bad about drugs and alcohol," barging into Stewart's room to command him to get moving. Gary said, "Marlow, I'm really sick—can you give me a few minutes?" Tackett barked, "You get your fuckin' ass onstage or I'm gonna knock your fuckin' teeth out." Sonny had to get between them. "Marlow was 250 pounds, Gary was 130. In ten minutes I had Gary onstage." Stewart went on to play a two-hour set and nearly an hour encore, but the damage had been done. From then on he refused Marlow's calls, telling Sonny, "I'll never play Marlow's again as long as I live." And he never did.[63]

A great song would come out of these Kentucky trips, and not one of Gary's—John Preston's "I've Just Seen the Rock of Ages." It "came from the hills of the Kentucky / Virginia state line, the Appalachian Mountains," said Stewart. I played a couple of gigs up there, went to a couple parties and people were playing that song—hey, *everybody* was singin' it—and I said, 'Lord!' It sounded like it was a standard a hundred years old and I was like, 'I want to record this.'" Tackett said that the party in particular was "at the local pot dealer's, one mile below Marlow's." Preston did the song and "Gary said, 'Get my recorder.' He captured the soulful backwoods spiritual on his little Memorex and promised Johnny he was gonna record it."

John Brenton Preston was a songwriter and harmonica player from Salyersville, Kentucky, who'd run afoul of the law, probably for drugs. "Johnny was just one of those restless souls," said Sonny. "When he got out of prison he went straight to Marlow's and played in the band for the summer. Marlow called him 'Johnny Smoke-A-Bowl.' He had a wooden leg. We would stash our pot in it on the way home." Preston would write a handful of songs for Ralph Stanley, who first cut "I've Just Seen the Rock of Ages" in 1977. It was one of the first songs cut during sessions for Stewart's next album, 1979's *Gary*, which stretched from October 1978 into February 1979. This mournful number about a mother's dying moments was perfect for Stewart, and in performing it he expresses an eerie awareness of death, the finality of it, the crippling sorrow it leaves in its wake.

63 Stewart also played a honky-tonk owned by Sonny's family, Star Musicland in Paintsville, Kentucky, and hung out in Wise, Virginia, with a band called Fallen Stars, sitting in on their gigs and attending their recording sessions at Bradley's Barn (singer Thomas Countiss contributed uncredited background vocals on Stewart's next album, *Gary*). Another member, Danny "Tuck" Robinson, would travel with Gary on the road.

When Gary hits the high and low notes in the third verse—"Pine breeze blowing on the mountain / Where forever she will lay / There she'll rest beside the fountain / There she'll sleep beneath the clay"—it chills the blood. You forget the other versions of the song, of which there have been many, Stanley's included.

"I loved the song, and when Gary sang it for me, because of my roots, I just kept thinkin' Staple Singers, Staple Singers," said Roy Dea. "When I got in the studio I took guitarists Jerry Shook and Dale Sellers and said, 'I want to make this like a Staple Singers record. Give me a lick." Dea thought it was a whole new direction for Gary, although he was cognizant it was still "a religious song and I'd never get that by 'em as far as a single. This is what they would tell me: 'Get somebody to rewrite it and make it a drinkin' song.'" Dea felt it was the greatest performance he'd ever produced. "I can sit there all morning and listen to 'Rock of Ages,'" he told me.

The album's second outstanding song is "Shady Streets." Gary had come by the song hanging around with the Allman Brothers.[64] Both Dickey Betts and Gregg Allman had become acquaintances since their chance airport meetings years earlier. Betts was sitting around with songwriter Billy Ray Reynolds and guitar player "Dangerous" Dan Toler when the trio broke into "Shady Streets," a song they'd written together. As Gary recalled, "They were sittin' around playin', guitar pullin', and I said, 'I *like* that, I'd like to cut that."

This mournful, affecting ballad about a wandering couple grabs you from the opening couplet: "Shadows fallin', on a Sunday afternoon / We go walkin', seems like the only thing we have to do." Are these two winners? Losers? "Some day the sun will shine, just for me and you," he sings, and you want to believe it. "Shady streets and shiny shoes." For Stewart, dreaming is the important part of the journey, not the destination. Now thirty-five, Stewart already knew plenty about turning away from opportunity, turning his back on success, and he sounds like he's had enough.

64 The Stewarts attended Gregg's marriage to Julie Bindas in 1979. "I got to bartend the wedding," said Shannon. "I was ten."

The studio cut is sublime, with beautiful guitar from Reggie Young ("he's so...precise," said Steve Hinson), but in live performances it became something worthy of Van Morrison. Gary would play it on the road with the Toman Brothers, Russ Toman trading licks with Gary. "We'd do it as a fifteen-minute jam," said Stewart. "Y'know—everybody takes it." Gary would explore the dynamics of the song, "whispering some words, and then, all of a sudden, he would scream some," said Randy Toman. It became a high point of his live sets.

The last great cut on *Gary* is "The Next Thing You Know" by Sonny Throckmorton and Curly Putman. Maybe the bleakest relationship song in Stewart's oeuvre, it begins at love's end and works its way down from there. "The next thing you know/Our love will be history/A total mystery/You can read back home." Throckmorton and ace background singer Dennis Wilson contribute background vocals. "The bridge will fall down/And sink in the ocean," wails Gary,

Gary with Thomas Countiss, who sang backup on 1979's *Gary*. (Shannon Ashburn collection)

the stein-swinging oompah tempo providing strange counterpoint to all the despair. Throckmorton, who penned "Middle Age Crazy" for Jerry Lee Lewis among many other hits, was a big fan of Stewart's and played a few shows with him. "We played in Texas one time. He played for about an hour and a half. And when Gary got through, he was wringing wet with sweat. He blew me away. Gary was the hardest-working artist I've ever worked with."

Released on Valentine's Day 1979, *Gary* has little else to recommend it. Stewart contributed only two songs, "One More," a good drinking song written with Bob Melton that doesn't feel fully realized, and "Everything a Good Little Girl Needs," which is as wince-inducing as the title suggests. Stewart covers the great Leon Payne song best known by Hank Williams, "Lost Highway," something he should've nailed, and fails to engage. Zero excitement. There's not much to say about the rest. It's all kind of rote—Gary sings, the players play. I guess you could say it's a fair album, decent enough, but if you're a Stewart fan, that's the kiss of death. One thing you don't expect Gary to be is boring, and aside from the three glittering jewels, this is one forgettable collection. "Shady Streets" climbed to sixty-six on the country charts, while the poppy annoyance "Mazelle" only hit seventy-five.

Dea sounded pained recalling the sessions. "There was just no communication between me, Gary, and the musicians. Everything was just to get it over, really. Get out of the situation and go home. It's awful when you're sitting there with a bunch of pickers and they're frustrated. They don't know what to play and you don't know what to suggest, 'cause you've got a guy that's in never-never land. I used to tell him, 'When the day comes when you can't get high on the music, it's over.'"

* * *

This would be Gary's last RCA album with Roy Dea. "RCA had grown. There were a lot more people involved in operations. The New Yorkers startin' comin' in, sittin' there, payin' attention, passin' judgment." He claimed even the accountants were "'tellin' you what type of songs to cut." Dea noticed that songs on which Jerry Bradley owned the publishing were getting preferential treatment, whether good or bad. I have heard also rumors of financial improprieties uncovered by Roy and an RCA promotion man, but they remain unconfirmed. Dea was also saddened by the way RCA treated Chet Atkins at the end. "Roy worshipped Chet," said his wife Delores, and Roy felt "they just kind of shuffled him out."

"A whole bunch of stuff went on that people don't know about," said Dea, comparing it to the fall of Rome. "There were other things goin' on at RCA that didn't have anything to do with Gary," Dea said, adding that certain people "didn't like me for my stand...makin' waves. I thought the tide had turned on me then." He suspected that some of Gary's later records weren't promoted because he was already in the doghouse on these other issues. "I had to be made to look bad—in other words, not have hit records." Paranoia? We may never know. I had intended to sit down and discuss it further with him one day, but Roy passed before that could happen.

In any case, Roy was removed as Stewart's producer, and not long after was shown the door. "I told Jerry, 'You'll have to fire me, because I won't quit.'" And that's exactly what happened. "He was a producer and he wasn't producing any hit records, not just on Gary, but other people," said Bradley matter-of-factly.[65]

Gary Stewart's biggest champion at RCA was history. He may not have understood the weirder, raggedy edges of Gary's talent, but he had harnessed the Stewart whirlwind in a way no one else had. Or would again. Chaos ahead.

65 For the record, in 1979 Dea produced a number-twelve hit on Dottsy, as well as "The Old Side of Town" by Tom T. Hall, which hit number nine.

12

GHOST TRAIN SLIDE

We only pass this way once, might as well pass by in a Cadillac.
– Maury Dann (Rip Torn), *Payday*

Gary Stewart needed a new producer, and one appeared: Lincoln Wayne "Chips" Moman. Georgia-born Moman had been an integral part of Memphis's fabled Stax Records, finding the label its movie-theater recording location and producing such spare, stunning records as William Bell's "You Don't Miss Your Water" as well as cowriting classic soul songs like "The Dark End of the Street" and "Do Right Woman—Do Right Man" with Dan Penn. He went on to run his own studio, American Sound, where he produced the first Elvis Presley album recorded outside of RCA studios, *From Elvis in Memphis*.

By the mid-seventies Moman had relocated to Nashville, where he co-wrote "(Hey Won't You Play) Another Somebody Done Somebody Wrong Song" for B.J. Thomas and, with frequent collaborator Bobby Emmons, he penned "Luckenbach, Texas (Back to the Basics of

Love)," a number-one country hit for Waylon Jennings in 1977, which he also produced. Chips had a long, rich history of producing American roots music, not to mention a knack for writing hit songs, and must've seemed like a great choice for Stewart. When I asked Jerry Bradley whose idea it was for Moman to produce *Cactus and a Rose*, Gary's next album, he was vague. "I imagine it was Chips. Chips has a way of callin' people when he wants to produce somebody. He called me when he wanted to produce Waylon."

While Moman certainly had the musical pedigree, this was not a match made in heaven. Gary "was real strange," Moman told Edd Hurt during a 2012 interview, the only time I know of that he discussed working with Stewart. Moman described being in the studio trying to capture a vocal that was sounding "muffled. I couldn't figure out what it was. I went back there, and he was layin' down on the floor. And that's the way he was. That explains everything. He was just a funny guy." According to Sonny Tackett, early on "Chips made a statement that put a sour note on the whole sessions. He said, 'This ain't gonna be another Roy Dea session,' and Gary happened to overhear it. Chips and Gary never got along."

"It was a lot different from the sessions for all my other albums," Stewart told Bob Allen. This was not a Music City three-hours / three-tracks situation. The fact Chips owned the studio meant there was no clock. A session booked for six might start at eight. Maybe they went out to eat instead. Or "just sat around and talked," said Gary. Moman called the shots. "We'd lay around and when that feeling would come to him, he'd turn on the tapes and start rolling...Sometimes it'd go two days. It was real relaxed...it'd get to where I'd have passed out on the couch. It took a long time to do the album...nine months. Like having a baby."

Was such a loosey-goosey set up good for an entity as spontaneous, immediate, and ethereal as Gary? Halfway through the sessions Dea was still at RCA, using keyboard player Bobby Emmons for a studio session. "Bobby Emmons, he's Chip's right-hand man," noted Dea, who said Emmons took him aside and told him, 'Hey, Chips sends you a message. He said to tell you you're a genius for ever getting anything out of Gary in the first place. And you're a bigger genius for getting out when you did.' Chips didn't get anything out of Gary, and it shows on that record. He couldn't figure out how we cut any records. Gary was running wild with him like he did with me."[66]

The recording of *Cactus and a Rose* started sometime in 1979, with Nashville press reporting that Gary was still in the studio in February 1980. By all reports it was by far the most expensive Stewart record ("I never seen any figures, but I'll kiss your ass if Chips Moman has ever done an album for $36,000," said Roy Dea, apparently indicating what his Stewart albums cost). *Cactus and a Rose* was cut in Moman's studio in Nashville, utilizing some of the same players Dea was fond of: Reggie Young, Pig Robbins, and Jerry Carrigan, as well as the aforementioned Bobby Emmons. That's where any common ground ended, however. *Cactus and a Rose* would sport an amorphous pop/rock sound and, although barely detectable, featured a couple of guest superstars that somehow helped spin it in an even more opaque direction: two of Gary's heroes, Gregg Allman and Dickey Betts.

* * *

The Allman Brothers were in tatters, having split up in 1976 following Gregg Allman's grand jury testimony in a drug investigation involving (among others) Allmans road manager John "Scooter" Herring. Gregg was labeled a snitch, with Dickey Betts proclaiming, "There is no way we can work with Gregg Allman again. Ever." But they patched up their differences in 1978 and recorded *Enlightened Rogues*, which was released in February 1979. Two months later they'd begin an extended tour of the States. Betts invited Stewart to the rehearsals. "Dickey got my phone number somehow. And asked me

66 In the eighties Red Ash Records label owner Dave Jordan was in Nashville having lunch with Roy Dea one day when Chips Moman came over to their table. "He says, 'Roy, I don't know how you did it. I don't know how you were able to get a performance out of this kid. We spent thousands of hours in the studio, and I only got two performances out of all those sessions.' He was talking about *Cactus and a Rose*."

did I want to come to the dress rehearsals—LORD, YES!" exclaimed Gary, who admitted he was more excited by this "than anything in the world."

Although the rehearsals were held in Jacksonville, Florida, a scant three-hour drive from Fort Pierce, Stewart decided to charter a plane that he ended up using again during their upcoming tour. Besides recording *Cactus and a Rose* sporadically in Nashville, Gary "wasn't doin' nothin' else but just laying around the house," he told Kirk West, the Allmans' tour photographer, who'd strike up a friendship with Gary.[67] Due to the Moman sessions, Stewart "couldn't go out and work the road because I had to be on call," but no way was Gary missing out on an invitation from the Allman Brothers. "I spent all the money I had in the savings account getting to them gigs, because, hey, that was *it*." Jerry Bradley was dumbfounded. "I was curious—I said, 'Well, how much are they payin' ya?' He said, 'Nothin'.' 'And you're rentin' an airplane, just so you can go *play*?' Hell, one time he missed the damn airplane he rented."

Once in Jacksonville, Gary became part of the rehearsals. "We did 'Ramblin' Man,'" he told West. "I sang a verse of it—the second verse—and boy, that thing started gelling. It took ahold of everybody, son. It took 'em on a magic carpet [ride]." "He was a great person, easy to become friends with," said Dickey Betts. "He loved fried green tomatoes, he even carried 'em on the road... Gary was just totally wide open, he'd give his heart to you in a second." Stewart's sartorial splendor made a big impression on Gregg Allman. Kirk West recalled getting some hats made and asking Gregg what style he wanted. "I want one like Gary Stewart wears, goddamn it!" demanded Allman. "I want to look like a fuckin' hustler."

67 West had an extensive archive of unreleased Allman Brothers tapes, and in the interview Kirk did with Gary it's amusing to hear him work on West to get some of his bounty, much the way he'd do with me years later. He tells Kirk how he was after some rare Amos 'n' Andy tapes and, this being the early days of VHS, he took his Quasar VCR on the plane to Nashville—"bought a seat for it and everything"—then took it to a motel where he met the other trader and figured out how to tape what he had. "So what I'm saying is that this stuff means so much to me that I will come to your house and bring some tapes and seriously sit there. 'Cause, son, nobody loves the Allman Brothers more."

Stewart would join the band intermittently for about fifteen of their tour dates, singing "Ramblin' Man" on the encores, doing background vocals with special tour guest Bonnie Bramlett, and occasionally doing a song of his own on piano. But the big thrill was joining in now and then on guitar. "Me, Gregg, and Dickey were in a bathroom, ready to go on in Jacksonville," Stewart told West. "I didn't want to come right out and say it—Dickey finally said, 'You want to play guitar, don't you?' 'Just one song.' He said, 'Okay, but hey—it's like a hurricane. I mean you jump in there, you got to hold on.' And son, I'll tell you...being onstage with 'em, I mean, there was a *force* there, boy. *Oh*, the *feelin'*!" When Stewart would join Bramlett at the mic for background vocals, he'd beat her leg "black and blue with a tambourine...Oh man, I got out there...I was in a trance."

Gary, Georgia, Gregg Allman, and Gerald Stewart. (Gina Stewart collection)

Although Gary was just one blip in the traveling Allman carnival—actor Don Johnson came out onstage in Atlanta, as did Southern gospel-rocker Mylon LeFevre—he couldn't have cared less. He loved being any part of this music, however fleeting. "Me and Dickey, always after the gigs, we'd go to a motel room, have two flat top guitars, and just set there and play Jimmy Rogers...hey, those guys are *country*," Stewart told West. "Gregg would be singin' 'Long Black Veil.'" Gary drew great inspiration from these informal jams. "Dickey Betts loves to write," Stewart told Bob Allen. "You don't sing a song that you wrote last year. You create on the spot."

That Easter, Stewart and Bramlett joined the band for a live radio show from a Savannah, Georgia, hotel room. Dickey was reading a press account of an infamous recent incident where Bramlett had backhanded Elvis Costello for referring to James Brown and Ray Charles in derogatory racial terms. Betts "got to the part where I said something disarming, to say the least," recalled Bramlett. "Hysterical laughter" among the group ensued, "and then we realized it was Easter Sunday." The group then broke into an impromptu "Amazing Grace," Gary leading the way. "The sun was rising, and it was all live on the radio," Bramlett recalled. "Beautiful harmony between me, Dickey, Gregg, and Gary." A tape exists of the performance, the only recorded evidence of how well Stewart fit in with this crew.

That day Gary called home to Lou—a big Gregg fan—and said, "Hey, I want you to talk to somebody." He handed Allman the phone. "Will you fry me some taters?" he asked Lou. A few hours later she got another unexpected call from Gary, who was at a nearby airport. He and Gregg had chartered a plane home and, much to Lou's panic, were ten minutes from the house. Once there, Allman, who, according to Lou, "had the dirtiest laugh," made the mistake of asking her to refrain from using the word "man" at the end of her sentences because she was "too much of a lady." Lou shot back, "I'm a musician's old lady. Musicians say that a lot. It's a habit. I will never stop saying 'man.' You just got to accept me as I am." Mary Lou wasn't going to rein it in for anybody, including her favorite rock star. Allman was knocked out by Gary's collection of artifacts and memorabilia. As Lou put it, "Gregg used to tell people, 'I would buy a ticket to go to Gary Stewart's house.'"

Allman's Fort Pierce visitations—there were several over the years—would set the town abuzz. As Laurie Rastrelli, the Stewarts' babysitter, remembered, "Mary Lou called me one night. I was probably sixteen. She goes, 'Lolo, can you come watch Shannon?' I said, 'I'm sleepin'.' And she's like, 'Well, I'll be pullin' up any minute, just come on.' So I got up, hair all messed up, and she pulls up in a Mercedes." When they arrived at the house, "I walk in and Gregg Allman is standing there. I said, 'Oh my gosh!' He's like, 'Honey, I'm just a person.'" Gregg was a favorite of Georgia's and would visit her house as well. When Larry Munson got into promoting concerts, Stewart suggested he get Gregg to do a show. Munson had no idea how to contact him. Gary gave him the number of the Beachcomber lounge in Daytona and suggested he call at 11 a.m. "His girlfriend will be there, tell her you want to speak to Gregg. Gary Stewart told you to call." Larry did as instructed and five minutes later Gregg Allman was on the line. "He said, 'Send me $10,000 in a cashier's check and we have a deal.'"

Drugs were de rigueur with this crew. When Gregg sat in with Gary at a Fort Pierce show in October 1980, he and another Allman band member pulled up "in a bright blue *Smokey and the Bandit* car," as Bob Melton recalled. "They came inside, and Gregg had a bag of cocaine that would've choked a mule, it was so big. They commenced to get into it." According to Melton, "Gary and Gregg would check in to someplace in Palm Beach so they could tell their record labels they were drying out. Then they'd sneak out at night, score, raise hell all night, and check back in come morning."[68]

Throughout the rest of his life Gary had high praise for Dickey Betts. One night when they visited an unnamed superstar to jam at some

68 In the Stewart archives is a treatment plan for a six-week stay at the Palm Beach Institute in West Palm Beach. It's dated October 30, 1979, and the cost was $4,810.00. I have no idea if Gary completed the rehab as we never discussed it.

club, Dickey declined to join in because the big shot's people wouldn't allow Gary through the door. Stewart admired Betts's old-school ways, telling Kirk West that Dickey always made a point of introducing people, whether celebrity or civilian. "Bonnie Bramlett summed him up to a T—Dickey is a Southern gentleman. He is the Rhett Butler of today, a man's man," he told West. Gary noted admiringly that when Betts got mad he'd refrain from punching somebody out and "take it out on a lamp. He could hurt somebody! He's *bad*."

Dickey Betts and Gary, up to no good. (Tommy Schwartz collection)

Stewart and Betts were a more volatile combo than Gary and Gregg. "Dickey loved Gary, Gregg was a little afraid of him," said West. "Gary was a fireball. Dickey and Gregg had completely different personalities when they were real high. Gregg would get subdued, Dickey would get pretty wild. He and Gary shared that." Upon staying at a Nashville establishment called Close Quarters, aka the "Rock & Roll Hotel," the duo was determined to make the joint live up to the name. "That was a wild night," Stewart told West, laughing. "We just had a good time... with the furniture. We redecorated." Next day when Stewart checked out, "they had a whole list—so much for this, so much for that...I wrote a check, I didn't have enough money on me!"

"We had some wild parties, with women and stuff," confessed Betts. "We were playing the Kentucky Derby. I had a bunch of women up in the room...I called Gary and said, 'We're having a party in my room. I need your help.' He said, 'Okay.' So he shows up at the door in a white cowboy hat, a pair of white cowboy boots, a silk white-on-white Western shirt, and he didn't have any pants on...actually, he was overdressed. We took care of that situation." Betts chuckled. "Gary Stewart, what a guy."

Bonnie Bramlett recalled some of their antics on the Enlightened Rogues tour. "It was daylight, we were coming out of the hotel room to get back on the bus," said Bramlett. "And evidently Dickey and Gary had a quite a night in their hotel room. As I was walkin' on the bus, Gary said to Dickey, 'I just can't call her Trigger, Dickey.'" Bramlett paused, letting that sink in. "Maybe they were bein' cowboys...?" She burst out laughing.

One night while sitting around with Gary and a few other pickers, Dickey asked him the secret to singing. "When you take your ride, you never play it the same way twice, do you? So don't ever sing it the same way twice." The advice registered. And when Betts mentioned he wasn't happy playing slide on his Les Paul, Stewart brought out a red SG that had been one of his favorites. As he told West, "When it was time to say goodbye, when I was going home and they're gonna go off somewhere, I said, 'Dickey, take this little guitar here and try it for a while, it's a pretty good slide guitar...if you like it, just keep it.' He burned the thing up!" For a time Betts and the red SG were inseparable on the road. "It tickles me every time I see a picture," said Stewart, proud of his contribution to the Allman legacy.

He also gave Dickey a Martin D-28 and a "1927 double-ought Gibson, the kind of guitar Robert Johnson played," said Betts. "Gary found it in a pawn shop for fifteen bucks and thought, 'Dickey, he'd like that.'" Surely the most unusual appearance Gary Stewart ever made as a guest star was on an acoustic blues medley Betts recorded in 1991 with Warren Haynes and harmonica player Thom Doucette called "Willie and Poor Bob." There are no vocals save for some distant whooping and hollering. "Gary did the moanin', like a train about twenty miles away," said Betts. Stewart is credited with "field hollers."[69]

Most of the music Gary made with the Allmans wasn't documented; they were just impromptu jam sessions out on the road like the one after a gig at a Georgia club called Bananas. As "Boogie" Bob recalled, "I remember sitting in a hotel with Gary and Dickey Betts in Macon, jamming acoustic guitars all night until the sun came up. There was a lot of George Dickel, marching powder, and everything else..."

* * *

As evidenced by the one recording of "Amazing Grace," *Cactus and a Rose* certainly could've amounted to something special had the sessions gone in a more downhome direction akin to Delaney & Bonnie's *Motel Shot*. But Gregg and Dickey are barely perceptible presences on the album, just a little superstar frosting on a cake already top-heavy with too many ingredients.

Four songs on the album were written by Chips Moman and Bobby Emmons, and while they might've succeeded in padding their publishing company credits, they are all substandard works. The first song on the album, "Okeechobee Purple," must've been inspired by Stewart's potent weed of the same name, but it was actually just a bland pop ballad, as were the other three—"Cactus and a Rose," "Staring Each Other Down," and the truly execrable "We Made It as Lovers (We Just Couldn't Make It as Friends)." A demo exists of Gary doing the songs accompanied solely by Emmons on keyboard, and

69 In later years Gary avoided Betts, who was a little out of control in the late '90s. The Allman Brothers fired him in 2000. "They let 'em go by email," said Stewart (others said it was by fax). "Dickey gets to drinkin', and he can be a handful."

his singing is wonderful. But by the time they finished tinkering with the studio takes, his delivery had grown labored and more mannered than ever before. He sounds desperate to breathe life into this tepid material, but all that registers is how hard he's trying.

The rest of the songs not penned by Gary aren't any better. All that needs to be said about "Lover's Knot," penned by pop/rock songwriter Richard Supa, is that Anne Murray's version is better. "Are We Dreamin' the Same Dream" was cowritten by Billy Burnette, a pop-rocker being produced by Moman at the same time as Gary, who fell for the number and talked Moman into cutting it. Unfortunately, the cloying production overwhelms the track. Toni Wine's background vocals are all over the album (she was married to Moman at the time), and while she's a strong stylist with a voice as distinctive and idiosyncratic as Stewart's (she is one of the singers who contributed "meow, meow, meows" to a long-running Meow Mix cat food commercial), she just clashes with Gary.[70]

"Roarin'" is a rocker that covers ground Stewart already excavated effortlessly in songs like "Honky-Tonkin'." It was written by Johnny Cobb and Mike Lawler, musicians who were writing for publisher Acuff-Rose at the time. Cobb, who had played bass for Ronnie Milsap, noted how when they'd walk into an auditorium, "people would just be yelling and screaming for Ronnie, kind of like they were roaring." That led to the song, which he and Lawler cut at an Acuff-Rose demo session with a few other players, including Hargus "Pig" Robbins. Cobb laid down the vocal live. The track made its way to Moman's studio. "Gregg, Dickey, and me all got pantin', the track was so hot, " Stewart told Bob Allen. A day or two later, "a song plugger at Acuff-Rose called and said, 'Well, congratulations—you got a cut with Gary Stewart and Chips Moman," recalled Cobb.

Not only that, but Moman simply took their track and "had Gary learn the song the way I sung it," then had him overdub a vocal that copied it closely. Moman "released it on RCA, but we got no credit,"

70 Charlie Rich's version of "Are We Dreamin' the Same Dream" hit number twenty-six in 1981.

said Cobb, laughing. (Cobb and Lawler are listed in the credits as being on the album, but that's it). Cobb's original vocal—cut live with the band—smokes Stewart's, who should've just recut the song with a band rather than huffing and puffing his way through the manufactured excitement of an overdub. And that's how an uncredited demo production wound up on *Cactus and a Rose*.[71]

* * *

Stewart cowrote three songs on the album. Much better in a band demo Stewart had cut on his own, the faintly amusing "How Could We Come to This After That" was cowritten by Waylon Jennings guitarist, songwriter, and sometime Dickey Betts crony Billy Ray Reynolds. The demo jumps; here it's a turgid blues.

"Ghost Train," the only song I know of credited to Gary Stewart and Gregg Allman, is an ambitious but half-baked misfire, with unconvincing self-reverential blather about "gypsies on the run" and "a man of the song and a man of the night" that crassly invokes the gone-too-soon triumvirate of Duane Allman, Hendrix,[72] and Presley, the track itself veering uneasily between chugging rock and space ballad. Stewart seems to want to say something about life on the road but conveys little more than rock star clichés, although one couplet jumps out, given Stewart's future: "It's a long hard ride when your ticket's fame/It's a downhill slide on the ghost train." I know of no greater Gary Stewart fan than Sonny Tackett, who describes the performance this way: "Gary was doing everything in his power to impress Gregg and Dickey...he was a little stoned on that session, and you can hear it on 'Ghost Train.' And what you hear is Gary almost trying to emulate Gregg. Goin' just a bit too far."

71 According to Cobb, Dickey Betts later cut an unreleased version of the song with Moman. Dickey's actor pal Don Johnson wanted to record it as well, but management nixed the idea due to drug references in the lyric.

72 Somewhere in a press clip I've been unable to locate, Stewart says the Jimi/Jimmy in question is not Hendrix but Reed.

There was one number on *Cactus and a Rose* that even Moman's bloated production couldn't desecrate, "Harlan County Highway." The song is credited to Stewart and Dickey Betts, who, according to what Gary told me, wrote the last verse. When I asked Dickey about it, he begged off any credit. "I don't think we wrote any together, but he gave me credit for a bunch of stuff. Hell, Gary would give you half the song if you said somethin' he liked." He told me how Stewart's publishing company called him specifically about "Harlan County Highway," asking if he'd written half. "No," he told them. "I didn't write any of it!"

A Kentucky boy quits school, leaving his home and a mother grieving over a father killed in the mines, gets married, runs moonshine, and drifts into an uncertain fate: "Temptation lurks on every corner / Seven corners every mile." His future is all used up. "What started off as heaven / Got lost along the way." There exists a slow, spartan demo of "Harlan County Highway," only three minutes long and without the final verse of the released recording. It's perhaps my favorite Gary Stewart recording of all. Nothing fancy, just a local Florida band he took to Nashville for the demo session, with acoustic and electric guitar, bass, and Gary's brother Gerald on drums. But Stewart's vocal will chill your blood. It is permeated with dread, the instinctual knowing an awful fate awaits. "As dramatic a recording as Hank Williams's 'Ramblin' Man,'" writes musician Dale Lawrence, who called the song "a hill-country soul ballad....The song sounds both a hundred years old and like it's writing itself on the spot. The performance is so stark, so still, that whole lives seem to pass between snare shots. Every line is sadder than the last."

Characteristically, Stewart didn't have much to say about the song. "I seen all this being from mining country—kids that grew up without a father, lost 'em to the mines...I had a second cousin in Louisville, she'd married a guy that played the horses all the time...I just pick up little pieces from here and there," he said with typical humility. Gary told Bob Allen that he wrote it en route to the hospital one day, thinking about his recent trips back to Kentucky. He referenced an old gospel song known to most due to Ralph Stanley's performances of it. "Old Baptist is the religion up there, and their singing is haunting—'Oh, Death.'" There's a lot of hard times up there, not many opportunities—coal mines, moonshine."

In 2024, shortly after I had finished an emotional interview with Shannon concerning her father's last days, a video materialized out of nowhere on YouTube of Gary, dressed in black (including hat), doing the song solo with an acoustic guitar on a Kentucky public TV show in 1979. As there are few videos of Stewart floating around, it came as a shock, and hearing such an unexpected and absolutely riveting performance so long after he was no longer on earth was startling, to say the least. It was as if Gary was tapping me on the shoulder, letting me know there would always be another surprise left. "It's like he's right here," whispered Shannon.

* * *

As for the wreck on the highway that is *Cactus and a Rose,* it was unleashed on the world in July 1980. RCA finally opted for a hip, rock and roll cover that Roy Dea would've died for, featuring high-contrast shots of Gary by Alan Messer in that smudgy Norman Seeff style popular at the time. On the back, Stewart thanks band members, Roy Dea, and at least two drug dealers/smugglers—Stormin' Norman and "The Florida Suitcase" (a reference to Ed Barber, who had a younger brother known as "Briefcase").

Cactus and a Rose is not a popular album among the Stewart fanatics I know. "It was real dark," said Steve Hinson, an admirer of many of the musicians involved in cutting the record. "It didn't sound like anybody was havin' fun. When you make records, you're supposed to have fun...I didn't hardly listen to it." A local Florida reviewer aptly declared it "songs about a man with no direction." There was one positive review by Art Fein in the *Los Angeles Times,* who maintained the album was "a mixture of Elton John's accessibility and Jimmy Buffett's languor. And it isn't country." (Apparently he saw these as positive attributes.) According to Randy Toman, RCA promotion man Wayne Edwards told Gary, "This isn't country. I don't know what we're going to do with this album." Toman said some at RCA were high on "Roarin'," but *Cactus and a Rose* only made it to forty-eight, and the split single "Are We Dreamin' the Same Dream"/'Roarin'" stalled at sixty-six. Stewart's most direct commentary on the album was to Sonny Tackett—that he loved recording with the Allmans, but hated the end result: "I didn't pull it off, Sonny."

One night in his trailer a decade and a half later I expressed my own disappointment over the record. I took its failure personally and let Gary know. He got testy.

"When you start getting a few hits and you start getting out there in the world and you're exposed to all this worldly knowledge, all these people, you change. Hey, my music changed. I was tryin' to take it a step farther, but I was taking it away from what the people had accepted. And yeah, it *didn't work.*

"So I just ran off and left the audience. But I ran off to nowhere, because what I had wasn't too much, y'know? I had to try it or I'd never been happy. Chips Moman made an album with Gregg, Dickey, Bonnie Bramlett that was really a completely different album, *completely different*. But I wouldn't have had it any other way. I'm happy with my career!"

The young upstart in me wouldn't leave it alone. "I've heard all the demos you cut at the time and that 'Amazing Grace' you recorded with the Allmans. You could've made a better record just sitting around with a couple of flat tops. But the album, I don't hear it. I mean, those keyboards..."

"I know! I had me a talk with the keyboard man [Bobby Emmons]—'How am I going to do this on the road? I ain't got no keyboards. I'm a guitar picker.' Chips was chief. Hey, I'm going to obey. He's the boss.

"I tried a bunch of things to find out 'Whoa, where are we going?' Finally we hit 'Lover's Knot' and okay, that sort of led us in a direction..." His voice trailed off, then he concentrated on the positive. "Chips Moman is a great producer, now. He wanted to do another one and, hey, we might've got somethin' then...but hey, *Cactus and a Rose*, there's a couple good things on there."

"WHAT???" I inquired. "What??"

Gary was getting frustrated. "I don't know!"

"What???" I, the twerp, repeated.

"'Are We Dreamin' the Same Dream'!" He didn't sound convinced.

"I'll listen again," I said dismissively. The song was far better when he performed it live. "I don't think it's a successful album."

Now he was annoyed. "NO, it wasn't successful."

"The album stiffed when it came out? Fair to say?"

"Yeah, definitely."

I rubbed it in. "A bomb?"

He looked murderous. "Sure."

* * *

Gary playing unknown acoustic gig, a bleary Gregg Allman and Julia Bindas in the background. (Tommy Schwartz collection)

If I'm harsh regarding the failure of *Cactus and a Rose*, it's because Gary was at the absolute peak of his abilities at the time he recorded it. There's ample evidence in unreleased recordings scattered everywhere. Here are three (there are more in the source notes):

—"It's True." Stewart wrote this song with the two sisters who had cowritten "Your Place or Mine" and "(I Can't Be) Your Backdoor," Carol and Mary Beth Anderson. The Andersons were driving around Nashville one day when they spotted Stewart walking down the street and invited him to help finish a song they'd been working on. Gary hopped in the car and "of course, on the way he lights up a joint," said Carol, laughing. "He was smoking it through his nose to save his voice." Once at the studio (Anderson thought it might've been Moman's), they finished the number and cut it, Gary singing his heart out on this old-school gospel-style ballad while pounding the eighty-eights, with Carol and Mary Beth adding knockout backing vocals. The song was later cut by sightless keyboard player Terri Gibbs for her 1981 album *Somebody's Knockin'*.

—"East Virginia Blues." Right before he cut *Cactus and a Rose*, Stewart recorded a pair of tracks out in California. Stewart wound up in the studio of Glen Castleberry after a gig at the Palomino and Glen played him some tracks he'd cut with a bunch of stellar musicians—bass and fiddle player Bill C. Graham, who worked with Glen Campbell; drummer Bartholomew Eugene Smith-Frost, aka "Frosty" (famous for being the other half of Lee "Do You Know What I Mean" Michaels's two-man band); and vocalist Spanky McFarlane (Spanky and Our Gang). They'd cut a striking instrumental track on the traditional murder ballad "East Virginia Blues," first recorded by Buell Kazee (as "East Virginia") in 1927. "Y'all mind if I sing that?" inquired Stewart, who immediately straddled a stool and tore through a pair of vocal takes. "He was singing so good it was incredible," said Castleberry. Yes, indeed. Gary's electrifying vocal doesn't opt for respectful distance to the familiar lyric as he lunges into the song's fatality—this is no quaint, old-timey museum piece—and he adds some dramatic, stuttering piano to the track, along with a breathy, mysterious whisper at the start of the vocal. Despite this being an overdub, Stewart sounds relaxed, spontaneous, and *in it,* as opposed to the heavy lifting on *Cactus and a Rose*. You wouldn't know this was a murder ballad as those verses are omitted from this version, but Stewart's menacing, sinister delivery spills blood anyway. "I'd rather live in some dark holler, where the sun never shines," he wails, going high, low, and everywhere in between. It is a virtuoso performance, with the kind of roller-coaster dynamics found in a Billy Sherrill Tammy Wynette production. Dea, who was still at RCA at the time, offered Castleberry and his partner Graham a thousand bucks to buy the master. To Glenn's dismay, Graham turned Dea down.[73]

—"Silver Cloud." "Jesus make up my dying bed / For I've been stung with the kiss of death" goes the opening couplet of this hillbilly Gothic, a grim ballad about lovers reuniting in heaven. Gary recorded a demo version of the song, which he'd written in a graveyard outside of Houston, on piano. Sonny Tackett was present. "Gary told me, 'Sonny, old graveyards will give you so much inspiration.' We were in Texas with the Toman brothers in a white van with no AC, two o'clock, three o'clock in the morning. Up comes a graveyard on the left and Gary goes, 'Hey, buddy, turn around and go back.' And here's me and Gary takin' a flashlight, an ink pen, and a guitar, goin' through these graves." Gary dusted off one old stone and "had the song. He started singing lines of it right then...as I was writin' it down, he was singin' 'em." As good as the recorded version is, "you should've heard the version in the graveyard," declared Tackett. The verse Stewart nicked off the tombstone is one that was fairly common on English and Scottish markers dating back to the 1700s (others claim earlier): "Remember me whenever you pass by / As you are now / So once was I / As I am now / So will you be / Prepare for death / and follow me."

73 Castleberry has released the song online. Unfortunately Gary's piano, opening whisper, and a few vocal flourishes were lost preparing it for release and this version just doesn't have the spook of the original, a tape of which exists.

Sometime in 1979, Stewart played a benefit for June Appal Recordings, a local label specializing in vintage and contemporary traditional music, at Clinch Valley College in Wise, Virginia. He and Sonny Tackett stopped by Whitesburg to tape songs and an interview for a local show called *Headwaters*, including "Silver Cloud."[74] Gary's sitting on a couch in a drab paneled room with an innocuous framed landscape hanging behind him. Bedecked in black, Stewart throws his whole scrawny body into the number, forcefully strumming the guitar, his quavering voice vulnerable, yet deliberate. His eyes are closed for most of the song, but he stares into the camera as he sings, "Prepare for death and follow me." The image fades out as Stewart leans into the shadows, looking solemn and a bit gutted by such a naked declaration. Watching this performance, one realizes this is exactly the inevitable ending Gary envisioned—he'd exit the planet first, Lou right behind him. "And I'll kiss your cold, cold lips with a burning kiss of fire." In the end it wouldn't go down that way.

* * *

1980 was the year it fell apart for Gary Stewart. Not only would it see the release of his worst album ever, his personal life unraveled in the wake of two back-to-back calamities.

First came the drug bust on April 15, 1980. "Me and Lou were just havin' a dispute. And the cops came." The police escorted Mary Lou out of the house. "She asked police to be present while she packed her clothing," according to the newspaper. As luck would have it, a friend had given Gary a fresh-picked ounce of pot the night before, and some of it was peeking out of its container on a coffee table. One of the officers spotted it. "After Lou left they said, 'Well, we hate to add to your problems, but what's this?'" I said, 'What does it *look* like?'" Now they wanted to look around further. "I didn't have nothin' to worry about—well, I didn't *think* I did. But someone who was there

74 The aforementioned live version of "Harlan County Highway" also comes from this show.

the night before had left a little stash which I wasn't aware of. And they went straight to it, I mean, it was right at the fucker's foot." Half an ounce of cocaine. "I didn't tell 'em that it wasn't my coke, neither, because what the hell good would've that done, y'know? That it was somebody else's stuff? That would've been another big argument, so I just said, 'Hey, charge me.' They told me it would cost my career. I said, 'So what?' My wife—my *life*—had just walked out the door. What did I have to lose?"

Gary was arrested, charged with possession of "cocaine, a plastic bag of pot, a mirror, a razor blade, and a straw." When Grandal asked how the arrest went, Gary told him, "Hell, man—they treated me like a king. Didn't even lock me up. They went and bought me a damn hamburger. I had to sign autographs."

They did grill him on where the cocaine came from, however. "Wanted to know where I got it—'Everything will be forgotten...' They put guys in the room with me after they took me downtown—slip 'em in, slip 'em out. Fortunately, I was real cool about it. I didn't clam up, it didn't scare me at all. 'I can't tell you where I got that stuff. Someone gave it to me. Now, why should I tell and get someone in trouble? You want me to be a RAT?'" He spat the word out like there was no worse fate for a Stewart.

Gary would be released on a $10,000 bond. Who bailed him out? Lou, who was also accused of having set up the bust. "Word travels fast in this town, especially when I'm seen in a cop car," said Gary. Charles Sullivan, Gary's lawyer, fought the arrest on the grounds that the police had no warrant. The charges would be dropped that December pending Stewart's "successful completion of a five-month pretrial intervention program." Still, the charges were plastered all over the local papers and for most of the rest of the year his fate was uncertain. RCA must've been thrilled.

Then, on May 1st, two weeks after the bust, Stewart got into a car accident driving the black '68 Cougar he'd bought for his son Joey, then a teenager. Lou had disappeared and Gary was on the hunt for her, checking the local motels. "He just took his eyes off the road for a minute, hit the brakes, and he just plowed right into the back end of a van," said Lou. The van passengers were a group of African Americans, one of whom would turn out to be Stewart's nurse during his hospital stay. "Totaled my brother's car," said Shannon. "It was a bad wreck."

Gary's leg was broken in three places, one of them right above the knee where it was split "completely in two," according to Lou. He was in the hospital for thirteen days and the leg was initially set wrong. Lou, who had been hiding out at her sister's place in California and was monitoring the situation from afar, was unhappy with the choice of doctor. But it wasn't until she returned home that she realized how bad the situation really was. "Gary walked with his leg kind of slewfoot. His right leg was halfway around his back! And I would tell the doctor, 'That is not right.' He said, 'That's the way he walks.' I said, 'No!' Gary could take his right leg and wrap it around the back of his head, that's how awful it was."

A year later Lou found Gary a new surgeon in nearby Stuart. "The specialist said, 'My God, your leg is sixty degrees off!' They had to go in, pull the plate and pin that was in there, cut his leg in two about eight inches higher,[75] turn it around, and put another plate and pin in. And another year later, he had to take that plate and pin out." In the meantime, Gary was gobbling pain pills to get through the situation, the start of his most serious drug dependency. He claimed unending pain in his back, his legs, his mind. It never went away.

* * *

On his birthday, May 28th, Stewart was back on the road, hobbling around on crutches to promote *Cactus and a Rose*, back in Texas at the Belle Starr in Dallas. "Survival," Stewart told Bob Allen. "I'd been off

75 "They saw it in half with a saw—just like bone in a butcher shop," Gary enthused to one reporter. Robert "Cotton" Payne recalled one scene backstage where Stewart was visiting with a fan couple backstage who were asking about the accident. Gary, who wasn't wearing any underwear, dropped his pants and, schlong hanging out, proceeded to show them his scar. "They were embarrassed as hell," said Cotton.

the road a year." The Honky-Tonk Liberation Army had fallen apart, so he resumed working with the Drugstore Cowboys.

But the Gary they encountered was not the one they knew and loved. "I could spend a week telling you about those first few years," said Randy Toman. "Especially in the beginning, it was just great, a fantasy situation—great vibes, the partyin', the girls...the crazy, ambulatory Gary was the one that was best, the most fun." The new Gary could be a moody character who instead of giving his all to a performance would "practically just mail in his stuff." Toman never knew which Stewart would show up. Or if he'd even make the flight.

One time they went to the airport and watched everybody get off the plane he was supposed to be on. Although Gary was known for being the last one off, Randy finally asked an airline rep if there was anybody left on board. Yes, came the answer. One person. Waiting for a wheelchair. "Sure enough, a skycap went on the plane with the wheelchair, and Gary comes out. And I was like, 'Oh, brother, how are we going to play tonight?' Gary kind of hobbled around and gave me a little hug. And he just whispered in my ear—'I just didn't want to walk.'" He got around fine once the skycap was out of sight.

Right after the car accident Stewart couldn't walk easily, and for a few months he "didn't play guitar at all, just an electric keyboard that we traveled around with," said Toman. They played a handful of dates opening showcases for Alabama, who were on their way up, just as Stewart headed for uncharted waters. The one good thing that came out of that brief union was that Alabama cut an unreleased Stewart song. "I was in the room when Gary pitched 'Hollywood' to Randy and Teddy," Toman recalled. The song wound up on Alabama's 1981 quadruple-platinum album Feels So Right, which stayed on the charts three years. Being coauthor of the song must've netted Stewart more than a few bucks in royalties.

* * *

Another bright spot in 1980 came on October 9th, when Gary played a hometown show at the St. Lucie County Civic Center with Hank Williams Jr. to a sellout crowd of four thousand. Stewart had a little surprise for the audience—after the fourth song he brought Gregg Allman out to join the band for "Midnight Rider" and "One Way Out." Toman had met Allman briefly backstage, where the singer was sitting in a chair like a zombie, catatonic. "He just barely raised his hand up, his eyes closed. I just thought he was wasted." But Allman rose to the occasion. When he slipped onstage and started into "Midnight Rider," Toman "got shivers down my back. The place came unglued." I can't imagine the joy Gary must've felt unleashing an Allman brother to his Florida crowd.

One person wasn't too happy about the unannounced guest—the headliner, who shared Gary's booking agent, Shorty Lavender. "Hank Jr. got pissed," said Toman. "Because it kind of stole the show." Gregg and Gary joined Williams for his encore to help appease matters. ("That's Gary's hometown," said Randy. "Did Hank Jr. really think he was gonna steal the show from a hometown favorite?") But the band still got a backstage talking-to from Williams's then-manager Merle Kilgore. Although Stewart would go on to play many a gig with Hank Jr., Gary was prevented from any future show-stealing shenanigans by a contractual agreement that he couldn't go over his allotted time as opening act. "They would fine us for every minute that we would go over," said Toman.

* * *

On November 6th came the Lone Star Cafe New York City gig described in the intro of this book, followed by Stewart and band turning up on the *Austin City Limits* show on November 30th, one-half of an episode that also featured Tony Joe White. Gary was annoyed at having to supply a set list and song timings to the TV people, and right before the taping told the band he'd ingested psychedelic mushrooms. "I didn't *really* take them," he confessed to me later. "I just wanted to keep everybody on their toes." (Others maintain he did imbibe, with a member of Joe Ely's band.) He also blew out his voice early in the taping. No matter, Gary and the boys come out swinging with "Honky-Tonkin'," letting rip a fiery set of five numbers: a desperate "Drinkin' Thing," "She's Actin' Single (I'm Drinkin' Doubles)," a demonic "Little Junior," and a carnal, shambolic "Your Place or Mine" that features some wild phrasing from Gary. Eyes hidden under the wide, downturned brim of a brown hat that barely contains his bushy black hair, Stewart looks ornery and more than a little screw-loose. He bobs and weaves before the microphone, stretching out some words with a snarl while abbreviating others for dramatic effect. This was a very different character from the joyful devil-may-care upstart who had appeared on the Luckenbach special just four years before. Pivoting around on a bum leg, saturated with drugs, he'd become the dark prince of the honky-tonks—inscrutable, uncontrollable, and, at age thirty-six, already world-weary beyond repair.

There are three guitar players on hand: Stewart, Dub Robinson, and a wild card from the past, Riley Watkins, who'd been invited back to the fold from the long-gone Imps days to be Gary's driver, road companion, and man Friday for a couple of years. "Gary always had somebody, whether it was his brother Greg or Riley, any of these different guys," said Randy Toman. "I can only imagine what kind of errands Gary sent them on." Amazingly, Toman felt the *Austin City Limits* performance was a dud, and he blames Watkins—who, according to Randy "didn't like country music. Riley was screwing up those songs...that night, he wore suspenders and a big old cowboy hat. He never dressed like that at any other gig!" Suspenders aside, *Austin City Limits* might not be the most polished performance, but I know many music fanatics who cherished the fuzzy VHS tape that made the rounds back in the day. It's far more memorable than many an episode of that show, and essential evidence of what we all loved about Gary—excitement, dynamics, and the tingle of not knowing where the hell he might land on the next note.

RCA released two more Stewart singles in 1981. The first, "She's Got a Drinking Problem" backed with "Memories Swim in Whiskey," is serviceable if not especially exciting. Although the label must've been relieved to have a couple of predictable booze tunes they could easily market, neither side of this 45 was "Drinkin' Thing," and it went no higher than thirty-six on *Billboard*. The record was produced by Eddie Kilroy, a former rodeo rider—and a fellow who deserves some kind of monument for reigniting the career of Jerry Lee Lewis in 1968 by producing his first hardcore country hit, the majestic "Another Place, Another Time."[76] But Kilroy worked no such wonders for Stewart, although he'd stick around for the beginning of the next chapter in Gary's career. Which wouldn't be pretty.

Stewart was in a precarious place as the eighties unfolded. He'd lost the producer most sympathetic to his cause and hadn't found anyone worthy of replacing him. His records were tanking, adding to the increasingly fraught relationship with his label. He didn't give a shit about commercial success, never had been good at playing the game, and now that he was bereft of hits, the pressure ratcheted up a few notches further. Stewart was not cut out for the role of "team player."

"The A&R guys that would travel around with Gary, they'd get him whatever he needed, legal or illegal," said Randy Toman. They'd expect something in return, however, and as Toman could clearly see, "Gary wasn't really cooperating too much." One A&R rep offered to take Stewart and the band out to eat if they could stop by a record store so Gary could sign autographs for thirty minutes. Stewart said, "Let's eat first, and if I'm not too tired, *then* I'll go sign records." *Poof* went the signing. Toman watched Gary blow off opportunity after opportunity. "There were so many times that my own thought was 'Wow, Gary, you're just simply not going to do anything?'" Motivating Stewart to tend to his career in any meaningful way was like pushing

76 Kilroy, then a promo man at Mercury Records, produced the record, but due to contractual obligations it was credited to Jerry Kennedy, who became Jerry Lee's primary producer at the label, assisted by none other than Roy Dea.

a rope. "The more pressure they put on him, the more he backed out," said "Boogie" Bob. "Gary was either canceling stuff—or RCA was."

Plus there was the undeniable oddness of Stewart himself. As Toman put it, "I think a lot of Gary's reputation comes from people mistakin' his weird ways—and Gary can be weird—for bein' drunk or stoned. He can talk a certain way or move awkward onstage and people would get the wrong idea." The honky-tonk audience found his eccentricities confounding, and presumed the man responsible for "Drinkin' Thing" had to be on the sauce. John Vann, one of the band's sound mixers, recalled many a fan coming up to the board asking, "'Is Stewart gonna show tonight? I'll bet he's drunk!' The truth was Gary drank mostly water, but I didn't want to ruin their image of him. What they thought Gary was and what he really was were really two different things."[77]

"It was that tragic traditional thing passed on through the years, expecting him to be too messed up to play, a No-Show Jones," said Gary's first sound mixer, Steve Cureton. As Dub Robinson put it in 1987, "Honest to God, there would be more times than not the guy would be straight as an arrow and we'd get off the stage and the club owner or promoter would say, 'He's really wasted tonight' and we'd say, 'No, that's the way he is.' Gary's just wild, and people want to see that act. Only thing is: it ain't no act."

While booze remained an occasional vice for Stewart, drugs were now a factor in everything. Those close to him point to the car accident as the line of demarcation: Gary before and Gary after. Pain pills and downers would now be constant companions. Yes, he had a high tolerance for drugs and had taken plenty of them, but that had been for recreation, not as a vocation. With his pain from the accident, his floundering career, not to mention unending conflicts with Lou,

77 These rumors persisted until the end of Stewart's life. Road manager Terry Porter recalled reporting to Gary that some fan in the club was trashing him for being drunk. "You want me to straighten his ass out?" Porter asked. Gary responded, "No, son. Sometimes bad publicity is better than no publicity at all." Nineties manager Richard McCroan maintained Stewart used this in his live act. "Gary was so smart—he'd have the stage lined with beer bottles and shot glasses. They just went to waste. He'd put his thumb over the lip of a Coors bottle and pretend he was swiggin' it and that crowd would roar. He wasn't drinkin' that shit!"

obliteration became the name of the game. Larry "Mouse" Munson didn't like what was happening to his friend. "Gary got miserable... everything was kinda snowballin'. It was painful to watch." "Boogie" Bob agreed. "After the wreck, Gary changed a lot. He got darker and more into drugs...the drugs had just taken over a big part of his personality. I hated it." Stewart wound up in the hospital three times due to overdoses. He was frequently frustrated and depressed out on the road as well as at home. "You never knew who was gettin' off that plane," said Lou. "My sweet lil' Gary or some mean sumbitch."

You can hear all this misery in "Honky-Tonk Man," a song buried on the B-side of "Let's Forget That We're Married," the second of the two orphan singles released in 1981. Nakedly autobiographical, there's nothing like it in the rest of Stewart's work. The song originated with Ron Coleman, one of the pickers who had played on "East Virginia Blues." When Stewart asked him if he'd been working on any songs, Coleman proceeded to sing him a number he'd started writing that day: "Dream of a Honky-Tonk Band." Gary liked it and told him to send a tape. "I loved the chord progression," said Stewart.

Shortly after receiving the tape, Gary hopped into an old black Mercury and showed up on "Boogie" Bob Melton's doorstep. "It was unusual, because he hardly ever drove himself anywhere. He didn't even tell me he was coming. He drove over there in his own car, all by himself, and said, 'I've got this song, we need to rewrite and finish it.'"[78] Thus "Dream of a Honky-Tonk Band" became "Honky-Tonk Man." "I just wrote about honky-tonk pickers and the life that I'd seen," said Gary.

The song was cut on October 13, 1978, the same day as "I've Just Seen the Rock of Ages," and features the usual stellar lineup of musicians: Dale Sellers on guitar, Jerry Shook on rhythm, Hal Rugg on steel, Buddy Harman on drums, Harold Strzelecki on bass, and Hargus "Pig" Robbins on piano. Roy Dea didn't care for the end

78 Stewart forgot to credit Melton on the song and it took years (and the help of Jerry Bradley) to get it corrected. Lacy J. Dalton cut a version of "Honky-Tonk Man" on her 1980 debut album. Perfectly respectable, it's more uptempo, a bit wistful, and possesses none of the desperation. You still might want to be a honky-tonk man after hearing it. Not so after Gary's evisceration.

result—he found Stewart's vocal too mannered. Gary didn't like it either. "It sounds like I'm bragging—that I'M the Honky-Tonk Man, some big star," he confessed. I nearly fell out when he told me this. Bragging?! This dirge? Johnny Horton had a 1956 hit with the same title, an exuberant ode to the honky-tonk life. It's as if Gary sticks a knife into Horton's classic, killing it dead. To hell with Stewart and Dea. This is one of Gary's greatest performances.

The song is in 3/4 time, done at a death crawl suitable for a Ray Charles ballad. The opening notes of Rugg's mournful steel sobs land you right in the black car leading this funeral procession. From the first couplet of this confession Gary grabs you by the throat and doesn't let go. "Singin' in bars/They say one day he'll be a star." He lurches into the words like a drunk off a diving board, braying with utter contempt for the fabulous world of country music. "*Him*, and his honky-tonk band." An awkward line only Stewart would come up with, he spits out the words with bile. "And it happened sure enough/The world fell in love/With the songs of the honky-tonk man." Gary reserves special venom for the words of the title, indicating his complete disgust for this cubic-zirconia "star." Here we have some of the most extreme singing of his career, more Charlie Feathers than Gary Stewart, and it guts me every time. "There's all the parties that come with the fame/And all the ladies that swoon at his name," he wails, rendering such rewards into horrors. "And they all come around/Every time he hits town/Just to see/The honky-tonk man." Stewart had been the animal in a cage, the main attraction at the Music City freak show, and he found it unbearable as well as inevitable. "Satisfaction guaranteed/They hate it when he leaves/Tonight, they saw their honky-tonk man." He's describing a wake, a requiem for how tawdry life could be beneath the big hair, rhinestone suits, and cowboy hats. Honky-tonking was all Gary knew how to do—and he'd go right on doing it, despite knowing the score. There was no other choice but to sing for his supper. And head for the next bar.

* * *

Nobody knew it at the time, but the golden era of Gary Stewart was over. He'd now hole up in his Fort Pierce sanctuary for weeks on end. If he didn't feel up to doing a show, he canceled. The long run of great songwriting was over, and at times he'd even lose interest in honing his guitar skills. The days of spontaneously recording new songs also faded away.

On the night in the trailer when I grilled Stewart about *Cactus and a Rose,* I needled him about the aftermath. "What did RCA say? 'Man, Gary, this is a turkey. You better write ten drinking songs by nine a.m. tomorrow and put your Pridesman leisure suit back on'?'"

He immediately shot back, "Yeah, so me and Dean Dillon were put together then." Jerry Bradley, the man who'd made Gary the king of the honky-tonks, had a new idea, a last-ditch effort to keep him on the charts. The Outlaws had been a huge hit for RCA, so why not pair Gary with a young up-and-comer as an outlaw duet team?

This ridiculous concept would demolish what was left of Stewart's RCA career, leaving Gary banished to the honky-tonk wilderness. And there would be drugs, drugs, and more drugs on the way down. Fucking up not only Gary, but other members of the Stewart clan. Like crazy, mustachioed brother Gerald, the most polarizing member of the clan, who'd nearly die in a dope smuggler's plane crash on October 12, 1981. But that's far from the only disaster involving Gerald Douglas Stewart...

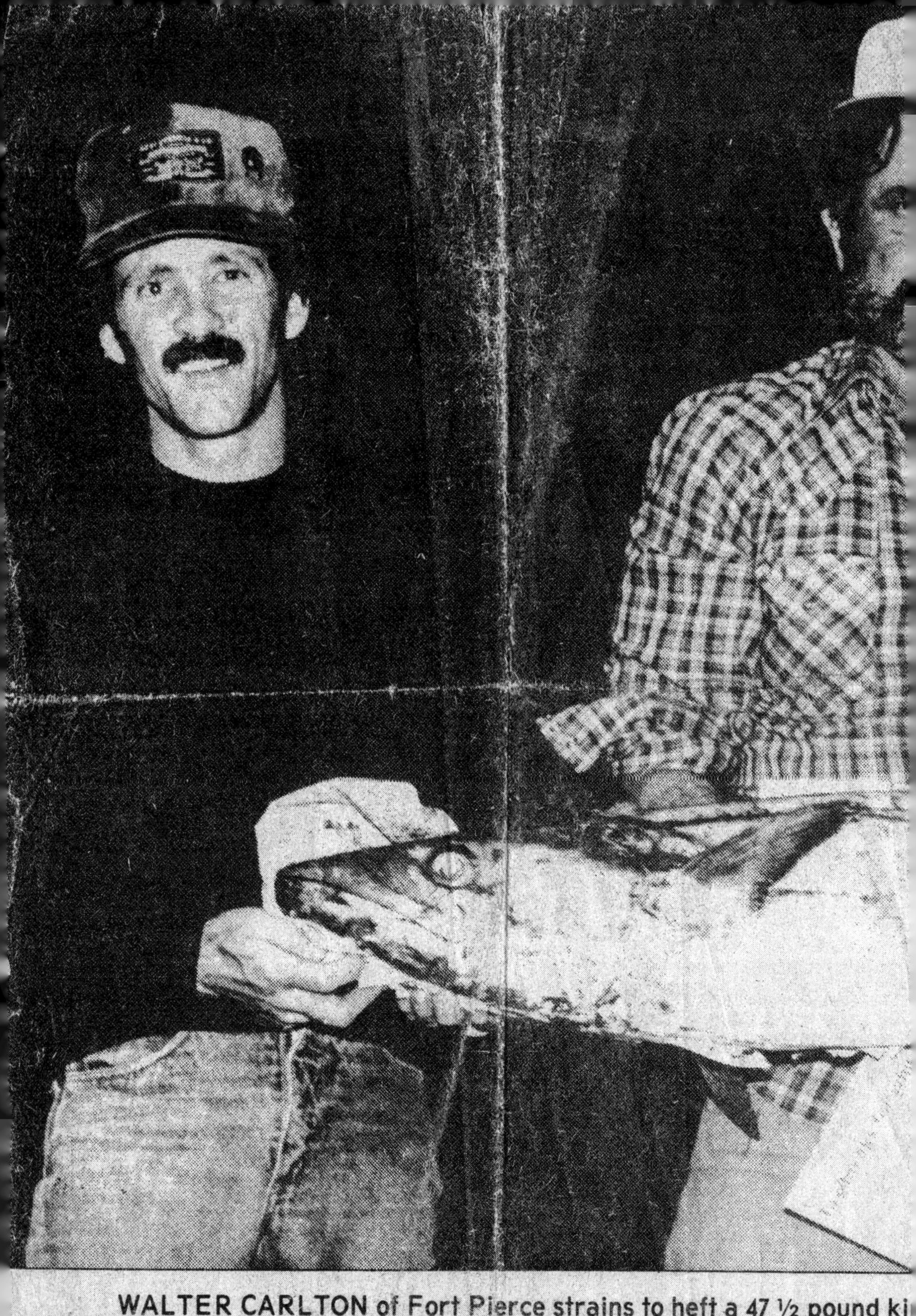

WALTER CARLTON of Fort Pierce strains to heft a 47 ½ pound ki
off the South Beach while fishing with Dr. Calvin Browning. The b

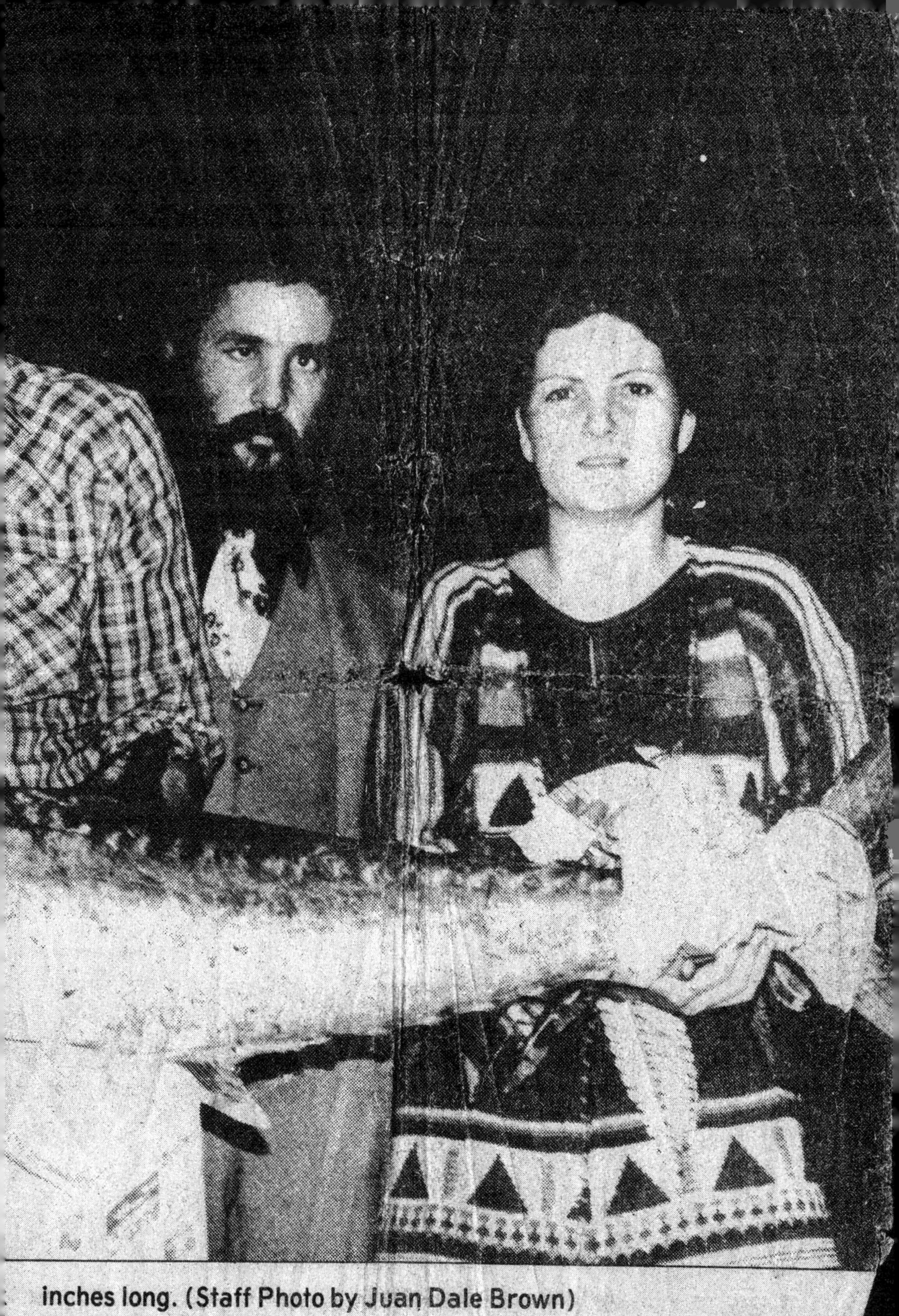

inches long. (Staff Photo by Juan Dale Brown)

13

GERALD

NICK STEWART: Gerald was a pistol. Ol' Magnum. Gerald was a good-looking guy before all that stuff happened to him. I remember standing next to him one time at one of the family funerals. He looked like a damn movie star. Gerald was an athlete. When he went to Little League tryouts, he'd hit a home run. Of course, nobody in his family cared anything about that. He wasn't a big guy, but was more muscular than the rest of the Stewarts, especially when he was young. Man, Gerald was the devil on two feet, but the nicest guy that you'd ever meet. Gerald had that Stewart charm. A super charmer. He had some big demons.

SHANNON ASHBURN: We all loved Gerald. Because he was so damn funny. Gerald took care of my dad. I can remember times when my dad would come off the road and in the kitchen would be Gerald makin' my dad cornbread, buttermilk. Gerald could cook. My dad went through this phase where he wanted fruit salad. And Gerald would come over, cut up all these oranges, citrus, apples, and grapes and make gallons and gallons of fruit salad for Dad.

JASON STEWART: Gerald was the youngest. The baby of the family. He was always getting in trouble. Gerald always had something going on, because he was "Gary's little brother." That was his way into things.

LAURIE RASTRELLI: He was the black sheep of the family. Gerald stole his mother's pocketbook one time. He was at my dad's house. Gary came over—"Gerald, give Mommy back her pocketbook." Gary got her purse back. And the money. Crazy. My sister's funny—she said to Gerald, "You dirty crook, dirty crook, you stole your momma's pocketbook."

STAN SPENCE: Georgia would always slip Gerald money. Gerald was Georgia's favorite, you ask any of 'em. Gerald would go over and rub his mama's back and he would say, "Mama, I need some money." And she'd say, "Oh, Gerald...I'll give you some." She'd always flip him some money, and then me and Gerald would go out. He was crazy as shit. Gerald was hyperactive, like on steroids, man. He was a left-handed drummer.

GEORGIA STEWART: Gerald's a good drummer! Gerald can play the piano, too. He's really got rhythm.

JIMMY SMITH: Gary was very particular about drummers. His favorite drummer was Gerald. Gerald was the baddest motherfucker. Gary said when Gerald was on, nobody could touch that fucker.

TRAMPAS STEWART: We used to hear him drum all the time. His drum set was in the barn. Gerald thought he was going to be the next Gary. We thought he was gonna be the next thing. Gerald really had the potential to do it. But once his marriage didn't work, that's when Gerald said, "Screw all this normal stuff. I'm just going all out bein' a rock star."

GINA STEWART: Gary said he was the best drummer he ever heard. If he could've stayed off drugs and kept his dick in his pants, Gary woulda kept him out on the road.

TOMMY SCHWARTZ: Gerald was an excellent drummer. He was just hard to be around all the time. You never knew what he was gonna do. Gary said, "You can't have Gerald around, because he'll try to fuck your dog."

DALE THOMAS, guitar player: When we played Frankie n' Johnny's, Gerald would come in with Gary, and after a while he played drums with us. And we lived upstairs, there was a big apartment. Every break Gerald would go around and pick up all the chicks and take them upstairs. And give 'em coke. I go upstairs on a break and there'd be, like, fifteen or twenty chicks up there. He's just gettin' 'em all high. And I just thought that was absolutely insane. There was cops all over the place, looking for that kind of stuff. Nothing ever happened for some reason.

Gary was the older brother, and I think he felt like that it was his job to keep Gerald in line. Gary and him used to fight like little kids. I remember one time, I think it was about Gerald bringing the chicks upstairs. Gary didn't think it was a smart thing, and he was jumping up and down on the bed just yelling at Gerald. He looked like a six-year-old kid havin' a tantrum.

RANDY TOMAN: Gerald was the biggest pain in the ass. He'd say to Gary, "Hey, listen, Mr. Big Star, you're just my brother." Gerald made Gary look like Mary Poppins.

BRUCE HUNTER, singer, friend: Roy Dea told me one time he come down to Gary's in Fort Pierce. He just got to the back door and heard a bunch of hollering and screaming. The door's open, and there was Lou. Gary and Gerald was on the floor going at it. And Lou's standin' there tellin' Gary, "Watch your throat, Gary, watch your throat!"

STAN SPENCE: Did they tell you why they called Gerald Magnum? That sucker had a twelve-inch cock. I ain't lying. Gerald was a monster.

ROBERT BATTAGLIA, friend: The Stewarts are notoriously known for having Kentucky Derby–sized cocks. If Gerald turned a corner, he knocked over a glass. Like, a foot long or something.

NICK STEWART: He probably had the biggest white dick in history. He outdid all of 'em.

JIMMY SMITH: Gerald had no fuckin' couth about it. He'd just whip that motherfucker out in front of anybody. I mean, we'd be sitting in the Rialto's bar—"Take a look at this!" "I don't want to see your fuckin' dick, Gerald, you make me feel insignificant."

ROBERT BATTAGLIA: Gerald and I should have been arrested a thousand times. I mean, he would bring me girls.

STAN SPENCE: Gerald was a pussy hound. I mean to tell you he would not stop. That guy was just all over every woman he ever met. Gerald, he'd get in a world full o' shit. One time we were at this motel and the manager called me and said, "Stan, you gotta get ahold of your drummer. He's chasing my maids around." Before he got his face crushed in, Gerald would go to any girl, just walk right up there and start feeding them a line. Just a natural talent. Very rarely would they get offended. He'd usually get the phone number. Every night. Yeah, his number-one priority: go out and get laid. Gary had women throwing themselves at him. But Gerald, he'd seek and destroy.

Georgia, Gary, Grandma Easter, and Gerald Stewart at José Pena's pool. (Gina Stewart collection)

BARBARA ANNE PETERS: Gerald could be a little bit eccentric. Mary Lou said he would come in her house and take stuff. She said, "I don't care if Gerald tells you he's about to shit himself. You tell him I got you locked in this house. I locked you in when I left, and you can't open it." She just about wouldn't let Gerald come in if Gary wasn't home.

LAURIE RASTRELLI: Gerald came to see Mary Lou in the hospital one time and he just whips it out and starts jerkin' off. His brother's wife! Then she picked Gerald up in her car once and he started again. She said Gerald would just do that all the time. So she told him to stop. And she said that he wouldn't. She pulled over to the side of the road, opened up the passenger-side door, and kicked Gerald out of the car, with his pants down to his knees. I said, "You did not." She said, "I did, too. And I went home and told Gary. Gary said, 'Well, where's my brother?' He's on the side of the road with his pants down to his ankles." Mary Lou was a tough one.

SHANNON ASHBURN: That character from *Tommy,* Uncle Ernie, who sang "Fiddle About"? That's what my mom always called Gerald, "Uncle Ernie."

POLLY DAVIS: I don't know what to tell you about Gerald. He was a species of his own. I don't think he really had any real morals. I mean, he just didn't care who he did or what he did. He didn't care whose wife he was fucking, or whose girlfriend or anything else. He just loved drugs. Any way he could get them.

SONNY TACKETT: The boy had something wrong with him. Psychologically-wise, because there is nothing on earth that he wouldn't screw.

BRENDA CASEY: Gerald was crazy. Seriously crazy. Gerald tried to put the moves on me. First time I met him. It was like, "Get away from me. Or I'll kill you." I meant it.

LAURIE RASTRELLI: I was sixteen, and my sister and I walked to a 7-Eleven. And Gerald was there in his van. And he's like, "Hey, y'all want to go do some coke?" Of course, I'm like, "Yeah." So he's like, "Well, come on, let's go to my house and we'll do some coke." Took me and my sister there—didn't have any coke, but he grabbed my arm, pulled me in his room. Dead-bolted the door. Turned the music up full blast. My sister is beatin' on the door. I kind of, like, freaked out. Well, anyways, he raped me.

JIMMY SMITH: Gerald chummed her up with a sack of coke, raped her, then he passed out. So she got out of the room and run all the way to this guy Ricky Ray. A mile run. Ricky Ray was a Hells Angel. A bad motherfucker.

TOMMY SCHWARTZ: Ricky Ray was a crazy son of a bitch.

LAURIE RASTRELLI: Ricky Ray's mom woke him up. I told him what happened. He didn't say anything except, "Mama, take care of her." He had a real big, high four-wheel-drive truck, and took off. He went to Gerald's. Busted out the jalousies where he was at, picked him up out of bed with a knife, and slit his throat.

JIMMY SMITH: Ricky Ray sticks a Buck knife under Gerald's chin and says, "Did you rape Laurie?" He says, "Yeah." And he sliced that motherfucker from ear to ear.

LAURIE RASTRELLI: I went back down to my dad's. When I walked in, I see Gerald, and I'm going, "Oh my God." Gerald's sitting in my dad's kitchen with a white towel that was dripping with blood. The towel was red, with probably an inch of blood on the floor. I mean, a lot.

JIMMY SMITH: There was a puddle of blood, blood, blood...it was fuckin' terrible. I'm still tryin' to get it out of the floor.

Ricky Ray said to my dad, "Well, Jimmy, you want me to go ahead and finish him off? Motherfucker raped your daughter." He said, "FUCK NO, get that motherfucker out of my house!" So Ricky Ray dragged Gerald back out to his truck by the hair on his head, took him to Lawnwood Hospital, and kicked the motherfucker out. They saved his ass. He coulda died.

LAURIE RASTRELLI: No, I didn't think about going to the police. We did it the old-fashioned way, I guess.

Gina was goin' with Walter Carlton, and they show up in my dad's front yard. Gina starts comin' towards me and swinging—"My brother didn't rape you. You're lyin'!" So Walter beat the shit out of Gina.[79]

I heard they put a hit out on Ricky Ray. You hear things, I don't know. But that ain't how Ricky Ray died. I heard he got poisoned in prison.

Gerald tried to make a pass at me again after that. Gerald was sick. He really was. Because my friend Kim Carlton said he raped her, too.

KIM CARLTON, Walter's daughter: Gerald was a beast. I'm telling you, he was a total sicko. He tricked me to come into the house. I had gone by looking for Tommy Schwartz. So I came into the living room.

---

79 Gina didn't recall this fight, and maintained the first she'd ever heard of the rape accusation was when I asked her about it. She also claimed that Ricky Ray left her brother in a garbage can after slitting his throat.

And Gerald goes "Shhhhhhhh" and pulls me into the bedroom. The next thing I know, the guy turns up music and throws me on the bed. I could not get away from the guy. I mean, he pawed all my clothes off and was slammin' me on the bed so hard. I was out of breath. And I couldn't scream louder than the music, either. I was afraid. I never told anyone. I knew if my father had ever known that, he would have killed Gerald.

JIMMY SMITH: One time Gerald put on a ski mask and stole Gary's purple buds—it was the absolutely best shit you ever smoked, fuckin' purple—and that's what made Gary put bars on his windows. We knew right away who did it. Another time Gerald went to Larry Munson's house all fucked up and was trying to get in the front door. Mouse geeked out and shot Gerald with a little automatic. But Gerald was invincible!! That fucker had nine lives!!

JO ANN GREGORY (Larry Munson's wife): It was in the middle of the night. We were all in bed. There was a pounding on the door. Larry didn't wake up, I did. I could hear yelling. There might have been a headlight in the window, like a car was out there. And I woke up Larry. He picked up a gun. It was a time when a lot of drugs were around and it was not unusual for a home invasion. And people beat up, harmed, whatever. That was not an unusual thing around here.

LARRY "MOUSE" MUNSON: Anybody that would come to my house knew to go around back. Gerald had been to my house two million times, man. Why he ever went to that front door I have no idea. I was worried about another situation. I was worried about getting robbed. By somebody else.

JO ANN GREGORY: Larry went to the door, and when he went to open it, he said Gerald pushed it.

LARRY "MOUSE" MUNSON: I was just going to crack the door a bit. When I opened it, it was Gerald, and he pushed that door right in on me. And I just shot, pulled the trigger. He said, "Man, what did do you do that for?" I hit him twice.

Gerald was all dressed up, man. In a white cowboy hat, boots, one of those white fancy cowboy shirts with embroidered pockets and pearl buttons. I mean he's decked out, man. I said, "Oh fuck, Gerald, get in here, man." He was stunned, it knocked him back a bit. I just snatched him through the door and got a bunch of towels. I pulled off his shirt. He was leakin' bad, man. Two shots—both of them through 'n' through shots. Put four holes in him, his arm and side, in and the out.

JO ANN GREGORY: I had grabbed my son and hid for a little bit. And when I got up the courage to come out, Gerald was just bleeding profusely. They were standing there. I think they were both kind of in shock. Larry wasn't doing much, he was just letting Gerald bleed. It was right in his stomach. I said, "Oh my God, he's gonna die. You gotta get him to the hospital." The whole time I'm thinking, "Gerald is gonna die right here."

LARRY "MOUSE" MUNSON: I said, "We gotta get you patched up, brother." So I load him up in the car and took him to the hospital. Of course, the police had been called. I didn't know what to tell them, so I said it was a hunting accident. And here Gerald is all dressed up in his boots, hat, pearl-button shirt. It looked way, way out of place. There were all kinds of questions: "What were you hunting?" I said, "Hogs."

JO ANN GREGORY: On their way to the hospital they decided to say it was a hog-hunting accident. I guess Gerald went along with it. I went along with it.

Gerald Stewart of South 35th St was hunting with his friend Larry Munson of Indian River Drive about 7PM when they spotted a hog and started chasing it. Munson's .22 cal. rifle allegedly discharged while the men were running after the hog. The shot grazed the right front side of Stewart's chest, then struck him in the right front forearm and exited at the upper portion of the elbow.

—*St. Lucie News Tribune*, February 21, 1981

LARRY "MOUSE" MUNSON: It really wasn't too bad. I think Gerald spent the night in the hospital. Gerald was as crazy as Gary, he just didn't get any notoriety. One time I heard a bang and tires squealin'. I look out the front window and Gerald's layin' in the front yard. And I said, "God damn, Gerald, what happened to you, brother?" "Oh man, these two guys beat me up." I said, "Oh shit, let me help you." He said, "Don't worry about it, man. They were amateurs."

Inspectors with the Federal Aviation Administration (FAA) said Ben Masters and Gerald Stewart were "probably poaching and looking for wildlife" when their Piper Cub crashed on the Adams Ranch Monday night.

—*Palm Beach Post*, October 14, 1981

STAN SPENCE: I'll just tell you the truth. Ben had a plane. He was pilotin' it.[80] Gerald was pushing bales out, they were flying low. They was doing this at night, dropping the bales on Raulerson's ranch. And Ben clipped a tree and flipped the plane upside down. They were lucky they didn't catch on fire. They were spotted by a helicopter pilot takin' a student for a ride or something who spotted it down there. And they were both still alive. Ben was paralyzed, but he miraculously came out of that—he broke his back then he got better. Gerald lost his right eye.[81] His whole right side of his face was crushed, and his right ankle got broken so bad, it was twisted around backwards, he was lucky they didn't have to amputate his foot.

---

80 This was the third airplane crash involving pilot Ben Masters. At the time, he was under indictment (along with other members of his family) in Operation Bancoshares, a case charging a network of approximately forty drug smugglers dubbed "the Mullet Mafia" that was run by Donald Raulerson, a one-legged Fort Pierce drug kingpin who had "shot himself in the foot with a shotgun to keep himself from goin' to Vietnam," according to one source. In 1985 Masters—plus his mother and father, the latter of which was an ex–Fort Pierce cop—pleaded guilty to trying to kill an FBI agent. While serving time at the Atlanta Federal Penitentiary, Masters and another inmate murdered William Bright, also incarcerated. Henry Benjamin Masters was transferred to a high-security supermax prison in Florence, Colorado, where he remains. According to this source, at one point Ted Kaczynski was in the cell to the left of Masters, and in the cell to his right was Timothy McVeigh. Masters is alleged to be a kingpin in the white supremacy movement.

81 Gerald isn't the only one-eyed Stewart. His brother Greg also lost an orb. "I was twelve, bicycle tire. I was puttin' air in it and it blowed up on me. Gerald lost his at twenty-seven. We both had plastic eyes. I still got mine." At least one of the one-eyed Stewarts was known to offer an eye as collateral to drug dealers until he could make payment in full. I won't say which.

JIMMY SMITH: I asked him, "Gerald, did you lose a nut?" He said, "No, it just fucked me up down there for a long time." I think they had to sew his dick back on or somethin'. It took a whole spool of thread.

NICK STEWART: I was in the hospital same time as Gerald was after the plane crash. I had a knee operation. Everybody had said that his testicles have been ripped off by the joystick in the airplane. And I got on my crutches, went down, and I said, "All right, Gerald—show me your fuckin' pecker. Because I heard it ripped your damn balls off." There was a hole, I forget if it was on the left side or right side. Where that joystick had went up right in him.

STAN SPENCE: The joystick did go up into his ball sack.

LAURIE RASTRELLI: Karma.

TOMMY SCHWARTZ: When Gerald got out of the hospital he was over at Garna's upholstery shop, pulling it out to show everybody. The damn thing look like Frankenstein's head.

JIMMY SMITH: I got me a job at Walmart. And every day I'd go over to Georgia's after work, maybe buy a couple Percocets [laughs]. Georgia said, "Jimmy, Gerald needs a job." I was in good with the boss, me and him were tight. I said, "You know Gerald ain't gonna do a good job. He's gonna fuck it up. It's gonna make me look bad."After about six months of her hammering me, I buckled under pressure and got him a job at Walmart. Gerald was trying. He really was. And while he was working at Walmart with me, some old freaky guy came in and was messing with the garden center cashier, being frisky with her. And Gerald popped that glass eye out and he said, "I got my fuckin' eye on you." That guy hauled ass outta there. Gerald always had fun with that eye.

STAN SPENCE: I'd set my beer down on the bar and say, "Gerald, keep an eye on that beer for me." He said, "Okay, I will" and he'd pop out his glass eye and put it on a napkin on top of my beer bottle.

NICK STEWART: All I remember about that eye was Gerald stickin' it in my drinking glass one night. He thought that that was so fun. He stole one of my trucks one time. Ford Bronco.

SHANNON ASHBURN: Among many other vehicles Gerald pawned. He'd pawn anything that wasn't tied down.

NICK STEWART: It took me about a week to get the Bronco back. I'd looked for him for two or three days. I wouldn't call the police on him. I finally found him and wanted to kill him.

TRAMPAS STEWART: After the plane wreck Gerald was not the same as before. Definitely a different person. A complete, 100 percent addicted crackhead.

SHANNON ASHBURN: We lost Gerald to drugs. Addiction runs in the family.

GINA STEWART: Gerald was sweet as can be, but buddy, get him on meth, you did not want to be around him. Gerald hocked his truck. Hell, he hocked his eye one time.

JO ANN GREGORY: Gerald was always doing crazy things. He went to another friend of mine, neighbor a couple doors down. She barely knew him, and he asked her if he could go in and use the bathroom and she said, "Sure." He locked himself in the bathroom for about an hour. She had to come and get Larry to get him out. She swore up and down Gerald was in there sniffing panties, because she had her hamper in there—"My daughter's panties! Jesus! Get him out of here!"

Suspect/defendant entered the store via the north entrance and walked to the lingerie dept. He then took two (2) pair of panties from the rack and placed them in a black Radio Shack bag. The suspect/defendant then began to walk speedily to the exit doors with no intentions of paying for the concealed merchandise. The suspect/defendant was stopped and detained and the merchandise recovered with a total value of $16.00. On officer's arrival the suspect/defendant was advised of his arrest and transported to the County Jail.

—Gerald Stewart arrest report, August 1, 1998, retail theft

TRAMPAS STEWART: He was so screwed up towards the end. His lips were cracked up and you could just see that he's been up for days. And he was just looking for a place to do the next bump, the next rock, and we had to push him away two or three times. It's like, "Please don't do this here."

STAN SPENCE: Shannon met me at the hospital in Fort Pierce. Gerald was in a coma, he's got tubes in him. Gina and Shannon both witnessed this, the nurse, too. I says, "Gerald, wake up. It's Stan, come on. We got places to go, women to do." And I swear to God, his one eye opened up. He come out of his coma right then and Gina's screamin', "It's a miracle, it's a miracle! Stan, I knew you could do it!" Gerald lived another two or three years after that.

JIMMY SMITH: He had horrible seizures, wasn't supposed to live many a night. Gary and Lou would call me and tell me to pray for him. I would sometimes drive to the hospital two towns over and sneak into the hospital at four in the morning and lay hands on him and he would get out the next day. Not because of me but because of faith. I do not take credit for that! I was in jail the last time. And he passed away.

GINA STEWART: When Gerald passed, honey, he was purple. And Bill Yates from the Yates Funeral Home couldn't fix him up enough. To where we put a net over the casket.

I still got his eye, I ain't shittin' ya. His girlfriend Dotty wanted to make a necklace with it. I said, "Fuck you, that's my baby brother."

JIMMY SMITH: Me and Gerald, we were brothers, man. I mean, I couldn't hate him. Even after what he did to my sister. I still just love the guy.

SHANNON ASHBURN: We were inseparable. Gerald was a very funny guy. And a sex pervert. He had his dark side, like all the Stewarts.

Gerald Stewart died January 16, 2002, at Lawnwood Regional Medical Center. The obituary from the local St. Lucie News Tribune *had a picture of Gerald in a cowboy hat, playing his drums in front of an American flag. His death certificate lists his occupation as: "Professional musician, drummer."*

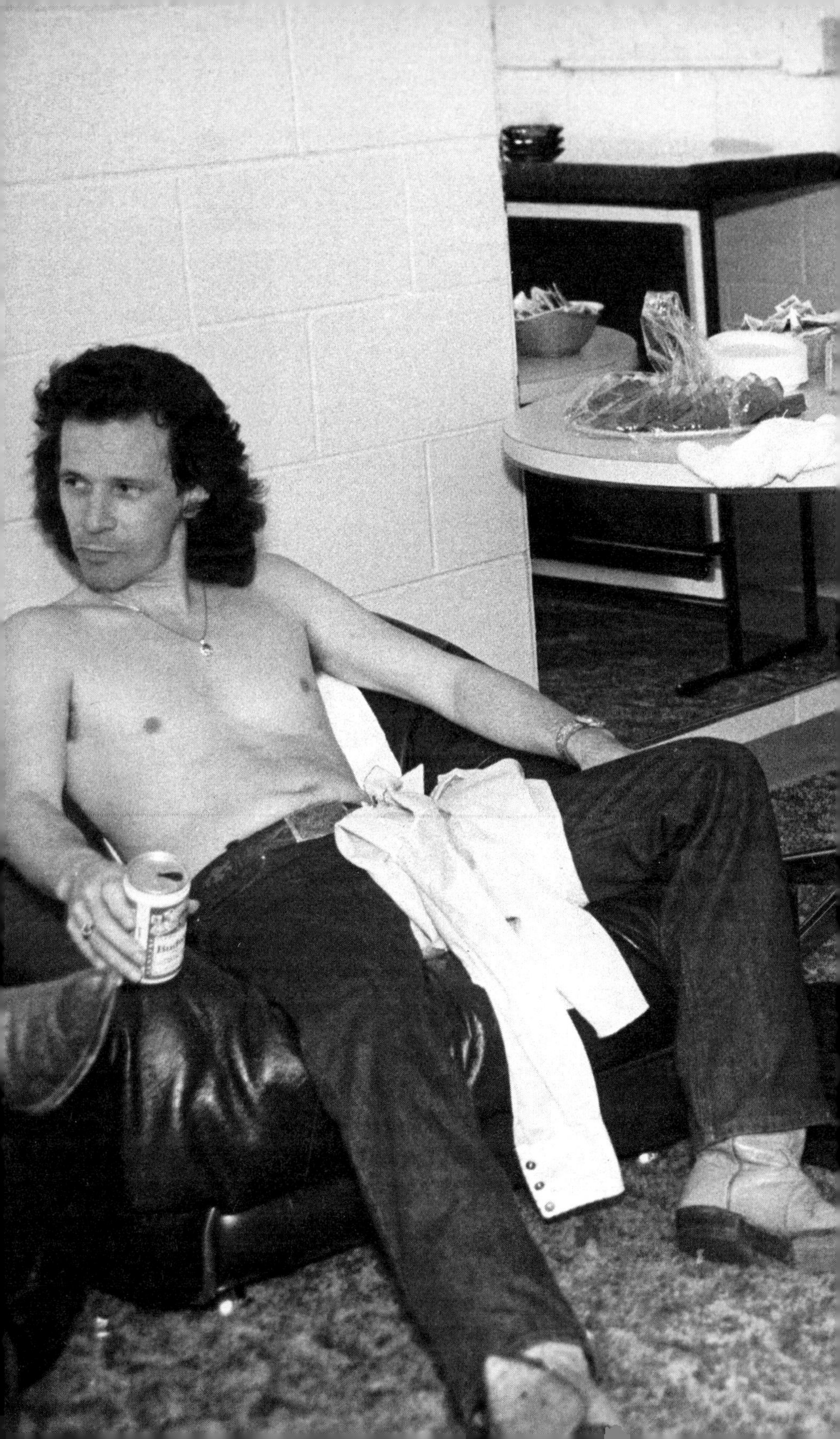

TENNESSEE

14

AN IRREVERSIBLE DESCENT INTO MAJOR SEVENTHS

Man, the raunchier, the weirder, the crazier, the wilder – that's where Gary wanted to be.

– Dean Dillon

Elvis Presley was often a reference point with Gary Stewart. No surprise there. He'd grown up on Presley's early Sun/RCA material and knew it backward and forward. Every Christmas at the Stewart Manor came a ritual—decorating the tree to "Blue Christmas." But Gary was extremely critical of the King as well. With very few exceptions, he thought Presley was truly great only "up until the first album he did comin' out of the army—*Elvis Is Back!*"

I maintained there was good later Elvis stuff, you just had to dig.

"You have to dig pretty damn *deep*, though," Stewart countered. "The plan was to do a movie, and pull a song—he wasn't recording to make records, he was recordin' to make fuckin' *movies,* and they were pieces of *shit*. Which Elvis even admitted himself! Hey, the fuckin' Colonel was his problem. He couldn't get out of doin' the movie shit. *That* is what happened to Elvis."

Gary got very worked up discussing this. Angry about bad Elvis! I told him I felt the same way about his duets with Dean Dillon. And I was just as pissed off. He didn't argue. "Jerry Bradley gave me *another chance*," he said wearily. "Hey, I wasn't makin' any money. It wasn't workin' out, okay? I was given another chance—'Okay, try it with you and Dean.'" Gary knew the score.

* * *

Pardon me, dear reader, for the revulsion I am about to express over the cover of Stewart's next album, *Brotherly Love*, his first effort with Dillon. Keep in mind that in the years just before first seeing it I had discovered those great albums cut by Roy Dea, then witnessed Gary's ferocious live performances at the Lone Star and on *Austin City Limits*. Furthermore, his most recent release in this period had been 1981's *Greatest Hits*, a stellar collection whose cover featured Stewart in all his dark, malevolent glory. And the majestic B-side "Honky-Tonk Man" was the last thing he'd released.

So to be confronted with this bland, drippy cover picturing Gary standing next to a purported honky-tonk buddy was definitely a shock. Stewart didn't need a baby-faced sidekick—a Robin, a Tonto, a Sammy Petrillo. He was Gary Goddamn Stewart, King of the Honky-Tonks. I thought *Brotherly Love* sported the worst RCA album cover since Hank Snow teamed up with an equally superfluous partner, Kelly Foxton (look it up). And once I heard the music within that sleeve, I'd detest the whole thing even more. *Cactus and a Rose* might have been a well-intentioned misstep, but *this*? *Brotherly Love* made me embarrassed for Gary. A king should not be treated this way.

Now, don't get me wrong. Dean Dillon, a fine songwriter. He wrote/cowrote many a hit, including a string of number ones for George Strait. And there's no doubt he loves Gary Stewart—he praises

Gary to the skies whenever his name comes up—"the greatest honky-tonk singer to ever take a breath." But he certainly wasn't a match for Stewart as a singer, and he's a very orthodox songwriter, with none of the weird turns of lyric nor music that you find in Stewart. Their pairing made little sense.

"Gary was like a prizefighter," said Steve Hinson. "You don't put him with some young coming-up guy. Their music is so different—Dean is a great ballad writer and his stuff always sounded current and contemporary, up-to-the-minute. Stewart, on the other hand, was kind of a throwback to an earlier time." Over 1982–83 they recorded and performed live as a duet, writing one song together ("An Empty Glass") that can stand with Gary's previous work. A certain softness and sentimentality crept into Stewart's songwriting with Dillon's arrival and—though I absolutely hate to say this—Stewart's music became a little boring and predictable, two words that should never be associated with him.

Gary was generous in his praise of Dillon, but he didn't seem particularly proud of the two records they'd done together. "Hey, I learned so much from Dean. That little fucker had a lot of valuable information about songwriting. That was a different stage of life, I guess...major sevenths." Gary repeatedly referenced that particular chord when it came to his work with Dillon, and he credited Dean for introducing it to him. "It's a different little chord progression...we used a lot of major sevenths."

Referencing dreaded seventies crowd-pleasers Chicago, musician Dale Lawrence maintains this particular chord "makes anything sound like 'Color My World,'" and it became a byword of mediocrity when I'd spar with Gary. Whenever Stewart mentioned a song I felt was a little more turkey-legged than the rest, I'd blurt out, "MAJOR SEVENTHS!" Sometimes he'd laugh, others, he'd want to throw a knife in my direction. Eventually Gary let slip that he "got that chord out of my system." "Good," muttered this nut.

* * *

Nearly ten years younger than Gary, Dean Dillon was born March 26,1955, in Lake City, Tennessee. His early influences were Merle Haggard and Sweet Baby James. During a discussion at the Country Music Hall of Fame with Michael Gray, Dillon laid it out, admitting that he wanted to "try to weld the two together—the James Taylor melodies and honesty of the Haggard stuff, and see what you can get out of it." He recorded for Shelby Singleton's Plantation Records as Dean Dalton in the mid-seventies before Jerry Bradley heard him on some demos and signed him to RCA. It was Bradley who renamed him Dillon, pouncing on the surname from an impromptu opening of the phone book. "He liked names with two of the same letters—y'know, Waylon Jennings had two *N*s in it," Dillon told Gray. Once again, the inspiration was outlaw. "Dillon was a bad guy...bank robber," Bradley told Paul Leslie, perhaps muddling John Dillinger with US Marshal Matt Dillon of *Gunsmoke*.

Dillon quickly made a name for himself as a songwriter—he and writing partner Frank Dycus are credited with the first hits of George Strait's career, "Unwound"[82] and "Down and Out" in 1981, leading off a long string of smashes they'd write for him. Dycus, who'd grown up poor as one of thirteen children in Hardmoney, Kentucky, told David Dawson, "Dean Dillon is a walking song title index, he'll open his mouth and a song title will come out without him even knowing it." As a solo artist Dillon recorded a handful of singles for RCA, all cowritten by him, most of them produced by Bradley himself, like Dillon's initial foray for the label in 1979, "I'm into the Bottle (To Get You out of My Mind)," which hit thirty on the country chart. They were good honky-tonk efforts, unlike, strangely enough, the direction he'd head into with Stewart. That same year, Moe Bandy and Joe Stampley released a novelty duet single "Just Good Ol' Boys," which went to number one and led

82 "Unwound" had been written in 1981 for Johnny Paycheck, but he'd been arrested for statutory rape, so when producer Blake Mevis went over to Dillon's house hunting for songs for "a new kid from Texas," they gave it to Mevis and he cut it with Strait.

to a succession of hit albums for the pair. Dean Dillon has said repeatedly that this was the inspiration for Bradley pairing him with Stewart.

Bandy and Stampley "were the hottest duet in country music—Moe and Joe. And Bradley was trying to combat that with two villains," Dillon told Gray. How Bradley saw this as an apt concept for Stewart eludes me. Bandy and Stampley were likeable oafs who would even squeeze cheap laughs out of their disbelief over Culture Club's success ("Where's the Dress"). It appears Bradley thought Stewart and Dillon could deliver a less comedic "outlaw" alternative, but they'd come up short. Truthfully, I can't imagine Stewart singing duets with *anyone*, except maybe...Dolly Parton?

"Boogie" Bob Melton first introduced Dillon to Gary at the annual Nashville Fan Fair in 1980 or so. He and Dillon were running buddies at the time. "It was right after Dean signed with RCA. Dean was just a super Gary Stewart fan." Dillon was also friends with Wayne Carson. "Wayne would go, 'Listen to this song I wrote,'" Dillon told Gray. "I would go, 'Man, the song's awesome. But the singer's more awesome.' I just thought [Gary] was phenomenal." As he elaborated to me, Dillon thought Stewart "was really different from mainstream country, and I was attracted to that because I love anything different." Sadly, the untamed edge he so admired would get sanded away as soon as Dillon entered the studio with his hero.

* * *

Once Jerry Bradley dreamt up the concept, Gary and Dean were off to write songs at Spence Manor, an infamous Music City hotel featuring Webb Pierce's lovably garish guitar-shaped swimming pool as part of their grounds. Spence Manor was known as a hangout for Elvis as well as numerous country stars, songwriters, and assorted Music City flotsam. There, in Room 607, the pair started "writin' and writin'," as Stewart recalled. "Finally—at last—we came up with *one* song. It was about four o'clock in the morning and Dean says, 'Listen, we've got to get to bed, because we got a picture session tomorrow.' I says, 'Dean, if we ain't got no records, son, there ain't gonna be no need for no fucking picture session.' So we came up with a couple things that weren't...that... great, but it was a start. Later on, we did write some good songs." Those elusive good songs...

"I never got the impression that Gary was very impressed with Dean," said "Boogie" Bob. "I don't think being pushed into the duet deal sat well with Gary. That happened around a time when he was not getting the best treatment from RCA." Steve Hunter, a Kentucky musician close to both Stewart and Dillon, agreed. "I think Gary kind of resented the fact that they had paired him up with Dean. Not the fact that it was Dean—just with *anybody* else." Due to his songwriting success, Dillon would manage to survive the union. Gary wasn't so lucky. "He had a great career before we hooked up," Dillon deadpanned to Michael Gray.

* * *

Eddie Kilroy was chosen to produce *Brotherly Love*. He'd been cutting Jerry Lee Lewis, Mickey Gilley, Faron Young, Roy Head, and Billy Joe Shaver. He'd produced solo singles on both Gary and Dean in 1981 as well. "Jerry Bradley called and asked me to do it. He never mentioned Moe Bandy and Joe Stampley. It was just putting two wild people that he had on the label—'These guys are nuts, what happens if we put them together?'"

The immediate result was a truckload of substance abuse. As Dillon readily admits, "Back in those days, man, I was just wide open—drinkin' a fifth of Jack a day and snortin' all the cocaine I could get my hands on, and Gary was pretty much the same way." Putting the two of them together was like "pouring gasoline on gasoline." RCA was finally marketing Stewart as an outlaw, with the back cover of *Brotherly Love* showing the disheveled duo deep in conversation at a table littered with beer cans and whiskey bottles. Unfortunately, the music within the album made Gary and Dean seem about as dangerous as a pair of Music City jaywalkers.

* * *

The eighties, a hollow-eyed cultural dead zone. The loose free fall of the seventies had ended in a chilly dawn with a gray hangover. Reagan was captain of the ship, with his First Lady bequeathing such gifts to the public as her infamous "Just Say No" campaign when not posing for giggly photo-ops in Mr. T's lap. There was a sense of dislocation to it all. Mainstream rock music was lost in a cloud of big hair and power ballads, with even Bob Dylan succumbing to gated drums. Compact discs were unleashed in 1982, and the unending technological advances of digital recording left the warm world of analog in the dust. The videocentric dimension known as MTV would create a glittering universe of opportunity that made the music itself more of a high-stakes commodity than ever.

Country music was also becoming bigger and bigger business, with the inevitable slide into mainstream pop/soft rock rapidly accelerating. "Inspired by the dramatic pop chart accomplishments of Crystal Gayle, Kenny Rogers, Dolly Parton, Jimmy Buffett and others, the country music industry has tasted the honey of the high reaches of pop success...and it wants more," Gerry Wood had written in *Billboard* in January 1978. Hollywood had also come a-calling, releasing a trio of big-budget country-centric movies in 1980: *Honeysuckle Rose, Coal Miner's Daughter,* and *Urban Cowboy*.[83]

83 Funnily enough, Stewart's music was initially supposed to be featured in *Urban Cowboy*, but rock mogul Irving Azoff packed the soundtrack with Joe Walsh, the Eagles, Bonnie Raitt, Boz Scaggs, and Dan Fogelberg instead. In a 1980 article, music supervisor Becky Shargo said that actual honky-tonk music by Stewart and Joe Ely "was originally the direction in which I was going. But when we got locked into the stuff Irving wanted to put on the album, we didn't have room." Who knows how being on that triple-platinum double album would've impacted Gary's career.

RCA Nashville was flying so high in this environment that RCA's president declared the office autonomous from its New York headquarters, partially due to such crossover smashes as a TV show theme by Waylon Jennings—"Theme from The Dukes of Hazzard (Good Ol' Boys)"—and a movie soundtrack hit, Dolly Parton's insanely catchy "9 to 5," both in 1980. With uncanny prescience, Jerry Bradley had experienced a vision at the end of the seventies, and its name was Alabama. "The disc jockey was changing...he was driving a Cadillac or brand-new pickup truck. He wasn't into his older-model used car, a seersucker suit. He was beginning to dress sporty... And I took notice of that. Music was changin', and that was one of the reasons that I signed Alabama... I gave it a lot of thought... And I saw a void in what [disc jockeys] were picking to play." Jerry's new breed of deejay helped turn Alabama into a monstrous hit-making machine with twenty-seven number-one eighties hits, their bland records frequently oozing onto the pop charts. "Oh, play me some mountain music / Like grandma and grandpa used to play," they belted out in ebullient, everybody-clap-along three-part harmony, a bullseye of unrelenting earwormery. Rock enough for the kids, mild enough for Mom and Dad, this was the kind of act RCA knew how to package and sell to the whole world, not just Joe Six-Pack nursing a honky-tonk beer in Muleshoe, Texas. "Country music in the eighties—was there such a thing?" wondered ace steel guitarist Robby Turner. "Even though there were country records being made still, the majority was this new kind of poppish sound."

"We're looking for total entertainers, not just acts that sing on-key," Joe Galante announced in a 1981 *Billboard* article entitled "Platinum, Gold Gild RCA Nashville: Label Stresses Pop Crossovers, Career Development." "My first country product presentation back to New York after I came here consisted of Hank Snow, Skeeter Davis and George Jones. Now when I take a presentation up to New York, it's a multi-format project like Alabama or Razzy Bailey or Steve Wariner." How did a downhome upstart like Gary Stewart fit into this new showbiz empire? Not at all.

* * *

Brotherly Love was recorded at Music City Music Hall (formerly RCA Studio B) and featured many familiar players from Stewart's sessions with Roy Dea, including Dale Sellers, Weldon Myrick, and Jerry Shook. But instead of the hardcore honky-tonk sound he captured for Jerry Lee Lewis, Kilroy went for bright, inoffensive, and generic. Ace session players are great when inspired, but this was dialed-in Nashville wallpaper, a limp, country-pop sound spawned in the suburbs of Margaritaville. Eddie felt he had little help from Stewart and Dillon. "Both of them were severely into drugs. Gary was in la-la land, laying on the couch, Dean was doing a lot of coke, and he was scratching his balls like a cat... I said, 'Boys, we're not gonna do vocal overdubs today. Tomorrow y'all get on the same drug, come back, and maybe we can do it.'"[84]

Still, despite the druggy haze, Eddie thought that "Gary's performance was very good. Dean was just typical Dean...Dean was a great writer and not a good singer." Kilroy felt that Stewart checked out early on and didn't really care what the end result was. "You couldn't help but like Gary Stewart. At the same time, he seemed pitiful to me. Certainly not because of lack of talent...he seemed like a lost soul. Gary was easygoin', he'd go along with anything too quickly. Musically, if we were talking about a song, anything I suggested it would be like, 'Yeah, that'll be fine, do that, Kilroy.' There was never any discussion about his views." The days of Stewart being a collaborative partner in the production as he had been with Roy Dea were long gone.

Dillon found it a challenge to vocalize with Gary. "He never sings the same way twice, you just have to watch him and guess," he told Ben Holland. Finding Stewart and Dillon's harmony duets unusable, Kilroy maintained that, without telling either one, he brought in a singer by the name of Larry Keith, known for his background work for Kenny Rogers, B.J. Thomas, and others. "He could sing any part

84 Kilroy said he'd been told Stewart was shooting heroin during the sessions. I don't believe this. Gary told me he had a fear of needles and had never shot any drugs intravenously, let alone heroin.

from the high third to the lowest. What made it so unusual was that he could temper his voice to fit the person he was singing with. So he came in and did all the harmonies on that album." Once it was done, Eddie called Gary and Dean for a listen. "They loved it. And Dean said, 'Kilroy, I told you we could do those harmonies. Listen!'" Keith's name fails to appear in album credits.

Dillon made abundantly clear that he wasn't Kilroy's biggest fan. "I had an extreme dislike for Eddie Kilroy. I didn't like him, I didn't like his production. I don't think he got it—I *know* he didn't get it, because of comments he said about Gary." When the album was done, Dillon said Eddie "called me in his office and said, 'Man, you need to get rid of Gary Stewart.'" Dillon said he marched over to Kilroy's desk and angrily cleared the top of it. "I said, 'You dumb son of a bitch, *he's* why we are who we are.' And he actually pushed me up against the wall. I said, 'Go ahead and hit me, motherfucker, you're just gonna make yourself look like the piece of shit you are.'" Kilroy confirmed the conversation, if not the physical altercation. "I just went off pretty heavy on Dean about how he should have a better role model. He said, 'Kilroy, you don't understand, Gary is my idol.' That's the way he felt about Gary Stewart."

If only the album was half as exciting as the backstage drama. *Brotherly Love* "was thrown together real fast....It was supposed to be an album of us doing all duets, but it had to be out so soon that some were just me singing and some just Dean singing," Stewart told David Dawson. Only two songs were written by Stewart and Dillon together, one of them the first single, an insufferable piece of nonsense the album's named for. In the song, Gary and Dean are siblings pursuing siblings, a pair of so-called "honky-tonk ladies." "I love the way she fills her jeans," coos Gary of sister Alice. The chorus is particularly execrable, topped off with a degrading call-and-response. "Hear they like to party," mews Dean in a timid wail. "So do you and I" is Gary's brilliant response. "Well, let's lay a little bit of that *brotherly love* on those sisters tonight," they chime together. Shopping-mall banality, it makes my skin crawl. The titan responsible for such feral boasts as "Little Junior" and "Flat Natural Born Good-Timin' Man" reduced to flaccid *Urban Cowboy* bro-country? O death, where is thy sting!

There are only four actual duets on the album, and none of them stand out. In the past, once Gary covered a song, it was nearly always definitive. But "Honky Tonk Crazy," a Dillon–Dycus number, was later vastly improved upon by George Strait. The best of Gary's solo numbers is "Cold Turkey," a rocker whose title hijacks drug lingo to crow about romantic obsession. The concept obviously appealed to Stewart, as the number features some of his loosest, loopiest singing, although the arrangement borrows heavily from "Flat Natural Good-Timin' Man."[85] "She Sings Amazing Grace," a classic Jerry Foster–Bill Rice song later cut by Jerry Lee Lewis, gets a near-great Stewart vocal but sounds slightly half-hearted compared to Gary's live performances of the number. The last solo Gary cut is "Body Shop," a truly lame paean to woman-as-car cowritten by Bobby Borchers and tailor-made for strip-club rotation. "It's so hard to defeat the curves / I can hardly put it into words," growls Stewart over a flaccid yakety sax. Alas, even this brain-dead novelty number is better than any of the duets. I should note that Stewart raved about one outtake from the sessions: an impromptu cover of the Fats Domino hit "Blue Monday," vividly recalling the guitar player (Dale Sellers, I'm assuming) deftly transposing Fats's piano solo from keys to frets note for note. The recording has never surfaced. There is another fine (if unfinished) Gary solo outtake floating around, "If This Is Our Last Time," an Orbison-dramatic Dallas Frazier ballad also cut by Brenda Lee, Tammy Wynette, and Percy Sledge.

* * *

85 "Cold Turkey" was written by legendary music business crackpot Gary S. Paxton, who produced both "Alley-Oop" and "Monster Mash." He was also repeatedly shot by hitmen some claim were hired by hard-country singer Vern Gosdin over a bad contract. Paxton won a Grammy for gospel music (sample gospel title: "Jesus Is My Lawyer in Heaven"). "Cold Turkey" was cowritten by Paxton's then-wife Karen, who left him over his alleged affair with evangelical supernova Tammy Faye Bakker. How cold that particular turkey was, I do not know.

Despite whatever bumps were going on with Stewart's career, he was hotter than ever on the road. The success of *Urban Cowboy* meant a proliferation of new places for Stewart to play in Texas and elsewhere. The movie was "the greatest thing that ever happened" to honky-tonks, said singer Richard McCroan, who'd later manage Gary. "The money doubled overnight. Everybody had a big feather at the end of their hat."

"So many clubs opened up," marveled Randy Toman. While the loot was great, Gary did not always care for these flashy new nightspots with their mechanical bulls. Singer Henson Cargill—who'd enjoyed a 1968 hit with the mournful, disquieting "Skip A Rope"— owned one such palace in Oklahoma City, Henson's Saloon, which Gary played in August 1982. "It was a swanky spot, not a joint," noted Toman. "It was almost a little too fancy. And Gary did not enjoy that gig whatsoever—'Okay, I'll play the songs, but this ain't my idea of a honky-tonk. And they don't want a fifteen-minute 'Shady Streets.' I don't ever want to play this place again.'"

The Gary-and-Dean road show entered the fray with a rough start. "We played at the Opry, RCA set it up, it was our big exposure day," said Dillon. "We show up stoned out of our minds on coke and whiskey. We get ten seconds into our first song, Gary stops—'Man, this is the wrong intro to this song!' He starts the whole thing all over again. I've got a baseball cap on, and my hair is down to my waist. So I jerk the cap off, shake my hair out, and we go at it." The Music City audience didn't know what to think. "The people in the first five rows, I looked at them and they're in shock—like, 'Who in the hell *are* these guys? What *is* this???' It was awesome."

RCA was set to give *Brotherly Love* a big push: five thousand postcards of Gary and Dean were mailed to distributors, there was a sales meeting attended by the artists, plus a TV appearance on *Nashville Alive*. The pair did quite a bit of press, most of it focused on their bad-boy reputations. "We met at a cockfight. His rooster beat my chicken," Dillon quipped to one scribe. Robert K. Oermann evoked the Stewart maelstrom while describing the Music City press performance he attended—"Gary gets a wild look in his eyes at one point and announces, 'I can feel the sea and the wind and the graveyard. I get so I scare myself to death.'"

Momentum for the album derailed almost immediately at an invitation-only listening party at the Stock-Yard Restaurant in Nashville. As Eddie Kilroy recalled, Gary and Dean came in "so fucked up. RCA people from New York were there. And of course, Jerry Bradley. RCA had a $250,000 marketing plan in place for the album. And I could see 'em kind of looking at each other—they're thinking, 'We're going to spend *this* money? Can we even send these guys to radio stations and be comfortable that they're even gonna be straight?'" A picture ran in *Billboard* of a smiling Bradley embracing Gary and Dean onstage at the event, a morose, wasted Stewart staring off toward some unknown horizon. When I asked Bradley about their booze-and-drug-fueled antics, I could practically hear him grinding his teeth. "Nobody thought it was funny. I guess if the whole world had been doin' what they were doin', it would've been great...The people that paid for the product, promoted it, and sold it, *they* didn't think it was too funny." According to Kilroy, RCA "flushed the album, the whole thing...I bet they didn't press five thousand albums. If they had just straightened up....The boys blew a great opportunity."

Joe Galante, who oversaw promotion for Stewart/Dillon, took issue with the amount Kilroy named—"We didn't spend that kind of money in '82"—but concurs that Gary and Dean's hard-partying ways were "an issue" that tanked marketing for the album after a five-city showcase tour with Stewart and Dillon backed by the Toman Brothers, the band augmented by Dillon on guitar, and steel guitar great Randy Reinhard, who'd played with Charley Pride, Johnny Bush, and others. "We stopped after New York City," said Galante, who was present for the infamous last date. Stewart and Dillon blew into the Big Apple on May 6th for a showcase at Sundown, a short-lived Midtown country venue. Bob Summer, RCA's president, attended at Galante's request, "which he never normally did. He walked in there in his three-piece suit and I'm thinking, 'Oh, my career's over.'" Joe knew that Gary and Dean were already three sheets to the wind.

Before the show, Galante had jumped into their limo and when he put his hand down, "a cloud of cocaine came up. I got a secondhand high there, just from breathing." By the time they went onstage, Gary and Dean were "feeling no pain. They were staggering, trying to sing into the microphone, bobbing and weaving." Toward the end of the set, "appearing onstage by impulse rather than design," as noted by *Billboard* reviewer Robyn Wells, a new running buddy joined them—Tanya Tucker. She charged into "Shady Streets" with Gary (she'd also cut the song in 1979). It was a wildly disorganized spectacle. "Her insistence on audience participation was a ploy not in keeping with the duo's more laid-back approach," wrote Wells. As far as Galante was concerned, Tucker "saved the night, because we were kind of sinking badly from everybody being a little high."

Excited about another ultra-rare Stewart sighting in Manhattan and looking forward to another fierce performance, I attended this mess of a show. But it possessed only fleeting moments of the intensity I had previously witnessed. This was a goofier Gary, more of a passive participant in a traveling carnival than one leading the charge. The duet songs were rough and raggedy, although Stewart did his best to inject excitement into his solo numbers, particularly "She Sings Amazing Grace." Partial video of the show exists and it's not quite as abysmal as memory serves, although Gary and Dean are as pale as ghosts and Dean looks like he might keel over at any moment. The best part of the show was the finale, when Stewart sat on the edge of the stage with an acoustic guitar and sang "Your Cheatin' Heart." I spoke to him briefly for the very first time as he made his way out of the club. Even in passing, his presence was electric. After a few minutes he disappeared into the night with his cohorts. When Galante and his associates hit the hotel lobby at 5 a.m. for their flight out, Gary, Dean, and Tanya were just pulling in. "They rode hard," said Joe.

Brotherly Love was a dud. The title single only hit forty-one, and Gary's solo follow-up, "She Sings Amazing Grace," stalled at eighty-three, the lowest-charting single thus far of his career. None of Dillon's three solo efforts from the album cracked the top fifty. *Brotherly Love* got mediocre reviews, with *The Tennessean* declaring it "half-hearted honky-tonk...the production is lifeless...the music doesn't kick." Veteran country music reporter Jack Hurst opened his nationally syndicated article on the album by coldly describing it as "an effort to revive the distinguished but faded career of singer-songwriter Gary Stewart."

Despite the *Brotherly Love* disaster, Gary and Dean managed to stumble on at RCA. Dillon insisted it was because of one person—Jerry Bradley. "I think there were some people at the record label who thought we shouldn't be on the label, I'm not gonna mention any names. But Jerry was like, 'No, no, no, we're not gettin' rid of *those* guys.'"

* * *

Gary, Russ Toman, Randy Toman, Dean Dillon, Ray Wilburn (Ray Wilburn collection)

It was far easier getting into Gary Stewart's trailer than speaking to Tanya Tucker for this book. We'd make an appointment to talk, she'd be a no-show, then I'd get funny, dramatic texts detailing what calamity had beset her. Somebody broke into my ranch! Or, I cut my foot badly! Complete with photographic evidence of a mangled appendage. Eventually her publicist demanded I stop responding to her texts and deal only with him. Yeah, right—*I'm* gonna ignore Tanya Tucker? As amusing as these exchanges were, after fifteen months of chasing her, enlisting the help of her management and more blown appointments, I finally called Tucker and left an exasperated voicemail telling her "no more, I give up." And just like that, she was on the phone. Besides the talent, Tucker's a wild one who seems comfortable with chaos. No wonder Gary was so fond of her.

Tanya was a fiery twenty-four when she met Gary and Dean. She had already survived an intense round of stardom as an adolescent, belting out provocative numbers produced by madman Billy Sherrill like "Delta Dawn" and "Would You Lay with Me (In a Field of Stone)." She was a magnetic figure, a passionate little oracle in a cowboy hat. "Her voice belied her chronological age," notes singer and Tucker admirer Tammy Faye Starlite. "It knew secrets. Her voice had experienced psychological pain and profound rapture beyond her years on earth." By 1982, Tanya was struggling to reinvent her career as an adult following a tempestuous relationship with Glen Campbell that had been tabloid catnip. While recording her one album for Arista, she spent a month at the Spence Manor—or "the S&M" as Tucker called it for the many oddballs that hung there—so she wouldn't have to drive to her family's ranch from the studio every night. She was kicking back in her room with her buddy Lorell Hughes when they heard a bit of a ruckus outside their door.

Peering through the peephole, Hughes spied two guys in "rock and roll jackets" entering the room across the hall. Intrigued, Tanya got on the phone and had the hotel operator put her through to the mystery guests. When some guy "with a drawl" answered, Tucker, not knowing it was Gary Stewart on the line, asked if they had any beer. "And I don't drink beer," added Tanya as an aside. "We were just bored out of our minds." "Well, I don't know," said Gary. "Are you good-lookin'?" With that, "we threw our tight jeans on, put a little makeup on, and got our hair lookin' fairly good. And we were *hot*. So we crossed the hall there and knocked on the door."

When the door opened, the room "was full of solid smoke," as Tanya recalled. "Everybody was smokin' cigarettes—Gary didn't smoke, but Dean smoked more than all of us." The room was also packed with songwriters—Gary, Dean, Frank Dycus, most likely Buddy Cannon, God knows who else. Tucker recognized Stewart right away. "I've always loved his music, so I was excited to meet him," she wrote in her autobiography. "It was exciting just to look at Dean Dillon, because he's a fox." Gary and Dean told her they were preparing material for their next album—at that moment a song about Natalie Wood, improbably enough. Tanya, who'd never written a song in her life, jumped right in. "I sat down and said, 'Naw, I think you need to change that line. I think it could be stronger.'[86] It's funny, because I got to thinkin' back, and that's an unwritten rule that everybody knows: don't mess with a gambler when he's gambling or songwriter when he's writin'." But Tucker butted in and Gary and Dean "didn't even care. We instantly became friends." They spent the rest of the night "drinking beer and writing songs."

According to Tanya, the trio wrote three other songs that night, including "I Owe It All to My Heart," which Gary eventually recorded on his 1988 album *Brand New*, and an unrecorded number called "Not Tonight, I've Got a Heartache." "Kind of a beer-drinkin', belt-buckle-

86 Stewart and Dillon would never record "Natalie," easily one of the worst songs ever to bear Gary's name. Not only does the lyric cry over Natalie, it throws Judy Garland, Jayne Mansfield, Marilyn Monroe, and Jean Harlow onto the pyre: "Judy's yellow brick road led to heaven." It's a nothing song, full of the kind of easy platitudes and cheap sentiment found on that immortal public-access vanity project *Skip E. Lowe Looks at Hollywood*, but for the heterosexual universe. Most amusingly, that notorious touring cohort from Stewart's Charley Pride days recorded it—Dave "Rings 'n' Things" Rowland, lead singer of Dave & Sugar, who featured it on his first (and only) album without his two lovely singing partners, the expressively titled *Sugar Free*. For the record, Dillon says the song was Tucker's idea. "Tanya loved Natalie Wood. She was adamant that we should write a song about her."

rubbin' song," explained Tanya. But the most commercial creation of the night was yet to come. In the wee hours the group thinned out. "It was just me and Gary and Dean. And for some reason, we went to another room, a really big one. They were kind of fried, y'know, just trying to come up with more ideas." Tanya, who was pacing around the room, went off on a rant about George Jones, who was in deathly shape at the time. His videotaped drunken encounter with police, in which Jones, looking absolutely demented, resisted arrest and kicked the cop interrogating him, had been plastered all over the news. "And I said, 'Man, they ought to leave that boy alone, let him sing his songs.' Gary went, 'Hey, T, that's it! That's the song, let's write *that*!'" They spent the rest of the twilight hours writing verses for "Leave Them Boys Alone." Tucker recalled they wrote "some really funny, stupid stuff—'Willie's got a ponytail about a mile long.' I wrote a verse that went 'George Jones is the king of soul.'"

Tucker was so excited about what they'd crafted that she demanded Gary and Dean accompany her to Tree Publishing, which was right down the street. It was early morning, they were trashed, and she didn't want to stagger over there in public, so Stewart and Dillon "put me on a luggage rack," pushing her discreetly down an alley to Tree. Tanya "rolled in looking like God knows what and shouted, 'Hey, guys, I wrote this song!'" Tanya and Dean took "Leave Them Boys Alone" personally to Hank Williams Jr., who changed the lyric to make his father the "king of country soul." Then came the phone call. "They said, 'Hank wants a quarter of the writers' publishing,'" Tucker recalled. "And I went, 'Well, fuck him!'" She relented after those around her informed her a quarter of a hit was better than no hit at all. Hank Jr. cut the song—with Ernest Tubb and Waylon Jennings providing guest vocals—and it went to number six. "So I was bitten by the songwriter's bug," said Tucker, who credits Gary Stewart for making it happen.

Although Tanya had hung with plenty of other songwriters, "Gary could bring something out in me. I don't know what, but he did. I didn't try to figure out what it was. And I loved being around him." From that moment on, Gary, Dean, and Tanya "were joined at the hip. We were the Three Musketeers." The reason she joined them for the showcase in New York was because she'd seen the one in Los Angeles and they'd invited her to come. Tucker was moving house at the time and agreed, on one condition—they had to help her unload a few of her things. "Gary Stewart and Dean Dillon are not musclemen by any means," she wrote. After they got over the shock of seeing her overstuffed moving van "they unloaded the whole truck." The trio then flew to New York, did that infamous show, and spent the rest of the night drinking tequila out of the bottle with *Country Music* writer Patrick Carr in tow.

They were still up the following morning in a hotel room on 58th Street, "all just totally fucking wired," as Carr recalled. "Tanya was crazed. She was very insistent about knowing how beautiful we thought she was. She kept asking us, 'Am I really beautiful?' It was just nasty drug hell." Tucker got a bee in her bonnet to confront Clive Davis, head of her current label, who was pissing her off by making her record songs she didn't want to cut. So the whole bunch, Gary included, piled into a limo. "We're all sitting around waiting for Clive to pay attention," said Carr. He never came out of his office. "That was the kind of dumb stunt you pull when you party all night," said Tanya.[87] Fortunately she wasn't carrying the piece she was toting for the trip—a .357 Magnum. "Loaded," said Tanya, oblivious to the fact it was illegal to take firearms on a plane. "I ended up leaving the gun in a drawer in the hotel. I couldn't call back and say, 'I left my gun.' I'd go to the penitentiary!"

Although there would be no romance between Tucker and Stewart, there was a short fling with Dillon. "I loved him, but not that way. Kind of like the way I loved Elvis." The vibe was more brotherly love: as Tanya put it, "Forget I'm a girl—I'm one of the boys." Whenever Dillon and Tucker would squabble, Gary would

87 Although Tanya enjoyed a Top Ten hit off her Arista album ("Feel Right"), she left the label over the matter. She says her father, Beau, intervened on her behalf with Davis. "My dad told him, 'You let my daughter go or you're gonna need a new dentist.'"

serve as peacemaker. "I had a temper and Dean sure had a temper," said Tucker. Gary was "a ref—'Okay, y'all, come on now, let's be friends, don't fight.'" During one writing session at Stewart's home, Tanya mused aloud that Gary wasn't a great singer but a stylist like Johnny Cash. She meant it as a high compliment, but Dillon wasn't having it. "Boy, Dean got so mad because I said that. Gary understood what I was saying. But Dean, he wouldn't speak to me for a whole day." There was one special detail Tucker loved about Gary's home—the fact that he had "bars on the windows, man, *bars on the windows*! I thought, 'How cool.'"

Just about everybody had a Gary and Dean cocaine story. Songwriter/musician/producer Buddy Cannon—famous in recent years for his production and cowriting with Willie Nelson—wrote with the duo and sang backup for them. He recalled being with Gary and Dean in a taxi en route to the airport after a show in Dallas that had led to an all-nighter and they "still had lots of cocaine left. We were all three in the back seat of the taxi, slumped down so the driver couldn't see us so we could snort all that cocaine up before we got to the airport."

Tanya was another who maintained that "Gary didn't like cocaine. Of course, I liked it. And Dean liked it, too. A lot. Crank was his choice. I never got into that like he did." Gary had gotten into meth in the waning days of the Honky-Tonk Liberation Army, and it was another vice that stuck around the rest of his life.

Whatever the poison available at the moment, Gary hoovered it up. One night Stewart and Dillon were in New Mexico on their way to a reservation gig. "Gary crawled in the back seat like he always did and went to sleep," said Dean. "I always was navigator." After about three hours he asked their road manager and cohort Rex Huston where they were and he said lost. Dillon got out the road atlas "lookin' for New Mexico and the whole damn page is gone. I said, 'Junior, wake up—have you seen the New Mexico page?'" Gary came to, announcing that he and a bandmate had smoked it the night before. "They rolled a joint using the New Mexico page and smoked it! I said, 'Couldn't you have smoked *Ohio* or some other state instead of the one that we're in?'" Dillon was yet another witness to Stewart's unbelievable capacity for drugs. "He would not give up the ship. We'd go and go and go and go and go—until he couldn't go anymore."

Dillon worried about Gary "a lot." Everybody worried about Dean as well. As Buddy Cannon saw it, "they weren't takin' care of each other. They may have *thought* they were. None of us were takin' care of the other one. It's a wonder any of us lived through that."

* * *

Rex Huston was a big part of the group during this period. The band loved Huston and often stayed at his house in Grapevine, Texas. He's even credited as cowriter on a few Stewart and Dillon songs. "Rex would pick us up on Wednesday in Dallas, and then we'd drive in his Cadillac to all our dates," said Dillon. "He'd been workin' with Gary, gettin' him paid, gettin' him to shows on time—which was extremely hard to do at times. Gary was like a little kid, you had to stay on top of him...

"In all honesty, Gary was helpless. You had to constantly stay on him about taking care of hisself, about eating. We'd make him eat a Whataburger. Rex did a whale of a job with Gary. Rex was a fun-lovin' guy. He had this great laugh and he took care of us—whatever we needed, he made sure we had." Randy Toman did not envy Rex. "Being Gary's so-called babysitter, that was a job. It was a little bit of—'*No*, you can't do that, Gary. We're not doing *that*, Gary.' He'd say, 'Oh, oh, let's stop here, I want to get me a candy bar.' He'd want to pull over, even though we'd just stopped. I'd say, 'Hey, Gary, let's put a few miles on it. We'll stop at the next place.'" Stewart invariably talked somebody into doing his bidding.[88]

---

88 According to Gina Stewart, things crashed to a halt with Rex after Gina, who'd partied with Huston in Florida, flew out to Texas in her "big-ass" white mink coat to deliver an ounce of cocaine to him. "Gary jumped on me for flying out there with that shit. Said I wasn't his damn mule." Then Rex got mad at Gary for calling his wife "honey." "Gary called everybody 'honey,' all of us hillbillies do." After that, "they just quit doing with each other."

Gary with Rex Huston. (Gina Stewart collection)

Dillon loved being out on the road with Stewart and the Toman Brothers, plowing through honky-tonk after honky-tonk. "We played them with chicken wire strung out in front of the stage. We played them where you walk in and if you didn't have a gun or a knife, they'd give you one. That was a whole new eye-opener for me, like being back in the wild, wild West. 'I get to be part of this, with the best damn honky-tonk singer that ever lived?'" Dillon would look out into the audience and "it was nothing but a damn sea of cowboy hats swaying, and most of it was due to Gary. You could feel every note by the movement in his body—tense and then loose, tense and then loose. It was just amazing." Buddy Cannon concurred. "When Gary strapped that guitar on, his whole body went into motion when he was playin' and singin'. It was like he was one with everybody in the audience, communicating what he was feeling to everybody in the room. It's one of the most unusual things I've ever seen." By the end of the show Gary would be "sweating like a whore in church," said Tanya Tucker in amazement. "Soaking wet."

No matter if he was late, high, or not even there, they all loved Gary and his endless quirks. Buddy Cannon tells a story about Stewart appearing out of nowhere at his studio one day wearing an Allman Brothers T-shirt and carrying an old suitcase. "He says, 'Buddy, do you mind if I change clothes? I've been out here walking around and I'm all sweaty, man.'" Stewart popped open his bag, which was nearly empty. Then, "skinny as Hank Williams," Stewart stripped off his T-shirt, pulling another one out of the suitcase "exactly like the one he just taken off," marveled Cannon. "He was good then." And off Gary went.

* * *

Another strange superstar intersection happened around this time—Stewart, Dillon, and that singular and unhinged cosmic blowhard genius David Allan Coe. The first evidence of Stewart/ Coe interaction is Gary's uncredited appearance on Coe's amusing "Bad Impressions" from 1977, in which David impersonates Hank Snow, Ernest Tubb, Marty Robbins, and Jerry Lee Lewis before Gary swoops in from out of nowhere for one line: "Forever didn't seem to last too long." Coe dedicates another song on *Family Album* to Mickey Gilley, Jerry Lee, and Gary. How all that came about is a mystery (Coe ignored requests to be interviewed, sadly).

During the Gary-and-Dean days, Coe reappeared. Ace guitar slinger Warren Haynes, in Coe's band at the time, recalled showing up for a 10 a.m. session at Columbia that Billy Sherrill was producing. David announced they weren't going to cut the song they had planned. "David, Gary, and Dean had been up all night at Spence Manor writing a song called 'Graveyard for Lovers,'" said Haynes, and Coe had brought Stewart and Dillon with him.

"Initially David was gonna do a duet. He was gonna sing half and Dean Dillon was going to sing the other half. We recorded the track, then Dean started singin' his vocal and his voice was shot. I still remember Gary pushing the talkback button and saying, 'Dean, your voice is trashed, man...we'll do it another time.'

"Then David said, 'Gary, why don't you sing it instead?' So Gary went out and put a vocal on it. And Gary's vocal was really good." There was just one problem: Stewart was on another label. "I remember Billy Sherrill saying to David, 'Are you sure that RCA is gonna give us permission to have Dean or Gary on this record?' And David said, 'Oh, it'll be fine.' A few days later word came in that it wasn't fine, so Coe recut it as a duet with Warren Haynes. It never got released. "So it started out as a duet with Dean, then a duet with Gary, then a duet with me. And somewhere in the vaults, all three of those versions exist." A David Allan Coe / Gary Stewart duet on a song called "Graveyard for Lovers" produced by Billy Sherrill? Mind-boggling.[89]

* * *

After *Brotherly Love*, Stewart and Dillon started to write together in earnest, sometimes at Stewart's place. "When you walked into Gary Stewart's home you definitely got the vibe, man. It's hard to explain, but it overcame you." The only other time Dillon had felt such a strong presence was at Johnny Cash's abode. Dean maintained he and Stewart were disciplined when it came to their craft. "When Gary and I were writing we were like mules with blinders on. That's all we thought about, all we cared about. And Lou gave us all the

89 One other night after another Nashville recording session, Coe had his bus parked outside the Hall of Fame Motor Inn. "Dean Dillon came on board and wanted to play a new song for David he had just written," said Coe's bass player, Mickey Hayes. "He told us the title was 'Tennessee Whiskey.'" Dillon popped in a tape of the song, which he'd written with Linda Hargrove. David thought it was a great song and told Dean it would be the title of his new album and single. "We were passing the guitars around a bit when George Jones and Gary Stewart came on board. David told them about the new song Dean had written, so of course George wanted to hear it. George liked the song and told us he would cut it as a single also." Coe's version went to number seventy-seven in 1981; Jones had a number-two hit with it in 1983. Interesting that Hayes puts Stewart at this event as Dean and Gary were not yet working together in 1981. Hayes also claimed that not long after this, Stewart visited Coe at a property he had outside of Dickson, Tennessee, called Ruskin's Cave. "David had invited Gary out to work on some songs." A tantalizing idea, but who knows if any songs were ever finished. There are no Stewart–Coe songwriting efforts listed in Gary's BMI entries.

room we needed." During one mammoth session, he says they wrote thirteen songs, the most notable of them being "An Empty Glass," which Stewart would release on his 1988 album *Brand New*.

Dillon noted that Gary was "appreciative of my songwriting," but these sessions didn't always go smoothly. One night at Spence Manor, Stewart, Dillon, and Rex Huston were writing songs when "Gary goes and locks himself in the bathroom." Stewart had abruptly decided he'd write solo. "Well, he leaves me and Rex out there and we write that big George Strait hit, 'Famous Last Words of a Fool.'[90] Gary finally comes out of the bathroom and plays us what he has, and it's a bad psychedelic trip song—you could tell the trip was bad. We play him what we wrote, he's like, 'Naah.'" Dean felt there was some "jealousy" over his success as a songwriter. "Who goes into Spence Manor and locks himself in the bathroom when you got two guys out there, and one of 'em is known to write a great song every now and then? Gary was out to prove a point—that he didn't need anybody to write great songs."

* * *

Those Were the Days, the next Stewart/Dillon release, was intended as a full-length album, but RCA had other plans. Jerry Bradley had stepped down as head of RCA Nashville and picked Joe Galante as his successor. "Though some found his direct, outspoken ways abrasive" goes the entry on him in the Country Music Hall of Fame *Encyclopedia of Country Music*, "Galante applied pop promotion techniques to country music and greatly expanded its commercial horizons....Galante established a reputation for his aggressive, relentless approach to finance, marketing and merchandising."

"A great guy," said Randy Toman of Galante, but Stewart didn't have the kind of relationship with him he'd enjoyed with Bradley. "Gary didn't get along with him," said another source. Galante would

90 Dillon released a solo RCA single of "Famous Last Words of a Fool" in 1983 that only went to number sixty-seven. George Strait wouldn't record it until 1987, and his went to number one. It's a perfectly fine hit, but I, for one, would rather hear Gary's "bad psychedelic trip song."

be instrumental in the careers of many new country artists such as the Judds, Vince Gill, Brad Paisley, and many others. And he'd help turn Nashville more successful, more mainstream, and more like the worlds of rock and pop. Not everybody was crazy about him. Joe was "a rare specimen: an Italian good ol' boy," wrote Dorothy Carvello, who worked under Galante at RCA. "When he first arrived in Nashville, no one liked him. He was a New Yorker, a numbers man and a pencil pusher who didn't have an ear for music." According to Carvello, Joe's name was the punch line for a Music City joke: "What has two arms, two legs and no ears?"

In 1983 Galante launched a mini-LP series at RCA, budget-priced at $6.98 and containing only six cuts. "We see this as a developmental program for artists who have proven themselves with two or three records but still aren't selling at the album level," Joe told *Billboard*. Thus it was decided *Those Were the Days* would be shortened to EP length. For Gary, who'd been putting out RCA albums since 1975, it must've felt like another demotion.

Produced by Blake Mevis, who'd produced George Strait since the beginning, *Those Were the Days* featured six songs all cowritten by Stewart and Dillon. The cover shows Gary and Dean below a neon hotel sign with a bright red '57 Chevy, while on the back some anonymous female leans out the car window to paw at Dillon as a hatless Stewart stands by looking like the crazy uncle. The packaging projected the sad atmosphere of an ersatz fifties diner with Sha Na Na on the jukebox and Marilyn Monroe prints on the wall. The cherry on this tasteless cake was a back-cover endorsement by Teddy Gentry, a member of then-ubiquitous Alabama. Hit producer, original songs, none of it made any difference, because *Those Were the Days* was just as weak as its predecessor. Too much James Taylor, not enough Merle Haggard, and only trace amounts of *Little Junior*. Stewart still sounds great, but he just cannot transcend the banal material and eighties-pastel production.

The title song, written en route to a gig according to Stewart—"we'd meet at an airport, head for a honky-tonk, buy a guitar, and write a song along the way"—is a saccharine ballad whose "drive-

in movies"/"fake ID" nostalgia is perhaps even less compelling than the album cover. (Gary does manage to slip Lou's name into the lyrics, though. Dillon considers it "a great song" so maybe you should listen to him.) "Smokin' in the Rockies" is a generic rock non-anthem just as dire as the title would indicate, another lazy laundry list of country greats à la "Leave Them Boys Alone." It took four geniuses to come up with this one—Stewart and Dillon, plus Frank Dycus and Buddy Cannon. Dycus, who was brave enough to take credit for the idea in an interview with David Dawson, recalled some amusing background behind the number, which features the names of Waylon and Willie, Hank Jr. and Jerry Lee.

"By then Dean and Gary were into the sauce pretty heavy, and they wanted to put Johnny Paycheck in it. At that time Paycheck was in the headlines for having sex with a 12 or 13 year-old girl. I said '[B]oys, we can't put Paycheck in that song, because his career is over as far as America is concerned.' I had to fight them all to keep him out of the song—they wanted to title it 'Smokin' in the Rockies with Johnny Paycheck.'" "Smokin' in the Rockies" has the dubious distinction of being performed on TV by grating country-pop band Sawyer Brown during their $100,000 win on *Star Search*. "Losers and Lovers" was another four-way cowrite, this one bearing the imprint of wild man Mack Vickery, author of fabulous songs for Jerry Lee Lewis and a cowriting partner of the underrated Wayne Kemp.[91] Featuring close-harmony singing influenced by, according to Stewart, "that sound of the Everly Brothers," this is another limp, forgettable ballad. "Lovers are losers when nobody wants them," the boys wail against tired key changes, bland strings, and eighties keyboard. "Meat Man" it isn't. "Misfits," the most interesting cut musically, is a jaunty self-referential tune about what kooky badasses Stewart and Dillon were supposed to be. "We've been told we don't

91 I spent a crazed night with Vickery in Nashville decades ago. Allegedly it was an interview, but Mack was so blitzed he could barely form a sentence. He made a point of taking me on a tour of his home, which featured a painting of an ex-wife gazing down over his bed ("so she knows what I'm up to these days") and, for reasons unexplained, a dentist's chair. Seek out his 1970 album, *Live at the Alabama's Women's Prison*, if only for the suitably bombastic cover.

know when to quit." The public agreed. "Those Were the Days" hit number forty-seven and "Smokin' in the Rockies" number seventy-one. Gary's last release for RCA, he went out with a whimper.

Dillon lamented that they were "maybe an album away from being extremely successful." Perhaps—there are Stewart/Dillon-penned outtakes lost in the switch to a mini-LP that point to a more honky-tonk sound —"Smooth Shot of Whiskey" and "I Lost the Best Thing Going." There is also a live recording of Lefty Frizzell's "Mom and Dad's Waltz" from a November 1982 Opryland radio broadcast that's simply incredible, with Gary singing the low part under Dean, turning the song into a stately hymn. The studio recording of this, which I haven't heard, was also cut from the second record. Nothing went right when it came to this duo.

* * *

Out on the road with Stewart and Dillon, the problem child was invariably Gary. They had a promotional date playing a listener appreciation day for a radio station in Phoenix. "We're the headlining act," said Dean, who arrived to find that Gary hadn't shown. "I'm waiting and waiting, and the guy at the radio station, he's waiting. Then he's pacing. Then he's sweating. Then he's chewin' my ass out, because Gary Stewart ain't there. I called Gary and he ain't comin', because there was no money involved. And I'm left there holdin' the bag." Dillon performed solo, valiantly doing a few of Stewart's songs on his own. There were more than a few of Gary's rabid, now disgruntled Native American fans in the audience from various Arizona reservations. "It was a disaster," said Dean.

Then there was the string of dates through Kentucky and the Carolinas. "It snowed four feet overnight," Dillon recalled. "We were tryin' to get over the Shenandoah Mountains. We told the highway crew Willie Nelson was on the bus and they actually cleared the road. When we got to the other side of the mountain one of them said, 'You think Willie will maybe come out and give us an autograph?' I said, 'Man, I'm sorry, but he's sound asleep right now.'" Dillon and company had escaped a blizzard, but not the effects of Hurricane Gary. Dean got a call from him announcing, "'There's a storm out there, I ain't comin'.' Then I get the dreaded phone call from RCA. Joe Galante—'Why the fuck is Gary not out there?'" Dillon felt the real reason for Stewart's no-show was simply a lack of drugs: "Not having any ammunition in his body, God rest his lovin' soul."

As their troubles continued, people saw a rift develop between Stewart and Dillon. "Something happened," said Steve Hunter. "Nobody knows what. Gary had lost somethin' for Dean." I'd heard tales of drug money lifted from socks, misappropriated song credits, purloined girlfriends, and more. Not true, according to Dillon. "There was no fallin' out," he insisted, maintaining that the real problem was that Stewart was barely keeping himself afloat financially. "I always felt like there was a money issue with Gary. I got to see it firsthand the first time I went home with him to Fort Pierce. We get home, and this cousin's got his hands stuck out for money, and this one needed money for that, and poor ol' Gary, he's dolin' out money, and by the end of the day he's damn near broke again. Because the guy would give you the shirt off his damn back."

According to Dillon, Stewart started to resent having to pay Dean out on the road. Gary "felt like all the shows we played were because of him. I didn't quite see it that way, but as time went on that's the way he felt about it. I'm out there on the road with him—hell, I gotta get right, I ain't gonna do this shit for nothing. I could tell that he was uncomfortable with the situation, man."

At some point, Lou turned against Dillon. As family friend Bill Hardman relates, "Mary Lou had a revolver that held five bullets. She had taken a Sharpie, took the bullets out of the gun, and wrote Dean Dillon's name on all five of them. She said, 'If I ever see him, I don't care what happens—all five of these are going into Dean Dillon." But in 1987, when Lou was going through rough times, she contacted Dean for $175 to pay her car insurance and he sent it. "I had Dean all wrong," she wrote in her diary. "He really does care. Dean's OK."

Complicating the situation were the chemicals being ingested at the homestead. "Drugs, if you do enough of them, they cause psychosis, and I think he'd done enough of them for so long that it actually had a mental effect on him," said Dillon. "Gary wasn't thinking right or clearly. You get paranoid on that shit. I was in the same shoes until I got help." Dean Dillon went to rehab in 1984, and it stuck, albeit with a couple of minor slips over the years. Tanya Tucker checked herself into the Hazelden Betty Ford Foundation in 1988, the day after an intervention by friends and family that included Dean. Tanya held her breath when Dillon spoke, "because I certainly didn't want him telling my folks we'd done drugs and had sex," she wrote. Dean tried to lighten the mood at the intervention by telling her he'd bought a new hat sober—"You can buy things when you get off drugs." "Dean probably thought it was the perfect pitch at the intervention of a world-class shopper." Tanya at one point offered to pick up the tab for Stewart to go to Betty Ford, but he never took her up on it.

Tensions between Gary and Dean grew until inevitably "it just came to a halt," said Dillon. "We played a show in Lawton, Oklahoma. Gary said 'I'm outta here.' And I got the message. It wasn't mean... Gary was as meek as a lamb. I understood, because I thought this was coming for a little while. To be honest with you, I was ready for it. I had the innate ability to bounce back on my feet pretty quick and, man, I was having a lot of success writin' songs. My stream of income from writin' songs was a hell of a lot more than it was playin' shows with Gary. I just dove back into the writing headfirst."[92]

As Dillon's star rose, Stewart retreated into the honky-tonks, and he'd do so without a label. The kind of rebel Stewart represented became way less fashionable in glitzy '80s Music City. Waylon Jennings recalled how late in the decade Joe Galante wanted him to meet an

92 Dillon would eventually abandon his solo recording career as well. "I'd cut something, it'd go to twenty-five, George Strait would cut it the next year, it'd go to number one. It only took a few of those to realize that my place in this world is to write songs."

up-and-comer named Clint Black to share some of his Waylon-and-Willie war stories. They all met for lunch, where Jennings regaled Black with numerous "coked up" tales. "After a while it got a little quiet," said Waylon. Black said, "Well, I'll tell you one thing... I've got to get rid of this Goody-Two-Shoes reputation." Galante quickly broke in to disabuse him of that notion. "Joe was scared to death that Clint would become like me," Waylon told Bruce Feiler. "A new crop of more clean-cut artists, led by George Strait and Randy Travis, arose to supplant the bad boys of the seventies," wrote Feiler.

Sometime in 1983 Gary got a call from Joe Galante telling him he was being dropped from RCA. When I asked how that affected him, he feigned indifference. "I just hung up the phone and went back to watching TV." Stewart told Bob Allen that "it didn't mean nothin' to me because I knew it was comin'." He blamed no one. "Hey, if Jerry Bradley didn't like me, I'd never have lasted as long as I did. Jerry was for me. Roy Dea was for me. Maybe I wasn't for me."

I wondered what Bradley thought about the situation, if he felt any responsibility for the inane duet records. "It was mostly what Gary wanted. They were his ideas, and he got a chance to distribute them through the RCA setup. I don't think anything was crammed down his throat." Although Bradley was newly retired from RCA when Stewart was dropped, he remained active in the music business and was Gary's publisher until the end of Stewart's life. Jerry grew philosophical over RCA cutting Gary loose. "It's like your loved one dying of a disease, a slow death. You know what's going to happen. And so when it *does* happen, it's not near as bad... I don't think anybody didn't expect it, including Gary.

"After sellin' as many records as Gary was, the artist gets his way. If he's right, it's a continuing relationship. If he's wrong, it's adios. Nobody's mad about it, it just didn't work out. Gary probably had three or four attempts at what he wanted to do and they did nothing.[93]

93 Hard to say what failures Bradley's referring to here. I could never ascertain if the Chips Moman album was Jerry's idea or Gary's. The Gary/Dean albums were certainly instigated by Bradley.

"Put yourself in a position of any record label. What happens is, you sit there and tell people, you try to communicate with them, you bend over backwards, usually. And when they don't want to listen, you go to somebody that does, because you're the captain of the ship. When people cease to listen, you let them go on until they burn it out, and people aren't interested anymore. When that happens, you give 'em their walking papers. Gary didn't listen. Wasn't anybody's way but his way."

If Stewart had been on any other label than RCA I believe the future might've turned out differently. Had he come up on a funky little label like Shelter or Bearsville or a more adventurous major like Warner/Reprise he could've made all sorts of great music, not just country. But it didn't happen that way.

It must've been rough for Gary. His records tanking, the only recent success had come from cowriting a novelty hit for Hank Jr. One day in Stewart's trailer, full of youthful ignorance, I probed into the matter further by callously asking, "Okay, 'Gary Stewart, washed-up has-been'—how did that make you feel?"

"Yeah, I never thought much about it," Gary shot back, the anger in his voice dissipating as quickly as it had risen. "I knew things couldn't go on forever. Things change. And I was *ready* for it. So it didn't blow me away. It didn't make me scared or nothin'. I had expected it before I went to Nashville. I had expected that all my *life,* 'cause I studied up on it. When I was a kid, y'see? By reading up on it in country music magazines. It's just plain ol' street knowledge, man. Look at the charts today and the charts in '49. They ain't got the same people! Times change, artists change. Hey, look how many artists have a hot span and then...pffft. I *knew* it wasn't goin' great. That's life. There are no free rides."

At one point when I told him it felt like he was prostituting his music, I saw him flinch. Later I asked if that had struck a nerve.

"Yeah. Because I used to say 'I will not prostitute my music.' I mean, those were the *exact* words. That's why it really hit."

"So is it fair to say there was a period at the end of the RCA years where you got far away from the kind of music you wanted to make?"

"Yeah. *Yeah*. I was prostitutin' myself and my music." There was no joy in hearing him utter these words.

* * *

Did Nashville appreciate Gary Stewart? "Never, never," said Tanya Tucker. "He was just too crazy. Musically he was just out there. He had his own agenda. You had to play the game, walk the walk if you wanna be successful. And if you don't, they'll scratch you off the list. That's kinda the way it goes."

Dean Dillon agreed. "Y'know, people didn't get Gary," he told me. Yeah—and in 1983 I'd say that included his producers, his label, the man who signed him and, unfortunately, many of those around him.

Dean Dillon is in the Country Music Hall of Fame. So is Tanya Tucker. And, bless his heart, Joe Galante. Gary Stewart is not in the Hall of Fame. And after being dropped by RCA, he would never record for a major label again.

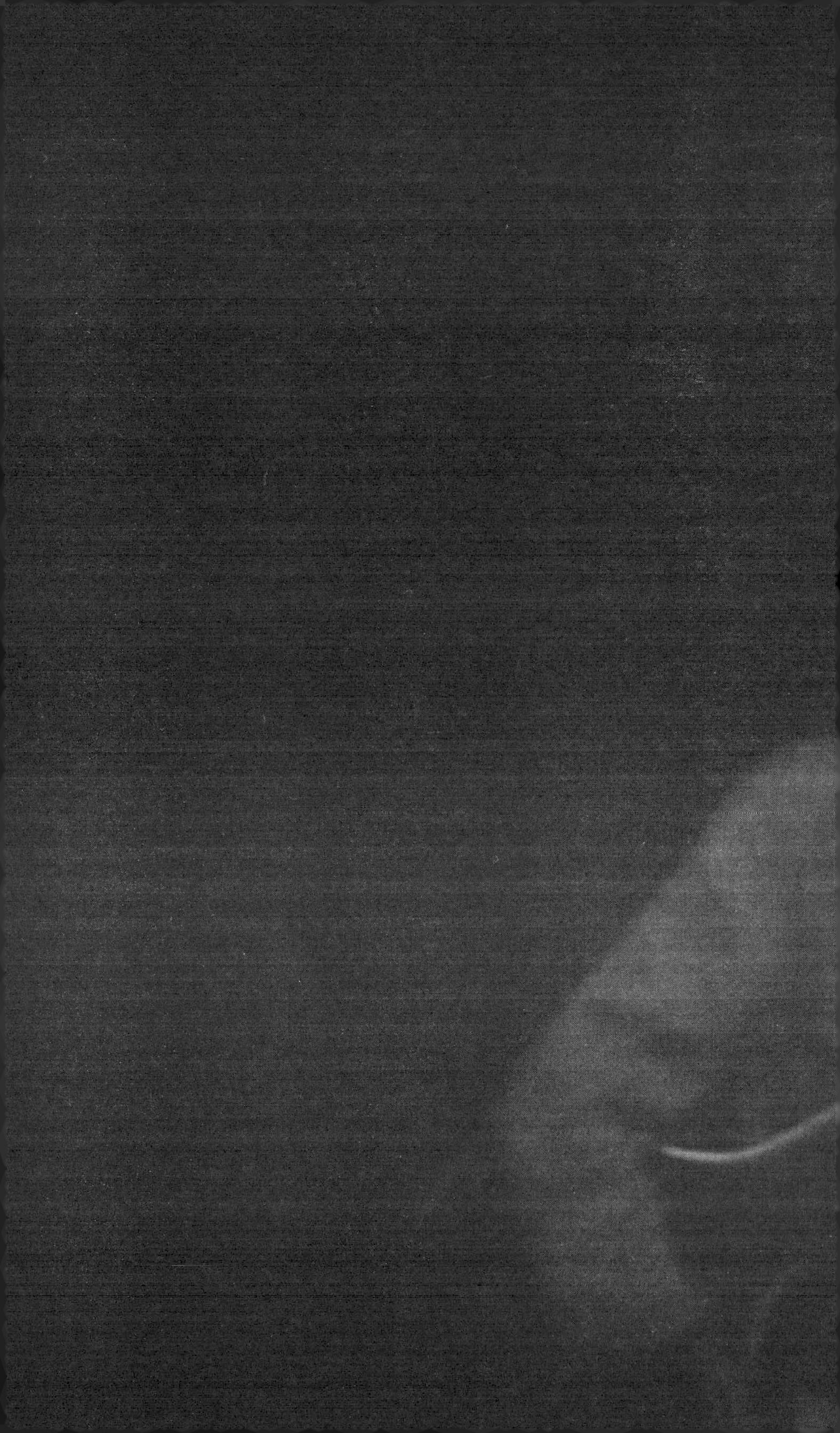

15

BAD ATTITUDE

I was surprised by the success that I had. I was not surprised when it went away.

– Leon Russell to David Fricke, 1992

Music, drugs, chaos—in the early eighties the Stewart house was a hive of activity. Gary was hitting it hard on the road, and Joey and Shannon were now teenagers. The Stewarts were a "modern-day hippie country family," as Tommy Schwartz told Charles Passy. "If there was any discipline, it was probably the kids trying to apply it to the parents." Shannon stressed that "my mom tried to keep it as normal as possible. We had dinner, you said grace—'Who's gonna say it tonight?' Dad, Mom, me, Joey—that was the seating. And you cleared the table."

As parents, Gary and Lou were lively and fun when things were up. "My mom taught me how to jitterbug, we used to dance all the time in the living room," Shannon recalled. MTV's *The Osbournes*—

later a favorite in the Stewart household—is a frequent reference point when Shannon discusses growing up. "We were a very open family, we didn't keep anything from each other. We were very boisterous, and we kept it real. My parents didn't hold anything back. Truth, no holds barred. If it hurts your feelings, *sorry*. That's just the way it was."

When Gary was writing a song at home, you didn't dare disturb him. "Everybody had to back off, leave him alone...he would be in the living room for days." One day Shannon complained to her parents that she had trouble studying due to the endless jam sessions. Music also kept her awake at night. "Every time my dad would play, he'd tap his heel on the hardwood floors. I went in there and told him, 'You gotta stop. I gotta go to school tomorrow!' And he goes, 'Listen, let me make you a deal. I can't quit pickin' and playin' music, so if you quit school, I'll buy you a car.'" This was an offer Shannon couldn't refuse. "What do you do at sixteen years old? You're like, 'Okay!'" Gary got her a burgundy Mustang—"an old one, nothin' extravagant"—and a job at the Tape Deck, a local music store. School versus music? No contest for Gary.

Mary Lou worked hard keeping loose ends together, the loosest being Gary. Just getting him home from the road with the money he'd earned was a challenge. Stewart never had credit cards, and his wallet contained only a picture of his family and a strip of rawhide.[93] "One time he called my mom and told her that he lost a whole weekend's worth of working money for a twenty-five-cent game of *Pac-Man*," said Shannon. Gary had sat down for a game between flights and spaced out picking up his cash bag when he left. "He lost the whole freakin' weekend money. My mom was disgusted. I don't think they talked for a week after that." At one point Lou hired a guy to take Gary to and from the airport. His name was Early. "An older gentleman, and that was his job," explained Shannon. And when Early deposited Gary

93 Gary loved to tie intricate, distinctive knots in strips of rawhide. They were all over his house. Tommy Schwartz still has a bunch of them, and they are sacred. "Everybody at my house knows you do not untie the fuckin' knot—that's a *Gary Stewart knot*."

A young Shannon matches her daddy. (Grandal Stewart)

back home after a trip, "my mom would always wait at the door with a loaded .38, because my Dad would have wads of fucking cash." This was a new discouragement tool for any of those looking to receive a handout from soft-touch Gary. "Everybody knew not to come around," said Shannon. "You didn't want to mess with Mary Lou."

Gary remained enigmatic, even to his family. One day Stewart had a yard sale that wasn't. "Me and my brother had to run it," said Shannon. "Dad had us put everything out on the front yard. Then he wouldn't let us sell none of it! Whenever people came in the yard to buy things, they'd be like, 'How much is that?' And he'd be like, 'Oh, that's not for sale.'" None of his family was allowed to sell anything, either. "People would come by, ask, and we had to tell them, 'It's not for sale.' He'd watch us! Like, what was the point behind *that*? I don't know if he was punishing us or getting off on it. So crazy. That was when he was doing quaaludes." Gary mentions this "yard sale" in a 1981 interview with Bob Allen. It seems that a neighbor was mad at him because somebody's dog kept going through Gary's garbage and dragging it onto the neighbor's immaculate lawn. To yank his chain,

Stewart dragged everything out of the house and "decorated the whole front yard like the carnival...like a gypsy camp." Shannon was surprised to hear this, because he never explained it to his family[94].

Shannon had an ironclad bond with her father. "One time we got in an argument—a pretty intense argument. With him being gone all the time, it was hard for him to be the disciplinarian...I think he had a hard time with that. He came in my bedroom, threw something and hit a mirror. And I remember I grabbed him and I pulled him into me. And I was gritting my teeth. And he looked at me. He goes, 'Oh my God, you're just like *me*.' And that stopped the whole argument." They never really battled again. "I was always daddy's little girl. My dad was my hero."

Joey had a rougher ride. He'd grown into a handsome, popular kid who was supernaturally close with his mother and frequently clashed with his dad. It didn't help that Gary had wrecked the car he'd given his son in the accident that mangled his leg, the infamous black Cougar. "They were never the same after that," said Shannon. "Joey never forgave him....Joey would pick me up from private school in that car, with the best stereo money could buy jamming Van Halen's 'Jamie's Cryin'' while waiting in the long pickup line. Back then I was so embarrassed, but now I look back and think, 'Hell, yeah.'"

There would be another juvenile delinquent hanging around the Stewart house during this time, sort of a bonus family member: Jimmy Smith.

* * *

When I think of Fort Pierce, I see Jimmy Smith's face. Jim-Bob, as Gary dubbed him. Ever watch *Teletubbies*? You know the Sun Baby that hovers over the inhabitants below? Well, if there was a *Piercebuddies* show, Jimmy's tanned, round, bearded, cowboy-hatted face would beam down on the town's denizens, laughing, crying,

94 Stewart also expressed to Allen how happy he was somebody had run over his mailbox, which he didn't put back up. "The mailman brings bills, son!"

maybe offering a little blow with a gleam in his eye. Jimmy makes me laugh harder than just about any human being on the planet. He's a fabulous guitar slinger. And, it must be said, a legendary self-abuser. At one point in the late eighties I tracked him down at the local hospital. Inebriated, depressed, and crazy, he had "tried hari-kari" by stabbing himself in the chest, missing his heart by a quarter inch but puncturing a lung. "I bled like a stuck hog." Then there was the time he went on a bender with Sonny Tackett. "I fuckin' pawned all my equipment—my fucking Strat, every amp. I said, 'I am goin' to drink myself to *death*. Fuck it." Jail, failed marriages, broken bands...somehow he has managed to survive it all with a grin on his face and guitar in hand. Often I get a bombardment of texts from him in the middle of the night. "Love you, brother," he'll say, with a link to some new musical discovery he just had to share. If I ever stop getting these drunken missives, Fort Pierce will cease to exist for me, for he is the town's spirit, in all its fucked-up, ragged glory.

James Carroll Smith Jr. was born March 20, 1959. His father was an electrician, and a person Gary sometimes came to—"my dad would loan him money, and he didn't do that too often." James Sr. was another Fort Pierce character. "Me and Daddy were more like friends than father and son. We'd pass girls to each other 'n' shit—'You wanna fuck this one over here?' And he was that way in his seventies, right up until the end. We'd come over to bring him food, I opened the door and a naked whore ran to the back—'Oh shit, Daddy, we didn't mean to interrupt your party.'"

James Sr. had always wanted to be a musician, and when he found a guitar on a trash heap, he got Gary's old running buddy Bill Eldridge to fix it up for his son. Since the guitar was mangled before Bill rebuilt it, Jimmy had no idea of the make. "I called it my Eldridge." But Jimmy Sr. wouldn't let Jimmy Jr. play it at first. "My dad stuck it up in the closet in my bedroom where I couldn't get to it—'No, you're not old enough yet.' I'd just stare at it every night. He was psychologically making me want to play guitar." Jimmy had his first lesson on his seventh birthday and was soon in a trio with neighborhood kids Felix Moss and Gary Abercrombie. "We sounded like shit. Our name was the Vibrations. They weren't good vibrations!"

Jimmy rode the school bus with Joey Stewart, and they became pals. Joey would sneak buds of Okeechobee Purple out of Gary's freezer jars for Jimmy. "That was *really* appreciated." Did Stewart care? Hell, no. According to Jimmy, he knew the Purple would "keep us out of his hair." It was after Joey heard the Vibrations practice that he went home and reported this new kid band to his dad, adding, "Would you show them how to play your songs right? 'Cause they're really fuckin' 'em up." By this point Jimmy's dad had bought him a Gretsch Tennessean—"like my hero, Chet Atkins. Gary come over, grabbed my ol' Gretsch, and right off the bat said, 'You need to change the strings. They're all rusty.'" Jimmy was clueless that his friend's dad was a big star. "I had no fucking idea." Jimmy became a long-term Stewart project, and with Gary's guidance the group would eventually morph into the Easy People Band and back Stewart up at local shows. "Gary took me under his wing. He was my mentor. The first album he gave me was *Layla*. And I got hooked on Allman Brothers, of course. I had no idea Gary *knew* them!"

Until one day when Jimmy and Joey, tooling around in Joey's old Impala, pulled up to the Stewart home. "There's Gary walking by with some lanky hippie and it was fucking *Dickey Betts*. And Gary wanted me to meet Dickey." Jimmy, who was sixteen at the time, asked "Mr. Betts" if he had any advice for a young fellow just learning how to pick. "Dickey walks around the car, puts his hand on my arm, looks me in the eye, and says, 'Okay, Jimmy, you remember when you first started gettin' pussy? You remember how you just jumped in there, gave it all you had, and in two seconds it was done?'" Jimmy nodded in the affirmative, then Betts asked him who he thought was the most beautiful woman in the world. Marilyn Monroe, said Jimmy. "Okay, picture you're in the sack with her. And you're wanting to give her your best shit. You don't just get up there like a rabbit, you take it easy. And give her a *little* bit—build it up and *tease*. That's the way you play your guitar." Words of inspiration for Jimmy Smith. "It worked! I learned how to play from my soul like that."[95]

Just before he turned sixteen, Smith pretty much moved in with the Stewarts after his parents split up, a trauma for Jimmy. Gary and Lou "kinda adopted me. Set me up with a forty-dollar tab at the corner store so I could go get me some food. And never batted an eye." By the early eighties Jimmy was in his twenties, and was now Gary's partner not only in music but drugs, part of the "very select few that got to party" at the Stewart home.

Gary was still deep into 'ludes. "He'd eat 'em like Chiclets," said Jimmy. What was the appeal? "They made you not think about eternity. They'd just blank it out." Stewart would be so out of it, "we had to tote him around the house. It was fucked." And he'd get ornery. "He'd be frothin' at the mouth, fallin' all around, he'd want to fight. Gary was a tough little bastard, and strong as a bear on them things." On quaaludes, Gary turned into Superman and would often take it out on Joey. "It was gladiator school with the quaaludes...I had to separate them many times," said Jimmy. As Shannon recalled, one day Gary "jumped out of a bedroom window onto my brother's back, because his shoes weren't tied...I had to pull them two apart. They were both beatin' the fuck out of me, tryin' to get to each other." Mary Lou stood on the stairs watching, unwilling to step into this particular brawl. "Nobody got hurt," said Jimmy. "Gary would thank me later for not letting anyone call the police."

Quaaludes were banned by President Reagan in 1984, but by then Stewart had graduated to another trashhead high—Soma, a

95 Years later Smith would jam with Betts after a big benefit for a cancer nonprofit. "We pull up at the Holiday Inn and Mary Lou is right there in the parking lot. She said, 'Come on, Jim-Bob, you're goin' with me, motherfucker!' She takes me up to fucking guitar heaven on the second floor of the Holiday Inn! All these monster players, especially Dickey." Impressed by Jimmy's playing, Betts started calling him Lightning Boy, after the whiz-kid guitarist in the *Crossroads* movie. Smith would also serve as gofer when Dickey needed coke. "Before he started playing, we'd have to go find him some shit, like a quarter of an ounce of it," said Bruce Hunter, singer in the Easy People band. "He'd do about half of it before he got up to play."

powerful muscle relaxant and pain blocker. Known by some as the "Houston cocktail," Soma imparts a heroin-like high that puts the user in an uncoordinated haze. "They'd make a grown man fall off a toilet" is how Shannon put it. "Gary would take so many friggin' Somas," said Laurie Rastrelli. "He'd start playing with his lips with his fingers and start going 'buh-buh-buh-buh-buh.'" The Somas had another side effect: binge eating. "It increases appetite insanely," said Shannon. "So he'd be up all hours of the night, which he was anyway, but eating just ridiculous shit. One time I came in and he was eating Kentucky Fried Chicken. Then he ate the coleslaw using the chicken bone leg as a fork." Gary went through a period where he had to have Breyers ice cream. For a while it could only be blueberry, then it was strawberry. After a few days Lou and Shannon would have to invade his room to clean up all the ice cream cartons scattered across the bed and floor.

Stewart would continue to abuse Somas on and off for the rest of his life. Sometimes Mary Lou joined in, sometimes not, but she remained unfazed by Gary's intake. Jimmy remembers a woman Stewart was staying with out on the road calling the house frantic to inform Mary Lou that her husband "had OD'd on Soma and probably wouldn't make it." Lou's reaction? Anger. "That fucker better not die, he's gotta write me one more song. I can't live on this shit!"[96]

Gary continued to bring trinkets home from the road for the kids. After one trip, he unpacked Roho and Jojo, a pair of garish, orange-and-purple marionette bird puppets that provided greater amusement for Gary and Jimmy than for the kids. The names were inspired by "a song about a badass fightin' rooster Gary used to sing."[97] Jimmy and Gary would put on a record and Roho and Jojo would dance. "We'd

---

96 Blasé when it came to Gary's overdoses, Lou instructed one panicked friend on the phone to "slap him around! Throw ice on him! Throw water!" It took an ambulance to the emergency room to revive him.

97 The song in question is "The Cockfight," an obscure 1967 novelty record by Archie Campbell, spoken-sung from the point of view of a rooster who has to face an infamous adversary: "I've come to kill a big rooster called Roho/Doin' it all for chicken feed." Complete with Spanish guitar and clucking humans in the background, it is the sort of oddity only Stewart could love.

make 'em hump 'n' shit," said Jimmy, laughing. Adding to the mirth, no doubt, was the fact that they were "tripping our brains out."

Blame it on the acid, another of Stewart's party favors at the time. Gary had an indirect connection to John C. Lilly, the infamous California physician/psychoanalyst/author most notorious for his research on interspecies communication between dolphins and humans, who'd send Stewart extremely potent blotter acid called Golden Dolphin. "It came in the mail in sheets," said Jimmy. "Gary wouldn't even use scissors—he'd tear off a corner and pop it in his mouth. He did about twenty-five or thirty hits once." (When Shannon quizzed Gary on what tripping was like, he said, "It's like dreaming, but while you're awake.")

Gary and Jimmy had their own LSD band of sorts—a psychedelic duo called Dolphins on Microdots. "We played for hours and hours." What kind of music was this? "Hard to explain," mused Jimmy. "Magic." But Smith did not possess the superhuman tolerance Gary did and Stewart "took me to places I didn't want to go," said Jimmy, shaking his head. They'd listen to music while tripping, like the Moody Blues' cosmic *On the Threshold of a Dream* album—"very good, but a bit creepy," declared Jimmy. "Still have trouble listening to it—flashbacks!" Another lysergic favorite was *Martha Carson's Greatest Gospel Hits*. Kentucky-born Carson was a singer, guitar player, and distant relative of Gary's who could really belt out an old-timey spiritual. One night when they put on the Carson album, "all of a sudden lights started flickering and the turntable slowed down," Smith recalled. "It freaked me the fuck out." Gary said ominously, "I'll bet this house is *glowing*." "Sometimes the trips with Gary got very scary...when they were bad, they were *bad*."

But it wasn't just the acid that scared Jimmy. Smith recalled a secret trip up to the Stewart attic, where Joey showed him a copy of *The Satanic Bible* and books about the occult. Joey whispered to Jimmy that his great-grandmother on Mary Lou's side "was a practicing witch." One day Smith woke up to discover Gary had put all his tiki-god statues and bones all over his front yard, including "a human skull that came from an Indian burial mound. Gary swore it was possessed...I promptly put them back. Little bastard." Jimmy also claimed that on one drug-fueled night at the Stewart residence one of his sisters watched a cat's head twist around à la *The Exorcist*. "Fear and loathing in Fort Pierce," said Jimmy.

But the night that really spooked Smith was the time "Stormin'" Norman Hamilton offered to buy Jimmy's soul. "That was fuckin' freaky," said Jimmy with a shudder. "I don't even like to talk about it." Norman grew Okeechobee Purple and dealt in "all kinds of hallucinogens—he had this shit called Mean Green—they take parsley and put some kind of chemicals on it....Norman grew good weed, but he was also into this hoodoo-black-magic shit. He was a very dark figure. I know Gary paid Norman $5,000 for 'spiritual help.' Lou was pissed off about it."

Jimmy was over at Gary's one day visiting with Joey and playing one of Stewart's vintage guitars. Gary and Norman were off in another room conspiring. "They were trippin' and so was I—it was my birthday. Gary gave me a little somethin'. I'm sitting there pickin', and a beer mug, a big ol' thick one—that son of a bitch exploded! It didn't fall from a cabinet, it fucking *exploded*. It slung glass all over Joey, his face was cut up. And I heard Norman and Gary in there laughing. I'm goin', 'What the fuck?'" And that's when Stormin' Norman waltzed out and asked Jimmy a question. "'What you want, Jimmy? What do you want?' I said, 'What do you mean?' He said, 'What do you want for your *soul*?' It freaked me out. I said, 'Fuck this, I'll see y'all later.' I went out the fucking door."

Smith hopped into his little '69 hatchback and tore back home. On the way, he passed a bad accident where cops were pulling a man out of a car. One officer left the scene to chase after Jimmy, no doubt due to his psychedelic driving—"I was fucking all tripped out, and the road is fuckin' peeling open like a banana." The cop pulled him over. "I said, 'This is my birthday, I'm legal!' My eyes were nothin' but pupils. He said, 'Get your ass back home, and don't come out of your house until tomorrow!' So I went...and the evil shit attacked me." The acid really kicked in. "I'm praying, I'm praying, and I had an out-of-body experience. I felt God come around me, and I felt so much joy. By this time, I'm butt-ass naked. And ready to run out and tell the world about Jesus!" From then on Jimmy avoided Stormin' Norman. "That was the scariest night of my life, I ain't shittin' ya. Gary was my friend and brother, but sometimes that house was like *The Addams Family.*"

* * *

No major labels courted Gary Stewart after he left RCA. As always, it wasn't Gary's style to beat his own drum. As he told Bob Allen, "I couldn't call somebody and say, 'Hey, can I record for you? I'm lookin' for a label. Y'all need any *artists*?'"

Dave Jordan entered the picture in 1983. At the time, he ran Raven Red Ash Coal Company, which had a hundred employees. He had his own helicopter at the time. Jordan had grown up in Grundy, Virginia, little over an hour's drive from Jenkins, where Gary was from, loved Stewart's music, and followed his career. He attended a Gary show at Marlow Tackett's Country Palace in 1981 and had been wowed. Dave got to talking to the band and arranged for them to play a show in the town he was living in, Richlands, Virginia. He'd quickly learn that Dean Dillon was no longer in the picture. "Gary didn't want anything to do with him. He wouldn't answer his phone calls...Gary was just drifting without a rudder. He was lost."

Jordan was savvy enough to recognize how instrumental Roy Dea had been in Stewart's success. He'd sense lingering acrimony between the two. "I think Gary blamed Roy and Roy blamed Gary. They weren't speakin' to each other." Dave decided to grab the bull by the horns. "Out of the blue, I said, 'Gary, what do you think about getting back with Roy?' and he said, 'Well, I'd be okay with that.'"

Jordan got on the horn to Dea. "Dave Jordan was a Gary Stewart *freak,*" said Roy. "Knew every lick. He called me a bunch of times, and I wouldn't return his calls—'I don't cut Gary Stewart no more.'" At the time, Dea and his partner Pat Carter had invested in singer-songwriter Steve Earle and were trying to get his career off the ground. But Jordan kept calling. "Finally one day I answered the phone. I said, 'What do you have to do with Gary?' And he said, 'Nothin', really, I just want to help him.'" Impressed by Dave's sincerity, Dea agreed to a meeting with Jordan and Stewart in Nashville.

Roy had heard through Music City rumor mills that Stewart's voice had been faltering due to the muscle relaxants and pain medications he'd been downing since his car accident. Roy suggested that Jordan send Stewart to a doctor to check out his vocal cords. Dave managed to slip him in to see Charley Pride's personal physician. "There's nothing wrong with his voice, except that he's lost an octave," the doctor told Jordan. He also threw in some personal advice: "Gary Stewart is one of the greatest singers in the history of country music. But you'll never make a dime off him. I advise you not to fool with it."

Jordan ignored that warning and plunged ahead. Once Dea took a gander at Stewart in the flesh, his fears subsided somewhat. "Gary looked really good. I said, 'Gary, are you *straight*?' He said, 'Yeah, man.' 'Can you *sing*?' He said, 'Yeah.' 'Are you gonna *try*, Gary? You gotta give it all you got. This man's gonna put a lot money into you, you owe it to him.' 'Yeah, yeah, yeah.'"

A plan was hatched to do a couple of singles and at least one album, all to be put out independently by Jordan, who had no experience in the music business. Dea, who believed in Dave, said he'd contribute 50 percent himself. "I won't charge anything for what I'm doing," Roy told him. The three of them rode around in a limo listening to the classic RCA sides. "I got all high again, charged up," Dea admitted.

Jordan even sent his CPA to Nashville to try to straighten out Gary's debt to the IRS, an ongoing headache. He bought Stewart a brand-new Thunderbird as well. "Gary didn't have a car. I don't think he even had a driver's license." Stewart showed up at Jordan's house one day with a friend who drove it back to Florida for him. "Gary couldn't afford any insurance, so I had to carry it. He never even changed the title over."

Dave also met with Jerry Bradley, who still held certain recording rights on Gary and from whom Dave had to get a release. Jordan was impressed by how protective Bradley was of Stewart but noticed "a chill" between Jerry and Roy when they were in the same room together. Nevertheless, Dea was fine with confronting his old boss when Bradley appeared a bit skeptical of their plans, telling him, "Well, what do you got, Jerry? You're not really doing nothing for Gary." Bradley relented.

For the next three years Jordan would bankroll Stewart and Dea, spending over fifty grand in the process. "All I was ever doing was writing checks," he cracked. The sessions were cut at LSI, a Nashville studio partially owned by Roy's partner, Pat Carter, which was "more of a demo place than a finished product place," according to Jordan. "Roy wanted to give Pat some business and help him out. He got criticized for that later by several people, including Jerry."[98] It certainly wasn't RCA, but Bill Lyerly, who recorded an album for Jordan produced by Dea, thought it was funky and great. "They had Isaac Hayes's Hammond B-3 and Leslie in there. Painted black, both of 'em, and they said 'I.H.' for Isaac Hayes!"

Jordan's label was christened Red Ash Records, after "the red ash seam of coal—high-quality metallurgical grade coal used to make steel." The mining connection must've pleased Gary. Dea put together an all-star cast of players from Gary's RCA sessions: Pete Drake, Jerry Shook, Dale Sellers, David Briggs, Harold Bradley, and others. Background vocals were done by the Whites, a Fort Worth family known for their country and gospel, along with highly regarded former Mother Earth singer Tracy Nelson. Having never been in a recording studio, Jordan attended the first few recording sessions, but soon lost interest. "It's like watching somebody make sausage. It would be like me taking somebody into a coal mine."

---

98 Dave nearly bought the fabled studio where Gary had recorded most of his hits—Music City Music Hall, aka RCA Studio B—as it was on the chopping block at the time. He had a $400,000 check to Jerry Bradley waiting when Roy told him, "Don't buy it—it's all analog, there's no digital equipment." This being the eighties, analog was considered obsolete.

The first Red Ash single, "Hey, Bottle of Whiskey," was a Don Singleton lament Gary had learned off a 1982 album he truly loved, *Waitin' on a Southern Train*, by John Starling, a bluegrass picker and singer who'd been a member of the Seldom Scene. No doubt chosen for its alcohol content, Stewart's version of the song is perfectly respectable, fine, even, but it does not eclipse Starling's recording. The flip, "Roadhouse Romances," is a jaunty but forgettable uptempo number that manages to work the phrase "your place or mine" into the lyrics. Released in May 1984, Stewart's return as a solo artist went to a mere number seventy-five on the charts. Not an auspicious start.

The following month came the best of the three Red Ash singles: "I Got a Bad Attitude," a tough little blues number written by W.T. Davidson that spoke volumes to Stewart's current status. "I got a whole lot of people/Disappointed in me," he snarls, unrepentant. It was backed with "Life's a Game," a superb, world-weary ballad credited to Gary, Rex Huston, and old Wagon Wheel buddy Hubert Thomas that Stewart sings the hell out of. "If you don't gamble, you can't win," Stewart wails mournfully, cognizant that the dealer's already taken his chips. According to Jordan, the single did well initially and was jumping up the charts when "people started playin' the back side," splitting airplay on the record. It went to number sixty-four.

In October came the third and last Red Ash single, "Red Georgia Clay," an old-school murder ballad written by the trio of Hal Bynum (most famous for penning the Kenny Rogers megahit annoyance "Lucille") and "Wild" Bill Emerson and his wife Jody. "He is a *Southern boy*, Lord, I'm tellin' you," exclaimed Stewart when Wild Bill's name came up, and Gary would cut a number of his songs late in his career. Emerson had been a running buddy of George Jones and was known to sell a song for quick cash. "Anytime you met Wild Bill he was completely broke," said Sonny Tackett, who watched his uncle Marlow supply Emerson handout after handout. "He was a great big presence, like 250 pounds, six foot six. Native American. You couldn't look him in the eye, because one eye looked at you and one looked down the road." One beer and Wild Bill was blotto, "and Gary hated that," Tackett said. One night they were having dinner at a fancy steakhouse where the patrons threw their peanut shells on the floor. "Bill had a big piece of steak he didn't eat. He picked up that steak and threw it on top of those peanuts. The waitress come by and Bill said, 'Honey, I hope you don't mind. I lost my meat.'"

The B-side of "Red Georgia Clay" was "Leaona," (later rerecorded as "Hey Leona"), the kind of woman's-name blues boast Stewart could write in his sleep (Rex Huston again gets cowriting credit) and whose main excuse for existing appears to be so Gary can reference one of his favorite cars in the chorus—a Cadillac Coupe DeVille. "Red Georgia Clay" did not crack the Top Hundred, and Jordan, who felt it was the best of the three singles, was deeply disappointed. Roy Dea was dismayed that John Anderson put the song out as an album cut at the same time. But they continued to record, the "Red Georgia Clay" single announcing it was "from the Red Ash album *Good-Timin' Man*."

Jordan said there were plans to cut a blues album, a collection of country gospel numbers à la "I've Just Seen the Rock of Ages" and much more. Among the songs cut at this time were the first version of "An Empty Glass"; a stark, no-frills remake of "Backslider's Wine"; and a left-field version of a Beatles classic that came about when Gary was jamming with fellow Red Ash artist Bill Lyerly. "They just started playing 'We Can Work It Out' super-uptempo bluegrass style, a cappella without guitars or anything," Jordan recalled. "It knocked me down." The magic failed to be recaptured once they attempted to record it without Lyerly. "I think it got half-assed done," said Jordan. "We had many wasted sessions." Unfortunately, we may never hear most of this material. "All the tapes are lost," said Jordan. The LSI studio got sold and the masters were apparently scattered in the process.[99]

99 Jordan noted cryptically that the Red Ash album still may see release, albeit minus Dea's title and with a cover photo by Tim Cox, who shot the *Gary* cover, of Stewart playing live in Colburn, Virginia, that "Gary didn't like—'That looks like a dead man...some kind of a monster.'"

Whenever I brought up the Red Ash recordings, Stewart grimaced. He didn't think it was his best work and blamed it on health problems that started right after the second album with Dillon. "I was sick, I couldn't sing, it was pitiful. I had eye trouble...it was my glasses." He claimed an incorrect eyeglass prescription "affected my right eye and down my right side. My neck muscles and my back would get real tense." He turned to the pain pills, which, as Dea had suspected, dried out his throat for "two and a half, three years." Gary struggled to deliver in the studio. "I was hopin' I might land on one, get one straight enough for a single. Only one song came off—'I Got a Bad Attitude.'" Whether real or imagined, he felt the relationship with the pickers he'd worked with at RCA wasn't quite the same now that he was off the label. "Gary told me he was in fear of the whole Nashville process by that time," said Randy Toman. "He'd get in there and feel like those studio musicians were almost lookin' through him, a has-been artist on a non-major label tryin' to shoot for one more hit...he just loathed the situation."

The sessions got worse as time went on. It wasn't like before, where he was off in never-never land, he "just wasn't physically capable," said Dea. "The voice was gone." The pills also sapped Stewart of energy. "He'd come to the house and sleep—sleep all night, all day...go to the studio, sleep all the way to the studio. I said, 'Gary, this ain't right.' And he'd say, 'Oh man, these pain pills, I gotta get off 'em.'"

Stewart played two of Dave Jordan's annual Christmas parties for Red Ash employees, but at the last minute, failed to play the third. Sound man/bodyguard John Vann worked the gig. "Gary wasn't looking too good." On the way to the stage with Jordan, "Gary stops and says, 'I'm just not goin' on.' Dave Jordan started to bargain with him—'Gary, if you just go up and do half your set, I'll still pay you a full paycheck.' 'No, I just don't want to go on.'" Finally Jordan tried to get Stewart to agree to just one song. "We got to the point where we were walkin' across to the stage, and Gary just stopped. He wasn't doin' it."

Jordan maintained that the showdown happened in the motel across from the steakhouse he'd rented for the gig. "The Toman Brothers opened the show, then Bill Lyerly did some numbers, and Gary was supposed to come on with the Tomans for a final set...I got word he was sick, so I went over to his room to talk to him. After thirty minutes of friendly back and forth, I was thinking about all the employees that had come to see Gary because they had never got to see him in the prior years. So I offered him more money. But he said that wasn't it—he had just played three straight nights and his throat was too sore to go on. I had heard him use this excuse on other people, but not on me. My final plea was for him to do one song, we would then make apologies to the crowd, and he could go back to the room." Gary refused.

Bill Lyerly said Jordan sent him over to the motel as well "to see if I could talk him into coming out." Gary "was drinking and doin' downs," and Lyerly maintained there was another reason Gary wouldn't go on. "He was really upset, because he just found out that his wife had lupus.[100] I hung out with him for about fifteen minutes. It's not that he didn't want to go, he couldn't. I knew Gary loved the blues. I said, 'Well, come on, man—you don't even have to sing, we'll just jam some blues. He almost went for that." But Gary didn't. "It was left to me to explain and apologize to the hundred or so people who had come to see him," said Jordan. "I was not happy about it."

Things degenerated further the next day when Jordan got an angry call from Mary Lou, who accused him of somehow "not doin' the Tomans right. It really just pissed me off and caught me wrong. All the money I poured into Gary, and you're bitching to me about something you have nothing to do with? And here you got a brand new $30,000 car and you can't even put it in your own name? We had a knock-down, drag-out and I just let her have it." It was the last time

100 Lou's lupus diagnosis was apparently an unofficial one. "I don't know if that was something she just created in her mind," said Shannon. "She ended up getting her breast implants out and she was one hundred percent better—one of her implants busted and that's what was making her feel so bad. We ended up thinking she never had lupus."

Dave ever spoke to her.[101] "After that, Gary and I got a little cold for each other." The union of Gary Stewart and Red Ash Records faded away. He wouldn't release any more music until 1988.

* * *

Gary Stewart stayed afloat the only way he knew how—honky-tonks. Hitting the road with the Toman Brothers Band, he made the rounds in Texas, Oklahoma, New Mexico. Stewart had gained a hardcore following in these joints, with some rabid fans following him from gig to gig. Not only that, "club owners loved him," said John Vann, as a Gary Stewart show meant tons of liquor sales. Rumors of drunkenness continued to follow him. Randy Toman maintained it got so bad, "the minute Gary would get up there and forget the words to somethin', the crowd turned."

Besides making sure Gary didn't drop any hundreds, the hard part was corralling Gary to the gig on time and making sure his sugar cravings were satisfied. Vann recalled how Stewart would be comatose in the back seat of whatever vehicle was transporting him and suddenly "pop his head up—'Hey, Johnny, you think they got some coconut cream pie back at that town? Can we go see?'" One night Vann turned around on the way to a gig and drove twenty-six miles back to find Gary his pie. "I told him I'd go in and get it, because if he goes in there, it's gonna be another hour. We barely got to the job in time." Russ Toman recalls the time Gary stayed with him and failed to get his ice cream allotment. Toman was going to make a cake for his mother's birthday and had bought a can of ready-made icing. He awoke to find Gary had "ate the whole can of Pillsbury frosting." Just the empty can with a spoon in it remained. "I guess his sweet tooth got the best of him."

One time Gary asked Randy if he had any porno movies. He had a few, but his brother had a lot more, so Russ set Gary up with a pile of tapes and a VCR. Toman then crashed, having driven all night from a

101 Jordan compared Mary Lou to Hank's infamous ex and tone-deaf duet partner, Audrey Williams. A little harsh, to say the least. Mary Lou never warbled a tune!

gig. When he awoke hours later, Gary was frozen in front of the tape machine, eyes glazed, remote in hand. On the TV "two people were fuckin'," said Randy. "He had it on fast scan, so they looked like a sewing machine." Gary muttered, "I'm just fixin' to hit the sack." When Gary stayed over, it "was like having an extra kid in your house," said Russ.

The topper came one night Randy and Russ were driving back from another gig. Gary was sprawled in the back seat, asleep as usual. The two brothers passed the time by swapping stories about women they'd met on the road and the various sexual shenanigans that had resulted. All of a sudden Gary rose up from the back seat and drawled, "Boys, my wife has got the *best pussy* out of *everybody*!" Randy and Russ just looked at each other dumbfounded. What do you say to the boss after such a declaration? "I didn't know where to go with it from there," said Randy.

* * *

It was during this period that Stewart started collecting a particular breed of maniac fan—married Texas couples who would cart him to gigs, buy him things, put him up at their homes, and pay his expenses. It never ended well. "They were the starstruck, take-it-too-far people," said Randy. "They reveled in the fact that all of a sudden people at Billy Bob's would have to take them seriously because they were Gary's so-called 'road managers.'"

Robert and Judy Austin, who hung around from July 1983 to the following January, founded a Stewart fan club before they started accompanying him to gigs. Robert soon left his job at a local Safeway supermarket to take care of Gary full time. "Many times he come in and he didn't have clothes to wear, we'd take him to buy clothes," said Austin. "My wife would take him to the beauty shop, fix his hair. It was just like babysittin'. If he wanted to run up to Skaggs and get a cream puff we took him, no matter. Gary really liked them cherry turnovers at Arby's because they had the glaze on top of 'em. If he wanted to go there at four or five o'clock in the mornin', we'd do it."

Gary (sporting eyepatch) with two fans backstage at Billy Bob's, February 1984. (Dave Jordan)

At first, Toman was relieved that Gary had a handler and a place to stay. "They bought a lot of nice gifts, things that Gary wanted. And Robert was trying to keep riffraff out of the backstage area, people that were going to give Gary cocaine. But it got to where Robert took it too seriously." Things soon soured between Stewart and the Austins. "Gary was depressed a lot," said Robert. "He didn't have a lot of ambition at the end. His mood would go minute to minute dependin' on who he was with. If you wanted to eat, he wanted to eat; if you wanted to see a movie, he wanted to see a movie. An' if you wanted to jump off a cliff, *he* wanted to jump off a cliff."

An aggressive new couple eased the Austins out of the way—Ray and Dana Marr. Like the Austins, they were thrilled to be in the limelight, or at least in close proximity. "It was really good for us, because they would just wait on us hand and foot," said Toman. The Marrs would even venture to Gary's home in Fort Pierce—"Dana and Ray were here a lot," said Shannon. But they, too, got too big for their britches and much tiny intrigue followed. According to Randy Toman, Dana, whom Randy merely considered Gary's "babysitter of the week," suddenly turned boss lady and barked at Toman she'd "fire his ass" if he were late. "Let's just see who's out first," Randy mused to himself. Then came disagreements over money, "and all of a sudden I remember Mom not liking Dana anymore," said Shannon.[102]

Soon enough, Dana was threatening to divorce her husband if Gary wasn't out of their lives. By the time I caught up with her in 1987, the party was over, and she had endless complaints about Stewart. Gary told a reporter he had Alzheimer's. Gary wouldn't do anything he promised he'd do. "People expect that from musicians," Stewart told Dana matter-of-factly. "He's the sorriest son of a bitch I've ever met," she hissed. "He's a user, he's rude, he has no respect for other people's feelings or their property. He takes every goddamn thing, he don't give a fuckin' thing back, and he never will. And when he gets through with you, somebody else will come along." As far as money went, Gary "don't ever know what he spent. If he had ten million dollars in his travel bag, he would still be broke."

* * *

By the mid-eighties Gary Stewart's live performances were beginning to falter. The shows became more erratic. "Gary got so sick of doing 'Drinkin' Thing,' and yet he knew he had to do it," said Toman. "He'd goof up and sing the words to 'She's Actin' Single,' so we'd act like it was a medley, but it wasn't. He just got on the wrong track. Gary hadn't really learned any new songs for a while, and he would find himself coming up onstage grabbing at straws." Usually they'd open with "Flat Natural Good-Timin' Man," but suddenly Gary would "want to do a song that we had never done before, like '(Now and Then There's) A Fool Such as I,' the Elvis Presley hit. He was like a batter in a slump."

---

102 The Marrs did one very special thing for Gary. They were the ones who, at Lou's insistence, called Dylan's people and got Gary an invitation to the 1986 Dallas show discussed earlier where Stewart met Dylan.

There were still stellar shows—like one night at Billy Bob's where "Gary just brought the house down," according to Toman. "We played an hour over the time we were supposed to, and it was one of the record crowds at the club—in spite of the fact that George Strait and Hank Jr. way outdrew Gary, he still held his own at a has-been status in his life." But those moments were getting few and far between. "It wasn't a sudden death," said John Vann. "The big money started becoming less and less and less." Additionally, Stewart's many ailments proved more and more challenging for those dependent on making a living. Said Toman, "I got to the point where I started thinking, 'Well, is he in pain or is he a hypochondriac?'"

But Randy had learned you could never predict what Gary might do or what he was capable of at any given moment. "The minute you think you're dealin' with this ol' stupid-ass country boy with all sorts of drug and medical problems, he'll do something absolutely unexpected and brilliant. He loved to pull the wool over people's eyes with that dumb hillbilly routine." Toman recalled some unwanted guest irritating the hell out of Stewart one night backstage. "Hey, motherfucker," drawled Gary. "I'm an in-breed, and us in-breeds are real ignorant when we get mad." They slunk off, tail between their legs.

As always, Gary felt things deeply. Shannon recalled that when John Lennon was murdered in 1980 he "locked himself in the bedroom for about a week because he took it so bad." Dana Marr remembered driving Stewart to a gig when Floyd Cramer's ambling 1960 piano instrumental "Last Date" wafted out of the car radio. Gary, conked out in the back seat, suddenly came unglued. "Turn that off! Turn that off!" The number conjured up memories of a musician friend who'd killed himself.

Out on the road with the band another night, traffic was backed up due to a car crash. "It was a really bad accident," said John Vann. "There were cars kind of scattered over the interstate, and as we crept closer, Gary just laid down and hid his face. And he said, 'I just don't want to see any dead bodies!' He was freaked out. There weren't any dead bodies to see, but he made sure he didn't see one. Gary was a very complex person."

On August 28th—the anniversary of Griselda's suicide—Hubert Thomas, Gary's old running buddy from the Wagon Wheel days, died in an ambulance en route to the Fort Pierce hospital. "That blew Gary away," said Lou. "He was in shock." Hubert's death was an unwanted milestone for the Florida crowd. Everybody I talked to held him in high regard, not just Gary. "To live your whole life and have nobody say nothin' bad about you? That's a hell of a man," said Lou. "That's how Hubert was." Said Tommy Schwartz, "Hubert once told me that if it is Saturday night and you are a picker... you are supposed to be picking somewhere, even if it is at home alone. Until this day, I think of that every Saturday night." The death of Thomas sent Gary further into a tailspin. "He took it very bad," said Shannon.

Stewart started missing shows—the Red Ash Christmas party in Virginia, another in Oklahoma. The Tomans had stopped by Gary's hotel room before the gig to check in and he told the guys he'd see them at the gig. He had his cronies there to take him—Ray and Dana Marr, plus a Knoxville doctor who'd buddied up to Gary named Hall Worthington. But after the Tomans played their opening set, Stewart never showed. "As it turns out, he left town," said Randy. "We were facing irate crowds—no-show Gary. We ended up not making any money at all off that road trip. And he had skipped town, just because he was just too afraid to go on."

It came to a head somewhere in Texas in December 1985, when Gary had a breakdown. "I went out on the road and I says, 'I'm not gonna take another pill, not even a sleepin' pill or anything.' I stopped, and you're not supposed to stop takin' 'em all at once. I went into shock, couldn't sleep for a whole week...it was scary. It's just like losin' your mind. You're scared of everything in the world, scared that this is the end. It was death all around you, the scarin' of *death*."

Lou made a rare trip out on the road to help him. "He was in real bad shape. We'd have to sit out in the car until it was time to go on 'cause he was so nervous. He couldn't face the audience. It was bad.

So I told the bookers, 'I'm takin' him home.' They said, 'You can't. He's got contracts, shows to play.' I said, 'Watch me.' Let 'em sue me....I told Gary, 'I'll dig ditches, I'll do any damn thing, but you ain't goin' out there.'"

For the next few years Gary was practically invisible—barely playing shows, not making records, a nonentity in Nashville and the rest of the world. He became reclusive and would lay in his bed for days, comatose. Old friends would call only to get a busy signal, and when they reached him, it wasn't always good news. "He was gettin' preoccupied by death, weird things, drugs," said Bob Melton.

It was at this point I began searching for Gary Stewart. Having loved his music, I wanted to know what the hell had happened to the guy. The hunt began the way it always did—picking up the phone and making inquiries. After much digging, I got to someone who knew Stewart well. This party warned me I'd be better off not finding Gary. Holed up in a double-wide, doing massive amounts of drugs, he and Lou were goners. "They live in the dark and don't eat any food, just like Count Yorga."

Oh really, I said, squeezing him for Gary's number.

Then I called.

16

JUKIN'

There's ten little me's in me. Hey, I'm serious, then I'm crazy and insane. But I try to do everything with a good heart. I have good intentions, y'know?

– Gary Stewart, 1987

I caught my first glimpse of Gary and Mary Lou Stewart as my bus rolled into Fort Pierce. Pale, jittery, dressed in black and wincing into the sun, they looked like zombie movie extras desperately in need of a cast lunch. We awkwardly said our hellos, hopped into Speed, the black T-Bird Dave Jordan had bequeathed Stewart, and set off, with Mary Lou manning the wheel, albeit erratically.[103] She'd later admit she could get lost a block from home.

There was a whiff of citrus in the air, the last vestige of Fort Pierce's extensive groves—chronic insect infestation had driven business

103 Speed was named after the horse Jack Nicholson rides in the 1978 movie *Goin' South.*

elsewhere. The town was no longer the mecca of honky-tonks and drive-in burger joints of Gary and Lou's youth, as the drug trade had taken its toll. "Fort Pierce is the crack capital of the world," a local drug squad sergeant would declare later that year. There were lots of bars on windows now, not just at Gary's. The week before I got there, some Uzi-toting thug had shot up a nearby convenience store that had been dealing coke under the counter. Stewart shuddered recounting the tale, one more reason to never leave the trailer. On Mary Lou's last trip to the gas station, some stranger had the nerve to ask if Gary "had suffered brain damage from all the coke." Aside from such violent intrusions, Stewart seemed blissfully unaware of the outside world. I got the sense Gary didn't know who the current president was. Nor did he care.[104]

We pulled in alongside a double-wide located not far from the home where they'd raised their two kids. With Lou's health battles, it had become too much, so they gave the house to Joey (Shannon was living behind it) and his old trailer became their new home. It was disorienting entering the place. Gary kept it dark, but as my eyes adjusted I tried to take in all that was crammed inside. There were vintage rugs, beaded curtains, mojo bags, cow skulls, and a wagon-wheel chandelier.

Pictures crowded the walls: Chief Rain-in-the-Face, Jesse James, Civil War scenes,[105] with pictures of the Stewart clan interspersed. "I could change these walls three times a day," said Stewart the restless curator. Playing on the TV was *The White Buffalo*, a 1977 Charles Bronson film that Gary loved. The sound turned down, at any given moment you'd look over and see a ghostly, mythical beast lumbering slow-motion through the snow. Stewart had covered several windows

---

104 Although when told about the crimes of Bin Laden by a friend, Gary declared fighter pilots should fly over his hideout, drop some boxes of Viagra, "and when that prick stands up, blow him away."

105 Years later I'd learn Stewart was a Civil War buff. According to his cousin Brenda Casey, "We would sit and talk about different battles, different strategies, and just all kinds of crazy stuff about the uniforms, the food that they used to have to eat. Gary was well-versed in the major battles of the Civil War." According to his drummer (and fellow Civil War aficionado) Ray Wilburn, when it came to the war's history, Stewart knew "a lot about the North and the South...a very smart dude."

with a giant painted stage backdrop of an eagle landing on a branch, which he'd freed from an old El Paso bar he played, taking an old bed apart to get pieces of wood long enough for the frame. "Dad would build his own frames," said Shannon. "He would always joke around and say, 'I'm not gonna play music anymore, I'm gonna open me up a framin' shop.'"

Gary's curious leather knots were everywhere, as were countless old, esoteric things he'd collected on his travels. At one point he pulled out a letter home from a Native American performer appearing as an "Indian Princess" in a Buffalo Bill Wild West show. A battered, taped-up phone lay on the floor, handset off the hook. And there were many, many albums stacked on the floor. Gary wasn't much for radio ("it influences me too much"), but he was definitely vinyl-crazy and would happily preach on the subject. "It gets me that a lot of musicians don't listen to music—y'know, *other* people's music. Hey, give me some RECORDS! Music, *music*!!! Yeah, I make it, but there's so many people that I listen to, that I respect, I don't get tired of listenin' to it." Guitars both valuable and cheap were never out of reach. Gary gave away as many as he kept. "Gary told me to bring my son over one day," said cousin Brenda. "They sat and played together. My son was thrilled. And at the end, Gary gave him the guitar. Gary told me that he believed there were only so many songs in a guitar for each person—'This guitar has given me all the songs it's going to give me. Maybe it'll give Brian some songs.'"

Between interviews we listened to records. He'd put a Brother Claude Ely 45 or a disc from a mammoth Bear Family Jerry Lee Lewis box set on the turntable, unscrew another bulb from the wagon-wheel chandelier to make the place even darker, then sprawl on the couch like a malnourished Gumby, albeit one wearing shades at 2 a.m. We'd ruminate on the music. And argue. And laugh.

* * *

Music had been my ticket into the trailer. The first time I called, I ranted and raved about Stewart's records and he'd recognized what they meant to me. This led into a discussion of our many obsessions. Even at this age I had accumulated a massive collection of crazy stuff, and Gary zeroed right in. Did I have any Allman Brothers? Audio, video, or both? Could I get him Dylan's *Eat the Document* or *Renaldo and Clara*? What about *Blonde Venus*, did I have a clean copy? "*Anything* with Marlene Dietrich," he stressed. (Gary and Lou both loved her.) We talked gospel, soul, country, bluegrass—getting worked up trading the names of those we loved like a couple of kids at a record swap. When I broached the idea of an interview, he told me there was one record he was looking for, and if I found it, yes, he'd do one—"Harlan County" by Wild Bill Emerson on Ace of Hearts Records. I got the feeling Stewart thought it such an obscure request he was off the hook. But within days a friend trawling dusty shops on his way through Pittsburgh had located a copy. Which I insisted on delivering myself.

* * *

There we sat in the trailer. Gary was forty-three. I was twenty-eight. Already jaded, hopelessly naive, I was a red-hot combination of utter certainty and gnawing self-doubt. I'd been hanging out in Times Square—a period of doom, destruction, and heroin. As a result, I'd become vociferously anti-drug, almost comically so. I saw things pretty much in black and white, which would prove problematic in a world as murky as Stewart's. Living in Hoboken, I was working in the film business while writing at night.[106] I talked an editor at New York City's influential *Village Voice* into doing a Stewart profile. This would be my first big story. I had barely been to the South and knew little of the machinations of Nashville, but I had a voracious appetite to learn. My mission was to tell the world how talented this guy was and somehow get him back in action in the process. Despite my being

106 Stewart was fascinated by my industry tales and expressed the desire to do a soundtrack more than once. "I'd love to do something for the movies."

Gary and the author. (Carole Nicksin)

new at the game, not to mention his own reticence, Gary made me feel like I belonged in that trailer. I fired away with the questions, many of which drove Stewart nuts. "This boy *questions* me, he questions my answers," he'd say to Lou. "I can't get complicated!"

At one point we discussed the tragedy of King Elvis. "I don't want to end up that way. Nobody would want to end up that way," he murmured in a suitably hushed tone. Then a crooked little smile crept across his lips. "But, y'know, I am the same age Elvis was when he died." To which I replied that this tin-box trailer wasn't exactly Graceland, nor had he really cut his Sun records as of yet. "If you went right now, who would give a shit, besides your friends, family, and me?" He cackled. "Y'know, pal, you got a point." Our interviews were often amusing, though a hint of malevolence always hung in the air.

Acoustic in hand, he'd prowl the trailer as he pontificated on his life, lunging into whatever song struck his fancy.[107] He'd get animated and loud when excited by the subject or belting out a song, but his slow drawl rarely rose much above a whisper so distinctive that just about everybody who knew Gary could slip into an impression. At first, drugs were done clandestinely, off in the bedroom away from the reporter's eyes, but soon enough he was snorting speed off album covers where he sat. "Hey, I ain't done a line in eight hours." He'd go and go and go, then collapse and take to bed. I wouldn't see him for days.

* * *

While the honky-tonk vampire lay comatose in his tomb, I'd run errands with Lou. She added a bit of smoky glamour to the festivities, and I was drawn to her. Gary could be very courtly to Lou, offering to put on her favorite Jimmy Reed record, then seconds later he'd be pissed that she had interjected an opinion he didn't care for. It changed like the wind.

Lou filled a shopping cart with Dr. Chek cola (a steal at nineteen cents a liter) and assorted sweets, the drug addict diet. Gary and Lou's son Joey, a stylish, handsome kid who had turned his parents' old home sleek with pink walls and Warhol Marilyn prints, met us at the store to make sure his mother had enough to cover the tab. "It's hard to do without once you've had it, y'know," muttered Lou. The Stewarts were broke, and Lou struggled to make it work. "Roy Dea told me once, 'Every family has to have an asshole, the one who does the dirty work.' Well, in this family the asshole's me." She joked about Gary's recluse ways, saying she had to turn him over every once in a while to avoid bedsores. Lou seemed weary of the drug life, but unable to break free.

* * *

107 It should be noted somewhere in this book that Gary was known to sing Prince's "Purple Rain" around the house. I'd give his brother Gerald's plastic eyeball to have heard that one.

While Stewart had only played live erratically following his 1985 "breakdown," he still did shows here and there, like a local extravaganza on June 28th, 1987, at the St. Lucie Fairgrounds that featured Stewart, Dickey Betts, and John Anderson—along with Jim "Ernest" Varney, making his singing debut. Whenever Varney's name came up, Gary would point out that he was "real intelligent," as if it were a surprise. One reason Stewart didn't like interviews: he was loath to criticize anyone. "He didn't talk bad about nobody," said friend and employee Barbara Anne Peters. Stewart could be sensitive to the point of inertia. He'd tell Peters he wouldn't call Dickey Betts or Gregg Allman out of fear that if he called one and not the other, feelings would be hurt.

* * *

Gary had not been completely idle during his time off the road. He proudly told me he'd written a bunch of new songs—"twenty or thirty," some going back a few years—and wanted to record again. There had been demo sessions in Nashville and scores more in home studios belonging to Tommy Schwartz and Fred Bogert in Fort Pierce. One session, overseen by Forrest Hills song plugger Glenn Middleworth for Jerry Bradley, produced a handful of recordings Roy Dea liked so much that he'd use the tweaked demo tracks on a couple of Gary's next albums—"Brand New Whiskey," "Empty Glass," "I Get Drunk," and "Delia."[108]

One of the most infectious new songs was a rolling, brokenhearted, old-timey lament, "Rainin', Rainin', Rainin'," a number Gary wrote on the spot over at Tommy Schwartz's house after his wife popped in to alert Tommy, Gary, and drummer Ed

108 Another Nashville Forrest Hills demo session happened not long after I started talking to Gary, but it was disastrous. Stewart's old writing partner Wayne Carson, who was supposed to produce, arrived "with a whole case of booze—whiskey, vodka, and tequila," said Glenn Middleworth, who was there to "babysit" Carson. By the end of the session "most of it was gone. He was so drunk, he literally passed out and fell on the console."

Smith of a thunderstorm outside. "Lee made it happen," said Tommy. "She walked into the studio and said, 'It's raining, raining, raining outside' and that we may want to unplug everything due to the lightning. Gary ran with that, and within an hour or so we had a great demo." Some of these songs dated back to the Red Ash period, like "Born a Rebel," a spirited declaration of all things Southern ("The heart of the South beats deep within me / I was born a child of Mother Dixie"). "Tommy, I've just wrote the best song I've ever written," Stewart told Schwartz.[109]

The solo Fort Pierce demo recordings are the most beguiling. Just Gary on guitar or electric piano, sometimes accompanied by a drum machine and reverb, and boy, are they hot stuff. He charges through the new songs, sometimes doing multiple takes at different tempos (usually "fast" and "faster"), interspersed with impromptu versions of such fifties hits as "I'm Walkin'," "All Shook Up," and "When My Blue Moon Turns to Gold Again."

Stewart sounds like he is speeding his brains out and, untamed and unencumbered by session players and Nashville-style demands to deliver, he cuts loose. You get the feeling he's doing it just to please his weird old self, nobody else. "Son of a Honky Tonk Woman" and "Let's Go Jukin'" are rockabilly boasts à la Jerry Lee that benefited greatly from Stewart's unruly, unrehearsed vocals and piano. The fact that Gary surrounded the new songs with beloved oldies from his youth is apt, for (by and large) these were not the intense, idiosyncratic numbers he'd written in his prime—there's not a "Harlan County Highway" or "Single Again" in the bunch. These are simple, lively rockabilly / R&B / rock and roll numbers that harken back to another age, the reflections of an older, more playful, slightly less crazed Stewart. "I'm wild in my mind now," he told me. "I want to write like Thomas Hart Benton paints."

Gary had a new cowriter on many of these songs: Mary Lou. She'd watched Gary write with Dean Dillon when he'd come to

109 According to Bill Hartman, Gary wanted to self-release an album of his outtakes called *Born a Rebel* at the end of his life. On the cover would be Stewart standing in front of a Confederate flag.

Fort Pierce, and when Gary left for the road during one visit, Dillon coaxed her into giving it a try. "Dean said, 'Let's write a song, Lou' and I said, 'I can't write, Dean!' He said, 'I *know* you can.'" Although they never finished that number, the encouragement was all Lou needed to start with Gary. "Sometimes we'll stay up for three days straight writin'," Lou told me proudly. "We might work on a song for two or three years." She cowrote at least nine songs with Gary in this period.[110] "Nothing Cheap About a Cheap Affair" came from a line a black preacher at a nearby Pentecostal church had used during an anti-cheating sermon Lou had attended. "I'm Guilty," a slow, sad ballad I could imagine James Carr tearing up during his Goldwax heyday, had come out of a quip Hubert Thomas used on his ex-wife, according to Lou. "He would say, 'Mary Lou, Carolyn's accusing me of lookin' at all the pretty girls, bettin' on horses, and spending all the money and gettin' drunk—and you know what? I'm *guilty*.'"[111] Unfortunately, this number and an eerie ballad Stewart gave Dickey Betts cowriting credit on, "She's Takin' Me Down"—two of Stewart's very best efforts—were never recorded outside of rough demos. Gary was proud of this new material, anxious to record (as he put it) one last album. "A singer only has so many years," he'd inform me. Stewart did bits and pieces of these new songs over the phone the first few times we talked and it was gripping.

* * *

110 Stewart's representatives at Forrest Hills were a little cynical about Mary Lou's writing credits. "Me and Jerry Bradley always thought if Mary Lou's name was on there, Gary had put it on just to get a piece of the publisher's share," said Glenn Middleworth. "He didn't have a copublishing deal with Jerry, he just got the writer's share." Gary's publisher had been Forrest Hills Music since the beginning, but Roy Dea had set Mary Lou up with her own publishing company, Blue Day. "So with Mary Lou's name on a song he also got copublishing through their own company. That would piss Jerry off!"

111 There is a fascinating tape of Gary and Lou writing "I'm Guilty." Gary reads bits of the Bible (Ecclesiastes 3:15, Song of Solomon 2:19) while Lou tries to sell Gary on the nearby church she's been attending. "Pentecostal is not a hypocrite church," she tells Gary, but he doesn't bite.

Word that Gary was ambulatory spread fast through Fort Pierce. Various pickers stopped by, thrilled that Stewart was even answering the door. At night the music flowed. It was thrilling. Fueled by adrenaline and speed, he'd jump from one song to the next, rat-a-tat-tat. Sometimes he'd just sing a line or two before moving on to the next number. While discussing Elvis, I had mentioned how much I loved his version of "Little Cabin Home on the Hill." A day later Stewart was performing it—"I'm learnin' that for you, Jimmy." He did the same with the old Lead Belly ballad "In the Pines," another personal favorite. Gary was so giving when it came to his music. He wanted you to feel it!

Some nights we'd head to Rialto's, a honky-tonk located at 3006 Orange Avenue, five minutes away from Stewart's house. Gary would dawdle for a few hours as he got ready, the shirts flying on and off that bone-thin frame when he wasn't obsessively combing his long black hair. This one night he chose a shiny black silk cowboy shirt, a black belt studded with buffalo nickels, tinted shades, and of course a black cowboy hat, which he'd held over a steaming teakettle to shape it just so. The look? Wasted hillbilly gangster. "He's a trendsetter in fashion, Gary is," said Lou. "And I am, too." Going out the door, Gary grabbed dinner—a fistful of Reese's Peanut Butter Cups (Gary's version: "Ree-See Cups"). He was wired. "C'mon, boy—let's go jukin'."

Rialto's was a dump, a large nondescript box containing the sweaty and drunken. There were fingerprints on the windows, paneled ceilings, cafeteria tables, vinyl seats, and a deer head on the wall. This was a honky-tonk—rough, tough, a den of sin, and a million miles from Nashville in every way.[112] The Easy People Band was onstage,

---

112 The wildest Rialto's tale happened in May of 1988. Ricky Ray—"one of our local redneck troublemakers" and the man who'd slit Gerald Stewart's throat—got into it outside the club with a couple of wannabe gangsters from south of the border who were trying to crash a wedding party the Easy People Band was playing. They came back to the club and shot up the joint through a little glass window in the rear door, hitting Ricky Ray, who wound up "with a colostomy bag on his side," said Tommy Schwartz, Easy People's bass player. Another bullet went through the leg of a bridesmaid, bounced off the floor, and hit bandleader Felix Moss in the ribs as he was singing "Marie Laveau." According to Tommy, "From that night on, every time someone requests that song Felix will say, 'Hell no, the last time I sang that song some Mexican shot me.'"

churning through numbers by Marshall Tucker and the Georgia Satellites. Named for the Stewart–Eldridge tribute to Kentucky holler life, this band of locals knew all of Gary's songs, having been instructed on their finer points by the master himself before they were old enough to shave, and he'd been sitting in with them since 1979 or so. This zero-prestige gig was perfect for Stewart. No pressure—he could blend into being just another picker in the band or charge into any song "that came to his mind," said their guitar player Jimmy Smith. When Stewart played with Easy People, "he turned us into a different band. All of a sudden we'd just become cool."

The crowd parted as Stewart made his way to the stage. Hometown boy. Some clapped, others just stared. The dance floor was packed. An old potbellied letch boogied around a barefoot teenager, occasionally grabbing her ass. She just laughed. A young cowboy did the gator, a big ol' Buck knife falling from his pocket with a thud. Nobody cared. A fight broke out in the corner, a couple of bottles flew. Gary just took it all in, a crooked grin the only thing visible beneath the hat.

A random drunk scolded Stewart for the beer bottle in his hand—"You could've made it real big if you'd quit that stuff"—then demanded to hear "Drinkin' Thing." Gary obliged, but slowed the number down, transforming it into a mournful, existential dirge, leaving the one who requested it perplexed. As soon as the song ended, Jimmy Smith lunged into a snakelike riff, the band crashing in behind him as Stewart began howling "Little Junior." Jimmy was having a big time on the strings. Gary laughed at the kid's flash and fired back an answer on his guitar. "Playin' next to him, I would feel these tingles—and I wasn't even trippin'," Smith told me later. "His energy...it was fucking incredible. A couple times I about blacked out." Lou, making a rare honky-tonk excursion, elbowed me in the ribs, happy to see Gary back in action. "It's been a long time since guitar playing has meant much of anything to him."

* * *

That first trip to Fort Pierce left me ecstatic. I told Roy Dea about Gary's new songs and he wanted to cut another album. I thought: We're gonna pry him out of the trailer to make his greatest record ever! We're gonna save Gary! But Stewart didn't want to be saved. From anything. By anyone.

* * *

In September came a suicide attempt. There had been a bad fight with Lou, and after she left, Gary swallowed a mountain of pills. He left a note saying, "I killed Gary" before hitting his head on a coffee table as he fell. His sister Gina found him and rushed him to the hospital, enlisting her parents to throw her brother's stash out the car window en route. He'd spend five days in the care of doctors and nurses. When he came to, he asked Gina, "Why'd you have to find me?" The only time Gary mentioned the attempt was to note that he couldn't pay the hospital bill. "I said, 'I ain't got no money, I'm broke. Shit, y'all better let me go.' They never did charge me. Even gave me my jewelry back."

In October Gary headed up to Memphis, meeting Roy Dea over potential recording plans. He'd jumped onstage to join Linda Gail Lewis—Jerry Lee's rambunctious, high-spirited sister—to do a few numbers.[113] I happened to be driving cross-country and met him there. He and Lou had gotten into a fight on the freeway and in a hair-raising moment she'd pulled the car key from the ignition. All that was quickly forgotten as we headed to pay respects at Graceland with Gary as our tour guide. Lou had never been.

That night we convened at a cheap motel. Gary seemed jittery and fragile at first, but I noticed him eyeballing my recorder like Casey at the bat. *Here we go,* I thought. He picked up a cheap guitar with a bum string he'd brought along for the ride, then stood in the corner with his back to us and started doing fragments of songs. He begged me to

113 "I was a big fan of Gary Stewart," said Linda Gail, who recalled no details from the gig. "I was going through a divorce and starting my solo career. I was drinking a lot during that time. Bartenders on Beale Street gave me free drinks."

rewind and delete his first attempt—"Erase that one, will ya, buddy? I don't like to embarrass myself, I really don't"—and then plowed through some numbers.

In rapid succession he went from "Hand Me Another of Those" (a wonderful Mickey Newbury song tailor-made for Gary—"Look how I'm shakin' from all that I'm takin' / She's tearin' me right away from my heart") to Johnny Horton ("Honky Tonk Hardwood Floor") to John Starling ("Waitin' on a Southern Train") to Lefty Frizzell ("Long Black Veil") to an Elvis quartet ("Love Me" / "Paralyzed" / "I Want You, I Need You, I Love You" / "Let It Be Me"). On and on it went—Fats Domino, Charlie Rich, Buddy Holly, Hank Snow's "Miller's Cave," Bobby Fuller's "I Fought the Law"...he was in magnificent voice. We sat in stunned silence when he stopped.

* * *

In January 1988 came another trip to Fort Pierce, this time with infamous photographer and soon-to-be filmmaker Larry Clark in tow to nab shots of Gary for the *Voice* article. I thought his documentary style would be perfect, since Fort Pierce and Tulsa seemed like two parts of the same neighborhood. With his immaculate white muscle T-shirts and shades, Clark turned a few heads in Fort Pierce, but he quickly fit in with the Stewarts due to his knowledge of old rock and roll—as well as quaaludes, which he and Gary discussed in detail.

Snapping a photo proved to be a challenge, however. Stewart was holed up in the bedroom when we got there, the vibe in the trailer was not good, and Clark got antsy—"Where is this guy?" I was sheepish. Joey Stewart told his mother we should just storm in, throw on the lights, and Larry could click away. Finally, after coming back from breakfast, we noticed the Confederate flag over the entrance to Gary's bedroom was fluttering slightly in the breeze, indicating that he was potentially among the living. The excitement was akin to a Bigfoot sighting. Stewart eventually shuffled out, commenting on how his bedhead resembled Little Richard's.

We rode over to George and Georgia's house for a celebration of their fiftieth wedding anniversary. On the way Gary brought us up to date on his sex life, regaling us with tales of an all-female country band that had taken him to bed. Those days were over, Gary insisted. He was faithful to Lou now.[114] He'd even tested himself with some knockout model on the road. "I took her to a motel room just to see if I could *not* be with her. I rolled around in bed with her, teased her all night long." There was no actual sex, however, Gary proudly informed us. "Lou and I, we have such a great sex life—and it just makes it so much greater knowin' that you're the *only* one." Gary reminded me of Brian Wilson in these strange, unguarded moments. Bizarrely childlike, full of wonder.

Arriving at his parents' house, which overflowed with relatives—brothers, sisters, aunts, and uncles—Gary took in all the Stewarts. "Rebels, every one," he said proudly. It would take me decades to unravel the weight of that statement. Meanwhile, George and Georgia held court, dishes of downhome food coming and going. Wearing a cockfighter's cap, George gave us a tour of his chicken coops, taking out a bird for our inspection. Boisterous and welcoming, Georgia regaled us with tales from Gary's childhood, but a concern for her son's present state lurked not far beneath the surface. You could tell Gary hadn't been visiting as much as Georgia would've liked. Seeing them together made me think of a story Roy Dea revealed only after I pressed. It's a tale I would subsequently hear told by others, with many variations, but it went like this:

At some point in the eighties, Georgia loaned Gary a large sum of money—the figure I was usually told was thirty grand (some say it was IRS debt). Eventually Georgia wanted her money back. Or her son's house. Since Gary was on the road, Georgia rang up Lou, giving her hell. More than once. Lou taped one of the calls and played it for Gary when he returned home. He grabbed a pistol

114 Despite his claims, Stewart would have many more girlfriends out on the road throughout the end of his life.

and headed to his mother's, where he strolled into the living room and asked, "Momma, who are your favorite people in the world?" Georgia thought it over, then named relations back in Kentucky. Pulling out his gun, Gary said, "Well, Momma, don't you *ever* say anything bad to Lou *again* or I'm gonna go up there with this gun and kill 'em BOTH." Then he turned and walked out. "See, that's the perfect Gary Stewart story," said Dea. "He has not jeopardized himself, because he ain't threatened his momma. He's just gonna kill somebody else."[115]

* * *

Stewart was back in the saddle. There was endless music both in the trailer and at Rialto's during that second trip. Donnie Coleman, Gary's old bandmate from Rockfish Railroad/Train Robbery days, came by and lent dobro and high tenor harmony to many a number there in the trailer. Larry Clark coached Gary on the words to the Presley hit "Tryin' to Get to You," a sight to behold.

At some point Stewart ripped through "One Night," the 1956 Smiley Lewis song that Elvis had not only recorded but absolutely demolished during his *'68 Comeback Special*. When I mentioned how great it must've been to be Presley at that very moment—to not only be "back," but blasting through the stratosphere like a rocket—Gary didn't miss a beat. "Man, it's a great feelin', bein' out there," he muttered without a trace of ego. "The best feelin' in the world. Better than any damn pain pill."

The high wouldn't last. Clark left,[116] and that night we headed to Rialto's. Gary was all revved up about a keyboard he'd just gotten, a Roland RD-300. He'd coveted the thing for weeks, and was determined to unleash it at the show that night.

115 Gary begged me not to include this tale in the *Voice* article, so I didn't. A few years later he asked me what got cut from the story. I told him this story was, at his request. Suddenly he was disappointed it hadn't been in there.

116 Clark later used two of Stewart's songs in his 2002 film *Ken Park*—"Out of Hand" and "Shady Streets." In what is surely the most unsavory use of a Stewart song in a movie, the latter is background music for a three-way sex scene.

After we got to the club, there was another detour to make. I hopped in a car with Stewart as some third party Gary seemed vaguely familiar with drunkenly drove us out in the sticks somewhere so Stewart could score. "Hey, I hope you got money for this," he said to the driver. "'Cause I'm broke." The guy handed Gary some cash and Stewart disappeared into a dilapidated trailer.

The wind rustled through the palms as I sat in the dark with the driver. "Boy, if Gary could get off that shit, he'd be bigger than ever. Bigger than Hank Williams." This from the guy who gave him the funds to cop. Gary and Fort Pierce was a doomed union. It seemed half the town enabled him.

Eventually we made it back to Rialto's. Stewart had a bad time getting a handle on the keyboard, although near the end of the night he slipped into a slow, mournful version of "In the Pines" that nearly had me weeping. The Rialto's crowd chatted all the way through his anguish. "In the Pines" wasn't ZZ Top.

Gary was dejected when we returned home. Silent. He had a bit of a cold from running himself ragged. He barked at Lou to return the keyboard and ambled off to the bedroom. I wouldn't see him for another five days. Lou tried to entertain me; Jimmy Smith came by and we whispered jokes in the living room. But mostly I sat and waited. *Do all celebrities do this sort of thing?* I'd of course find out they were capable of much crazier, but at the moment I was stressed. A friend had given me the money to make this trip and I was envisioning returning home empty-handed. There were still questions to ask.

Every once in a while Stewart would stumble out to the refrigerator to chug some cola and grab a little candy, muttering a sentence or two as he returned to his crypt. Madness. At one point I stood outside the trailer with Donnie Coleman, pontificating on Gary's fate as he lay comatose mere feet away. "I guess it's like Elvis," he mused, invoking a clichéd comparison that seemed inevitable but apt. "You can't save a man from himself."

But it was actually Gary who'd shortly utter the most ominous line in reference to Presley. "He needed to *escape*. I know how he felt, 'cause I've felt the same way and gone through some of the same things. I just haven't lost my wife. That would kill me."

* * *

In the middle of this graveyard quiet I had noticed a few worn boxes of 1/4" tapes and cassettes peeking out from a box in one corner of the trailer. Inspecting them, I deduced they were Gary's session recordings and outtakes. *Well, if that motherfucker isn't coming out of the bedroom, I'm going to imbibe.* I found a nearby friend of Stewart's to loan me a reel-to-reel machine, strapped on some headphones, and took the plunge.

Talk about a revelation. Piles of outtakes, each more compelling than the last. By 5 a.m. on the fifth day in the double-wide gulag, I'd listened to everything but a box labeled "Lenny Dee."[117] Having little else to occupy my thoughts, I threaded it up. *Might as well.*

I was unprepared for what came next. Here was the Rosetta stone—perhaps the most spellbinding and mysterious recording Gary ever made. His anguished vocal soars over a raggedy four-piece band, the piano anchoring a distorted, howling guitar and a weird, twitchy mandolin that buzzes around like an out-of-reach mosquito. So otherworldly...it took me a second to recognize "Williamson County." There's a fine Music City rendition on Stewart's first album—polished, jaunty, Nashville-perfect. This was something else entirely. It sounded like a Kentucky murder ballad from another planet, with Gary, who might be a little high, setting out on a long lazy march toward Hades after strangling his lover—a working girl who's fallen for another. "Now the same hands that catered to her/ Are clutching at her throat." The killer is damned for all eternity for what he's done. "And I ride this nightmare all over Williamson County/The devil waits on my soul for his payment/I await the

117 This tape is now lost.

hunter of my bounty." Gary practically screams the "devil" line, then pulls back, accepting his fate, making way for a long, keening guitar coda, like a junkyard ghost whistling down the tailpipe of a dead Plymouth Duster. The song evokes the chaos, tragedy, and soul of the Stewart clan like nothing else, the performance an unholy hybrid of rock, country, bluegrass, blues, and even psychedelia. Sitting there alone in the dark, I felt the full measure of Stewart's talent for the first time, and reckoned with how deep that well was, how he'd been in the right place and time to absorb all that had come before him. It coursed through his veins completely and authentically, enabling him to alchemize all those genres into something utterly new and completely his own.

By the end of it I was in a trance. This bleak, unsettling hill country drone was a glimpse into the abyss equal to Dylan's "Not Dark Yet," the 13th Floor Elevators' "May the Circle Be Unbroken," or Reverend Julius Cheeks and the Four Knights' "The Last Mile of the Way."

Just then Gary shuffled out from the bedroom yawning. I ripped off the headphones. "Listen to this!" Stewart seemed just as shocked as I was. Who played on it? He couldn't tell me. When was it recorded? He didn't know, although he thought it had been done during his tenure at Bradley's Barn, before RCA. He listened intently, traveling back there in his mind. The tape ran out, the loose end flapping around on its plastic spool as we sat in silence. Gary, staring into space, said softly, "I thought we were going to make records like that all the time—y'know, round up some pickers and *play*."

* * *

That night Gary spun some Chuck Willis records as I wasn't too familiar with his oeuvre at the time. He excitedly paced around the trailer, offering me any album I liked for keeps. Then we headed off to Rialto's, where Gary closed his set with a Willis medley—"Born to Lose," "Betty and Dupree," "It's Too Late." Stewart had been a little obsessed with that last one all the while I'd been down there, and when he got to it in the medley, he just erupted. "She's gone, she's gone—

where can my baby *be*?" he screamed, bringing the medley to a violent close. He poured everything we'd discussed back in the trailer into the performance, and left the stage breathless, bathed in sweat. A crowd of sixty or so had been mulling about the club. Some of them even clapped.

* * *

Gary writing. (Tommy Schwartz collection)

My last day in Fort Pierce, Stewart was in a foul mood. I was pissed off from being cooped up in the motionless trailer, and as I provoked him with more questions, resentment oozed out. I mocked him, calling him Moleman and Howard Hughes, and informed him that he was a drug fiend, a shut-in, and just plain nuts.

For a moment he looked at me like he was about to fly across the room and pull my eyeballs out with his fingers. "I'm forty-three years old an' still a child—ain't that *great*?" he snarled. "I'm a musician, a singer, a songwriter, a husband, and a human being—music ain't the *only* thing in my life. I don't owe my life to a damn guitar!"

Foolishly, I asked what value he offered to his family—or anyone else—by being conked out for days on end, telling him he didn't care about anybody but himself. His long face, which on this particular day shone with the embalmed elegance of a Jerry Lee Lewis, got cloudy. "I tell you what...why don't you stay a few more days and I'll go back there and I'll get *down* and then I'll come out here and *be* with you when I'm down like that and you will *never* want to come back here. I stay away when I can't do any good."

Shortly thereafter Gary threw the knife in my direction, then scuttled off for the scroll he angrily read aloud, declaring his allegiance to the hills of Kentucky. All I knew was that I wanted to slither out of that trailer and run for it.

And just like that, the storm passed. I had to catch a train home, but Stewart was going to leave a gift on my recorder first. Lording over me with his acoustic, practically on fire, Gary sang "Williamson County." Boom. "I've Just Seen the Rock of Ages." Boom. "Silver Cloud." Boom. Then "There Ain't No Grave Gonna Hold My Body Down," the Brother Claude Ely song he learned as a kid. As if sensing my anxiety over my friend's travel loan, he laid down a Dickey Betts song in her honor—"Nancy," the icing on the cake being a spoken thank-you to her for getting me to Fort Pierce.

* * *

Georgia tagged along when we headed off to the station, Gina Stewart at the wheel. Gary and Georgia sang mountain songs as the car flew down the highway. Outside the car window a vivid tropical sun set on Florida, Gary's craggy, sunglassed profile standing in relief. "This was the time of day I'd get real homesick out on the road," he murmured. Before we said goodbye Stewart gave me the cheap gold bracelet he'd had on his wrist ("Gypsy," it said) then encouraged me to write the story as I saw fit. "Don't puss out on me, bud. Tell it the Jimmy way," he said, giving me my identity in those last five words. It took me many years to realize the significance, and Gary would no longer be around to thank when I did.

Although it was by no means easy for him, Gary had invited me into his life, and shared it all, good, bad, and ugly. I'm ashamed to say I took much of it for granted at the time. Only now, nearly forty years later, do I recognize the extent of his kindness.

* * *

A week later I called. Mary Lou had left. For good, Gary informed me. He was in great pain, and muttered about an open whiskey bottle by his side. Stewart admitted he had no clue how to change his ways at this late stage of the game. He also let me know how much shit my interrogations had stirred. "I need a friend who's not a reporter," he said, begging me to find Lou.

Four days after that, Lou called. Seeing the *Elvis and Me* TV movie had sparked her to call Gary. She was giving him one last chance, provided they exit Fort Pierce forever. They were going to leave in one week.

Three days later Lou called back. Gary Joseph Stewart, known to all as Joey, had taken his life. The police had broken into his room at the Scottish Inn, a motel out on Okeechobee Road, and found him dead on the floor with a gun in his hand, victim of a self-inflicted shot to the head. He was twenty-five years old.

17

JOEY

TOMMY SCHWARTZ: Gary did an interview on his old Roberts tape recorder with Joey when he was just a little kid. It's so funny, oh my God.

GARY: *What jokes have you learned at school lately?*

JOEY (around 5 years old): *None.*

GARY: *Did I ever tell you the one about this guy riding on a train? This guy was riding on a train, and he wore a toupee—that's a wig, see. And he was sleepin' in his bed—y'know, they have, like, bunk beds, lower berth and upper berth? And his wig fell off and fell down there into the lower bed. And he reached down, and he was in the dark...he reached all around, heard this woman sayin' [Gary does a falsetto woman's voice], "Yeah, yeah, that's it! That's it! Yeah, that's it!!!!" He said, "No, ma'am, that's not it. I part mine on the side." Don't you get it?*

JOEY: *No.*

GARY: (chuckling): *Maybe in a few years you will.*

[In the background you hear Lou admonishing her husband: "Gary! He's just a boy!"]

TOMMY SCHWARTZ: But there is a morbid section to this interview.

GARY: *What do you think is going to happen in the next twenty years?*

JOEY: *Me die.*

GARY: *In twenty years? That's a short time.*

JOEY: *Me know.*

TOMMY SCHWARTZ: Joey died pretty much twenty years after that.

SHANNON ASHBURN: Joey was the best big brother that any girl could ever ask for. He protected me. Joey was loved—by everyone. He didn't have an enemy. Not one person never said anything bad about my brother. 'Til this day. Twenty-five, that's just too young. It's like we didn't get enough time together, y'know? Because he was so awesome. Joey was so much fun.

JIMMY SMITH: When we were young'uns, Joey was just one of them ADHD or ADD kids. He needed Ritalin, but they didn't diagnose him. Joey was a live wire. One time he was running through the house and Mama got the belt and beat his ass. Man, he freaked out. He didn't run through the house no more.

LAURIE RASTRELLI: Joey was *our* brother, too, he wasn't just Shannon's. Jimmy's dog would go over to their house, Mary Lou would cut the first slice of meatloaf...we were family. Mary Lou talked my dad into putting me in private school with Joey. Because she knew Joey and I were so close that we could go to school together. I went all the way through school with him. We were best, best friends. Joey called his mom Lulu and he called me Lolo.

JO ANN GREGORY: I think Joey was born smiling. He was so handsome and beautiful. Joey had a good heart. Even though he was Stewart, he wasn't like the Stewarts. I don't think he thought any evil, or would try to manipulate. Joey was just a kind, handsome kid.

GINA STEWART: When Gary went to London, Mamaw kept Joey. At six years old I was up getting a bottle, because that baby sat with me. At six!! He was my baby. Gary and Mary Lou were in the *back*.

GRANDAL STEWART: Mama practically raised Joey. Because Gary was gone a lot and Lou was runnin' wild. That changed a lot of the tension between Mom and Lou.

Gary and Joey. (Shannon Ashburn collection)

TRAMPAS STEWART: Joey was shining. I mean, *shining*. I'm telling you, he was the shining star that all the cousins looked up to. He was the first, and he was in charge. He was a leader. And he had so many friends.

GAIL STEWART: I loved him. He would go, "Pretty, pretty, Gail Trina"—I used to be pretty when I was young. Joey was wonderful, flamboyant. He was just all that and a bag of chips. He was handsome, tall. Joey was beautiful, inside and out.

JIMMY SMITH: We were, like, brothers, man. Joey was so good to me. I'd be working at Pitts Furniture store and Joey would have the house just clean and perfect for me. I'd come home to a fucking castle. He knew I was by myself. Joey was right there, man. He cared about me. He was a precious spirit. I loved my little brother. He had a heart of gold.

TRAMPAS STEWART: Joey was more like his mom than his dad.

SHANNON ASHBURN: Joey was my mom, and I was my dad, y'know what I mean? I think Dad was jealous of Joey. Because my dad wanted Lou to himself. Pancho and Cisco—that was his partner. And Mom loved her Bubala, that's what she called Joey. It was tough for my mom. 'Cause she was torn. That was her son and her husband, and they just didn't mesh well. I don't know why. I still don't know why.

GINA STEWART: Gary used to make Joey pick up cigarette butts out on the front lawn. Gary hated cigarette butts. And Gary better not go out there and find a new one. 'Cause then Joey would get a whuppin'.

MARY LOU STEWART: Gary was jealous of Joey's looks, jealous we were so close.

SHANNON ASHBURN: My dad and brother knocked heads a lot. I mean, they would have fistfights. It got pretty violent.

FRED BOGERT: Conflict, father-son.

MARY LOU STEWART: Joey wanted so bad for Gary to love him. And Gary never paid no attention to him. Everybody but Joey. *Everybody*. Gary gave more to Jimmy Smith than he ever did to Joey.

SHANNON ASHBURN: Joey used to hang out at this bar Duke's. Him and his friends would hang out there, and he paid somebody at the door to get me in. I was about sixteen. I just thought that was the coolest thing—I actually got to get in and go dancin' with my brother. Joey loved to dance. And so do I. That was our thing.

RANDY TOMAN: Joey was always an uptempo guy, not a stoner guy. Whatever shortcomings Gary or Lou had, their kids came out of it good. Joey and Shannon never treated us like, "Oh, our dad is your boss." I couldn't believe how well brought-up they were.

SHANNON ASHBURN: Joey had a Dodge Dart with leopard-skin seats. He used to always play chicken with everybody. You think my dad drove bad? Joey got in three wrecks in one week.

TRAMPAS STEWART: Joey was a punk rocker, a headbanger, a surfer...Joey was everything. He was all over the place.

SHANNON ASHBURN: Joey went through different fads in his life, different fashions and stages. He was just always so fashionable, always dressed to the nines, man. Very stylish. He worked at the jewelry store and had the Flock of Seagulls hairdo. He went through the punk rock stage, where he had the mohawk and the safety pin in his jaw. Then he'd have the surfer look. Everybody was like, "What's Joey going to do next?" He was just that dude. *The* dude. I mean, he could've been a model. I even wonder what he'd be doing right now. Probably be wearing Gucci loafers, jeans, and a suit blazer. Joey was just so ahead of his time.

TRAMPAS STEWART: Joey had a million girlfriends, man.
SHANNON ASHBURN: All the girls would just flock to him. All the girls loved Joey.
JIMMY SMITH: I made sure Joey got plenty of pussy. I hooked him up a lot with girls around here. Me and him had a threesome with this poor little ol' girl named Jenny Fuckalot. That was her name. Even her mother called her that.
MARY LOU STEWART: Gary would get Joey's girlfriends...take his girlfriends away from him. Just to fuck with him.
JIMMY SMITH: Deidre Hall, that was Joey's girlfriend.
SHANNON ASHBURN: You know what Deidre told me every time we talked? She said, 'I will never love anybody like I loved your brother. Your brother was the love of my life.' She would iron his clothes every night before he'd go out and do the shopping. She took good care of Joey.
TRAMPAS STEWART: I don't think Deidre was very good for Joey. Deidre was more into drugs and stuff. And she just kind of pulled Joey into it more. It killed his whole personality.
JIMMY SMITH: One night here comes Dickey [Betts] and Gary says, "Man, he needs blow real bad." And see, Joey was sellin'. I slipped and said, "Joey might know where you can get some." Uh-oh, *bad* fucking mistake. Gary went off the fucking chain. It just slipped out, y' know?
LAURIE RASTRELLI: Joey was selling a little bit of dope. Which I knew, because I bought some from him.
JIMMY SMITH: One time I went out and bought a little bit of coke. And a little bit of heroin. I'd mix 'em together, make a speedball. I never done it before. I shot that shit and went *out*. Fell on the bathroom floor. I'm laying there, going out of body, deader than a motherfucker. And true story, I swear—the Lord come to me and said, "It ain't your time. You got to help Joey. You gotta go help Joey." I know it sounds crazy. Anyway, Deidre, she told Mary Lou, "Well, that Jimmy Smith, he's been doing heroin."

So I'm sitting in my house and here comes Gary and Lou. Lou had fire in her eyes and a .38 Special in her fucking hand. She stuck that

Joey and Shannon, sitting under a portrait of Mary Lou. (Shannon Ashburn collection)

motherfucker in my face and said, "You motherfucker, if you've ever given Joey any heroin."...I said, "I swear to God, I *never* gave Joey any heroin. Never, ever!"

Lou wasn't comin' to threaten me, she was comin' to KILL my ass. Gary was there, standin' behind her. Gary's back there wavin' his arms, goin' "No, no, no!" And Lou has this fucking gun pointed right at my head and it's *cocked*.

I said, "Go ahead, Mary Lou. Shit, I'm miserable, anyway." I was really in a bad place—it was "Go ahead, do me a favor." Then she knew I was real. She woulda done it if I woulda said too much more! That motherfucker about took me *out*. I never gave Joey that shit. He never asked for it.

Shannon and Joey. (Shannon Ashburn collection)

SHANNON ASHBURN: Mom and Dad were at the mall goin' to the record store, 'cause Dad liked to go record shoppin' when he was home. They were walking in the mall, and all of a sudden they passed my brother all in black leather, with a six-inch mohawk and safety pin in his jaw. My dad was floored. He wasn't happy, to say the least.

STAN SPENCE: The last time I saw Joey was at Frankie n' Johnny's. He was doin' this gothic thing, wearing black, puttin' fishhooks through his lips. I said, "Joey, you doin' okay?" He said, "Yeah, I'm doin' okay." I said, "Well, you need to get rid of all that shit on your face. You look like you fell into a tackle box."

LAURIE RASTRELLI: I was Shannon's babysitter. She said to me, "Lolo, I need you to come with me to Lakeland to find Andy." Mary Lou had a son named Andy.[118] Joey, Mary Lou, Shannon, and I went. Mary Lou got a hotel. That was when I did my first line of cocaine.

118 Andy was the son Mary Lou gave up for adoption after marrying Gary.

Mary Lou put a line on the back of the toilet and I snorted. I was probably fifteen. They left me with Shannon and they set out to go find Andy. Well, she found him. Brought him back to Fort Pierce. I don't know what Gary thought about that.

SHANNON ASHBURN: Mom brought Andy around. He came around a lot. I loved Andy. He was gay, he was fun, and he looked just like my mother. He had the high cheekbones and the curly, coarse hair. I mean, he was Mary Lou all over. He looked up to my mom. And then him and Joey became really good friends. Andy used to come and stay with us—me, Mom, and Joey—when my dad was out of town. She was doing this a lot behind my dad's back, I'm sure.

JIMMY SMITH: Andy comes in, flamin' out, man, with a hot-pink fedora and purse around his shoulder. I'm goin', "Well, what the fuck?!?" Joey loved him, that was his long-lost brother. And Joey idolized him. It was kind of weird. Joey wasn't the same after that. That's when he painted the house pink. And all of a sudden Joey starts going down to Miami on the weekends with Andy. He'd just disappear.

LAURIE RASTRELLI: Andy was a very nice person. Andy was definitely gay. Very skinny and very prissy. He and Joey went out to California. I don't know what happened there, but I know Joey came back and said he was sick. I said, "Well, go to the fuckin' doctor and get some antibiotics." He said, "Laurie, I've been to the doctor. I've taken so many antibiotics I got a yeast infection." He thought he had AIDS.

MARY LOU STEWART: Joey went to clinics and stuff...so did some doctor tell him that? I don't know, *I'll never know*!

JIMMY SMITH: Andy was in the hospital. Mary Lou and Joey watched Andy die of AIDS.

LARRY "MOUSE" MUNSON: I know that Gary was worried about Joey. He knew that Joey was kind of experimenting with lifestyles. I believe it didn't sit well. I said, "Hey, a lot of people experiment with that type of stuff." But Gary didn't like it. He was old-fashioned in a lot of ways. That kind of ate him up. He didn't really talk about it. Gary just kept it bottled up inside.

MARY LOU STEWART: Joey tried to talk to Gary, but Gary was...Gary.

SHANNON ASHBURN: Mom felt like Andy came into the picture and kind of drug Joey down to that Miami scene, brought him into a whole other different lifestyle. And she blamed Andy for that. Because my brother was always a ladies' man. Always. So all of a sudden, Andy came around and then Joey was gay, y'know what I mean? So my mom always blamed Andy for it.

JO ANN GREGORY: There was a point in time when I wanted to look for this child that I had that was adopted. And Mary Lou was the only one that I ever talked to about it. We talked, and then she encouraged me not to do it. That I would be sorry if I did it.

GAIL STEWART: I don't think Gary was very comfortable about Joey being bisexual or gay, number one. I think that smacked him in the face, because that was something you just didn't talk about at that time. Gary loved his son, don't get me wrong, but his parenting skills weren't that great. My mother and father's parenting skills weren't that great. It would suffice for the time, but was totally lacking by today's standards. He did the best he could. A lot of it is from the upbringing that we had. Because our father never showed us loving and Mother never really showed you much love, either. There was no hugs and "I love you. Oh, I can't wait to see you," no nothin'. I think it stems from that. I do.

LARRY MUNSON: None of us really knew how to be fathers at that time. My father sure wasn't like Beaver Cleaver's dad, y'know. Most everybody I knew didn't really know the things you were supposed to do. They just weren't taught by their dad. We were taught to get up in the morning, work your ass off, put some bread on the table, and do the same the next day. So you got to look at that and say, "How the hell does Gary even know how to be a father?" There's no trainin', no pattern to follow, nothing. You just got up and winged it.

JIMMY SMITH: I lived out in White City and Joey comes over with a frickin' mohawk this tall and he's got a fucking safety pin runnin' through his cheek. Freaked me out. He said, "I'm not feeling good, man." I didn't get it. I didn't put two and two together...he never said AIDS. He said, "I'm really sick, Jimmy, I'm gonna die." I said, "No, you're not, you look great, man." He pulled his shirt up and there were, like, swellings. I don't know what it was. Didn't look good.

MARY LOU STEWART: Near the end we went ridin' every day in the car and just talked and talked. He told me things about hisself that I had no idea of. I knew more about him in those two weeks than I knew about him in twenty-five years. I think he had a homosexual thing and I think it ate him up. The guilt. He just couldn't handle things. He thought he had AIDS. And he didn't.

SHANNON ASHBURN: Joey called me and asked me to meet him at Searstown Plaza. I was eighteen. I didn't think nothin' of it, I just thought it was a normal day. I went, met him, and he gave me an envelope and told me, "Don't open it until I leave." I was like, "Why?" And he was just like, "Don't open it until I leave." I was eighteen, on my way somewhere. I didn't have time for all that. But it was pretty much a goodbye letter.

Shannon, Mom, Dad, Mamaw and Jenna,

So please, please know in your hearts that mine is breaking. I know these things don't seem large enough to die for. But I can't live with it. Without my skin being clear, I am a nervous wreck. To the point to where I live in fear. I hate it. Nightmares and all that goes with it. Shannon, baby, I love you so very much. As much as I know you love me. It hurts so bad to leave you the most. I mean it. I mean, it's like we finally grew up to be the same age.

And then I got sick. I leave you everything I got. And I know you want me instead of it. And me saying I am sorry is not good enough. But try hard to understand. I hurt so bad that I'm cracking inside. I know at your age you don't know what that means. And at any age. I hope you don't have to. I love you. Stay away from drugs, Shannon. They're so very damaging to your body and God only gives us one body. Remember that, help Mom and Dad through this.

I love you, Joey

MARY LOU STEWART: The day before he killed hisself he came over. I helped him get dressed—black slacks, black shirt, red satin bow tie, white satin suspenders. I don't know where he was goin'. When he had walked in, Gary said, "I was more of a man at twenty-five than you'll ever be." And Joey said, "Well, Daddy, like you always told me—don't judge a man 'til you walk in his shoes. You don't know me." Gary went back to bed. I said, "Go give your dad a hug." He just looked down and said, "No." When he got ready to go, Joey stopped at the door of the trailer, and stood there for about a minute lookin' down at the ground. He said, "I love you, Daddy." Gary said, "Yeah."

Son of Country Music Star Dies: Gary Joseph "Joey" Stewart, the 25-year old son of country singer songwriter Gary Stewart of Fort Pierce, died Saturday of a self-inflicted gunshot wound, according to the St. Lucie County Sheriff's Department. Stewart was found dead in a locked room at the Scottish Inn, 7050 Okeechobee Road, around noon Saturday. According to Sheriff's spokesman Lou Ericsson, Stewart checked into the motel in the early evening on Friday and when he did not check out Saturday morning, maids at the motel knocked several times at the door, but received no response. Deputies were sent to the motel and had to cut the chain lock on the door to gain entrance, Ericsson said. They found Stewart's body on the floor and a handgun in his hand.

—*St. Lucie News Tribune*, February 14, 1988

DAVE BROOKS: I was a brand-new detective. It was a single shot right to the temple of his head with a .38 caliber. There was a two-page note apologizing to his family and warning first responders to be aware of the possible contaminations.

SHANNON ASHBURN: The next day I was getting ready to go to a wedding, and we couldn't get ahold of my brother. Deidre called and she's like, "He didn't come home last night," and I was like, "Oh my gosh....well, I got this letter." We start calling hotels. I was like, "You start from the bottom and work your way up and I'll start from the

A's and work down." We were workin' on that phone book until I got a knock on the door. It was a cop. And that's when he came in and gave me my brother's driver's license. I knew right then.

I had to get in my car and drive over to the trailer to tell my mom and dad. All I remember is walking into the trailer—they were in the back bedroom—and when I told my mom, she literally took her whole body and threw it into this big glass mirror and shattered the whole mirror.

MARY LOU STEWART: I knew he was gonna do it, but it was still a whammy when it happened.

LAURIE RASTRELLI: When Griselda killed herself, Joey and I went to her funeral. They had patched her up and had open casket. Joey and I was standing over her. And he said, "I would never do that." Well, when he did do it, I just started screaming and crying. I said, "You promised me! You promised me you wouldn't! And you *did* it!"

JIMMY SMITH: I remember when I found out. This is fuckin' weird. Dickey Betts was coming to town, we were all excited. We were going to go play, I was on cloud nine. I'm like, "Holy shit, man, Dickey's here." I went up, shook his hand, and less than five minutes into talking, here comes Bruce Hunter. He says, "They just found Joey dead out at the Crossroads." It was like, *What the fuck???* No one seen it coming.

STAN SPENCE: The funeral was horrible. *Horrible.* Gary was bawling and Mary Lou and everybody was cryin' and it was just... bad. I don't know how many times I went to Fort Pierce because somebody had died. There was a lot of tragedy with that family. So much tragedy.

BILL HARDMAN: The guy that owned the local funeral home told me, "I refused to take him because I didn't want nobody at my funeral home that had AIDS."

LAURIE RASTRELLI: I went with Mary Lou to Joey's funeral. Gary went separately.

SHANNON ASHBURN: Mom and Dad requested to be in a room that no one could see them in. I remember Dad not wanting to ride in the car to the service.

JO ANN GREGORY: There was a service. Gary and Lou were secretive and in a separate room. It was all too overwhelming for them. For everybody, I think. And the Stewarts, like most people from Kentucky, were wailers.

TOMMY SCHWARTZ: It was at Haisley Funeral home. Fred Bogert played "Candle in the Wind" on piano.[119] The place was packed, I had to stand in the outer room. At the cemetery portion, Gary walked over to me and said, "Tommy, we need to get back in the studio."

JIMMY SMITH: All that was a fog, man.

MARY LOU STEWART: They did a two-week investigation on Joey. I told the detective, "What I tell you is strictly confidential." That's how the story of AIDS got around. There was a kid who worked at the coroner's office. Joey said to make sure he wasn't there for the autopsy. Well, they made sure this kid was out of the room when they did the autopsy, but he had access to the records, pulled Joey's file, and showed a lot of Joey's friends pictures of Joey on the slab.

BILL HARDMAN: I remember pictures of his body going round.

SHANNON ASHBURN: Mom knocked the headlights out of the coroner's car and she went to jail. Because they put on the death certificate that Joey had AIDS. And the autopsy came back that he was negative. He was healthy as a horse.

MARY LOU STEWART: They even run the test through twice on Joey for AIDS and he didn't have anything! For him to die February 12 and then for them to call me up March 7th to say they had made a mistake? I beat the headlights out of the coroner's car.

I had to write a letter of apology saying the reason I did it was my son died February 12 and I was informed March 7th that he did not have AIDS.[120] It still says it on his fuckin' death certificate. They said, "It's changed in Jacksonville, but it ain't changed here." That's public record.

SHANNON ASHBURN: That was all bullshit. Andy died of AIDS. Joey didn't.

---

119 The Elton John song was a favorite of Joey's. Fred changed "Goodbye, Norma Jean" to "Goodbye, Gary Joe."

120 Joey's autopsy does indeed note that he was retested and did not have AIDS.

RANDY TOMAN: Lou called me and wondered if the band could help pay for his tombstone. I said, "Hey, our band is only three guys." She kind of hung up. Gary rang and said, "I'm sorry about Lou calling. She's not herself right now."

MARY LOU STEWART: I got Joey's stone ordered. It's real pretty—gray, about three feet high, same size as my mom's. His picture's gonna be at the top, a real pretty picture taken about two months before he died. Then, in real pretty scroll, I want to have "Joey" written really big. On the back there's gonna be a pink flamingo, 'cause he liked that. It's gonna say, "God only loans our child to us. God gave him to us not for an hour, but twenty-five years. Thank you, Jesus. Thank you for Joey. My Bubala."

JIMMY SMITH: I don't want to be cremated. I told Nick, "Would you make sure I'm buried?" He said, "Yeah, where do you want to be buried?" I said, "As close to Joey as you can get me." I go to his grave all the time. I clean his grave. Sometimes I take a guitar over there.

SHANNON ASHBURN: After Joey died, Dad felt so bad and guilty...I know he wished he could've took it all back. He was so heartbroken....I don't think Dad ever forgave himself for that.

I remember he walked to Joey's grave sometime after Joey died and slept on his grave. He walked home the next day and told us, "I cried and cried and begged for forgiveness. I don't know if he's ever going to forgive me." Dad was in a really dark place.

18

DARK PLACE

They call me the Killer, but Jerry Lee never killed anybody but himself.

– Jerry Lee Lewis to Elaine Dundy, 1991

Thus far, Gary and Mary Lou had managed to survive career failures, financial problems, overdoses, and infidelities, but the death of Joey proved nearly insurmountable. They blamed themselves, they blamed each other. His suicide "drove a deep wedge," said Jo Ann Gregory. "I think it almost killed them both."

"When my mom and dad lost Joey, everything changed," said Shannon. "I don't even know how to explain it. It just got dark. Bad." When you called the trailer, the phone would be busy for days on end. Lou would leave Gary, Lou would come back. "I never knew what to expect," said Shannon, who would come check on her parents and was mystified why they didn't move back into the house. Shannon found the trailer "dark and depressing...that place was horrible." She felt both her parents were suffering from major depression—"it would bounce back and forth from my dad to my mom, from my mom to my dad." Shannon and her boyfriend Royce Ashburn tried to get her parents out into the world, but "we couldn't get them to do anything. Nothing. We were scared to even call over there. We'd get Mom in trouble. Dad was just so mean. Mad at the world."

I didn't talk much to Gary in this period. He'd sleep for days, and when he was conscious, he was often in a haze or too high to form a sentence. "Gary just hid out in that trailer," said Bill Hardman. "He wouldn't eat, he wouldn't talk to anybody. Nobody could get to him. He went into seclusion, just fucking buried himself in there." The situation was so dire that even George came to check on his son. "Gary had a big fork, and run the ol' man out of his house—with a damn fork," said Grandal.

The next time I did visit, Gary literally didn't utter a word to me, he just lay on the couch and stared at the TV, not even looking in my direction. I spent the whole visit talking to Lou. When I called Gary after the trip, he remained impenetrable. "You can't understand me, nobody can understand me."

* * *

Late one night in May 1988, Lou called. "Ever since Joey died, man, I am just losin' my fuckin' mind. I just hear a voice in my head—'You gotta kill yourself, you gotta do it.' I ain't gonna leave no notes, I ain't gonna tell nobody. I just gotta be with Joey...if I couldn't help my son, what good am I?"

I asked how Gary was coping. "He can't talk about it...he gets pissed, because I sit and look at pictures of Joey for hours. Hey, I know I'm crackin' up." She sounded near-catatonic until she started talking about Gary. Then anger came. "Nothin' can change him." She said Gary had taken her name off some of the songs they'd written together, giving the credits to his friends, along with the publishing.

Roy Dea was setting up Lou on a $200 a week songwriting salary, but she was already over it. "Why should I feed Gary lines?" With Joey gone, nothing mattered.

Lou spoke about how hard Gary had been on Joey. "He's gotta be in everybody's business. You don't do it his way, it's wrong. If you talk, you're stupid. He's a self-centered, spoiled, motherfuckin' son of a bitch. Put *that* on his epitaph. Hey, I raised him—*I* spoiled him. But I sure don't like him."

Worse yet, Gary was taking it out on her physically. He'd sleep for days, then come to and start "slappin' the shit outta me because he's comin' down." Lou admitted she was "hidin' bruises on my arms and head."[121] Out of desperation she reached out to Bill Hardman, their detective friend. "Gary was so wired up, when I walked in the door, he looked at me and screamed, '*Get the fuck outta here*!'" said Hardman. "I don't know how many times I went over there just to get her through it and calm him down, which was hard to do."

Lou knew Gary was haunted by Joey's death, but felt he was just using it as another excuse. "I said, 'Come on, Gary. Knock it off. Before that, it was somethin' else. Who you gonna blame it on next? It's you, Gary. It's *you*.'"

Hearing this from Mary Lou was crushing. And the reason I didn't return to this story for many years. It had gotten so grim. All I could think at the time was that Lou had to get away from Gary.

* * *

"Honky-Tonk Man," my *Village Voice* profile, came out in the spring of 1988 and got people talking about Stewart's music again. Despite the ongoing madness in Fort Pierce, Roy Dea moved forward with recording plans. By way of Gary, he stumbled onto

121 Grandal Stewart witnessed one of these attacks. "Lou was standin' by the coffee table and said something Gary didn't like. He jumped across the damn coffee table and just slapped the shit out of Lou. Knocked the hell out of her."

HighTone Records, a small, well-respected independent label out of Oakland, California, that specialized in roots music. Stewart regularly ordered records from a legendary outfit in that state, Down Home Music in El Cerrito. Sometimes he'd gab with the owners on the phone and, according to owner Frank Scott, "the person who suggested that Gary might be interested in recording for HighTone was my wife, Nancy Scott-Noennig." HighTone's owners, Larry Sloven and Bruce Bromberg, were big fans. "The people at Downhome kept telling me about these friends of theirs who had a record label," said Gary. "I asked Roy to call and check HighTone out."

When Dea called HighTone, Sloven thought it was a prank by his partner. Dea "was a figure that I kind of idolized as a producer." Once he got on the phone, he realized it was no joke: Roy was indeed looking for a label for Gary Stewart. HighTone made their pitch, and Gary liked the fact there was little pressure. "The people at HighTone just said, 'We don't care if you ever tour again, we just want you,'" he told Bob Allen. "I said, 'That's what I want to hear.'"

Sloven was thrilled. "I've always said that before I started the label, if there were four artists that I could have on my label, it was the Blasters, Joe Ely, Merle Haggard, and Gary Stewart."[122] He soon made a deal with Roy that included a small advance against royalties—"we were a tiny company, we didn't have money to throw around"—and Dea was given free rein. "In many cases what we did at HighTone, either the artist or the producer just said, 'This is what we're gonna do' and we said, 'Okay.' I don't think we gave Roy any input at all, really." Dea was high on the label—he'd also produce Johnny Rodriguez for them, reuniting him with his old buddy Jerry Kennedy[123]—and Sloven was instantly fond of Dea. "Roy was about the nicest person that I ever met in the record business. He smoked a

---

122 As HighTone would release albums by Stewart, Ely, and Dave Alvin (plus reissue the Blasters' first album), Sloven nabbed everybody on that list but Haggard.

123 Sloven declared Johnny's version of Robert Earl Keen's "Corpus Christi Bay" on this 1996 album—*You Can Say That Again*—to be "the best track we ever released on our label."

lot and liked Jack and Coke immensely. Roy was really dedicated to Gary." Sloven was such a Stewart fan he and his wife Valerie would name their daughter Leah after hearing Stewart do the song live in Austin in August 1990.

* * *

There's no question HighTone treated Stewart well during his three-album tenure there—they briefly got him back on the charts, reissued his first RCA albums, and did two anthologies (an uneven collection of RCA/HighTone material and a HighTone best-of). But there was little imagination in the way he was presented, and as much as it pains me to say it, Roy would rely on old formulas, cutting tracks with many of the same players from the golden era at Stewart's old stomping grounds, RCA Studio B (by then an independent studio known as Music City Music Hall), and releasing a drinkin' song for the single. I sensed Gary would've enjoyed trying something different, but never in a million years would he address such an issue with Roy. HighTone released three Dea-produced albums between 1988 and 1993, and they'd all suffer from a certain '80s/early '90s country-pop sheen that proved an unfortunate update on the hard country sound Stewart and Dea were famous for. "You can't really fault them, that was the sound of that decade," said Steve Hinson. "They were just trying to sound like what was 'going on,' like the other records on the radio. You gotta do it. It's a business."

* * *

On July 17 came a bright spot for Gary in the bleakness of 1988. Tanya Tucker, who'd gone through rehab at the Betty Ford Center just five months earlier, played the Port St. Lucie Civic Center, twenty miles from Gary's house. She told the local paper she was looking forward to playing "Gary Stewart country." After the show, there was Stewart backstage, waiting to say hello. They caught up, with Tucker confiding that she'd fallen for a new guy and had been writing a song about it. She showed Gary the verses and they proceeded to write a chorus together. "I want to demo this now!" said Tanya, so Stewart took her over to Fred Bogert's home studio, where they recorded "There's a Tennessee Woman/Ben's Song." "We went until about two o'clock in the morning," said Bogert. Before Tanya hopped on the bus to her next tour date, she told Stewart the song "was going to be the title of my next album." *Tennessee Woman* came out in 1990.

* * *

Brand New, the first album for HighTone, was largely recorded in July 1988. Pianist and longtime Dea session man David Briggs was the musical director, Dale Sellers came back on guitar. Other studio hotshots this time around included Larry Paxton on bass, Jerry Kroon on drums, Kenny Bell on rhythm guitar, and Sonny Garrish on steel, with Buddy Cannon and Carla Hunter on backing vocals. Warren Haynes was enlisted to overdub slide guitar. Work after those first sessions continued in fits and starts depending on what shape Stewart was in. When Roy wanted Gary to redo some of the weaker vocals, he couldn't even get him on the phone.

"Roy had to come here and get Gary," said Lou. "Gary wouldn't talk to him. Roy told me, 'I've got my life savings, everything, even my marriage on the line, the son of a bitch better not do this to me. Can't you get him on a plane, Lou?' I said, 'This time I can't. Because if I go in there and say anything to him, he's gonna knock me across the floor.' Roy said, 'He ain't seen the bad side of me.' I said, 'Well, maybe he should.'"

So Roy flew down to Fort Pierce. Mary Lou didn't tell Gary he was coming. When Dea walked in, "the couch potato was on the couch," as Lou put it. When she tried to get Gary's attention, he literally growled at her like an animal. Suddenly there stood Roy. According to Mary Lou, he said, "Get up, take a shower, shave, get your clothes on. We're goin' to Nashville. You ain't gonna do this to me, you son of a bitch." Caught by surprise, Stewart did as he was told and the album was finished.

* * *

Once *Brand New* was completed, Gary's life continued to unravel. His drug intake even further out of control, Stewart was making life hell for Lou. Another physical attack was detailed in a July journal entry. "He went crazy—or crazier than ever...The pain is bad."

The pair moved back into their old house. The trailer had mysteriously burned down. Lou suspected Georgia was behind it, along with one of her offspring. A detective wanted her to testify. "I told him, 'They got a bad family. If I say something, hey, they might really hurt me.'" She suggested he serve her with a subpoena so she'd be legally obligated, but no charges were ever filed. Ironically, Lou had sold the trailer before the arson. "I got cash. Gary didn't even know." And if Georgia was involved, she got nothing out of it, much to the amusement of Lou. "My friend Jo Ann said, 'Man, you got the old witch again.'"

By the end of August, Lou could take no more. Stewart had gone on another rampage, attacking her in her sleep. "He doesn't even remember what he does anymore, that's how dangerous he gets." This time Lou managed to call 911. "Gary didn't see me do it. They got there in, hell, less than five minutes. That's how I got out of the house." Shannon "begged me to put Gary out—'Dad's gone crazy,'" Lou wrote in her diary. On August 28 she filed a restraining order, and the cops dragged Stewart away. Gary pleaded with Lou to call off the wolves, but she wouldn't budge. "I know what you're gonna be like when the shit wears off," she told him.

I spoke to her a few days later. "To me he's dead, deader than Joey. I had all the locks changed. If he shows up, I'll call 911 and they'll take him to jail. After he goes to jail a few times, maybe then he'll stay away. I'm through...I hate him. If he kills hisself, it's not my fault. I really don't think he's got the fuckin' guts to do it." Despite the chaos, Lou sounded invigorated, stronger than she had in a long time. As much as I cared about Gary, Lou had to get out of there, and I told her she had a hideout in Hoboken if she needed one. "I'll make it," she assured me. "You know me, I'm a survivor."

Meanwhile, Gary wandered around Florida and Kentucky staying with a succession of friends, all the while pining for his wife to return. "Lou was more able to climb out of that hole than Gary," said Jo Ann Gregory. "I'm not saying he was a weak personality by any stretch of the imagination, but she was a stronger one—and even though she was equally addicted to drugs, she did not have as addictive a personality as he did. Lou could overcome things.

"I think Gary had a lot more ghosts—ghosts about decisions that he made. Pile the drugs on top of it… It was always easier to find Lou straighter than Gary, willing to do something, go out. But Gary, you always just found him in his room, huddled under the covers."

* * *

Brand New was released that November. The cover was a moody close-up of Stewart's face. "He's not smiling on that album cover," said Bill Hardman, who said Gary told him, "That's for Joey."[124] The album was a mixed collection of numbers drawn mainly from the recent demos—eight of the ten cuts were cowritten by Stewart (Mary Lou his cowriter on five), the most Gary songs ever on an album, excluding the collection of demos and Kapp singles on MCA. Four cuts were just sweetened versions of the demos Forrest Hills executive Glenn Middleworth had cut previously.

Two songs stand above the rest. "Rainin', Rainin', Rainin'" is maybe the catchiest number Stewart ever wrote, a song so simple and infectious that even the lack of Gary's piano-playing can't sink it (Stewart plays

124 Eerily, Stewart is also wearing one of Joey's shirts, although he didn't realize it until Lou pointed it out.

piano on the demo cut at Tommy's Easy People home studio, which is superior). It features one of the more impassioned vocals on the album, although it never truly catches fire. "An Empty Glass" had been kicking around at least since 1983—Stewart demoed it both at Tommy Schwartz's house and for Red Ash. Despite it being unreleased, he'd even played it out on the road with the Toman Brothers.

"Russ Toman is actually the one that came up with the signature guitar lick—da-daa, da-da," said drummer Ray Wilburn. This angst-ridden number about a barstool loser had been inspired by Garna Stewart's split with his wife Lydia, who'd been a dancer at a local fleshpit, Evil People Lounge. Tommy Schwartz remembered working in Garna's shop to fix up a "'60 Falcon convertible, black with a red top" that Garna gifted Lydia, to no avail. "That's what she left town in," said Tommy. Soon thereafter, Gary encountered his brother at Rialto's, drowning his sorrows. "Garna was sitting back there sulking, with a drink and a cigarette," said Tommy. "That's where the song came from." Dean Dillon helped Gary finesse the lyric, and while it only reached number sixty-four on the charts, "every band in Texas plays that song," Dillon maintained. "To this day, when you close a show in Texas, it's 'An Empty Glass.'" The chorus is Stewart at his dramatic, desperate best. "With an empty glass / And a last cigarette / Closing time / And I'm drunk again."[125]

"Brand New Whiskey," the first single, is an exuberant if unremarkable drinking song with some clever wordplay (it was later cut by Brooks & Dunn on their 1998 album *If You See Her*). The amusingly boastful "Son of a Honky Tonk Woman," originally a Jerry Lee Lewis–style piano-thumper, lost most of its charm without Gary on the keys. "I Get Drunk" (cowritten with Steve Hunter) is a forgettable novelty number not unlike throwaways George Jones would pad his later albums with. "I Owe It All to My Heart" is a poppy ballad from the dreaded major-sevenths period written by

125 Randy Toman felt the released version of "An Empty Glass" missed the mark. "Man, almost every night, that was a better song live than the studio session." He found the demo cut for Red Ash was superior. "Gary's voice and just the feel is way better than the HighTone record."

Gary, in a Gary Stewart shirt, looking unhappy to be photographed. (Gina Stewart collection)

Stewart, Dillon, and Tanya Tucker, albeit beautifully sung by Gary. "Lucretia," another clichéd number about a predatory female, verges on generic hair-metal.

Lastly are two songs Gary had no hand in: "Murdered by Love" is an overwrought four-minute-plus blues that is more Blueshammer than juke joint and lacks the humor of the version cut by one of the song's three writers, Don "Poobah" Mealer. "Looking for Some Brand New Stuff" is a Sonny Tackett number that I retrieved from a cassette in Gary's trailer and sent to Dea. A sly, lusty song that could've slid off Stewart's *Little Junior*, when Tackett penned it, he instantly thought, "Bam! This is perfect for Gary. He must've wrote this, and then it come into my mind." Tackett's freewheeling, funky acoustic demo is tremendous. Stewart's version is leaden. Sonny, who would also contribute "Make It a Double" to the last HighTone album, felt that both could've been better. "I thought Gary would just absolutely kill them, and he did not. I couldn't understand why—if it was Gary, or if it was Roy, letting him get by?"

Where Gary and Roy had been trailblazers, they were now settling for weakly imitating the past. Plenty of people love Gary's HighTone Records—numerous industry potentates like *The Tennessean*'s Robert K. Oermann[126] put *Brand New* on their best-of-the-year lists—so listen and make up your own mind. But I never play them. They just aren't exciting to me, with too much huffing and puffing in the vocals, many of which have a cloudy chemical haze reminiscent of 1970s/1980s Jerry Lee Lewis. Stewart himself was later critical of his delivery, telling Bob Allen, "I went from a year of not singing at all into the studio and that was tough! I had a hell of a time hittin' some of them high sharps and flats!" Hell, I'd heard Gary blasting away on his acoustic guitar in the trailer and live in the Fort Pierce joints. I knew he was still a vital artist and felt he deserved better than one last mediocre pat on the back before being shuffled off to the retro boneyard.

I almost did something about it. The following year I started hanging around the Neil Young crowd, beginning my tortured ten-year journey to complete my biography, *Shakey*. I played Stewart for Neil as well as his firebrand producer, David Briggs,[127] and they were both knocked out. Briggs had recorded Young's inebriated 1975 classic *Tonight's the Night* by knocking a hole in the wall of a Los Angeles rehearsal hall and recording the album on the fly like a drunken, one-take wake. I thought Stewart would benefit from such a raw approach and, as Briggs was a crazed maniac who didn't accept second best, sparks would've definitely flown. I pitched the idea to David, and he was interested. But he quickly got sucked back into the Neil Young/Crazy Horse vortex. Plus, Roy had plans to do more HighTone albums and I held him in too much awe to butt in with my ten-cent notions. It's one of my greatest regrets, because I feel the results could've been far more original and less stale than any of the HighTone material Gary cut.

126 When Oermann profiled Stewart for the paper the previous year, his opening sentence gave indication of how Gary's reputation had continued to grow despite his lack of presence on the country charts: "If there's any honky-tonk star living today that conjures up the tortured spirit of the immortal Hank Williams, it's Gary Stewart."

127 Not to be confused with the Nashville David Briggs who played on many a Stewart album, including *Brand New*.

Not wanting to rain on anybody's parade, I kept my opinions to myself, although I did have an amusing encounter with Larry Sloven the one time Dea introduced us. The conversation was rather brief. "So you're the guy obsessed with Gary Stewart," I said by way of an introduction. Larry seemed a bit taken aback. "I'm not obsessed with anybody," he replied. That was it for this young hothead. I walked away, thinking, "Yeah— and that's the problem. Nobody's obsessed."

* * *

There is no denying *Brand New* invigorated Stewart's career and got him back to doing regular gigs.

In addition, it earned him his last appearances on the country charts—"Brand New Whiskey" hit number sixty-three, "An Empty Glass" sixty-four, and "Rainin', Rainin', Rainin' seventy-seven. "Several chart singles off of one album," said Sloven. "It's pretty unusual in those days for an independent label." But while Stewart continued to record for HighTone, his enthusiasm quickly waned. "He had his hopes about the first one," said Randy Toman. "And then, not so much. We hardly did any of those songs, just 'Brand New Whiskey' and 'Rainin', Rainin', Rainin'. It got to the point where if people even asked for those other songs, Gary said no. He never said, 'Y'know what, we better learn that one.'"

* * *

Funnily enough, Gary cut a handful of fascinating recordings on the sly during this time, although he never mentioned them and I only learned of their existence years later when they popped up online. They were recorded at the home of then-medical student Jay Haskett, a transplanted guitar-playing Kentuckian living in Vero Beach. He had been in Russell Music, one of Gary's Fort Pierce hangouts, talking guitars with owner Wallace Parr when Parr pointed and said, "That's Gary Stewart." "Who's Gary Stewart?"

replied Jay, completely unaware. Haskett struck up a conversation with Gary, which ended with Stewart inviting him to the trailer. "He immediately gave me a 1964 Gibson ES-335! Just gave it to me. Such a valuable guitar!"

Stewart took to calling when he was short on cash. "He'd call me and say, 'Jay, can you buy some of my stuff, I need money.' He sold me a bunch of guitars, some old Fender amplifiers." Haskett would visit Gary's place now and then, always bringing imported LU cookies that Stewart coveted. Haskett's first encounter with Mary Lou left an indelible impression. "She said, "Well, you're a doctor, Jay. Look, what do you think of my breast implants?' She showed me and said, 'What do you think?' I said, 'They seem nice to me.' But it never went any further than that! That's Gary's wife!"

Haskett was an unusual player who called his slightly hallucinatory style a "syncopated pedal staccato style of lead guitar with a 'B' bender...I learned from Charlie Christian and Joe Pass and Clarence White. I could make it fit into Gary's stuff. He said, 'I never heard anything like that.'" Haskett played a few gigs with Gary and the Easy People Band, "then he started asking me to come record on his albums with him." Gary was so taken with his sound, he wanted Jay to play on *Brand New,* but Haskett didn't want to leave his medical career.

Haskett had Stewart over for dinner in Vero Beach. He had a home recording studio, and asked Gary if he'd throw some vocals down on some tracks he'd recorded with his brother Brenan on a four-track machine. "I was organized for Gary. I would put all the tracks together and had the lyrics written out, because, I mean, he's a celebrity guy, y'know?" Over the next few years Stewart would overdub one-take vocals on five songs on the fly. Haskett wasn't in the music business, wasn't in awe of Gary or even aware of his history—"I didn't really appreciate him"—so there was no pressure. These numbers were just done on a whim, and Stewart's loose, freewheeling vocals are far better than anything he was laying down in Nashville.

On the Dave Dudley hit "Six Days on the Road" Gary's near-rockabilly delivery recalls his screwball uptempo numbers from the Kapp days. There's a heartfelt version of "Long Black Veil," plus a somewhat hokey attempt at a country ballad written by Haskett, "Leave the Note" (that actually required two takes because of a flub). Improbably enough, the two knockouts are mournful versions of Rolling Stones chestnuts—"Wild Horses" and "No Expectations." Gary renders them like songs from the darkest holler, particularly "No Expectations," which he Stewartizes instantly by mangling the opening: "Take me to the airport and put me on a train." As Haskett recalled, "Gary got the words mixed up. But it was so good I'm like, 'We ain't changin' this.'" You hear this material and want ten more albums of it. But it was just another little mystery Gary left by the side of the road, never to be revisited.

* * *

At the time *Brand New* came out, Gary was staying with musician friends Steve and Carla Hunter in Ashland, Kentucky. "Lou had run his ass off," said Steve. "Gary called me from Knoxville, wanting to know if I could come get him. He had no place to go." Stewart stayed for "probably three months, maybe longer." According to Carla, Stewart "was part of the family. He was like our adopted son." Since both Hunters had day jobs, Gary was alone in the house during the day. "To try to keep him busy, I gave him projects—sweep the walks and the deck, do a little housework," said Steve. "Lotta times he'd come up with excuses—his knees were too bad." Stewart wreaked havoc on the kitchen while the Hunters were away. One night Steve came home intent on having a Lean Cuisine frozen dinner. "That's what I had for lunch," said Stewart. When he offered to fix Gary a burger, "No, I ate them 'em all, too." Another night Gary took a big Tupperware bowl, "dumped in a can of peaches, threw four Klondike bars on top of it, and then went back upstairs to bed," said Hunter. The concoction wound up all over the bed, and Gary. "I had to peel the sheets off him."

Suffice to say Stewart was not in good shape. "He was brokenhearted," said Hunter. Fueled by various medications and desperate to reconnect with his wife, Gary would stay up for three days, then take something to knock him out for the next three. "He had a darkness," said Steve. Stewart was also drinking. "He acquired a taste for the Crown Royal."

One day they were driving down the Bluegrass Parkway headed for Nashville to attend a listening party for *Brand New* when they pulled off the side of the road so Stewart could relieve himself. "Gary never wore underwear and didn't have a belt on," said Steve. "He got tangled up in his pants, which dropped to his ankles." They had been parked on a steep incline, and Gary fell down the hill, "rollin' and tumblin' end over end," said Steve. "His pants come completely off. I had to go down there and help him back up." And yet when they made music, Stewart snapped to. "When he played a song, his whole body played it," said Carla. "It was almost impossible to sing harmony with him. You didn't know which way to go." Sometimes they'd take Gary to Hanging Rock, a place across the river in Ohio where you could look out over the Ohio River Valley. According to Steve, "He'd get out there and holler, 'Lou! Lou, I love you!" his forlorn cries echoing through the hills. "Gary was a tortured man," said Carla.

* * *

Stewart's next stop was Sonny Tackett's place outside Prestonburg, Kentucky. Although the Hunters loved Gary, they sounded relieved to have him out of their hair. Sonny said Gary stayed about six months. He didn't sleep in a bedroom as there was a couch next to Tackett's considerable collection of vinyl. "We played music all night," said Sonny. "I don't think we even slept." Gary's habit of blasting albums at 2 a.m. irritated Tackett's wife, who had a job to go to in the morning.

Realizing this couldn't go on forever, Sonny hatched a plot to get Gary back home. Without telling Gary, he called Mary Lou and told her, "Gary wants you to meet him at the Hyatt Regency hotel in

Nashville tomorrow." She went for it. So then he told Gary that Lou had called and wanted to meet him at the Regency the next day. "For the first time since he'd been there, Gary was happy," said Sonny. "Right that minute, he started packin'—and everything he was packing was my records. He took a whole suitcase!" Tackett loaded Gary into the car and drove to Music City. "We walk in through the front doors of the Hyatt and there's Lou, standing by the desk. Gary just jumped into her arms. And that's how they got back together."[128]

No one was surprised. "Mom and Dad always found their way back to each other," said Shannon. "Always." Given Stewart's state, I worried about what might happen next, but Lou assured me something had changed in Gary, and while he'd still have moments of utter lunacy, the physical abuse had stopped.

A new arrival had come into their lives that gave them hope—a grandson. Shannon gave birth to Joseph on June 25, 1989. When I asked Shannon who picked the name, she said, "I had nothing to do with that. My mom did that, because of Joey." At first, Gary was resistant. "My dad was like, 'I don't want nothing to do with him. I don't want nothing to do with that baby, I know what you're tryin' to do, and he ain't Joey.' Two days later I look around the corner and my dad's in there going, 'Googoo, gaga.'"

Gary and Lou doted on the child. Said Shannon, "I wasn't allowed to leave with my son until he was about six months old. Mom kind of took Joseph." One day Lou called me giddy with excitement, telling me she'd had a dream that Joseph cut a record—"Baby Joseph Sings the Blues." When he was a little older she started creating costumes for him—first it was Elvis, then Frank-N-Furter from *The Rocky Horror Picture Show*. "Honey, I dressed him up in black nylons, a garter belt, and red heels," said Lou with a cackle. Gary got Joseph a set of drums. "You'd go in there and Joseph's banging on them," said Jay Haskett. "I'm goin', 'Why in the hell would you ever buy a little kid a

---

128 Stewart's prolonged visit took a toll on Tackett's own marriage, however—Sonny's wife of ten years took their baby and fled to her parents' home in Indiana. "My wife left me, my dog left me, and if I'd had a horse, he would've left me."

set of drums?' Gary loved that kid." Lou "spoiled me rotten," said Joe Peavy. "There was nothing really I could've ever have done wrong in that house. I learned a lot from Lou, like, 'Yes, ma'am' and 'No, ma'am.'" And to never go into a woman's purse. One day Lou was smoking in the house. "She's like, 'Here, go ahead.' And I mean, I was young, under ten for sure. Since then I've never, ever once wanted to smell it, taste it, hit it. I mean, I'm a cigarette Nazi!"

Lou would tell Shannon more than once that Joseph's arrival had saved their lives. "Joseph's funny," Lou gushed to me. "We enjoy him so much...he really turned our lives around for the good. Gary even keeps the phone on the hook, Jimmy!"

* * *

Mary Lou and Gary with grandson, Joseph, 1990. (Shannon Ashburn)

Battleground, Stewart's second HighTone album, came out in 1990. This album had less to recommend it than *Brand New*, and sported the absolute worst Gary Stewart album cover—a shot of Gary looking deflated and glum in a leather jacket, the lackluster image adorned with ten-cent graphics. There were no singles released from *Battleground*, which opens with a half-baked cover of Robert Cray's generic "Nothin' but a Woman" and sputters along from there. Four songs were cowritten by Gary, two of them memorable, but the versions here are substandard. "Let's Go Jukin'" was written with Dickey Betts for Jason D. Williams, a goofy Jerry Lee Lewis acolyte Roy Dea was producing for RCA. This was another number that needed Gary on piano—as did "Nothing Cheap About a Cheap Affair." There was also an unwise remake of a classic unreleased Stewart recording, "Woman in Demand." How Gary felt having to match his younger, incandescent self is anyone's guess. The only thing I return to on *Battleground* is a spirited, unexpected cover of Bobby Darin's 1963 hit "You're the Reason I'm Living." The do-or-die lyrics would prove sadly prescient in Gary's case.

That year Stewart made a rare TV appearance on *Nashville Now* (alongside the great Faron Young) and performed a half-hour live set for a TNN show called *On Stage*. Not easy to track down, the *On Stage* show is the one great document from the HighTone years. Backed by a group of Nashville pros led by David Briggs, Stewart is in great form, charging through six songs from *Battleground*. They are far livelier than the album, and Gary delivers a performance with Elvis-like authority, extracting the humor from "Ol' Hank's Lovesick Blues," adding swagger to "You're the Reason," and making "Nothin' but a Woman" his own.

During the *Battleground* promotion, Stewart was also interviewed by his old press buddy Bob Allen, and an ominous exchange took place about another Kentucky talent, Keith Whitley, who'd killed himself just months before. "That mother could sing," said Stewart, who was touched to learn Whitley had opened his shows with "Flat Natural Good-Timin' Man." Gary empathized with Whitley's suffering and condemned those who judged. "Bein' in the limelight, Lord, it's darkness many times, it's *so* dark in there..." And when it came to Whitley's fatal ending, Stewart admitted, "I've been right there, son."

* * *

Stewart's career puttered along, Gary putting in minimal effort. As long as he could play a few gigs and pay some bills, fine. As Gary wrote to Lou in a 1991 note, "If it wasn't for you and the kids I'd probably work just as hard at not working, and I could always scratch and get by, 'cause the world is always ready for one more troubadour. But you all are worth all the shit that's foreign to my nature."

I'm a Texan,[129] the third and final HighTone album, came out on October 15, 1993. It featured only one song Gary had cowritten, and it was another inferior recreation of a fantastic unreleased demo from the distant past, "It's True." The bulk of the recordings are half-hearted covers, although the opening cut, a "Wild" Bill Emerson song written with wife Jody, "Come On In," has more swing than the rest and features a wry, inspired vocal from Gary. This would be Stewart's last studio album, and he went out with a whimper.[130]

The arrangement with HighTone "just sort of sputtered out," according to Larry Sloven. "Sales declined over the three albums. There were a lot of diminishing returns." Gary would never work with Roy Dea again. Dea's last years were rough. Sonny Tackett, who worked with Dea on a solo album, recalled a late-night phone call. "Roy was really, really drunk. He was angry at Nashville, angry at RCA, angry at Gary...it must've been an hour and a half, just ranting and raving." Roy drank and smoked 'til the end. Dea had been in the Marine Reserves, and a big joy at the end of his life was "hanging out

129 "Gary hated the title," said his cousin Nick Stewart. "He wasn't a Texan." But the title paid unexpected dividends, as Governor Ann Richards made Gary an honorary Texan on May 24, 1994.

130 One good thing came out of *I'm a Texan*: Steve Hinson got to make a record with two of his heroes—Stewart and Dea. When Roy asked if he wanted to play steel on the record, he said, "How much do I have to pay?" They did the sessions in a day. "I don't like that record. I don't think I did a good job on it. But I got to do it!"

at the American Legion club," according to his wife Delores. "Roy loved all of the veterans. They were his heroes, so he would hang out down there and buy them drinks." Roy Dea died on August 22, 1997, two days after suffering a heart attack.

I'd planned on visiting Gary and Mary Lou around this time. I'd just gotten married and my wife Natalia was a big Gary Stewart fan. I wanted them to meet. Everybody was excited about the trip and arrangements were made. But Lou called at 2 a.m. and announced, "Gary said he doesn't want you to come to Florida," then abruptly hung up. The next day she called back, apologizing, and they both got on the line, imploring me to visit. Weary of such shenanigans, I declined. Who knows which Gary I might encounter down there, I thought. We should've gone, as I'd never see him in person again, although we kept in touch by phone. Out of the blue he'd send me noteless audio tapes in the mail where he'd do "Little Cabin Home on the Hill" or something equally close to my heart. His packages would be return-addressed from either Mike Love or Howard Hughes.

Turns out this period was another rough patch, with the couple splitting for yet another time (no one can recall just why). Stewart went off to Texas to stay with Joey Floyd, fiddle and banjo player for Toby Keith.[131]

Gary had no label, no Lou, and nothing on the horizon. But two wild Texas characters would soon enter the picture to inject new energy into his life on the road, ushering in the last golden period of Gary Stewart's time on earth. Their names are Terry Porter and James Willingham.

131 When Stewart wore out his welcome with Floyd, Joey used the same playbook Sonny Tackett had. "He played both Gary and Lou, saying they each missed the other in order to get Gary to go home," said Stewart friend Barbara Anne Peters.

19

HONKY-TONK BANDITS

It's like my own fate was chasin' me into the grave.
– Wild Bill Hickok (Charles Bronson), *The White Buffalo*

Some entertaining new players entered Gary Stewart's life in the early to mid-nineties. One was Richard McCroan. A Texan in his early thirties, McCroan worked as a body shop manager by day and crooned the songs of Haggard, Price, Mel Street, and Gary Stewart—what he calls "Texas dance hall music"—in honky-tonks at night. Stewart had been working at a big Dallas club called Cowboys Dancehall in an ill-advised attempt by the club to make him a regular with their house band. Donnie McDuff and Gary "Breeze" Hogue, both of whom would go on to play with Gary intermittently, introduced Stewart to McCroan. Like many others before him, Richard became hooked on helping Stewart, and he started driving Gary to gigs, running his many errands, pressing his clothes, and even, upon occasion, washing his back.

McCroan and Stewart were an odd couple. Richard, a forceful personality with a slick, clean-cut professional air, was irretrievably locked into that classic 4/4 Texas shuffle beat and didn't care for the funkier, far-out side of Gary. "I was so different from him," McCroan admitted. "I was diametrically opposed to every value he had, every fashion." Richard wore fine business suits under his cowboy hats, taking extra care to get spiffy for honky-tonk nights. "That drove Gary nuts about me. He'd ask, '*Why* do you *blow dry* your hair? Do you even *own* a T-shirt?'"

Nonetheless, McCroan was a go-getter determined to revitalize Stewart's career, which led him into booking Stewart's gigs. "I got permission from Gary to put a new band together, take over everything," said McCroan, who soon realized he'd have to do it all in spite of Stewart. "I wasn't gonna change Gary. There was no changin' Gary." At the time, Stewart was getting gigs through a Nashville booking agent, Dan Wojcik, as well as longtime friend and bodyguard Henry Esparza—a short, heavyset Mexican American beloved by all of Stewart's Texas circle. McCroan felt these two were at best treading water and at worst letting Stewart's career slide into the toilet with bookings like a $1,500 appearance at the grand opening of Wild Wet Willie's strip club in Aledo, Texas. "I didn't want Gary to play no more damn VFW clubs or strip joints."

Richard set his sights on trying to wean Gary off the Toman Brothers Band. "As long as I had been watching Gary play, it never sounded like the damn record. It was like a *rock band*," judged McCroan, lamenting that there was no steel player.[132] So Richard lined up musicians who could duplicate the Nashville arrangements: "Everything that we did, it had to sound just like the record," he

132 Randy Toman noted that while Gary had played live with many great steel players, including Buddy Emmons, many of them, as great as he knew they were, just weren't suitable for his music. "Gary didn't want one of those old-school steel players. He wanted somebody that was a little bit more ready to jam and not just play the fills on old Ray Price songs. Gary didn't want to play that kind of country." A steel player could definitely tilt things in the wrong direction when they were playing, say, the Allman Brothers' "One Way Out," and it would drive Stewart nuts. "He'd say, 'I don't want it to sound like a country band playing rock!'"

insisted. McCroan next did the unthinkable—he enforced a set list, something Stewart had pointedly ignored the rest of his career. It was built around Gary's hits, although Richard begrudgingly let him open with "Little Junior." As Richard conceded, "I got that out of the way, because that gave Gary his groove."

McCroan also sought to tighten up Gary and his band sartorially. "Randy would wear a hot-pink shirt, Russell a wifebeater, and Gary would just wear the sloppiest shit," crowed McCroan. So he decreed that band members dress all in black to highlight Gary, who was even dragged to a hairstylist for a photo shoot, polishing him up to look like an over-earnest Porter Wagoner. "It was all about the presentation," said McCroan, and while this wouldn't necessarily result in great Gary Stewart music, Richard was soon delivering better shows and bigger fees. "The money came back. I got so many compliments from club owners who had booked Gary previously. I really upped the game tremendously."

Stewart attracted the cream of the crop when it came to Texas musicians, allowing him to draw from a changing pool of ace pickers. The unnamed band that originated at Cowboys[133] was led by guitarist Donnie McDuff, son of Texas songwriter Eddie McDuff and "totally crazy," according to steel player Steve Palousek, a frequent witness to the chaos that seemed to follow McDuff wherever he went. "From his wife trying to run him over with a car, to where we'd be in a hotel, you'd hear this ruckus, and the elevator opens and McDuff's in there wrestling with the singer Bobby Smith, and he'd knocked Bobby's toupee off." McDuff and Stewart were not the best combo. Donnie "had this deal about wanting to control everything," said Palousek, a lost cause with Gary. The end came when McDuff got blitzed on tequila at Cutters nightclub in Beaumont and started throwing shot glasses at Stewart's head from the audience.[134]

133 "Gary was always wantin' to name the band Hurricane Pony," said sometime pianist Jeff Williams with a sigh.

134 One version of the Cowboys band with McDuff and Hogue can be seen on a 1992 episode of TNN's *On Stage*. McCroan calls it Gary's "comeback performance"; I call it dull.

Randy Toman watched these comings and goings with a grain of salt. "Gary had a way about him—when the new guy came along he acted like, 'Whatever you need, tell me what you want me to do and I'll make you feel good about it.' Donnie was not the first or the last guy that thought he was in charge." The same would go for McCroan.

These bands all bled together somewhat. McDuff had played with the Tomans, as had another another on-again, off-again player—drummer Randy "Panda" Woolery, not to mention later band members Curtis Randall and Jeff Williams. Harmonica player Tim Harris sat in with all of Gary's bands, while many other musicians came and went, like guitarists Rusty Burns,[135] Buddy Whittington, and Michael Jeffrey, steel guitarist Junior Knight, drummer John Phillips and others. Sometimes Stewart would want a piano, sometimes steel, sometimes you wouldn't hear from him for nine months. "Gary was fickle that way," said Steve Palousek.

For a brief second Jeff Williams stepped in as leader of Stewart's band. A fabulous piano player, "Jeff always seemed like he was into something shady," said Palousek. "If you roomed with him you wanted to sleep with one eye open." Williams had no illusions about being bandleader for Little Junior. "What that means is you're the wet nurse," he explained. "I had to iron his fucking underwear." Jeff got so tired of Stewart's demands, one night before a show he put Ben-Gay in Gary's shorts. "By the third song in he was sweatin' and doin' Elvis moves." Jeff would drive Gary to some of the gigs and would be amazed by Stewart's back-seat guitar picking. When Williams asked Stewart why he didn't play like that onstage, Gary drawled, "Well, Jeff, then they'd expect it *every night*." Williams proclaims that being in Stewart's band was "the most real gig I ever did. Everything about it was real. Everybody in the band was real."

---

135 Rusty Burns was a blues and Southern rock guitarist who "played left-handed, upside down like Hendrix," said McCroan. "Gary loved him." One night Burns got popped for weed en route to a Stewart show and rang McCroan to inform him he wasn't going to be able to play. "I called a good friend in law enforcement who was in my wedding," said Richard. "He got Rusty out with a phone call."

Williams recalled playing a Native American event somewhere in Florida. The tribal chief wanted to hear "Cactus and a Rose" and he was insistent, despite the fact that Stewart hadn't played it for years. According to Williams, who'd be Gary's sole accompanist on the number, somebody got ahold of the album and "we pulled it out of a hat. The chief came up there and put a chair on the stage right in front of Gary's microphone. And he sat there in his war bonnet and listened to 'Cactus and a Rose.' Every Indian there was standin' in front of that stage, swayin' back and forth." Williams made a dramatic exit from the band in 1998. "The main reason I left is because I was strung out on meth," admitted Jeff, who pawned one of Gary's guitars after Stewart had been a no-show for several gigs (Williams, long clean, now drives a truck).

Guitarist Glynn Fleming stepped in as bandleader of what would later become the Texas Honky-Tonk All Star Band. Fleming and bassist Curtis Randall had played with Gary at Cowboys and would work with him off and on when they weren't on the road with LeAnn Rimes.[136] They were joined by steel player Steve Palousek, pianist Dickie Taylor, and drummer Dick Dunn. "The most emotional singer I've ever worked with," Dunn said of Stewart. "He was like a walking, exposed nerve end." Randall and Dunn were a great rhythm section that, as Tim Harris pointed out, gave the band "a certain lope. You don't hear it in every country band. It's almost a bluesy kind of a country feel. Not complicated, just a real nice groove. It fit Gary to a T." The Texas Honky-Tonk All Star Band[137] was a very slick outfit that fulfilled McCroan's edict to sound "just like the record." But is that what you want to hear from Gary?

---

136 Curtis had played on the smash-hit demo of "Blue" for Rimes, who was thirteen at the time. When it started getting airplay, her dad asked Randall to go on the road. He was playing with Stewart at the time, and when he got to the honky-tonk a while later, "Blue" was wafting out of the jukebox. Gary, who had gotten there early, was eating a steak as he listened. Curtis didn't know how Stewart would take his leaving the band, but Gary was excited for Randall, telling him, "You need to go...milk that thing for as long as you can." Stewart said there'd be a spot for him whenever he returned. LeAnn came with her family to see Gary perform one night, but she "just didn't get it," according to Randall.

137 The name came from Richard McCroan's old band. To keep out the riffraff, Richard also instituted blue-and-red backstage passes for Gary that featured a horseshoe motif he lifted from his friend Marty Stuart's passes.

"The sound changed when Randy and Russell Toman left," said Jeff Williams. "To me, *that* was the Gary Stewart sound." There was no spontaneity. As Craig Turley, who recorded many of the later Stewart shows, noted, "When he played with the Tomans, they changed the set list all the time. With the Honky-Tonk All Stars, they played the same show...it got so boring."

* * *

Turley was another new face in the Stewart entourage. Part of an underground circuit of tapers and traders, in 1989 the young Texan had been asked to record Gary shows for Stewart's old Allman Brothers friend, Kirk West. Kirk promised Craig a case of Allman Brothers soundboards for every Gary show he taped. With that, Turley headed over to Billy Bob's in Fort Worth, his black Walkman WM-D6 in hand. "I wasn't necessarily a country and western music lover. I couldn't have told you who Gary was to save the moon." When he got to Billy Bob's, Craig was "blown away" to find a crowd of four thousand. "I never ever would've guessed that many people would like this guy. The venues that Gary played usually held three to four thousand-plus people, and they always seemed sold out or close to it. Cowboys in Dallas, a huge place, was always so packed that it was hard to move around the club. Billy Bob's was always packed to the rim."

Turley became a fan, and when he bumped into the Tomans on a return visit to Texas, they invited him backstage to meet Stewart. When Gary learned of Craig's Allman Brothers tape collection he flipped, giving Turley his phone number and address and instructing him to call. He did, and eventually got a 2 a.m. "Hey, bud..." return call a few days before Stewart's next Texas gig. Gary insisted on coming to Turley's house in Mansfield after the show. Once there, Turley popped in a live Allman Brothers tape and Gary sat there "mesmerized by the music." Suddenly he pulled off one cowboy boot, turned it upside down, and shook it. "Out comes a wad of bills that would choke a mule. All hundreds," recalled Turley. Gary announced that even though it would cost a fortune, he was changing his flight home. The next morning they went and bought blank cassettes, then commenced copying Craig's tapes, with Gary offering musical insights about the Allmans as they listened.

Stewart became a frequent guest in the Turley abode, staying as long as two weeks at a time when his back went out. Craig's wife Karen would make Gary pies and fried green tomatoes, Stewart would park the dirty dishes "outside the door for us to clean up, like he was at a hotel. He never, not one time ever, called Karen by her name." He also rifled through their medicine cabinets. But Craig laughed off Gary's eccentricities. The Turleys had been bitten by the Stewart bug, even flying to Fort Lauderdale to attend a July 7, 1990, Allman Brothers show with Gary. Although Stewart had no license at the time, he drove them to the show in Speed, Lou's Thunderbird. "Gary scared us just driving from the hotel to the airport" said Craig. "He took all these albums with his picture on them. He said, 'If I get pulled over, I'll just show the police officer these so they know who I am.'" Gary was sitting in the front row with Craig when "Dickey walked over to the edge of the stage and helped Gary up," said Turley. Stewart jumped in for two impromptu verses of "Ramblin' Man."

Craig was thoroughly entertained by the behind-the-scenes antics at Stewart's shows. "As I've told a lot of people, it's a lot wilder backstage with Gary Stewart than it is with Allman Brothers." Despite his being pale, frail, and just about fifty, "the young girls loved Gary," said friend Kim Willingham. "It was the weirdest thing." Women would routinely show up backstage demanding autographs in all the wrong places. "I've seen him sign many a boob," said Turley. "All these women were whippin' their boobs out. Gary did it so smooth... you could tell this wasn't his first rodeo." One woman begged him to sign her panties, but Gary refused, "so she dropped her pants and he signed her butt." When Craig inquired why he didn't sign undies, Stewart let him in on a nonsensical rule: he would sign actual skin, but no bras or panties. "You can get beat up for signing those, but if you just sign on the butt or the boob, they don't get mad at you." I'm like, 'Okay...'" Nor would Stewart always sign his own name. Bass player Curtis Randall was hanging in Gary's motel room when some crazed beauty whipped off her top. "Her titties were hard as a rock. They were bought," noted Randall. "Gary goes, 'Curtis, you never sign your own name on these titties.' And he reached down and signed my name!" Boob-signing proved highly contagious among band members. According to Steve Palousek, "We kept a Sharpie on us at all times."

* * *

Despite a lack of hit albums, singles, or videos and zero presence in Nashville, Gary was, as Turley put it, "making a crapload of money" in the last years of his life, selling out huge honky-tonks and dance halls across Texas. Clubs that had balked when McCroan demanded a new, higher rate for Stewart acquiesced once he started pressing for a cut of the alcohol sales. "When you played Billy Bob's, they booked you on tiers—'We'll pay $4,500 for the first 1,000 people, we'll pay $5,500 for the next 750, and $6,500 if we get 2,000,'" explained McCroan. "I hated it, because I never trusted their numbers...it would look to me like we'd hit 6,000 people. And at the end of the night, they'd say, 'We hit 4,500 tonight.' They wouldn't even consider talking about liquor sales. And I knew I hit a nerve, because it wasn't just one club owner, it was everyone." Using that as his wedge, Richard got Stewart's rate up, getting top dollar if Gary played a casino or racetrack—$12,000.[138]

Wherever Gary played, the booze definitely did flow. "Gary told me multiple times how proud he was for holding the record for the most liquor sold in one night at Billy Bob's," Craig Turley recalled.[139]

138 Two places Richard couldn't get Gary booked: the Broken Spoke in Austin and Gruene Hall in New Braunfels. Both were run by old-school guys and McCroan "could not get either one of those places to even consider Gary, because they thought he was a drug-addled, wino drunk."

139 The flip side of that was "sometimes Gary got down because he played in bars and his music made people drink," said Lou. "I said, 'No, people would be drinking anyway. You bring happiness into their lives.'"

Randy Woolery was Stewart's drummer the night Billy Bob's "sold out of beer. And that's a 147,000-square-foot beer joint that holds 3,500 to 4,000 people. I walked out the back door and saw eleven beer trucks backed into that motherfucker, unloading beer. It was that way everywhere we played with Stewart. Gary was a beer-joint icon."

Stewart sold a ton of alcohol at the Coupland Dancehall in little Coupland, Texas, a regular stop. Barbara Worthy, who ran the place with her husband Tim, would also book him at their other club, the River Palace in Johnson City. Stewart loved the chicken-fried steak and peach cobbler at the Dancehall and "was like a son to us," said Barbara. One night Stewart did $30,000 in liquor sales there; on another they sold out of beer before he even hit the stage. "Twenty-seven cases of beer and eleven kegs," noted Tim. Barbara recalled a night they had 1,100 people in the Dancehall and "two or three fights broke out." She told Stewart to quit playing, but he had his own way of handling it. "Gary went up to the mic and said, 'Hey, ya'll—let's not fight, let's fuck.'"

* * *

An unexpected demographic Stewart killed in? College students. "Gary was the Ozzy Osbourne of the college market," boasted McCroan, saying that colleges were "gold mines you could just bank on. Nobody had that—not Johnny Rodriguez, nobody. People who didn't listen to country music loved Gary Stewart." Case in point: Richard's own sister Shannon, a rock fan he caught singing along to "Single Again." When asked how she knew the song, Shannon quipped, "Richard, when you go to college in Texas, if you don't have a Gary Stewart CD they issue you one when you get there."

Any increase in revenue came in handy, because ongoing tax problems weighed heavily on Gary's mind. "The IRS can take lots or everything we got, but not our love," he scribbled in a little note to Lou in 1991. According to Steve Hunter, at one point Stewart had "to go pay thirty-some thousand dollars. I think it's the only time I've ever seen Gary cry." Stewart was paranoid the government would pounce on his assets, as they had done with Willie Nelson in 1990. "He would always be complainin', 'Any day they're going to come and get me,'" said cousin Nick Stewart, who assured him he was comparatively small potatoes. "I said, 'Gary, they don't give a shit about you.'" Nick actually got Stewart on a payment plan, while others around him who shall remain nameless came up with novel financial solutions out on the road that enabled Gary to chip away at the debt.

Nick spent a lot of time with Gary and Lou as a bit of an adopted son. Like Joey, he was a rarity—a blond Stewart. "I looked so much like Joey, I think I was like a replacement." Gary would routinely call him at 1 or 2 a.m. to shoot the shit.[140] Nick even managed to get busted with Gary. In 1993 they were driving the Florida back roads inland to Kissimmee in Nick's green Mercedes when they stopped at a convenience store in Yeehaw Junction to get Gary a Yoo-hoo. As usual, Stewart made an impression. "He got out and staggered around. I could see this deputy lookin' at him." (Cops were always on Stewart's case, according to Richard McCroan. "Law enforcement loved Gary and they loved his music, but they knew what went along with it. His reputation was so bad.")

Shortly after Nick and Gary drove off, the police pulled them over. "I was worried about what Gary had in his little bag," said Nick, but they were more interested in the (unloaded) 9 mm pistol Nick had in the car. Nick was busted for his gun and Gary for pills. The matter was eventually settled, and rather unglamorous as it was, this was Stewart's last run-in with the law.

* * *

140 Many of us got late-night phone calls from Gary in the nineties, including his old bandmate "Boogie" Bob Melton. "This is No-Nook of the North, and I need some nookie," he'd announce, then talk for hours. "He'd go on until he passed out." Patrick Carr, who hadn't been in contact with Gary since 1982, got a middle-of-the night phone message nearly twenty years after that, saying only, "Paddy, you need a friend?" Carr, who was recently sober, never called him back as he'd heard about the shape Gary was in and wanted to stay clean. "I should've just told him. I've always regretted that."

Now middle-aged, Stewart was farther out than ever. "He woke up in a different world every day," said Steve Palousek. Out on one road trip, Gary, who had taken to carrying a magnifying glass, whipped it out to peruse his favorite magazine of Old West culture, *Cowboys & Indians*. He was "in the back seat, all folded up like a contortionist, holding the magazine upside down, studying those pictures," said McCroan, his then-driver. When Richard asked him what the hell he was doing, Stewart replied that he liked to study the minute details of the photographs. "He don't want to see the main character in the picture. He wants to look on the walls and on the floor and on the shelves!"

Interesting way of looking at things, thought McCroan. And as soon as they checked in to the cheap motel that was their destination, "Gary gets his magnifying glass out and walks over to the wall. And he's looking at the wallpaper. I said, 'Gary, what are you searching for?' He said, 'Phallic symbols.'" Stewart then proceeded to point out all sorts of phalluses and vaginas in the floral design on the wall. "I'll be damned," thought Richard. "Gary convinced me if you look deep enough in somethin', you're gonna find a damn dick in it."

Stewart turned each lonely motel room into a secret clubhouse. He'd drape scarves over the lights, hide contraband in the shower curtain rod, and deny the housecleaners entry. He also liked taking the knobs from light fixtures and TVs. "He'd have 'em all in a bag in his luggage," said Jeff Williams, who recalled booking a room for Gary in Texas where he could wind down after a series of gigs there. When he returned a few days later to pick him up, the room was quiet. No Gary. "It looked like rhinoceroses had run through there. The mattress was off on the floor, he had dismantled everything." Williams found Stewart "in the tub, passed out, Snickers bars in his hair. I thought, 'Oh my God, he's fuckin' dead.'" But no, after confirming that he had a pulse, Jeff managed to rouse him.

Gary had a routine whenever the band checked in to a motel after a long day on the road. "The first thing he would do was get buck naked and take a hot bath," said Randy Woolery. One particular time Gary got on the phone and forgot the water was running. Woolery, who was in an adjoining suite, opened the doors to Stewart's room and "stepped into a puddle of water. This motherfucker had flooded the whole bathroom, half of his room, and it was starting to float into my room. The next morning the manager said, 'I really don't need y'all back here ever again.'" (Gary flooded the bathroom of at least one other Texas home he was staying in, causing massive damage to the floor below.)

A bathtub is also central to what is perhaps the craziest Stewart story of this era. It happened in Mexia, Texas, after Stewart and the band had checked in to one of what Curtis Randall nicknamed "Gary Stewart Inns," which meant "motels where you can pull your truck up to the door."

The band had a few hours to relax before showtime at the Cowboy Western Club, an old honky-tonk Stewart had been playing for years. "I'm in my room, already got my shoes off and I'm laying on the bed, flipping through the TV channels," said Randall. "Glynn comes in and says, 'Gary needs to see everybody in his room.'" When Curtis inquired why, "Glynn goes, 'Well, he wants everybody to get together and pour hot water on his balls.' I said, *'Excuse me?'"*

They went to Stewart's room to find him sitting in the tub naked, eating a slab of pizza out of a cardboard box on the toilet. "He was fucked up. Higher than a Georgia pine," said Randall. ("All Soma-tabbed, speeded, and beered out of his mind," added Jeff Williams.) "And Randy Panda's sitting on a chair there in the door of the bathroom, and he's got a bucket full of hot water. Randy looked at me and said, 'Curtis?'" Randall was stunned. When he refused to participate, somebody fulfilled the brief. Although no one wants to cop to it now. "I was standin' in the doorway goin', 'This isn't happenin'—*is it*? What exactly are we tryin' to *achieve* here?'" Curtis wondered. "And I could hear Gary in the bathroom goin', 'Yeah! Yeah! Yeah! Oh *yeah*!'" Jeff Williams added with irony, "Evidently the water was a little too hot. It burned his balls."

No one could come up with a precise explanation for this puzzling escapade, which left his grizzled band of Texas road dogs shaking their heads. "He got off on it," mused Woolery. "That's the only thing that I can come up with." At some point Woolery suggested that Gary write a song about the watery-balls saga. "Gary kind of looked at me, almost with that 'Oh my God, that's a great idea' look. He said, 'Really?' I said, 'NO! Just kidding!'"

* * *

Stewart continued to ingest massive amounts of drugs—Somas, Xanax, painkillers, coke, speed, and whatever else got slipped to him by fans. He even took to wearing a T-shirt with "WHERE'S MY FUCKIN' MEDICATION?" emblazoned across it. Lou eventually stole it —"to wear to the beauty parlor," he informed a friend. At one point Gary took some time off the road, and when he came back, Jeff Williams couldn't believe how healthy he appeared to be. "Gary always looked like a corpse, and he even had a little bit of a suntan. Somebody said, 'You look good, man.' To which Gary replied, 'Yeah, well, it won't be long 'til I'll be back to my old self.'"

On the last day of March 1996, Stewart OD'd at Randy Woolery's house. "We come off a three-day weekend," Randy recalled. "I decided I was gonna run down to the barbecue joint." Where he ran into a couple of women he knew. They got excited when he informed them Gary was at his house, and he instructed them to go to the house and keep him company. But when they arrived they found Stewart "laying in my bed, shaking and foaming at the fucking mouth," said Woolery. "It just freaked those girls, scared the fuck outta them. They didn't call me first, they called the fuckin' ambulance."

Woolery returned home to find a fire truck, police car, and ambulance lined up in front of his house. When he found out what was going on, he rang Lou. "The first question out of her was 'Oh, is he foaming at the mouth?'" She pleaded with Woolery not to let them haul Gary to the hospital. "I can't stop 'em, it's the fuckin' law," he told Lou. "Especially with the shape he was in—slobbering, with his fucking eyes all rolled back in his head. It scared the emergency people." They managed to deduce Stewart had overdosed on Somas, which earned him an overnight stay at the hospital. He flew home the next day. "The guy who sold him crank took him to the airport," noted Randy. "The next weekend it was 'Here were go again,' like nothin' ever happened...that little son of a bitch, I don't know how he lasted as long as he did."

"In the time that I was with him, Gary died three or four times," claimed Jeff Williams. Somehow doctors and nurses always managed to bring him back. "I've always thought that Gary had a death wish." Williams recalled Gary showing him a wooden box in his bedroom containing a Geronimo Colt .45 "in a leather holster, man.[141] I mean, it was the fucking real deal. Gary looked at me and goes, 'If anything ever happens to Lou, I'm gonna end it all. Right here.'"

Drug-induced craziness continued back home in Fort Pierce. According to Lou's January 11, 1996, diary entry, Gary got mad at her for stepping outside to talk with a friend and chased off her visitor. "Then the fun really began," wrote Lou. "He was wanting me to have a shootout." Gary ordered her to take a painting she liked off the wall, then pack her clothes, "all the time waving the loaded .38 pistol I got him for Christmas." He was going to throw Lou out and board up the door. Stewart had been off the road for two weeks and, according to Lou, had "stayed in his room most of the time. Nothing pleased him." She eventually managed to hustle him onto a plane headed for Texas. "Gary's mood swings are more than I can handle anymore...the little shit."

* * *

141 Apparently Geronimo was carrying a .45 when he surrendered, but that resides in a Fort Sill, Oklahoma, museum. I'm assuming this was one of the commemorative "tribute" handguns made in recent years. Stewart would tell Richard McCroan he had made two serious attempts at suicide. When Richard asked what happened during one of these attempts, Gary said, "The phone rang." What happened then? "I answered it," muttered Gary.

On April 14, 1996, George Stewart died. He was seventy-seven, and black lung from his years spent working in the mines had finally done him in. "George Stewart was a hell of a man," wrote Lou in her diary. "When Gary and I got married in '61, he hated my guts. And did for a lot of years. Then after 16 years he liked me." Gary didn't attend the funeral. He claimed to have pneumonia, but he'd also avoided visiting George at the hospital. "Gary said, 'I just can't face the old man,'" recalled Gina. "Gary could see he was passin' and couldn't handle it." Stewart "couldn't do it," confirmed Shannon. "He couldn't even go to his father's funeral."

* * *

Gary Stewart loved renegades of every stripe, and there was an endless supply in his orbit during the nineties. McCroan recalled one such character, a Harley dealer with a Nazi museum over his showroom we'll call Jack. "This guy had a custom van, and it had 'Out of Hand' custom-painted on the front of the hood. And on the wheel cover it had 'Drinkin' Thing.'" Jack would bring the bikers, and he'd station them outside the doors when he'd come see a Stewart show. "It was like a *Sons of Anarchy* episode," said McCroan, who was pressured into a meeting with Jack by Gary. "I walk in and he's got an AK-47 and a pistol laying out, and he proceeded to tell me how he was taking over Gary's bookings."

Richard somehow managed to dodge that particular bullet, but more threats awaited. "There were these dudes that lived at a place called Lake Tawakoni. Dixie Mafia. Happy, Smiley, Skinny...they didn't go by real names." Gary loved going there, particularly for the drugs.[142] McCroan was childhood friends with Glenn "Dog" Shindler, a bruiser who ran a wrecking yard and was intertwined

142 Jeff Williams remembers Lou calling up a few times and announcing somewhat imperiously, "'This is Mary Lou, Gary Stewart's wife. I need you to go down to Tawakoni and get an eight ball, and I need you to mail it to me.' I would say, 'Okay,' and never do it."

with this bunch.[143] Shindler and Gary hit it off, and when Stewart had problems with yet another fly-by-night character booking his gigs, Glenn suggested Porter, who had collected money for a bookie operation he ran on the side. "Terry was a badass," said McCroan. "Six foot four, 240 pounds, built like a brick shithouse." Porter had been sergeant at arms in the Dorsai Motorcycle Club.

A meeting was arranged between Gary and Terry. "Gary goes, 'What do you know about country music?' I said, 'Nothing.' He says, 'Good. I'm gonna hire you. You're gonna go with me to Houston and help me take care of some business.' Some people were jacking him around down in South Texas." When Stewart and Porter hit Houston, Terry invited these folks to stay at their hotel, which they assumed was a big party Gary was paying for. "I set up this big free dinner because that's what kind of people they were...they'd take all the free shampoos and towels and stuff...all the bills was going home to Gary." There at dinner, "Gary sits down at the table like the Godfather. I said, 'Which one of these guys was in charge of the money?' Gary pointed the guy out and I said, 'You no longer work here.'" Porter paid everybody whatever they were owed and told them they could take their meals in to-go boxes as the party was now over. Off-duty sheriffs were waiting in the wings. Threats were implied. They were to check out in the morning and have no more to do with Gary Stewart.

A close friendship developed between Stewart and Porter, who seemed to have a sixth sense about handling him. Terry was the type of guy that, if Gary wanted to hunt for Hawaiian shirts at Walmart, instead of taking Gary over there to wander the aisles for hours and endure the stares of strangers, he'd convince the store to let him push a whole rack of shirts over to the hotel so Stewart could peruse them at his leisure. A man of action. Their bond grew deeper after Terry lost his son Rance in a 2001 auto accident. "Gary helped Terry as much as Terry helped Gary," said Lee Schwartz.

---

143 Dog and Gary were fast friends. He kept Stewart's *Little Junior* Western suit framed on the wall, a gift from Stewart. "I think Gary owed him for an ounce of damn crystal," said Tommy Schwartz.

Right around the time of Porter's trip to Houston, McCroan hired Terry to go on the road as Gary's bodyguard. "They got me to go take care of stuff whenever they was in trouble, to collect money." Almost immediately, things started going sideways between McCroan and Stewart. "My percentage was ten percent of the booking and $300 a night as road manager. It worked out really good—so good that Gary started questioning, 'Hey, why am I paying you $300?'" When McCroan ticked off the many things he did for him, Stewart, accustomed to civilians handling his needs for nothing, muttered, "I've never paid anybody to do that before." Nonetheless, "Gary was very, very dependent on Richard," said McCroan's friend, deejay and music historian Joe Bielinksi. "And he expected a lot of Richard. If Richard didn't produce, Gary chewed on him."

On some level McCroan expected Stewart to become a slick, professional hit-spewing machine and make the most of all the new opportunities laid before him. Gary, on the other hand, just wanted to be left in peace. "Richard is a perfectionist," said Bielinski. "And he's a perfectionist to the point where it's almost psychotic." Gary wasn't the only one that McCroan drove crazy. Jeff Williams recalled going to a copy store to pick up a fax from Richard only to find three hundred pages waiting. "A fucking three-hundred-page fax! All I wanted was a set list!"

McCroan saw Stewart as a "savant" who lived in a twilight zone and "couldn't write a check." One night, the pair were at an airport motel after a show and McCroan, who was bored, emptied the paper bag of gig money and began stacking it, "putting the fives in a pile, the tens in a pile, the twenties in a pile...I even turned the presidents' heads the same way." This excited Stewart, who had a eureka moment and exclaimed, "Richard, now *that's* the kind of stuff I want you doin'!" McCroan was dumbfounded. "He was dead serious. I thought, 'Have you lost your fucking mind? All the shit I've done for you and you want me to just stack your damn money and put a rubber band around it?'"

Thus it was predestined that the McCroan–Stewart union would implode, and Terry Porter was right there to catch a falling star when it did. "Terry Porter was smooth," said McCroan. "He was so smooth, he kicked me out. Terry took over." So just as McCroan had hijacked Gary from Henry Esparza, Porter poached Stewart from McCroan. Terry had good things to say about his predecessor, with one reservation. "Richard was a good guy, a solid dude. He increased Gary's gigs up in the money. But Richard was too clean. He wasn't outlaw enough for Gary."

Porter was plenty outlaw, as evidenced by an escapade involving a stolen tour vehicle. Not long after a white van was purchased from Terry's aunt, the van, full of equipment, was stolen from under their noses while they slept at the Dallas Radisson down the street from Cowboys. The alleged thieves were quickly apprehended—not by police, but by Porter, determined to find out who'd hired them. The desperate hombres were detained in a boat storage unit until Terry could figure out what to do next. "Gary was freaked about how we handled that," said Porter. "He sent somebody to McDonald's—'We gotta feed their asses, we can't have 'em die in there!'"

Curiously, they decided that McCroan might be the criminal mastermind behind the heist ("What would I do with a raggedy-ass van?" mused Richard), so they decided to parade him in front of the captives to see if they'd ID him. Gary summoned Richard to their hotel on some bland pretext and he was shown to the suspects, now handcuffed in the back of a van. Unfortunately they took one look at McCroan and laughed. It became apparent they had no idea who Richard was, so he was off the hook—and the prisoners were whisked away, never to be seen again. Although Terry never figured out who planned the job, he did get most of the stolen gear back.

The story only gets weirder from there. Richard, still in shock over being suspected of thievery, went back to the hotel to see Gary, who suddenly announced he wanted to learn how to use a manual razor. Stewart relied on an electric shaver, which he'd pop out on the road while in the back seat. McCroan didn't have a blade on him, so he walked to a convenience store to get a Bic disposable and travel-size shaving cream, then returned to the room to give Gary a crash course, complete with hot towel. "I shit you not, I *shaved* Gary," recalled McCroan, who, in hindsight, feels it was simply Stewart's strange attempt to calm Richard's panic over the van escapade. "Gary was a damn shrewd guy."

Things got no better between the two after Vangate. The final straw came when Stewart berated McCroan for taking his $400 booking fee up front for a gig in Denton, Texas. Gary dressed Richard down "in front of the whole band, it was embarrassin' as hell," said McCroan. When the gang took off for Oklahoma City the next day, Richard bowed out. Gary rang McCroan en route, telling him, "Richard, I'm not tryin to run you off." To which McCroan responded, "Then why are you?"

And just like that, *poof*! Another Stewart handler gone—although he continued to book gigs for Gary with bandleader Glynn Fleming. "I liked the money."

* * *

The Terry Porter regime kick-started a wild new chapter in Gary's life, and with Porter came his longtime running buddy and hunting partner, cabinetmaker James Willingham ("We met in kindergarten detention," said James). James drove an almost-new gleaming white Caddy and, as Porter recalled, "Gary liked ridin' in that Cadillac, so he said, 'Hey, let's hire James.'" Willingham had zero clue as to who Stewart was. "I remember asking him, 'So, you're, like, in a band or somethin'?' And Gary says, 'Oh, not much, son. Just a little country music.' I thought, this ol' fucker's playin' in some garage band, y'know?"

Porter and Willingham were brawlers. Bassist Curtis Randall recalled traveling to North Dakota for a gig at the Standing Rock Reservation. After the band checked in, they hit a nearby bar, where a couple of Native Americans near the elevator were "givin' us some pretty go-to-hell looks. These Indian dudes decided they were gonna whip our asses." Curtis was about to throw a punch when "the elevator opens and there was a guy sitting on the floor in the elevator. James already knocked him out. And then the other elevator opened, and here comes Terry. He just stepped in front of me and says, 'Which two?' I said, '*Those* two.' Wham wham! He knocked one guy out and started on the other one. That's how James and Terry took care of us. They're bad boys...*bad* boys. They can whip your ass and send you on your way really fast." They instilled fear in Richad McCroan. "Those cats are dangerous."

The three amigos: Terry Porter, Gary, and James Willingham (James Willingham collection)

Stewart bequeathed Willingham with the moniker "Wheelman." He was a salty character who didn't have a problem delivering some blunt honesty when needed. "James was the voice of truth," said Porter. "He could tell Gary if he looked ridiculous in an outfit or whatever—'Hey, Gary, comb your hair!'" Willingham drove like a bat out of hell. As Porter recalled, "Neither one of us wanted to tell James he was drivin' too fast, so we stopped at a truck stop and bought a radar detector. We thought that would kind of give James the idea." Unfortunately all it meant was that Willingham still drove like a maniac, only now he'd slam on the brakes whenever the radar alarm went off, and Gary, reclining in the back seat, would go flying. "Gary said, 'Throw that damn radar away!'" Into the trash it went.

Both Porter and Willingham were nearly twenty years younger than Gary and injected new energy into Stewart's scene, becoming his personal road crew and bodyguards for the last years of his life. "We actually lived together, Thursday through Monday every two weeks," said Porter. "I talked to him like he was my dad, and he treated me like I was his son. Gary called us his 'boys.' He was showing us the ropes. What he taught us was how to be real." Stewart would fly in from Florida, often arriving in a wrecked state. "Different color shirt, checkered britches, wrong belt," said Porter. "We would put all that together and make it happen. The transformation, that was always the major deal."

They'd convene at Willingham's house in Carroll, Texas, where Stewart had his own room. ("Everything we got still has got some kind of Gary stain on it," said Porter, chuckling.) Once Stewart had achieved some kind of equilibrium, they'd pour Gary into the back of the Caddy and roar off, first hitting the gigs farther away, then working their way back home. James drove, Terry commandeered the passenger seat, while Gary sprawled in the back, wearing reading glasses enhanced by an oversized pair of shades balanced over them. Frequently his black-silk-stockinged feet would be sticking out the window.

One time they pulled in for a show at the River Club in Comanche, Texas. Gary was comatose in the back seat, feet out in the breeze. The security guard took one glance and said, "I'm telling you right now, that guy's too drunk to come in here." Porter stopped him. "Hey, wait a minute, man—that's *Gary Stewart*. We're playin' here tonight!"

Unlike McCroan, Porter was canny enough to realize that it was pointless to push Gary, demand he be on time or even show up. And since he and James both had money, it didn't make much difference to them either way. "When we got with Gary, we enjoyed every bit of it, because we didn't have to be *professional*," said Porter. "We were runnin' up the road like a bunch of banshees, gettin' paid cash money, not havin' to answer to nobody. We made it into a game. All them gigs were like banks—'Let's go rob these motherfuckers and see how fast we can get out of there.'" Since Stewart hated hanging around after a show anyway, James would have the Cadillac running and "we'd try to get in the car and leave before the band was even offstage," said Porter.

The end result was that Gary "started doing stuff that was fun instead of work," said Terry. "That was why he did so good those last years, because there was no pressure on it. You could tell. Gary started dressing better. He was takin' home ten grand a month!"

Said Shannon, "I think the most fun Dad ever had on the road was with Terry and James. They used to do the funniest shit."

* * *

Some of that funny shit:

One night Porter and Willingham were tearing through Texas when Gary rose up from the back like the living dead as his sensors detected a Dairy Queen out in the middle of nowhere. Although he had been completely conked out for some time, Stewart was suddenly coherent and incredibly specific when it came time to order. "He tells the girl, 'I want a banana split, but I want the bananas firm, and I don't want no green banana. *I need a firm banana.*'" Since Gary lived on donuts, chocolate milk, and Snickers, actual meals could be an adventure. "When he poured salt, he'd hold the saltshaker above his head, and when he shook it, it'd be like a snowstorm," said Willingham's then-wife, Kim. "I'd say, 'Gary, lower it and you might get it on your food.'"

Stewart was constantly losing his dentures, which he kept in a little Tupperware container. One time when they had left Dallas on their way to that night's gig, "we've made it, like, two hundred miles down the road and Gary woke up and said, 'Where's my teeth?'" recalled Porter. Back to Dallas. No teeth. They crawled into the hotel dumpster. No choppers. Showtime was looming a considerable distance down the highway. "Okay, I gotta make me some teeth out of masking tape," decided Gary. He instructed Terry and James there was just one song he absolutely couldn't do with the fake teeth due to the sibilance—"Blue Christmas."

"Well, hell, it was Christmas time. That's what everybody wanted to hear and Gary sang it a bunch," said Porter. "First thing the owner said—'Will you have Gary sing 'Blue Christmas' for my wife and friends?'" Terry didn't know what to do until he remembered the pair of cute girls in front of the stage who'd been holding up request signs. Gary had been bantering with them during the show. Terry and James grabbed a piece of cardboard, scrawled "Blue Christmas" on it, and passed it to the women, who promptly held it up. Stewart's face dropped. Cornered, he sang the number, albeit with his back to the audience. "You sorry sons of bitches," he muttered to Terry and James as he exited the stage.

More fun was extracted from the undercover cop who showed up one night in Coupland. "Good-looking gal, she was *hot*," said Porter. "She was keyed in, lookin' around—we was thinkin' 'Holy shit, we got a tail.'" The Stewart entourage was hanging out in an RV behind Coupland Dancehall with Johnny Rodriguez. "Rodriguez is like, 'Let's smoke a joint.' I said, 'Hey, man, that girl over there, she's undercover drug task force.' He's like, 'What the hell's she doing here?'" Everyone was paranoid—except Gary, who suddenly acted like the new sheriff in town. "He said, 'Y'all need to let me handle this,'" recalled Porter. "We're lookin' at each other like, 'No. *Bad idea*.'"

Gary and the cop exchanged numbers, and soon thereafter Stewart and Porter were out at a hunting ranch Terry kept in the country with his cousin Virgil when a surprise guest showed up. "My cousin comes out," Porter recalled. 'He goes, 'Hey, man, there's a cop car parked out front!' I go, 'Yeah, I know. That's Gary's girlfriend.' Virgil goes, 'What???'"

Stewart instructed his hosts to fetch two of their Aunt Jo's coconut cream pies. They got the pies and gave them to Gary, who proceeded to retreat inside the house with the officer—still in full uniform. He told them to come back later. And locked the door.

When they returned, the cop was gone and Gary was covered in coconut cream. "He hit that bitch in the pussy with coconut pie!" said Terry. "Her little police britches had the crotch tore out of 'em and they was throwed over in the trash. Gary had that damn coconut pie in his hair, it was everywhere. We had to hire a cleaner to come in. I guess Gary slayed her with sex."[144]

Terry and James had quickly cottoned on to just how slippery a character Stewart could be. Once they were in Dallas when Gary got the impromptu notion to round up a bunch of local pickers and deejays for a "Midnight Ramble" show. As Terry recalls, Gary went as far as calling "the radio station in Dallas and all these big clubs" to recruit musicians, and Porter helped put it together. The night of the supposed event, "all of them were downtown in a motel. Well, somewhere during the middle of all of that, Gary changed his mind." Not that Stewart told him. "Gary would take these Somas, man, and just knock hisself out if he didn't want to do nothing. He didn't argue with you—he just took his medication and it was like *Weekend at Bernie's*. He was luggage." With Gary unconscious, Terry was on the hook to inform everybody there wasn't going to be any "Midnight Ramble." "These people was hounding me," says Porter.

This time Terry exacted revenge. He crept into Stewart's motel room with a can of Wolf Brand Chili (a favorite) and tossed back the sheets. He then emptied the can down by dead-to-the-world Gary's ass and returned to his room to await the phone call. Sure enough, an agitated Stewart soon rang, imploring Terry to come right away. Alone. When he knocked on the door, Gary, who "had that chili all over—even in his hair, which was standin' up like Billy Idol," glumly whispered to Porter, "Man, I think I shit myself in my sleep...don't worry, it don't smell bad. It smells like chili!" They laughed about it later, but Gary had learned there were consequences with his new compadres.

144 Lady Undercover showed up at another Coupland Dancehall gig and had some sort of freak-out after the show, unnerving Gary, who pleaded with Barbara Worthy, "Honey, go get her. Look, she's running around out there naked!" Worthy, unmoved, responded, "I ain't gonna get that bitch."

Chaos inevitably followed this trio. When Stewart played an antique tractor show somewhere in South Central Texas, a young lady tried to spirit him away to show him her personal animal farm. As Porter recalled, "Gary goes, 'I would *love* to ride a zebra.' I looked at James. I said, 'Gary, we're not goin' to these people's house so you can *ride a fuckin' zebra*.'" "By that time I figured out she was underage," said Willingham. "Her daddy was dragging her out of the car and Gary's goin', 'Leave that girl alone!' I said, 'Gary, that's her daddy!'" They drove off, and minutes later a tractor blew up right where they'd been standing, injuring several enthusiasts.

The stories are endless. There's the cross-eyed hooker Gary and James bought Terry for his birthday. Or the time Gary played hillbilly doctor ("we do abortions, we pull teeth, we take bullets out"), removing a stubborn splinter from Willingham's finger while applying an OxyContin compress to the wound. When Stewart started sewing up the cut with dental floss, "James starts turnin' white," said Porter. "He fell out on the way to the bathroom." James's wife Kim was coming down the hallway and inquired as to what was going on. "Oh, you better ask Terry," said Gary nervously. For a moment they thought James was a goner. Videotape evidence exists on which you can hear Terry saying, "How do you turn this off? We've got to get rid of this!" Willingham said that when he came to, "Gary was standing over me, fanning me with a towel."

One night when they stopped for gas in San Antonio, Terry went in to pay as James got impatient waiting for the attendant to release the pump. "I walked in there, got a case of beer, walked up to the clerk, and said, 'What the fuck is the holdup here?' Terry said, 'They are negotiating.'" Suddenly James realized an actual armed holdup was in progress, right before his eyes. "I said, 'Well, fuck me running...if they want to negotiate, put this on their tab'"—pointing to the thieves—"'we don't got time to negotiate. Come on, Terry. Let's go.' We walked right out with everyone looking at us, including the guys that was robbing the place."

As they were pulling out, four cop cars tore in. "Gary had this wide-eyed look and said, 'You boys are the toughest road crew in the business.'"

* * *

On August 29, 1998, an unexpected honor came from out of the blue. Kentucky had renamed US 23, a scenic highway running through seven counties in the eastern part of the state, the Country Music Highway, with commemorative signs honoring ten country stars who'd been born in the Bluegrass State, among them Loretta Lynn, Dwight Yoakam, Patty Loveless—and Gary Stewart, whose sign was going up in Jenkins. According to Terry Porter, receiving an honor from Kentucky was "the biggest deal" to Gary, much more personal than any Nashville honor. After local officials unveiled the large brown marker bearing his name, Gary spoke to the crowd, giving a brief but rambling history of his career during which he mentioned Texas, Oklahoma, and finally Kentucky. Clearly humbled and honored as well as nervous, Stewart searched for words before closing with a quiet, "Hey, what else can I say but thank you, folks."[145]

Perched on the back deck of a neon-yellow Plymouth Prowler in a cheap black Hawaiian shirt festooned with roses, Stewart served as grand marshal for the Jenkins Homecoming Festival parade that day, waving to the crowd and signing autographs. That evening Gary, a bit well-oiled on the moonshine passed around backstage, played to a crowd of five thousand. "There wasn't a parking place within a half mile of the city park," noted then-mayor Charles Dixon. "People were standing elbow to elbow just trying to get to see Gary. Not only was the park full, but there were hundreds standing on the roads trying to get a peek at him."

145 Porter noticed a bunch of geologists were in the audience. They'd cut a new section of the highway through the mountains around Jenkins and "it exposed a million years of earth."

Tommy Schwartz and Gary, 1997. (Meghan Pollard)

As the band left town, an officer stopped Jeff Williams's van. It was a relative of Gary's. "Have you got any contraband?" Williams said no. "You want some?" With that, the officer hoisted "a case of Mason fruit jars full of white lightnin' in my van."

* * *

Stewart worked on a song in these last years that seemed to bedevil him, one he never finished. "Jesse's Last Ride" is a tribute to the kind of complicated, unsavory character Stewart loved—Missouri-born bank and train robber Jesse James. Long romanticized as the embodiment of the Robin Hood 'Rob from the rich and give to the poor' legend, historians in recent years have painted a more intricate portrait of the Confederate sympathizer. "Had Jesse James existed a century later, he would have been called a terrorist," wrote biographer T.J. Stiles. I doubt any of this would've damped Stewart's interest. "Jesse's Last Ride" is only a couple of verses, but one wishes Gary had cut a whole album of this stuff: *Gary Stewart's Ghosts of the Old West.*

The song was cut at least three times—once with a band in Texas, once in Tommy Schwartz's home studio, and, best of all, live on the radio during a rousing 2001 performance on KPLX 99.5 The Wolf in Dallas, with sometime cohort Michael Jeffrey joining in on guitar and chorus. "Shot in the back, hangin' a picture," wails Stewart, all too familiar with outlaws and their shabby finales. "Now that same ol' train that brought Jesse fame is takin' Jesse home." The mood is dread. "Jesse's Last Ride" is a haunting number, the last song Stewart was known to write, and he sings it like someone who knows his own time is just about up.

* * *

There were no more Texas ODs once Terry and James arrived on the scene. They were both well aware of Stewart's intake and what lurked in his "Elvis Presley Starter Kit," as Terry called his toiletries bag.[146] "Man, you could hear him rattling those bottles in the back seat like a rattlesnake, makin' sure they wasn't empty." No strangers to a little contraband themselves (namely weed), Porter and Willingham knew it was pointless to try to stop Gary from taking drugs. "That wasn't what he hired me to do," said Porter. "My job was to get him to the honky-tonk dressed well, get his paycheck, make sure nobody seen him in a bad way—*and* protect him with my life. That's what I did." The pair managed to curtail Stewart's use while in Texas by keeping him moving from town to town, making it trickier to replenish his supply. "We didn't try to stop him," said Porter, who tried instead to limit his intake to "enough to get by." Although Stewart seemed aware of their efforts to keep his drug intake under control, the subject of actually quitting wasn't broached. "As far as Gary was concerned, we *was* rehab," said Porter. "He told us, 'You boys are close as I'm gonna get to rehab.'"

Up until this time in his life, Gary had managed to juggle massive amounts of muscle relaxers, speed, and painkillers, as well as the occasional line of cocaine, but in the mid-nineties he would meet his match. OxyContin—or "hillbilly heroin," the media nickname Gary preferred—was unleashed on the public in 1996 and gripped Gary and Lou like no other substance, Gary in particular.

* * *

Although no one can say exactly when Stewart was first prescribed OxyContin, they all mention one doctor's name: Asuncion Luyao, a Filipina who had run a practice in nearby Port St. Lucie since 1977. Beloved by many patients who would testify for her in court, Dr. Luyao's patient roster expanded dramatically when she started doling out oxy. According to Jimmy Smith, "You

146 Also in the bag were prescription suppositories, as Stewart was continually constipated by all the drugs. Lou used to joke that she had to take a spoon to pry the crap out of him.

could tell her you had a headache and that was good for ninety fuckin' OxyContin. She was just writin' scripts for everybody. She gave my sister ninety 80-milligram OxyContins a month. That's enough to kill a horse, dude."

His sister Laurie Rastrelli maintained, "You would go into Dr. Luyao's office and she would prescribe you 80-milligram OxyContins, then she would ask you if you wanted the kicker—which was the 30-milligram oxycodones. When the 80s wore off you would take the 30 milligrams. Everybody was on it back then. It was a mess."[147]

Since Stewart was forever searching for relief from his back pain, Rastrelli sent him to Dr. Luyao, whose prescription certainly did help. Shannon recalled how crowded the waiting room was when she took her parents there. "There was people standing outside to get into her office." Despite paying $1,800 a month in insurance, Gary and Mary Lou always paid Dr. Luyao—whose casino gambling would later be brought up in court—in cash. "They never had to wait, because she knew that they would pay her cash money," said Shannon.

Gary told friends he'd been assured the drug was not addictive. To be fair, Purdue Pharma, the manufacturer, was supplying doctors like Luyao with misleading information and hiding evidence of morphine-like dependency issues. "Less than 1 percent of patients taking opioids actually become addicted," advised a 1998 promotional video, but eventually the death and destruction from OxyContin became so widespread that Purdue Pharma—and the Sacklers, the family running the company—had to face the music. Purdue would plead guilty in 2007 to conning the public and would pay $600 million in fines, one of the largest pharmaceutical settlements in US history. The state of Kentucky sued them next.

147 OxyContin abuse became epidemic, with pill mills popping up all over the country. From 2000 to 2010 the total number of opioid analgesic prescriptions in the United States increased by 104 percent, from 43.8 million in 2000 to 89.2 million in 2010.

In the late nineties, abuse of the drug was raging, and the Stewarts found themselves right in the middle of it. "Them OxyContin would make him lay on the floor and cry like a baby," said Porter. "There was no way he could quit." On one trip Gary arrived in Texas empty-handed. "He got on an airplane, flew all the way back home for one pill, turned around an' flew back," said Porter. Stewart was even put on methadone for a brief spell. ("Gary said, 'This is the devil, right here,'" said Willingham. "He didn't want no more of it.") James has held on to an empty prescription bottle all these years as a reminder of the bad old days, telling Terry, "I'm saving that for anybody who thinks our job ain't tough." It seems Gary got tired of fighting with the childproof cap on this particular bottle so he "took a pair of fingernail clippers and scraped a hole in the side of it," Terry recalled. "I seen him take seven 80s," said James. "Gary tried to overdose on 'em, but he couldn't," said Jimmy Smith. "He had such an incredible tolerance to drugs."

The situation became grimmer after Dr. Luyao was arrested in 2002. "Mom called me and said, 'Hurry up and go fill every prescription you got before they put a freeze on the pharmacy, because Dr. Luyao just got busted.'"[148] The hunt for willing doctors became constant. At first Shannon was naive—"I just saw Mom be happy after taking the pills." She'd drive both parents to doctors, sometimes out of state, and see long, desperate lines extending out of the waiting rooms. "I was ignorant. I didn't know they were pill shopping."

Gary and Lou "got so bad that I had to pretty much dispense their medications, because it got to the point that Dad thought Mom was trying to kill him," said Shannon. "And she thought the

148 Luyao was charged with several counts of manslaughter in the overdose deaths of eleven of her patients. "People started dyin' like fuckin' flies," said Jimmy Smith. Her first trial in 2004 ended in a hung jury. She was convicted of one count of manslaughter in 2006 and given a fifty-year prison sentence, but that conviction was overturned on appeal and she left prison a free woman in 2007 after serving less than two years. A final plea agreement dismissed the manslaughter and racketeering charges, along with all but two charges of oxycodone trafficking. Luyao was permanently barred from practicing medicine and paid over $100,000 in fines. As of 2023 she still appeared to be living in Fort Pierce.

same thing about him." Lou accidentally OD'd and had to be taken to Lawnwood Hospital. Another day when Shannon went to check on Gary, she found him "sitting in a chair, comatose." She tried to slap her father awake; when that failed, off he went to Lawnwood ICU, with Lou just below on the second floor. With both parents in the hospital, "I was goin' back and forth from the second floor to ICU, second floor to ICU, second floor to ICU....for, like, a week." One day when Shannon visited Lou, Lou told her to "go whisper in Gary's ear, 'Come back to me.'" The line is the first one the Elise McKenna character speaks in *Somewhere in Time* before she dies in her sleep and is reunited with her lover. Gary and Lou, deathbed romantics.

Mary Lou decided to check herself into a Port St. Lucie rehab after her overdose. "She promised me: 'Shannon, I wanna get clean for you...I'm sorry. I'm done.'" That left Gary. "I had to convince my dad to check himself into rehab, which he did. He wasn't happy, but he did. He didn't talk to me for months. I even went up there to drop clothes off. Nothing. Silent treatment. He didn't wanna participate in group or anything like that. He wanted to hurry up and get back home, and he wanted to know where Lou was. I'd say, 'Lou's gettin' clean.' When Mom got out she felt revived. She was doing great. She loved it. Dad came out and he was just pissed."

For a while, the pair appeared to have their drug intake under control. "Everybody was on the same page. We were all happy," said Shannon. "We had a great Christmas." Gary took to drinking a limited-edition chocolate port wine with a festive purple, gold, and blue label called Danielle, which friend and sometime assistant Barbara Anne Peters would order from Pappy's Wine. "He wanted to make sure they had it on hand regularly." All these years later, Peters still has a voicemail Gary left. "Hey, Babs, it's me, Gary," he whispers. "Hey, honey, I need some wine. Real bad!"

* * *

Stewart had one last album to go. *Live at Billy Bob's* was just that, a fifteen-song greatest hits collection derived from a December 21, 2002, show with the Texas Honky-Tonk All Star Band, although they are not credited on the album. Which is a crime, as the smooth, accomplished playing has had many online aficionados debating who's on it.[149] Unfortunately, Stewart does not fare as well on this clean, bloodless recording. This is feeble, by-the-numbers Gary. He talk-sings his way through the performance, with some bum notes hanging out there for all to hear. The harmony vocals were stripped off the recording, no doubt to facilitate Stewart's labored overdubs. The original live recording sounds "way better than the overdubbed one," according to Tommy Schwartz, who's heard both. He maintains that Gary "never listened to the album."

There was a noble cause behind Gary's participation in the project, however. Stewart confessed to Kentucky friend Ardell Taylor the only reason he made the album was that he needed ten grand so Lou could get her leaky breast implants removed. "His health insurance wouldn't pay for it," said Taylor. Although Stewart looks rather morose on the cover of *Live at Billy Bob's,* even sadder is the ghastly illustration on the CD itself, where Gary looks like a self-satisfied Milton Berle in pink lipstick (he hated the image). Unfortunately, this is how Gary Stewart's recording career fizzled out, not that many noticed.

* * *

For a brief moment, things were on something of an even keel. Gary was killing it out on the road with the Texas Honky-Tonk All Star Band. He'd won a "King of the Honky-Tonks" contest in Plano a few years in a row and the title stuck. Everybody in the Lone Star State wanted to see Gary Stewart. Said Terry Porter, "We nearly sold out every place that we played."

149 For the record, the band on *Live at Billy Bob's*: Glynn Fleming, guitar; Curtis Randall, bass; Steve Palousek, steel guitar; Dick Dunn, drums; Tim Harris, harmonica; and Dickie Taylor, piano. The album was released on March 11, 2003, by independent label Smith Music Group.

Back in Fort Pierce, Gary spent his days hanging out with grandson Joseph, buying cheapo Hawaiian shirts down at Walgreens, and framing old pictures, writing notes about Lou on the back. "Tonight I named my new guitar Mary Lou," he scribbled on one. "I sang her that song first night I met her. Her loving husband, Gary." "He was so precious at the end," said Shannon, who grew particularly close to her parents during this period.

Lou would stress to me during phone calls that Gary's crazed werewolf days were long gone. "Since 1996 and now my life with Gary Stewart has turned like night and day," she wrote in her diary in 2000. "Every once and [sic] a while he acts up, but he works so hard, and he does it for Joseph, Shannon, and me. He is in pain all the time. He does more for Shannon and Joe than any father or Paw-Paw I know."

Things were looking up. But a new player slipped into Gary's life who would throw a final wrench into it all: Johnny Shepherd. "The only thing I regret in the years I knew Gary is that I didn't shank Johnny Shepherd and feed him to the hogs," said James Willingham. "That just sprung the trap on everything."

20

FIND ME

There is worse things than death.
– Billie Jean Horton, widow of Hank Williams

"I have a lot of dark issues," Johnny Shepherd informed me. Johnny is "a watermelon man," as Tommy Schwartz put it, and he's made his living in South Florida harvesting and shipping the fruit. He's also pushed drugs, and would be given a six-year sentence for amphetamine trafficking in 2006. Shepherd was a Gary Stewart fanatic who claims to have first seen him perform in Texas when he was a teenager. In the wake of the Stewart deaths, he had Gary and Lou's names tattooed on one leg and the Gary logo from *Your Place or Mine* burned into his shoulder. Johnny was that lethal combination: a rabid fan offering unlimited contraband. As he's well aware, he's not a popular guy with the Stewart crowd. "They ain't gonna tell you nuthin' good about me," he accurately predicted. "But I don't give a rat's ass."

According to just about everybody else, John Emmanuel Shepherd came into Gary Stewart's life sometime after July 4th, 2002. According to Johnny, he met Gary at shows many times over the years, and was thick as thieves with Stewart at the end.[150] "The last five years of his life, I was probably with him most every day. Most of the time I stayed at his house." This does not line up with anyone else's account, nor does much of what Johnny has to say. Mr. Shepherd is a curious one. I've been interviewing people for forty years now, everyone from kings to kidnappers, and in the dubious hall of unreliable narrators, Johnny Shepherd stands alone. Very little of what he has to say have I been able to verify. According to one source who knew him then, Shepherd "lives in a fucking fantasy world."

"If Shepherd said it, don't believe it," said Bill Hardman. "Johnny is a tremendous storyteller. The guy could be a stand-up comic." Hardman recalled being on the road with Johnny and some of the Stewart clan. "I had to pull over, I was laughing so hard. Every fucking syllable that came out of his mouth was hilarious. I *like* Johnny. Johnny is a horrible fucking person, but he was entertaining to be around.

"Johnny got blamed for a lot of stuff, and I don't know how much ever was really his fault. To blame Gary's death on him is so unfair. Look, Johnny Shepherd was never significant enough to cause anybody's death. If Johnny wasn't supplyin' Gary, somebody else would've. I'll tell you who I blame for Gary's death—Gary."

* * *

In July 2002 Gary Stewart played a big outdoor show for the Seminole Tribe at the Fred Smith Rodeo Arena in Brighton, Florida, a unique gig that had both his Texas band and the Easy People Band onstage. "They hired Gary for $14,000," said Tommy Schwartz. "We had a ball. It was a giant party." A short time later, Stewart returned to

150 Shepherd came up briefly during a phone call with Stewart in December 2003. He gave me the impression he'd met Johnny recently.

the Brighton arena to play for a Seminole named Johnny Tucker, who was dying of cancer and threw a birthday party for his son with Gary and the Easy People Band as the main entertainment. Afterward, Tommy Schwartz headed over to the Duck Pub in Okeechobee. Stewart had gone home.

It was at the Duck Pub that Schwartz first encountered Johnny Shepherd. Johnny, who had been at the Brighton show, announced that he wanted to buy the cheapo off-brand guitar Stewart had played that night for ten grand as a gift for his girlfriend Betty Kester.[151] Tommy said he'd relay the offer to Gary, which he did a day or so later. "Gary says, 'I couldn't do that, that guitar ain't worth five hundred dollars! I'll tell you what, Tommy—I'll give you the guitar, you sell it to him.'" Tommy wasn't interested, and forgot about it.

A month or so later, Stewart "got to where he was a little broke," according to Schwartz. "He said, 'What about that guy who wants that guitar?' I hooked him up...I kinda wished I never had." Johnny "started coming over to Gary's, and spending a couple days at a time," said Schwartz. "He was always toting crystal meth, so that probably helped him wiggle his way in." Shepherd went on a road trip to Texas with Gary and the Schwartzes. "Johnny was busy slinging lots of big dollars," said Lee Schwartz. "Next thing you know, we got Johnny around all the time. As nice as he was, he was a little shady. I don't think Gary saw that."

What Stewart saw was an individual who would supply him with drugs. Shepherd boasted to me of paying off Gary's dealers. One individual in particular was hounding Stewart—"Only time I'd seen Gary scared," said Shepherd—so Johnny said he tracked him down, paid him off, and told him, "If you fuck with [Gary] one more time, you gonna wish you hadn't...somebody's going to be dead." Shepherd maintained that from then on, he was Stewart's connection. "Whatever he wanted, I'd get it for him." Shepherd claimed that everybody was taking advantage of Gary financially except him.

151 An alias.

Johnny blandly rattled off drug deals he made for Stewart and the money spent. "We had this guy that worked at the VA hospital in West Palm. A thousand in a bottle and they wanted seven dollars apiece, so that's $14,000 for two bottles of oxy, compared to $50 to $60 on the street." Johnny also brought over "two or three ounces of some good crank that I got from the Hells Angels out of Fresno." He said Stewart hid it atop a brick under the floorboard in his bedroom.

I asked Shepherd to tabulate Gary's intake at the time. "When I tell you the amount, you're gonna wonder how he functioned... It was three 40-milligram OxyContin from sunup to noon. From the afternoon to whatever time of night, it was four 80-milligram OxyContin. This is *every day*. Four 80 milligrams is enough to kill a load of elephants. Two-thirds of the time you couldn't tell he was on it. There was nothing wrong with him." Augmenting this at any given time was "four to eight Somas, Xanaxes, a couple grams of crank, and beer." Shepherd claimed that Gary tried to get him on the oxy train, but the painkiller made him ill. "I wouldn't take one, and it kind of pissed him off...he was like a kid if he didn't get his way sometimes." Johnny said he'd pretend to take the pills, palm them and "when I got a handful, I'd put them back in the bottle." In addition to the drugs, Shepherd said that he'd drive Gary to a convenience store to get beer "every night at 11:39." Stewart had made friends with the kid working the counter, and when Gary would pull up he'd put an "Out to Lunch" sign on the door. For the next forty-five minutes or so, "Gary would walk around the 7-Eleven in his fuckin' pajamas like he was Elton John at Macy's."

"Once Johnny got around Gary, he got to where he was kinda being Gary's right-hand man," said Tommy. "He was there all the time for a couple of months." Shepherd brought his then-girlfriend Betty Kester, and they both stayed at the house. "They were all doin' meth together," said Jimmy Smith. "They were all messed up." (According to Shepherd and others, Kester was not a drug user and quite naive. She's said to have been completely unaware of the drug use going on in the house.)

There was "some weird stuff going on," said Royce Ashburn, Shannon's then-boyfriend. "When Shepherd came into the picture, nobody was allowed over ever again. They would never talk with nobody no more. They would never, ever open the doors—they wouldn't even let Shannon in. He turned her mom and dad against her.[152] It just kept going downhill from there."

* * *

For better or worse, Shepherd was one of the last people to spend time with Gary, so I wanted to know: What did Shepherd witness? He said Gary and Mary Lou were livelier than ever—up one minute, down the next. Stewart couldn't walk by her room without wanting to "kiss her or piss her off, and he liked to do both." Johnny felt death was never far away. "They were two fabulous people that happened to live a dark life." According to Shepherd, Lou had no patience for any suicide talk from Gary, telling him, "If you want to shoot yourself, go outside, 'cause I don't wanna clean the mess up." He alleged that he was shown two special pills set aside for final exits—"if somethin' happened to one, the other one takes the pill." Johnny felt that Gary "knew Satan well," yet "sometimes at night he'd sit there and play gospel music with a piano or guitar. Gary had to believe in God to sing that music...he lived both sides of the fence, God and the devil. He had zero fear of dyin', I think he kind of looked forward to it. Almost like he'd been on the other side and wanted to go back."

* * *

An endless supply of drugs at home meant that Stewart had little motivation for heading to Texas, where a work schedule forced him to be on somewhat of an even keel. James Willingham recalled the exact

152 Shepherd claimed there was a meeting with Shannon and her parents over mishandling of finances. Both Shannon and Royce were dumbfounded by such a claim, and said they'd never met with Johnny about anything. "Never," said Royce. "Never."

moment he realized things were heading south. Stewart flew into Texas and casually mentioned that while cleaning up on the plane he discovered an ounce of speed he'd forgotten about in his shaving kit. "The whole time I knew Gary, I never known him to have any of that on his own, ever," James recalled. "All of a sudden he had an ounce of it." It only got worse from there. Porter said Gary "canceled two big gigs in Texas" because he didn't want to leave home. Or his drugs.

"We were regulatin' Gary's intake, and Johnny just come on the scene," said Terry Porter. "Gary wasn't physically able to keep up with the amount that they were taking. Johnny led Gary into a drug stupor that we just never could get him out of." Willingham agreed. "Everything that was regulated got undone, and there wasn't a way for us to control things in Florida from Texas... I feel some guilt, 'cause that was our job, to protect him—and we failed."

Despite these setbacks, the Gary/Terry/James train rolled on throughout Texas for much of 2003. Stewart played a lucrative gig for the Standing Rock Sioux Tribe in South Dakota, where the band members were bequeathed with handmade blankets and Gary was presented with an ornate rifle commemorating Crazy Horse. "Damn, son, we done took over the whole Sioux nation," Porter told me. "The chief gave us his credit card."

Stewart nearly got busted after a gig at Linda's Lounge in Fort Worth. Gary was in the back of the Cadillac changing his shirt, illuminated by Porter and Willingham's lighters as the dome light was out. Some cops were driving by, saw the flickering lights, and suspected weed was being smoked, so they came knocking on the car window. Once they figured out Gary Stewart was inside, "boy, they had a hard-on for him," said James. "That was going to be a feather in their cap." The police searched the vehicle for forty-five minutes, ignoring a piece of crank-burnt tinfoil (Willingham: "They asked, 'What's all this burnt tinfoil?' I said, 'I don't know—does it have a tortilla in it?'") to pounce on a half joint wrapped in cellophane. They were putting the cuffs on Gary when a former booking agent/bodyguard buddy who'd been along for the ride piped in to take responsibility for the contraband. "They had no choice but to uncuff Gary," said James. "A million miles with Gary Stewart and that's the only run-in we had with police."

* * *

James Willingham witnessed a more reflective Gary in that last year or so of his life. Stewart had a quirky habit where he'd lie on his hotel bed and beckon whoever was present to come lie under the covers where he slept so they could "see what it feels like to be me." He used the same line on James during a big racetrack show in Houston. "The attendance for that day was eighteen thousand. Gary delivered a wonderful show and was getting a standing ovation." Stewart saw James standing offstage and motioned for him to come join him. "As the crowd is going crazy, Gary put his arm around me and whispered in my ear, 'See what it feels like to be me?'"

One late night they were heading back to the hotel after a post-gig autograph session, Stewart sitting silently in the back of the Caddy. James asked Gary what he wanted him to tell people when they asked him about Gary Stewart in the years to come. Stewart thought for a long moment, the passing streetlamps throwing light and shadow on his face. Then he issued a simple request. "James, just tell them I was your friend."

* * *

To some degree, Stewart was thinking about his health. Kim Willingham was in the living room one day while Gary was staying with them. "All of a sudden he gets all these pill bottles out and starts dumping all these pills out on the table." Willingham expressed her disbelief. "Oh, honey, I take this about three times a day," said Stewart. "That's gonna kill you," Kim told him. Later, Stewart pulled her aside. "He said, 'You know, I've been thinking about what you said, and the look on your face when you saw me dump out those pills. It just struck a chord with me. I'm going to have to see what I can do about my back and managing my pain differently. It just takes more and more and more, and it's not workin'.'"

The Willinghams took him to see James's sister Irene, a neurosurgeon. "Her specialty is spinal surgery," said James. When an intake doctor asked for Gary's pain medication tally during a twenty-four-hour period, James wrote it down: 240 milligrams of OxyContin. "She read that and she said, 'You mean 24 milligrams?' I said, 'No, ma'am. I mean 240, and I'm being conservative.'" The doctor was stunned. Then they met with Irene. "Gary was real up front with my sister—he said, 'Doctor, I got to work. The doctor tells you to take these pills, and to take another one before you start hurting. Then they give you a pill to wake up...and the next thing you know, ten years has gone by.'" Irene felt she could help Gary solve his back pain. "Well, schedule my surgery," said Stewart. He was going to have it done after the Christmas holidays.

* * *

Gary had the future on his mind. He'd called Randy Toman on Toman's birthday, September 13th, telling him that he hated the fact that they hadn't been playing together, and that he wanted to start using the band again after the New Year if they were interested. Toman enthusiastically said yes, and they agreed that his son Randy Jr. would play rhythm, returning the band to a three-guitar lineup. Apparently Gary thought he had enough work to keep both of his bands going. Curtis Randall had become part owner of the Old Top Rail, a legendary Dallas honky-tonk that had been around forever—rumor had it that Jack Ruby once owned a stake in the club—with the intention of making it home base for Stewart and the Texas Honky-Tonk All Stars. "We all thought, 'We got another twenty years giggin' here.' Gary was going to have a home place."

As far as new music went, Gary was itching to record "I'm Guilty" and "Jesse's Last Ride." According to Willingham, he also fancied having a small club where he could "sing the blues without his teeth." Most tantalizingly, Stewart was contemplating recording Black Sabbath's "Changes" after playing the song one night in Fort Worth during an unlikely jam with Rusty Young and Pantera guitarist Dimebag Darrell.

New dreams that Gary wanted to make real. He told James the only regret he had was the fact that everything he'd achieved in his musical career had come to him without trying. "Gary said he wanted to try, and see how that worked. Gary had visions of the future...if we had another five years together he would have pulled another rabbit out of that hat."

* * *

On October 18, 2003, Stewart played one of his last gigs, at the Ponderosa in Abilene, Texas. "The sleek Cadillac appeared through a cloud of dust," wrote local reporter Charles Chupp describing Gary's arrival. Stewart was in the back, "his sock-clad feet protruded through the right rear window." Willingham pulled the Caddy into the club and Stewart emerged from "the billowing dust cloud...not only was he in socks, he was shirtless, and his hair was in great disarray." By Chupp's account, Stewart tore the joint up that night. "The King of the Honky Tonks reigned supreme, and at the top of his voice."

Stewart went on to play the Texas Hall of Fame in Bryan, Texas, on November 6th, but Porter says things began to go very wrong that month. Lou had pneumonia and Gary worried constantly about her. "He was so messed up, we didn't even let him get out in public," said Terry.

There was one more appearance at the Old Top Rail in Dallas that nearly didn't happen at all. This is perhaps the most contentious gig of Stewart's career. Depending on who you talk to, he was either booked to play a pre-reopening gig or he did a loose guest appearance right before that Thanksgiving of 2003. Everybody agrees Gary was going to return for the grand reopening of the club around Christmas.

Whatever the particulars for this event in November, Stewart didn't appear the Friday he was expected to play. "Gary no-showed me," said Curtis Randall with a dark chuckle. "The place was packed. I'm calling him and he's not answering. Y'know, he's doing the Gary Stewart thing. Just being himself!"

While Stewart blew off the performance that night, Randall says the next day Gary got on a plane and showed up, ready to go. Terry Porter maintains Stewart was already in Texas but didn't want anybody to know it and that he just stopped by the club to sit in and reassure Curtis, who was worried Stewart wouldn't make the grand reopening a month later. Gary explained the reason he was a no-show was because Lou was sick. Now that Stewart was there, Randall plunged ahead. "I went to the radio station and said, 'Gary's here. He's gonna be at Top Rail tonight.' And you know what? The place packed out, everybody came in. It saved my ass." Thomas Pablo, who worked at the club that night, noticed the much younger crowd Stewart drew.

Pablo recalled a jittery Stewart concerned about his wife and wanting to get back home. He said Gary needed help getting dressed for the show, and watched "his old, frail hand reach for his beer on the desk. Instead of grabbing the beer with the palm of his hand, he stuck his pointer finger into the top of the beer bottle and slowly drug it into his lap where he could get a better grip on it, then shakily brought it to his mouth." Teresa McCandless, also working that night, was another who felt Stewart was struggling to get through the show. "You could definitely see the sadness in him." Dressed in a simple black suit and white shirt, Gary still gave a performance that left the audience hollering for more. And then he hopped a plane back home, where he'd left Lou in the care of Johnny Shepherd and Betty Kester. "Gary was not in good shape at all," said Porter. "He was really worried about Lou."

* * *

Exactly what happened next (and through the following weeks) at the Stewart house is difficult to ascertain. When it comes to the details, "there's a lot of cloudiness," said Porter. Johnny Shepherd's recollections once again run contrary to everyone else's, but as he was one of two people still alive that were there, I am including his version of events to some degree. (Betty Kester, whom Shepherd insisted was present for everything, would not go on the record despite my many phone calls, texts, and letters requesting an interview.)[153]

"My mom had pneumonia and she was very sick," maintained Shannon. Family friend Jo Ann Gregory concurred. "The last phone call I got from Mary Lou, she had pneumonia. The doctor wanted her to go to the hospital—and she was not going to the hospital, by God."[154] Hospitals made her feel bad, and they took your drugs away. Gary would tell me later that December that Lou had pneumonia "about six weeks...but she was over it."

Other friends maintain Lou was still sick and weak and using a nebulizer to breathe. Kester took her to her doctor's office but she refused to go in. The doctor came out to the car and told her it sounded like she had fluid in her lungs. She spent her last days in bed, watching the musical *Chicago* over and over with Betty.

Shepherd's version: Despite the testimony of others here, Johnny insisted that Lou wasn't sick, that it was a story concocted after the fact. He claims he took Gary and Lou to "the ER a week before. Both

153 In March of 2004 Kester filed domestic violence charges against Shepherd. On July 23 of that year he was arrested and charged with aggravated assault with a deadly weapon after ramming her vehicle repeatedly, according to the police report. "Shepherd again struck [Kester's] truck with his vehicle and forced her into oncoming traffic...[Kester] was in fear for her safety at the time of the incidents. There were approximately six other people in [Kester's] car at the time of the incident, including five juveniles. Shepherd called several times earlier in the day threatening to harm [Kester]." Facing a five-year maximum sentence, Shepherd pleaded nolo contendre to the offense, spent thirty-one days in jail, surrendered his firearms, submitted to random drug testing, and completed a Batterer's Intervention Program (he changed his plea to not guilty after that).

154 Lou made plans with Jo Ann before she hung up. "She said, 'I gotta get better so we can go out to the new porn store in town.' That's Mary Lou—'We're not gonna go out shopping for a new dress, honey, we're going to the porn store.'"

got a checkup, got their scripts refilled. They hadn't gone, because they didn't have the money to pay." Shepherd says he paid $150 for the visit. "Lou was fine. She didn't have pneumonia, she wasn't sick."

* * *

Worried about her mother, Shannon had gone to the house in an attempt to get her to a doctor. She didn't get a friendly reception from her father. "That's when he came out and ran me off. He wouldn't let me in the house. Dad got really mean when he would hang out with Johnny Shepherd, because he would be up for days on end on crystal meth." As far as Lou went, Betty "was taking care of her—that's the excuse Dad was giving me." Shannon was told Kester was a nurse. She wasn't.

At some point Shannon and Royce went to the house together. Complicating matters was the fact that Royce was not Gary's favorite person at the time, as he was young, wild, and not treating their daughter well. "He was really shitty to Shannon," said Lee Schwartz. "Royce was a ladies' man around town." (Adding another layer of tension to the situation in the house, Lou didn't like the way Johnny treated Betty. "Mary Lou wasn't a big fan of Johnny there towards the end," said Lee. "She realized what Johnny was all about.")

When Royce and Shannon went over, they "couldn't get nobody to answer," said Royce. "I was banging on the front door." Finally, the door opened, and there were Gary and Johnny standing behind a screen door, which they refused to open. "I said, 'Man, I'm just trying to get Shannon's mom to talk to her, and y'all are keeping everybody held hostage.' Gary had his .38 pistol and said, 'Royce, if you knock on my door again, I'm gonna shoot you.' Johnny Shepherd's shifty little ass was hidin' behind Gary." They left without seeing Lou.

Shannon, who was used to keeping in touch with her mother by phone, was getting more and more alarmed. She possessed a key to the house, so on Friday, November 21, she went over about noon and just "pushed my way in." She walked right past Gary and Johnny, who were doing "some kind of music thing" in the living room. As she walked down the hallway to her mother's room, "everything started moving in slow motion." The door was shut, which was no surprise, as Lou would shut it when Stewart was playing, but "when I went to turn the doorknob, the doorknob was cold." Looking back, she feels her mother was sending her a message, preparing her for what she was about to encounter.

"From the door to the bed is probably four steps, but in those four steps I knew something was wrong." Lou "had the sheet clenched in her hand. I looked at her and knew. That's when I started screaming, 'Dad! Dad! Dad!'" Gary ran down the hallway, "jumped on the bed, and started shaking her," said Shannon, who yelled for Betty, asleep elsewhere in the house.

A 911 call was made. Gary was "hugging me, hugging me, hugging me," said Shannon. "He wasn't crying or anything. He was in total shock." Gary told her he'd been checking on Lou all night and she'd been fine. He'd held her hand and sung to her, and later that night he put a picture of her in a leopard-skin frame "so when she woke up, I had a present for her."

Shannon got ahold of their friend in law enforcement, Bill Hardman. "I was a detective at the time. I was at lunch. Shannon called me and I could tell something was wrong. She said, 'Bill, can you come to house?' and I said, 'Is everything okay?' She said, 'No.' I was working undercover at the time and driving a Z28 Camaro. I didn't stop at a red light, didn't slow down for turns. I drove that motherfucker, man." He arrived at the house to find Lou unresponsive, with only Gary and Shannon there at that moment.

Gary did not want an autopsy. Hardman said Gary took him aside. "He said, 'Bill, I don't want an autopsy done on her. They cut 'em all to pieces.' I said, 'Let me see what I can do.'" Hardman conferred with the other officers and it was decided that the family would refuse the autopsy for religious reasons, which is legally permissible in the state of Florida. The cause of death given the next day was heart disease. Due to the way her mother was clutching the sheet, Shannon felt that her mother might've died of a heart attack. In December, after first telling me it was pneumonia, Gary said, "It was her heart." Rumors would swirl around Lou's demise due to the rampant drug use in the house. As Terry Porter put it, "Sometimes them damn OxyContins would get you in a place where you didn't want to live, especially if you didn't have any more, you know what I'm sayin'?" By the time Tommy Schwartz got to the house, the body had been removed. "They did that thing so fast, I always wondered, but being that it was already gone and done, I just kind of stayed out of it." Mary Lou was cremated within days.[155]

Shannon remembers huddling in the West Wing[156] with Gary while they removed her mother's body from the house. "You could hear the gurney—click, click, click." She tried to talk over it so Gary wouldn't hear. "I just felt so bad for my dad at that point, because I knew it was over, and that my days were numbered with my dad. It was just a matter of time before he was going to go."

* * *

Hardman was also summoned to the West Wing. "Gary said, 'Come with me.' We went in the back room, he locked the door. Gary had some guitars in there. We're just sitting there on the couch, side by side. I deal with death all the time—I was in the business. But it was killing me to see Gary hurt like this. He was a fuckin' wreck. A zombie.

"Gary didn't say a word, he just walked over, picked up a guitar, sat down on the couch, and put it on his lap. And he just started

155 In an attempt to ascertain the facts of the situation, I tried to get police reports on both Mary Lou's and Gary's deaths. "The Fort Pierce Police Department has no records responsive to your request," a spokesperson for the department told me.

156 The back end of the house was fixed up so Mary Lou could hang out there and do her crafts away from the music. Everybody called it the West Wing.

singing 'He Stopped Loving Her Today.'"[157] Stewart did a verse or two of the grim George Jones ballad, then handed Bill the guitar, the Les Paul TV Junior that appears on the cover of *Your Place or Mine*. He told Hardman the guitar was now his.

"I don't know how to play it," demurred Bill, politely declining the offer. Gary suddenly leapt to his feet, demanding that he take the guitar. "He grabbed it like a baseball bat, raised it up over his head, and said, 'Either you tell me you're gonna take this home or I'm gonna smash it on the floor in a million pieces.'" Hardman reluctantly put the guitar in his car.[158]

* * *

Johnny's version of events, particularly of the night before Lou was found, have proven impossible to verify. Suffice to say they include drugs and an overdose. He said Betty Kester was present for this, but sources tell me that not only was she not there, she knew nothing about Lou's death until Shannon came in to alert her.

Johnny insists he was the one who found Lou as they were getting ready to leave for a Texas trip,[159] and he had Betty call 911, then gave

---

157 For those who don't know, "He Stopped Loving Her Today" is the George Jones hit from 1980 written by Bobby Braddock and Curly Putman, widely considered to be the greatest country song of all time. It concerns a man who remains obsessed with his dear departed for the rest of his life, keeping all her old letters and photos, hoping she'll return. Only his death ends his love for her.

158 Hardman, who still has the guitar, said he's been offered a million dollars for the instrument. He is keeping the Les Paul for Gary and Lou's grandson Joseph.

159 Shepherd also claimed he and Stewart were leaving for Texas the next morning to play Billy Bob's, then Gary was going to get on Willie Nelson's bus so Gary could write with Willie and Toby Keith. "No to any of that," said James Willingham, adding, "Johnny Shepherd is more of a liar than I thought he was." (Willie Nelson did play a few dates with Toby Keith, but they had ended in October.) And Gary was planning on appearing at a show in nearby Felda, Florida, on the 22nd—the Easy People Band had a gig opening for the Charlie Daniels Band, and Stewart had planned to join them unannounced. "He was just going to tag along, see Charlie, and get up and play with us," said Tommy. Unlike any of the unverified plans that Shepherd describes, this gig was advertised in the local paper and actually happened. Asleep at the Wheel subbed for Gary at the Billy Bob's gig in Texas, which was on November 29th.

Lou CPR until police and some paramedics showed up. "I thought, 'What's the fuckin' cop doin' here?' And he shook me. He said, 'Son! You done all you could...it's over. It's done.'"

Shepherd also claimed that he dispensed of any autopsy being done by bribing the officials involved to the tune of $15,000. "I had to pay all these people off," he said. "Shit, that's against the law." Hardman was rather amazed by this claim. "Hmm, how interesting. That's not the way Detective Bill remembers it. *I* talked them out of an autopsy because Gary didn't want one," said Hardman. "And Johnny Shepherd didn't pay nobody, no money changed hands...it wasn't necessary." Shepherd's version? "Just a bullshit story," said Bill.

* * *

Friends and family began to arrive at the house. Terry Porter flew in from Texas, James Willingham soon followed. Everybody was in shock. "We always figured Gary was the one who was gonna go first," said Tommy. "We weren't prepared for Mary Lou." Jimmy Smith, who had been excommunicated by the Stewarts over some bad shenanigans, came by. "I sat with Gary and held hands with him on the porch. We were both weepin'. He just broke down. He said, 'Jim-Bob, what the fuck am I gonna do? I don't think I can make it.'"

Gary and Shannon made the sad trek to the Yates Funeral Home to make arrangements for Lou's ashes. "Dad wanted to pick out the urn by himself," said Shannon, who waited in the other room as Gary settled on a marble container. An obituary was prepared that ran in the *St. Lucie News Tribune* the following Tuesday. At the bottom were the lyrics for an unreleased song Gary and Lou had written together, "Touch of You," slightly modified by Gary to read, "Lou, getting over you is the hardest thing I've tried to do." It was signed "Cisco."

There was a small memorial in Gary's yard for friends and family on the 22nd. "My dad wouldn't let a funeral happen," said Shannon. "I said, 'Dad, I have to put closure to it. I have to do something for my mother.'" She arranged some of Lou's scarves along with some pictures on a table and people came by to pay their respects. After a couple of hours, Gary summoned Shannon inside the house. "He goes, 'I don't like this. I want everyone to leave.' That's when I went out there and just kind of wrapped it up. Honestly, I think he was ready to be alone and mourn." Terry Porter recalled Stewart getting testy when the people in the yard got a little too wasted and rowdy. "I remember him comin' out of the house goin', 'This isn't a celebration, this is a *death*.' I looked at James and said, 'He's not in the clouds right now, he's serious.' I'm telling you, after Lou died, I never seen Gary that straight. When she passed away, reality set in on Gary's ass. He got real quiet, real sober."

A decision was made to remove the guns from the house, which meant the Crazy Horse rifle the Sioux had given Stewart as well as the .38 that had been a gift from Lou. Tommy thought it was a bad idea as he knew Gary would get upset. "I said, 'Don't get the gun, just take the bullets out.'" He was overruled. Friends were concerned about Stewart's state of mind. "I think Gary blamed himself for having Johnny in there and Lou dyin'," said one. And they worried about the suicide pact he'd made with Lou. Said Porter, "We knew what he was thinking—'I got to keep up the deal with Lou. She's gone and I gotta kill myself.' I go, 'No, you don't.'" When the subject of suicide came up, James and Terry tried to make light of it, telling Gary that if he was going to go, shooting himself wasn't the way to do it. Instead, they should get into Willingham's Cadillac and smash it into the Ryman. "If we're gonna do it, let's go out in style," said Porter, an idea Gary found appealing.

James and Terry hung out with Gina Stewart for a bit while they were down in Fort Pierce, and she escorted them over to Georgia's house one night at 2 a.m. "to get weed," according to Terry. The matriarch of the Stewart clan was up, but "in a wheelchair and on oxygen. She gave us the nod. She was like, 'I hear good things about you boys.'" On their way back to Texas, Terry and James were so concerned about Johnny Shepherd that they asked Glenn "Dog" Shindler, who had also come over from Texas, to roust him out of there. Shepherd was gone—"until Gary called him again," said Willingham, who had a feeling of dread over the situation.[160] "We all knew the writin' on the wall. I knew there wasn't anything you could do to stop it."

Gina Stewart agreed. One thing she said stuck with Terry and James. "You know what's gonna happen, right? Nothin' you can do about it. That's what us Stewarts do."

* * *

Everybody rallied around Gary. "We did everything we could to make sure life was great while he was alive," said Terry. Family members stopped by, particularly Gina, while Shannon and Tommy checked on him daily. Friend Ardell Taylor came to stay with Gary for a bit. Taylor was a regular guy from Kentucky who "didn't even know who Gary Stewart was," said Schwartz. Ardell would help Stewart frame pictures and was the perfect hang-out buddy, as he knew nothing about the country music business or Gary's role in it. Taylor simply learned of Mary Lou's passing and showed up at the house. Stewart loved a shrimp-and-peppers dish Ardell made and he made it a lot in the last few weeks of Gary's life. "It was all his stomach could handle," says Shannon.

Stewart demanded to have a gun back in case anybody broke in—"to protect *mi casa*," he insisted. He assured those close to him that he wasn't going to turn the weapon on himself. "Gary was just like, 'Hey, I could kill myself anyway, I got enough OxyContin,'" Porter

160 Shepherd would continue to be a thorn in everyone's side after Stewart passed. Terry Porter went on to manage the Luckenbach Dance Hall in Texas and Dale Watson played there one night. Porter was alerted that someone was inside selling Gary Stewart T-shirts and hats. Lo and behold, it was Johnny Shepherd. Terry had him thrown out. "He threatened me with his Mexican cartel connections and shit," said Porter, adding that Shepherd made the mistake of calling the corporate office and making the same threats. It is fair to say that Johnny Shepherd is not Porter's favorite person. "I'd drive across the country to whip his ass." Shepherd insists that any Gary Stewart merchandise he's made, he's given away for free. He adds, "I never sold a fucking thing of Gary's." I asked Shepherd if he'd threatened to sic the Mexican cartel on Porter. "That's possible," was his reply.

recalled. "He kind of put the guilt trip on us." Shannon tried to brush it off, but her father insisted—"I want my fucking guns." The .38 Lou had given him was returned. Gary also demanded his house key back from Shannon. "He said, 'I want my privacy. You can't just be poppin' in here.' That's when I knew he didn't want me to be the one to find him." Shannon gave the key back, not telling her father she'd had another made. "I pulled a Mary Lou on him."

Despite anger over the firearms, Stewart seemed to be on an even keel, making plans for after Christmas. In the last week or so Tanya Tucker called to check up on him, inviting him to a remote island a billionaire friend of hers owned off the Florida coast. "I said, 'Junior, you gotta come down to this place. You can only get there by airboat. This would be a great place for us to write.'" She was going to invite John Anderson to collaborate with them. Bill Hardman said Gary asked him to come along, and he was going to take his grandson Joseph on at least part of the trip. "He even booked an airplane ticket for him and my son to go fly out to Texas," said Shannon.

At the same time, Stewart was gently coaxing people out of his house. Terry Porter, who'd come back to check on him, was sent home by Gary, who instructed him to start booking gigs and making plans, adding that he was bringing Joseph there for Christmas. "I didn't question him, because he seemed normal. Anytime he involved his grandson it was pretty serious."

Stewart nudged Ardell to head back to Kentucky for his daughter's birthday. "The day I left, he was sittin' in the kitchen, singin' that song 'Swing Low, Sweet Chariot.' Then he said, 'I'll see you soon, baby.' I said, 'Gary, I didn't hear that right, did I?'" He assured Taylor that he needn't worry. "Gary told me everything was gonna be good." They hugged goodbye. "He got me convinced, but in my heart I knew it wasn't gonna be okay. It's bothered me ever since." In retrospect, Porter feels that Stewart had "made up his mind about what he was gonna do. He was getting all the ducks in a row." Shannon agreed. "He was fooling everybody." Gary did hint at his plans to one person, oddly enough—Royce. Ashburn was in such bad shape at the time "it was hard for me to grasp exactly what Gary was sayin'... He told me he was going to be gone soon, and to make sure that I take care of his daughter."

* * *

On December 3, Gary called me. I had been immersed in a book project, hadn't talked to him in a while, and hadn't heard about Mary Lou's passing. "You were her favorite, so I thought you should know," he said. It was such a caring thing to do. Typical Gary. I tried not to lose it. We talked about Lou for a while. "Soulmates, we truly were," he told me, admitting he found it hard to believe she was gone. "Her room still smells of vanilla." He related a story about Lou and some running buddy out on the town in their youth. "Out of the club comes this guy, he has a truck." Apparently this guy made the mistake of telling Lou she would be incapable of driving such a rig. "Lou said, 'I can drive anything, including drivin' you crazy,'" said Gary, chuckling. "That's Lou." He told me she had been working on a new song called "A Woman's Intuition." The only line he could recall was "It drives a man nuts."

He spoke of how proud they were of their grandson Joseph and what a little gentleman he was becoming. He assured me he was fine and that Shannon and others were checking on him regularly. I asked him if he'd get out of bed if I came and visited. He assured me emphatically that he would, shooting back with "I'm no longer in the bed...except for *a few days*. I've seen the light, the sunshine that Mike Love sings about."

That had me laughing. "Jimmy, come and see me. Jump a freight train. It's just me and a big ol' house." I promised I'd be down soon. There was an emotional goodbye. I'd never speak to him again. One thing that would haunt me: while he was talking about Lou, he belted out a line that chilled my blood. "When I cross the creek, with my last moan I'll cry her name."

* * *

On Saturday, December 6th, Tommy stopped by on his way home from work. Gary said, "You wanna go get a beer?" Schwartz thought he meant going to the store for a six-pack. "Next thing I know Gary's combin' his hair and is dressed to the nines. He's got his ostrich coat on." Although Tommy wasn't really dressed for a night on the town, there was no way he was going to miss an opportunity to get Gary out of the house. They wound up at a bar on Highway 1—Pineapple Joe's Grill. Tommy cased the joint and everything seemed fine until he got back to the car. "That's when Gary says, 'Tommy, I forgot my teeth.'" They drove all the way back to Stewart's house, then returned to Pineapple Joe's.

They snagged the last two seats in the place, right by the cash register, and sat there 'til the last set of a local band called Moonshadow. Billy Smith, their guitarist, had played in Easy People during one of Jimmy Smith's firings. "Everybody knew what happened with Gary, and they were giving him space," said Tommy. Shannon called while they were there. She'd driven by her dad's house and called Tommy when she found Gary missing. When he told her where they were, "she about shit her pants." Relieved that her dad was out in the world, Shannon was there "five minutes later." Shortly after her arrival, one of the guys in the band said, "Well, we got Gary Stewart in the house. Maybe he'll get up and do a couple." Stewart waved it off, but the crowd wouldn't relent. "Gary grabbed me and said, 'If I'm going up, you're going up,'" said Tommy. Shannon was sitting at a table right in front of her father.

Stewart did three numbers, reaching back to his childhood for a couple of mid-fifties love songs: Jimmy Reed's "Honest I Do" and "So Glad You're Mine," best known by Elvis Presley. And then he sang his own tale of heartbreak, "An Empty Glass." The audience went nuts. This impromptu performance, Gary's last ever, was videotaped. You can see Shannon reaching up in the air, "trying to grab my mom because I felt like there was hope. Hope that he might push through this."

* * *

Saturday, December 13th, Tommy came by. They had planned on hitting the town again that night, but Gary, "he'd been over at his mama's house and couldn't find his keys when he got back," said Schwartz. He said Stewart was a bit sideways because he'd gotten into it with one of his brothers over an unpaid debt.

When Tommy arrived, Gary was particularly dismayed because Lou's room was locked and he didn't have the key. "He used to keep all of his medicine in Mary Lou's bedroom. That was 'the Pharmacy.' You had to get down under the bed and pull it out. And it looked like a damn pharmacy." The door was deadbolted, but Schwartz offered to drill it out. While Tommy ran home to get his tools, Jo Ann Gregory showed up to check on Stewart. She left feeling that Gary might actually survive Mary Lou's passing. "He was conversational. I thought, 'Maybe this is gonna have a different ending than I thought.' I was elated."

By the time Tommy had drilled out the lock, Gary and Tommy had decided to simply get dinner at a joint called P.P. Cobb's. Shannon and Royce joined them. Shannon had been over earlier that day to clean the house and take her dad grocery shopping, buying him ham-and-cheese Hot Pockets, Breyers ice cream, and beer. It was the night of the annual boat parade, people were out, and they enjoyed a nice dinner together. As far as the shape Gary was in, Shannon felt her dad "seemed fine. He told me he was going to take the phone off the hook and get some sleep."

Tommy and Gary tooled around town for a bit on the way home. He mentioned he liked that new song by Joe Nichols, "Brokenheartsville." Stewart wasn't much for any new country music, and Tommy knew it was only due to the fact that there was a line in the song about a Cadillac, his favorite ride.[161] They made their way to Stewart's house. "Gary told me how hard it was to go back to the house with nobody in it, how lonely it was."

161 A new set of wheels had been on Stewart's mind at the end. "He was gonna find him a late '69, early '70 Cadillac," said Ardell Taylor.

The next morning Schwartz got a panicked 6 a.m. call from Gary, who was clearly discombobulated. "He was freaking out—'I spilled my pills all over the floor,'" he told Tommy, who immediately drove over to help. "Gary was a total wreck. I got him to go back to bed." Tommy hung around reading the paper and watching news broadcasts of Saddam Hussein's capture the day before. When Stewart woke up, he maintained he was feeling a whole lot better. Schwartz had to get back home, so he asked if Gary had enough food. Stewart popped open the freezer to show Tommy his voluminous collection of Hot Pockets. Satisfied that Gary was doing all right, he said goodbye. "I hugged his neck, like you would a kid."

Stewart went to his brother Garna's house to visit his mother, who was ailing and lying in a hospital bed. According to Gina Stewart, who taped the visit with a camcorder, Gary stood by her bed and serenaded Georgia with a few songs, including "I've Just Seen the Rock of Ages." He did not seem troubled at the time. "I don't know if, in his mind, it was his moment to say goodbye to Mama," said Gina.

Gary phoned a few people that Sunday. He called Bill Hardman, expressing his great frustration over his daughter's boyfriend and asking him to bump off Royce. "Promise me you'll kill him," said Gary.[162] Hardman declined the request, but said he'd keep an eye on Shannon. They talked about their upcoming travel plans, then Gary "gave me a speech about what a great friend I'd been over the years." Looking back, Hardman realized it was a goodbye. "I'm a fucking cold-case homicide detective, I should've picked up on the clues."

Stewart also called Terry Porter to place a bet on a football game taking place on Monday—Philadelphia Eagles versus Miami Dolphins. This was out of the ordinary, to say the least. Gary was not a sports fan in the slightest and "never gave a shit about football," according to Porter. Gary wanted Terry to place a bet for him—$150 on the Eagles. "I was like, 'Who is this?'" Stewart would win the bet,

---

162 Gary asked at least three people to take Royce out—Hardman, Ardell Taylor (Stewart found out Ardell had been in the Teamsters "and he associated that with the Mafia," said Ardell), and Johnny Shepherd. Only Shepherd agreed to do it. "I said, 'Yeah, but you better make sure, 'cause you can't undo that shit once it's done.'"

as the final score was Eagles 34, Dolphins 27. In hindsight, Porter thinks Gary did this so Terry would call to tell him the news and once he'd gotten no answer, he'd alert everyone.[163]

When Tommy had arrived the night before, Stewart had been looking for Lisa Sutton's phone number. Sutton, the daughter of Lynn Anderson and Glenn Sutton, was art director on the *Live at Billy Bob's* album. Stewart had given Sutton a call, then regretted his demeanor and misplaced her number. "When I talked to her, I sounded like I was having too much fun," Gary told Tommy, feeling it wasn't appropriate for a grieving widower. Schwartz tried to explain that people wanted him to be happy, wanted him to survive this tragedy. He told Stewart that he had Sutton's number on his work computer in Vero Beach and that he'd call with the number Monday morning.

To my knowledge, no one heard from Gary after that. What did Stewart do the last hours of his life? Play guitar? Write a song? Watch TV? Eat a Hot Pocket? Did the whippoorwill cry, the hoot owl hoot? Mundane questions that haunt the mind. Had he already planned what he was going to do, or had something sent him into a tailspin? Gary was alone, presumably in pain. He reached out to no one.

That Monday at 10 a.m. Tommy called with Sutton's number. No answer. He called throughout that Monday. Fearing the worst, he stopped by Stewart's house after work. "I beat on all the doors. I beat on all the windows." He called Shannon. As Schwartz remembered it, Shannon and Royce were in Palm Beach and wouldn't be back until morning. Tommy tossed and turned all that night.

* * *

The events of Tuesday the 16th are remembered slightly differently by everyone involved. Shannon and Royce didn't recall being away, or Tommy's call. Royce remembers having a crew of guys over at the Stewart house doing landscaping. One of the workers had made the

163 Perhaps it will come as no surprise, but Johnny Shepherd claims to have been Gary's final call. "He called me at midnight. I was the last one he talked to."

mistake of mowing close to Gary's window and Ashburn thought it was odd that Stewart, who slept all day, hadn't opened the window to tell him to stop. He knocked at the door and got no answer, so he entered the house, calling Gary's name. Nothing. "I pushed the bedroom door open, and there he was. He'd put the pistol in his mouth. The pistol was actually laying on his chest."

Royce went out in the yard to call Shannon. Bill Hardman and Tommy Schwartz were also alerted. "I got a phone call from Royce. And he says, 'I'm in. It ain't good.'" Schwartz left work immediately. First, he rang Terry Porter. "I said, 'The king of the honky-tonks is gone.'"

Hardman must've alerted the police department, as Rob Perkins, a brand-new local cop, was having lunch with his partner about a mile and a half away when a "shots fired" came over the radio. They arrived at the Stewart home to find Royce "sitting on the front stoop visibly distraught. I just remember him saying, 'He did it. He did it.'" The two cops cautiously entered the house, not knowing what to expect. They quickly realized what the situation was, and when they came out of the house Shannon drove up "over the sidewalk, right up into the front yard, and hopped out way distraught, trying to get in the house. We wouldn't let her in."

Shannon insists she was the first one to find her father. Both Royce and Shannon agree on how she responded when she saw her father lying there and noticed something dark oozing from Gary's mouth. "I turned around, buried my head into Royce's chest, and said, 'Please tell me it's blueberries.'" Royce rushed her out of the house.

Hardman arrived and "started making phone calls, trying to take control of the situation," said Royce. Detectives Bill Hall[164] and Joe Coleman arrived to survey the crime scene. While they were there, no one could enter, so family gathered to one side of the house. "Everything got kind of chaotic," said Ashburn. "Bill was trying to keep the press away."

164 Hall told me even though it's been over twenty years, every time he hears "Empty Glass," Gary's death flashes through his mind. "All I can think about is that scene."

"There were cameras in the yard," said Shannon. "I'm like, 'Jesus Christmas.'" It became a "frenzy of fucking people," said Hardman, who "went out to the front porch, telling these motherfuckers, 'Go away, go away!'" Someone recalled Bill talking the media out of shooting the removal of the body by handing them 8x10s of Gary and coaxing them to leave. Papers across the country would soon carry Gary's obituary.

As the body was being taken away, Shannon ran out and tried to "tackle the gurney. Royce held me back. Because I knew that was going to be the last time that I seen him. I knew that was it, that was the end of my family." She had lost them all—Joey, Mary Lou, and now her father. Shannon's best friend Tina Corley pulled up just as "they were carrying Gary out with a sheet over him. Shannon just fell to her knees and she was screaming—I hear it like it was yesterday—'Daddy, no! Daddy, you promised!'"

Close friends and family continued to arrive. Garna, the brother closest to Gary, came by the house but couldn't bring himself to go in. Inside, people were consoling themselves by watching a 1998 video of Gary at Billy Bob's. "We'd watched that damn Billy Bob's tape ten or fifteen times," said Tommy, who always stopped the tape after the set was over as Gary wasn't one to do encores. This time he just let it play. Suddenly there was Gary on the TV, his shirt covered in sweat as he ambled out for a surprise encore, singing "Cactus and a Rose" accompanied only by piano. "It brought a tear to everybody's eye," said Tommy.

That Thursday there was a private viewing at the Yates Funeral Home. "Seemed like for a long time we lived there," said Shannon. She brought Yates an outfit for Gary— pressed jeans, a leather jacket—and "they dressed him real nice." "You could not tell by looking at the man that he shot himself in the head," said Tommy. "I remember playing with his hair," said Shannon. "Dad had a beautiful head of hair and I used to always play with it. They told me to be careful." Only immediate family members, Tommy, Terry, and James were allowed in. "I didn't want nobody to gawk at my dad," said Shannon.

Gary had been adamant that he didn't want a service when he died, and Shannon had planned to adhere to his wishes. But Gary's brother Glenn insisted they had to do something—for Georgia. "So I compromised," said Shannon. There was a closed-casket visitation on Friday open to the public, Gary's music playing softly in the background. Flowers arrived "from all over the world" and Native Americans from the Brighton Seminole Reservation showed up "in full headdresses," said Shannon. "There were a ton of people outside in the street tailgating, playing Gary Stewart music for blocks and blocks."

Georgia arrived to say goodbye to her son, the sixth child to leave the planet before her. "They wheeled Mamaw in with a wheelchair," said Shannon. She let loose with a Kentucky wail that sent shivers down everyone's spines. Georgia would never know the real cause of death. "We kept Mamaw out of it," said Shannon. "The brothers and sisters refused for her to find out that Dad committed suicide." They told her he died of pneumonia. "She just cried and cried and cried and cried." James Willingham remembers Georgia moaning, "Get up, Gary," over and over.

Possessing an aversion similar to Gary's to such events, I did not come to pay my respects, something I now regret. I just sat in a dark room, playing "Pretend I Never Happened" over and over. Funny what goes through your mind. I thought about all the records I never played him, the many things I didn't thank him for. I never asked Gary about the Civil War.

* * *

After the service, Shannon invited Terry and James to each take a souvenir, something to remind them of her father. James took one of Gary's infamous strings of leather, as "Gary was always tying something with a strip." Terry surveyed the house of memorabilia, but he didn't want souvenirs—he had his memories. But he suddenly thought of one item. "I said, 'Hold on a minute. I *do* want something. I'm tired of looking for them fucking teeth after every gig. I want them sumbitches. I never want to look for them again.'" So Terry got Gary's dentures, which now reside in Texas.

Shannon also gave Terry and James some of her dad's ashes. She felt some of Gary should end up in the Lone Star State. When they got to the airport, Terry and James were taking the ashes through security. Security was eyeballing them and the container. As Porter recalled, "They go, 'What's in the box?'" James, who was already emotional, said, "I've been to a funeral." Security did not catch on, and repeated the question more forcefully: *"What's in the box?"* James blurted out, "Gary Stewart!" The two men cried like babies getting on the plane.

When the pair got to Texas, they spread a bit of the ashes at the Stockyards Hotel, one of their old stomping grounds. And they headed to the Old Top Rail, where Gary had been booked to play the grand reopening. "Well, Gary showed up all right," said Porter. "We brought his ashes. We said, 'You want to do a number with Gary? He's right there onstage.'" Nobody could say Stewart failed to make his last gig.

* * *

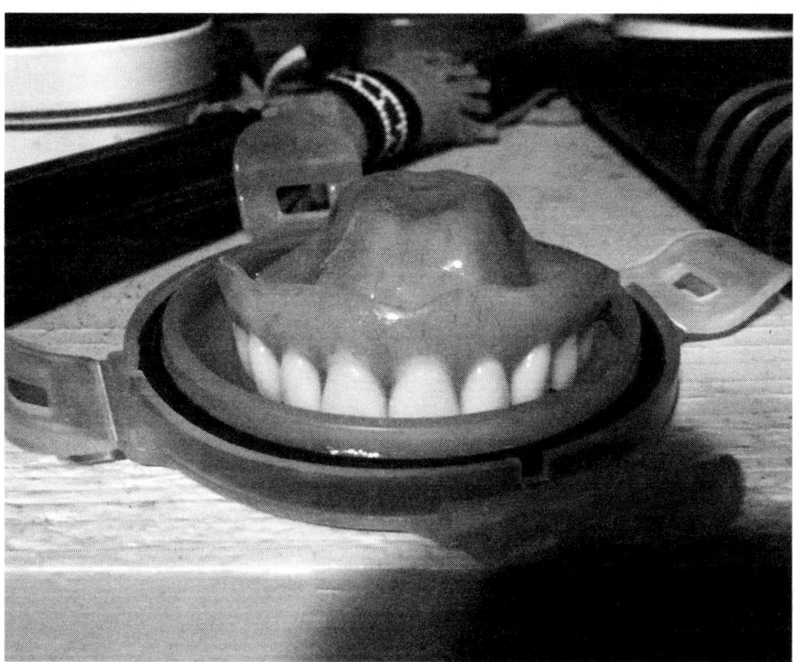

The teeth of Gary Stewart. (James Willingham)

Over the years, Mary Lou's death nagged at me. All the accounts sounded so vague and inconclusive. I had been told repeatedly that no autopsy had been done. When I sent the medical examiner a request for the autopsies done on Gary and Joey—something I do routinely if a book subject has passed away—I added Mary Lou's name to the list. I was stunned to get a report back.

An "external autopsy" had been done on Mary Lou. Dr. Charles A. Diggs[165] had examined her at 7:30 a.m. the day after her death, listing as cause of death atherosclerotic cardiovascular disease. "In other words, blocked heart arteries and heart attack," as the doctor I asked to review the results put it. Diggs also listed hypertension but had crossed it out. He based his findings on his visual inspection of her body. But Diggs also drew blood from Mary Lou, and he wrote the cause of death without knowing the results of the toxicology report, which came back on January 12, 2004. Apparently, since a full autopsy was declined, they had languished in a file since that time.

To see these results over twenty years after the fact was a shock. Mary Lou had taken oxycodone, but that was the least of it. The predominant drug in her system was Sinequan, a brand name for doxepin. I'd only heard it mentioned in passing, and only in reference to Gary. "That was his sleeping pill," said Terry Porter. "He'd take the Sinequan and Somas." Mostly everyone appeared to be ignorant of the drug, including Johnny Shepherd. It's a tricyclic antidepressant used to treat both depression and insomnia. By 2003, tricyclic depressants were already being phased out for the treatment of depression by serotonin reuptake inhibitors, a safer group of antidepressants that "you can't overdose on," according to the doctor I consulted. People who have experienced suicidal thoughts are at risk on doxepin. Mary Lou had 1,735 milliliters in her body,

165 Diggs, a highly respected African American medical examiner who also performed the autopsy on Gary, died in 2019, before I learned of his involvement in the case. He can be seen in a 1996 episode of the TV show *Forensic Files* discussing the case of serial killer Bobby Joe Long. Diggs had examined one of Long's victims.

nearly seven times the maximum therapeutic dose.[166] She also had the sedatives Miltown and Xanax in her system, as well as Gary's favorite muscle relaxant, Soma. "All of these drugs can depress breathing," said the doctor, who felt that "if the medical examiner had the blood toxicology available at the time, he/she would have listed the cause of the death as a drug overdose." This information stunned me. I dreaded having to share it with Shannon.[167]

What had happened? Royce and Shannon lived down the street from her parents, and Lou came over one day a few months before she passed. "She would always bring us money and try to help us, she knew we were struggling," said Royce. "We had a serious conversation in the driveway. And she had really laid it out for me. Because being a drug addict, it's a very exhausting life. She was like, 'I don't want to do this anymore. I'm tired. I don't want to get no older.'" Mary Lou told at least one other friend the same thing. But she had said similar things to me after Joey died and hadn't acted on those impulses. Sources tell me Lou wasn't distraught in the days before her death, just weak.

I leave the last word on that subject to Shannon, who is adamant that her mother was delirious from illness and other drugs, and that her death had been a horrible accident. "I know that she would not have done it on purpose. She would never do that to us. She would have never ever left me, much less Joseph."

Everybody assumed that OxyContin had been the major villain in Gary and Lou's end days. But Gary's autopsy showed eerily similar results to Lou's. Not only did he have oxycodone and morphine in his system, there was three times the therapeutic dose of doxepin, making him "more likely to commit suicide if depressed," said the doctor I consulted.

---

166 To complicate matters, "Toxic level of a TCA (tricyclic antidepressant) can build up in the body if the TCA and other medicines interact," according to the Mount Sinai Hospital website. "This interaction can affect how well the body can break down the TCA." They add, "Tricyclic depressant overdoses are very toxic and difficult to treat. Many people have died from TCA overdose, even with aggressive medical treatment."

167 After a few agonizing, emotional calls discussing the results with her, Shannon charged right into helping me uncover any remaining details concerning her parents' deaths. I was amazed, and told her so. "What can I say? I watch a lot of crime TV, it is my passion. I would love to go back to school and become a detective."

How did they have so much doxepin? Did something more nefarious occur? Was Gary aware of the toxicology report coming back on Lou and did that influence his actions? (He'd never know the results, as they came back nearly a month after his death.) Would things have been different if there hadn't been so much excess at the very end, or if they hadn't had doxepin in their systems? What had been intentional, what was provoked by drugs?

Endless questions remain, and they all turn to smoke. Aside from Betty Kester, who apparently witnessed nothing, the inhabitants of this house had been lost in a fog of drugs and were not in their right minds. The answers lie with the dead.

Gary and Lou were fierce, incandescent souls, flawed like the rest of us, caught up in something they felt they couldn't escape. It could happen to you. Or me. Late some restless nights I turn to that haunting demo of "Williamson County" few have heard, with its ghostly guitars and Gary howling bloody murder. And I wonder—did he know way back at the beginning what the end would be?

Remember: Gary and Lou saw their union as a fatal love story, and drugs or not, they had written this finale long before. If one goes, the other will follow—this was their romance. "They truly, truly loved each other—to death," said Royce.

When they found Gary, there was a cheap little notepad with a brown cover by his body. It contained lyrics, reminders, and what Shannon described to me as his "suicide note." In a large, crazed scrawl, Gary had scribbled down an incomplete, barely legible version of that haunting line that he had moaned to me on the phone a little over a week earlier—"When I cross the creek, with my last moan I'll cry her name." I have no doubt that's exactly what he did before pulling the trigger.

In slashing penmanship on the page before this, he wrote:

Lou, if you find this
Please find me
Look
I'm lookin' for you

epilogue

SOMEWHERE IN TIME

The aftermath of Gary and Lou's deaths cast long, black shadows. Stewart might've been erratic and reclusive, but without their crazy captain at the wheel his crew was lost, particularly Shannon and Royce. "Things got even worse," said Royce. "Because once that happened, we continued to indulge in a lot of cocaine. We drowned ourselves in it for a long time after that, to numb the pain."

It took forever for Shannon to rid her parents' house of OxyContin. She found pills everywhere—under mattresses, on bookshelves, in the couch. The house reeked of them, an odd scent she could only compare to Cheetos. "Maybe it was something coming out of their pores. To this day I won't eat a Cheeto, because it reminds me of the smell."

Still, she felt it difficult to escape the place. "I remember Royce tryin' to get me out of the house. And I told him, 'I can't, I just can't.' I couldn't leave. I was so fixated with staying here and I don't know why. For years after they died I was still feeling like I was redecorating the house for them."

Shannon went through a particularly rough period with Xanax. "My mom is to blame for that," she said with a wry laugh. "I had been going through a really bad time with Royce. Mom found me in the front yard, pulling up the grass with my hands. She said, 'Here, take this little pill. This is going to help you eat.' It helped so much that I fucking fell in love with them." For Shannon's thirtieth, Mary Lou had taped a Xanax bar to her birthday card.

The drug provided diminishing returns. After Mom and Dad passed, her friend Tina Corley watched as Shannon wasted away. "It got to the point where I put her in front of the mirror—'Look at you. You're gonna die, too. And I don't want you to die. I need you." Tina drove her to rehab.

Royce had gone off the rails as well. "I was a drug dealer turned into a drug user turned into a piece-of-shit drug addict," he told me. Bill Hardman recalls a freaked-out Shannon and Tina showing up at his house after Royce slashed Shannon's tires. "She was shaking," said Hardman. A restraining order was filed. Hardman, who had promised to Gary he'd watch over his daughter, paid Royce a visit, where he tried to talk sense into him and told him to leave Shannon alone. "I promise you, I'm gonna send you up to the state prison." "My whole life Hardman tried to arrest me and put me in jail," Royce admitted. "Because I always had drugs, women, and money—and he was a *cop*."

At one point Shannon wound up in the hospital. "She wasn't eating, she wasn't drinking," said Tina, who drove her there. "We were all the way in the back in the emergency room. Shannon was hooked up to IVs because she was extremely dehydrated." Royce showed up. "He went to jail for violating the restraining order," said Corley. "I wrote warrants for him," said Hardman. "He wound up gettin' eight years." Somewhere amid this chaos Royce "kicked the windows out of the police car," according to Lee Schwartz.

Ashburn was sent to Taylor Correctional Institution,[168] a grim prison nearly five hours north. Shannon refused to give up on Royce. "He's my Gary," she told me. "Shannon, she's a beast," said Royce. "She just held on, she never let go. We had all these accumulating bills. The whole time I was gone, she had, like, three jobs waitressing. She's a strong woman, and she was very determined to move forward from all the past."

His third year in prison, Royce underwent a transformation. He was awakened at 3 a.m. by an entity he called "Denial." He heard no voices and saw no visions—there was just "a tap on my shoulder that told me to go to the bathroom and look in the mirror. It hit me like a sheet of rain: I'd been in denial my whole life. I realized everything that had happened and was happening was my own fault. It was *all* my fault. That right there was the changing point in my life. I knew I was supposed to be more of a provider and helper than a person of hindrance. I said, 'When I get out of here, I will never be lost in drugs again. And I will never have to ask people for anything again, and I'll never be broke again.'" It took a year or so to adjust once he got back home, but he managed to escape the cycle of drugs, violence, and incarceration. "He came out of prison a changed man," said Lee Schwartz. "We are so proud of Royce. He's very devoted to Shannon." None of this came easy for the couple. "They've been through hell and back," said Tina.[169]

Shannon and Royce married on September 8, 2018. They lead a busy but uncomplicated life. Shannon does clerical work for a local mining company while Royce runs his own landscaping business. Joseph Peavy, the grandson much loved by Gary and Lou, earned a bachelor's degree in biology (a first for the family), and is the

---

168 Taylor Correctional has one inmate review on Yelp, and it's one star. "Where do I start...Guards will literally beat you till [you're] not moving," writes Yee Y. "Place is like being in a very bad dream. If your family calls to ask about you they will punish you. If you don't wake up on time for work they will put you in confinement....[a lot] of bugs and especially sand fleas....Place should be shut down."

169 What would Gary, the protective father, think of the incredible turnaround Royce has made? I asked Bill Hardman. "Here's what he would say: 'I sure like the way Royce is doing things now...But I *still* don't trust that fucker.'"

operational manager of a medical testing lab, with a son, Kash, that "Mom and Dad would be crazy about," Shannon noted.

* * *

"Fort Pierce is known for eating people alive," Royce told me. He admitted it was challenging to remain there and not get sucked back in. Drugs remain the scourge of the town. Many of his old friends are either addicted or dead. He mentioned accompanying Mary Lou on drug runs as a kid. "Watching that, y'know, kind of led me into the life that I lived," he states with no judgment.

Did Fort Pierce eat Gary and Lou alive? Yes, in a sense, said Ashburn. "They just had more money, more access, and more freedom to do what they wanted inside this house. All they had to do is make a phone call and whoever it was, they would rush over here to the door to give Gary and Mary Lou whatever they needed. But nobody really cared about them. They just wanted the money."

* * *

A day or so after Gary passed in 2003, Shannon rang me. Everyone was gathered at the house, telling Gary and Mary Lou stories. "So, you want to make a book out of this? You're the only one that my dad trusted." No time wasted. It was a move worthy of Mary Lou. Given the circumstances, it left me a bit speechless. I had a hunch how bad the end of the story was, and I had no desire to dig deeper—or cause anybody further pain. Particularly Shannon. But she stayed on me, reassuring me that she could handle the results. "Don't ever think that you're going to get me upset. Or you're walking on eggshells, because it's not like that with me. My mom and dad raised me to be a very strong person."

I felt no need to go back to Music City. The Nashville that briefly embraced Gary is long gone, and these days, for the most part, it cranks out slop that could originate anywhere, a bland, generic, tasteless, pop-rock gumbo seasoned with whatever the popular flavors of the moment are, diluting its sound even further. "In their quest to make everybody like [country music], they ruined it," wrote Steve Hinson. When I told Joe Galante, surely one of the chief engineers of the current Music City empire, that there was nowhere in Nashville for a Gary Stewart anymore, he disagreed. "I can imagine Gary Stewart in today's world being with a hip-hop act," he enthused. Now, that was a funny idea. Stewart hated anything connected to rap.

But mysteries remained in Fort Pierce, and in July 2021 I returned. Much of the old gang was still there, like Tommy Schwartz. I'd found Tommy intimidating when I first met him in 1987. Schwartz is a no-bullshit guy. He once told me a story about some dame who wanted to join the Easy People Band. "I told her, 'You're a good-looking girl, you sing great, you play good guitar, but you are a bitch. Nobody wants to put up with your shit.' She pretty much agreed with me." That's Tommy. He reminded me of Sam Peckinpah in the role of drill instructor—at any moment I thought he was going to bark at me to drop and give him twenty. I do believe Tommy has mellowed over the years. He feels things deeply, I've discovered. He just doesn't tell anybody.

One day he took me out to his garage to show me the box of bullets that had held Gary's last shot. "I don't know why I have these," he said a bit sheepishly. But I knew why. If it pertained to Gary, Tommy thought it belonged to history. Tommy is the Gary Stewart archivist and he has saved everything—tapes, photos, suitcases full of handwritten lyrics. I've known plenty of people in this position—friends to the star who wind up with the treasures—and 95 percent of them are a pain in the ass. They lord over their collections, determined to make life miserable for anyone who wants access. Not Tommy. If it benefits Stewart, he's all for it, and he's exceedingly generous. The day of the viewing at the funeral home, he leaned over Gary's body and whispered, "I won't let the world forget you." As Shannon, who heard that vow, will tell you, "Tommy has kept his promise."

Shannon arranged for all the local Stewart family members to come to the house to be interviewed for the book. This was no easy task with such an idiosyncratic, iconoclastic group—some didn't want to talk, some wanted money—but through sheer force of will Shannon made it happen. "As I see her age, I see Mary Lou in her so much more," said Lee. "I'm like, 'You go, Lou.' Shannon stands her ground."

And so they all made the pilgrimage to Shannon's house—courtly Grandal, blunt Gail, taciturn Garna, and wild child Gina, who showed up completely soused the first day. The last of the wild Stewarts, Gina has aged into a lovable old rogue, albeit one who occasionally shoots the moon—literally. "It was too damn bright," she said she told the officers. "And I was tryin' to dim the son of a bitch." The Stewarts were all stars to me. They had survived.[170]

Sadly, the Stewart matriarch wasn't present—Georgia passed away in 2004, just months after Gary. So the clan all gathered at Yates Funeral Home once more. Gina, the last to arrive, brought a departing gift for her mother. "She had a big ol' shopping bag with her, and she reaches in the bag and pulls out a pistol—her mama's pistol—and sticks it up under her mother's body," said Tommy. Gina explained she wanted Georgia "to shoot her way into heaven." The reported $300,000 Georgia left to her children was the source of many a squabble. Money may be the root of all evil when it comes to the Stewarts.

One night we all went out honky-tonking. The Fort Pierce scene has mostly faded away, but Tommy and Jimmy Smith were playing in a band called Whiskey Trip in nearby Vero Beach at a short-lived bar called Center City Tavern. It was a small but lively joint, packed to the gills with rednecks and ancient hippies. There were couples in full Western regalia, others in tie-dye shirts, even one old coot in an American flag suit. Drinking, dancing, and fighting—one dame came barreling out of the ladies' room yelling

170 Including Greg Stewart, who was living in Tennessee at the time.

after clobbering some younger chick (friends held them apart). It was rather heartwarming to see that in some respects nothing had changed in the honky-tonk life.

The band ripped through several Stewart songs, with Smith laying down some tough licks. Jimmy's had a hard time with it. Drugs, prison, madness... He veers from barroom to Bible on a daily basis. Hand him a guitar, though, and he'll bring down the house, that shit-eating grin plastered across his face. In between sets I hugged his neck. Back on my first trip to Fort Pierce he'd saved my sanity by hanging out with me in the trailer when Gary was zonked out in the bedroom. When Jimmy goes back to the Stewart house now, "memories come flooding back to me. It's bittersweet." Jimmy has a heart the size of Texas, and often wept recounting the past. Like the rest of us, Smith has a wound that won't quite heal.

Shannon has remained in the house where her parents lived and died. Back around 2015, she decided to redo the kitchen. "I'm finally gonna make it my own," she said. It was a momentous decision. "Shannon just wanted the dark out of the house," said Lee Schwartz. Shannon's home, which she now calls Stewart Manor, is full of light and has become a much less gloomy place. "It's one hundred percent night-and-day difference," said Royce. "Because I still have all the memories of how this house was lived—and how this house is lived. The only thing that's the same is we don't let nobody come over, either."

There is a room in the house Shannon calls the Shrine Room, and there on display are pictures of her parents, their wedding license, and both her parents' ashes intermingled in one urn "so they're together." Shannon keeps some of these ashes in a trinket she wears around her neck.

On October 26, 2024, I accompanied Shannon to Mt. Vernon, Kentucky, where Gary was inducted into the Kentucky Music Hall of Fame. Wearing her dad's leather jacket and her mother's earrings, Shannon slayed the crowd with a raunchy couplet from "Flat Natural Born Good-Timin' Man." Somewhere her mother and father were chuckling. It was deeply moving to see Gary finally get some respect. Neither of us will rest until all his unheard music gets a proper release.

To say Shannon is devoted to keeping her parents' memory alive does not begin to convey her dedication. "Shannon is Gary and Mary Lou all day, every day," said Royce. "She makes her decisions on what she thinks they would say or what they would think. She values them to this day like they were still here." And sometimes they are.

"It's the weirdest thing," Shannon told me. "I'll get all dog-tired, and have to go lay down and take a nap. And they will come to me in my dream and they'll tell me something. Something that I need to know.

"I hope I'm still going to see them again," she says. "Mom, Dad, and Joey. I feel like they're all together. On top of that silver cloud."

OU
ONCA

HERIFF
ARRIAGE PARLO
STICE'S COURT
AND INSPECTOR
CK CONTROL
SAYER'S OFFICE
S. MARSHAL
NY EXPRESS
RONER'S OFFICE
AP

ACKNOWLEDGMENTS

The infidels that occupy current-day publishing would not put this book out. Only one person undertook the cause, and he's done it with Pentecostal fervor: Chris "The Champion" Campion. He is the reason you hold this tome in your hands, and I am eternally grateful to him. We have more things planned. May they all happen.

You work on a book for nearly forty years, there are a lot of people to thank.

My thanks to all the interviewees. They are listed in the source notes. Thank you to my anonymous sources (you know who you are).

There is no way I can adequately thank Gary's daughter Shannon Ashburn. She opened doors in every way possible. What a jewel you are. Shannon has a website for her dad: *garystewartstore.com*. Thanks to Royce Ashburn and Joe Peavy as well.

Tommy Schwartz was an invaluable resource for this work. He answered (literally) thousands of emails and made everything he had available to me. There is no one more devoted to the cause of Gary Stewart. Thank you, Tommy. Thanks also to Lee Schwartz. Thanks to Dale Lawrence, who introduced me to Gary Stewart's music in a swampy Bloomington, Indiana, apartment with colorful, photorealistic wallpaper over four decades ago. That was the beginning of it all. Thanks to Carole Nicksin, who was there at the start.

Thanks to Kit Rachlis, who first believed in this tale. He taught me a great deal about telling a story. Thanks to Nancy Beyda for funding one of my first trips to Florida back in 1987; it never would've happened otherwise. I could fill a book with praise for Nancy. An extraordinary person.

For transcription work, thanks to Stephanie Kreutter, Chris Ryan, and Jil Heimensen. Thanks to Otter.ai, which has been an invaluable tool for my work.

Randy Toman of the Drugstore Cowboys / Toman Brothers Band was a fantastic help. The great "Boogie" Bob Melton was always there when I had a question. RIP, Roy Dea.

Trampas Stewart was a great help with genealogical information about the Stewarts, as was Nick Stewart. Gina Stewart (my favorite) helped with many, many things. Love you, Huet. Brenda Casey (RIP) was another invaluable source on the Stewart history.

In Fort Pierce: Jimmy Smith, Laurie Rastrelli, Bill Hardman all went the extra mile. Angela Beecham, thank you. Grandal Stewart, what an amazing guy. He took the most indelible pictures of Gary. Thanks to Candy and Jason Stewart as well. And Trish Powers. Thanks to Jo Ann Gregory. Special thanks to the fantastic Larry "Mouse" Munson. Big thanks to Kentucky Kate.

Thanks to the Texas Two: Terry Porter and James Willingham. What a duo! In Kentucky: thanks to Lee Adams for showing me around Letcher County, and to Mike Rose for giving me a tour of Gary's old home. In Nashville: a big thank you to the great Steve Hinson. Country Music Hall of Fame: thanks to Michael Gray for providing invaluable interviews and Kathleen Campbell for Hall of Fame materials.

Mark "Media Mail" Linn has rescued many Gary recordings from oblivion and been a great help. Diana Darby assisted with session sheet information. Author Bob Allen gave me access to all his interviews with Gary. Brad Swiger provided some rare materials as well. Dave Jordan provided great information and photos. Thanks to soul brother #1 Kirk West for insight, photographs, and live tapes. Thanks to Craig Turley for tapes. Thanks to Mia De Sousa and Rosie Flores.

Thank you to the people who provided other rare images of Gary for the book: Ray Wilburn, Juan Dale Brown, and Gary Stewart's #1 fan Meghan Pollard. And Masumi Kobayashi for her stellar retouching work.

PEN America gave an emergency grant for this project through their US Writers Aid Initiative just when I needed it the most. They are a fantastic resource for writers.

Thanks to Susan VanHecke for an immaculate copyediting job. A lethal mind. I am humbled.

Thanks to Eric S. Reid, Jaishanker Nautiyal, Stephanie Saffer, and Cindy K. Girres for saving my life. Teeth by Dr. Mary Fischer. Hair by Jerry Ripley. Shades by Sara Lassiter-Burgoyne. Thanks to Sarah at Elmer's. Thanks to Melissa and Melissa at Tualatin Hills Aquatic Center.

Legal by the fabulous Bart Day, my lawyer for life. Thanks as always to David K. Frasier.

Thanks as well to Joel Selvin, Lucy Fur, Josh "Clifford" Lewellen, Bob Mehr, Liz Main, Keiley Mynk, Nicki Walters, B.S., Alex DiSanto, Alison Auerbach, Margaret Dollrod, Mara Stevenson, Lisa Petrucci, Rudolph Grey and Lisa Pan, Yara Cluver, Bill Bentley, Lucy Lucio, Dave Dawson, Holly Gleason, Martha Spencer and Jonathan Penner. Billy Q. Smith, thank you for all the music. Thanks to John McDonough and Mary Jo Berner. Special thanks also to John Kopf and Kier-La Janisse.

Sarah Heldman did some incredible sleuthing when it came to court documents. She unearthed all sorts of information I wouldn't have found otherwise. Thank you, Sarah!

Tammy Faye Starlite, my own personal Angela Lansbury, offered much encouragement throughout my work on this project. It usually ended in three exclamation points.

As always, thanks to Frank "Poncho" Sampedro, who has been an incredible friend over the years. Thanks to the wonderful Ipo Sampedro as well! Shout-out to Wolf Boy.

Thanks to my agent, David McCormick. He never gave up on this book. Thanks as always to Bridget McCarthy for taking care of the details.

Molly Scott, my favorite writer, read the manuscript and offered many suggestions, not the least of which was to stand my ground. Her opinions were invaluable.

As with all my books, Charlie Beesley went over the manuscript, made corrections, and provided many ideas. He went as far as to rewrite a few sentences when mine were crap. He also did photo restoration on quite a few images in this book. Charlie has the most incredible collection of vernacular photos known on earth. It's about time somebody publishes a collection of this singular archive.

Natalia Wisdom McDonough, who loves Gary's work as much as anyone in this world, educated me on the music, contemplated all my theories, and talked me down from the ledge many a time. This is her book as much as mine. She lived it with me, and for that and so many other things I will love her forever.

– Jimmy McDonough, 2025

PHOTO CREDITS

Front Gary and Mary Lou (right) honky-tonkin', early sixties. (Shannon Ashburn collection)

12-13 Gary in his Fort Pierce lair, lost in the music. (Grandal Stewart)

18 Gary blasting away in a honky-tonk, mid-to-late seventies. (Shannon Ashburn collection)

24-25 Georgia and George Stewart and their boys. Back row: Gregory, Grandal, Gary. Front row: Gerald, Glenn, and Garna. (Gina Stewart collection)

44-45 Glenn, Gerald, Gina, Gail, Gregory, Garna, Griselda, Grandal, Gary, and Georgia Stewart. (Grandal Stewart collection)

66-67 Gary and fellow Tom Cat, Joe Parker. (Author's collection)

88 Gary and Lou, the scandalous young lovers. (Shannon Ashburn collection)

96 Imps-era publicity shot. (Shannon Ashburn collection)

112 Gary Stewart, Music City songwriter. (Gina Stewart collection)

136-137 Charley Pride, Gary, Roy Dea. (Shannon Ashburn collection)

151 Early RCA publicity shot. (Author's collection)

158-159 Tammy Wynette, Gary, Mary Lou, Willie Nelson. (Shannon Ashburn collection)

179 Gary in London, 1975. (Doug MacKenzie/Country Music People magazine)

196-197 Gary sporting some serious jewelry, date unknown. (Shannon Ashburn collection)

214-215 Gary and the Drugstore Cowboys, L to R: Dub Robinson, Robert "Cotton" Payne, and Randy Toman. (Author's collection)

218 Mary Lou boudoir shot sent to author. (Grandal Stewart)

232-233 Griselda Stewart on the night she died. (Gina Stewart collection)

240 Evil skull and suave Gary: *Little Junior* cover session outtake. (Grandal Stewart)

262-263 Dickey Betts and Gary (with "Boogie" Bob Melton in the background), Macon, Georgia, approximately 1981. (Gina Stewart collection)

274 Gary and Bonnie Bramlett, singing backup for the Allman Brothers, 1980. (Kirk West/Retro Photo Archive)

294-295 Greg Stewart, Walter Carlton, Gerald and Gina Stewart, 1981. (Gina Stewart collection)

308-309 Gary and Dean Dillon backstage, 1982. (Kirk West/Retro Photo Archive)

336 Gary Stewart, 1982. (Kirk West/Retro Photo Archive)

344-35 Punk rock Joey, eighties. (Shannon Ashburn collection)

370 Gary and the King. (Tommy Schwartz collection)

392-393 Punk rock Joey, eighties. (Shannon Ashburn collection)

408-409 Gary lost in some nameless hotel, date unknown. (Shannon Ashburn collection)

430-431 A fully McCroanized Gary with Richard McCroan, early nineties. (Stephanie Piras)

464-465 Gary and Mary Lou. Tommy Schwartz: "This photo was almost never seen unless you were at Gary and Lou's. He was adamant that this picture was to never leave his house. He was afraid that something might happen to it." (Grandal Stewart)

499 Gary on his way to nowhere, date unknown. (Shannon Ashburn collection)

508-509 The Stewarts: Mary Lou, Gary, Shannon, and Joey. Shannon Ashburn: "We were on our way to Colorado for our first real family trip. All the Stewart brothers came anyway. My mom fried potatoes every night. That's all them Stewart boys eat." (Grandal Stewart)

SOURCE NOTES

intro
TRAILER WITH BLACKED-OUT WINDOWS

Interviews: Gary Stewart, Mary Lou Stewart, Shannon Ashburn, Tanya Tucker, Buddy Cannon, Terry Porter, Dale Lawrence, Mike Smith, Joe Nick Patoski, "Boogie" Bob Melton, Randy Toman, Richard McCroan, Curtis Randall, Robert Gallagher, other sources.

"kick it in...do these boys": Stewart to unknown, "S.A. Boys to Hit the Roadhouse," *Action*, July 1977. **Longhorn Ballroom amplifier anecdote:** Post in "Longhorn Ballroom—Dewey Groom Era 1958 Thru 12-31-1985" Facebook group. **"There ain't no big goals...that got lucky":** Julie Bartlett, "Gary Stewart Comes Home," unidentified publication, March 25, 1976. **"It was as if... offspring together":** Dwight Yoakam, courtesy Bill Bentley. **"that made you...professional criminal":** Bob Dylan, *Chronicles: Volume One* (Simon & Schuster, 2004). **"Too country for country and too rock for country":** Jay Orr to Charles Passy, "Gary and Mary Lou," *Palm Beach Post*, March 14, 2004. **"I am from the honky-tonks":** Joe Nick Patoski, "Gary Stewart: Rock vs Country-Western," *American Statesman*, January 18, 1976. **"The electricity around...sparks flying off":** Marty Stuart to Bill DeYoung, "Fans, Friends Pay Tribute to Honky-Tonk Legend," *Indian River Press Journal*, December 18, 2003. **"Just remember there's a tape of me in Pikeville":** Gary Stewart to Bob Allen, "Gary Stewart on the Road Again," *Country Song Roundup*, January, 1981. Note: I have never found this tape and have no idea what's on it. It appears Stewart referenced this session again in an interview with Holly Gleason: "I remember this one time in Pikeville, Kentucky. I got so much energy that it was like I was going out into space." Gleason, "Roadhouse Musical Meltdown," *Pulse*, October 1988. **"My wife understands...and drugs":** Gary Stewart to Christopher Allfirst, "Scotch Tape and Spit: An Off-the-Wall Talk with Gary Stewart," *Honky-Tonk*, December 1981. **"My Appalachia"** by Muriel Miller Dressler courtesy of W. L. Eury Appalachian Collection, Applachian State University.

1
GEORGIA AND GEORGE

Interviews: Terry Porter, Georgia Stewart, George Stewart, Gary Stewart, Jimmy Smith, Trampas Stewart, Karen Parker, Brenda Casey, Jason Stewart, Nick Stewart, Gregory Stewart, Shannon Ashburn, Bill Stewart, Gina Stewart, Garna Stewart, Grandal Stewart, Candy Stewart, Kim Carlton, Tommy Schwartz, Dale Thomas, Jo Ann Gregory, Barbara Anne Peters, family friend, relative, Gail Stewart, other sources.

2
LONG WAY OUT OF THIS HOLLER

Interviews: Gary Stewart, Nick Stewart, Bill Stewart, Jake Stewart, Trampas Stewart, Brenda Casey, Georgia Stewart, Grandal Stewart, Ernie Elkins, Terry Porter, Lee Schwartz, Louise Hudson, Gary Gallant, other sources.

General genealogical information on the Stewarts: "A Place Called Long Fork" Facebook group; James Chris Fleming, *Stewart: Ancestors and Descendants of Robert "Bob" Stewart and Mary (Mullins) Stewart*, published by the author, Fleming Family History website. **John Stewart information:** "Stewart," Stewarts of Alexander website; "Dr. John Stewart," genii.com; "Dr. John Stewart File," "A Place Called Long Fork" Facebook group. **The Highland Clan and bagpipes information:** "Bagpipe History," Scotia Pipers website. **"a number of Indians...with**

common savage usage": Daniel Boone to Francis L. Hawks, *Life of Daniel Boone* (1856) (reprint, Kessinger, 2009). **"I returned home...a second paradise":** Hawks. **"a road with no painted lines":** Shane, "The Appalachian Project" Facebook group, January 5, 2021. **"A holler has...stream of water":** Jim Cornett, "What Is a Holler?," *Mountain Eagle*, May 23, 2018. **"also has plenty...likely taken notice":** Shane, "The Appalachian Project." **Kentucky was the sixth poorest state:** Oleksandra Mamchii, "Top 12 Poorest States in America," bestdiplomats.org, April 15, 2024. **"In eastern Kentucky, everybody...do after work":** "'I Wanna Make Art': Sturgill Simpson's Twisting Path to Nashville," npr.org. **"The thing that I found... and to listen":** Thomas E. Gish in *Kentucky Life*, season 6, episode 13, produced/directed by Charlee Heaton Pagoulatos, 2000. **"The companies that...was totally dependent":** Harry Caudill, BBC documentary clip used in *Stranger with a Camera*, directed by Elizabeth Barret, 1999. For more on Caudill, a somewhat controversial character, see the KET documentary *Harry Caudill: A Man of Courage*, produced by Dave Harl, 2017. **"the courthouse...go his bond":** Megan Rosenfeld, "Killing in Kentucky: Out-of-Focus 'Camera,'" *Washington Post*, July 10, 2000. **"It should read 'A City Built on the Backs of Miners'":** Thomas Daniel Anderson, "Put a Roof on Whitaker Music Shop" GoFundMe, January 20, 2016. **"the one who may have started the music in us":** uncredited, "Abraham Stewart," "Robert Winfield and Bethane Burke-Stewart (1875-1975 Era)" Facebook page. **"was a preacher on the side for a spell":** uncredited, "Abraham Stewart." **"walked everywhere...white pressed shirts":** uncredited, "Abraham Stewart." **"forced to stare death directly in the face":** Macel Ely II, *Ain't No Grave: The Life and Legacy of Brother Claude Ely* (Dust-to-Digital, 2010). **"He would put everything...really belt it out":** Raymond Williams, in Ely, *Ain't No Grave*. Garna Stewart does not think his father is in the image of Consolidation Coal workers in this chapter. Gary did. I went with his notes on the back of the picture.

3
FLORIDA MAN

Interviews: Gary Stewart, Shannon Ashburn, Grandal Stewart, Candy Stewart, Trampas Stewart, Wallace Parr, Bill Hardman, Tommy Schwartz, Jason Stewart, Ronnie Baird, Gina Stewart, Kim Carlton, Polly Davis, Jo Ann Gregory, Lee Schwartz, Joe Parker, Karen Parker, Katherine "Kitty" Parr, Jake Stewart, other sources.

The chapter title comes from an obscure local hit "Florida Man" by Chuck Penny from 1972 on Tim Records. Find it! Reverend Billy C. Wirtz (aka William Wirths), "Function at the Yeehaw Junction," 2021, commissioned by the author. **"least racist":** Gary loved black music. And he enjoyed playing with black musicians. But he was known to use the n-word on occasion. Richard McCroan, who road-managed Gary in the late nineties, was also a singer, and one night driving to a gig, McCroan played Stewart a live tape of one of his shows. "Gary listened, then he said, 'Richard, hey, man, you need to start singin' like a nigger. You're phrasin' things like you're a damn character. It don't have no damn emotion to it. It's not genuine.' And I immediately started singing better." What can you say about that line of instruction? Gary was far from alone among his peers in using the word. Lou told me when Gregg Allman stepped inside their house for the first time, he "dropped his bags and said, 'The nigger is home!'" **Details on John Wesley Davis case:** Rollin Rogers, "Miamian Arrested; 75000 Bond Set," *St. Lucie News Tribune*, March 13, 1964; Ray Washington, "No Limits to the Excesses of John Wesley Davis," Cracker Florida (column), *Fort Pierce Tribune*, January 22, 1984. **"I just sat down...what I knew":** Stewart later told Ralph Emery, 1978 radio interview. **"It brought in a lot of action":** Josie Tobin to Gloria Weinberg, "Memories of Nightlife Fun in Fort Pierce," *Fort*

Pierce Tribune, January 1, 1995. **"She had even seen Little Richard":** Gary recalled Mary Lou seeing Little Richard at the Showplace. No one I've talked to in Fort Pierce recalls a club by that name. Mysterious!

4

HELLO, MARY LOU

Interviews: Mary Lou Stewart, Shannon Ashburn, Royce Ashburn, Larry "Mouse" Munson, Jo Ann Gregory, Gail Stewart, Gina Stewart, Grandal Stewart, Ed Teague, Mel Briggs, Riley Watkins, Darrell Dawson, Ron "Radar" Griffith, Tommy Schwartz, "Boogie" Bob Melton, David Thomas, Georgia Stewart, Fred Burch, Billy Swan, Chris Parker, Karen Parker, other sources.

"skull orchards...wild ones": Gary Stewart, Lee Arnold radio interview, *Country Cookin'*, New York City, 1975. **"could change clothes...skinny as Hank!":** Mel Tillis to Charles Passy, "Gary and Lou," *Palm Beach Post*, March 14, 2004. **"a little like Montgomery Clift":** Patrick Anderson, "The Real Nashville," *New York Times*, August 31, 1975. **"My first record...she got bumped off":** Gary Stewart to Ralph Emery, radio interview, 1978. **"saw an old Negro...wrote itself":** Ann Wilder, "Gary Strikes Pay Dirt with Guitar and Song," *Miami Herald*, January 9, 1966.

5

MUSIC CITY ASSEMBLY LINE

Interviews: Gary Stewart, Bill Eldridge, Jimmy Smith, Fred Burch, Jerry Bradley, Tommy Schwartz, Shannon Ashburn, Riley Watkins, Jim Snead, Henry Hurt, Mary Lou Stewart, Brenda Casey, Rick Durrett, other sources.

"I took the songwriting...have many friends": Gary Stewart to author, 1987 interview. **"I'm not a...songs I could":** Jerry Bradley to Paul Leslie, *The Paul Leslie Hour*, October 8, 2020. **"He didn't have...by remote control":** Waylon Jennings with Lenny Kaye, *Waylon: An Autobiography* (Warner Books, 1996). **"He never knew...step of the way":** Jennings with Kaye, *Waylon*. **"He could dress... your pal later":** Jerry Bradley to John Rumble, Country Music Hall of Fame interview, 2012. **"turned to me...the hell I think":** Bradley to Rumble, Country Music Hall of Fame. **"about ten new...just know it":** Claire Pottopff, "FP Cop Pounds Beat with a Guitar," *Fort Pierce Tribune*, February 9, 1969. **"I thought we were gonna raise cows":** Bradley to Rumble, Country Music Hall of Fame. **"We got so busy...a hot little studio":** Bradley to Rumble, Country Music Hall of Fame. **"Making records was...playing much better!":** Walter Haynes post on the Steel Guitar Forum thread "Who is Walter Haynes?," October 24, 2000. **"Recording was accidental... as a songwriter":** Gary Stewart to uncredited, "Country Star of the Month: Gary Stewart," *Song Hits*, October 1975. **Stewart first seeing the Allman Brothers:** Gary could not recall the date or venue to me, but in 1985 he told Kirk West he saw them in Clarksville, Tennessee, around 1971. There is no record of the band playing Clarksville. They played Cookeville, Tennessee, May 13, 1971, and this seems to be the correct date based on the other particulars Gary mentioned (the Allman Brothers also played Vanderbilt University in Nashville on October 30, 1970, but this date seems too early). **Coven:** Rick Durrett (and the rest of Coven) did not play on "One Tin Soldier (The Legend of Billy Jack)." Jinx Dawson, the band's singer, cut it with an orchestra for the soundtrack. She insisted Coven be credited.

6

BETTER THAN GUNSMOKE

Interviews: Roy Dea, Tanya Tucker, Jerry Kennedy, Steve Hinson, Delores Kennedy, Joe Galante, David Briggs, Charlie McCoy, Jim Isbell, Bill Harris, Bruce Hunter, Jerry Carrigan, Bobby Wood, Buddy Harman, Dale Sellers, Chip Young, Harold Bradley, other sources.

I quote Delores Kennedy simply as "Delores" to avoid confusion; she later married Jerry Kennedy, Roy's best friend, in 2013 (Roy passed away in 1997). A twist worthy of a country song. **"the goofy guy jumpin' around":** Jerry Kennedy to Tom Roland, "Record Producer Roy Dea Dies," *The Tennessean*, August 22, 1997. **"a very, very closed...'Kenny Chesney?'":** Joe Galante to Kane Harrison, "Music Business Week: Joe Galante Part 1 (of 4)—Early Days of Nashville Music," *Talkapolis*, September 11, 2013.

7

NUMBER ONE WITH A BULLET

Interviews: Roy Dea, Gary Stewart, Steve Hinson, Jerry Bradley, Bruce Carter, David Briggs, Ann Stuckey, Jim Snead, "Boogie" Bob Melton, Fred Bogert, Mary Lou Stewart, Jerry Bradley, Joe Galante, Randy Toman, Larry "Mouse" Munson, Charley Pride, Rozene Pride, Shannon Ashburn, Steve Cureton, other sources.

"I never set out...never went lookin'": Gary Stewart to Bob Allen, 2/27/90 phone interview, CMHOF Digital Archive (all other non-print Allen interviews that follow are from there as well). **"I didn't set out...tolerance than indignation":** Charley Pride with Jim Henderson, *Pride: The Charley Pride Story* (Quill, 1994). **"I'm no color...on their blackness":** Charley Pride to Joe Sornberger, "No Color Hang-Up for Charley Pride," *Edmonton Journal*, February 20, 1976. **"like maybe Hollywood...longhandle... hunchback":** Gary Stewart to Ralph Emery, *The Ralph Emery Show*, 1976. **"I call Charley up...just gettin' it!":** Stewart to Emery, *The Ralph Emery Show*. **"stomped, shouted, and strummed... gyrating, always vocal":** Don Rubincam, "Waterloo Festival: Traditional Country Music Challenged," *Courier-News*, August 4, 1975. **"drew a standing ovation":** Rubincam, "Waterloo Festival." **"One of the classy joints... song to write":** Wayne Carson to Michael Gray, Country Music Hall of Fame interview, 2011. **"He was making...off the radio":** John Morthland to Joe Gross, "Saying Goodbye to a True Texas Honky-Tonker," *Austin-American Statesman*, December 25, 2003. **"return to the roots...against that domestication":** John Rockwell, "The Pop Life," *New York Times*, June 20, 1975. **"Don't be misled...a little crazy":** Robert Christgau, "Consumer Guide," *Village Voice*, May 12, 1975. **"One of the greatest honky-tonk albums ever recorded":** Bill C. Malone, *Don't Get Above Your Raisin'* (University of Illinois Press, 2002). **"how traditional...on the recording":** Charlie Crockett in "The Next Waltz and Western Fidelity Present: Gary Stewart's *Out of Hand*," *The Next Waltz*, May 28, 2024. **"Driven by the crying steel...Magic Fingers":** Reverend Billy C. Wirtz (aka William Wirths), "Function at the Yeehaw Junction," 2021, commissioned by the author. **"layin' around the house...gettin' high with my friends":** Gary Stewart to Julie Sneed, "Big-Time Singer Gary Stewart Still Loves Fort Pierce," *Fort Pierce News-Tribune*, March 16, 1975. **"Some night when...the whole audience!":** Gary Stewart to Christopher Allfirst, "Scotch Tape and Spit: An Off-the-Wall Talk with Gary Stewart," *Honky-Tonk*, December 1981. **"Sometimes I feel...seems so phony":** Gary Stewart to Bob Allen, "Can Gary Stewart the Faded Honky Tonk King Find His Second Wind?," *Country Music*, December 1980.

8

ANIMAL IN A CAGE

Interviews: Grandal Stewart, Gary Stewart, Roy Dea, Jerry Bradley, Mary Lou Stewart, Larry "Mouse" Munson, Reggie Young, Eddie Kilroy, Willie Nelson, Georgia Stewart, "Boogie" Bob Melton, Charley Pride, Carol Anderson, Kim Willingham, other sources.

"I feed off...as they are": Gary Stewart to Bob Allen, "On the Road with Gary Stewart," *Country Music*, March 1979. **"I never got to know him but I considered him kindred":** Danny O'Keefe, "Danny O'Keefe, Songbird

Foundation," *Grist*, December 19, 2003. **"Me and my mama...on the plane":** Gary Stewart to Bob Allen, interview at RCA Nashville, June 12, 1980. **"I did a laid-back...arrangement than mine":** Sterling Whipple to Bob Allen, interview, October 15, 1976. **"I did it for love!":** Beverly Shoemaker to uncredited, "Prisoner of Love," *National Enquirer*, October 11, 1988. **"through a personal ad":** Shoemaker to uncredited, "Prisoner of Love." **"I hate myself... back row again":** Matt Yancey, "50,000 a Year, He Hates Self," *Atlanta Journal*, September 3, 1975. **"a poor man's music...a simple man":** Gary Stewart to David DeVoss, "A Honky-Tonk Man," *Time*, September 27, 1976. **"About the closest...on Music Row":** Waylon Jennings 1988 *Spin* interview quoted in Casey Young, "Waylon Jennings Once Famously Said the Most Outlaw Thing Willie Nelson Ever Did Was 'Double-Park on Music Row,'" whiskeyriff.com, August 10, 2024. **"about the dumbest thing I ever heard":** "Waylon Jennings Interview!," *Down Home Down Under Show* #2. **"a good merchandiser":** Waylon Jennings with Lenny Kaye, *Waylon: An Autobiography* (Warner Books, 1996). **"the heretic sons of Bill Monroe":** Patrick Carr, "Good Time Gary: Honkytonkin' Homelife and the Hot Lick Kid: Gary Stewart Gets It On," *Country Music*, January 1976. **"from midnight...be that big":** Charley Pride with Jim Henderson, *Pride: The Charley Pride Story* (Quill, 1994). **"I wanted to get up...music is all about":** Gary Stewart to Jon Bream, "Gary Stewart Is a Rocker at Heart," *Minneapolis Star*, November 10, 1978.

9
CHECK MY STRIDE

Interviews: Gary Stewart, "Boogie" Bob Melton, Darrell Dawson, Roy Dea, Grandal Stewart, Ron "Radar" Griffith, Gail Stewart, Shannon Ashburn, John Kopf, Jo Ann Gregory, Steve Hinson, Dale Sellers, Dub Robinson, Randy Toman, Robert "Cotton" Payne, Leonard Yazzie, other sources.

"It's not an easy life...and wrecks and teardrops": Charles Portis, "That New Sound from Nashville," *Saturday Evening Post*, February 12, 1966. **"I love for people...around the floor":** Gary Stewart to Leon Black, *Country Music Scene*, USA, October 1980. **"alcohol-fueled, teetering...hard honky-tonk thing":** Rodney Crowell to Bill DeYoung, "Fans, Friends Pay Tribute to Honky-Tonk Legend," *Indian River Press Journal*, December 18, 2003. The details of Gary's meeting with Dylan remain hazy as I've lost the interview in which we discussed it. Some people (including Grandal) stated that Dylan (with Petty) came to Gary's house during their tour, but I've encountered no evidence of this. **Stewart divorce filing:** St. Lucie County court filing, case # 77-309 FR, May 12, 1977. **"He could sing...his face turn red":** Hank Beach, "The Past with a Personal Touch: Gary Stewart," *Nashville Music Guide*, September 12, 2011.

10
GRISELDA

Interviews: Trampas Stewart, Tommy Schwartz, Stan Spence, Nick Stewart, Greg Stewart, Mary Lou Stewart, Gina Stewart, Jimmy Smith, Laurie Rastrelli, Grandal Stewart, Candy Stewart, Kim Carlton, other sources.

11
ONLY GOIN' THROUGH ONCE

Interviews: Gary Stewart, David Thomas, Trampas Stewart, Larry "Mouse" Munson, Gail Stewart, Grandal Stewart, Jimmy Smith, Tommy Schwartz, Royce Ashburn, "Boogie" Bob Melton, Dee Moeller, Roy Dea, Steve Hinson, Dale Sellers, Ralph Profeta, Darrell Dawson, John Whalen, Michael Ochs, Mia De Sousa, Rosie Flores, Ray Wilburn, Sonny Tackett, Randy Toman, Sonny Throckmorton, Delores Kennedy, Dub Robinson, Mary Lou Stewart, other sources.

"Life ain't worth living...of hand sometime": Gary Stewart to Ray Washington, "Cracker Florida," *St. Lucie News Tribune*, March 4, 1979. **"Whenever I get...like a tranquilizer":** Gary Stewart to Bob Allen, interview at RCA Nashville, June 12, 1980, Country Music Hall of Fame. **"a place where your...of one another":** Coyote Wallace, "The Legend of Marlow's Country Palace," *Medium*, June 25, 2023.

12
GHOST TRAIN SLIDE

Interviews: Gary Stewart, Jerry Bradley, Sonny Tackett, Roy Dea, Dave Jordan, Jerry Bradley, Dickey Betts, Kirk West, Bonnie Bramlett, Mary Lou Stewart, Laurie Rastrelli, Larry "Mouse" Munson, "Boogie" Bob Melton, Steve Hinson, Johnny Cobb, Shannon Ashburn, Art Fein, Randy Toman, Carol Anderson, Glen Castleberry, Grandal Stewart, John Vann, other sources.

"was real strange...a funny guy": Chips Moman to Edd Hurt, "Chips Moman: The Cream Interview," *Nashville Scene*, August 17, 2012. **"It was a lot...having a baby":** Gary Stewart to Bob Allen, interview at RCA Nashville, June 12, 1980. **"There is no way… Ever":** Dickey Betts in John Rabb, "Allman Bros. Reunion," *Washington Post*, April 11, 1979. **"wasn't doin' nothin' else but just laying around the house":** Gary Stewart to Kirk West, unpublished interview, October 19, 1985. **"Dickey Betts...on the spot":** Gary Stewart to Bob Allen, interview at RCA Nashville, June 12, 1980. **"a hill-country soul...than the last":** Dale Lawrence, "Rebel to the End," *Chicago Reader*, January 15, 2004. **"Old Baptist is... coal mines, moonshine":** Stewart to Allen, RCA, June 12, 1980. **"a mixture of Elton...it isn't country":** Art Fein, "Stewart: Countrified Rock," *Los Angeles Times*, August 24, 1980. **"They saw it…a butcher shop":** Gary Stewart to Christopher Allfirst, "Scotch Tape and Spit: An Off-the-Wall Talk with Gary Stewart," *Honky-Tonk*, December 1981. **"Survival... road a year":** Stewart to Allen, RCA, June 6, 1980. **Two more songs from Gary's stunning songwriting run during the *Cactus and a Rose* period:** "Devil's Triangle" was an obscure song released on Berry Hill Records in 1975 by Buzz Cason (who wrote it with Dan Penn). Stewart recorded it during the 1979 Gary sessions but the band version remains unreleased (I only know the demo). Before recording it in Nashville, Stewart walked into a nearby Vero Beach studio owned by a friend of his brother Gerald and laid down a demo of the song to send to Roy Dea. "He never paid me for the session," said Mike Gerbhardt. "Typical for Gary." This classic Stewart recording only surfaced because Gebhardt emailed me out of the blue a few years ago and the demo he shared is more evidence of Gary's stone genius. He takes this familiar tale of infidelity, slows the arrangement down, simplifies the song by omitting some of the hokier lines about Satan (not Stewart's style), emphasizes the heartbreak, and wrings every last bit of pathos out of the lyric. To hear Stewart at the height of his vocal powers, unadorned by anything but his acoustic guitar—well, it stops your clock. He manages to invest so much feeling in just about any shopworn cliché that he makes it sound real, like it's happening to you. "Lost in the devil's triangle /Three hearts all in a tangle." A bittersweet, loping ballad with a wistful edge, "Where Does a Rolling Stone Go" evokes the world-weary path Gary had taken that "Ghost Train" failed to capture: "Where does a rolling stone go, when it goes, it's gone/ What do you do when the shadows you're casting are too damn long." It's an incomplete demo not unlike "Harlan County Highway," but it's fantastic. **"Hey, if Jerry Bradley...wasn't for me":** Gary Stewart to Larry Crowley, "Time in a Bottle: After Decades of Drinkin' and Thinkin', Hondy-Tonk Maverick Gary Stewart Has Trouble Getting Mellow," *Phoenix New Times*, January 15, 1992.

13
GERALD STEWART

Interviews: Nick Stewart, Shannon Ashburn, Jason Stewart, Laurie Rastrelli, Stan Spence, Georgia Stewart, Jimmy Smith, Trampas Stewart, Gina Stewart, Tommy Schwartz, Dale Thomas, Randy Toman, Bruce Hunter, Robert Battaglia, Barbara Anne Peters, Polly Davis, Sonny Tackett, Brenda Casey, Kim Carlton, Jo Ann Gregory, Larry "Mouse" Munson, other sources.

"Gerald Stewart of...of the elbow": uncredited, *St. Lucie News Tribune*, February 21, 1981. **"Inspectors with the...Ranch Monday night":** uncredited, *Palm Beach Post*, October 14, 1981. **"Suspect/defendant entered...the County Jail":** Gerald Stewart arrest report, case # 98-03470, August 1, 1998. **Gerald Stewart obituary:** *Fort Pierce Tribune*, January 19, 2002.

14
AN IRREVERSIBLE DESCENT INTO MAJOR SEVENTHS

Interviews: Gary Stewart, Dean Dillon, Tanya Tucker, Eddie Kilroy, Steve Hinson, Dale Lawrence, "Boogie" Bob Melton, Steve Hunter, Richard McCroan, Randy Toman, Joe Galante, Tammy Faye Starlite, Patrick Carr, Buddy Cannon, Warren Haynes, Mickey Hayes, Bill Hardman, Jerry Bradley, other sources.

"try to weld...Ns in it": Dean Dillon to Michael Gray, Country Music Hall of Fame "Poets and Prophets" series, 2008. **"Dillon was a bad guy... bank robber":** Jerry Bradley to Paul Leslie, *The Paul Leslie Hour*, October 8, 2020. **"Dean Dillon is...even knowing it":** Frank Dycus to Dave Dawson, "Dave's Diary—16 November 2011—Frank Dycus Interview," nucountry.com.au. **"a new kid from Texas":** Blake Mevis to Dixie Reid, "Strait Talk: Songwriters Like Working with George," *Sacramento Bee*, September 19, 2002. **"were the hottest...with two villains":** Dean Dillon to Michael Gray, Country Music Hall of Fame "Poets and Prophets" series, 2008. **"Wayne would go...thought [Gary] was phenomenal":** Dillon to Gray, "Poets and Prophets." **Room 607:** Jack Hurst, "RCA Put Gary Stewart and Dean Dillon Together...and Got a Pleasant Surprise," *Waterloo Region Record*, July 8, 1982. **"Inspired by the...and it wants more":** Gerry Wood, "Crossover Country's Magic Key for 1978," *Billboard*, January 7, 1978. **"was originally the... didn't have room":** Becky Shargo to Yardena Arar, "Album Skimps on Country Music," *News-Journal*, July 13, 1980. **"The disc jockey... picking to play":** Jerry Bradley to Paul Leslie, *The Paul Leslie Hour*, October 8, 2020. **"Country music in...of poppish sound":** *Robby Turner, Willie Nelson & Family*, episode 3, directed by Oren Moverman and Thom Zimmy, 2023. According to a forum thread entitled "Dickey Betts NIGHT album" on allmanbrothers.com, Gary played on an unreleased 1981 Dickey Betts solo album, *Night*, produced by Chips Moman. An unnamed musician who played on the album, CrossEyedCat, states Gary sang on "Whole Lotta Memories" and played guitar on the sessions. Gary later performed a Betts song from these sessions, "Nancy," in his trailer for me. **"We're looking for...Steve Wariner":** Joe Galante to Kip Kirby, "Platinum, Gold Gild RCA Nashville: Label Stresses Pop Crossovers, Career Development," *Billboard*, July 4, 1981. **"He never sings...him and guess":** Dean Dillon to Ben Holland, RCA promotional interview with Gary Stewart and Dean Dillon, 1982. **"was thrown together...some just Dean singing":** Gary Stewart to David Dawson, "Dave's Diary—21 December 2003—Gary Stewart—Q & A," Nu Country TV. **"We met at...beat my chicken":** Dean Dillon to Vernell Hackett, "Gary Stewart: The King of the Honky-Tonks," *Country Hotline News*, April 1982. **"Gary gets a...'myself to death'":** Gary Stewart as quoted by Robert K. Oermann, "Gary Stewart and Dean Dillon Living on the Ragged Edge," *Country Song Roundup*, December 1982. **"appearing onstage**

by…laid-back approach": Robyn Wells, "Talent in Action: Gary Stewart and Dean Dillon," *Billboard*, June 19, 1982. **"half-hearted honky-tonk...music doesn't kick":** Walter Carter, "For the Record," *The Tennessean*, May 8, 1982. **"an effort to revive…Gary Stewart":** Jack Hurst, "RCA Put Gary Stewart and Dean Dillon Together...and Got a Pleasant Surprise," *Waterloo Region Record*, July 8, 1982. **"I've always loved… he's a fox":** Tanya Tucker with Patsi Bale Cox, *Nickel Dreams: My Life* (Hyperion, 1997). **"a rare specimen…ear for music":** Dorothy Carvello, *Anything for a Hit: An A&R Woman's Story of Surviving the Music Industry* (Chicago Review Press, 2018). **"What has two arms, two legs and no ears?":** Carvello, *Anything for a Hit*. The joke also opens this story: Kay West, "They Barked, He Bit Back," *Nashville Scene*, November 6, 2003. **"We see this...the album level":** Joe Galante to uncredited, "RCA Launches Mini-LP Series," *Billboard*, January 8, 1983. **"By then Dean...'Johnny Paycheck'":** Frank Dycus to Dave Dawson, "Dave's Diary—16 November 2011—Frank Dycus Interview," Nu Country TV. **"Joe was scared...become like me":** Waylon to Bruce Feiler, *Dreaming Out Loud: Garth Brooks, Wynonna Judd, Wade Hayes, and the Changing Face of Nashville* (Spike Books, 1998). **"A new crop...of the seventies,":** Feiler, *Dreaming Out Loud*. **"I just hung up...mean nothin' to me":** Gary Stewart to Bob Allen, "Gary Stewart: A Different Perspective," *Country Song Roundup*, September 1990. The quote is a bit of a mash-up as he said a slightly different version to me, adding the "because I knew it was comin'."

15
BAD ATTITUDE

Interviews: Gary Stewart, Shannon Ashburn, Tommy Schwartz, Jimmy Smith, Laurie Rastrelli, Dave Jordan, Roy Dea, Randy Toman, John Vann, Bill Lyerly, Russ Toman, Robert Austin, Dana Marr, other sources.

In his interview concerning the Red Ash period, Dave Jordan told me several things that I was unable to confirm. He said that Vince Gill stopped by Stewart's hotel room to pitch a song they later recorded. "I've never been aware of Gary cutting one of my songs—I hope it's true!!" Gill said through his representative, Alison Auerbach. Jordan also said that Gary had told him to sign Dwight Yoakam, claiming he was a distant relative. Yoakam, through his publicity person Bill Bentley, said he was unaware of Stewart being a relation. Jordan also said that Steve Earle pissed everybody off by playing too long at Jordan's company party, the one and only time Stewart and Earle played on the same bill. No one else present for the show remembers this. Jordan also told me how Gary had given him his father's mining helmet, claiming Stewart told him his father was deceased. Dave was shocked when I told him George was alive at the time. **"modern-day hippie...to the parents":** Tommy Schwartz to Charles Passy, "Gary and Mary Lou," *Palm Beach Post*, Sunday, March 14, 2004. **"decorated the whole front yard...like a gypsy camp":** Gary Stewart to Bob Allen, July 29, 1981. **"The mailman brings bills, son!":** Stewart to Allen, July 29, 1981. During the mid-eighties period and beyond, Forrest Hills tried to get Stewart into cowriting with other writers, the vogue in Nashville at the time. All attempts failed. One person Gary actually wanted to write with was Dennis Robbins, who'd cowritten singles for Highway 101, Shenandoah, and Garth Brooks. Stewart, who rarely showed up anywhere by himself, went as far as appearing at Robbins's hotel room for a writing session. They never managed to finish a song.

16
JUKIN'

Interviews: Gary Stewart, Mary Lou Stewart, Jimmy Smith, Shannon Ashburn, Brenda Casey, Barbara Anne Peters, Glenn Middleworth,

Tommy Schwartz, Felix Moss, Linda Gail Lewis, George Stewart, Georgia Stewart, Roy Dea, Donnie Coleman, Dennis Robbins, other sources.

"Fort Pierce is...of the world": Sergeant Roy Hudson to Niles Graben, "Special Unit Organized to Fight Drug War in Streets," *Fort Pierce Tribune*, December 20, 1987. **"He didn't talk bad about nobody":** Bill Hardman told me an amusing tale related to this subject. Hardman was driving Stewart to the airport one day and refused to get him there on time until Gary bad-mouthed somebody, anybody. Stewart finally relented, telling Bill about a time he, Jerry Lee Lewis, and Johnny Rodriguez were together after or before a gig, having a little party and feeling no pain. Jerry Lee mentioned in passing that he had lost a lot of personal memorabilia in a recent fire. Gary offered to replace his early records from his own collection. Jerry Lee somehow got offended by this charitable offer and soon had his hands around Gary's neck. Rodriguez intervened by (allegedly) putting a knife to Jerry Lee's throat, getting the Killer off Stewart. Gary admitted to Hardman that this incident made him less than fond of his hero. I have heard many variations on this tale from others but was not able to verify it. By the time I heard it, Gary and Jerry Lee were gone and Johnny Rodriguez ignored my requests for an interview. Linda Gail Lewis couldn't recall any fire involving her brother's memorabilia. One other country star Stewart apparently didn't care for: Reba McEntire. As Kim Willingham recalled, "We go in this hotel room one day and there's some magazines laying there and one of them had Reba McEntire on the front of it. Gary goes, 'Oh, Rita, that cunt.'" It appears Stewart didn't care for the way he thought McEntire treated her band (the author has no evidence regarding such claims). Gary apologized to Kim for his salty language.

17
JOEY

Interviews: Shannon Ashburn, Mary Lou Stewart, Jimmy Smith, Tommy Schwartz, Laurie Rastrelli, Gina Stewart, Jo Ann Gregory, Grandal Stewart, Trampas Stewart, Gail Stewart, Fred Bogert, Randy Toman, Stan Spence, Larry "Mouse" Munson, Dave Brooks, Bill Hardman, other sources.

"Gary Joseph 'Joey'...in his hand, Ericsson said": "Son of Country Music Star Dies," *St. Lucie News Tribune*, February 14, 1988.

18
DARK PLACE

Interviews: Gary Stewart, Mary Lou Stewart, Shannon Ashburn, Jo Ann Ramsey, Frank Scott, Larry Sloven, Grandal Stewart, Steve Hinson, Tanya Tucker, Fred Bogert, Bill Hardman, Carla Hunter, Ray Wilburn, Tommy Schwartz, Dean Dillon, Sonny Tackett, Jay Haskett, Steve Hunter, Carla Hunter, Joseph Peavy, Delores Kennedy, Nick Stewart, Steve Hinson, Barbara Anne Peters, other sources.

A note on the diary passages: Mary Lou had offered me use of her diaries when I was working on my first article about Gary in 1987. I didn't rely on them then, but encouraged her to keep writing. It was a jolt thirty-five years later to see a passage that began with "Jimmy McDonica [sic] always told me I should keep a journal on my life with Gary. I have always hated to write." I feel she gave me permission to use this material. Gary's brief diaries from his early years in the music business (used earlier in the book) contained just factual dates and events, so I felt no qualms about including this material. **"They call me...anybody but himself":** Jerry Lee Lewis to Elaine Dundy, *Ferriday Louisiana: Portrait of a Remarkable American Town That Can Boast of the Likes of Jimmy Swaggart, Jerry Lee Lewis, Mickey Gilley, Howard K. Smith, and General Claire Chennault* (Donald I. Fine, 1991). **"The**

people at...want to hear'": Gary Stewart to Bob Allen, "Gary Stewart: A Different Perspective," *Country Song Roundup*, September 1990. **"I went from...sharps and flats!":** Stewart to Allen, "Gary Stewart." **Oermann put *Brand New*:** "Country's Countdown for '88: The Best of the Year," *The Tennessean*, December 31, 1988. **"If there's any... it's Gary Stewart":** Robert K. Oermann, "Gary Stewart Doesn't Have Time for the Pain," *The Tennessean*, April 1, 1989. **"That mother could sing...right there, son":** Gary Stewart to Bob Allen, February 27, 1990. **Order of protection:** St. Lucie County Court, case # 88 955 FR-11, August 25, 1988.

19
HONKY-TONK BANDITS

Interviews: Gary Stewart, Mary Lou Stewart, Richard McCroan, Terry Porter, James Willingham, Randy Toman, Steve Palousek, Jeff Williams, Dickie Taylor, Dick Dunn, Craig Turley, Kirk West, Curtis Randall, Randy Woolery, Barbara Worthy, Tim Worthy, Steve Hunter, Nick Stewart, "Boogie" Bob Melton, Gina Stewart, Joe Bielinksi, Shannon Ashburn, Kim Willingham, Jimmy Smith, Laurie Rastrelli, Tommy Schwartz, Ardell Taylor, other sources.

Gary's band lineups from the early nineties onward get extremely convoluted. Apologies for any errors; corrections welcomed. **"There wasn't a...peek at him":** Charles Dixon to Ked Sanders, "Stars Align for Jenkins Festival," *Mountain Eagle*, September 3, 2008. **"Had Jesse James...called a terrorist":** T.J. Stiles, *Jesse James: Last Rebel of the Civil War* (Vintage, 2002). **"Less than 1 percent...actually become addicted":** 1998 Purdue Pharma marketing video. **Details about the Purdue Pharma conviction:** Purdue Pharma: "2007 Guilty Plea," *Wikipedia*. **Luyao hung jury, 2006 manslaughter, fifty-year sentence:** Derek Simmonsen, "US FL: 'Saddened' Luyao Gets 50-Year Prison Term," *Press Journal*, April 29, 2006. **Luyao verdict overturned:** "US Judge Shows Mercy to 85-Year-Old Fil-Am Doctor Convicted of Drug Crimes," *GMA News*, January 26, 2013. **"From 2000 to 2010...89.2 million in 2010":** Brian D. Sites et al., "Increases in the Use of Prescription Opioid Analgesics and the Lack of Improvement in Disability Metrics Among Users," *Regional Anesthesia & Pain Medicine* 39, no. 1 (2014):6–12.

20
FIND ME

Interviews: Gary Stewart, Mary Lou Stewart, Shannon Ashburn, Royce Ashburn, Johnny Shepherd, Bill Hardman, Tommy Schwartz, Lee Schwartz, Terry Porter, James Willingham, Kim Willingham, Randy Toman, Curtis Randall, Thomas Pablo, Teresa McCandless, Jo Ann Gregory, Jimmy Smith, Ardell Taylor, Tanya Tucker, Lisa Sutton, Bill Hall, Tina Corley, other sources.

"There is [sic] worse things...": Billie Jean Horton, *Honky Tonk Blues: Hank Williams*, 2005 documentary. Directed, produced, and written by Morgan Neville. **"The sleek Cadillac...of his voice":** Charles Chupp, "One Discordant Note," I Got No Reason to Lie (column), *De Leon Free Press*, November 20, 2003. **"The Fort Pierce...to your request":** Jocelyn Gephardt, records specialist, *City of Fort Pierce*, email, March 26, 2024. When Tommy Schwartz arrived at Gary's house the day he died, he noticed a package sitting on the porch behind the police tape. It was from me. On our last phone call Gary had asked for a copy of my Neil Young biography *Shakey*. For the record, there have been individuals who have committed suicide via doxepin. Arnold Friedman, convicted of child abuse in a case examined by the 2003 documentary *Capturing the Friedmans*, intentionally overdosed on the drug while in prison in 1995. "*Capturing the Friedmans* (TV) Summary," paleycenter.org.

epilogue

SOMEWHERE IN TIME

Interviews: Shannon Ashburn, Royce Ashburn, Tina Corley, Bill Hardman, Jimmy Smith, Gina Stewart, other sources.

"In their quest...they ruined it": Steve Hinson, Facebook post, February 10, 2025. **"Where do I...be shut down":** Yee Y., Taylor Correctional Institution Yelp review, January 15, 2020. Jessica Blankenship, executive director of the Kentucky Music Hall of Fame, who got Gary Stewart into the museum, called Shannon one day all excited that she'd found an album signed by Gary to put in the display case for his upcoming October 2024 induction. When Shannon and I saw a photo of this acquisition we realized Gary had autographed the album to one of the doctors he scored drugs from, we both felt it was an appropriate addition.

Some of the material in this book appeared in my *Village Voice* article "Honky-Tonk Man: Up and Down the Lost Highway with Gary Stewart" in their *Rock & Roll Quarterly* supplement, Spring 1988.

BIBLIOGRAPHY

Carvello, Dorothy. *Anything for a Hit: An A&R Woman's Story of Surviving the Music Industry.* Chicago Review Press, 2018. **Caudill, Harry M.** *Night Comes to the Cumberlands: A Biography of a Depressed Area.* Little, Brown, 1962. **Cash, W. J.** *The Mind of the South.* Vintage, 1941. **Cooper, Deborah Adams.** *Images of America: Letcher County.* Arcadia Publishing, 2011. **Country Music Hall of Fame.** *The Encyclopedia of Country Music.* Michael McCall, John Rumble, and Paul Kingsbury, editors. Oxford University Press, 2012. **Dickerson, James L.** *Mojo Triangle: Birthplace of Country, Blues, Jazz and Rock n' Roll.* Schirmer Trade Books, 2005. **Dickerson, James L.** *Chips Moman: The Record Producer Whose Genius Changed American Music.* Sartoris Literary Group, 2020. **Ely, Macel, II.** *Ain't No Grave: The Life and Legacy of Brother Claude Ely.* Dust-to-Digital, 2010. **Feiler, Bruce.** *Dreaming Out Loud: Garth Brooks, Wynonna Judd, Wade Hates and the Changing Face of Nashville.* Spike Books, 1998. **Freeman, Scott.** *Midnight Riders: The Story of the Allman Brothers Band.* Little, Brown. 1995. **Hayes, Mickey.** *My Life on the Road with David Allan Coe: The Early Years.* Self-published, 2021. **Jessings, Waylon, with Lenny Kaye.** *Waylon: An Autobiography.* Warner Books, 1996. **Johnson, Larry.** *Historic Photos of Outlaws of the Old West.* Turner Publishing Company, 2010. **Kaserman, James, and Sarah Kaserman.** *Florida Pirates: From the Southern Gulf Coast to the Keys and Beyond.* History Press, 2001. **Malone, Bill C.** *Don't Get Above Your Raisin': Country Music and the Southern Working Class.* University of Illinois Press, 2002. **Monroe, Gary.** *The Highwaymen: Florida's African-American Landscape Painters.* University Press of Florida, 2001. **Nager, Larry.** *Memphis Beat: The Lives and Times of America's Musical Crossroads.* St. Martin's Press, 1998. **Pride, Charley, with Jim Henderson.** *Pride: The Charley Pride Story.* Quill, 1994. **Rodriguez, Johnny, with Austin Teutsch.** *Desperado: A Piece of My Soul.* Independently published, 2023 **Stiles, T. J.** *Jesse James: Last Rebel of the Civil War.* Vintage, 2002. **Stoll, Steven.** *Ramp Hollow: The Ordeal of Appalachia.* Hill and Wang, 2017. **Tillis, Mel, with Walter Wager.** *Stutterin' Boy: The Autobiography of Mel Tillis, America's Beloved Star of Country Music.* Rawson Associates, 1984. **Tucker, Tanya, with Patsi Bale Cox.** *Nickel Dreams: My Life.* Hyperion, 1997. **Williams, Ada Coats.** *Images of America: Fort Pierce.* Arcadia Publishing, 2003. **Wilson, Jean Ellen.** *Legendary Locals of Fort Pierce.* Arcadia Publishing, 2014. **Wolfe, Charles K.** *Kentucky Country.* University Press of Kentucky, 1982.

DISCOGRAPHY

This is a bare-bones discography. For instance, no reissue singles are listed, nor are writing credits, producers, session players or place of recording. Country chart positions for the singles are listed in brackets. Songs with an asterisk indicate works Gary either wrote or cowrote. Dates of recordings mentioned in the book are from RCA session sheets. Release dates are (mostly) courtesy the online database I have found most reliable, SecondHandSongs, and other sources. Corrections are welcome.

STUDIO ALBUMS

OUT OF HAND—Drinkin' Thing/Honky-Tonkin'/I See The Want To in Your Eyes/This Old Heart Won't Let Go/Draggin' Shackles/She's Actin' Single (I'm Drinkin' Doubles)/Back Sliders Wine/Sweet Country Red/Out Of Hand/Williamson County*. (RCA Victor APL1-0900) January 1975.

YOU'RE NOT THE WOMAN YOU USED TO BE—You're Not the Woman You Used to Be*/Sweet-Tater and Cisco*/Here Comes That Feeling Again*/Big Bertha, the Truck Driving Queen*/Little Old Love Light*/Merry-Go-Round*/You're Everything (God Meant Woman to Be)*/The Snuff Queen*/Lesser of Two Evils*/Caffein, Nicotine, Benzedrine. (MCA 488) August 1975.

STEPPIN' OUT—Flat Natural Born Good-Timin' Man*/Quits/Trudy/I Still Can't Believe You're Gone/Lord What A Woman*/Oh Sweet Temptation*/If You've Got the Money (I've Got the Time)/(I Can't Be) Your Backdoor/Hank Western*/Easy People*/In Some Room Above the Street. (RCA Victor APL1-1225) January 1976.

YOUR PLACE OR MINE—Your Place Or Mine/Rachel/Leah/Drinking Again/The Blue Ribbon Blues/Pretend I Never Happened/I Had to Get Drunk Last Night/I Ain't Living Long Like This/Broken Hearted People/Ten Years of This*/Dancing Eyes*. (RCA Victor APL1-2199) April 1977.

LITTLE JUNIOR—Whiskey Trip/Little Junior*/Stone Wall (Around Your Heart)/Can't You See/Single Again*/Tequila After Midnight/I Got Mine/If My Eyes Touch You/Honky-Tonkin'/You're Running Wild. (RCA Victor APL1-2779) April 1978.

GARY—Mazelle/Shady Streets/Next Thing You Know/Everything a Good Little Girl Needs*/The Same Man/The Blues Don't Care Who's Got 'em/I've Just Seen the Rock of Ages/Walkaway/Lost Highway/One More*. (RCA Victor AHL1-3288) February 1979.

CACTUS AND A ROSE—Okeechobee Purple/Cactus and a Rose/Staring Each Other Down/Lover's Knot/Ghost Train/Roarin'/Harlan County Highway*/Are We Dreamin' the Same Dream/How Could We Come to This After That/We Just Couldn't Make It as Friends. (RCA Victor AHL1-3627) July 1980.

GARY'S GREATEST—Drinkin' Thing/Out of Hand/She's Actin' Single (I'm Drinkin' Doubles)/Flat Natural Born Good-Timin' Man*/Quits/Ten Years of This*/Whiskey Trip/Single Again*/Your Place or Mine/Let's Forget That We're Married*. (RCA Victor AHL1-3981) May 1981.

BROTHERLY LOVE (with Dean Dillon)—Brotherly Love*/Cold Turkey (Gary solo)/You to Come Home To (Dean solo)/Honky Tonk Crazy/Body Shop (Gary solo)/Suburban Life/Play This Old Working Day Away (Dean solo)/She Sings Amazing Grace (Gary solo)/Firewater Friends/Let's Start a War (Dean solo). (RCA Victor MHL1-8602) April 1982.

THOSE WERE THE DAYS (with Dean Dillon)—Those Were the Days*/Misfits*/Hard Time for Lovers/Living on the Ragged Edge/Losers and Lovers/Smokin' in the Rockies (Note: not a full-length album). (RCA Victor MHL1-8602) February 1984.

BRAND NEW—Brand New Whiskey*/Son of a Honky Tonk Woman*/I Owe It All to My Heart*/Lucretia*/An Empty Glass*/Rainin' Rainin' Rainin'*/Looking for Some Brand New Stuff/Ramona*/I Get Drunk/Murdered by Love. (HighTone HT-8014) November 1988.

BATTLEGROUND—Nothin' but a Woman/Bedroom Battleground/Let's Go Jukin'*/Nothing Cheap About a Cheap Affair*/Ol' Hank's Lovesick Blues/Woman In Demand/Hey Leona/You're the Reason I'm Living/Delia/Seeing's Believing. (HighTone HT-8023) August 1990.

I'M A TEXAN—Come On In/I'm a Texan/Stompin' Grounds/Hand Me Another/Draggin' Leather/It's True*/Honky-Tonk Hardwood Floor/Dark End of the Street/Make It a Double/One Night/Those Memories/Two More Fools. (HighTone HT-8050) October 1993.

LIVE ALBUMS

IN CONCERT—Gary appears on one track: Out of Hand. (RCA– CPL2-1014) 1975

LIVE FROM GILLEY'S—Gary Stewart with the Toman Brothers Band: Louisiana Man (Randy Toman singing)/Honky-Tonkin'/Drinkin' Thing/I Had to Get Drunk Last Night/Rachel/Backslider's Wine/Little Junior/Leah/Flat Natural Born Good-Timin' Man*/Cactus and a Rose. Rest of the cuts are by Ernest Tubb. (Westwood One 81-4) 1981.

LIVE FROM GILLEY'S—Gary Stewart with the Toman Brothers Band: Honky-Tonkin'/Drinkin' Thing/Out of Hand/She's Actin' Single (I'm Drinkin' Doubles). The rest of the cuts are by Moe Bandy. (Westwood One LG 83-35) 1983.

THE SILVER EAGLE CROSS COUNTRY RADIO SHOW—Gary Stewart with Dean Dillon: Livin' On The Ragged Edge*/Hard Times for Lovers*/Mom and Dad's Waltz/Those Were the Days*/Smokin' in the Rockies.* The rest of the cuts are by George Jones. (ABC Radio Networks SE 078) 1983.

LIVE AT BILLY BOB'S TEXAS—Little Junior*/Flat Natural Born Good-Timin' Man*/Whiskey Trip/An Empty Glass*/She's Actin' Single (I'm Drinkin' Doubles)/I See the Want to in Your Eyes/Out Of Hand/Ten Years Of This*/Quits/Drinkin' Thing/In Some Room Above the Street/Single Again*/Your Place or Mine/Are We Dreamin' the Same Dream/Brand New Whiskey. (Smith Music 5015) March 2003.

GUEST APPEARANCES

FAMILY ALBUM, David Allan Coe, 1977. Gary makes an uncredited appearance singing a verse of the Coe song "Bad Impressions."

LET'S GET TOGETHER/THE COLLECTORS VOLUME I, Dickey Betts and Great Southern, 1991. Gary is credited with "Field Hollers" on the track "Willie and Po' Bob." Note: Gary also contributed to the 1979 Betts album "Night," as yet unreleased.

GRANDMA'S ROADHOUSE, Riley, 2010 (recorded approximately 1970): Grandma's Roadhouse*/Picture/Daddy's Come Home/Daddy's Come Home/Love, Love You Lady*/Listen to My Song/You Been Cheatin' on Me Honey/Easy People*/Field of Green/Drinkin' Them Squeezins*/Funky Tar Paper Shack/Grandma's Roadhouse alternate-digital only/

Gotta Get Away-digital only. Gary contributes songs, vocals, guitar, harmonica, and piano to this album.

COLLECTIONS

20 OF THE BEST (RCA NL 89372/Germany) 1984. **BEST OF THE HIGHTONE YEARS** (Shout Factory 8141) 2002. **ALL AMERICAN COUNTRY** (SBME Special Mkts) 2003. **GARY'S GREATEST** (WEA/Atlantic/Rhino/HighTone) 2006. **THE ESSENTIAL GARY STEWART** 2007. **RCA COUNTRY LEGENDS** October 2011. **THE ESSENTIAL** (Sony digital) 2015 (highly recommended by the author).

CD TWOFER REISSUES

BROTHERLY LOVE/THOSE WERE THE DAYS (Raven) 2007. **OUT OF HAND/YOUR PLACE OR MINE** (Morello) 2013. **OUT OF HAND/BRAND NEW** (Floating World) 2013. **I'M A TEXAN/BATTLEGROUND** (Floating World) 2013

SINGLES

I Love You Truly/Walk On Boy (Cory) 1964. **Merry-Go-Round*/Here Comes That Feeling Again*** (Kapp, K934) 1968. **Sweet-Tater and Cisco*/Little Old Love Light*** (Kapp, K2008) **You're Not the Woman You Use to Be*/The Snuff Queen*** (Kapp, K2089). **She's the Next Best Thing*/Something to Believe In*** (Decca, 32880). **Ramblin' Man/Williamson County*** (RCA, APB0-0144) 1973 [#63]. **The Lesser of Two Evils*/Big Bertha the Truck Driving Queen*** (Kapp, K2065). **Drinkin' Thing/I See the Want To in Your Eyes** (RCA, APB0-0281) 1974. **Drinkin' Thing/I See the Want To in Your Eyes** (RCA, APB0-0035) (piano overdub version) 1974 [#10]. **Out of Hand/Draggin' Shackles*** (RCA, PB-1061) 1974 [#4]. **She's Actin' Single (I'm Drinkin' Doubles)/Williamson County*** (RCA, PB-10222) 1975 [#1]. **You're Not the Woman You Use to Be*/I Owe It All to Mama*** (MCA, 40414) 1975 [#15]. **Flat Natural Good-Timin' Man*/This Old Heart Won't Let Go** (RCA, PB-10351) 1975 [#20]. **Oh, Sweet Temptation/Hank Western*** (RCA, PB-10550) 1976 [#23]. **In Some Room Above the Street/Easy People*** (RCA, PB-10680) 1976 [#15]. **Your Place or Mine/Lord, What a Woman*** (RCA, PB-10833) 1976 [#11]. **Ten Years of This*/I Ain't Living Long Like This** (RCA, PB-10957) 1977 [#16]. **Quits/Dancing Eyes*** (RCA, PB-11131) 1976 [#26]. **Whiskey Trip/Williamson County*** (RCA, PB-11224) 1978 [#16]. **Single Again*/Little Junior*** (RCA, PB-11297) 1978 [#36]. **Stone Wall (Around Your Heart)/I Got Mine** (RCA, PB-11416) 1978 [#41]. **Shady Streets/Everything a Good Little Girl Needs*** (RCA, PB-11534) 1979 [#66]. **Mazelle/One More*** (RCA, PB-11623) 1979 [#75]. **Cactus and a Rose/Staring Each Other Down** (RCA, PB-11960) 1980 [#48] **Roarin'/Are We Dreaming the Same Dream** (RCA, PB-12081) 1980 [#66]. **Let's Forget That We're Married*/Honky-Tonk Man*** (RCA, PB-12203) 1981 [#72]. **She's Got a Drinking Problem/Memories Swim in Whiskey** (RCA, PB-12343) 1981 [#36]. **Brotherly Love*/Firewater Friends*** (RCA, PB 13049) 1982 [#41]. **She Sings Amazing Grace/Cold Turkey** (RCA, PB-13261) 1982 [#83]. **Those Were the Days/Drinkin' Thing** (RCA, PB-13401) 1982 [#47]. **Smokin' in the Rockies*/Hard Time for Lovers*** (RCA, PB-13472) [#71]. **Hey, Bottle of Whiskey/Roadhouse Romances** (Red Ash, RAS-8403-1 NSD) 1984 [#75]. **I Got a Bad Attitude/Life's a Game*** (Red Ash, RAS-8406-NSD) 1984 [#64]. **Red Georgia Clay/Leaona *** (Red Ash, RAS-8410) 1984. **Brand New Whiskey*/Son of a Honky-Tonk Woman*** (HighTone 506) 1988 [#63]. **An Empty Glass*/Lucretia*** (HighTone 507) 1988 [#64]. **Rainin', Rainin', Rainin'*/I Get Drunk** (HighTone 509) 1989 [#77]. **Let's Go Jukin'*/Let's Go Jukin'*** (HighTone 601) 1990. **Nothin' but a Woman/Nothin' but a Woman** (HighTone 602) 1990. **Baby I Need Your Lovin'/Yester-Me, Yester-You, Yesterday** (Delmore, DEO-28) 2018. **I'm Guilty*** (Singing Hearts) 2025, 1992 recording.

UNRELEASED/OUTTAKES

The Tom Cats (Uncle Jake Tape, circa 1959): Let the Good Times Roll/Johnny B. Good/Shortnin' Bread/Lonely Weekends/Is a Blue Bird Blue/ three instrumentals. **Wagon Wheel Radio Show:** The Fugitive/Charlotte (Bill Eldridge lead vocal)*/Let's Forget That I'm Married*/ Hello Josphine. **Live at The Wagon Wheel:** Working on a Railroad/Here Comes That Feeling Again*/Joe and Mable's 12th Street Bar and Grill/Last Thing on My Mind/Susie Q (note: crude, 18-minute tape). **Cedarwood demos:** Kings and Queens*/Big Bad Train*/ I've Been Known to Get a Little Stoned*/ Nothing Left to Do but Say Goodbye*/Mark My Words*/Spare Me*/Let's Forget That I'm Married*/There Goes the Girl*/A Woman Can Tear the Heart Out of a Man*/Have You Forgotten*. **Forrest Hills demos:** The Poor Hand*/She's All I Live For*/Forever On*/Her Apple Pie*/Once More*/Our Love*/She's a Woman Alone*/Three Fingers High*/Tonight We're Drunk*/Brewer's Art*/A Bigger Man Than Me*/It Takes Me All Night Long*/Your Secrets*/99 Bottles*/You Can't Housebreak a Tomcat*/Living the Life of Dog*/Californy*/ Every Day*/If You Come Back Darlin'*/My Woman Knows*/What Kind of Love Is This*/ There's a Whole Lot About a Woman (A Man Don't Know)*/Morbid the Great*/My Lips Are on Hers*/Something's Always Coming Between Us*/Big Jet Plane*/Gold Barstool*/ Snuff Queen (demo)*/Putt Putt Here, Putt Putt There*. **Early Nashville tapes:** Williamson County*/Ballad of Corsey and John*/Beautiful River*. **Motown demos still unreleased:** I Can't Help Myself (Sugar Pie Honey Bunch). **Early RCA unreleased:** Red Necks, White Socks and Blue Ribbon Beer/I Love You/She's Actin' Single alternate/I'm Ready/Woman in Demand/Play It Boys/I Love You/Easy People* alternates 1&2/Blue Ribbon Blues alternate. **Bradley's Barn session with Rockfish Railroad:** Hollywood*/Stella Mae*/Let It Burn*/4th of July*/Bedtime Stories*/Hollywood*/Ballad of Corsia and John*. **Later RCA unreleased:** Who You Been Givin' It To*/How Could We Come to This After That*/Where Does a Rolling Stone Go*/Harlan County Highway (demo)*/ Devil's Triangle (demo)/Devil's Triangle (RCA version)/Riders in the Rain/Single Again (demo)*/Running Wild (demo)/East Virgina Blues/Lovelight/This Boy's Leavin' Town*/ Shoulda Coulda*/If This Is the Last Time/Silver Cloud*. **Gary Stewart/Dean Dillon unreleased:** Blue Monday/Mom And Dad's Waltz/I Had the Best Thing Going (But the Best Thing I Had Is Gone)*/Smooth Shot of Whiskey*/Heartbreak Haven*. **1980s–2003 unreleased:** Moonshine Mountain*/A Touch of You*/If You Can't Use It Give It Back*/You Can't Make Me What I Ain't Out of What I Am*/Champagne World*/ Hand Me Another/Man on the Run/Torture/ All the Boys Want to Dance With Barbara*/ I'm Guilty*/Born a Rebel*/Baby You're So Square/Long Black Veil (heavy metal version)/ He's History*/Moonshine Mountain*/Spanish Harlem/C.C. Rider/ No Expectations/Leave the Note/Wild Horses/Six Days on the Road/ Ride on a Tear Drop*/She's Takin' Me Down*/ Jesse's Last Ride* /It's True*/In The Pines/.

Note: There are many, many demos of the HighTone material, including Empty Glass*/ Rainin', Rainin', Rainin'*/Let's Go Jukin'*/ Son of a Honky Tonk Woman.* Various other live tapes exist, the bulk of which are from the 1990s–2000s. Some of these outtakes (with notes by me) can be heard at: https://bynwr.com/ posts/gary-stewart

This list is by no means complete as unreleased songs still are surfacing...

INDEX

A

"A Woman Will Tear the Heart Out of a Man" 110, 121
"A Woman's Intuition" 487
Aberdeen Rockfish Railroad; Rockfish Railroad; Rockfish 208-210, 216-217, 221, 225-228, 249, 385, 529
AC/DC (band) 227
Ace of Hearts Records 374
Acuff-Rose Music 275
The Addams Family (TV) 356
AFM Local 257 148
All About Eve (film) 14
"Alley-Oop" 86, 320n
Allman Brothers Band, the; Allman Brothers; Allmans 19, 61, 81, 132-133, 139, 144, 167-168, 171, 182, 249-250, 258, 266-273 (also: 267n, 273n), 279, 332, 351, 374, 433n, 437, 438, 514, 517, 525
Allman, Duane 132, 276
Allman, Gregg 167-168, 242, 258 (also: 258n), 266-271, 273, 275-276, 279, 280, 287, 377, 516
Alvin, Dave 413n
Akeman, David "Stringbean" 47
American Sound Studio 147, 153, 264
AMI jukebox 97
"An Empty Glass" 312, 334, 360, 377, 418, 421, 488, 492n, 527-528
Anderson, Carol and Mary Beth 201, 212, 212n, 281, 518, 520
Anderson, John 360, 377, 486
Anderson, Lynn 155, 491
Anderson, Tommy 57
"The Appalachian Project" (FB group) 46n, 516
"Are We Dreamin' the Same Dream" 275, 279, 280, 526
Armstrong, Louis 119
Ashburn, Royce 75, 90, 243, 411, 472 (also: 472n), 479, 486-487, 489, 490-493 (also: 490n), 497-498, 500-503, 506-507, 510, 517, 519, 524, 525
Ashburn, Shannon (Shannon Doah' Stewart) 25, 30, 32-35, 38, 40, 51, 56, 68, 90, 126, 144, 184-185, 208, 219-220, 239, 243, 258n, 259, 270, 278, 285, 296, 300, 306-307, 346-349, 352-354, 362n, 365-368, 372-373, 395-407, 410-411, 416, 425-426, 440, 446, 453, 461-463, 465, 472 (also: 472n), 478-495, 497-498 (also: 497n), 500-507, 510, 514-525
Asleep at the Wheel 216, 482
Austin City Limits (TV) 287-288, 311
Austin Municipal Auditorium 21
Austin, Robert and Judy 364-365, 522
Autumn Records 244

B

Baez, Joan 119
Baird, Ronnie 73, 78, 516
Baker's Flamingo Grill 72, 99
Bakker, Tammy Faye 320n
"The Ballad of Corsia and John" 133, 209, 529
Bananas (club) 251
Bandy, Moe 313-315, 527
Barber, Ed "The Suitcase" 73-74, 278
Battaglia, Robert 298-299, 521
Battlefield Trailer Park 119, 134
Battleground (album) 427, 527, 528
Beamsturfer, Cecil 82
"Beautiful River" 133, 529
Bell, Kenny 415
Bell, William 133
Ben-Gay incident 435
Bendectin 246
Benihana 236
Benton, Barbi 178
Benton, Thomas Hart 378
Bear Family Records 373
Berinati, Lea Jane 155, 199
Berry, Chuck 64, 85, 91, 100, 141
Betts, Dickey 168, 201-202, 251, 258, 266-273, 273n, 275-277, 279, 351, 352n, 377, 379, 390, 398, 405, 427, 438, 514, 520, 527
The Beverly Hillbillies (TV) 33
Bielinski, Joe 448
Bic razor incident 450
"Big Bertha, the Truck Driving Queen" 121, 133, 254, 526, 528
"Big Train" 109
Billy Bob's 23, 364-365, 366, 437, 439-440, 464 (also: 464n), 482n, 491, 493, 527
Billy Jack (film) 134, 517
Bin Laden 372
Bindas, Julie 258, 280
Bishop, Hayward 152
Blasters, the 413 (also: 413n)
Bloody Bucket Bar 65
Blonde Venus (film) 374
Bloomin' Onion 24
"The Blue Ribbon Blues" 221, 526, 529
"Blue Suede Shoes" 83
Bluegrass Parkway 424
Blueshammer 419
Bogert, Fred 79-80, 116n, 169-173, 175, 193-194, 377, 397, 406, 415, 518, 523
"Body Shop" 320, 526
Bonds, Gary U.S. 100
Boone, Daniel 49, 516
Boot Heel Records 117
Borchers, Bobby 320
"Born a Rebel" 378, 529

Boss Chorus (pedal) 174
Bourke, Rory 212
Box Tops, the 160
Braddock, Bobby 482n
Bradley, Jerry 115-117, 119-120, 122-123, 129, 133, 135, 143-145, 154, 162, 165, 167, 173-174, 181, 188, 199, 200, 204-205, 206, 207, 210, 261, 265, 267, 291n, 293, 311, 313, 314, 315, 317, 322, 324, 334, 341-342, 358, 377, 379, 517, 518, 520, 521
Bradley, Harold 115-116, 117n, 154-155, 157, 247, 358, 517
Bradley, Owen 115, 116n, 119, 120n, 123, 128-131, 148, 154n, 155-156 (also: 156n), 173, 183
Bradley's Barn 119, 121, 126-129, 134, 157, 168, 208-209, 249, 255, 257n, 388, 529
Bramlett, Bonnie 268-269, 271-272, 279, 514, 520
Brand New (album) 326, 334, 415-424, 427, 524, 527, 528
"Brand New Whiskey" 377, 418, 421, 527, 528
Breyers (ice cream) 185, 353, 489
Briggs, David (Nashville) 108, 130, 146, 148, 152-153, 154n, 156 (also: 156n), 163, 212, 247, 358, 415, 427, 517, 518
Briggs, David (California) 420 (also: 420n)
Briggs, Mel 98, 100, 103, 517
"Broken Hearted People (Take Me to a Barroom)" 222-223, 526
Broken Spoke, the 439n
Bromberg, Bruce 413
Brooks & Dunn 418
"Brotherly Love" 319-320
Brotherly Love (album) 311, 315, 318-322, 324, 333, 526, 528
Brown, Ronnie and Donny 82 (also: 82n)
Browning, Tod 47
Buck Jones Bar 73
Buckley's Discount Record Shop 91
Buffett, Jimmy 246, 278, 316
Burch, Fred 107-110, 115-116, 517
Burnette, Billy 275
Burns, Rusty 435 (also: 435n)
Buttrey, Kenny 108, 152
Bynum, Hal 359

C

Cabooze, the (club) 251
Cadillac Coupe DeVille 360
"Cactus and a Rose" 273, 436, 493, 526-528
Cactus and a Rose (album) 265-267 (also: 266n), 273, 275-282, 285, 293, 311, 520, 526
Caldwell, Toy 246
Cale, J.J. 119, 152, 222
Cannon, Buddy 15, 326, 329, 330-332, 337, 415, 515, 521
"Can't You See" 246, 526
Cargill, Doug 236, 239 (also: 239n)
Carlos 'n Charlie's (club) 252
Carlton, Kim 35-36, 39-40, 43, 76n, 239n, 301-302, 515-516, 519, 521
Carlton, Walter Lee 40, 75-79, 114-115, 236-237, 239n, 301 (also: 301n), 514
Carr, James 379
Carr, Patrick 191-192, 208, 328, 441n, 519, 521
Carrigan, Jerry 130, 152-153, 157, 266, 517
Carson, Martha 60, 354
Carson, Wayne 160-162, 185, 199, 201, 209, 223, 246, 248, 314, 377n, 518
Carter, A. P. 50
Carter, Pat 356-358
Casey, Brenda 31-34, 36, 38, 53-55, 133, 134n, 300, 372n, 373, 511, 515, 517, 521-522
Casses, Chris 208, 217
Caudill, Harry M. 52, 516, 525
Cayce, Edgar 47
Cedarwood Publishing 107, 109-110, 115, 221, 529
Center City Tavern 505
"Champagne World" 76n, 529
Chappell Music 212
"Charlotte North Carolina" 117
Cheetos 500
Chevrolet Styleline Special Business Coupe 200
Chiclets 352
Chilton, Alex 19, 160
Clark, Guy 221-222
Clark, Larry 383, 385 (also: 385n)
Clash, the 19
Clooney, Rosemary 47
Coal Miner's Daughter (film) 316
Cobain, Kurt 15
Coe, David Allan 107, 212, 222, 255, 332-333 (also: 333n), 525, 527
"Cold Turkey" 320 (also: 320n), 526, 528
Coldwater Cattle Company (club) 251
Cole, Jack 231
Coleman, Donnie 208, 385-386, 522, 523
Coleman, Joe 492
Coleman, Ron 291
Collins, Joan 72
Collins, Nick 105
Collins, Tommy 140
Colter, Jessi 189, 207-208
"Come On In" 428, 527
Conlee, John 161
Conley, Arthur 108
Consolidation Coal Company 51, 56-57, 60
Cooder, Ry 247-248
Cooke Duet, the; the Singing Cookes 61
Corley, Tina 493, 501, 524-525
Cory Records 107
"Cotton-Eyed Joe" 19
Country Music Hall of Fame 20, 313, 334, 343, 511, 517-518, 520-521

Country Music Highway (Kentucky) 457
Coupland Dancehall 440, 454, 455n
Cowboy Western Club 443
Cowboys & Indians (magazine) 442
Cowboys Dancehall 432
Crazy Horse (band) 17, 420
Crazy Horse (person) 473, 484
Creedence Clearwater Revival 128-129
Crockett, Charley 190, 518
Crowe, J. D. 47
Crown Royal 424
Crowell, Rodney 220-222 (also: 220n), 251, 519
Cureton, Steve 213, 290, 518
Cutters (nightclub) 434

D

Dalton, Lacy J. 291n
Dan McCarty High School 84
Dance Town USA (club) 251-252
"Dancing Eyes" 221, 229, 526, 528
Danielle (port wine) 463
Dann, Maury (character) 264
Darin, Bobby 427
Dave & Sugar 205, 326n
Davis, Clive 328 (also: 328n)
Davis, Jesse Ed 89
Davis, John Wesley 75, 78-81, 516
Davis, Polly 75-76, 79-81 (also: 80n), 300, 516, 521
Davis, Skeeter 47, 122, 147, 317
Dawson, Darrell 99, 169, 208, 217, 249-251, 517, 519
Dawson, David 247, 313, 319, 337, 512, 521-522
Dawson, Jinx 517
Day, Jimmy 246
D.B.M. Studios 130
Dea, Roy 138-150 (also: 142n, 143n), 152-157, 160-161 (also: 161n), 163-165, 168-169 (also: 168n), 173-175 (also: 173n), 177-178 (also: 177n), 185-192, 195, 199-200, 202-203, 206, 210, 212, 221, 225, 244-248, 258, 260-261 (also: 261n), 265-266 (also: 266n), 278, 282, 289n, 291-292, 298, 311, 318, 341, 356-358, 360-361 (also: 360n), 376-377, 379n, 382, 384-385, 412-416, 419, 421, 427-429 (also: 428n), 511, 514, 517-520, 522-523
Dee, Lenny 387
Delaney & Bonnie 273
Deleonibus, Dottie 247
"Delia" 377, 527
DeShannon, Jackie 47
De Sousa, Mia 252-253, 511, 519
Dickel, George 273
Dickens, Little Jimmy 63, 120, 122
Dietrich, Marlene 374
Diggs, Charles A. 496 (also: 496n)
Dillon, Dean; Dean Dalton 150, 293, 310-316 (also: 313n), 318-335 (also: 326n, 333n, 334n), 337-340 (also: 340n), 341n, 343, 356, 361, 378-379, 418-419, 514, 521-523, 526-527, 529
Dimebag Darrell 476
Dinah! (TV) 178
Dinning, Mark 108
Dirty Cop No Donut (film) 72
Dixon, Charles 457, 524
Dottsy 138, 261n
Doucette, Thom 273
Down Home Music 413
Dr. Chek (soda) 376
"Draggin' Shackles" 167, 231, 526, 528
Drake, Roddis Franklin "Pete" 154-156, 162, 178, 186-187 (also: 187n), 212, 224-225, 358
Draughty, Buster 41
"Drinking Again" 221, 526
Dressler, Muriel Miller ("My Appalachia") 25, 515
Drifting Cowboys 17
"Drinkin' Thing" 19, 160, 162-164, 173-175, 177, 180, 182, 192, 200, 231, 288-290, 366, 381, 446, 526-528
Drugstore Cowboys 17, 127n, 226-228 (also:227n), 231, 248-249, 286, 511, 514
Duck Pub (club) 470
Duel in the Sun (film) 89
Dunn, Dick 436, 464n, 524
Durrett, Rick 134, 168, 517
Dycus, Frank 313, 320, 326, 337, 521-522
Dylan, Bob 17, 19-20, 152, 155, 225, 316, 366n, 374, 388, 515, 519

E

Earl Barton Music 160
Eason, Willie 72
"East Virginia Blues" 281-282, 291
"Easy People" 53, 128, 202-203, 223, 526-529
Easy People Band 176, 351, 352n, 380-381 (also: 380n), 422, 469-470, 482n, 488, 504
Easy People (studio) 418
Eat the Document (film) 374
Edenton, Ray 203
Edwards, Stoney 226
Eldridge, Bill 86, 103, 113-115, 116-122, 124-125, 127-135, 165, 168n, 202, 243, 350, 381, 517, 529
Electrolux vacuum cleaner 34-35
Elkhorn coalfield 52
Elkins, Ernie 57-58, 63, 515
Ely, Brother Claude 61-62, 373, 390, 516, 525
Ely, Joe 231, 288, 316n, 413
Ely, Macel, II 62, 516, 525
Emerson, "Wild" Bill 359, 374, 428
Emerson, Jody 359, 428
Emery, Ralph 83, 108, 122, 180, 516-518

Emmons, Bobby 153, 264-266, 273, 279
Emmons, Buddy 246, 433n
Empire of the Ants (film) 72
Erickson, Roky 20
Escobar, Pablo 75
Esparza, Henry 433, 449
Esquerita 180
Everly Brothers 47, 82, 248, 337
"Everything a Good Little Girl Needs" 260, 526, 528
Evil People Lounge (club) 73, 418

F

FAME Recording Studios 107, 109, 148, 152
Fan Fair 193, 314
Feathers, Charlie 292
Ferry, Bryan 20
Fireballs, the 113
"Flat Natural Born Good-Timin' Man" 198-200, 231, 246, 320, 506, 526-527
Flatt, Lester 64
Fleming, Glynn 436, 450, 464n,
Flores, Rosie 252-253, 511, 519
Florida East Coast Railway 79
Floyd, Joey 429 (also: 429n)
Flynt, Larry 47
Fogelberg, Dan 208, 316n
Folcarelli, Howard "Bingo" 169-170, 175, 249
Forensic Files (TV) 496n
Forrest Hills Music 115-119, 124, 377 (also: 377n), 379n, 417, 522, 529
Fort Pierce Hotel 172, 193, 219
Foxton, Kelly 311
Frank-N-Furter (character) 425
Frankie n' Johnnie's (club) 73, 170-172, 193, 298, 400
Frazier, Dallas 320
Fred Smith Rodeo Arena 469
Frey, Glenn 252
Fricke, David 346
Fricke, Janie 155
Frizzell, Lefty 201, 338, 383

G

Galante, Joe 145-146, 173n, 178, 317, 322-323, 334-335, 339-341, 343, 504, 517-518, 521-522
Gallagher, Robert 23, 515
Gallant, Gary 63n, 65, 515
Garland, Judy 326n
Garrish, Sonny 415
Gary (album) 257-260 (also: 257n)
Gayden, Mac 222
Geronimo Colt .45 445 (also: 445n)
"Ghost Train" 276 (also: 276n), 520, 526
Gibbs, Terri 281
Gibson ES-335 422
Gill, Vince 19, 335, 522
Gilley, Mickey 251-252, 315, 332, 523
Gilley's (club) 178, 251, 527
Gimble, Johnny 155
Gish, Thomas E. 48, 516
Glaser Brothers 125
Glaser, Tompall 207
Glock 45 (weapon) 255
"Goin' Up" 109
Gordy, Berry 129
Gosdin, Vern 320n
The Gospel Ranger Show (radio) 62
"Grandma's Roadhouse" 126-128, 527
Grandma's Roadhouse (album) 126-130, 165, 527
Grandpa Jones 47
Graves, Josh 203
Green Acres (TV) 39
Green, Roy 125-126
Greene, Jack 105, 118-199, 124, 210
Gregory, Jo Ann 37, 79, 89, 92, 93, 94, 100, 224, 302-303, 306, 395, 402, 406, 410, 417, 478, 489, 511, 515-517, 519, 521, 523-524
Griffith, Ron "Radar" 99, 217, 517, 519
Griggs, Jimmy 117
Gruene Hall 439n
Grumman (factory) 98
Guerriero, Frank 171-172
Gunsmoke (TV) 157, 313

H

Hager Brothers 61
Haisley Funeral 406
Hall, Bill 492 (also: 492n), 524
Hall, Deidre 398, 404
Hall, Tom T. 47, 261n
Hammond B-3 358
Hampton, Lionel 47
Hanging Rock 424
"Hank Western" 73n, 86, 201-202, 526, 528
Harden, Bobby 247
Hardman, Bill 71, 73-74 (also: 73n), 76, 78, 339, 405-406, 411-412, 417, 469, 480-483 (also: 158n), 486, 490, (also: 490n), 492-493, 501, 502n, 511, 516, 521, 523-525
Hargrove, Linda 333n
"Harlan County Highway" epigraph, 277-278, 283n, 378, 520, 526, 529
Harlow, Jean 326n
Harman, Buddy 152-153, 247, 291, 517
Harris, Emmylou 61, 221-222
Haskett, Jay 421-423, 425, 523
Hawkins, Dale 124
Hawkins, Ronnie 92
Haynes, Walter 120 (also: 120n), 122, 521
Haynes, Warren 273, 332-333, 415, 517
Hazelden Betty Ford Foundation; Betty Ford Center 340

Hee Haw (TV) 155, 178
Hells Angels 471
Helms, Jimmie 188 (also: 188n)
Hendrix, Jimi 276n
Henson, Cargill 321
Henson's Saloon (club) 321
"Here Comes That Feeling Again" 120, 124, 526, 528-529
Herring, John "Scooter" 266
"Hey, Bottle of Whiskey" 359, 528
Hickok, Wild Bill 432
HighTone Records 413-415 (also: 413n), 418n, 419-421, 427-428, 527-529
Higgs Drive-In 73, 91
Hillcrest Memorial Gardens 24
Hinson, Steve 139, 146-147, 150, 153-155, 161-162, 168, 174, 182, 186, 187n, 202, 223-225, 246-247, 259, 278, 312, 414, 428n, 504, 511, 517-521, 523, 525
Hogue, Gary "Breeze" 432, 434n
Holyfield, Wayland 221
"Hollywood" 209-210, 252, 286, 529
Hollywood Argyles, the 102
Honeysuckle Rose (film) 316
"Honky Tonk Crazy" 320, 526
Honky-Tonk Liberation Army 250-251, 286, 329
"Honky-Tonk Man" 291-292 (also: 291n), 311, 528
"Honky-Tonkin'" (Seals) 188, 231, 275, 288, 526-527
"Honky-Tonkin'" (Williams) 248
"How Could We Come to This After That" 276, 526, 529
"How High's the Watergate, Martha" 107
Hood, David 108
Hopper, Edward 47
Hornsby, Walter "Fly" (aka Rockin' Ricky) 104, 169, 172-173, 219
Horton, Billie Jean 468, 524
Horton, Johnny 383
Hot Pockets 489, 490
Houghtaling, John Joseph 72
Hudson, Louise 55, 59 (also: 59n), 515
Hughey, John 168
Hunter, Bruce 150, 161n, 163, 298, 352n, 405, 517, 521
Hunter, Carla 415, 423-424, 523
Hunter, Steve 315, 339, 418, 423-424, 440-441, 521, 523-524
Husky, Ferlin 155
Hussein, Saddam 490
Hurston, Zora Neale 72
Hurt, Edd 265, 520
Hurt, Henry 130, 143 (also: 143n), 517
Huston, Rex 329-331 (also: 330n), 334, 359-360

I

"I Ain't Living Long Like This" 221-222, 526, 528
"(I Can't Be) Your Backdoor" 201, 281, 526
"I Get Drunk" 377, 418, 528
"I Got a Bad Attitude" 359, 361, 528
"I Got Mine" 247-248, 526, 528
"I Had to Get Drunk Last Night" 222, 526-527
"I Love You Truly" 107-108, 528
"I Owe It All to My Heart" 326, 418, 527
"I See the Want To in Your Eyes" 160-164, 526-528
"I Still Can't Believe You're Gone" 201, 526
Idol, Billy 455
"If My Eyes Touch You" 248, 526
"If You've Got the Money (I've Got the Time)" 201, 226, 526
"I'll Go Stepping Too" 64
"I'm a Texan" (song) 527
I'm a Texan (album) 428 (also: 428n), 527-528
"I'm Guilty" 379 (also: 379n), 475, 528-529
Impacts, the (aka the Imps) 98-103, 109, 128, 180, 288
"In Some Room Above the Street" 202, 226, 526, 528
"In the Pines" 15, 61, 380, 386, 529
Invasion U.S.A. (film) 72
"Is a Blue Bird Blue" 85, 529
Isbell, Jim 149, 152, 154, 203, 517
Ison, Hobart 52
"It Takes Me All Night Long" 118, 529
"It's True" 281, 428, 527, 529
"I've Been Known (to Get a Little Stoned)" 103n, 109, 529
"I've Just Seen the Rock of Ages" 257-258, 291, 360, 390, 490, 526

J

James, Etta 108
Jans, Tom 177
Jeffrey, Michael 435, 459
Jenkins, Mike 238
Jenkins Homecoming Festival 457
Jenkins Theatre 57, 59
Jenkins, Tiny 98 (also: 98-99n)
Jennings, Waylon 19, 116, 144, 171, 207, 208, 222-223, 246, 251, 265, 276, 313, 317, 327, 337, 340, 517, 519, 522, 525
Jennings, Will 177n
"Jesse's Last Ride" 459, 475, 529
J.M. Fields (store) 235
Jobete Music 130, 143
John R (DJ) 91
"Johnny B. Goode" 64, 85
Johnson, Carl 84
Johnson, Don 269, 276n

Jones, George 20, 61, 146, 189, 246, 317, 327, 333n, 359, 418, 482 (also: 482n), 527
Jordan, Dave 266n, 356-358, 360-363 (also: 363n), 365, 371, 511, 520, 522
Jordanaires, the 155-156 (also: 156n), 188, 199
Judds, the 47, 335
June Appal Recordings 283

K

Kaczynski, Ted 304n
Kapp Records 119-123, 130, 157, 163-164, 417, 423, 528
Kazee, Buell 281
Keen, Robert Earl 413n
Keith, Larry 318
Keith, Toby 429, 482n
Ken Park (film) 385n
Kendalls, the 139
Kennedy, Delores (formerly Delores Dea) 140, 143-144, 261, 429, 517-519, 523
Kennedy, Jerry 138, 140-143, 150, 154, 289n, 413, 517-518
Kentucky Music Hall of Fame 506, 525
Kershaw, Rusty and Doug 141
Kester, Betty (alias) 470, 477-470, 478n, 482, 498
Kilgore, Merle 287
Kilroy, Eddie 206-207, 289 (also: 289n), 315, 318-319 (also: 318n), 322, 518, 521
King, B.B. 141
"Kings and Queens" 109, 529
"Kiss an Angel Good Mornin'" 21
Klondike bar 423
Knight, Junior 435
Kool-Aid 237
Kopf, John 222, 512, 519
KPLX 99.5 The Wolf 459
Kroon, Jerry 415

L

Lady Long Legs (club) 251
Ladysmith (band) 212
Larson, Nicolette 220
Lavender, Shorty 287
Lawnwood Hospital; Lawnwood Regional Medical Center 105n, 307, 463
Lawrence, Dale 17, 277, 312, 510, 515, 520-521
Lead Belly 15, 124, 380
"Leah" 208, 221, 231, 526-527
"Leaona" (aka "Hey Leona') 360, 527, 528
"Leave the Note" 423, 529
LeBlanc, Leo 221
Lee, Dickey 139
Leech, Mike 154
LeFevre, Mylon 269
Leigh, Danni 146
Les Paul (guitar) 17, 42, 182, 225, 272, 482 (also: 482n)
"The Lesser of Two Evils" 121, 526, 528
"Let's Forget That We're Married" (formerly "Let's Forget That I'm Married") 124, 291, 526, 528-529
"Let's Go Baby" 113
"Let's Go Jukin'" 378, 427, 527-529
Levi's 183, 191
Lewis, Jerry Lee 19-20, 61, 82, 85, 98-99, 105, 110, 122-123, 142, 190, 247, 252, 255, 260, 289 (also: 289n), 315, 318, 320, 332, 337, 373, 378, 382, 390, 410, 418, 420, 427, 523
Lewis, Linda Gail 382 (also: 382n), 523
Lewis, Smiley 385
"Life's a Game" 359, 528
Lightfoot, Gordon 119
Lilly, John C. 354
Linda's Lounge (club) 473
Linn, Mark 110, 130, 143n, 511
Little Anthony 98
Little Beaver 170
"Little Junior" 244, 288, 320, 381, 434, 526-528
Little Junior (album) 240, 244 (also: 244n), 246-248, 335, 419, 447n, 514, 526
"Little Miss Hideaway" 109
"Little Old Love Light" 121, 526, 528
Little Richard 47, 72, 91, 383, 517
Live at Billy Bob's (album) 464 (also: 464n), 491, 527
Lone Star Cafe (club) 16, 287
Lone Star Texas Music Special (TV) 231
"Long Black Veil" 269, 383, 423, 529
Long, Bobby Joe 496n
Longhorn Ballroom (club) 17n, 226, 251, 515
"Looking for Some Brand New Stuff" 419, 527
"Lord What a Woman" 201, 526
"Losers and Lovers" 337, 527
"Lost Highway" 260, 526
Louisiana Hayride (radio/TV) 140
Love Me Tender (film) 59
Loveless, Patty 47, 457
"Lover's Knot" 275, 279, 526
LSI (studio) 358, 360
LU (cookie brand) 422
Luckenbach Dance Hall 231, 485n
"Luckenbach, Texas (Back to the Basics of Love)" 264-265
"Lucretia" 419, 527-528
Luyao, Asuncion 460-462 (also: 462n), 524
Lyerly, Bill 358, 360, 362, 522
Lynn, Loretta 47, 61, 119, 155, 165, 167n, 177n, 224, 457

M

M16 (weapon) 255
"Make It a Double" 419, 527

"Man of Constant Sorrow" 60n
Mansfield, Jayne 326n
Marlow's Country Palace 253-257, 520
Marr, Dana 365-368, 522
Marr, Ray 365-368
Martin D-28 (guitar) 272
Masters, Henry Benjamin; Ben 304 (also: 304n)
Masters, Howard 74, 77
Maxwell, Tommy 83, 92
"Mazelle" 260, 526, 528
McCall, C.W. 189
McCandless, Teresa 477, 524
McClain, Charly 228
McCoy, Charlie 148-149, 153, 155, 517
McCroan, Richard 22, 290n, 321, 432-436 (also: 434n, 435n, 436n), 439-442 (also: 439n), 445n, 446-452, 514, 516, 521, 524
McDuff, Donnie 432, 434-435 (also: 434n)
McDuff, Eddie 434
McFarlane, Spanky 281
McKenna, Elise (character) 463
McMillan, Terry 155, 246
McPhatter, Clyde 110
McVeigh, Timothy 304n
Mealer, Tom "Poobah" 419
Memphis Boys, the 147-148, 153
Melton, "Boogie" Bob 20, 104, 169-173, 175, 208-210, 216, 219, 229-230, 249-250, 260, 270, 291 (also: 291n), 314, 369, 441n, 511, 514-515, 517-521, 524
"Memories Swim in Whiskey" 289, 528
Meow Mix 275
"Merry-Go-Round" 120, 526, 528
Merry-Go-Round, the (club) 73, 85-87, 91, 114, 201
Messer, Alan 278
Mevis, Blake 313n, 335, 521
Michaels, Lee 281
Middleworth, Glenn 377 (also: 377n), 379n, 417, 522
Miller, Tommy Ray ("T-Ray") 249-250
Miltown (drug) 497
Minarchick, Tom 75
"Misfits" 337-338, 527
Moeller, Dee 244n, 519
Mo-Fok Records 129
Moman, Lincoln Wayne "Chips" 147, 153, 264-267 (also: 266n), 273, 275, 276n, 277, 279-281, 341n, 520-521, 525
Monroe, Bill 47, 61, 208, 223, 519
Monroe, Charlie 61
Monroe, Marilyn 326n, 335, 351
Montgomery, Earl "Peanutt" 108
Moonshadow (band) 488
Moore, Bob 154 (also: 154n)
Moore, Scotty 140
Moss, Felix 351, 380n, 523
Mother Earth 358
Mr. Lucky's (club) 251
"Mr. Peanut Man" 109
Mullins, Kevin 48
Munson, Larry "Mouse" 90, 98-103 (also: 98n), 180, 182-183, 192, 204-205, 209, 211, 242, 250, 270, 291, 302-304, 401-402, 511, 517-521, 523
"Murdered by Love" 419, 527
Music City Music Hall (studio) 318, 358n, 414
Myrick, Weldon 118, 155, 202, 209, 212, 249, 318

N

Nashville Alive (TV) 321
Nashville A-Team 150
Nelson, Connie 181
Nelson, Tracy 358
Nelson, Willie 19, 34n, 61, 144, 147, 171, 181, 201, 206-207, 216, 222-223, 226, 234, 327, 329, 337-338, 341, 441, 482n, 514, 518-519, 521
"The Next Thing You Know" 259-260, 526
Newbury, Mickey 383
Niece, Jasper "Hoss" 53, 55, 60
Night Comes to the Cumberlands: A Biography of a Depressed Area (book) 52, 525
"No No No" 109
"No Expectations" 423, 529
Norris, Chuck 72
"Nothin' but a Woman" 427, 527-528
"Nothing Cheap About a Cheap Affair" 379, 427, 527
Noveskey, Jim 128-129
Nubrume, the 127
Nudie suit 16

O

Oates, Warren 47, 154
O'Connor, Hugh 52
Oermann, Robert K. 321, 420 (also: 420n), 521, 524
O'Lunney's (club) 212
Okeechobee Purple (marijuana) 206-207, 302, 351, 355
"Okeechobee Purple" 273, 526
O'Keefe, Danny 201, 518
Odyssey (perfume) 35
"Ol' Hank's Lovesick Blues" 427, 527
Old Top Rail (club) 475-476, 495
On Stage (TNN show) 427, 434n
"One More" 260, 526, 528
"Only a Woman Like You" 118
Operation Bancoshares 304n
"Orange Blossom Special" 39
Orbison, Roy 20, 98, 147, 320
Orr, Jay 20, 515

Osborne Brothers 47, 119
The Osbournes (TV) 346
Osbourne, Ozzy 440
"Out of Hand" 155, 177-178 (also: 177n), 180, 446, 526-528
Out of Hand (album) 187-190, 193, 199, 518, 526, 528
Outback Steakhouse 24
OxyContin; oxy, oxycodone 456, 460-462 (also: 461n, 462n), 471, 475, 481, 485, 496-497

P

Pablo, Thomas 477, 524
Pac-Man (video game) 347
Palomino Club (Fort Pierce) 78
Palomino Club (North Hollywood) 251-252, 281
Palousek, Steve 434-436, 439, 442, 464n, 524
Pappy's Wine 463
Parker, Chris 111, 517
Parker, Cliff 224-225
Parker, Joe 82-86, 91-92, 110-111, 514, 516
Parker, Junior 141
Parker, Karen 31, 83-86, 515-517
Parr, Katherine "Kitty" 84, 516
Parr, Wallace 71, 421, 516
Parsons, Gram 20
Patoski, Joe Nick 21, 515
Paxton, Gary S. 320n
Paxton, Karen 320n
Paxton, Larry 415
Payday (film) 264
Payne Gap School 58, 62
Payne, Jimmy 168
Payne, Leon 260
Payne, Robert "Cotton" 19, 127n, 205n, 217, 226, 230-231, 252-253, 285n, 514, 519
Peavy, Joseph; Peavy, Joe 425-426, 465, 482n, 486-487, 502-503, 510, 523
Peckinpah, Sam 504
Pena, José; Pena, Joe 76n, 242-244 (also: 242n, 243n), 299
Perkins, Rob 492
Peters, Barbara Anne 37, 299, 377, 429n, 463, 515, 521-523
Petrillo, Sammy 311
Philco 61
Phoenix (band) 169-173, 175, 183, 187, 193, 204, 208, 249
Pickett, Wilson 108, 153, 254
Pierce, Webb 63, 106, 314
Pineapple Joe's Grill (bar) 488
Piper Aircraft 98, 99
Plastic Man (comic book) 213
Ponderosa Ballroom (club) 476
"Poor Red Georgia Dirt" 109
Pop! Goes the Country (TV) 180, 200
Porter, Terry 21, 28, 58, 290n, 429, 447-457 (also: 457n), 459, 462, 464, 473, 476-477, 481, 483-486 (also: 485n), 490-496, 511, 515, 524
Posey, Sandy 108
Potter, Bill 64
P.P. Cobb's (restaurant) 489
Preston, John Brenton 257
"Pretend I Never Happened" 223, 494, 526
Price, Ray 63, 146, 188, 190, 433n
Pride, Charley 19, 21, 107, 116, 145, 156, 165, 175-186 (also: 177n), 187, 195, 200, 204-205, 208, 210-211, 213, 226, 293, 322, 326n, 357, 514, 518-519, 525
Pride, Rozene 181, 518
Pridesmen, the; Pridesman 176, 178, 182-183, 211, 226, 293,
Profeta, Ralph 208, 249, 250, 252, 519
Pruett, Jeanne 120
Publix 185
Purdue Pharma (Sackler family) 461, 524
Putman, Curly 259, 482n

Q

Quasar VCR 267n
"Quits" 201, 231, 526-528

R

"Rachel" 222, 526-527
Radisson (hotel) 449
"Rainin', Rainin', Rainin'" 229, 377-378, 417-418, 421, 528-529
Raitt, Bonnie 316n
Rally candy bars 35
"Ramblin' Man" (Allman Brothers) 168, 187, 267-268, 438, 528
"Ramblin' Man" (Hank Williams) 277
Randall, Curtis 22, 435-436 (also: 436n), 439, 443, 450-451, 464n, 475, 477, 515, 524
Rastrelli, Laurie 236-238, 270, 297, 299-301, 305, 353, 395, 398, 400-401, 405, 461, 511, 519-524
Raulerson, Donald ("Big Potatoes Man") 74, 77, 105n, 304 (also: 304n)
Raven, Eddy 228
Raven Red Ash Coal Company 356
Ray, Ricky 300-301 (also: 301n), 380n
Red Ash Records 266n, 358-363, 368, 378, 418 (also: 418n), 522, 528
"Red Georgia Clay" 359-360, 528
Reed, Jimmy 85, 91, 190, 276n, 376, 488
Reese's Peanut Butter Cups 380
Reeves, Del 118
Reinhard, Randy 322
River Palace (club) 440
Renaldo and Clara (film) 374

Reverend Julius Cheeks and the Four Knights 388
Reynolds, Billy Ray 258, 276
Rheem Roberts 133
Rialto's (club) 73, 298, 380-381 (also: 380n), 385-386, 388, 418
Rimes, LeAnn 436 (also: 436n)
Rio Palm Isle (club) 251
River Club (club) 452
"Roarin'" 275, 279, 526, 528
"Roadhouse Romances" 359, 528
Robinson, Danny "Tuck" 257n
Rhodes, Dusty 33, 71
Robinson, Dub 226-227, 230-231, 288, 290, 514, 519
Robbins, Dennis 522
Robbins, Hargus "Pig" 153, 247, 266, 275, 291
Robbins, Marty 167
The Rocky Horror Picture Show (film) 425
Rodriguez, Johnny 142-143 (also: 142n), 413, 440, 454, 523, 525
Roland RD-300 385
Rowland, Dave 205, 326n
"Rub-A-Dub-Dub" 61
Rubik's Cube 178
Rugg, Hal 155, 246-247, 291
Russell, Leon 346
Russell, Marie 71n
Russell Music 71, 421

S

7-Eleven 300, 471
Sanders, Ked 57, 524
Sawyer Brown 337
Scaggs, Boz 316n
Schlitz beer 97
Schwartz, Lee 58, 81, 447, 470, 479, 501-502, 506, 510, 515, 516, 524
Schwartz, Tommy 35, 41, 43, 58, 71n, 73, 76 (also: 76n), 78, 102, 104, 105n, 106, 111, 124-125, 127-128, 234, 236-237, 239, 243n, 244, 271, 280, 297, 300-301, 305, 346, 347n, 368, 377-378, 380n, 389, 394-395, 406, 418, 447n, 458-459, 464, 468-471, 481, 482n, 483-485, 488-493, 504-505, 511, 514-517, 519, 521-524
Scott, Frank 413, 523
Scott, Jimmy 20
Scottish Inn (motel) 391, 404
Scott-Noennig, Nancy 413
Scruggs, Earl 64
Seals, Troy 177n, 188, 248
Sears Silvertone (guitar) 63, 81, 140
Searstown 113, 403
Seeff, Norman 278
Seldom Scene, the 359
Sellers, Dale 150, 153-154, 212-213, 224-225, 247, 258, 291, 318, 320, 358, 415, 517, 519
Seminole 71-72, 469-470, 494
Seminole Wars 71
Sha Na Na 335
"Shady Streets" 154, 258-260, 321, 323, 385n, 526, 528
Shannon, Del 98
Shaver, Billy Joe 315
"She Goes Walking Through My Mind" 118
"She Sings Amazing Grace" 320, 323-324, 527-528
Shepherd, John Emmanuel; Johnny 465, 468-473 (also: 472n), 477-480 (also: 478n), 482-485 (also: 482n, 485n), 490n, 491n, 496, 524
Sherrill, Billy 282, 325, 332-333
"She's Actin' Single (I'm Drinkin' Doubles)" 19, 155, 161, 163, 185-187 (also: 187n), 200, 255, 288, 366, 526-529
"She's Got a Drinking Problem" 289, 528
"She's Takin' Me Down" 379, 529
"She's the Next Best Thing (To Being There)" 130, 528
Shindler, Glenn "Dog" 446-447 (also: 447n), 484
Shook, Jerry 130, 154, 247, 258, 291, 318, 358
Shupe, Carrie "Corsia" 34, 133-134 (also: 134n), 209, 529
Shupe, John 133-134 (also: 134n), 209, 529
"Silver Cloud" 90-91, 282, 390, 507, 529
Siman, Si 160-161
Simpson, Sturgill 47, 516
Sinequan (drug) 496
"Single Again" 247-248, 378, 440, 526-529
Singleton, Don 359
Singleton, Shelby 141, 313
'68 Comeback Special (TV) 385
"Six Days on the Road" 423, 529
Skinner, Jack 221
Sloven, Larry 413-414 (also: 413n), 421, 428, 523
Smash Records 122, 141, 150
Smith, Billy 488
Smith, Bobby 181, 434
Smith, Cal 118, 120
Smith, Connie 144
Smith, Ed 378
Smith, Emma 47
Smith, James Carroll, Jr.; Jimmy 29, 33, 35-37, 50n, 76n, 114, 134n, 235, 239, 242, 297-298, 300-302, 305, 307, 349-356 (also: 352n), 381, 386, 395-399, 401-402, 405-407, 460-462 (also: 462n), 471, 483, 488, 505-506, 511, 515, 517, 519, 521-525
Smith, Mike 17n
Smith, Warren 247
Smith-Frost, Bartholomew Eugene "Frosty" 281
Smith Music Group; Smith Music (label) 464n, 527
"Smokin' in the Rockies" 337-338, 527-528
Snead, Jimmy; Snead, Jim 128-130, 165-167, 181-182, 517-518

"The Snuff Queen" 118, 123-124, 526, 528-529
Soma (drug) 243, 352-353, 443-445, 455, 471, 496-497
"Something to Believe In" 130, 528
Somewhere in Time (film) 91 (reference to), 463,
"Son of a Honky Tonk Woman" 378, 418, 527, 529
Sons of Anarchy (TV) 446
Sony Walkman; Walkman WM-D6 15, 437
South Dixie Drive-In 73
Sovine, Red 105
"Spare Me" 110, 529
Spears, Billie Jo 189
Spence Manor 314, 325, 332, 334
Spence, Stan 55, 234, 237, 297-299, 304-305, 307, 400, 405, 519, 521, 523
St. Lucie Junior High 82
Stampley, Joe 313-315
Standing Rock Reservation 450
Standing Rock Sioux Tribe 473
Stanley Brothers 61, 203
Stanley, Ralph 60n, 257-258, 278
Star Musicland (club) 257n
"Staring Each Other Down" 273, 526, 528
Starling, John 359, 383
Starlite, Tammy Faye 325, 512, 521
Starr, Ruby 244
Stax Records 264
Steppin' Out (album) 73n, 200-203, 526
Stevens, Ray 100
Stewart, Abraham; Abe 60 (also: 60n), 516
Stewart, Alexander 48, 48n
Stewart, Bill 32, 64, 515
Stewart, Candy 33, 68, 111, 198, 238, 511, 515-516, 519
Stewart, Charlie 52
Stewart, Easter 50, 64-65, 299
Stewart, Gail 39-40, 93, 109, 220, 235, 242 (also: 242n), 396, 402, 505, 514-515, 517, 519, 521
Stewart, Garna 35, 38, 42, 58, 81 (also: 81n), 87, 97, 305, 418, 490, 493, 505, 514-516
Stewart, Gary Joseph; Joey; Bubala 25, 284, 346, 349, 351-352, 354-355, 372, 376, 383, 391, 394-407, 410-412, 416-417 (also: 417n), 425, 441, 493, 496, 497, 507, 514
Stewart, Gary Ronald
  album covers of 69, 189-190, 193, 199-201, 203, 225, 244, 248, 278, 311, 315-316, 335, 337, 360n, 378n, 417, 427, 482
  Allman Brothers, obsession with 61, 132-133, 144, 267 (also: 267n), 374, 437-438
  arrests of 283-284, 416, 441
  attire of (including hats) 23, 174, 189, 225, 244, 248, 278, 288, 371, 380, 477, 488, 493
  bird calls by 127
  bird puppets of (Roho and Jojo) 353-354 (also: 353n)
  birth of 56
  "Call her Trigger" incident 272
  car accident of 284-285 (also: 285n)
  canned chili "defecation" incident 455
  Civil War interest of 372 (also: 372n)
  death of 491-494
  dropped by RCA 341-343
  drug use of 15, 25, 75, 86, 102, 125, 134-135, 191-192, 206-207, 210, 213, 242-246, 256, 270, 283-285, 288, 290-291, 293, 315-316, 318 (also: 318n), 321, 339-340, 352-356 (also: 353n), 361-362, 365, 376, 382-383, 417, 441, 444-446, 455, 460-463 (also: 460n), 469, 470-475, 490, 496-498
  Dylan, Bob, meeting with 225
  extramarital affairs of 192-195, 217, 219, 252-253, 384 (also: 384n), 454-455
  false teeth of 453-454, 476, 488, 494-495
  food eccentricities of 127, 353, 363-364, 489-490
  Forrest Hills Music, signing with, 117
  guitar playing of 19, 21, 63-64, 82, 84, 91-92, 97, 110, 128-129, 171, 182, 187, 198-200, 251, 268, 278, 293, 331, 378, 381-382, 420, 470, 481-482
  Garyisms of 246
  influences of 61
  last live performance of 488
  Taylor, Mary Lou, and
    death pact with 283, 472, 484, 498
    initial meeting with 91-92
    marriage to 95, 97
  mental "breakdown" of 368-369, 377
  physical endowment of 219
  playing Native American reservations, 228-231, 338, 436, 469-470
  "pour water on my balls" incident 443-444
  Presley, Elvis, on 310-311, 375
  RCA, signing with 145
  record collecting of 16, 174, 184, 373-374
  songwriting of 103, 106, 109-110, 113-124 (also: 117n), 126-128, 130-131, 133-135, 168-169, 195, 198-201, 209-211, 223-224, 246-247, 276-278, 293, 312, 314, 319-320, 333-335 (also: 333n), 337, 359-360, 411-412, 417-419, 427-428, 517, 520
  Top Ten single appearances of 174, 178, 187
  unreleased recordings of 16, 22, 76n, 103n, 203, 221, 281, 418, 427-428, 520-521, 527, 529
  violent behavior of 219-220, 412 (also: 412n), 416
  vocal problems of 361
Stewart, George Robert; Papaw 23, 27-34, 37, 39-40, 42-43, 49-56 (55n), 58-59 (also: 59n), 63-65, 93, 95, 107, 133, 252, 384, 411, 446, 514-515, 522-523
Stewart, Georgia (née Niece); Georgie; Mamaw 23-24 (also: 23n), 28-40 (also: 28n, 34n), 43, 53-56, 58-65, 69,71, 81, 93-95, 97, 106, 133, 184, 187, 198n, 203, 207, 238-239 (also: 239n), 242-243, 268-270, 297, 299, 305, 384, 390, 395, 403, 416, 484, 490, 494, 505, 514-515, 517-518, 521, 523

Stewart, Gerald Douglas 24, 34, 36, 38, 81, 105, 115, 217, 268, 277, 293, 296-307 (also: 304n), 376n, 380n, 514, 520-521
Stewart, Gina 23-24 (also: 23n), 28, 31, 33-36, 38-40, 42, 69, 72, 76-78 (also: 76n), 81, 94, 131, 184, 205, 235-239, 242-243 (also: 242n), 254, 268, 297, 299, 301 (also: 300n), 306-307, 330n, 331, 382, 390, 395, 397, 419, 446, 484-485, 490, 505, 511, 514-517, 519, 521, 523-525
Stewart, Glenn 33, 35, 81, 494, 514
Stewart, Glenna Sue 55 (also: 55n)
Stewart, Gordon 23n, 31n
Stewart, Grandal copyright page, 33-34, 36-37, 39-40, 42, 51, 53, 55n, 56-59 (also: 59n), 61-65 (also: 63n), 68-69, 71, 77, 81-83, 85, 87, 89, 94, 97, 111, 133, 189, 198-200 (also: 199n), 203, 205, 217, 236-238, 242, 244, 284, 348, 395, 411, 412n, 505, 511, 514-520, 523
Stewart, Gregory; Greg 23n, 31 (also: 31n), 40, 42-43, 81, 105, 127, 234, 237, 288, 304n, 505n, 514-515, 519
Stewart, Greta Joe 55, 55n
Stewart, Griselda Nelson 24, 63, 81, 207, 231, 232-239, 244, 367, 405, 514
Stewart, Harlan McClellan; Clell 49-50, 64-65
Stewart, Isaac; Blind Ike 49
Stewart, Jake 50-52, 60, 85, 87, 515, 516, 529
Stewart, Jason 31, 40-42, 72, 297, 511, 515-516, 521
Stewart, John 48-49 (also: 48n, 49n), 60, 515
Stewart, Mary Lou (née Taylor) dedication, 14, 25, 30, 37, 50n, 87, 88-95, 97-100, 102, 108, 110-111, 132, 134-135, 145, 168-169, 172, 181, 183-185, 191, 195, 201, 203, 209, 220, 224, 234-236, 238-239, 242-243, 247, 252, 269-270, 283-285, 299-300, 307, 333, 339, 346-349, 352-354 (also: 352n, 353n), 362 (also: 362n), 363n, 368-369, 371-372, 374-376, 378-379 (also: 379n), 382, 384-386, 391, 394-395, 397-407, 410-412 (also: 412n), 415-417 (also: 417n), 422-426, 428-429 (also: 429n), 441, 444-445, 446 (also: 446n), 460n, 461-465, 472 (also: 472n), 477-487 (also: 478n, 481n), 489, 493, 496-498, 500-501, 503, 505-507, 514-515, 517-520, 522-523, 524
Stewart, Nick 31, 39, 41, 43, 48, 50, 74, 166, 234-235, 296, 298, 305-306, 407, 428n, 441, 511, 515, 519, 521, 523-524
Stewart, Samuel 49n
Stewart, Thomas, Jr. 49
Stewart, Trampas 30, 33-35, 39-43, 53-54, 69, 81, 234, 241-242, 297, 306-307, 396-398, 511, 515- 516, 519, 521, 523
Stiles, Jerry Lewis 82
Stiles, T.J. 459, 524-525
Stines, Shawn "Mickey" 48
Stockyards Hotel 23, 495
"Stone Wall (Around Your Heart)" 247-248, 526, 528
Stokes, Frank 247
Strait, George 311, 313 (also: 313n), 320, 334-335 (also: 334n), 340n, 341, 367, 521
Strzelecki, Henry 154, 247, 291
Stuart, Marty 20, 21n, 436n, 515
Stuckey, Ann 518
Stuckey, Nat 118, 121-122, 124, 165-167 (also: 167n), 182,
"Sugaree" 84
Summer, Bob 322
Sun Bank 234-235
Sunrise Theatre 73
Sutton, Lisa 491, 524
Sutton, Glenn 491
Swan, Billy 107, 110, 517
"Sweet Country Red" 177n, 188, 526
"Sweet-Tater and Cisco" 120, 165, 526, 528
"Sweet Thang"; "Sweet Thang and Cisco" 118, 121, 165
Swindall, Ron 249

T

13th Floor Elevators 388
39th Infantry 53
.38 Special (gun) 398
.357 Magnum 237, 328
Tackett, Marlow 253-257, 356, 359, 520
Tackett, Sonny 255-257, 257n, 265, 276, 279, 282, 300, 350, 359-360, 419, 424-425, 425n, 428, 429n, 519-521, 523
Tankersley, Don 246, 248
Taylor, Ardell 464, 485-486, 489n, 490n, 524
Taylor, Dickie 436, 464n, 524
Taylor Correctional Institution 502 (also: 502n), 525
Telecaster 84, 140, 224
Teletubbies (TV) 349
"Ten Years of This" 19, 161, 223-225, 526-528
"Tequila After Midnight" 244 (also: 244n), 247, 526
Texas Honky-Tonk All Star Band 436 (also: 436n)
Them Tasers Hurt (album) 73n
"There Ain't No Grave Gonna Hold My Body Down" 61-62, 390
"There Goes a Girl" 109
"There's a Tennessee Woman/Ben's Song" 415
"There's a Whole Lot About a Woman (a Man Don't Know)" 118, 529
"This Old Heart Won't Let Go" 188 (also: 188n), 526, 528
Thomas, B.J. 264, 318
Thomas, Dale 36, 298, 515, 521
Thomas, David 106, 241, 517, 519
Thomas, Hubert Daniel; Thomas, Hubert 104-106, 105n, 125, 359, 368, 379
Thompson, Bobby 203
Thompson, Hank 61

"Those Were the Days" 335, 337, 527-528
Those Were the Days (EP) 334-335, 337, 527-528
Throckmorton, Sonny 259-260, 519
Thunders, the 229
Tillis, Mel 105-108, 110, 113-114, 121, 249, 517, 525
Tobin, Josephine 85, 516
Toler, "Dangerous" Dan 258
Tom Cats, the 83-87, 92, 114, 529
Toman Brothers, the; Toman Brothers Band; Tomans, the 227 (also: 227n), 259, 282, 322, 331, 362-363, 368, 418, 433, 435, 511, 527
Toman, Randy 21n, 167n, 177n, 188n, 226-231, 259, 279, 286-289, 298, 321, 324, 330, 334, 361, 363-368, 397, 407, 418n, 421, 433n, 434-435, 437, 475, 511, 514, 518-524, 527
Toman, Russ; Toman, Russell 227, 229, 259, 324, 363-364, 418, 434, 437, 522
Tootsie's Orchid Lounge (club) 194
Top Ten, the 106, 176, 328n
Top Twenty, the 213, 248
Top Hundred, the 360
Torn, Rip 264
Town and Country Tavern (club) 73
"Touch of You" 483, 529
Train Robbery (band) 249, 251, 385
Trammell, Bobby Lee 20
Trans Am (car) 220
Tree Publishing 327
"Trudy" 201, 223, 231, 526
Tucker, Tanya 15, 19, 20, 138, 323-329, 331, 340, 343, 414-415, 419, 486, 515, 517, 521-525
Tupperware 35, 423, 453
Turley, Craig 437-439, 511, 524
Turley, Karen 438
Turner, Ike and Tina 72, 161
Turner, Josh 146
Turner, Robby 317, 521
Twitty, Conway 85, 162-163, 165, 167n, 168, 174
Twitty, Pat 247

U

Urban Cowboy (film) 316 (also: 316n), 320

V

Van Eaton, J.M. 110
Varney, Jim "Ernest" 377
"Vanishing Breed" 118
Vann, John 290, 361, 363, 367, 520, 522
Vaughan, Stevie Ray 99
Vickery, Mack 337 (also: 337n)
Vulco Records 113
Vulgamore, Irvin 113

W

Wagon Wheel, the (club) 103-107, 121, 124-125, 170, 359, 368, 529
Wagoner, Porter 146, 160, 434
Walden, Phil 139
Wallace, Coyote 253-254, 520
Wallace, Herby 165
"Walk On, Boy" 108
Walk the Walk (film) 169
Watkins (company) 59, 63,
Watkins, Riley 98, 100, 103, 109, 128-129, 288, 517
"We Made It as Lovers (We Just Couldn't Make It as Friends)" 273, 526
Weekend at Bernie's (film) 455
West, Kirk 202, 267 (also: 267n), 271, 437, 511, 514, 517, 520, 524
Whalen, John 249-250, 519
Whataburger 330
Wheeler, Billy Edd 141
Wheeler, Karen 166
"When a Man Loves a Woman (the Way That I Love You)" 118
Whipple, Sterling 202, 519
"Whiskey River" 147
Whiskey River (club) 251
"Whiskey Trip" 161, 198n, 246, 248, 526, 528
Whiskey Trip (band) 505
Whitaker Music Shop 62, 516
Whitaker, Cora 62
White, Buck 203
White, Tony Joe 287
Whites, the (vocal group) 358
Whitley, Keith 47, 71, 427-428,
Whittington, Buddy 435
"Whole Lot of Shakin' Going On" 61
Wilburn Brothers 105, 188n
Wilburn, Ray 254, 324, 372n, 418, 512, 519, 523
"Wild Horses" 423, 529
Wild Wet Willie's (club) 433
Williams, Audrey 363n
Williams, Dale 105
Williams, Hank, Jr. 287, 327, 337, 342, 367
Williams, Hank, Sr. 19, 61, 106, 138, 181, 210, 248, 260, 277, 332, 363n, 386, 420n, 427, 468, 517, 524
Williams, Jason D. 427
Williams, Jeff 434n, 435, 437, 442-445, 446n, 448, 459, 524
Williams, Mentor 177 (also: 177n)
Williams, Raymond 62, 516
Williams, Tommy 155, 203
"Williamson County" 134, 168, 387-388, 390, 498, 526, 528, 529
"Willie and Poor Bob" 273
Willingham, James 429, 450-457, 459-460, 462, 465, 472-476, 482n, 483-485, 494-495, 511, 524

Willingham, Kim 213, 438, 453, 456, 474, 518, 523, 524
Willis, Chuck 388
Wine, Toni 275
Wirtz, Reverend Billy C. (William Wirths) 71-72, 190, 516, 518
WLAC 91
Wojcik, Dan 433
WOKC 124
Wolf Brand Chili 455
"Woman in Demand" 211, 427, 527, 529
Wood, Bobby 147, 153, 161, 174, 212, 517
Woolery, Randy "Panda" 435, 440, 443-445, 524
Worthington, Hall 368
Worthy, Barbara 440, 455n, 524
Wray, Link 85
WTCW 62
WWF 33

Y

Yates, Bill 307
Yates Funeral Home 307, 483, 493, 505
Yazzie, Leonard 229, 519
"Yellow Rose of Texas" 19
Yoakam, Dwight 19, 47, 457, 515, 522
Yoo-hoo (beverage) 441
York, Rusty 84
"You Can't Housebreak a Tomcat" 188, 529
"You're Running Wild" 248, 526, 529
"You're the Reason I'm Living" 427, 527
Young, Chip 130, 138, 154, 517
Young, Faron 63 (also: 63n), 142, 157, 315, 427
Young, Reggie 150, 153-154, 202, 206, 212, 259, 266, 518
"Your Place or Mine" 19, 154, 212-213, 223, 281, 288, 526, 528
Your Place or Mine (album) 221-225, 468, 482, 526, 528
"You're Everything (God Meant Woman to Be)" 131, 526
You're Not the Woman You Used to Be (album) 123 (also: 123n), 526
"You're Not the Woman You Use to Be" (also "You're Not the Woman You Used to Be") 122-123 (also: 123n), 526, 528

Z

Zinkan, Joe 203
ZZ Top 19, 228, 386